IMAGE EFFECTS

True Impostors
Eric Risser
(University of Central Florida)
481

Baking Normal Maps
on the GPU
Diogo Teixeira
(Move Interactive)
491

High-Speed, Off-Screen
Particles
Iain Cantlay
(NVIDIA Corporation)
513

The Importance of
Being Linear
Larry Gritz
Eugene d'Eon
(NVIDIA Corporation)
529

Rendering Vector Art
on the GPU
Charles Loop
Jim Blinn
(Microsoft Research)
543

Object Detection by
Color: Using the GPU
for Real-Time Video
Image Processing
Ralph Brunner
Frank Doepke
Bunny Laden
(Apple)
563

Motion Blur as a Post-
Processing Effect
Gilberto Rosado
(Rainbow Studios)
575

PHYSICS SIMULATI

Real-Ti
Simulat
Takahir
(Univer
611

Real-Time Simulation
and Rendering of 3D
Fluids
Keenan Crane
*(University of Illinois at
Urbana-Champaign)*
Ignacio Llamas
Sarah Tariq
(NVIDIA Corporation)
633

Fast N-Body Simulation
with CUDA
Lars Nyland
Mark Harris
(NVIDIA Corporation)
Jan Prins
*(University of North
Carolina at Chapel Hill)*
677

Broad-Phase Collision
Detection with CUDA
Scott Le Grand
(NVIDIA Corporation)
697

LCP Algorithms for
Collision Detection
Using CUDA
Peter Kipfer
(Havok)
723

Signed Distance Fields
Using Single-Pass GPU
Scan Conversion of
Tetrahedra
Kenny Erleben
*(University of
Copenhagen)*
Henrik Dohlmann
(3Dfacto R&D)
741

Practical Post-Process
Depth of Field
Earl Hammon, Jr.
(Infinity Ward)
583

GPU COMPUTING

re
PU
s
)
r
785

AES Encryption and
Decryption on the GPU
Takeshi Yamanouchi
(SEGA Corporation)
785

Efficient Random
Number Generation
and Application Using
CUDA
Lee Howes
David Thomas
*(Imperial College
London)*
805

Imaging Earth's
Subsurface Using
CUDA
Bernard Deschizeaux
Jean-Yves Blanc
(CGGVeritas)
831

Parallel Prefix Sum
(Scan) with CUDA
Mark Harris
(NVIDIA Corporation)
Shubhabrata Sengupta
John D. Owens
*(University of
California, Davis)*
851

Incremental
Computation of the
Gaussian
Ken Turkowski
(Adobe Systems)
877

Using the Geometry
Shader for Compact
and Variable-Length
GPU Feedback
Franck Diard
(NVIDIA Corporation)
891

GPU Gems 3

GPU Gems 3

Edited by Hubert Nguyen

♦♦ Addison-Wesley

Upper Saddle River, NJ • Boston • Indianapolis • San Francisco
New York • Toronto • Montreal • London • Munich • Paris • Madrid
Capetown • Sydney • Tokyo • Singapore • Mexico City

About the Cover: *The image on the cover has been rendered in real time in the "Human Head" technology demonstration created by the NVIDIA Demo Team. It illustrates the extreme level of realism achievable with the GeForce 8 Series of GPUs. The demo renders skin by using a physically based model that was previously used only in high-profile pre-rendered movie projects. Actor Doug Jones is the model represented in the demo. He recently starred as the Silver Surfer in* Fantastic Four: Rise of the Silver Surfer.

Many of the designations used by manufacturers and sellers to distinguish their products are claimed as trademarks. Where those designations appear in this book, and the publisher was aware of a trademark claim, the designations have been printed with initial capital letters or in all capitals.

GeForce,™ CUDA,™ and NVIDIA Quadro® are trademarks or registered trademarks of NVIDIA Corporation.

The authors and publisher have taken care in the preparation of this book, but make no expressed or implied warranty of any kind and assume no responsibility for errors or omissions. No liability is assumed for incidental or consequential damages in connection with or arising out of the use of the information or programs contained herein.

NVIDIA makes no warranty or representation that the techniques described herein are free from any Intellectual Property claims. The reader assumes all risk of any such claims based on his or her use of these techniques.

The publisher offers excellent discounts on this book when ordered in quantity for bulk purchases or special sales, which may include electronic versions and/or custom covers and content particular to your business, training goals, marketing focus, and branding interests. For more information, please contact:

U.S. Corporate and Government Sales
(800) 382-3419
corpsales@pearsontechgroup.com

For sales outside of the United States, please contact:

International Sales
international@pearsoned.com

Visit us on the Web: www.awprofessional.com

Library of Congress Cataloging-in-Publication Data
GPU gems 3 / edited by Hubert Nguyen.
    p.   cm.
  Includes bibliographical references and index.
  ISBN-13: 978-0-321-51526-1 (hardback : alk. paper)
  ISBN-10: 0-321-51526-9
  1. Computer graphics. 2. Real-time programming. I. Nguyen, Hubert.

  T385.G6882 2007
  006.6'6—dc22

                                                            2007023985

Pearson Education, Inc.
Rights and Contracts Department
75 Arlington Street, Suite 300
Boston, MA 02116
Fax: (617) 848-7047

ISBN-13: 978-0-321-51526-1
ISBN-10:   0-321-51526-9

Text printed in the United States on recycled paper at Courier in Kendallville, Indiana.
First printing, July 2007

Contents

Chapter 7
Point-Based Visualization of Metaballs on a GPU 123

Kees van Kooten, Playlogic Game Factory
Gino van den Bergen, Playlogic Game Factory
Alex Telea, Eindhoven University of Technology

PART II   LIGHT AND SHADOWS   151

Chapter 8
Summed-Area Variance Shadow Maps 157

Andrew Lauritzen, University of Waterloo

Chapter 9
Interactive Cinematic Relighting with Global Illumination 183

Fabio Pellacini, Dartmouth College
Miloš Hašan, Cornell University
Kavita Bala, Cornell University

Chapter 12
High-Quality Ambient Occlusion 257

Jared Hoberock, University of Illinois at Urbana-Champaign
Yuntao Jia, University of Illinois at Urbana-Champaign

Chapter 13
Volumetric Light Scattering as a Post-Process 275

Kenny Mitchell, Electronic Arts

Chapter 20
GPU-Based Importance Sampling 459
Mark Colbert, University of Central Florida
Jaroslav Křivánek, Czech Technical University in Prague

PART IV   IMAGE EFFECTS   477

Chapter 21
True Impostors. 481
Eric Risser, University of Central Florida

PART V PHYSICS SIMULATION   607

Chapter 29
Real-Time Rigid Body Simulation on GPUs 611
Takahiro Harada, University of Tokyo

Chapter 32
Broad-Phase Collision Detection with CUDA 697
Scott Le Grand, NVIDIA Corporation

Chapter 33
LCP Algorithms for Collision Detection Using CUDA 723
Peter Kipfer, Havok

Chapter 34
Signed Distance Fields Using Single-Pass GPU Scan
Conversion of Tetrahedra 741
Kenny Erleben, University of Copenhagen
Henrik Dohlmann, 3Dfacto R&D

Chapter 41
Using the Geometry Shader for Compact and Variable-Length GPU Feedback 891
Franck Diard, NVIDIA Corporation

Foreword

Composition, the organization of elemental operations into a nonobvious whole, is the essence of imperative programming. The instruction set architecture (ISA) of a microprocessor is a versatile composition interface, which programmers of software renderers have used effectively and creatively in their quest for image realism. Early graphics hardware increased rendering performance, but often at a high cost in composability, and thus in programmability and application innovation. Hardware with microprocessor-like programmability did evolve (for example, the Ikonas Graphics System), but the dominant form of graphics hardware acceleration has been organized around a fixed sequence of rendering operations, often referred to as the *graphics pipeline*. Early interfaces to these systems—such as CORE and later, PHIGS—allowed programmers to specify rendering results, but they were not designed for composition.

OpenGL, which I helped to evolve from its Silicon Graphics-defined predecessor IRIS GL in the early 1990s, addressed the need for composability by specifying an architecture (informally called the *OpenGL Machine*) that was accessed through an imperative programmatic interface. Many features—for example, tightly specified semantics; table-driven operations such as stencil and depth-buffer functions; texture mapping exposed as a general 1D, 2D, and 3D lookup function; and required repeatability properties—ensured that programmers could compose OpenGL operations with powerful and reliable results. Some of the useful techniques that OpenGL enabled include texture-based volume rendering, shadow volumes using stencil buffers, and constructive solid geometry algorithms such as capping (the computation of surface planes at the intersections of clipping planes and solid objects defined by polygons). Ultimately, Mark Peercy and the coauthors of the SIGGRAPH 2000 paper "Interactive Multi-Pass Programmable Shading" demonstrated that arbitrary RenderMan shaders could be accelerated through the composition of OpenGL rendering operations.

During this decade, increases in the raw capability of integrated circuit technology allowed the OpenGL architecture (and later, Direct3D) to be extended to expose an

ISA interface. These extensions appeared as programmable vertex and fragment shaders within the graphics pipeline and now, with the introduction of CUDA, as a data-parallel ISA in near parity with that of the microprocessor. Although the cycle toward complete microprocessor-like versatility is not complete, the tremendous power of graphics hardware acceleration is more accessible than ever to programmers.

And what computational power it is! At this writing, the NVIDIA GeForce 8800 Ultra performs over 400 billion floating-point operations per second—more than the most powerful supercomputer available a decade ago, and five times more than today's most powerful microprocessor. The data-parallel programming model the Ultra supports allows its computational power to be harnessed without concern for the number of processors employed. This is critical, because while today's Ultra already includes over 100 processors, tomorrow's will include thousands, and then more. With no end in sight to the annual compounding of integrated circuit density known as Moore's Law, massively parallel systems are clearly the future of computing, with graphics hardware leading the way.

GPU Gems 3 is a collection of state-of-the-art GPU programming examples. It is about putting data-parallel processing to work. The first four sections focus on graphics-specific applications of GPUs in the areas of geometry, lighting and shadows, rendering, and image effects. Topics in the fifth and sixth sections broaden the scope by providing concrete examples of nongraphical applications that can now be addressed with data-parallel GPU technology. These applications are diverse, ranging from rigid-body simulation to fluid flow simulation, from virus signature matching to encryption and decryption, and from random number generation to computation of the Gaussian.

Where is this all leading? The cover art reminds us that the mind remains the most capable parallel computing system of all. A long-term goal of computer science is to achieve and, ultimately, to surpass the capabilities of the human mind. It's exciting to think that the computer graphics community, as we identify, address, and master the challenges of massively parallel computing, is contributing to the realization of this dream.

Kurt Akeley
Microsoft Research

Preface

It has been only three years since the first *GPU Gems* book was introduced, and some areas of real-time graphics have truly become ultrarealistic. Chapter 14, "Advanced Techniques for Realistic Real-Time Skin Rendering," illustrates this evolution beautifully, describing a skin rendering technique that works so well that the data acquisition and animation will become the most challenging problem in rendering human characters for the next couple of years.

All this progress has been fueled by a sustained rhythm of GPU innovation. These processing units continue to become faster and more flexible in their use. Today's GPUs can process enormous amounts of data and are used not only for rendering 3D scenes, but also for processing images or performing massively parallel computing, such as financial statistics or terrain analysis for finding new oil fields.

Whether they are used for computing or graphics, GPUs need a software interface to drive them, and we are in the midst of an important transition. The new generation of APIs brings additional orthogonality and exposes new capabilities such as generating geometry programmatically. On the computing side, the CUDA architecture lets developers use a C-like language to perform computing tasks rather than forcing the programmer to use the graphics pipeline. This architecture will allow developers without a graphics background to tap into the immense potential of the GPU.

More than 200 chapters were submitted by the GPU programming community, covering a large spectrum of GPU usage ranging from pure 3D rendering to nongraphics applications. Each of them went through a rigorous review process conducted both by NVIDIA's engineers and by external reviewers.

We were able to include 41 chapters, each of which went through another review, during which feedback from the editors and peer reviewers often significantly improved the content. Unfortunately, we could not include some excellent chapters, simply due to the space restriction of the book. It was difficult to establish the final table of contents, but we would like to thank everyone who sent a submission.

Intended Audience

For the graphics-related chapters, we expect the reader to be familiar with the fundamentals of computer graphics including graphics APIs such as DirectX and OpenGL, as well as their associated high-level programming languages, namely HLSL, GLSL, or Cg. Anyone working with interactive 3D applications will find in this book a wealth of applicable techniques for today's and tomorrow's GPUs.

Readers interested in computing and CUDA will find it best to know parallel computing concepts. C programming knowledge is also expected.

Trying the Code Samples

GPU Gems 3 comes with a disc that includes samples, movies, and other demonstrations of the techniques described in this book. You can also go to the book's Web page to find the latest updates and supplemental materials: **developer.nvidia.com/gpugems3**.

Acknowledgments

This book represents the dedication of many people—especially the numerous authors who submitted their most recent work to the GPU community by contributing to this book. Without a doubt, these inspirational and powerful chapters will help thousands of developers push the envelope in their applications.

Our section editors—Cyril Zeller, Evan Hart, Ignacio Castaño Aguado, Kevin Bjorke, Kevin Myers, and Nolan Goodnight—took on an invaluable role, providing authors with feedback and guidance to make the chapters as good as they could be. Without their expertise and contributions above and beyond their usual workload, this book could not have been published.

Ensuring the clarity of *GPU Gems 3* required numerous diagrams, illustrations, and screen shots. A lot of diligence went into unifying the graphic style of about 500 figures, and we thank Michael Fornalski and Jim Reed for their wonderful work on these. We are grateful to Huey Nguyen and his team for their support for many of our projects. We also thank Rory Loeb for his contribution to the amazing book cover design and many other graphic elements of the book.

We would also like to thank Catherine Kilkenny and Teresa Saffaie for tremendous help with copyediting as chapters were being worked on.

Randy Fernando, the editor of the previous *GPU Gems* books, shared his wealth of experience acquired in producing those volumes.

We are grateful to Kurt Akeley for writing our insightful and forward-looking foreword.

At Addison-Wesley, Peter Gordon, John Fuller, and Kim Boedigheimer managed this project to completion before handing the marketing aspect to Curt Johnson. Christopher Keane did fantastic work on the copyediting and typesetting.

The support from many executive staff members from NVIDIA was critical to this endeavor: Tony Tamasi and Dan Vivoli continually value the creation of educational material and provided the resources necessary to accomplish this project.

We are grateful to Jen-Hsun Huang for his continued support of the *GPU Gems* series and for creating an environment that encourages innovation and teamwork.

We also thank everyone at NVIDIA for their support and for continually building the technology that changes the way people think about computing.

Hubert Nguyen
NVIDIA Corporation

Contributors

Thomas Alexander, Polytime

Thomas Alexander cofounded Exapath, a startup focused on mapping networking algorithms onto GPGPUs. Previously he was at Juniper Networks working in the Infrastructure Product Group building core routers. Thomas has a Ph.D. in electrical engineering from Duke University, where he also worked on a custom-built parallel machine for ray casting.

Kavita Bala, Cornell University

Kavita Bala is an assistant professor in the Computer Science Department and Program of Computer Graphics at Cornell University. Bala specializes in scalable rendering for high-complexity illumination, interactive global illumination, perceptually based rendering, and image-based texturing. Bala has published research papers and served on the program committees of several conferences, including SIGGRAPH. In 2005, Bala cochaired the Eurographics Symposium on Rendering. She has coauthored the graduate-level textbook *Advanced Global Illumination, 2nd ed.* (A K Peters, 2006). Before Cornell, Bala received her S.M. and Ph.D. from the Massachusetts Institute of Technology, and her B.Tech. from the Indian Institute of Technology Bombay.

Kevin Bjorke, NVIDIA Corporation

Kevin Bjorke is a member of the Technology Evangelism group at NVIDIA, and continues his roles as editor and contributor to the previous volumes of *GPU Gems*. He has a broad background in production of both live-action and animated films, TV, advertising, theme park rides, print, and—of course—games. Kevin has been a regular speaker at events such as SIGGRAPH and GDC since the mid-1980s. His current work focuses on applying NVIDIA's horsepower and expertise to help developers fulfill their individual ambitions.

Jean-Yves Blanc, CGGVeritas

Jean-Yves Blanc received a Ph.D. in applied mathematics in 1991 from the Institut National Polytechnique de Grenoble, France. He joined CGG in 1992, where he introduced and developed parallel processing for high-performance computing seismic applications. He is now in charge of IT strategy for the Processing and Reservoir product line.

Jim Blinn, Microsoft Research

Jim Blinn began doing computer graphics in 1968 while an undergraduate at the University of Michigan. In 1974 he became a graduate student at the University of Utah, where he did research in specular lighting models, bump mapping, and environment/reflection mapping and received a Ph.D. in 1977. He then went to JPL and produced computer graphics animations for various space missions to Jupiter, Saturn, and Uranus, as well as for Carl Sagan's PBS series "Cosmos" and for the Annenberg/CPB-funded project "The Mechanical Universe," a 52-part telecourse to teach college-level physics. During these productions he developed several other techniques, including work in cloud simulation, displacement mapping, and a modeling scheme variously called *blobbies* or *metaballs*. Since 1987 he has written a regular column in the *IEEE Computer Graphics and Applications* journal, where he describes mathematical techniques used in computer graphics. He has just published his third volume of collected articles from this series. In 1995 he joined Microsoft Research as a Graphics Fellow. He is a MacArthur Fellow, a member of the National Academy of Engineering, has an honorary Doctor of Fine Arts degree from Otis Parsons School of Design, and has received both the SIGGRAPH Computer Graphics Achievement Award (1983) and the Steven A. Coons Award (1999).

George Borshukov, Electronic Arts

George Borshukov is a CG supervisor at Electronic Arts. He holds an M.S. from the University of California, Berkeley, where he was one of the creators of *The Campanile Movie* and real-time demo (1997). He was technical designer for the "bullet time" sequences in *The Matrix* (1999) and received an Academy Scientific and Technical Achievement Award for the image-based rendering technology used in the film. Borshukov led the development of photoreal digital actors for *The Matrix* sequels (2003) and received a Visual Effects Society Award for the design and application of the Universal Capture system in those films. Other film credits include *What Dreams May Come* (1998), *Mission: Impossible 2* (2000), and *Michael Jordan to the Max* (2000). He is also a co-inventor of the UV pelting approach for parameterization and seamless texturing of polygonal or subdivision surfaces. He joined Electronic Arts in 2004 to focus on setting a new standard for facial capture, animation, and rendering in next-generation interactive entertainment. He conceived the *Fight Night Round 3* concept and the Tiger Woods tech demos presented at Sony's E3 events in 2005 and 2006.

Tamy Boubekeur, LaBRI–INRIA, University of Bordeaux

Tamy Boubekeur is a third-year Ph.D. student in computer science at INRIA in Bordeaux, France. He received an M.Sc. in computer science from the University of Bordeaux in 2004. His current research focuses on 3D geometry processing and real-time rendering. He has developed new algorithms and data structures for the 3D acquisition pipeline, publishing several scientific papers in the fields of efficient processing and interactive editing of large 3D objects, hierarchical space subdivision structures, point-based graphics, and real-time surface refinement methods. He also teaches geometric modeling and virtual reality at the University of Bordeaux.

Ralph Brunner, Apple

Ralph Brunner graduated from the Swiss Federal Institute of Technology (ETH) Zürich with an M.Sc. degree in computer science. He left the country after the bear infestation made the major cities uninhabitable and has been working in California on the graphics stack of Mac OS X since then.

Iain Cantlay, NVIDIA Corporation

Iain started his career in flight simulation, when 250 polys per frame was state of the art. With the advent of consumer-level 3D hardware, he moved to writing game engines, with published titles including *Machines* and *MotoGP 3*. In 2005 he moved to the Developer Technology group at NVIDIA, which is the perfect place to combine his passions for games and 3D graphics.

Ignacio Castaño Aguado, NVIDIA Corporation

Ignacio Castaño Aguado is an engineer in the Developer Technology group at NVIDIA. When not playing Go against his coworkers or hiking across the Santa Cruz Mountains with his son, Ignacio spends his time solving computer graphics problems that fascinate him and helping developers take advantage of the latest GPU technology. Before joining NVIDIA, Ignacio worked for several game companies, including Crytek, Relic Entertainment, and Oddworld Inhabitants.

Mark Colbert, University of Central Florida

Mark Colbert is a Ph.D. student at the University of Central Florida working in the Media Convergence Lab. He received both his B.S. and his M.S. in computer science from the University of Central Florida in 2004 and 2006. His current research focuses on user interfaces for interactive material and lighting design.

Keenan Crane, University of Illinois

Keenan recently completed a B.S. in computer science at the University of Illinois at Urbana-Champaign, where he did research on GPU algorithms, mesh parameterization, and motion capture. As an intern on the NVIDIA Demo Team, he worked on the "Mad Mod Mike" and "Smoke in a Box" demos. His foray into graphics programming took place in 1991 at Nishimachi International School in Tokyo, Japan, where he studied the nuances of the LogoWriter turtle language. This summer he will travel to Kampala, Uganda, to participate in a service project through Volunteers for Peace.

Eugene d'Eon, NVIDIA Corporation

Eugene d'Eon has been writing demos at NVIDIA since 2000, when he first joined the team as an intern, spending three months modeling, rigging, and rotoscoping the short film "Luxo Jr." for a real-time demo that was only shown once. After quickly switching to a more forgiving programming position, he has since been employing the most mathematical, overly sophisticated models available to solve the simplest of shading and simulation problems in NVIDIA's real-time demos. He constantly struggles between writing a physically correct shader and just settling for what "looks good." Eugene received an Honours B.Math. from the University of Waterloo, applied mathematics and computer science double major, and is occasionally known for his musical abilities (piano and *Guitar Hero*) and ability to juggle "Eric's Extension." Research interests include light transport, scattering, reflectance models, skin shading, theoretical physics, and mathematical logic. He never drives faster than c, and unlike most particles in the universe, neither his position nor his momentum can be known with any certainty. He never votes for someone who doesn't have a clear stance on the Axiom of Choice. Eugene uses Elixir guitar strings.

Bernard Deschizeaux, CGGVeritas

Bernard Deschizeaux received a master's degree in high energy physics in 1988 and a Ph.D. in particle physics in 1991. Since then he has worked for CGG, a French service company for the oil and gas industry, where he applies his high-performance computing skills and physics knowledge to solve seismic processing challenges. His positions within CGG have varied from development to high-performance computing and algorithm research. He is now in charge of a GPGPU project developing an industrial solution based on GPU clusters.

Franck Diard, NVIDIA Corporation

Franck Diard is a senior software architect at NVIDIA. He received a Ph.D. in computer science from the University of Nice Sophia Antipolis (France) in 1998. Starting with vector balls and copper lists on Amiga in the late 1980s, he then programmed on UNIX for a decade with Reyes rendering, ray tracing, and computer vision before transitioning to Windows kernel drivers at NVIDIA. His interests have always been around scalability (programming multi-core, multi-GPU render farms) applied to image processing and graphics rendering. His main contribution to NVIDIA has been the SLI technology.

Frank Doepke, Apple

After discovering that one can make more people's lives miserable by writing buggy software than becoming a tax collector, Frank Doepke decided to become a software developer. Realizing that evil coding was wrong, he set sail from Germany to the New World and has since been tracking graphic gems at Apple.

Henrik Dohlmann, 3Dfacto R&D

From 1999 to 2002, Henrik Dohlmann worked as a research assistant in the Image Group at the Department of Computer Science, University of Copenhagen, from which he later received his Cand. Scient. degree in computer science. Next, he took part in an industrial collaboration between the 3D-Lab at Copenhagen University's School of Dentistry and Image House. He moved to 3Dfacto R&D in 2005, where he now works as a software engineer.

Bryan Dudash, NVIDIA Corporation

Bryan entered the games industry in 1997, working for various companies in Seattle, including Sierra Online and Escape Factory. He has a master's degree from the University of Washington. In 2003 he joined NVIDIA and began teaching (and learning) high-end, real-time computer graphics. Having studied Japanese since 2000, Bryan convinced NVIDIA in 2004 to move him to Tokyo, where he has been supporting APAC developers ever since. If you are ever in Tokyo, give him a ring.

Kenny Erleben, University of Copenhagen

In 2001 Kenny Erleben received his Cand. Scient. degree in computer science from the Department of Computer Science, University of Copenhagen. He then worked as a full-time researcher at 3Dfacto A/S before beginning his Ph.D. studies later in 2001. In 2004 he spent three months at the Department of Mathematics, University of Iowa. He received his Ph.D. in 2005 and soon thereafter was appointed assistant professor at the Department of Computer Science, University of Copenhagen.

Ryan Geiss, NVIDIA Corporation

Ryan has been a pioneer in music visualization for many years. While working at Nullsoft, he wrote many plug-ins for Winamp, most notably the popular MilkDrop visualizer. More recently, he spent several years as a member of the NVIDIA Demo Team, creating the "GeoForms" and "Cascades" demos and doing other GPU research projects.

Nolan Goodnight, NVIDIA Corporation

Nolan Goodnight is a software engineer at NVIDIA. He works in the CUDA software group doing application and driver development. Before joining NVIDIA he was a member of the computer graphics group at the University of Virginia, where he did research in GPU algorithms and approximation methods for rendering with precomputed light transport. Nolan's interest in the fundamentals of computer graphics grew out of his work in geometric modeling for industrial design. He holds a bachelor's degree in physics and a master's degree in computer science.

Larry Gritz, NVIDIA Corporation

Larry Gritz is director and chief architect of NVIDIA's Gelato software, a hardware-accelerated film-quality renderer. Prior graphics work includes being the author of BMRT; cofounder and vice president of Exluna, Inc. (later acquired by NVIDIA), and lead developer of their Entropy renderer; head of Pixar's rendering research group; a main contributor to PhotoRealistic RenderMan; coauthor of the book *Advanced RenderMan: Creating CGI for Motion Pictures*; and occasional technical director on several films and commercials. Larry has a B.S. from Cornell University and an M.S. and Ph.D. from The George Washington University.

John Hable, Electronic Arts

John Hable is a rendering engineer at Electronic Arts. He graduated from Georgia Tech with a B.S. and M.S. in computer science, where he solved the problem of reducing the rendering time of Boolean combinations of triangle meshes from exponential to quadratic time. His recent work focuses on the compression problems raised by trying to render high-quality facial animation in computer games. Currently he is working on a new EA title in Los Angeles.

Earl Hammon, Jr., Infinity Ward

Earl Hammon, Jr., is a lead software engineer at Infinity Ward, where he assisted a team of talented developers to create the multiplatinum and critically acclaimed titles *Call of Duty 2* and *Call of Duty*. He worked on *Medal of Honor: Allied Assault* prior to becoming a founding member of Infinity Ward. He graduated from Stanford University with an M.S. in electrical engineering, preceded by a B.S.E.E. from the University of Tulsa. His current project is *Call of Duty 4: Modern Warfare*.

Takahiro Harada, University of Tokyo

Takahiro Harada is an associate professor at the University of Tokyo. He received an M.S. in engineering from the University of Tokyo in 2006. His current research interests include physically based simulation, real-time simulation, and general-purpose GPU computation.

Mark Harris, NVIDIA Corporation

Mark Harris is a member of the Developer Technology team at NVIDIA in London, working with software developers all over the world to push the latest in GPU technology for graphics and high-performance computing. His primary research interests include parallel computing, general-purpose computation on GPUs, and physically based simulation. Mark earned his Ph.D. in computer science from the University of North Carolina at Chapel Hill in 2003 and his B.S. from the University of Notre Dame in 1998. Mark founded and maintains www.GPGPU.org, a Web site dedicated to general-purpose computation on GPUs.

Evan Hart, NVIDIA Corporation

Evan Hart is a software engineer in the Developer Technology group at NVIDIA. Evan got his start in real-time 3D in 1997 working with visual simulations. Since graduating from The Ohio State University in 1998, he has worked to develop and improve techniques for real-time rendering, having his hands in everything from games to CAD programs, with a bit of drivers on the side. Evan is a frequent speaker at GDC and he has contributed to chapters in the *Game Programming Gems* and *ShaderX* series of books.

Miloš Hašan, Cornell University

Miloš Hašan graduated with a degree in computer science from Comenius University in Bratislava, Slovakia. Currently he is a Ph.D. student in the Computer Science Department at Cornell University. His research interests include global illumination, GPU rendering, and numerical computations.

Jared Hoberock, University of Illinois at Urbana-Champaign

Jared Hoberock is a graduate student at the University of Illinois at Urbana-Champaign. He has worked two summers at NVIDIA as an intern and is a two-time recipient of the NVIDIA Graduate Fellowship. He enjoys spending time writing rendering software.

Lee Howes, Imperial College London

Lee Howes graduated with an M.Eng. in computing from Imperial College London in 2005 and is currently working toward a Ph.D. at Imperial. Lee's research relates to computing with FPGAs and GPUs and has included work with FFTs and financial simulation. As a distraction from education and to dabble in the realms of reality, Lee has worked briefly with Philips and NVIDIA.

Yuntao Jia, University of Illinois at Urbana-Champaign

Yuntao Jia is currently pursuing a Ph.D. in computer science at the University of Illinois at Urbana-Champaign. He is very interested in computer graphics, and his current research interests include realistic rendering (especially on the GPU), video and image processing, and graph visualizations.

Alexander Keller, Ulm University

Alexander Keller studied computer science at the University of Kaiserslautern from 1988 to 1993. He then joined the Numerical Algorithms Group at the same university and defended his Ph.D. thesis on Friday, the 13th of June, 1997. In 1998 he was appointed scientific advisor of mental images. Among four calls in 2003, he chose to become a full professor for computer graphics at the University of Ulm in Germany. His research interests include quasi-Monte Carlo methods, photorealistic image synthesis, ray tracing, and scientific computing. His 1997 SIGGRAPH paper "Instant Radiosity" can be considered one of the roots of GPGPU computing.

Alexander Kharlamov, NVIDIA Corporation

Alex is an undergraduate in the Department of Computational Mathematics and Cybernetics at the Moscow State University. He became interested in video games at the age of ten and decided that nothing else interested him that much. Currently he works as a member of NVIDIA's Developer Technology team implementing new techniques and effects for games and general-purpose computation on GPUs.

Peter Kipfer, Havok

Peter Kipfer is a software engineer at Havok, where he works as part of the Havok FX team that is pioneering work in large-scale real-time physics simulation in highly parallel environments, such as multi-core CPUs or GPUs. He received his Ph.D. in computer science from the Universität of Erlangen-Nürnberg in 2003 for his work in the KONWIHR supercomputing project. He also worked as a postdoctoral researcher at the Technische Universität München, focusing on general-purpose computing and geometry processing on the GPU.

Rusty Koonce, NCsoft Corporation

Rusty Koonce graduated from the University of Texas at Dallas with a degree in physics. He has worked on multiple shipped video game titles across a wide range of platforms, including console, PC, and Mac. Computer graphics has held his interest since his first computer, a TRS-80. Today he calls Austin, Texas, home, where he enjoys doing his part to "Keep Austin Weird."

Kees van Kooten, Playlogic Game Factory

Kees van Kooten is a software developer for Playlogic Game Factory. In 2006 he graduated summa cum laude for his master's degree at the Eindhoven University of Technology. The result of his master's project can be found in this book. His interests are closely related to the topics of his master's research: 3D graphics and real-time simulations. After working hours, Kees can often be found playing drums with "real" musicians.

Jaroslav Křivánek, Czech Technical University in Prague

Jaroslav Křivánek is an assistant professor at the Czech Technical University in Prague. He received his Ph.D. from IRISA/INRIA Rennes and the Czech Technical University (joint degree) in 2005. In 2003 and 2004 he was a research associate at the University of Central Florida. He received a master's in computer science from the Czech Technical University in Prague in 2001.

Bunny Laden, Apple

Bunny Laden graduated from the University of Washington with a Special Individual Ph.D. in cognitive science and music in 1989. She joined Apple in 1997, where she now writes documentation for Quartz, Core Image, Quartz Composer, and other Mac OS X technologies. She coauthored *Programming with Quartz* (Morgan Kaufmann, 2006) and *Learning Carbon* (O'Reilly, 2001). In her former life as an academician, she wrote articles on music cognition, musical acoustics, and other assorted topics.

Andrew Lauritzen, University of Waterloo

Andrew Lauritzen recently received his B.Math. in computer science and is now completing a master's degree in computer graphics at the University of Waterloo. To date, he has completed a variety of research in graphics, as well as theoretical physics. His current research interests include lighting and shadowing algorithms, deferred rendering, and graphics engine design. Andrew is also a developer at RapidMind, where he works with GPUs and other high-performance parallel computers.

Scott Le Grand, NVIDIA Corporation

Scott is a senior engineer on the CUDA software team at NVIDIA. His previous commercial projects include the game *BattleSphere* for the Atari Jaguar; Genesis, the first molecular modeling system for home computers, for the Atari ST; and Folderol, the first distributed computing project targeted at the protein folding problem. Scott has been writing video games since 1971, when he played a Star Trek game on a mainframe and he was instantly hooked. In a former life, he picked up a B.S. in biology from Siena College and a Ph.D. in biochemistry from The Pennsylvania State University. In addition, he wrote a chapter for *ShaderX* and coedited a book on computational methods of protein structure prediction.

Ignacio Llamas, NVIDIA Corporation

Ignacio Llamas is a software engineer in NVIDIA's Developer Technology group. Before joining NVIDIA, Ignacio was a Ph.D. student at Georgia Tech's College of Computing, where he did research on several topics within computer graphics. In addition to the exciting work he does at NVIDIA, he also enjoys snowboarding.

Charles Loop, Microsoft Research

Charles Loop works for Microsoft Research in Redmond, Washington. He received an M.S. in mathematics from the University of Utah in 1987 and a Ph.D. in computer science from the University of Washington in 1992. His graphics research has focused primarily on the representation and rendering of smooth free-form shapes, including subdivision surfaces, polynomial splines and patches, and algebraic curves and surfaces. Charles also works on interactive modeling and computer vision techniques. Lately, his efforts have gone into GPU algorithms for the display of curved objects.

Tristan Lorach, NVIDIA Corporation

Since graduating in 1995 with a master's in computer science applied on art and aesthetic, Tristan Lorach has developed a series of 3D real-time interactive installations for exhibitions and events all over the world. From the creation of a specific engine for digging complex galleries into a virtual solid, to the conception of new 3D human interfaces for public events, Tristan has always wanted to fill the gap between technology and artistic or ergonomic ideas. Most of his projects (such as "L'homme Transformé" and "Le Tunnel sous l'Atlantique") were presented in well-known exhibition centers like Beaubourg and Cité des Sciences in Paris. Now Tristan works at NVIDIA on the Technical Developer Relations team, based in Santa Clara, California.

David Luebke, NVIDIA Corporation

David Luebke is a research scientist at NVIDIA. He received an M.S. and Ph.D. in computer science in 1998 from the University of North Carolina under Frederick P. Brooks, Jr., following a B.A. in chemistry from the Colorado College. David spent eight years on the faculty of the University of Virginia before leaving in 2006 to help start the NVIDIA Research group. His research interests include real-time rendering, illumination models, and graphics architecture.

Kenny Mitchell, Electronic Arts

Kenny is a lead engine programmer at Electronic Arts' UK Studio. His Ph.D. introduced the use of real-time 3D for information visualization on consumer hardware, including a novel recursive perspective projection technique. Over the past ten years he has shipped games using high-end graphics technologies including voxels, PN patches, displacement mapping and clipmaps. In between shipping games for EA's flagship Harry Potter franchise, he is also involved in developing new intellectual properties.

Jefferson Montgomery, Electronic Arts

Jefferson Montgomery holds a B.A.Sc. in engineering physics and an M.Sc. in computer science from the University of British Columbia. He is currently a member of the World Wide Visualization Group at Electronic Arts, tasked with adapting advanced techniques to the resource constraints faced by current game teams and producing real-time demonstrations such as those at Sony's E3 presentations in 2005 and 2006.

Kevin Myers, NVIDIA Corporation

Kevin Myers is part of the Developer Technology group at NVIDIA, where he helps game developers make full use of the GPU. He regularly presents at GDC and has been published in a previous *ShaderX* book. He is native to California and received his B.S. in computer science from Santa Clara University. His favorite food is the sandwich, especially the Cuban Sandwich—but only if it's greasy enough.

Hubert Nguyen, NVIDIA Corporation

Hubert Nguyen works at NVIDIA, where he manages the developer education program, which helps developers push the graphical envelope of their applications. Prior to that, he spent his time on NVIDIA's Demo Team, searching for novel effects that showed off the features of the latest GPUs. His work appears on the previous *GPU Gems* covers. Before joining NVIDIA, Hubert was at 3dfx interactive, the creators of Voodoo Graphics, as a developer technology engineer. He had his first contact with 3dfx while working on 3D engines in the R&D department of Cryo Interactive, a video game company in Paris. Hubert started to program 3D graphics in 1991 when he was involved in the European demoscene, where he and his "Impact Studios" team ranked number one at the world's largest PC demo competition: "The Party 1994," in Denmark.

Lars Nyland, NVIDIA Corporation

Lars Nyland is a senior architect at NVIDIA, focusing on computationally related issues for GPU architectures. He earned his Ph.D. and A.M. in computer science at Duke University (1991 and 1983, respectively). He followed his graduate work with a 12-year research position at the University of North Carolina, working on parallel computing (languages, compilers, algorithms, and applications) and image-based rendering, where he developed the DeltaSphere range scanner device (now sold by 3rdTech). Prior to joining NVIDIA in 2005, he was an associate professor of computer science at the Colorado School of Mines in Golden, Colorado.

Oskari Nyman, Helsinki University of Technology

Oskari Nyman is an undergraduate student in the Computer Science and Engineering Department at Helsinki University of Technology. His roots belong to the mod scene, where he first started programming at the age of fifteen. His interests lie in real-time rendering and game programming in general.

Manuel M. Oliveira, Instituto de Informática–UFRGS

Manuel M. Oliveira is a faculty member at UFRGS, in Brazil. He received his Ph.D. in computer science from the University of North Carolina at Chapel Hill in 2000. Before joining UFRGS, he was an assistant professor at SUNY Stony Brook from 2000 to 2002. His research interests include real-time rendering, representation and rendering of surface details, surface reconstruction, and image-based rendering.

John D. Owens, University of California, Davis

John D. Owens is an assistant professor of electrical and computer engineering at the University of California, Davis, where he leads research projects in graphics hardware/software and GPGPU. Prior to his appointment at Davis, John earned his Ph.D. (2002) and M.S. (1997) in electrical engineering from Stanford University. At Stanford he was an architect of the Imagine Stream Processor and a member of the Concurrent VLSI Architecture Group and the Computer Graphics Laboratory. John earned his B.S. in electrical engineering and computer sciences from the University of California, Berkeley, in 1995.

Gustavo Patow, University of Girona

Gustavo Patow received a degree in physics from the Universidad Nacional de La Plata, Argentina, and earned his Ph.D. at the Universitat Politècnica de Catalunya at Barcelona, Spain, under the supervision of Xavier Pueyo and Àlvar Vinacua. His thesis topic was the inverse design of reflector surfaces for luminaire design, and his current research continues both in the inverse rendering set of problems and the efficient usage of modern GPUs to achieve real-time photorealistic rendering. He currently holds an associate professor position at the University of Girona, Spain.

Fabio Pellacini, Dartmouth College

Fabio Pellacini is an assistant professor in computer science at Dartmouth College. His research focuses on algorithms for interactive, high-quality rendering of complex environments and for artist-friendly material and lighting design to support more effective content creation. Prior to joining academia, Pellacini worked at Pixar Animation Studios on lighting algorithms, where he received credits on various movie productions. Pellacini received his Laurea degree in physics from the University of Parma (Italy), and his M.S. and Ph.D. in computer science from Cornell University.

Fabio Policarpo, Perpetual Entertainment

Fabio Policarpo is a senior software engineer working on Perpetual Entertainment's latest project: Star Trek Online. He graduated in computer science from Universidade Federal Fluminense in Rio, Brazil, and is the author of a few game programming books, including a chapter in *GPU Gems*. His main research interests are related to real-time special effects for games, including graphics, physics, and animation.

Jan Prins, University of North Carolina at Chapel Hill

Jan Prins is professor and chair of the Department of Computer Science at the University of North Carolina at Chapel Hill. He was a cofounder of Digital Effects Inc. and contributed to the film *Tron*. Prins received his Ph.D. in 1987 in computer science from Cornell University. He has been on the computer science faculty at UNC Chapel Hill since 1987 and is a member of the bioinformatics and computational biology program. He was a visiting professor at the Institute of Theoretical Computer Science at ETH Zürich from 1996 to 1997, in the area of scientific computing. His research interests center on high-performance computing, including algorithm design, parallel computer architecture, programming languages, and applications.

Eric Risser, Columbia University

Eric Risser is a graduate student of computer science at Columbia University. Previously he attended the University of Central Florida, where he had been involved with real-time graphics programming and research for the better part of four years. The bulk of his expertise is in the area of image-based, real-time rendering techniques centering on per-pixel displacement mapping. His research has been presented at the Symposium on Interactive 3D Graphics and Games, GDC, and SIGGRAPH. For more information, visit www.ericrisser.com.

Gilberto Rosado, Rainbow Studios

Gilberto Rosado is a graduate of DigiPen Institute of Technology, where he studied video game programming for four years. While at DigiPen, Gil was the graphics programmer on the 2005 Independent Games Festival finalist, *Kisses*. Gil is currently at Rainbow Studios, where he works as a graphics and technology programmer on killer new games. He has also been published in the book *ShaderX4*. When not playing the latest games, you might find Gil at the gym working out or at the local dance studio practicing his Salsa moves.

Christophe Schlick, LaBRI–INRIA, University of Bordeaux

Christophe Schlick is a professor in computer science at the University of Bordeaux 2 (France), where he has headed the Applied Mathematics and Computer Science Department during the last five years. He received his Ph.D. in 1992 for his work on BRDF models and Monte Carlo techniques, and his research interests have embraced many aspects of computer graphics, including participating media, procedural textures, spline and wavelet curves and surfaces, implicit surfaces, and more recently, point-based modeling and rendering. He currently holds a senior researcher position at INRIA, the French National Institute for Research in Computer Science and Control.

Elizabeth Seamans, Juniper Networks

Elizabeth Seamans completed her Ph.D. in computer science at Stanford University in 2005 before cofounding Exapath to write GPU-accelerated scanning libraries. She is now a software engineer at Juniper Networks, where she keeps parallel computing resources busy.

Shubhabrata Sengupta, University of California, Davis

Shubho is a Ph.D. student in the computer science department at University of California, Davis, where he is a member of the Institute for Data Analysis and Visualization. His current research focuses on parallel data structures and algorithms and their applications to various areas of computer graphics. Shubho received his M.Sc. and B.Sc. in mathematics from Indian Institute of Technology, Kharagpur, in 1998 and 1996, respectively.

Tiago Sousa, Crytek

Tiago Sousa is a self-taught game and graphics programmer who has worked at Crytek as an R&D graphics programmer for the last four years. He has worked on the "Far Cry: The Project" demo and most recently on *Crysis*, where he developed most of the visual effects, including water/underwater rendering and all post-effects, such as motion blur and camera environmental effects. Before joining Crytek, he cofounded a pioneering game development team in Portugal and very briefly studied computer science at Instituto Superior Técnico, which he hopes to finish one day. He spends his time mostly thinking out of the box, inventing original and creative techniques for making pretty images.

Yury Stepanenko, NVIDIA Corporation

In 1998 Yury graduated from Zaporozhye State Engineering Academy (Ukraine), Department of Electronics, where he specialized in microprocessor systems. As a student he became keen on computer graphics and low-level optimization and decided to make this hobby his trade. He now works at the NVIDIA Moscow office, where he is engaged in development of new graphics technologies.

Martin Stich, mental images

Martin Stich is a graphics software engineer at mental images in Berlin, where he works on rendering algorithms for the RealityServer product. His research interests include real-time rendering, rasterization, and ray tracing. Before joining the company in 2006, he developed real-time image generation software for air traffic control simulation systems. He holds a degree in computer science from the University of Ulm.

Hanqiu Sun, The Chinese University of Hong Kong

Hanqiu Sun received her M.S. in electrical engineering from the University of British Columbia and her Ph.D. in computer science from the University of Alberta, Canada. She has published more than one hundred refereed technical papers in prestigious VR/CG journals, book chapters, and international conferences. She has served as guest editor of MIT's *Presence* and *Journal of Computer Animation and Virtual Worlds*, program cochair of ACM VRST 2002, organization cochair of Pacific Graphics 2005 and CGI 2006, conference general chair of ACM VRCIA 2006, and a member of numerous international program committees. Her current research interests include virtual and augmented reality, interactive graphics/animation, hypermedia, computer-assisted surgery, Internet-based navigation, telemedicine, and realistic haptic simulation.

László Szirmay-Kalos, Budapest University of Technology and Economics

László Szirmay-Kalos is the head of the computer graphics group of the Faculty of Electrical Engineering and Information Technology at the Budapest University of Technology and Economics. He received a Ph.D. in 1992 and full professorship in 2001 in computer graphics. He has also spent some time at the University of Girona, the Technical University of Vienna, and the University of Minnesota as a guest lecturer or researcher. His research area is Monte Carlo global illumination algorithms and their GPU implementation. He has published more than one hundred papers, scripts, and book chapters on this topic. He is the leader of the illumination package of the GameTools EU-FP6 project. He is a member of Eurographics, where he served three years on the executive committee.

Sarah Tariq, NVIDIA Corporation

Sarah is a software engineer on NVIDIA's Developer Technology team, where she works primarily on implementing new rendering and simulation techniques that exploit the latest hardware, and helping game developers to incorporate these techniques into their games. Before joining NVIDIA, Sarah was a Ph.D. candidate at Georgia Tech, where she also got her master's degree in computer science.

Diogo Teixeira, Move Interactive

Diogo Teixeira is a computer graphics enthusiast with special interests in game development. His appetite for low-level 2D and 3D computer graphics grew while he was still in high school. Being an avid gamer eventually led him to start his game development career in early 2000, when he joined a pioneer Portuguese team creating a third-person action adventure called *Yamabushi*. In 2003 he was a project lead in a community game project called *RCmania*, a multiplatform racing game. In 2005 he interrupted his studies at the University of Lisbon to join Move Interactive and work on a game called *Ugo Volt* for PC and next-generation consoles.

Alex Telea, Eindhoven University of Technology

Alex Telea received his Ph.D. in visualization in 2000 from the Eindhoven University of Technology, where he currently works as assistant professor in the field of visualization and computer graphics. His main research interests are data visualization, texture-based rendering methods, numerical methods for image and data processing, shape simplification, and software visualization and reverse engineering. He has coauthored more than 70 papers in international publications.

David Thomas, Imperial College London

David Thomas received his M.Eng. and Ph.D. in computer science from Imperial College in 2001 and 2006, respectively. He likes Imperial so much that he stayed on, and is now a postdoctoral researcher in the Custom Computing group. Research interests include FPGA-based Monte Carlo simulations, algorithms and architectures for uniform and nonuniform random number generation, and financial computing.

Ken Turkowski, Adobe Systems

Ken Turkowski started his career by designing programmable hardware for graphics acceleration, and then developing algorithms that utilized the hardware well. An applied mathematician at heart, he then concentrated his efforts on developing efficient software for a variety of graphical applications: texture mapping, antialiasing, shading, panoramas, image processing, video transformations, camera/lens modeling, collisions, surface modeling, and outline fonts—at companies such as Ampex, Compression Labs, CADLINC, Apple, Media Machines, Fakespace Labs, Adobe, and Google. He specializes in algorithms that are faster, are more robust, and use less memory than traditional algorithms. He is active in SIGGRAPH as an Electronic Theater contributor, paper author, and Silicon Valley Chapter chair.

Tamás Umenhoffer, Budapest University of Technology and Economics

Tamás Umenhoffer is a Ph.D. student at the Faculty of Electrical Engineering and Information Technology at the Budapest University of Technology and Economics. His research topic is the computation of global illumination effects on the GPU. His submission was a finalist at the Graphics Meets Games Competition of EG 2006. He is an active member of the GameTools EU-FP6 project.

Gino van den Bergen, Playlogic Game Factory

Gino van den Bergen is lead programmer at Playlogic Game Factory. He holds a Ph.D. in computer graphics from Eindhoven University of Technology. He is the author of the book *Collision Detection in Interactive 3D Environments* (Morgan Kaufmann). Gino is the creator of SOLID, a software library for collision detection, which has been applied successfully in top-selling game console titles and CAM applications.

Carsten Wächter, mental images

Carsten Wächter studied computer science at Ulm University from 1998 to 2004. He then pursued his Ph.D. studies under the supervision of Alexander Keller; he started to work at mental images in 2007. His research interests include real-time ray tracing, global illumination, and quasi-Monte Carlo methods. He has been an active member of the European demo scene since 1999.

Takeshi Yamanouchi, SEGA Corporation

Takeshi Yamanouchi graduated from Kyushu Institute of Technology with a master's degree in computer science in 1995. That same year he joined SEGA Corporation and has since been engaged in the development of arcade games at AM R&D Dept. #2. His most recent work was on graphics, shaders, and network programming for *Virtua Fighter 5*. His latest interest is in the face of his daughter, who is now one year old. He wonders if he can implement this beautiful subsurface scattering in a 60 fps real-time game. While writing his chapter, he was helped with his English by Robert Gould, who belongs to AMplus R&D Dept.

Cyril Zeller, NVIDIA Corporation

Cyril Zeller works in the Developer Technology group at NVIDIA, where he explores and promotes all the new ways of leveraging modern GPUs in real-time graphics and simulation, as well as in all the new application fields opened up by CUDA. Before joining NVIDIA, Cyril was developing games at Electronic Arts. He received a Ph.D. in computer vision from École Polytechnique, France.

Fan Zhang, The Chinese University of Hong Kong

Fan Zhang received his B.S. and M.S. in computational mathematics from Jilin University, China, in 2000 and 2002, respectively. He is currently a Ph.D. candidate in the Department of Computer Science and Engineering, The Chinese University of Hong Kong. His main research interests include real-time shadow rendering and GPU-based rendering techniques.

Renaldas Zioma, Electronic Arts/Digital Illusions CE

Renaldas Zioma is working on rendering technologies for the upcoming *Battlefield: Bad Company* at EA/Digital Illusions CE. In the past he developed real-time strategy games, some previous-gen console games, and sensorless motion recognition software; he even coded a couple of small games using ZX Spectrum assembly when he was a kid. Currently he is wasting his spare time by rendering things on homebrew PSP devkit and Amiga 1200, mostly with guys from The Black Lotus demogroup. Otherwise he would go hiking! He has previously published articles in *ShaderX2*, *ShaderX4*, and *AI Game Programming Wisdom 3*.

GPU Gems 3

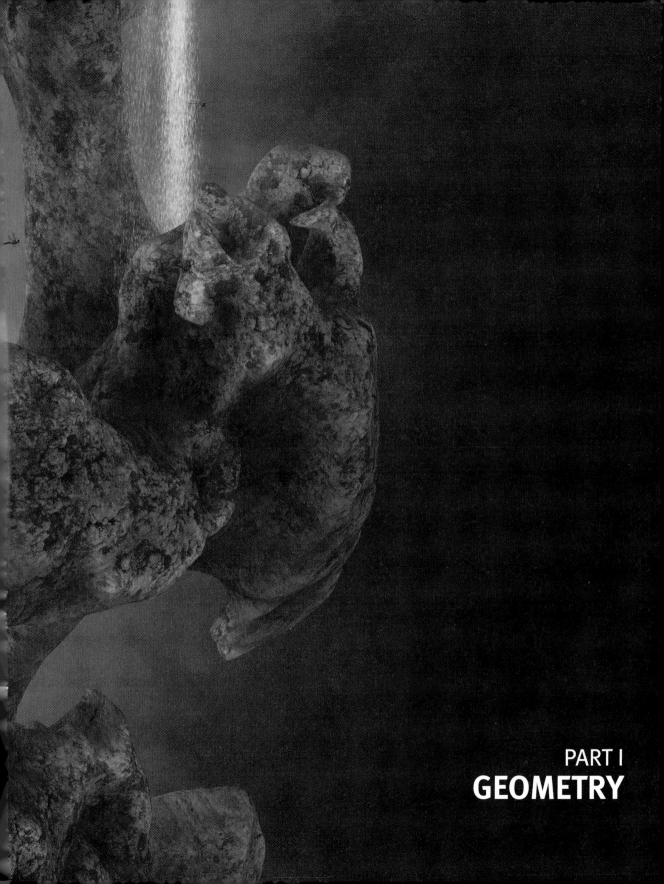

Although pixels and pixel shaders often get the attention, geometry is "where it all starts." Without geometry, we would find lighting, shadows, and reflections quite uninteresting. Why? Because raising the complexity of the underlying geometry also raises the quality of the pixel. Thus the theme for this part of the book could best be described as "complexity," because all its techniques use the GPU to enhance the complexity of the scene in ways that previously required CPU intervention. Most of these approaches are made possible by the recent advances in graphics hardware exposed by DirectX 10, with capabilities like the geometry shader, stream out, and buffer fetches. However, many topics also improve techniques already feasible with previous hardware.

Chapter 1, "Generating Complex Procedural Terrains Using the GPU," approaches geometric complexity from the aspect of procedural generation. **Ryan Geiss** of NVIDIA Corporation demonstrates how to utilize many of the new hardware capabilities to generate terrain with features typically not seen when procedural synthesis is used. Of particular interest, Geiss suggests how to control procedural terrains to avoid the single largest practical hurdle of procedural generation.

Chapter 4, "Next-Generation SpeedTree Rendering," covers rendering the geometry for another outdoor environment: trees. **Alexander Kharlamov, Iain Cantlay,** and **Yury Stepanenko** of NVIDIA concentrate on improving the detail in trees that are relatively close to the viewer. This chapter accounts for all rendering aspects, from enhancing the geometry to improving lighting and shadows.

Expanding the tree theme, **Chapter 6, "GPU-Generated Procedural Wind Animations for Trees"** by **Renaldas Zioma** of Electronic Arts/Digital Illusions CE, demonstrates how to upgrade the animation effects of trees. The procedural wind effects allow a developer to take trees beyond the simple rustling that many applications are limited to today for tree animations.

The ability to handle massive amounts of simpler animation is also important for improving complexity. **"Animated Crowd Rendering"** in **Chapter 2** addresses just this need. Here, **Bryan Dudash** of NVIDIA shows how to utilize DirectX 10 features to animate an entire stadium full of characters while keeping the CPU overhead manageable.

More ideas on improving characters are provided in the chapter on blend shapes, where NVIDIA's **Tristan Lorach** shows how new hardware capabilities are useful for creating rich animation. **Chapter 3, "DirectX 10 Blend Shapes: Breaking the Limits,"** focuses on the animation techniques used in the "Dawn" demo but updates them to remove the limits placed by previous hardware.

Rendering particular objects such as terrain, characters, and trees is extremely important, but no section on geometry rendering would be complete without a discussion of more-generic techniques like surface rendering. Thankfully, **Tamy Boubekeur** and **Christophe Schlick** of LaBRI–INRIA, University of Bordeaux, have provided a chapter on generalized surface rendering with their GAMeR algorithm. **Chapter 5, "Generic Adaptive Mesh Refinement,"** presents a technique that allows GPU acceleration of many surface types.

Finally, in addition to presenting surface techniques, this section offers a chapter on metaballs. **Chapter 7, "Point-Based Visualization of Metaballs on a GPU"** by **Kees van Kooten** and **Gino van den Bergen** of Playlogic Game Factory and **Alex Telea** of Eindhoven University of Technology, demonstrates an alternative to some more-popular methods of rendering metaballs, with the advantage that their approach can be accomplished completely on the GPU with just Shader Model 3.

With the broad range of topics and target hardware covered in this Geometry section, there is almost certainly something of interest for everyone. Whether the need is to add polish to technology already under development, or to learn how to utilize the new DirectX 10 features to maximize a project, valuable information is presented. Hopefully, you will enjoy reading these chapters as much as I have enjoyed editing them.

Evan Hart, NVIDIA Corporation

Chapter 1

Generating Complex Procedural Terrains Using the GPU

Ryan Geiss
NVIDIA Corporation

1.1 Introduction

Procedural terrains have traditionally been limited to height fields that are generated by the CPU and rendered by the GPU. However, the serial processing nature of the CPU is not well suited to generating extremely complex terrains—a highly parallel task. Plus, the simple height fields that the CPU can process do not offer interesting terrain features (such as caves or overhangs).

To generate procedural terrains with a high level of complexity, at interactive frame rates, we look to the GPU. By utilizing several new DirectX 10 capabilities such as the *geometry shader* (GS), stream output, and rendering to 3D textures, we can use the GPU to quickly generate large blocks of complex procedural terrain. Together, these blocks create a large, detailed polygonal mesh that represents the terrain within the current view frustum. Figure 1-1 shows an example.

1.2 Marching Cubes and the Density Function

Conceptually, the terrain surface can be completely described by a single function, called the *density function*. For any point in 3D space (x, y, z), the function produces a single floating-point value. These values vary over space—sometimes positive, sometimes negative. If the value is positive, then that point in space is inside the solid terrain.

Figure 1-1. Terrain Created Entirely on the GPU

If the value is negative, then that point is located in empty space (such as air or water). The boundary between positive and negative values—where the density value is zero— is the surface of the terrain. It is along this surface that we wish to construct a polygonal mesh.

We use the GPU to generate polygons for a "block" of terrain at a time, but we further subdivide the block into 32×32×32 smaller cells, or voxels. Figure 1-2 illustrates the coordinate system. It is within these voxels that we will construct polygons (triangles) that represent the terrain surface. The marching cubes algorithm allows us to generate the correct polygons within a single voxel, given, as input, the density value at its eight corners. As output, it will produce anywhere from zero to five polygons. If the densities at the eight corners of a cell all have the same sign, then the cell is entirely inside or outside the terrain, so no polygons are output. In all other cases, the cell lies on the boundary between rock and air, and anywhere from one to five polygons will be generated.

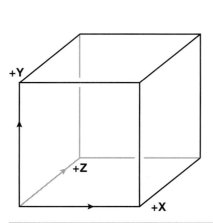

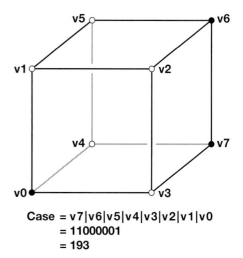

Case = v7|v6|v5|v4|v3|v2|v1|v0
     = 11000001
     = 193

Figure 1-2. The Coordinate System Used for Voxel Space
This conveniently matches our world-space and 3D-texture-space coordinate systems.

Figure 1-3. A Single Voxel with Known Density Values at Its Eight Corners
A solid dot indicates a positive density value at that corner. Each corner becomes a "bit" in determining the 8-bit case.

1.2.1 Generating Polygons Within a Cell

The generation of polygons within a cell works as follows: As shown in Figure 1-3, we take the density values at the eight corners and determine whether each value is positive or negative. From each one we make a bit. If the density is negative, we set the bit to zero; if the density is positive, we set the bit to one.

We then logically concatenate (with a bitwise OR operation) these eight bits to produce a byte—also called the *case*—in the range 0–255. If the case is 0 or 255, then the cell is entirely inside or outside the terrain and, as previously described, no polygons will be generated. However, if the case is in the range [1..254], some number of polygons will be generated.

If the case is not 0 or 255, it is used to index into various lookup tables (on the GPU, *constant buffers* are used) to determine how many polygons to output for that case, as well as how to build them. Each polygon is created by connecting three points (*vertices*) that lie somewhere on the 12 edges of the cell. Figure 1-4 illustrates the basic cases resulting from application of the marching cubes algorithm.

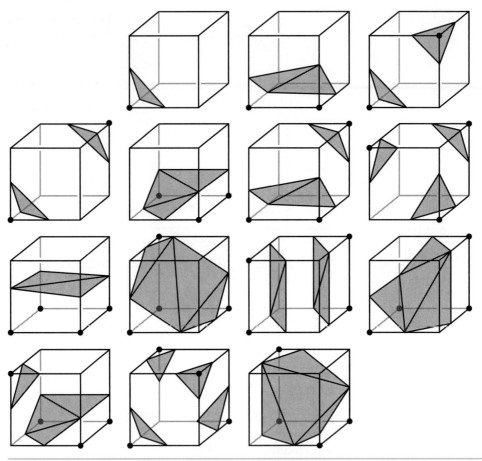

Figure 1-4. The 14 Fundamental Cases for Marching Cubes
The other 240 cases are just rotations or inversions of these base cases. Image courtesy of Martin Franc.

Exactly *where* a vertex is placed along an edge is determined by interpolation. The vertex should be placed where the density value is approximately zero. For example, if the density at end *A* of the edge is 0.1 and at end *B* is −0.3, the vertex would be placed 25 percent of the way from *A* to *B*.

Figure 1-5 illustrates one case. After the case is used to index into lookup tables, the blue dots indicate which edges must have vertices placed on them. Gray areas show

how these vertices will be connected to make triangles. Note that where the blue dots actually appear along the edges depends on the density values at the ends of the edge.

Our output is a triangle list, so every three vertices that are output create a triangle, and the next vertex output begins a new triangle. If a certain case requires that we generate N polygons, we will need to generate a vertex (somewhere along one of the cell's edges) $3 \times N$ times.

1.2.2 Lookup Tables

Two primary lookup tables are at work here. The first, when indexed by the case number, tells us how many polygons to create for that case:

```
int case_to_numpolys[256];
```

The second lookup table is much larger. Once it receives the case number, the table provides the information needed to build up to five triangles within the cell. Each of the five triangles is described by just an `int3` value (three integers); the three values are the edge numbers [0..11] on the cube that must be connected in order to build the triangle. Figure 1-6 shows the edge-numbering scheme.

```
int3 edge_connect_list[256][5];
```

For example, if the case number is 193, then looking up `case_to_numpolys[193]` would tell us how many polygons we need to generate, which is 3. Next, the

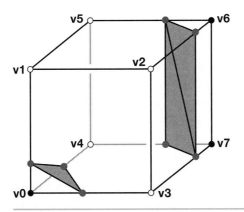

Figure 1-5. Implicit Surface to Polygon Conversion

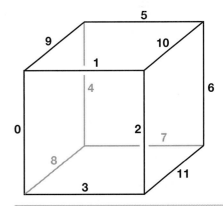

Figure 1-6. The Edge Numbers Assigned to the 12 Edges of a Voxel

`edge_connect_list[193][]` lookups would return the following values:

```
int3 edge_connect_list[193][0]:   11  5 10
int3 edge_connect_list[193][1]:   11  7  5
int3 edge_connect_list[193][2]:    8  3  0
int3 edge_connect_list[193][3]:   -1 -1 -1
int3 edge_connect_list[193][4]:   -1 -1 -1
```

To build the triangles within this cell, a geometry shader would generate and stream out nine vertices (at the appropriate places along the edges listed)—forming three triangles—to a vertex buffer for storage. Note that the last two `int3` values are −1; these values will never even be sampled, though, because we know there are only three triangles for this case. The GPU would then move on to the next cell.

We encourage you to copy the lookup tables from the demo on this book's accompanying DVD, because generating the tables from scratch can be time-consuming. The tables can be found in the file **models\tables.nma**.

1.3 An Overview of the Terrain Generation System

We divide the world into an infinite number of equally sized cubic blocks, as already described. In the world-space coordinate system, each block is 1×1×1 in size. However, within each block are 32^3 voxels that potentially contain polygons. A pool of around 300 vertex buffers are dynamically assigned to the blocks currently visible in the view frustum, with higher priority given to the closest blocks. As new blocks come into the view frustum (as the user moves around), the farthest away or newly view-cullable vertex buffers are evicted and reused for the newly wished-for blocks.

Not all blocks contain polygons. Whether they do or not depends on complex calculations, so usually we won't know if they contain polygons until we try to generate the blocks. As each block is generated, a *stream-out query* asks the GPU if any polygons were actually created. Blocks that don't produce polygons—this is common—are flagged as "empty" and put into a list so they won't be uselessly regenerated. This move also prevents those empty blocks from unnecessarily occupying a vertex buffer.

For each frame, we sort all the vertex buffers (their bounding boxes are well known) from front to back. We then generate any new blocks that are needed, evicting the most distant block whenever we need a free vertex buffer. Finally, we render the sorted blocks from front to back so that the GPU doesn't waste time shading pixels that might be occluded by other parts of the terrain.

1.3.1 Generating the Polygons Within a Block of Terrain

Conceptually, generating a block of terrain involves two main steps. We outline the steps here and then elaborate upon them in the following subsections.

- First, we use the GPU's pixel shader (PS) unit to evaluate the complex density function at every cell *corner* within the block and store the results in a large 3D texture. The blocks are generated one at a time, so one 3D texture can be shared universally. However, because the texture stores the density values at the cell *corners*, the texture is 33×33×33 in size, rather than 32×32×32 (the number of cells in the block).

- Next, we visit each voxel and generate actual polygons within it, if necessary. The polygons are streamed out to a vertex buffer, where they can be kept and repeatedly rendered to the screen until they are no longer visible.

1.3.2 Generating the Density Values

Rendering to a 3D texture is a somewhat new idea, and it's worthy of some explanation here. On the GPU, a 3D texture is implemented as an array of 2D textures. To run a PS that writes to every pixel in a slice, we draw two triangles that, together, cover the render portal. To cover all the slices, we use instancing. In DirectX, this means nothing more than calling `ID3D10Device::DrawInstanced()` (rather than the ordinary `Draw()` function) with the `numInstances` parameter set to 33. This procedure effectively draws the triangle pair 33 times.

The vertex shader (VS) knows which instance is being drawn by specifying an input attribute using the `SV_InstanceID` semantic; these values will range from 0 to 32, depending on which instance is being drawn. The VS can then pass this value on to the geometry shader, which writes it out to an attribute with the `SV_RenderTarget-ArrayIndex` semantic. This semantic determines to which slice of the 3D texture (the render target array) the triangle actually gets rasterized. In this way, the PS is run on every pixel in the entire 3D texture. On the book's DVD, see **shaders\1b_build_density_vol.vsh** and **.gsh**.

Conceptually, the PS that shades these triangles takes, as input, a world-space coordinate and writes, as output, a single, floating-point density value. The math that converts the input into the output is our density function.

1.3.3 Making an Interesting Density Function

The sole input to the density function is this:

```
float3 ws;
```

This value is the world-space coordinate. Luckily, shaders give us plenty of useful tools to translate this value into an interesting density value. Some of the tools at our disposal include the following:

- Sampling from source textures, such as 1D, 2D, 3D, and cube maps
- Constant buffers, such as lookup tables
- Mathematical functions, such as `cos()`, `sin()`, `pow()`, `exp()`, `frac()`, `floor()`, and arithmetic

For example, a good starting point is to place a ground plane at $y = 0$:

```
float density = -ws.y;
```

This divides the world into positive values, those below the $y = 0$ plane (let's call that earth), and negative values, those above the plane (which we'll call air). A good start! Figure 1-7 shows the result.

Next, let's make the ground more interesting by adding a bit of randomness, as shown in Figure 1-8. We simply use the world-space coordinate (ws) to sample from a small (16^3) repeating 3D texture full of random ("noise") values in the range $[-1..1]$, as follows:

```
density += noiseVol.Sample(TrilinearRepeat, ws).x;
```

Figure 1-8 shows how the ground plane warps when a single octave of noise is added.

Figure 1-7. We Start with a Flat Surface

Figure 1-8. Terrain with One Level of Noise

Note that we can scale ws prior to the texture lookup to change the *frequency* (how quickly the noise varies over space). We can also scale the result of the lookup before adding it to the density value; scaling changes the *amplitude*, or strength, of the noise. To generate the image in Figure 1-9, the following line of shader code uses a noise "function" with twice the frequency and half the amplitude of the previous example:

```
density += noiseVol.Sample(TrilinearRepeat, ws*2).x*0.5;
```

One octave (sample) of noise isn't that interesting; using three octaves is an improvement, as Figure 1-10 shows. To be optimal, the amplitude of each octave should be half that of the previous octave, and the frequency should be *roughly* double the frequency of the previous octave. It's important not to make the frequency exactly double, though. The interference of two overlapping, repeating signals at slightly different frequencies is beneficial here because it helps break up repetition. Note that we also use three different noise volumes.

```
density += noiseVol1.Sample(TrilinearRepeat, ws*4.03).x*0.25;
density += noiseVol2.Sample(TrilinearRepeat, ws*1.96).x*0.50;
density += noiseVol3.Sample(TrilinearRepeat, ws*1.01).x*1.00;
```

If more octaves of noise are added at progressively lower frequencies (and higher amplitudes), larger terrain structures begin to emerge, such as large mountains and trenches. In practice, we need about nine octaves of noise to create a world that is rich in both of these low-frequency features (such as mountains and canyons), but that also retains interesting high-frequency features (random detail visible at close range). See Figure 1-11.

Figure 1-9. One Octave of Noise with Twice the Frequency but Half the Amplitude of Figure 1-8
Note that the camera is in the exact same location as in Figure 1-8.

Figure 1-10. Three Octaves at High Frequency Generate More Details

Figure 1-11. Adding Lower Frequencies at Higher Amplitude Creates Mountains
Left: Six octaves of noise. Right: Nine octaves of noise.

Sampling Tips

It's worth going over a few details concerning sampling the various octaves. First, the world-space coordinate can be used, without modification, to sample the seven or eight highest-frequency octaves. However, for the lowest octave or two, the world-space coordinate should first be slightly rotated (by 3×3 rotation matrices) to reduce repetition of the most salient features of the terrain. It's also wise to reuse three or four noise textures among your nine octaves to improve cache coherency; this reuse will not be noticeable at significantly different scales.

Finally, precision can begin to break down when we sample extremely low frequency octaves of noise. Error begins to show up as (unwanted) high-frequency noise. To work around this, we manually implement trilinear interpolation when sampling the very lowest octave or two, using full floating-point precision. For more information on how to do this, see the comments and code in **shaders\density.h.**

Using many octaves of noise creates detail that is isotropic (equal in all directions), which sometimes looks a bit *too* regular. One way to break up this homogeneity is to *warp* the world-space coordinate by another (low-frequency) noise lookup, before using the coordinate for the nine noise lookups. At a medium frequency and mild amplitude, the warp creates a surreal, ropey, organic-looking terrain, as shown in Figure 1-12. At a lower frequency and higher amplitude, the warp can increase the occurrence of caves, tunnels, and arches. The effects can easily be combined, of course, by summing two octaves.

```
// Do this before using 'ws' to sample the nine octaves!
float3 warp = noiseVol2.Sample( TrilinearRepeat, ws*0.004 ).xyz;
ws += warp * 8;
```

Figure 1-12. Warping the World-Space Coordinate Creates a Surreal-Looking Terrain

We can also introduce a hard "floor" to the scene by very suddenly boosting the density values below a certain *y* coordinate. To some degree, this mimics sediment deposition in nature, as eroded sediment finds its way to lower areas and fills them in. Visually, it makes the scene feel less aquatic and more landlike, as shown in Figure 1-13.

```
float hard_floor_y = -13;
density += saturate((hard_floor_y - ws_orig.y)*3)*40;
```

Many other interesting effects can be accomplished by adjusting only the density value by the world-space *y* coordinate. We can make the adjustment by using either the pre-warp or the post-warp world-space coordinate. If we use the post-warp, then under its influence any effects that look like shelves or terraces will appear to melt and sag, along with the rest of the terrain. Figures 1-14 and 1-15 show two examples.

These are very basic techniques. Myriad effects are possible, of course, and can be easily prototyped by modifying **shaders\density.h.**

Figure 1-13. A Floor Level Can Be Introduced

Figure 1-14. Building Shelves
Generated by increasing the density value over a thin range of y values.

Figure 1-15. Repeating Terraces
Built by casting the y coordinate to an integer and then decreasing the density value by this amount.

1.3.4   Customizing the Terrain

All of the techniques we have discussed so far contribute to producing a nice, organic-looking terrain. However, for practical use, we must be able to domesticate the shape of the terrain. There are many ways to do this.

Use a Hand-Painted 2D Texture

Stretch a hand-painted 2D texture over a very large area (one that would take, say, 10 minutes to "walk across" in your demo or game). The density function could sample this 2D texture using ws.xz and use the result to drive the eight noise lookups. The red channel of the texture could influence the scaling of ws.y before using it for the lookups, resulting in the noise appearing vertically squished in some areas or stretched in others. The green channel could modulate the amplitudes of the higher-frequency octaves of noise, causing the terrain to look rocky in some places and smoother in others. And the blue channel could even modulate the warp effect discussed earlier, so that some areas look more "alien" than others.

Add Manually Controlled Influences

It's also possible to add manually controlled influences to the density field. So, if your game level needs a flat spot for a ship to land, as in Figure 1-16, you could pass data to describe it to the pixel shader in a constant buffer. The shader code might then look something like the following:

```
float distance_from_flat_spot = length(ws.xz - flat_spot_xz_coord);
float flatten_amount = saturate(outer_radius - distance_from_flat_spot)/
                       (outer_radius - inner_radius) ) * 0.9;
density = lerp(density, ws.y - flat_spot_height, flatten_amount);
```

Here, the density function will be 90 percent replaced by the "flat spot" function
within `inner_radius` world-space units of its center; however, by a distance of
`outer_radius`, the influence drops off to zero (`saturate()` clamps a value to the
0..1 range). In addition, many flat spots could be used across your terrain—at varying
heights, weights, and radii of influence. These flat spots are obtained for the cost of just
one flat spot, as long as there is enough distance between them that an individual block
of terrain will only be affected by, at most, one flat spot at a time. (Of course, dynamic
looping could also be used if you need more than one per block.) The application is
responsible for updating the constant buffer with the relevant information whenever a
block is to be generated.

Add Miscellaneous Effects

Other effects are possible by combining all the previous techniques—from caves, to
cliffs, to painted maps of rivers. If you can imagine it, you can probably code it. Want a
spherical planet, as in Figure 1-17? Instead of using the *y* plane as a ground, try this
(plus noise):

```
float rad = 80;
float density = rad - length(ws - float3(0, -rad, 0));
```

Or, for a never-ending 3D network of caves, try this (plus noise):

```
//This positive starting bias gives us a little more rock than open space.
float density = 12;
```

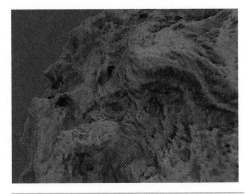

Figure 1-16. This "Man-Made" Flat Spot Creates an Ideal Landing Place for Aircraft

Figure 1-17. A Spherical Planet

The density function used in the demo can be modified by editing **shaders\density.h**, which is included by several other shaders in the demo. If you'd like to make changes in real time, do this: Run the demo in windowed mode (see **bin\args.txt**), edit the density function to your liking, and then press F9 (Reload Shaders) followed by "Z" (Regenerate Terrain).

1.4 Generating the Polygons Within a Block of Terrain

There are many ways to break up the task of generating a block of terrain on the GPU. In the simplest approach, we generate density values throughout a 3D texture (representing the corners of all the voxels in the block) in one render pass. We then run a second render pass, where we visit every voxel in the density volume and use the GS to generate (and stream out to a vertex buffer) anywhere from 0 to 15 vertices in each voxel. The vertices will be interpreted as a triangle list, so every 3 vertices make a triangle.

For now, let's focus on what we need to do to generate just one of the vertices. There are several pieces of data we'd like to know and store for each vertex:

- The world-space coordinate
- The world-space normal vector (used for lighting)
- An "ambient occlusion" lighting value

These data can be easily represented by the seven floats in the following layout. Note that the ambient occlusion lighting value is packed into the .w channel of the first float4.

```
struct rock_vertex {
    float4 wsCoordAmbo;
    float3 wsNormal;
};
```

The normal can be computed easily, by taking the gradient of the density function (the partial derivative, or independent rate of change, in the x, y, and z directions) and then normalizing the resulting vector. This is easily accomplished by sampling the density volume six times. To determine the rate of change in x, we sample the density volume at the next texel in the $+x$ direction, then again at the next texel in the $-x$ direction, and take the difference; this is the rate of change in x. We repeat this calculation in the y and z directions, for a total of six samples. The three results are put together in a float3, and then normalized, producing a very high quality surface normal that can later be used for lighting. Listing 1-1 shows the shader code.

Listing 1-1. Computing the Normal via a Gradient

```
float d = 1.0/(float)voxels_per_block;
float3 grad;
grad.x = density_vol.Sample(TrilinearClamp, uvw + float3( d, 0, 0)) -
         density_vol.Sample(TrilinearClamp, uvw + float3(-d, 0, 0));
grad.y = density_vol.Sample(TrilinearClamp, uvw + float3( 0, d, 0)) -
         density_vol.Sample(TrilinearClamp, uvw + float3( 0,-d, 0));
grad.z = density_vol.Sample(TrilinearClamp, uvw + float3( 0, 0, d)) -
         density_vol.Sample(TrilinearClamp, uvw + float3( 0, 0,-d));
output.wsNormal = -normalize(grad);
```

The ambient occlusion lighting value represents how much light, in general, is likely to reach the vertex, based on the surrounding geometry. This value is responsible for darkening the vertices that lie deep within nooks, crannies, and trenches, where less light would be able to penetrate. Conceptually, we could generate this value by first placing a large, uniform sphere of ambient light that shines on the vertex. Then we trace rays inward to see what fraction of the vertices could actually reach the vertex without colliding with other parts of the terrain, or we could think of it as casting many rays out from the vertex and tracking the fraction of rays that can get to a certain distance without penetrating the terrain. The latter variant is the method our terrain demo uses.

To compute an ambient occlusion value for a point in space, we cast out 32 rays. A constant Poisson distribution of points on the surface of a sphere works well for this. We store these points in a constant buffer. We can—and should—reuse the same set of rays over and over for each vertex for which we want ambient occlusion. (Note: You can use our Poisson distribution instead of generating your own; search for "g_ray_dirs_32" in **models\tables.nma** on the book's DVD.) For each of the rays cast, we take 16 samples of the density value along the ray—again, just by sampling the density volume. If any of those samples yields a positive value, the ray has hit the terrain and we consider the ray fully blocked. Once all 32 rays are cast, the fraction of them that were blocked—usually from 0.5 to 1—becomes the ambient occlusion value. (Few vertices have ambient occlusion values less than 0.5, because most rays traveling in the hemisphere toward the terrain will quickly be occluded.)

Later, when the rock is drawn, the lighting will be computed as usual, but the final light amount (diffuse and specular) will be modulated based on this value before we apply it to the surface color. We recommend multiplying the light by `saturate(1 - 2*ambient_occlusion)`, which translates an occlusion value of 0.5 into a light multiplier of 1, and an occlusion value of 1 to a light multiplier of 0. The multiplier can also be run through a `pow()` function to artistically influence the falloff rate.

1.4.1 Margin Data

You might notice, at this point, that some of the occlusion-testing rays go outside the current block of known density values, yielding bad information. This scenario would create lighting artifacts where two blocks meet. However, this is easily solved by enlarging our density volume slightly and using the extra space to generate density values a bit beyond the borders of our block. The block might be divided into 32^3 voxels for tessellation, but we might generate density values for, say, a 44^3 density volume, where the extra "margin" voxels represent density values that are actually physically outside of our 32^3 block. Now we can cast occlusion rays a little farther through our density volume and get more-accurate results. The results still might not be perfect, but in practice, this ratio (32 voxels versus 6 voxels of margin data at each edge) produces nice results without noticeable lighting artifacts. Keep in mind that these dimensions represent the number of voxels in a block; the density volume (which corresponds to the voxel corners) will contain one more element in each dimension.

Unfortunately, casting such short rays fails to respect large, low-frequency terrain features, such as the darkening that should happen inside large gorges or holes. To account for these low-frequency features, we also take a few samples of the *real* density function along each ray, but at a longer range—intentionally outside the current block. Sampling the real density function is *much* more computationally expensive, but fortunately, we need to perform sampling only about four times for each ray to get good results. To lighten some of the processing load, we can also use a "lightweight" version of the density function. This version ignores the higher-frequency octaves of noise because they don't matter so much across large ranges. In practice, with eight octaves of noise, it's safe to ignore the three highest-frequency octaves.

The block of pseudocode shown in Listing 1-2 illustrates how to generate ambient occlusion for a vertex.

Note the use of `saturate(d * 9999)`, which lets any positive sample, even a tiny one, completely block the ray. However, values deep within the terrain tend to have

Listing 1-2. Pseudocode for Generating Ambient Occlusion for a Vertex

```
float visibility = 0;
for (ray = 0 .. 31)
{
  float3 dir = ray_dir[ray];   // From constant buffer
  float this_ray_visibility = 1;
  // Short-range samples from density volume:
  for (step = 1 .. 16)   // Don't start at zero
  {
    float d = density_vol.Sample( ws + dir * step );
    this_ray_visibility *= saturate(d * 9999);
  }
  // Long-range samples from density function:
  for (step = 1 .. 4)   // Don't start at zero!
  {
    float d = density_function( ws + dir * big_step );
    this_ray_visibility *= saturate(d * 9999);
  }
  visibility += this_ray_visibility;
}
return (1 - visibility/32.0);   // Returns occlusion
```

progressively higher density values, and values farther from the terrain surface do tend to progressively become more negative. Although the density function is not strictly a signed distance function, it often resembles one, and we take advantage of that here.

During ray casting, instead of strictly interpreting each sample as black or white (hit or miss), we allow things to get "fuzzy." A partial occlusion happens when the sample is *near* the surface (or *not too deep* into the surface). In the demo on the book's DVD, we use a multiplier of 8 (rather than 9999) for short-range samples, and we use 0.5 for long-range samples. (Note that these values are relative to the range of values that are output by your particular density function). These lower multipliers are especially beneficial for the long-range samples; it becomes difficult to tell that there are only four samples being taken. Figures 1-18 through 1-20 show some examples.

1.4.2 Generating a Block: Method 1

This section outlines three methods for building a block. As we progress from method 1 to method 3, the techniques get successively more complex, but faster.

Figure 1-18. Long-Range Ambient Occlusion Only
Left: A strict (high) multiplier yields artifacts. Right: A fuzzy (low) multiplier yields smoother shading.

Figure 1-19. Both Long-Range and Short-Range Ambient Occlusion

Figure 1-20. The Regular Scene, Shaded Using Ambient Occlusion

The first (and simplest) method for building a block of terrain is the most straightforward, and requires only two render passes, as shown in Table 1-1.

However, this method is easily optimized. First, the execution speed of a geometry shader tends to decrease as the maximum size of its output (per input primitive) increases. Here, our maximum output is 15 vertices, each consisting of 7 floats—for a whopping 105 floats. If we could reduce the floats to 32 or less—or even 16 or less—the GS would run a lot faster.

Another factor to consider is that a GS is not as fast as a VS because of the geometry shader's increased flexibility and stream-out capability. Moving most of the vertex generation work, especially the ambient occlusion ray casting, into a vertex shader would

Table 1-1. Method 1 for Generating a Block

Pass Name	Description	Geometry Shader Output Struct
`build_densities`	Fill density volume with density values.	N/A
`gen_vertices`	Visit each (nonmargin) voxel in the density volume. The geometry shader generates and streams out up to 15 vertices (5 triangles) per voxel.	`float4 wsCoordAmbo;` `float3 wsNormal;` **Count:** 0/3/6/9/12/15

be worthwhile. Fortunately, we can accomplish this, and reduce our GS output size, by introducing an extra render pass.

1.4.3 Generating a Block: Method 2

The problems described in method 1—extremely large geometry shader output (per input primitive) and the need to migrate work from the geometry shaders to the vertex shaders—are resolved by this design, shown in Table 1-2, which is an impressive 22 times faster than method 1.

Here, the `gen_vertices` pass has been broken into `list_triangles` and `gen_vertices`. The `list_triangles` pass has much smaller maximum output; it outputs, at most, five marker points. Each point represents a triangle that will be fleshed out later, but for now, it's only a single uint in size (an unsigned integer—the same size as a float). Our maximum output size has gone from 105 to 5, so the geometry shader will execute much faster now.

The crucial data for generating each triangle is packed into the uint:

```
struct triangle_marker_point {
  uint z6_y6_x6_edge1_edge2_edge3;
};
```

Table 1-2. Method 2 for Generating a Block

Pass Name	Description	Geometry Shader Output Struct
`build_densities`	Fill density volume with density values.	N/A
`list_triangles`	Visit each voxel in the density volume; stream out a lightweight marker point for each *triangle* to be generated. *Use a stream-out query to skip remaining passes if no output here.*	`uint z6_y6_x6_edge1_edge2_edge3;` **Count:** 0–5
`gen_vertices`	March through the triangle list, using the vertex shader to do most of the work for generating the vertex. The geometry shader is a pass-through, merely streaming the result out to a buffer.	`float4 wsCoordAmbo;` `float3 wsNormal;` **Count:** 3

Six integer values are packed into this one uint, which tells us everything we need to build a triangle within this voxel. The x, y, and z bit fields (6 bits each, or [0..31]) indicate which voxel, within the current block, should contain the generated triangle. And the three edge fields (each 4 bits) indicate the edge [0..11] along which the vertex should be placed. This information, plus access to the density volume, is all the vertex shader in the last pass needs to generate the three vertices that make up the triangle. In that final pass, all three vertices are generated in a single execution of the vertex shader and then passed to the geometry shader together, in a large structure, like this:

```
struct v2gConnector {
    float4 wsCoordAmbo1;
    float3 wsNormal1;
    float4 wsCoordAmbo2;
    float3 wsNormal2;
    float4 wsCoordAmbo3;
    float3 wsNormal3;
};
```

The GS then writes out three separate vertices from this one big structure. This activity produces a triangle list identical to what method 1 produced, but much more quickly.

Adding another render pass is helpful because it lets us skip the final (and most expensive) pass if we find that there are no triangles in the block. The test to determine if any triangles were generated merely involves surrounding the list_triangles pass with a stream output query (ID3D10Query with D3D10_QUERY_SO_STATISTICS), which returns the number of primitives streamed out. This is another reason why we see such a huge speed boost between methods 1 and 2.

Method 2 is faster and introduces the useful concept of adding a new render pass to migrate heavy GS work into the VS. However, method 2 has one major flaw: it generates each final vertex once *for each triangle that uses it*. A vertex is usually shared by an average of about five triangles, so we're doing five times more work than we need to.

1.4.4 Generating a Block: Method 3

This method generates each vertex once, rather than an average of five times, as in the previous methods. Despite having more render passes, method 3 is still about 80 percent faster than method 2. Method 3, instead of producing a simple, nonindexed triangle list in the form of many vertices (many of them redundant), creates a vertex pool and a separate index list. The indices in the list are now references to the vertices in the vertex pool, and every three indices denote a triangle.

To produce each vertex only once, we limit vertex production within a cell to only edges 3, 0, and 8. A vertex on any other edge will be produced by another cell—the one in which the vertex, conveniently, does fall on edge 3, 0, or 8. This successfully produces all the needed vertices, just once.

Within a cell, knowing whether a vertex is needed along a particular edge (3, 0, or 8) is as simple as checking if the case number bits are different at the two corners that the edge connects. See **shaders\4_list_vertices_to_generate.vsh** for an example of how to do this, but note that it could also be done easily using a lookup table.

The render passes to generate vertices uniquely are shown in Table 1-3.

The previous passes generate our vertices without redundancy, but we still need to generate our index list. This is the most difficult concept in method 3. To make it work, we'll need a temporary volume texture, VertexIDVol. This is a 32^3 volume texture of the format DXGI_FORMAT_R32_UINT, so each voxel can hold a single uint.

The problem is that when generating the indices for a given (nonempty) cell, we have no idea where the indices are *in the vertex buffer*, that magical storage structure where all those streamed-out vertices have been consolidated for us. (Remember, only a small fraction of cells actually generate vertices.) The 3D texture is our solution; we use it to *splat* the vertex ID (or index within the vertex buffer) of each vertex into a structure that we can look up into randomly. Sampling this volume can then act as a function that takes, as input, a 3D location (within the block) and provides, as output, the vertex ID (or index in the vertex buffer) of the vertex that was generated there. This is the missing information we need to be able to generate an index list to connect our vertices into triangles. The two extra render passes are described in Table 1-4.

Table 1-3. Method 3 for Generating a Block

Pass Name	Description	Geometry Shader Output Struct
build_densities	Fill density volume with density values.	N/A
list_nonempty_cells	Visit each voxel in the density volume; stream out a lightweight marker point for each *voxel* that needs triangles in it. *Use a stream-out query to skip remaining passes if no output here.*	uint z8_y8_x8_case8; **Count:** 0–1 *Note: Includes an extra row of voxels at the far end of x, y, and z.*
list_verts_to_generate	Marches nonempty_cell_list and looks only at edges 3, 0, and 8; streams out a marker point for each one that needs a vertex on it.	uint z8_y8_x8_null4_edge4; **Count:** 0–3
gen_vertices	Marches vert_list and generates the final (real) vertices. VS does the bulk of the work to generate the real vertex; GS just streams it out.	float4 wsCoordAmbo; float3 wsNormal; **Count:** 1

Table 1-4. Method 3 for Generating the Index Buffer

Pass Name	Description	Geometry Shader Output Struct
`splat_vertex_ids`	Marches `vert_list` and splats each one's `SV_VertexID` to VertexIDVol.	(No stream output; pixel shader just writes out `SV_VertexID`.)
`gen_indices`	Marches `nonempty_cell_list` and streams out up to 15 uints per cell—the indices to make up to five triangles. Samples `VertexIDVol` to get this information.	`uint index;` **Count:** 15 *Note: Do not output any indices for cells in any final row (in x/y/z).*

The splat is accomplished by drawing a single point into a voxel of the 3D texture. The *xy* coordinates are taken from the block-space *xy* coordinate, and using the block-space *z* coordinate, the GS routes the point to the correct slice in the 3D texture. The value written out in the PS is the value that came into the VS as `SV_VertexID`, which is a system-generated value indicating the zero-based index of the vertex in our `vert_list` vertex buffer. Note that it's not necessary to clear the `VertexIDVol` prior to splatting.

When sampling the volume to fetch a vertex ID, note that if you need the vertex ID for a vertex on an edge other than 3, 0, or 8, you will instead have to sample the appropriate *neighbor* voxel along edge 3, 0, or 8. The mechanics for this actually turn out to be trivial; see **shaders\7_gen_indices.gsh** on the DVD.

You might notice that we would often be splatting up to three vertices per voxel, but we're only writing to a one-channel texture! Thus, if a single cell had vertices on edges 3 and 8, the `VertexIDVol` could hold the index for only one of them. The easy solution is to triple the width of the vertex ID volume (making it $3N{\times}N{\times}N$ in size). When splatting, multiply the integer block-space *x* coordinate by 3, then add 0, 1, or 2 depending on which edge you're splatting the vertex ID for (3, 0, or 8, respectively). (See **shaders\5b_splat_vertex_IDs.vsh**.) In the final pass, when you're sampling the results, adjust the *x* coordinate similarly, depending whether you want the vertex ID along edge 3, 0, or 8 within that voxel. (See **shaders\7_gen_indices.gsh.**)

Also note that in method 3, the `list_nonempty_cells` pass includes an extra layer of cells at the far ends of the *x*, *y*, and *z* axes. Sometimes vertices will be needed that fall on an edge other than 3, 0, or 8 in the final row of cells, so this ensures that the vertices are all created—even if the cell in which they *do* map onto edge 3, 0, or 8 happens to be in a neighboring block. In the `gen_indices` pass, which operates on `nonempty_cell_list`, index generation is skipped for cells that are actually beyond the current block. (See **shaders\7_gen_indices.gsh** for an example.)

Method 3 allows us to share vertices and, as a result, generate about one-fifth as many of them. This is quite a savings, considering that each vertex samples the complex density function 128 times (32 rays × 4 long-range occlusion samples per ray).

Using the density function and settings that ship with the demo for this chapter, an NVIDIA GeForce 8800 GPU can generate about 6.6 blocks per second using method 1, about 144 blocks per second using method 2, and about 260 blocks per second using method 3.

1.5 Texturing and Shading

One challenge with procedural generation of terrains, or any shape of arbitrary topology, is texturing—specifically, generating texture coordinates, commonly known as *UVs*. How can we seamlessly map textures onto these polygons with minimal distortion? A single planar projection, like the one shown in Figure 1-21, of a seamless and repeating 2D texture looks good from one angle, but inferior from others, because of intense stretching (see also Figure 1-23).

A simple way to resolve this is to use triplanar texturing, or three different planar projections, one along each of the three primary axes (x, y, and z). At any given point, we use the projection that offers the least distortion (stretching) at that point—with some projections blending in the in-between areas, as in Figure 1-22. For example, a surface point whose normal vector pointed mostly in the $+x$ or $-x$ direction would use the yz planar projection. A blending range of roughly 10 to 20 degrees tends to work well; see Figure 1-23 for an illustration of how wide the blending range is.

Figure 1-21. A Single Planar Projection Is Plagued by Distortion

Figure 1-22. Three Planar Projections of the Same Texture, Blended Together Based on the Surface Normal Vector

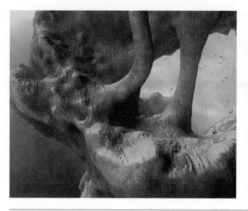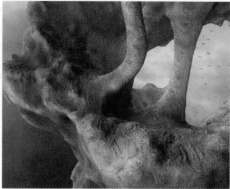

Figure 1-23. Triplanar Texturing
This illustrates where each projection is dominant and how broad the transition zones are.
Left: Each of the three source textures is highly colorized. Right: The screenshot without colorization.

When we use bump mapping with triplanar texturing, we need to make sure the tangent basis is generated from the normal separately for each projection. For example, for the x-projection, a very crude world-space tangent basis could simply be the vectors $\langle 0, 1, 0 \rangle$ and $\langle 0, 0, 1 \rangle$. However, we can do much better than this. Fortunately, it is very easy to generate the real tangent basis from the normal. Here, 90-degree rotations of vectors amount to just swizzling two of the components and flipping the sign on one of them. For example, for the x-projection, you might use the vectors $\langle normal.z, normal.y, -normal.x \rangle$ and $\langle normal.y, -normal.x, normal.z \rangle$. However, note that the location of the negative sign depends on the way the data is stored in the bump maps.

Triplanar texturing can be done in a single render pass, as shown in the pixel shader code sample in Listing 1-3. The sample fetches the color values and bump vectors for each of the three planar projections and then blends them together based on the normal. Finally, the blended bump vector is applied to the vertex-interpolated normal to yield a bumped normal.

Another convenient way to texture the terrain is by mapping certain height values to certain colors, creating striations. With graphics hardware, this translates into a 1D texture lookup that uses the world-space y coordinate—or, better, use a 2D texture lookup. In the texture, let the color scheme vary across the u axis, and let the v axis represent the altitude. When doing the lookup, use a single octave of very low frequency noise to drive the u coordinate, so that the color scheme changes as the viewer roams.

Listing 1-3. Texture Planar Projection

```
// Determine the blend weights for the 3 planar projections.
// N_orig is the vertex-interpolated normal vector.
float3 blend_weights = abs( N_orig.xyz );

// Tighten up the blending zone:
blend_weights = (blend_weights - 0.2) * 7;
blend_weights = max(blend_weights, 0);

// Force weights to sum to 1.0 (very important!)
blend_weights /= (blend_weights.x + blend_weights.y +
blend_weights.z ).xxx;

// Now determine a color value and bump vector for each of the 3
// projections, blend them, and store blended results in these two
// vectors:
float4 blended_color;  // .w hold spec value
float3 blended_bump_vec;
{
  // Compute the UV coords for each of the 3 planar projections.
  // tex_scale (default ~ 1.0) determines how big the textures appear.
  float2 coord1 = v2f.wsCoord.yz * tex_scale;
  float2 coord2 = v2f.wsCoord.zx * tex_scale;
  float2 coord3 = v2f.wsCoord.xy * tex_scale;

  // This is where you would apply conditional displacement mapping.
  //if (blend_weights.x > 0) coord1 = . . .
  //if (blend_weights.y > 0) coord2 = . . .
  //if (blend_weights.z > 0) coord3 = . . .

  // Sample color maps for each projection, at those UV coords.
  float4 col1 = colorTex1.Sample(coord1);
  float4 col2 = colorTex2.Sample(coord2);
  float4 col3 = colorTex3.Sample(coord3);

  // Sample bump maps too, and generate bump vectors.
  // (Note: this uses an oversimplified tangent basis.)
  float2 bumpFetch1 = bumpTex1.Sample(coord1).xy - 0.5;
  float2 bumpFetch2 = bumpTex2.Sample(coord2).xy - 0.5;
  float2 bumpFetch3 = bumpTex3.Sample(coord3).xy - 0.5;
  float3 bump1 = float3(0, bumpFetch1.x, bumpFetch1.y);
  float3 bump2 = float3(bumpFetch2.y, 0, bumpFetch2.x);
  float3 bump3 = float3(bumpFetch3.x, bumpFetch3.y, 0);
```

Listing 1-3 *(continued)*. Texture Planar Projection

```
// Finally, blend the results of the 3 planar projections.
blended_color = col1.xyzw * blend_weights.xxxx +
                col2.xyzw * blend_weights.yyyy +
                col3.xyzw * blend_weights.zzzz;

blended_bump_vec = bump1.xyz * blend_weights.xxx +
                   bump2.xyz * blend_weights.yyy +
                   bump3.xyz * blend_weights.zzz;
}

// Apply bump vector to vertex-interpolated normal vector.
float3 N_for_lighting = normalize(N_orig + blended_bump);
```

To make it even more interesting, make the low-frequency noise vary slowly on x and z but quickly on y—this approach will make the color scheme vary with altitude, as well. It's also fun to add a small amount of the normal vector's y component to the u coordinate for the lookup; this helps break up the horizontal nature of the striations. Figures 1-24 and 1-25 illustrate these techniques.

Planar 2D projections and altitude-based lookups are very useful for projecting detailed, high-resolution 2D textures onto terrain. However, texturing can also be done procedurally. For example, a few octaves of noise—based on the world-space coordinate—can be used to perturb the normal vector, adding a few extra octaves of perceived detail, as shown in Listing 1-4 and Figure 1-26.

Figure 1-24. The Striation Technique
Left: An aerial view. Right: A more ground-level view.

Figure 1-25. The Variable Climate Lookup Texture

Listing 1-4. Normal Vector Perturbation

```
// Further perturb normal vector by a few octaves of procedural noise.
float3 v = 0;
v += noiseVol1.Sample(ws* 3.97)*1.00;
v += noiseVol2.Sample(ws* 8.06)*0.50;
v += noiseVol3.Sample(ws*15.96)*0.25;
N = normalize(N + v);
```

Figure 1-26. Textured Terrain
Left: Without noise-based perturbation of the normal. Right: With noise-based perturbation of the normal.

The base surface color can also be generated or modified procedurally. For example, a simple marble texture can be created by warping the world-space coordinate by several octaves of lower-frequency noise, then taking $\sin(\text{ws.y})$, as shown in Listing 1-5 and Figure 1-27.

Texture projection and procedural texturing are very powerful tools that can be combined easily to achieve a large variety of effects. Used alone, procedural texturing tends to lack the high-resolution detail that a texture (such as a photograph or a painted map) can offer. On the other hand, texture projection used alone looks repetitive over a very large space. However, simple and creative combinations of both tools can solve these problems and create beautifully textured landscapes with impressive detail and variety.

Listing 1-5. Marble Texture Generation

```
// Use warped world-space coordinate to generate a marble texture.
float3 v = 0;
v += noiseVol2.Sample(ws*0.47)*1.00;
v += noiseVol3.Sample(ws*1.06)*0.50;
v += noiseVol1.Sample(ws*1.96)*0.25;
float3 ws_warped = ws + v;
float is_marble = pow( saturate( sin(ws_warped.y)*1.1 ), 3.0) ;
float3 marble_color = 1;
blended_color = lerp(blended_color, marble_color, is_marble);
```

Figure 1-27. Terrain with Marble Texture

1.6 Considerations for Real-World Applications

1.6.1 Level of Detail

In an ideal 3D scene, all polygons would show up at about the same size on the screen. In practice, though, this rarely happens. The terrain technique presented so far has created a tessellation that is somewhat uniform in world space, but definitely not uniform in screen space. As a result, distant polygons appear very tiny (one pixel or less in size), which is wasteful, and introduces aliasing artifacts. To alleviate this problem, we'd like to divide blocks into three groups: close, medium, and far. Blocks at close range will have polygons at a regular size, and blocks at a medium distance will have larger polygons (in world space). Finally, blocks at a far distance will have the largest polygons. To implement this approach, we can choose from two basic schemes: one in which lower-level-of-detail (LOD) blocks have fewer polygons in them, and another where lower-LOD blocks simply represent a larger space.

In the "fewer polygons" scheme, all blocks remain at 1×1×1 in world space, but faraway blocks have a smaller internal grid size (16^3 or 8^3 instead of 32^3). Unfortunately, this scheme causes the number of blocks to bloat very quickly, which rapidly decreases performance—for both the rendering and, especially, the generation of blocks.

The "bigger blocks" scheme is a better approach. Here, all blocks have a constant 32^3 internal grid size, but the world-space size of the terrain that the blocks represent changes, based on their distance from the viewer. Nearby blocks will occupy a cube that is 1×1×1 in world space, while larger blocks (for terrain that is farther away) will cover a 2×2×2 cube in world space and some even larger cubes (4×4×4) out to a great distance. At draw time, we draw the large (faraway) blocks first, then the medium blocks, then the fine blocks (1×1×1) overtop. Because the number of blocks remains manageable, this is the preferred scheme.

As with many LOD schemes, however, switching a section of terrain from one LOD to another creates a sudden, visual popping artifact. The easiest way to deal with this problem is to draw both LODs during the transition period. Draw the low LOD first and slowly alpha-fade the higher-LOD block in, or out, over some short period of time. However, this works well only if the z-buffer (depth) values at every pixel are consistently closer for the higher-LOD block; otherwise the higher-LOD block won't alpha-blend over the lower-LOD block.

Therefore, some small amount of negative bias on the z (depth) value should be used in the vertex shader when we're drawing higher-LOD blocks. Even better, we can generate the lower-LOD blocks by using a small negative bias in the density function. This approach isotropically "erodes" the blocks and is similar to shrinking the surface along its surface normals (but better, because it does not result in any pinch points). As a result, the higher-LOD chunks will usually encase the lower-LOD chunks, and will not have z-fighting problems when alpha blending over the top of them.

1.6.2 Collisions and Lighting of Foreign Objects

Collisions

In an interactive or game environment, many movable objects—such as insects, birds, characters' feet, and so on—must be able to detect, and respond to, collisions with the terrain. "Intelligent" flying creatures might need to cast rays out ahead of time (as the dragonflies do in the "Cascades" demo) in order to steer clear of terrain features. And surface-crawling objects—such as growing vines (a hidden feature in the "Cascades" demo), spiders, or flowing water—must stick to the terrain surface as they move around. Thrown or launched objects also need to know when they hit the terrain, so that they can stop moving (such as a spear hitting the ground), bouncing (as in a soccer ball), or triggering some kind of event.

These object-terrain interactions are easy to compute if the object's motion is primarily driven by the GPU from within a shader. It's easiest to do this computation using a geometry shader, where a small buffer containing a single element (vertex) for each moving object is run through the geometry shader for each frame. In order for the geometry shader to know about the terrain, the density function must be placed in a separate file that can be included (via `#include`) by other shaders. The geometry shader can then include the file and use the function, querying it when needed, to test if a point in space is inside or outside of the terrain.

For example, if a soccer ball were sailing toward the terrain, the geometry shader could test the density function at the previous frame's position and at the new frame's position. If the ball was previously in the air but the new position would be inside the terrain, then the exact location where the ball first hit the surface could be determined by an interpolation of the density value to find where it would equal zero. Or we could use an iterative refinement technique, such as interval halving. Once we find the exact point of collision, we can compute the gradient at that point (via six more samples). Finally, knowing the velocity of the ball and the normal of the terrain, we can compute the bounce direction, and then we can output the proper new position and velocity of the ball.

Lighting

If the soccer ball of the previous example falls into a cave, the viewer will expect it to look darker because of the general occlusion of ambient light that is happening inside the cave (assuming it's not a magical, light-producing soccer ball). Fortunately, this is easily accomplished by casting ambient occlusion rays out from the center of the object for each frame (if the object is moving), just like the ray casting when we generate a single terrain vertex.

The only difference is that here the density function must be used instead of the density volume, because the density volume data for this block is likely long gone. Using the density function is much slower, but if these occlusion rays are cast for only a few dozen moving, visible objects per frame, the impact is not noticeable.

1.7 Conclusion

We have presented a way to use the GPU to generate compelling, unbounded 3D terrains at interactive frame rates. We have also shown how to texture and procedurally shade the terrain for display, build a level-of-detail scheme for the terrain, allow foreign objects to interact with the terrain, plus light these objects to match the terrain.

We encourage you to try these techniques and build on them. The techniques we covered in this chapter are only the basics for, potentially, a new paradigm of GPU-powered terrain generation. What is fully possible now is largely unexplored, and what is possible with future generations of chips holds even greater promise.

1.8 References

Ebert, David S., F. Kenton Musgrave, Darwyn Peachey, Ken Perlin, and Steven Worley. 2003. *Texturing & Modeling: A Procedural Approach,* 3rd ed. Academic Press. Chapters 9–13 by F. Kenton Musgrave are recommended.

Geiss, Ryan, and Michael Thompson. 2007. "NVIDIA Demo Team Secrets—Cascades." Presentation at Game Developers Conference 2007. Available online at http://developer.download.nvidia.com/presentations/2007/gdc/CascadesDemoSecrets.zip.

NVIDIA Corporation. 2007. "Cascades." Demo. More information available online at http://www.nzone.com/object/nzone_cascades_home.html.

Chapter 2

Animated Crowd Rendering

Bryan Dudash
NVIDIA Corporation

With game rendering becoming more complex, both visually and computationally, it is important to make efficient use of GPU hardware. Using instancing, you can reduce CPU overhead by reducing the number of draw calls, state changes, and buffer updates. This chapter shows how to use DirectX 10 instancing with vertex texture fetches to implement instanced hardware palette-skinned characters. The sample also makes use of constant buffers, and the SV_InstanceID system variable to efficiently implement the technique. With this technique, we are able to realize almost 10,000 characters, independently animating with different animations and differing meshes at 30 frames/sec on an Intel Core 2 Duo GeForce 8800 GTX system, as shown in Figures 2-1 and 2-2.

2.1 Motivation

Our goal with this technique is to use DirectX 10 efficiently to enable large-scale rendering of animated characters. We can apply this method to crowds, to audiences, and generally to any situation that calls for drawing a large number of actors, each with a different animation, and distinct mesh variations. In such scenarios, some characters will be closer than others, and thus a level-of-detail (LOD) system is important. With instancing, game designers can realize large, dynamic situations previously not possible without pre-rendering or severely limiting the uniqueness of the characters in the scene.

Figure 2-1. A Crowd of Characters Animated Using Skinned Instancing
That's a lot of animated dwarves!

2.2 A Brief Review of Instancing

In this chapter, we assume a basic understanding of instancing; however, let's review the fundamentals. The term "instancing" refers to rendering a mesh multiple times in different locations, with different parameters. Traditionally, instancing has been used for static mesh objects such as leaves, grass, or other small pieces of mesh geometry that occur in great numbers throughout the scene. This is accomplished by binding a secondary vertex buffer that contains the custom per-instance parameterizations. At render time, the primary vertex buffer is looped over once for each instance, and the secondary buffer is incremented to parameterize each loop over the mesh. See Figure 2-3 for an illustration. In effect, this results in a much larger combined vertex buffer without having to manually create or transfer this buffer.

Under the DirectX9 API, using instancing is a little tricky, because the API requires an overloaded `SetStreamSourceFrequency()` function call. In addition, under DirectX 9, we are unable to index into constant memory based on the current instance; therefore, we must encode all the per-instance data into the vertex stream. This proves to be cache-inefficient as well as more difficult to integrate into an existing rendering engine.

Figure 2-2. A Close-up Shot of the Animated Crowd
With a level-of-detail system in place, character detail changes as the camera moves.

In the DirectX 10 API, instancing has been moved to the core of the API. There are new draw functions, `DrawInstanced()` and `DrawIndexedInstanced()`, which support drawing multiple copies of a mesh, and vertex declarations now contain a special type to identify attributes that are per instance data (`D3D10_INPUT_PER_INSTANCE_DATA`).

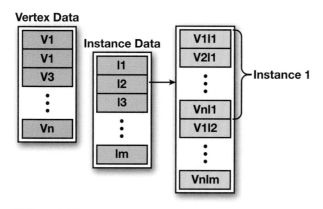

Figure 2-3. Instancing Basics

2.3 Details of the Technique

Traditionally using instancing, we have not been able to render animated objects efficiently. With the advent of DirectX 10, efficient skinned animated instancing became possible.

Skinned instancing is an extension of regular instancing. It renders each character using hardware palette skinning. Instead of using the standard method of storing the animation frame in shader constants, we encode all frames of all animations into a texture and look up the bone matrices from that texture in the vertex shader. Thus we can have more than one animation, and each character can be in a different frame of its animation.

We encode the per-instance parameters into a constant buffer and index into that array using the `SV_InstanceID`.

To achieve mesh variation per instance, we break the character into submeshes that are individually instanced. Such meshes would be different heads, for example.

Finally, to avoid work animating characters in the far distance, we implement an LOD system with lower-resolution polygonal mesh subsections. The decision of which LOD to use is made per frame on a per-instance basis.

What follows is a simple rendering flow. For details on each step, see the corresponding subsections of this chapter.

CPU

1. Perform game logic (animation time, AI, etc.).
2. Determine an LOD group for each instance and populate LOD lists.
3. For each LOD:
   a. For each submesh:
      i. Populate instance data buffers for each instanced draw call.
      ii. For each buffer:
         – Call `DrawInstanced()` on the submesh.

GPU
Vertex Shader

1. Load per-instance data from constants using `SV_InstanceID`.
2. Load bone matrix of appropriate animation and frame.
3. Perform palette skinning.

Pixel Shader

1. Apply per-instance coloration as passed down from vertex shader.

2. (*Optional*) Read a custom texture per instance from a texture array.

2.3.1 Constants-Based Instancing

The technique does not use the traditional method of encoding the per-instance data into a separate vertex stream. In testing, we found that reading per-instance data from a constant buffer using an index per instance was faster due to better cache utilization of the vertices. With the traditional method, vertex attributes increase by the number of per-instance data attributes. We chose instead to put the low-frequency data into constant memory.

SV_InstanceID

Under DirectX 10, there are a number of useful variables that can be generated automatically by the GPU and passed into shader code. These variables are called *system variables*. All system variables have a semantic that begins with "SV_". SV_InstanceID is a GPU-generated value available to all vertex shaders. By binding a shader input to this semantic, the variable will get an integral value corresponding to the current instance. The first index will get 0, and subsequent instances will monotonically increase this value. Thus every instance through the render pipeline gets a unique value, and every vertex for a particular instance shares a common SV_InstanceID value.

This automatic system value allows us to store an array of instance information in a constant buffer and use the ID to index into that array. Because we are injecting per-instance data into constant buffers, we are limited in the number of instances we can render per draw call by the size of the constant memory. In DirectX 10 there is a limit of 4,096 float4 vectors per constant buffer. The number of instances you can draw with this size depends on the size of the per-instance data structure. In this sample, we have the per-instance data shown in Listing 2-1.

As you can see, in this sample each instance takes up five float4 vectors of constant memory, which means we can store a maximum of 819 instances. So we split each group of instanced meshes into *N* buffers, where *N* = *Total Instances*/819. This is a very acceptable number, and it means that if we were to draw 10,000 meshes, it would take 13 draw calls. There is a difference in CPU overhead between 1 and 13 draw calls per frame, but the difference between 13 and 819 is much larger. Each draw call removed allows a reduction in CPU overhead and a possible increase of performance. Thus, there is often little effective difference in final frame rate between 1 and 13 draw calls.

Listing 2-1. Instance Data Structure and Constant Buffer

```
struct PerInstanceData
{
    float4 world1;
    float4 world2;
    float4 world3;
    float4 color;
    uint4  animationData;
};

cbuffer cInstanceData
{
    PerInstanceData g_Instances[MAX_INSTANCE_CONSTANTS];
}
```

On the CPU side, the data looks like Listing 2-2.

Listing 2-2. C++ Instance Data Structure

```
struct InstanceDataElement
{
    D3DXVECTOR4 world1;
    D3DXVECTOR4 world2;
    D3DXVECTOR4 world3;
    D3DXCOLOR color;

    // Offset in vectors (texels) into the whole data stream
    //   for the start of the animation playing
    UINT animationIndex;
    // Offset in vectors (texels) into the animation stream
    //   for the start of the frame playing
    UINT frameOffset;
    UINT unused1;   // pad
    UINT unused2;   // pad
};
```

2.3.2 Palette Skinning Using an Animation Texture

In traditional matrix palette skinning, you encode the transform matrices into vertex shader constants. In our case, each character has a different pose, and possibly a different animation. We use a texture to store the animation data because the amount of data required for all animation frames is too large to fit into constant memory. All DirectX 10-class hardware should have sufficient vertex-texture fetch capability to make this a fast operation.

As shown in Figure 2-4, we save each bone matrix for each frame for each animation linearly into a texture, and thus we can read it out in the vertex shader.

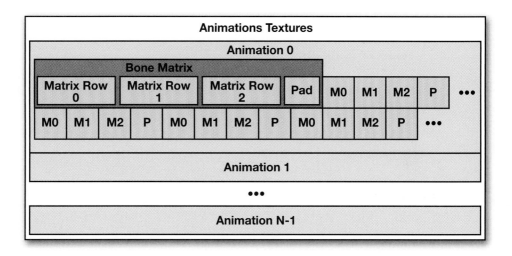

Figure 2-4. The Animations Texture Breakdown

Decode Matrices from a Texture

Listing 2-3 shows the function in HLSL that loads the matrix from the animations texture based on the animation offset and bone offset in texels. You can see that we divide and modulus to determine a UV from a linear offset into the animation. Then we point-sample three rows of the matrix and construct a float4x4 (the translation is encoded in w components for each row). The sampling from the animation texture uses the HLSL Load() method, which returns the texel unfiltered, and takes an exact pixel position as input, thus simplifying the lookup process.

Conditional Branching for Weights

As with regular palette skinning, vertices can have up to four bone weights, but not all vertices have four bones active. Thus we make use of conditional branching in the vertex shader to avoid unnecessary texture loads of matrices we won't use. Listing 2-4 shows this technique.

Listing 2-3. The `loadBoneMatrix()` HLSL Function

By restricting `g_InstanceMatricesWidth` *to a power of two, the computational overhead of the addressing logic can be significantly reduced. The power of two restriction allows the shader to use bitwise operations in place of integer divide and modulus operations. With GPUs just as with CPUs, integer divides are more costly than other operations.*

```
// Read a matrix (3 texture reads) from a texture containing
// animation data.
float4x4 loadBoneMatrix(uint3 animationData, float bone)
{
  float4x4 rval = g_Identity;

  // If this texture were 1D, what would be the offset?
  uint baseIndex = animationData.x + animationData.y;

  // We use 4 * bone because each bone is 4 texels to form a float4x4.
  baseIndex += (4 * bone);

  // Now turn that into 2D coords
  uint baseU = baseIndex % g_InstanceMatricesWidth;
  uint baseV = baseIndex / g_InstanceMatricesWidth;

  // Note that we assume the width of the texture
  // is an even multiple of the number of texels per bone;
  // otherwise we'd have to recalculate the V component per lookup.
  float4 mat1 = g_txAnimations.Load( uint3(baseU,baseV,0));
  float4 mat2 = g_txAnimations.Load( uint3(baseU+1,baseV,0));
  float4 mat3 = g_txAnimations.Load( uint3(baseU+2,baseV,0));

  // Only load 3 of the 4 values, and decode the matrix from them.
  rval = decodeMatrix(float3x4(mat1,mat2,mat3));

  return rval;
}
```

Listing 2-4. Conditional Branching in the Vertex Shader

```
VS_to_PS CharacterAnimatedInstancedVS( A_to_VS input )
{
  VS_to_PS output;

  uint4 animationData = g_Instances[input.instanceId].animationData;
```

Listing 2-4 (continued). Conditional Branching in the Vertex Shader

```
// Our per instance data is stored in constants
float4 worldMatrix1 = g_Instances[input.InstanceId].world1;
float4 worldMatrix2 = g_Instances[input.InstanceId].world2;
float4 worldMatrix3 = g_Instances[input.InstanceId].world3;
float4 instanceColor = g_Instances[input.InstanceId].color;

float4 finalMatrix;
// Load the first and most influential bone weight.
finalMatrix = input.vWeights.x *
                loadBoneMatrix(animationData,input.vBones.x);

// Conditionally apply subsequent bone matrices if the weight is > 0.
if(input.vWeights.y > 0)
{
  finalMatrix += input.vWeights.y *
                loadBoneMatrix(animationData,input.vBones.y);
  if(input.vWeights.z > 0)
  {
    finalMatrix += input.vWeights.z *
                loadBoneMatrix(animationData,input.vBones.z);
    if(input.vWeights.w > 0)
      finalMatrix += input.vWeights.w *
                loadBoneMatrix(animationData,input.vBones.w);
  }
}
}
```

A Few Important Points

- The animation texture must be a multiple of four. This allows us to calculate the row only once in the vertex shader and then simply offset along U to get the four lines for each matrix.

- We actually encode the matrix into three lines to save a texture fetch, but to avoid issues with non-power-of-two textures, we add in a pad texel.

- The linear offset in texels to the active animation, and the linear offset within the animation for the active frame, are specified per instance.

- The bone index and bone weight information are stored (as normal) per vertex for matrix palette skinning.

2.3.3 Geometry Variations

If all characters rendered had the exact same mesh geometry, the user would immediately notice the homogeneousness of the scene and her disbelief would not be suspended. To achieve more variation in character meshes, we break a character into multiple pieces and provide alternate meshes. In the case of this sample, we have warriors with differing armor pieces and weapons. The character mesh is broken up into these distinct pieces, and each piece is instanced separately.

The basic method involves understanding which pieces each character instance contains. Then, we create a list of characters that use a given piece. At draw time, we simply iterate over the pieces, inject proper position information into the per-instance constant buffer, and draw the appropriate amount of instances.

Figure 2-5 is from Autodesk's 3ds Max 9, where we can see that the source mesh contains all the mesh permutations for each character. Notice that all the weapons are included in the same file. They are exported as separate mesh objects but all are bound to an identical skeleton. Thus we can reuse the animations from the character for all the subsections. At load time, the system will generate random permutations of the subsec-

Figure 2-5. The Character Mesh in 3ds Max 9 Showing All Mesh Variations

tions to give each character a different appearance. The technique supports as many mesh variations as your artists can come up with. For a real game, you might want to have finer artist control over this (as opposed to random generation), which would require some work on tools or on the export path.

2.3.4 The Level-of-Detail System

Because characters in the distance take up fewer pixels on the screen, there is no need for them to be as highly tessellated as characters closer to the camera. In addition, distant characters do not need to sample from the normal map, or calculate complex lighting. Thus we implement an LOD system to improve performance. The technique for instancing breaks each character into a collection of mesh pieces that are instanced. We can easily create an LOD system by simply adding more pieces to the instancing system. Every frame, each character instance determines the LOD group that it is in by its distance from the camera. This operation happens on the CPU. Then at render time,

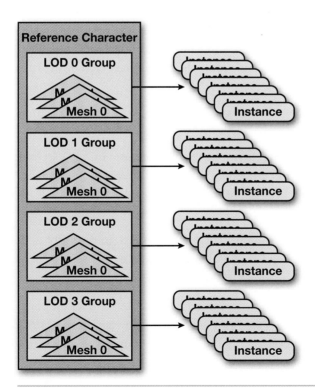

Figure 2-6. The Layout of the LOD Data

collections of each mesh piece in each LOD group are drawn. As we iterate through each LOD mesh piece, we consult which instances are in that LOD group and use that piece. Thus we can update the instance data buffers appropriately to render each character at the correct LOD level. See Figure 2-6. We also perform a simple view frustum culling on the CPU to avoid sending thousands of characters behind the camera to the GPU.

An additional benefit of an LOD system is to reduce geometric aliasing, which would result if you were to draw a highly tessellated object in the far distance such that vertices overlapped on a pixel.

2.4 Other Considerations

2.4.1 Color Variations

Each instance has a different "base" color, which is selectively applied to the mesh based on the alpha channel of the color map. The artists have painted an alpha channel that represents the amount of custom color to blend in. In the pixel shader, we lerp between the custom instance color and white based on this blend factor. This allows greater variation, and it is possible to define multiple instance colors to be used across the different mesh pieces.

2.4.2 Performance

As with any type of instancing, performance gains are seen on the CPU side. By using instancing, you free up CPU processing time for other operations, such as AI or physics. Thus, the importance of this technique depends on the CPU load of your game.

In general, any instancing technique will shift the load from the CPU to the GPU, which is a good thing, because the CPU can always do more processing of your game data.

Performance also depends on where you set the LOD levels. If all the characters are rendered at the highest LOD, then you can render many fewer characters. But as you bring the lines for far LODs closer to the camera, you may see artifacts. This is a judgment call for the graphics programmer.

Our sample in the instanced case runs at about 34 frames/sec for 9,547 characters on an Intel Core 2 Duo 2.93 GHz, 2GB RAM system with an NVIDIA 8800 GTX at 1280×1024 resolution. This is with the LOD level lines set to 20, 60, and 100 character radiuses, respectively. This setting results in 160 instanced draw calls, compared to 59,726 single draw calls if you were to draw the same character meshes in a more traditional way (albeit inefficiently).

Performance will also depend on the mesh data and the level of variety. You can increase performance with more aggressive use of LOD, and you can improve quality with less aggressive use of LOD. This sample is actually pixel/fill limited with so many characters; however, the balance is close and the GPU is fully loaded. As the resolution lowers, the bottleneck shifts to vertex processing due to the vast numbers of GPU skinned characters.

2.4.3 Integration

Integrating this technique is similar to the integration of a new rendering type. Most likely you would define a crowd class, or a background group of animated characters. The placement of the characters in the group can be specified by artists and used to populate the instance data buffer. Placement could also be defined by more-complex AI.

The mesh data and animation data are exactly the same as for a normal hardware palette skinning implementation. The only difference is that you need to preprocess the animation curves into a collection of bone matrices per frame. This should most likely be a preprocessing step.

2.5 Conclusion

Skinned instancing is an appropriate technique for rendering massive numbers of independently animating characters in real time. It makes use of many key features of the DirectX 10 API. It uses vertex texture fetch to read animation data that is stored in a single texture. It also uses SV_InstanceID to index into a constant buffer containing instance information (position, animation time). Finally, the system supports an easy-to-implement LOD system to allow polygonal/lighting detail to be higher when appropriate and lower in the distance.

2.6 References

Carucci, Francesco. 2005. "Inside Geometry Instancing." In *GPU Gems 2*, edited by Matt Pharr, pp 47–67. Addison-Wesley.

Dudash, Bryan. 2005 "Technical Report: Instancing." In NVIDIA SDK 9.5. Available online at http://developer.nvidia.com.

Dudash, Bryan. 2007. "Skinned Instancing." In NVIDIA SDK 10. Available online at http://developer.nvidia.com.

Microsoft. 2007. "DirectX Documentation for C++." In Microsoft DirectX SDK (February 2007). Available online at http://msdn.microsoft.com/directx.

Chapter 3

DirectX 10 Blend Shapes: Breaking the Limits

Tristan Lorach
NVIDIA Corporation

Rich animation is an important aspect of any modern game, and blend shapes are among the most effective techniques to drive this animation. With the capabilities introduced in DirectX 10 hardware, prior GPU-based implementations can be extended to support much more flexible blending scenarios. In this chapter we present two strategies for moving beyond the previous limitations on GPU-accelerated implementations of blend shapes. Figure 3-1 illustrates several facial expressions created from multiple blend shapes.

3.1 Introduction

Blend shapes are a well-known and useful deformer available in any digital content creation (DCC) application. These deformers can achieve rich animations by morphing the mesh between many different shapes. For this reason they are also known as *morph targets* (Beeson 2004).

Blend shapes are a very flexible tool, enabling many animation possibilities. A simpler animation sequence may use a series of poses through which the object is morphed. During a sequence such as this, the geometry is blended between only two of the targets at any instant in the animation. Alternatively, more-complex animations may combine several blend shapes to produce a new expression. On top of the opportunities for

Figure 3-1. This Character Has More Than 50 Blend Shapes

facial animation, blend shapes offer interesting possibilities in multiplayer games. Many of these games require that the character be configurable so that every individual can have a unique identity in the game. The blend shapes can be used to composite features to a mesh that is read back to the CPU for efficient processing, and they can also be used to produce variations in the animations for processing at runtime.

NVIDIA's past demo characters Dawn, Nalu, and Luna are examples of how blend shapes can be used to create facial expressions. Interactively changing the sliders controlling the expressions in these demos reveals that the flexibility is still restricted. The user can select only a base expression and use sliders to change some details of that base expression. These restrictions result from the limits on GPU capabilities when the demos were created.

GPUs prior to the NVIDIA GeForce 8800 required the additional blend shape data to be sent as vertex attributes. The limited number of attributes restricted the number of blend shapes the GPU could process simultaneously. This restriction led to a necessary trade-off: either the blend shapes were processed on the CPU (potentially bottlenecking the application), or the blend shapes were processed on the GPU, with restrictions on the flexibility of the animation.

When the Dawn demo was created in 2002, it was possible to pack only four blend shapes into the vertex attributes (Beeson 2004). In the demo, two of the shapes were devoted to drive the animation of the base expressions, while the other two were used to control orthogonal expressions such as eye blinking. For the two primary shapes, interpolation was done between the two shapes (A and B) until the animation was weighted 100 percent toward B. At this point, A would be replaced by the next shape in the progression (C). The animation would then continue gradually morphing toward C. Similar operations would occur with the orthogonal expressions, with these being applied on top of the base expressions.

DirectX 10 enables the blend shape algorithm to extend beyond the restrictive set of four inputs to an essentially limitless set. This clearly opens the door to more-complex and expressive animations. These improvements enable the following possibilities:

- Creating composite expressions by mixing several expression components such as a wink or a smirk
- Animating between different expressions each of which requires several components, such as a transition from a surprised look requiring seven subexpressions to an annoyed look requiring five subexpressions.
- Storing all the animation frames and blend shapes statically while restricting the per-vertex processing to the components of interest.

3.2 How Does It Work?

Mathematically, blend shapes are very simple. A blend shape is simply the per-vertex difference between a reference, or neutral, pose and the intended pose. This set of per-vertex differences can be thought of as a mesh of vectors. The difference vectors contained in this mesh not only cover the vertex positions, but they also cover other properties such as surface normals, texture coordinates, and tangent vectors. If $\mathbf{P}$ is a vertex in the mesh, then the following equation demonstrates how to compute the blend shape vector for the ith pose of $\mathbf{P}$:

$$\Delta\mathbf{P}_i = \mathbf{P}_i - \mathbf{P}_{neutral}.$$

Creating the final vertex is as simple as computing a weighted sum of all the blend shapes for the present animation:

$$\mathbf{P}_{final} = \mathbf{P}_{neutral} + \sum_{i=0}^{N} \mathbf{w}_i \cdot \Delta\mathbf{P}_i.$$

3.2.1 Features of DirectX 10

The blend shapes algorithm can take advantage of the following major DirectX 10 features:

- **Stream-out.** Stream-out allows a vertex shader to operate on a batch of vertices but write them back to a buffer instead of forwarding them down the graphics pipeline to become triangles and eventually pixels. This powerful capability allows an arbitrary number of processing phases for blend shapes.

- **HLSL buffer template.** This provides access to an unsized data buffer for holding blend shape data.

- **VertexID.** The VertexID system value provides a convenient reference to the vertex in the mesh that is currently being processed. This allows the shader to fetch additional blend shape data not in the vertex buffer.

3.2.2 Defining the Mesh

Some regions of the mesh are unaffected by the animations driven from the blend shapes. As an optimization, these regions are rendered separately without any of the blend shape shading.

For example, under this approach, we compute the expression on Dawn's face by providing the following to the GPU:

- **One neutral mesh.** This mesh contains the vertex positions, normals, tangents, and texture UVs.
- **Fifty-four expressions (blend shapes).** These shapes contain the differences that we need to add to the neutral mesh to reach each new expression. We typically store the positions, normals, and tangents (the binormal vector can be computed in the vertex shader). There is no need to store the attributes that do not change (such as texture coordinates).

We use Maya to create the blend shape data, and we export the final mesh in a custom format made of a sequence of blocks, as shown in Figure 3-2.

If we consider these blocks as DirectX 10 slots, slot 0 would contain the base mesh with interleaved data made of position, normal, tangent, and texture coordinates. Additional slots would be filled with the 54 blend shapes, with each slot containing position difference, normal difference, and tangent difference. This would result in 166 attributes per vertex, if all blend shapes were bound concurrently. Clearly this greatly exceeds the limits of DirectX 10 hardware, but even a small subset such as 4 active blend shapes, exceeds the 16 attributes available. The two methods presented next in this chapter offer solutions to this problem.

3.2.3 The Stream-Out Method

One way to work past the limitations on the number of attributes in DirectX 10 is to operate on the mesh in an iterative fashion. By combining a subset of the presently active blend shapes in each pass, we need only a small number of attributes in each pass. Each pass can select between one and four of the active blend shapes and place

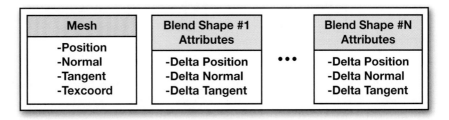

Figure 3-2. Each Blend Shape Encodes Delta Information Relative to the Original Mesh

them into slots. These blend shapes are added to either the results of the last blending pass, or for the first pass, they are added to the base mesh. While this method does require multiple passes over the data, in practice, the required number of passes is likely to be quite low (seven passes would be enough to apply more than one-half of the total blend shapes available for our Dawn model).

In our case, we could add four blend shapes, as shown in Figure 3-3 and Listing 3-1.

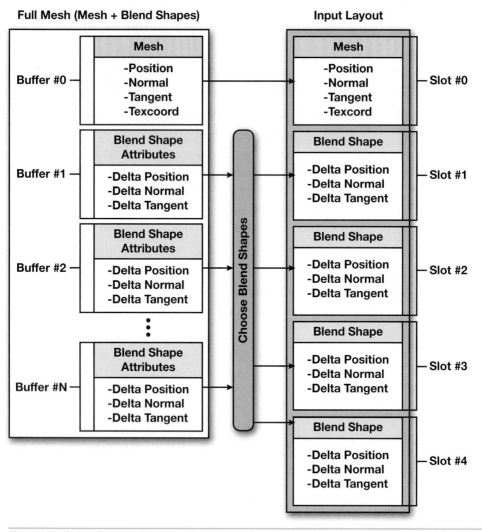

Figure 3-3. Only a Subset of the Total Blend Shape Set Is Used at Once

Listing 3-1. Vertex Structure Used to Contain the Mesh and Blend Shape Information

```
struct Face_VSIn
{
  float3 pos     : position;   // Neutral shape from slot 0
  float3 normal  : normal;
  float3 tangent : tangent;
  float2 tc      : texcoord0;

  float3 bsP0    : bs_position0; // Blend shape 0 from slot 1
  float3 bsN0    : bs_normal0;
  float3 bsT0    : bs_tangent0;
  .
  .
  .

  [Same for blend shapes 1, 2, and 3 bound to slots 2, 3, and 4]
};
```

- The first slot will contain the mesh attributes.
- Four other slots will be added to provide four facial expressions on top of the neutral one. For efficiency reasons, we try to avoid sending null expressions.

The maximum number of blend shapes applied in a single pass depends on how many fit in the 16 available attributes. More blend shapes can fit in a single pass if the data is compressed (for example, packing normalized vectors into 32 bits or using fewer components) or if the data has fewer components (such as no tangent vectors). For simplicity, the examples in this chapter use a maximum of four blend shapes on top of the main mesh.

The shader in Listing 3-2 demonstrates how the input data is processed for a single pass.

To iterate over the data, the algorithm must dump the results out after vertex shading. To facilitate this, the new DirectX 10 stream-out functionality allows the vertices to be written back to a buffer after the execution of the vertex shader, and it allows the geometry to (optionally) not be rendered during this pass. By binding the result of the nth pass as the base mesh for the $(n + 1)$th pass, the effects of the blend shapes for all passes can be accumulated. To maximize the efficiency of the operation, the algorithm needs two buffers to hold the stream-out results. This way, the shader can ping-pong between them, using the first buffer for output and the second buffer for input on odd-numbered passes, and vice versa on even-numbered passes. Before each of these passes, a constant buffer containing the weights (weightBS) needs to be updated with the

Listing 3-2. The Basic Blend Shapes Computation

```
Face_VSStreamOut VSFace(Face_VSIn input)
{
  Face_VSStreamOut output;
  output.pos = input.pos
                    + (weightBS[0].xxx*input.bsP0)
                    + (weightBS[1].xxx*input.bsP1)
                    + (weightBS[2].xxx*input.bsP2)
                    + (weightBS[3].xxx*input.bsP3);
  output.normal = [. . . similar equations as for pos . . .]
  output.tangent = [. . . similar equations as for pos . . .]
  output.tc = input.tc;

  return output;
}
```

proper weightings for the next set of blend shapes. Once all the blend shapes have been accumulated in this manner, this output vertex buffer is ready to be used as the input vertex buffer to render the scene as it normally would be done. Figure 3-4 illustrates the process.

Note that we never perform any CPU readback of our data: everything is kept within vertex/stream buffers. Therefore, you have to tell this buffer that it is a receiver for streamed data (D3D10_BIND_STREAM_OUTPUT) and a source for the Input Assembler (D3D10_BIND_VERTEX_BUFFER).

3.2.4 The Buffer-Template Method

An alternative to using the CPU to drive the iteration over the active blend shapes, as occurs in the stream-out method, is for the GPU to perform the iterations. DirectX 10 enables this by providing flow control in the vertex shader for managing the iterations along with the ability to bind a buffer as a shader resource view to provide access to the data. This buffer is available through a template in HLSL, which can be read by using the Load() method:

```
Buffer<float3> myBuffer;
. . .
float3 weight = myBuffer.Load(x);
```

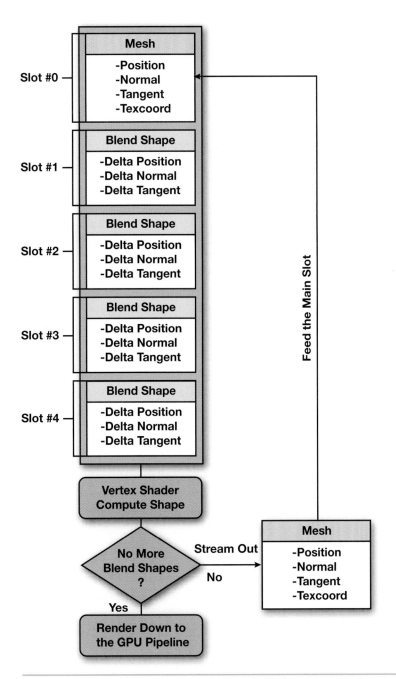

Figure 3-4. Stream Output Enables Multipass Blend Shape Computations

In the application, this shader resource view is created from any buffer that was created with the `D3D10_BIND_SHADER_RESOURCE` flag. Once the resource has been created, it is bound to the effect variable like this:

```
ID3D10EffectShaderResourceVariable *v;
. . .
v->SetResource(myRV);
```

Using a shader resource to hold the blend shape data, this method breaks the input data set into two types. The base mesh is read through the input assembler, while the blend shape data are all loaded explicitly in the shader from the resource view of the buffer. Utilizing loads from the buffer means that an effectively unlimited amount of blend shape data can be read in with a single invocation of the vertex shader.

In addition to the nearly unlimited loads, a buffer provides other advantages over alternative solutions. Textures are restricted to 8,096 elements in a single direction, and while 2D and 3D textures extend the total addressable size beyond the size of video memory, the extra arithmetic for computing row and column offsets is an undesirable complexity. On the other hand, buffers support more than sixteen million elements in a simple 1D package.

With this method, we use this type of buffer to store all the blend shapes in one single big buffer. As mentioned previously, creation of this buffer requires a special binding, `D3D10_BIND_SHADER_RESOURCE`, so we can create a 1D (`D3D10_SRV_DIMEN-SION_BUFFER`) shader resource view. Additionally, because blend shapes are not modified at all at runtime, declaring the buffer as immutable (`D3D10_USAGE_IMMUTABLE`) ensures that it is allocated in the most optimal way. See Listing 3-3.

To address the blend shape components, the shader can utilize the `SV_VertexID` semantic introduced in DirectX 10. This semantic provides the element number currently being processed. By combining this element number with the stride and pitch of the blend shape elements, the shader can easily compute the proper offset for the `Load()` function to retrieve the necessary blend shape elements.

Obviously, the shader must be restricted to process only those blend shapes currently in use. This is done by using an additional pair of buffers that store the indices and weights of the active blend shapes. The number of meaningful entries in these buffers is provided by the variable `numBS`. The index buffer, weight buffer, and the `numBS` variable are all updated every frame. To optimize this usage pattern, the buffers are declared with `D3D10_USAGE_DYNAMIC` (telling DirectX that it will be updated frequently) and `D3D10_CPU_ACCESS_WRITE` (telling DirectX that it will be updated directly from

Listing 3-3. Data Declaration and Resources Creation

```
D3D10_BUFFER_DESC bufferDescMesh =
{
  sizeBytes,
  D3D10_USAGE_IMMUTABLE,
  D3D10_BIND_SHADER_RESOURCE,
  0,
  0
};
D3D10_SUBRESOURCE_DATA data;
data.SysMemPitch = 0;
data.SysMemSlicePitch = 0;
data.pSysMem = pVtxBufferData;
hr = pd3dDevice->CreateBuffer( &bufferDescMesh, &data, & pVtxResource );

D3D10_SHADER_RESOURCE_VIEW_DESC SRVDesc;
ZeroMemory( &SRVDesc, sizeof(SRVDesc) );
SRVDesc.Format = DXGI_FORMAT_R32G32B32_FLOAT;
SRVDesc.ViewDimension = D3D10_SRV_DIMENSION_BUFFER;
SRVDesc.Buffer.ElementOffset = 0;
SRVDesc.Buffer.ElementWidth = numBlendShapes * vertexCount *
    (vtxBufferStrideBytes/(3 * sizeof(float)));
hr = pd3dDevice->CreateShaderResourceView( pVertexResource, &SRVDesc,
                                           &pVertexView );
```

the CPU). Listing 3-4 shows how the blend shapes are accumulated in this method. Figure 3-5 illustrates the process.

To get to the final vertex position, the vertex shader simply

- Loops over these two arrays of indices and weights
- Retrieves the corresponding vertex attributes in the blend shape pointed out by the index
- And finally adds these contributions to the final vertex

If you compare this approach with the previous method, you see that now the whole construction of the final shape is performed in one single draw call: we don't need to drive the iterations by sending additional draw calls. Instead, we stay in the vertex shader and loop in it depending on how many blend shapes need to be processed.

Listing 3-4. A More Flexible Way of Computing Blend Shapes

```
for(int i=0; i<numBS; i++)
{
  uint offset = bsPitch * bsOffsets.Load(i);
  float weight = bsWeights.Load(i);
  dp = bsVertices.Load(offset + 3*vertexID+0);
  dn = bsVertices.Load(offset + 3*vertexID+1);
  dt = bsVertices.Load(offset + 3*vertexID+2);

  pos += dp * weight;
  normal += dn * weight;
  tangent += dt * weight;
}
```

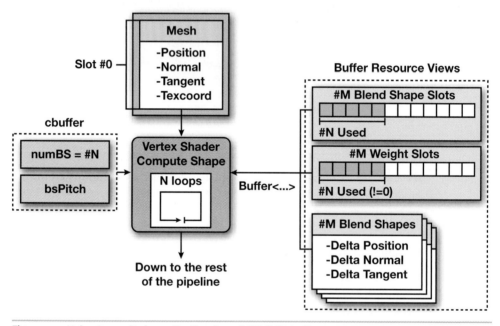

Figure 3-5. Using Loops Reduces the Number of API Calls to One

Listing 3-5 shows the final sample code for this vertex shader.

Although this method is more efficient, you need to be aware of a limitation in DirectX 10 when using buffers to read vertex data:

Listing 3-5. Initialization Code Surrounding the Loop Featured in Listing 3-4

```
Head_VSOut VSFaceBufferTemplate(Head_VSIn input, uint vertexID :
SV_VertexID)
{
  Head_VSOut output;
  float3 pos = input.pos;
  float3 normal = input.normal;
  float3 tangent = input.tangent;
  float3 dp, dn, dt;
  for(int i=0; i<numBS; i++)
  {
    uint offset = bsPitch * bsOffsets.Load(i);
    float weight = bsWeights.Load(i);
    dp = bsVertices.Load(offset + 3*vertexID+0);
    dn = bsVertices.Load(offset + 3*vertexID+1);
    dt = bsVertices.Load(offset + 3*vertexID+2);

    pos += dp * weight;
    normal += dn * weight;
    tangent += dt * weight;
  }
  . . .
}
```

- In the shader code, it is impossible to use a user-defined type for data (for vertex attributes) in the `Buffer<>` template. Only basic types such as `float`, `float3`, and so on can be used.

- In the application code, when we create a shader resource view to bind to the buffer, we face the same problem: only the types from the `DXGI_FORMAT` enum are available. There is no way to specify a complex input layout made of different formats in a resource view.

This issue is not a problem at all in our case because our blend shapes are made of three `float3` attributes (position, normal, and tangent). So we can simply declare a buffer of `float3` and step into it three by three. However, there is a problem if you want to read a set of vertex attributes made of different widths, say, `float2` for texture coordinates, `float4` for color, and so on.

The easiest workaround is to pad the shorter data. For example a `float2` texture coordinate will have to be `float4` in memory, and the shader will use only the first two components. But this trick requires us to prepare data with some "holes" in it, which is not very elegant and takes more memory. A more complicated workaround would be to read a set of `float4` values and to reconstruct the vertex attributes by ourselves in the shader. As an example, we may be able to use the third components of position, normal, and tangent to reconstruct another three-component vector. We didn't test anything related to this issue, and so we leave it to the reader to find some compression solutions.

3.3 Running the Sample

The sample available with this book shows how to combine 54 facial expressions on the face of the Dawn character. The demo starts with the animation turned on. This animation is simply reading a set of curves to animate a few weights.

We arbitrarily grouped these expressions two by two in 26 groups: you can play with two sliders to vary the 54 expression intensities. Note that if the animation is on, you may not be able to use the sliders that are being animated. However, check out the ones you can change (try Group 6, for example) at the same time the animation is running: this is a good example of how you can combine complex expressions. There is a combo box that allows you to switch between the two modes. Finally, some sliders are available so you can change the lighting of Dawn's skin.

3.4 Performance

Performance varies depending on how many expressions we use. The first technique, using stream-out buffer, is slower than the second, using buffer templates and shader resource views. The main reason for this slowdown is that the first is streaming out the data as many times as needed: the more expressions we have, the more times we will loop through the stream buffer, back on the CPU. In the second implementation, everything is performed inside the vertex shader and no intermediate data needs to be streamed out from the GPU pipeline.

The gap in performance between the methods increases as we add more blend shapes, as you can see in Figure 3-6. With 6 blend shapes, the second method is already 1.34 times faster than the first one. When we reach 50 blend shapes, the second method is 2.4 times faster.

Although the second implementation may appear to be the better choice, the first one is still an interesting technique as long as you use a reasonable number of blend shapes.

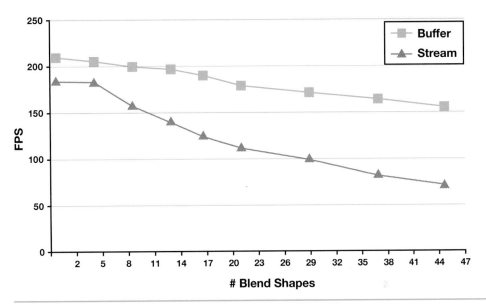

Figure 3-6. Frame Rate per Second for Various Numbers of Blend Shapes

In some situations, it could be useful to save the final result of a blend shape combination. For example, blend shapes could be used to customize a character and then you could save the result for the rest of the game, so you don't need to recompute it. The stream-out mechanism would be necessary for this operation, but we leave it to the reader to figure out how easy it is to integrate one technique versus the other in a particular engine.

3.5 References

Beeson, Curtis. 2004. "Animation in the 'Dawn' Demo." In *GPU Gems*, edited by Randima Fernando, pp. 63–72. Addison-Wesley.

Hagland, Torgeir. 2000. "A Fast and Simple Skinning Technique." In *Game Programming Gems*, edited by Mark DeLoura. Charles River Media.

Chapter 4

Next-Generation SpeedTree Rendering

Alexander Kharlamov
NVIDIA Corporation

Iain Cantlay
NVIDIA Corporation

Yury Stepanenko
NVIDIA Corporation

4.1 Introduction

SpeedTree is a middleware package from IDV Inc. for rendering real-time trees. A game that uses SpeedTree has great flexibility in choosing how to render SpeedTrees. We discuss several features of the GeForce 8800 that enable high-quality, next-generation extensions to SpeedTree. First, silhouette clipping adds detail to branch and trunk outlines. Next, shadow mapping adds realistic self-shadowing at the level of individual leaves. Additionally, we further refine the lighting with a two-sided-leaf lighting model and high-dynamic-range (HDR) rendering. Finally, multisample antialiasing along with *alpha to coverage* provide very high visual quality, free from aliasing artifacts.

4.2 Silhouette Clipping

Tree branches and trunks are organic, irregular, and complex. Figure 4-1 shows a typical, real example: although the branches are approximately cylindrical, the detailed silhouette is rough and irregular. A medium-polygon or low-polygon tree trunk mesh, say 1,000 polygons, cannot capture this detail. The resulting straight polygonal edges are a subtle but important cue that you are seeing a computer-generated image.

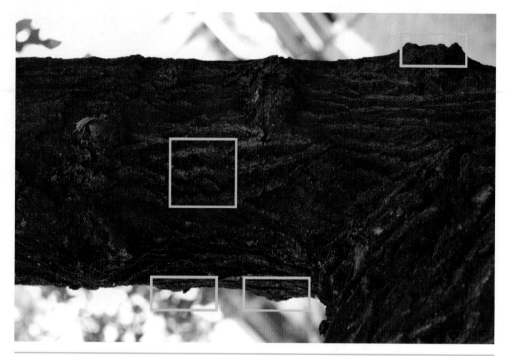

Figure 4-1. A Photograph of a Real Tree Branch, with an Irregular Silhouette

Many algorithms are available to help represent the large amount of detail seen in the branch depicted in Figure 4-1. The oldest and most widely implemented of these techniques is bump mapping. Bump mapping provides a reasonably good representation of the interior region of the branch, such as the region within the lime square in Figure 4-1. However, it is completely unable to handle the details of the silhouette highlighted in the blue squares. It also fails to handle the parallax a viewer should observe from the varying depth of the bark. Improving on bump mapping are a pair of related techniques: *relief mapping* (Oliveira and Policarpo 2005) and *parallax occlusion mapping* (POM)(Tatarchuk 2006). Both techniques perform shallow ray tracing along the surface of the object, which can add parallax and self-occlusion. (We use *relief mapping* as the generic term to cover both.) With parallax occlusion mapping, the effect is again limited to the interior of the object, and the silhouette is unchanged. Relief mapping offers several extensions, one of which supports silhouettes, but it requires additional preprocessing to enable it. Finally, tessellation of the model and displacement mapping can also be used, but they create a significant overhead in geometry processing that may not be worthwhile when trying to render a whole forest full of trees.

Our approach is to utilize relief mapping on the trunks of the trees to handle the interior detail, and to perform an additional pass to provide silhouette details. None of this is supported by the SpeedTree reference shaders, but they can be easily added because the tools, file format, and API allow for additional custom functionality, including extra texture maps.

For the silhouettes, we employ a technique that we call *silhouette clipping*. Although the technique differs significantly from the original described in Sander et al. 2000, the net effect is very similar. Our technique extrudes fins from the silhouette of the object in a direction perpendicular to the view vector. These silhouettes undergo a ray tracing of the height map similar to relief mapping to determine which pixels should actually be occluded by the silhouette. As with the relief mapping used on the branch polygons, this technique requires no additional preprocessing work.

4.2.1 Silhouette Fin Extrusion

The first step in rendering the silhouettes is to extrude the fins. We do this by using smooth, per-vertex normals to determine the silhouette edge within a triangle. If the dot product of the vertex normal and the view vector changes sign along a triangle edge, then we find a new vertex on that edge, in the position where the dot product of the interpolated view vector and interpolated normal equals zero. Figure 4-2 illustrates the procedure.

Finding silhouettes and fin extrusion can be performed directly on DirectX 10 hardware. We calculate the dot product between the vertex normals and view vector inside the vertex shader. After that, the geometry shader compares the signs of the dot products and builds two triangles at the points where the dot product equals zero, as shown in Figure 4-2c and Figure 4-2d. Because the two triangles are generated as a strip, the maximum number of vertices output from the geometry shader output is four. If the dot product sign does not change within the triangle, the geometry shader does not output anything. If a single vertex normal turns out to be orthogonal to the view vector, then our calculations will produce a degenerate triangle. Naturally, we do not want to waste time processing such triangles, so we check for this case, and if we find that two of the triangle's positions are the same, we do not emit this triangle from the geometry shader. Figure 4-3 shows an example of the intermediate output.

To ensure continuity along the silhouette, the algorithm requires smooth, per-vertex, geometric normals. This requirement conflicts with SpeedTree's optional "light-seam

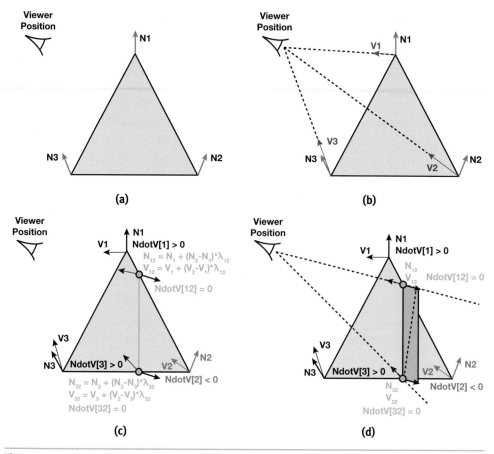

Figure 4-2. Side View of Silhouette Extrusion on a Single Triangle
(a) Triangle with smooth per-vertex normals. (b) View vector computations. (c) Computation of silhouette end points. (d) Fin extrusion.

reduction" technique, whereby branch normals are bent away from the geometric normal to avoid lighting discontinuities. To support both features, two different normals have to be added to the vertex attributes.

4.2.2 Height Tracing

Once the fins have been extruded, we use a height map to present a detailed object silhouette. The height map is the same one used by the main trunk mesh triangles for relief mapping, but silhouette fins need a more sophisticated height map tracing algorithm. We extrude additional geometry from vertices V_0 and V_1, as shown in Figure 4-4. For this fin we will need the following:

Figure 4-3. Tree Trunks with Silhouette Fins (in Wireframe)

- The tangent basis, to calculate diffuse lighting
- The vertex position, to shadow fins correctly
- The texture coordinates
- The view vector, for height tracing

There is no need to calculate new values for tangent basis and texture coordinates, for vertexes V_2 and V_3. V_2 attributes are equal to V_1 attributes, whereas V_3 attributes are equal to V_0 attributes, even though that is theoretically incorrect.

Figure 4-5 demonstrates how this works. It shows that we compute a different view vector for every vertex. In the pixel shader, we first alter the texture coordinate from the fin (point A) by making a step backward in the direction of the view vector (the view vector is in tangent space after the geometry shader). We clamp the distance along the view vector to be no more then an experimentally found value and we arrive at point B. It is possible that point B can be different for different fragments. After that, we perform the usual relief-mapping height-tracing search. If we find an intersection, then we calculate

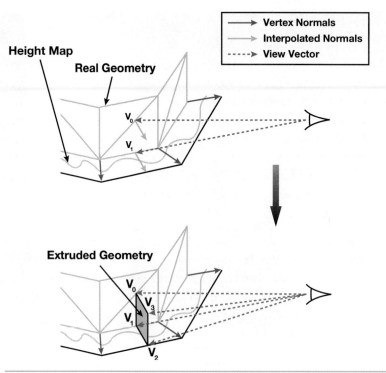

Figure 4-4. Vertex Attributes for Extruded Geometry

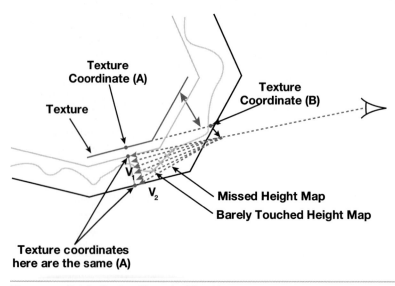

Figure 4-5. Height Tracing Along the View Vector

diffuse illumination and shadowing for this fragment. Otherwise, the fragment is anti-aliased (see Section 4.6.3) or discarded.

For silhouette fins, the search through the height map will trace along a longer footprint in texture space because, by definition, the view vector intersects the mesh at a sharp angle at the silhouette. Thus, the fins require more linear search steps than the relief mapping on the main trunk polygons. Fortunately, the fins are always small in terms of shaded screen pixels, and as a result, the per-pixel costs are not significant. We also clamp the length of the search in texture space to a maximum value to further limit the cost. Figure 4-6 shows a cylinder with attached fins. It illustrates how the fins are extruded from simple geometry. Figure 4-7 shows the same cylinder, textured. Relief mapping combined with silhouettes show realistic, convincing visual results.

Although the algorithm presented here produces excellent results, in many ways it is simply the tip of the iceberg. We rely on simple linear height map tracing for relief mapping. This can be improved by using a combination of linear and binary searches as in Policarpo 2004 or using additional precomputed data to speed up the tracing algorithm (Dummer 2006, Donnelly 2005). Additionally, self-shadowing can be computed by tracing additional rays.

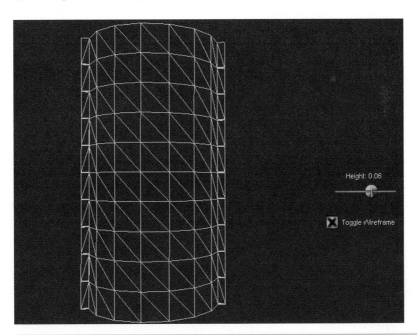

Height: 0.06

Toggle Wireframe

Figure 4-6. Wireframe with Silhouette Fins

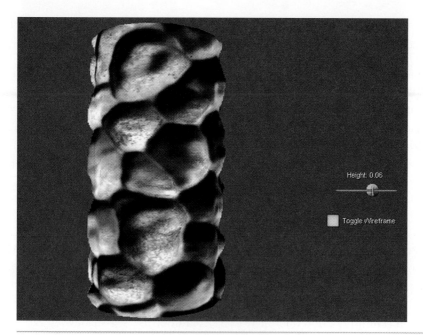

Height: 0.06

Toggle Wireframe

Figure 4-7. The Result of Relief Mapping and Height Tracing

4.2.3 Silhouette Level of Detail

Even with the optimizations, note that silhouettes are not required for most trees. At distance, silhouettes' visual impact is insignificant. Because they do require significant pixel and geometry cycles, we remove them from distant trees. For each tree type, there is a transition zone during which the width of the silhouettes, in world coordinates, is gradually decreased to zero as a function of distance, as shown in Figure 4-8. Thus they don't pop when they are removed. In practice, the number of visible silhouettes is limited to less than ten in typical scenes, such as those appearing in Section 4.7.

4.3 Shadows

With the tree silhouettes improved, we move on to raise the quality of the shadows. Because general shadow techniques are specific to each game engine, out-of-the-box SpeedTree shadows are precomputed offline and static—a lowest-common-denominator approach so that SpeedTree can work with many different engines. This approach has some drawbacks:

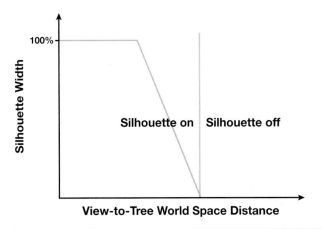

Figure 4-8. The Silhouette Falloff Function

- When the tree model animates due to the wind effect, shadow animation is limited to transformations of the texture coordinates: stretching, rotation, and so on.

- Precomputed shadows don't look as realistic as dynamic ones, especially shadows projected onto the tree trunks.

- The leaves do not self-shadow.

4.3.1 Leaf Self-Shadowing

Our second major goal is to make the leaves look individually shadowed within the leaf card. (SpeedTree uses both flat leaf cards and 3D leaf meshes; this section details leaf card self-shadowing.) Leaf self-shadowing is not straightforward, because leaf cards are simplified, 2D representations of complex 3D geometry. The leaf cards always turn to face the camera, and as a result, they are all parallel to the view plane. Figure 4-9 shows a tree with leaf cards. In this method, we use shadow mapping. (See King 2004 for an introduction to shadow-mapping techniques.) To make the shadows look visually appealing, we have altered both the process of generating the shadow map and the technique of shadow-map projection.

Our generation of shadow maps for leaves largely follows standard rendering. Leaf cards turn to face the view position. When rendering to the shadow map, they turn to face the light source and thus make good shadow casters. However, as Figure 4-10 illustrates, they rotate around their center point, which presents a problem. In the figure, the pale blue leaf card is rotated toward the viewer; the lime leaf card represents the

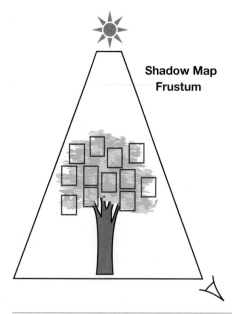

Figure 4-9. A Shadow Map Projected Vertically onto Leaf Cards

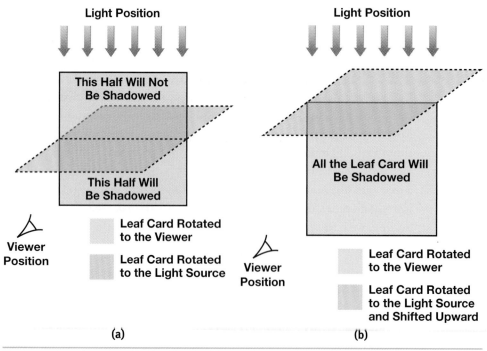

Figure 4-10. Leaf Card Positioning
(a) The leaf card in the standard position. (b) The same leaf card offset toward the light.

same leaf card, but now rotated toward the light source. In Figure 4-10a, note that the lime leaf card will shadow only the lower half of the blue leaf card during the shadow projection. To avoid this artifact, we simply translate the lime leaf card toward the light source, as shown in Figure 4-10b. We translate it by an arbitrary, adjustable amount, equal to approximately half the height of the leaf card.

The planar geometry of leaf cards poses a more significant problem when applying the shadow map. Applying a shadow map to a planar leaf card will result in the shadows being projected along the 2D leaf card as elongated streaks (see Figure 4-12). The only case that works well is a light source near the eye point.

To shadow leaf cards more realistically, without streaks, during the shadow application pass, we alter the shadowed position by shifting it in the view direction. (Note that we are not altering the geometric, rasterized position—the leaf card is still a 2D rectangle. We only shift the position used for the shadowing calculation.) The offset coefficient is stored in a texture and is uniform across each individual leaf inside the leaf card. Figure 4-11 shows the resulting texture. Using this new leaf position, we project the shadowed pixel into light space and sample the shadow map. Because this operation alters different leaves inside the leaf card independently, it has to be performed in a pixel shader. The function used for performing these operations is detailed in Listing 4-1.

Figure 4-12 shows the results of both types of offset. (Except for the shadow term, all other lighting and color has been removed to emphasize the shadow.) Two types of artifacts are visible in the Figure 4-12a: there are vertical streaks due to the projection of the shadow map vertically down the 2D leaf cards. There are also diagonal lines at the

Listing 4-1. Pixel Shader Code to Apply Shadow Maps with Offsets

```
float PSShadowMapFetch(Input In)
{
  // Let In.VP and In.VV be float3;
  // In.VP - interpolated Vertex Position output by VS
  // In.VV - View Vector output by VS
  // OCT - Offset Coefficient Texture
  // SMPP - Shadow Map Pixel Position
  // SMMatrix - transform to Shadow Map space
  float3 SMPP = In.VP + In.VV * tex2D(OCT, In.TexCoord).x;
  float3 SMCoord = mul(SMMatrix, float4(SMPP, 1));
  float SM = tex2D(SMTexture, SMCoord);
  return SM;
}
```

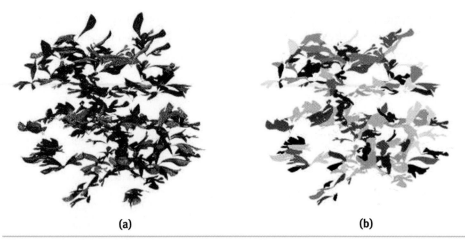

(a)   (b)

Figure 4-11. Leaf Texture and Accompanying Depth-Offset Texture
(a) The leaf card. (b) The depth offset texture for the leaf card.

(a)   (b)

Figure 4-12. The Impact of Leaf Offsets with Self-Shadowing
(a) Naive leaf card self-shadowing. (b) Self-shadowing with offsets.

positions of the leaf cards when the shadow map is rendered. In Figure 4-12b, these artifacts are eliminated. The result is very detailed and natural foliage. In our real-time demo, the self-shadowing of individual leaves varies as the tree moves due to wind.

4.3.2 Cascaded Shadow Mapping

Improving the shadowing behavior of the tree leaves unfortunately does not free the scene from other shadow-map artifacts. For vast outdoor scenes, a single shadow map is usually insufficient. *Cascaded shadow mapping* (CSM) is a common technique that addresses this problem by splitting the view frustum into several areas and rendering a separate shadow map for each region into different textures. (A description of CSM can be found in Zhang et al. 2006. Also, see Chapter 10 of this book, "Parallel-Split Shadow Maps on Programmable GPUs," for more on shadow maps and a technique that is related to CSM.)

To reduce CPU overhead, different cascades are updated with different frequencies:

- The closest cascade is updated every frame. All objects are rendered into it.
- The second cascade is updated every two frames. Fronds are not rendered into the shadow map.
- The third cascade is updated every four frames. Only leaves are rendered into the shadow map.

After the shadow maps are rendered, we have many ways to actually shadow our 3D world:

1. Render objects in the same order as they were rendered during shadow-map rendering, using an appropriate cascade.
2. Fetch pixels from every cascade and mix them.
3. Use texture arrays and choose the appropriate cascade in the pixel shader.
4. Split one render target into several shadow maps, using viewports.

Every approach has its own pros and cons. In SpeedTree, we chose the second option.

4.4 Leaf Lighting

Lighting plays an important role in viewers' perception. The latest versions of SpeedTree provide all the data necessary to perform per-pixel dynamic lighting on the leaf cards, including tangents and normal maps. Alternatively, leaf cards in SpeedTree can use precomputed textures with diffuse lighting only. Detailed lighting and shadows are prebaked into the diffuse textures. We have opted for the first solution, because it supports a fully dynamic lighting environment.

4.4.1 Two-Sided Lighting

In addition to the differences in specular lighting, we observed that leaves look different depending on the view's position relative to the light. Figure 4-13 shows two photographs of the same leaves taken seconds apart, in the same lighting conditions, with the same camera settings for exposure, and so on. (Look closely at the brown spots of disease and you can compare the same leaf in both photos. One leaf is marked by a red spot.) When a leaf is lit from behind, the major contribution is not reflected light; instead, the major contribution to the illumination is from transmitted light. As the light shines through the leaf, its hue is slightly shifted to yellow or red.

Based on this observation, we have implemented the following scheme to simulate the two-sided nature of the illumination:

- Yellow leaf color is generated inside the pixel shader as a `float3` vector with components (`Diffuse.g * 0.9`, `Diffuse.g * 1.0`, `Diffuse.g * 0.2`).

- Depending on the value of $\mu - angle$, as shown in Figure 4-14, between light direction and view vector, we lerp between the original color and the yellow version. Lerping occurs if μ is close to π, which means that we are looking at the sun, and if the tree is in our way, leaves will appear slightly more yellow.

Depending on μ, the specular component is reduced, because no light reflection should occur on the back side. This approach may seem naive, but it makes the picture more visually appealing. See Figure 4-15.

(a)   (b)

Figure 4-13. Real Leaf Lighting as a Function of View Direction
(a) Leaves lit from the front. (b) Leaves lit from behind.

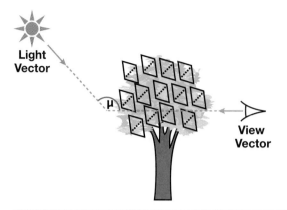

Figure 4-14. Back-Lighting of Leaves

Figure 4-15. Lighting Enhancement Comparison
(a) Precomputed diffuse map. (b) Shadows per-pixel lit. (c) Simple lighting. (d) Two-sided lighting.

4.4.2   Specular Lighting

In addition to the tweaks for two-sided lighting, we modify the specular illumination to enhance the realism. First, with normal specular lighting, distant trees tend to shimmer, so we reduce specular lighting according to distance. Next, we observed actual tree leaves to get some additional clues. Figure 4-16 shows some typical shiny leaves, and from it we observe three points. The specular reflection is dominated by a strong division of the leaf into two planes along its axis. Relative to the effect of these planes, the fine detail of the veins and other features is fairly insignificant. The specular power of the reflection is low: the reflections are not sharp, as they are on, say, a glassy material. Because we are interested in modeling on the scale of whole trees, not leaf veins, we use these observations to simplify our leaf specular model. To simulate the axial separation, we use a coarser V-shaped normal map to split the leaf into two halves. Finally, because too much detail in the specular contribution often results in shimmering, we bias the texture fetch to a lower mipmap level of the normal map. The end result is smoother, gentler specular lighting that does not introduce heavy lighting-related aliasing.

Figure 4-16. A Photograph of Leaves, Showing the Behavior of Specular Illumination

4.5 High Dynamic Range and Antialiasing

Our SpeedTree demo implements high dynamic range combined with multisample antialiasing (MSAA). We use a `GL_RGBA16F_ARB` format frame buffer, in conjunction with the `GL_ARB_multisample` extension.

High-range frame-buffer values come from the sky box, which is an HDR image, and from the tree rendering. SpeedTree supports overbright rendering. Our demo adjusts this so that it outputs values ever so slightly outside the [0, 1] range.

A post-processing filter adds "God rays" to bright spots in the frame buffer by using a radial blur. Otherwise, our use of HDR is not new.

4.6 Alpha to Coverage

Alpha to coverage converts the alpha value output by the pixel shader to a coverage mask that is applied at the subpixel resolution of an MSAA render target. When the MSAA resolve is applied, the result is a transparent pixel. Alpha to coverage works well for antialiasing what would otherwise be 1-bit transparency cutouts.

4.6.1 Alpha to Coverage Applied to SpeedTrees

Such 1-bit cutouts are common in rendering vegetation, and SpeedTree uses transparent textures for fronds and leaves. We apply alpha to coverage to these textures, and Figure 4-17 shows the benefits when applied to fronds. The pixelation and hard edges in the left-hand image are greatly reduced when alpha to coverage is applied. The benefits are greater when the vegetation animates (SpeedTree supports realistic wind effects), as the harsh edges of transparency cutouts tend to scintillate. Alpha to coverage largely eliminates these scintillation artifacts. Unlike alpha blending, alpha to coverage is order independent, so leaves and fronds do not need to be sorted by depth to achieve a correct image.

4.6.2 Level-of-Detail Cross-Fading

However, there is a problem. The reference SpeedTree renderer uses alpha cutouts for a different purpose: *fizzle* level of detail (LOD). A noise texture in the alpha channel is applied with a varying alpha-test reference value. As the reference value changes, differing amounts of the noise texture pass the alpha test. (For more details, see Whatley 2005.)

Figure 4-17. The Impact of Alpha to Coverage
The same scene without alpha to coverage (left) and with alpha to coverage (right). The pixelation and hard edges in the left-hand image are greatly reduced on the right.

To cross-fade between LODs, two LOD models are drawn simultaneously with differing alpha-test reference values. The fizzle uses alpha test to produce a cross-fade at the pixel level. All sorts of things went wrong when alpha to coverage was naively applied in conjunction with fizzle LOD (most obviously, the tree trunks became partly transparent).

Fortunately, alpha to coverage can also be adapted to implement the cross-fade. Alpha to coverage is not a direct replacement for alpha blending: large semitransparent areas do not always work well. In particular, alpha to coverage does not accumulate in the same way as blended alpha. If two objects are drawn one on top of the other with 50 percent alpha-to-coverage alpha, they both use the same coverage mask. The resulting image is the object that passes the depth test, drawn with 50 percent transparency.

We solve this problem by offsetting the alpha-fade curves of the two LODs. The result is not perfect: at some points during a transition, the overall tree is still more transparent than we would like. But this defect is rarely noticeable in practice. Figure 4-18 shows a tree in the middle of a cross-fade, using alpha to coverage.

4.6.3 Silhouette Edge Antialiasing

In our silhouette-clipping algorithm, height tracing is performed in the pixel shader. This means that the silhouette outline is determined only for each pixel, not for each sample. Because the visible edge is no longer the geometric edge, standard multisampling does not antialias the visible edge.

Figure 4-18. A Tree in the Middle of an LOD Cross-fade
Using alpha to coverage to implement the transparency.

Alpha to coverage can be used to antialias the silhouette edges. To do this, we generate a narrow border region, at the edge of the silhouette, across which the silhouette opacity fades from opaque to clear.

We store 1 or 0 in the view vector W component in the geometry shader. Vertices V_0 and V_1 store 0 and V_2 and V_3 store 1, as shown in Figure 4-19. This value will be interpolated across the fin and represent a smooth height change.

During height tracing, we remember the minimal miss against the height map and change the pixel opacity according to that value. We take *ddx*() and *ddy*() of the view vector's W component to determine height change per pixel. After that, we check the minimal miss (from view vector to height map tracing) against the footprint to determine pixel alpha as a linear function. The alpha value equals 1.0 if the view vector intersects the trunk height map. If we miss, we let alpha fade to 0 if the minimal miss is less than about 1.5 pixels in screen-space units. Otherwise, alpha is set to 0.

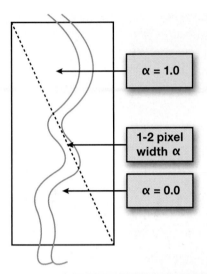

Figure 4-19. The Alpha Distribution on a Silhouette Fin

Figure 4-20 shows a silhouette without antialiasing and the same silhouette with our alpha-to-coverage border applied.

4.7 Conclusion

The figures in this final section show some typical results obtained using our techniques. They bring all of our GeForce 8800 SpeedTree techniques together in a high-quality demo. Figure 4-21 shows our two-sided leaf-lighting model interacting with high-dynamic-range effects. Detailed trunk silhouettes are also clearly visible. Close inspection of the trunk near the bottom center of Figure 4-21 shows some discontinuity artifacts between the trunk mesh and the silhouette. However, we find these artifacts small and acceptable.

Figure 4-22 demonstrates silhouette clipping applied to a quite different trunk type: the tall, thin trees. Note how the silhouette bumps correspond well with the relief-mapped bumps applied to the trunk mesh. The silhouettes also have a subtle effect on the thinnest trunks, for example, on the very right edge of the image. The effect is subtle, but it breaks up what are otherwise straight polygonal edges. Lighting and HDR effects are also visible, and all the trees show detailed self-shadowing.

Figure 4-23 shows a closer view of our shadowing. The foreground tree casts accurate shadows on the rock below and on its own trunk, including the silhouette fins. These

Figure 4-20. Alpha-to-Coverage Antialiasing on Extruded Silhouettes
Top: Visible edges without alpha to coverage. Bottom: Visible edges with alpha to coverage.

Figure 4-21. Two-Sided Leaf Lighting and Branch Silhouettes

Figure 4-22. High Dynamic Range and Two-Sided Lighting Plus Silhouettes
Note the two-sided lighting on the left and the silhouettes in the middle.

shadows move realistically as the tree sways due to SpeedTree's wind effects. The leaves in the very top right and in the center of the image demonstrate self-shadowing. This depiction is not strictly accurate, but it is realistic. The light source is almost directly overhead. Note how the shadowing of the leaves reflects this: in the center of the image, the clusters are lit at the top and in shadow at the bottom, with a realistic dappling in between.

Note also the effect of the cascaded shadow maps. A highly detailed shadow is visible in the foreground of Figure 4-23. Yet, just to the right of the center, shadows are cast by distant trees, to the limit of the view distance. All visible shadows are dynamically generated and move as the trees animate.

Figure 4-23. Detailed, Accurate Self-Shadowing

These images demonstrate that SpeedTree's shaders can be readily customized well beyond the standard reference implementation. They also demonstrate that the NVIDIA GeForce 8800 is capable of rendering extremely high quality, realistic vegetation.

4.8 References

Donnelly, William. 2005. "Per-Pixel Displacement Mapping with Distance Functions." In *GPU Gems 2*, edited by Matt Pharr, pp. 123–136. Addison-Wesley.

Dummer, Jonathan. 2006. "Cone Step Mapping: An Iterative Ray-Heightfield Intersection Algorithm." Available online at http://www.lonesock.net/files/ConeStepMapping.pdf.

King, Gary. 2004. "Shadow Mapping Algorithms." Presentation. Available online at ftp://download.nvidia.com/developer/presentations/2004/GPU_Jackpot/Shadow_Mapping.pdf.

Lloyd, Brandon, David Tuft, Sung-Eui Yoon, and Dinesh Manocha. 2006. "Warping and Partitioning for Low Error Shadow Maps." In *Proceedings of the Eurographics Symposium on Rendering 2006*, pp. 215–226.

NVIDIA Corporation. 2005. "Anti-Aliasing with Transparency." White paper. Available online at http://http.download.nvidia.com/developer/SDK/Individual_Samples/DEMOS/Direct3D9/src/AntiAliasingWithTransparency/docs/AntiAliasingWithTransparency.pdf.

Oliveira, Manuel, Gary Bishop, and David McAllister. 2000. "Relief Texture Mapping." In *ACM Transactions on Graphics (Proceedings of SIGGRAPH 2000)* 19(3), pp. 359–368.

Oliveira, Manuel, and Fabio Policarpo. 2005. "An Efficient Representation for Surface Details." UFRGS Technical Report RP-351. Available online at http://www.inf.ufrgs.br/~oliveira/pubs_files/Oliveira_Policarpo_RP-351_Jan_2005.pdf.

Policarpo, Fabio. 2004. "Relief Mapping in a Pixel Shader Using Binary Search."

Sander, Pedro, Xianfeng Gu, Steven Gortler, Hugues Hoppe, and John Snyder. 2000. "Silhouette Clipping." In *ACM Transactions on Graphics (Proceedings of SIGGRAPH 2000)* 19(3), pp. 327–334.

Tatarchuk, N. 2006. "Dynamic Parallax Occlusion Mapping with Approximate Soft Shadows." In *Proceedings of ACM SIGGRAPH Symposium on Interactive 3D Graphics and Games 2006*, pp. 63–69.

Whatley, David. 2005. "Toward Photorealism in Virtual Botany." In *GPU Gems 2*, edited by Matt Pharr, pp. 7–26. Addison-Wesley.

Zhang, F., H. Sun, L. Xu, and K. L. Lee. 2006. "Parallel-Split Shadow Maps for Large-Scale Virtual Environments." In *Proceedings of ACM International Conference on Virtual Reality Continuum and Its Applications 2006*, pp. 311–318.

Chapter 5

Generic Adaptive Mesh Refinement

Tamy Boubekeur
LaBRI–INRIA, *University of Bordeaux*

Christophe Schlick
LaBRI–INRIA, *University of Bordeaux*

In this chapter we present a single-pass generic vertex program for performing adaptive, on-the-fly refinement of meshes with arbitrary topology. Starting from a static or animated coarse mesh, this vertex program replaces each triangle with a refined triangular patch, chosen according to the required amount of local geometry refinement, among a set of pre-tessellated patterns stored in GPU memory. By encoding these patterns in parametric space, this one-to-many, on-the-fly triangle substitution is cast as a simple barycentric interpolation of a vertex displacement function, which is either user-provided or computed from existing data. In addition to vertex displacement, the same process can further be used to interpolate any other per-vertex attribute during the refinement process. The method is totally generic in the sense that no restriction is ever made about the mesh topology, the displacement function, or the refinement level.

Several illustrative applications are presented here, including full GPU implementations of (1) mesh smoothing with higher-order Bézier patches, (2) high-frequency geometry synthesis with procedural displacement functions, (3) animated free-form deformations, (4) standard displacement mapping with guaranteed shading and silhouette consistency, and (5) multilevel terrain rendering, to name only a few. But the technique is virtually applicable to any problem that uses predictable generation of geometry by refinement.

5.1 Introduction

Mesh refinement is a powerful technique for representing 3D objects with complex shapes. Rather than enumerate the huge number of polygons that would be required to get an accurate discrete approximation of such a complex shape, mesh refinement techniques split the surface representation into a coarse polygonal mesh combined with a continuous displacement function. Then, at rendering time, two successive operations are basically performed on the coarse mesh:

- **Tessellation**, for generating a refined mesh topology at the desired level of detail
- **Displacement**, for translating each newly inserted vertex to its final position, obtained by sampling the continuous displacement function

More precisely, the role of the tessellation step is to split each polygon of the coarse mesh into a (possibly huge) set of small triangles without performing any actual geometric deformation. The role of the displacement step is to add small-scale geometric details by moving the vertices of these triangles along a vector provided by the displacement function. Depending on this function, the displacement of each vertex can either be constrained along its normal vector or be performed along an arbitrary vector. While the former solution is more compact and easier to apply on an animated object, the latter allows the creation of much more complex shapes for a given coarse mesh. Popular displacement methods include bitmap textures (such as grayscale height-fields) and procedural 3D textures (such as Perlin noise).

Many existing computer graphics techniques can be expressed under this paradigm, such as spline-based or wavelet-based surface representation, subdivision surfaces, hierarchical height fields, and more. However, performing a full GPU implementation of this two-stage process remains a problem with current devices. Although the traditional vertex shader allows an efficient computation of the displacement stage, the lack of geometry creation on the GPU makes the tessellation stage really tricky. Recently a geometry shader (Blythe 2006) has been designed for geometry upscale, but it suffers from a strong limitation, as it can output 1,024 floats at most, which means that only two or three levels of refinement can be applied on each triangle. If deeper refinement is required, multipass geometry shading has to be employed, which obviously reduces overall performance.

On the contrary, the vertex program proposed in this chapter allows very deep adaptive, single pass mesh refinement even on three-generations-old GPUs. Basically, it relies on barycentric coordinates to perform a consistent, crack-free adaptive tessellation. One major advantage of such an on-the-fly implementation of mesh refinement is to deal only with low-resolution meshes at the CPU level, letting the GPU adaptively generate the high-resolution displaced meshes. With our method, this target mesh is never generated on the CPU, never transmitted on the graphics bus, and even never stored on the GPU; the only remaining bottleneck is the GPU's vertex-processing horsepower.

5.2 Overview

The generic adaptive mesh refinement (GAMeR) technique that we present in this chapter offers the following features:

- Standard geometry representations used by common rendering APIs (polygon soups or indexed triangle sets) can be employed as-is, without any preprocessing (such as global or local parameterization) and without any of the additional data structures often required by refinement techniques (such as half-edge structure).

- Only the coarse mesh is transmitted from the CPU to the GPU. The only additional data needed by GAMeR is a per-vertex scalar attribute, called *depth tag*, that indicates the level of detail required in the vicinity of each vertex. Note that this depth-tagging may be generated either automatically or under user supervision.

- Because the mesh refinement is performed on-the-fly, on a per-frame/per-triangle basis, arbitrary level of detail can be obtained, even for animated meshes.

- The whole two-stage adaptive mesh refinement (tessellation and displacement) is performed on the GPU by a single-pass vertex program, which totally frees the fragment shaders for including additional visual enrichments.

The workflow architecture used by GAMeR is presented in Figure 5-1. The key idea is to precompute all the possible refinement configurations of a single triangle, for various per-vertex depth tags, and encode them using barycentric coordinates. Each possible configuration is called an adaptive refinement pattern (ARP) and is stored once for all on the GPU, as a vertex buffer object. Then, at rendering time, the attributes of each polygon of the coarse mesh, as well as the attributes of the displacement function, are uploaded to the GPU (by using uniform variables, for instance) and the adequate ARP is chosen according to the depth tags. Finally, the vertex program simultaneously interpolates the vertices of the current coarse polygon, and the displacement function, by using the barycentric coordinates stored at each node of the ARP. The first interpolation generates the position of the node on the polygon (*tessellation*) and the second one translates the node to its final position (*displacement*).

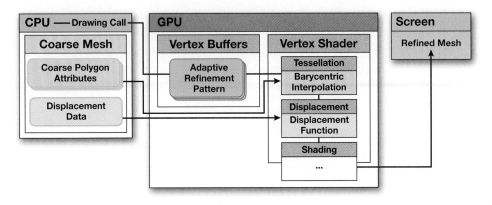

Figure 5-1. Workflow Architecture of Our Generic Adaptive Mesh Refinement

5.3 Adaptive Refinement Patterns

During the initialization step of GAMeR, all possible ARPs are computed once for all and stored in a 3D matrix, called the *ARP pool*, as shown in Figure 5-2a. An element $\{i, j, k\}$ of this matrix is the ARP corresponding to a triangle refined at depth i on its first edge, depth j on the second edge, and depth k on the last one. Since depth values are stored on a per-vertex basis, the order in which the edges are enumerated does not matter. The diagonal of the matrix corresponds to the case of uniform refinement (all edges are refined at the same depth). All other cases have to deal with adaptive refinement, because each edge may require a different depth.

A simple, but not optimal, way to generate the ARP for a nonuniform depth-tag configuration is to uniformly refine the initial triangle until reaching the minimum depth of the three edges. Then, in the neighborhood of the remaining edges, the border triangles are simply split to reach the correct refinement depth for each edge. The upper pattern in Figure 5-2b has been obtained with this simple algorithm applied on the $\{3, 4, 5\}$ depth-tag configuration. To get more equilateral triangles, a larger support for adaptive refinement may be employed. The lower pattern in Figure 5-2b shows an alternative topology for the same $\{3, 4, 5\}$ configuration.

5.3.1 Implementation

As already mentioned, each node of the ARP is encoded by using its barycentric coordinates. The very valuable benefit of this approach is that only a single pattern is required for a given depth configuration, whatever the position, orientation, and shape of any

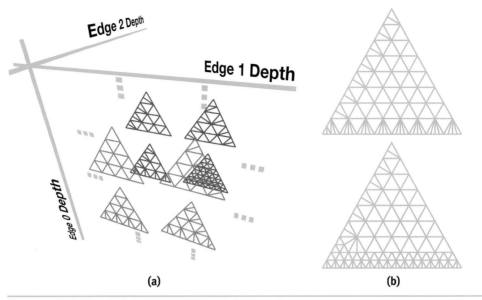

Figure 5-2. Adaptive Refinement Patterns
(a) The 3D matrix of precomputed ARP, stored in GPU memory as stripped indexed VBOs. (b) Two different refinement topologies for the same {3, 4, 5} depth-tag configuration.

coarse triangle it will substitute during the refinement step. Note, therefore, that in the vertex program, the barycentric coordinates of the refined vertices will take the place of the usual position (gl_Vertex). Thus, the geometric attributes of the coarse triangle have to be transmitted in another way. For deep enough refinements or recent graphics devices, uniform variables can be used safely with regard to performance.

The ARP is the central structure of our system. In order to achieve maximum performance at rasterization time, the ARP is encoded as an indexed vertex buffer of degenerated triangle strips, directly in the GPU memory. Moreover, because we use dyadic refinement, each refinement level is actually a superset of the previous one, so we can further reduce the global memory footprint by separating the geometry from the topology. A vertex buffer is used to encode all the geometry, as the set of barycentric coordinates for the nodes that belong to the deepest regular ARP. Then the topology of any given ARP is encoded by using an index buffer, as an indexed strip over this maximum configuration. So, at rendering time, the only action to perform is to bind the index buffer of the selected APR, while always keeping the same vertex buffer.

In restricted conditions, such as PDAs with 16-bit precision, this encoding allows a maximum refinement level of 256×256 for each coarse triangle. At the other extreme, with a modern GPU, we have experienced real-time performance when using 1024×1024 refinement per coarse triangle, in the context of procedural high-frequency geometry synthesis. Even higher resolutions can easily be obtained if required, because our kernel fully runs in object space and does not depend on the screen resolution.

5.4 Rendering Workflow

5.4.1 Depth-Tagging

The depth-tagging process provides an efficient and flexible solution to control the level of adaptive refinement of the input coarse mesh. At the CPU level, the application provides a per-vertex scalar attribute (a positive integer, in our implementation) that indicates the level of detail required in the vicinity of each vertex. In practice, common choices for computing the depth tag may include the camera-to-vertex distance, the local curvature, the semantic importance of the object, the saliency, or any combination of these values. Figure 5-3 presents two different mesh refinements generated by GAMeR on the same coarse mesh, by using either a distance-based tagging or a curvature-based one.

Note that, in some specific cases, the depth-tagging may also be performed at the GPU level, by using a preliminary rendering pass with render-to-vertex-buffer functionalities. However, we believe that this is usually not a good choice, mainly for two reasons:

- The depth-tagging is computed on the coarse mesh, which contributes little overhead at the CPU level.
- The depth-tagging may depend on various criteria, most of which are not easily available at the GPU level.

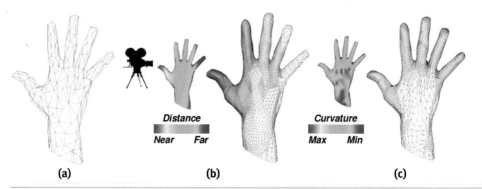

Figure 5-3. Adaptive GPU Refinement Control by Depth-Tagging
(a) The coarse mesh stored and depth-tagged on the CPU. (b) Distance-based tagging (color code) and the resulting refined mesh. (c) Alternative refinement by using curvature-based tagging.

Once the depth-tagging has been performed, the attributes of each coarse polygon are uploaded as uniform variables, and the depth-tag configuration is used to select the adequate ARP's index buffer. Note that edges are not explicitly represented in most real-time 3D engines. Thus we compute depth tags on a per-vertex basis, and then we convert these values to per-edge depth tags simply by using the mean value of the two adjacent vertices. This ensures a crack-free transition between neighboring triangles.

5.4.2 The CPU-Level Rendering Loop

At the CPU level, the application just has to maintain the per-vertex depth tags, bind the adequate index buffer from the ARP pool, and draw it, as shown in Listing 5-1.

Listing 5-1. Pseudocode for the Rendering Loop on the CPU

```
GLuint ARPPool[MaxDepth][MaxDepth][MaxDepth];
. . .
void render(Mesh M) {
  if (dynamic)
    for each Vertex V of M do
      V.tag = computeRefinementDepth (V);
    for each CoarseTriangle T of M do {
      sendToGPU(T.attributes);
      bind(ARPPool[T.v0.tag][T.v1.tag][T.v2.tag]);
      drawElement();
  }
}
```

Note that the number of bind operations can be greatly reduced by clustering coarse triangles according to their depth-tag configuration. Similarly, displacement attributes (such as standard displacement maps, parameters of procedural functions, or coefficients for spline-based or wavelet-based smoothing) are either uploaded once for all at initialization, or on a per-frame basis in the case of animated displacement.

5.4.3 The GPU-Level Refinement Process

The vertex program contains three stages: (1) a tessellation stage, which simply interpolates the vertices of the coarse triangle; (2) a displacement stage, which samples and interpolates the continuous displacement function; and (3) the traditional shading stage. In Listing 5-2, we use simple linear interpolation for both stages, but higher-order interpolation can be used, with possibly different orders for each attribute (for example, linear interpolation for vertex positions, coupled with quadratic interpolation for normal vectors).

Listing 5-2. Pseudocode of the Refinement Vertex Program on the GPU

```
const uniform vec3 p0, p1, p2, n0, n1, n2;

// User-defined Displacement Function
float dispFunc(vec3 v) {. . .}

void main(void) {

  // Tessellation by barycentric interpolation
  float u = gl_Vertex.y, v = gl_Vertex.z, w = gl_Vertex.x; // w=1-u-v
  gl_Vertex = vec4 (p0*w + p1*u + p2*v, gl_Vertex.w);
  gl_Normal = n0*w + n1*u + n2*v;

  // User-defined Displacement Function
  float d = dispFunc(gl_Vertex.xyz);
  gl_Vertex += d * gl_Normal;

  // Shading and Output
  . . .
}
```

5.5 Results

In this section, we present several examples created with GAMeR. Most of them use simple curvature-based and distance-based depth-tagging. Refinement depth ranges from 4 to 10 (that is, from 16×16 to 1024×1024 refined triangles). In Figure 5-4, a mesh smoothing is performed with triangular Bézier patches, using either curved PN triangles (Vlachos et al. 2001) or scalar tagged PN triangles (Boubekeur et al. 2005) to include additional sharp features. In this case, the displacement attributes transmitted on the graphics bus are reduced to a few Bézier parameters per coarse triangle.

Figure 5-5 illustrates another interesting feature of our generic refinement method: because no conversion or preprocessing of the coarse input mesh is required, it can be animated in real time, while always being consistently refined.

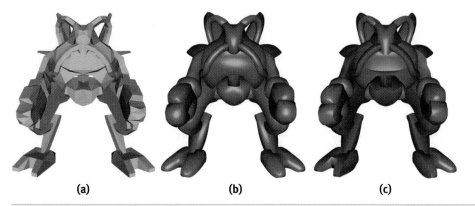

(a)   (b)   (c)

Figure 5-4. Mesh Smoothing
(a) Input CPU mesh (1,246 polygons). (b) Smooth GPU refinement using PN triangles.
(c) Additional sharp features using scalar tagged PN triangles.

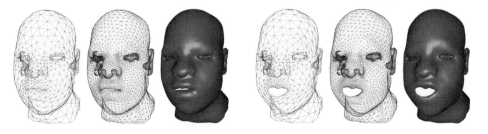

Figure 5-5. Animated Surface Refinement
A curvature-based adaptive tessellation and Bézier displacement performed with a single-pass vertex program.

As shown on Figure 5-6, this flexibility also ensures a consistent adaptive refinement of a surface with arbitrary topologies.

Another application of our refinement kernel is the use of procedural refinements. In this case, complex shapes can be represented as very simple meshes equipped with procedural functions. These functions may exhibit very high frequencies, requiring a deep level of tessellation for accurate sampling. Examples are shown in Figure 5-7.

With the use of vertex texturing, displacement maps can also be used with our kernel. Figure 5-8a shows a terrain rendering system using our kernel for refining coarse ground in a view-dependent fashion while displacing it with a height map. Figures 5-8b and 5-8c show a displaced refinement of a scanned human face.

Figure 5-6. Single-Pass Adaptive Refinement of Arbitrary Topologies

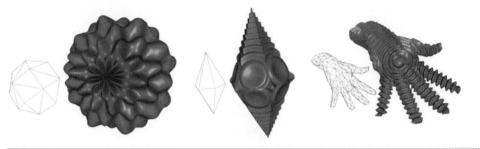

Figure 5-7. Procedural Refinement
The coarse lit meshes are created by applying our vertex program, which produces green refined ones.

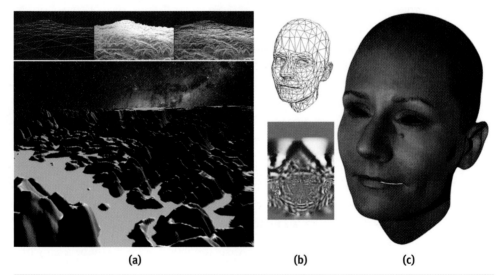

(a) (b) (c)

Figure 5-8. Adaptive GPU Mesh with Displacement Maps
(a) Adaptive terrain rendering. (b) Coarse CPU mesh (top) with high-resolution on-GPU displacement map (bottom), refined with our kernel. (c) Rendering with additional normal maps and shadow maps. Model courtesy of Cyberware.

In general, the best overall performance is obtained with the highest refined size versus coarse size ratio. The refinement can be about three orders of magnitude faster than its equivalent CPU implementation. With recent GPU unified architectures, vertex texture fetches can be performed very efficiently, which allows the use of more and more displacement maps in real-time applications. Our generic refinement technique is then a good candidate for saving CPU workload, graphics bus bandwidth, and on-board graphics memory. Table 5-1 illustrates the frame rates obtained by our implementation on an NVIDIA GeForce 8800 GTX for various models presented earlier.

Table 5-1. Frame Rates Achieved Using GAMeR

Model	Input (CPU) (Triangles)	Depth Tag	Displacement	Output (GPU) (Millions of Triangles)	Frame Rate (FPS)
Robot	1,246	Curvature + Distance	Bézier (STPN)	1.1	263
Hand	546	Distance	Procedural	2.1	155
Face	1,914	Curvature	Displacement Map	4.0	58
Terrain	98	Distance	Height Map	6.4	44

Globally, if the refinement depth is low and the input CPU mesh is large, the system is bottlenecked by the upload of coarse polygon attributes. At the other extreme, if the input CPU mesh is coarse and the refinement is deep, the system is bottlenecked only by the GPU horsepower. For instance, with a target mesh size of one million triangles, an input CPU mesh of 65,000 triangles results in an average GPU refinement depth of 2 and rendering performed at 38 frames/sec. With a CPU mesh of 4,000 triangles, the average GPU refinement depth is 4, and the rendering reaches 279 frames/sec. This makes the system particularly interesting for applications requiring a huge refinement depth, such as CAD or scientific visualization.

5.6 Conclusion and Improvements

We have presented an efficient single-pass vertex shading technique for performing real-time adaptive mesh refinement. This technique is particularly interesting when the input mesh is coarse and the refinement is deep. This technique can be combined with the geometry shader by using the geometry shader for low refinements (such as a depth of 1 or 2) and then switching to our kernel for deeper refinements. The tagging system makes our method generic and allows us to integrate it in a 3D engine by just adding a per-vertex attribute. The killer application of our method is clearly the case of dynamic coarse mesh (such as an animated character face or a soft body) equipped with a displacement function, where the CPU application just has to maintain the coarse mesh while still having very high resolution objects on screen.

Among the possible improvements of this technique, we can mention the use of alternative refinement patterns, with different polygons distribution, as well as the implementation of true subdivision surfaces, where the displacement function is based on their parametric form instead of their recursive definition.

5.7 References

Blythe, David. 2006. "The Direct3D 10 System." In *ACM Transactions on Graphics (Proceedings of SIGGRAPH 2006)* 25(3), pp. 724–734.

Bolz, Jeff, and Peter Schroder. 2003. "Evaluation of Subdivision Surfaces on Programmable Graphics Hardware." http://multires.caltech.edu/pubs/GPUSubD.pdf.

Boubekeur, Tamy, Patrick Reuter, and Christophe Schlick. 2005. "Scalar Tagged PN Triangle." *Eurographics 2005*.

Boubekeur, Tamy, and Christophe Schlick. 2005. "Generic Mesh Refinement on GPU." In *Proceedings of the SIGGRAPH/Eurographics Workshop on Graphics Hardware 2005*, pp. 99–104.

Boubekeur, Tamy, and Christophe Schlick. 2007. "A Flexible Kernel for Adaptive Mesh Refinement on GPU." *Computer Graphics Forum*, to appear.

Bunnell, Michael. 2005. "Adaptive Tessellation of Subdivision Surfaces with Displacement Mapping." In *GPU Gems 2*, edited by Matt Pharr, pp. 109–122. Addison-Wesley.

Shiue, Le-Jeng, Ian Jones, and Jorg Peters. 2005. "A Realtime GPU Subdivision Kernel." In *ACM Transactions on Graphics (Proceedings of SIGGRAPH 2005)* 24(3), pp. 1010–1015.

Vlachos, Alex, Jörg Peters, Chas Boyd, and Jason Michel. 2001. "Curved PN Triangles." In *Proceedings of SIGGRAPH 2001 Symposium on Interactive 3D Graphics*, pp. 159–166.

Chapter 6

GPU-Generated Procedural Wind Animations for Trees

Renaldas Zioma
Electronic Arts/Digital Illusions CE

In this chapter we describe a procedural method of synthesizing believable motion for trees affected by a wind field. The main goal of this approach is to enable the simulation and visualization of large open environments with massive amounts of vegetation. By introducing procedural animation calculations inside the vertex shader, this method works well with instancing and leverages the power of the GPU.

6.1 Introduction

Wind is an important element in creating believable and visually pleasant vegetation. The problem of simulating tree motion in a wind field is a complex, scientific topic. Most scientific approaches use physical simulation techniques based on motion equations that apply wind force to individual branches. Such simulations usually are prohibitive for time-constrained applications, and moreover, they can result in a less-than-natural look because of the inherent complexity of the underlying problem.

The actual motion of trees in a wind field depends on various factors, such as the stiffness and length of branches, the size and shape of leaf crowns, the conditions of the wind field, and turbulence inside the tree crown, as noted by Harker 2002.

Given the complexity of the forces affecting trees in the wind and actual observations of trees under natural conditions, we can observe that tree movements are random. Thus, a number of methods abandon physically correct simulations, instead modeling tree movement as a stochastic process.

6.2 Procedural Animations on the GPU

Given the large number of plants necessary to visualize natural environments, we need an efficient method for both simulating and rendering vegetation. And at the current rate of graphics hardware evolution, end users have come to expect simulated vegetation to be increasingly complex. The goals of our approach are (1) to offload motion simulation of trees from the CPU to the GPU, (2) to leverage hardware instancing to reduce the number of render calls, and (3) to allow seamless integration with GPU-based fluid simulation for an evolving wind field (Harris 2004).

6.3 A Phenomenological Approach

Physically correct simulation of tree motion is very complicated, and computational costs are too high for real-time applications. Instead, we choose to concentrate on a visual aspect of simulation. As Stam (1997) observed, motions of trees in a wind field are chaotic in nature. Thus, we can approximate complicated underlying dynamics using noise or a series of periodic functions. This observation forms the basis of our method. To increase the realism of existing approaches, we selected distinguishable visual phenomena and captured them into a set of simple rules. The final dynamics of the tree are synthesized by combining noise functions according to a set of those rules.

6.3.1 The Wind Field

In order to simplify the calculations, we define wind as a two-dimensional force field over terrain. The aerodynamics-based method for simulation of objects in fluid flows, presented in Wejchert 1991, defines the representation of force fields. Such fields define the direction and velocity of the fluid. Another commonly used name for such fields is *vector fields*.

A vector field can be stored as a sparse data structure. Global wind direction and velocity can be stored along with sparsely placed wind primitives, as in Di Giacomo 2001, or small vector grids to add details in the wind field—capturing phenomena caused by explosions or the rotors of a low-flying chopper, for example. A wind primitive is defined as an analytical function:

$$\mathbf{v} = G(\mathbf{x}, t),$$

where $\mathbf{x}$ is the two-dimensional vector representing position inside the wind primitive, and $\mathbf{v}$ is a wind vector at the given position. Time t represents wind evolution over time. A wind primitive allows us to calculate wind direction and velocity for each given point inside the field, for example, repulsion or vorticity.

6.3.2 The Conceptual Structure of a Tree

Conceptually, a tree consists of a main trunk, branches, and leaves. Such a structure can be represented as a simplified hierarchy of interconnected rigid segments with the trunk as the root of the hierarchy. Each branch is represented as a single rigid segment and can rotate around the joint that connects to its parent branch. Although branches of a real tree are not rigid and can bend, we do not represent branches with several segments as a number of other methods do (such as Kanda 2003). Instead, this property is left to the rendering, where it is applied as a purely visual effect.

A shallow hierarchy, two to three nodes deep, is usually enough to represent visually plausible tree motion. An example of a hierarchy representing a tree with branches is shown in Figure 6-1. Later in the chapter we present a framework for generating animation by modeling angular motion at the joints of the hierarchy.

For performance reasons, we omit the direct effect of leaves and small branches on the overall motion of the tree. However, such effects can be implicitly incorporated in the stochastic simulation.

We assume that the tree is initially in a state of equilibrium. Internal or constraint forces of the tree, such as branch elasticity force, are compensated for by gravity. Offline tools or modeling packages can provide solutions for these constraints.

6.3.3 The Two Categories of Simulation

Simulation levels of detail (SLODs) in animation are analogous to geometric levels of detail. Complex simulation in the distance can be replaced with a simplified version with minimal visual error. The motion of the tree trunk is the most important visual cue in the distance; in close proximity, the natural motion of the branches becomes more important. We choose to distinguish trunk and branches as two important simulation

Figure 6-1. Tree Structure Represented by a Hierarchy Three Nodes Deep

categories. Both categories benefit from the same stochastic simulation approach; however, each has its own implementation details.

Transitions between different SLODs exhibit visual popping; however, such side effects are partially concealed because of the chaotic nature of the small branch motion and the amorphous shape of the leaf crown itself.

Animating the Trunk

Trunk motion is mainly a result of the drag forces applied to the branches. In this chapter, we use *drag force* in terms of aerodynamics: a sum of external forces affecting a solid body in the direction of the flow. To simulate the dynamic motion of the trunk, we need to simulate the drag forces on each contributing branch and in turn propagated down the hierarchy toward the trunk.

However, it is hard to parallelize such an approach, because it would require finishing all branch simulations before the trunk could be processed. Thus, this approach would not suit implementation on the GPU. So we choose the opposite approach. We observe that the sum of all forces propagated from the branches to the trunk will result in a chaotic trunk motion. Thus, we omit the direct physical effects of the branches and instead implicitly include them in the noise function representing the motion of the trunk as a higher frequency noise.

Along with the main drag force, there are a number of other important phenomena affecting the look of the trunk motion. First, inertia resulting from the tree mass and the stiffness of the trunk will affect the amplitude and behavior of the motion. Second, because of the uneven distribution of branches, trunk motion will exhibit some movement perpendicular to wind direction along with a small amount of rotation along the axis of the trunk. And finally, turbulence in the wind field is very important, to avoid producing unnaturally synchronous movement in the tree clusters.

For performance reasons, we would like to combine all of these forces and simulate them as a single stochastic process. Luckily, there is a strong relation between external forces, the physical properties of wood, and the resulting motion of the branch (Ota 2003):

$$m\mathbf{a}(t) + c\mathbf{v}(t) + k\mathbf{x}(t) = \mathbf{f}(t),$$

where m is mass, and c and k are damping and stiffness coefficients, respectively. The force $\mathbf{f}$ accounts for an external load due to wind. Vectors $\mathbf{a}$, $\mathbf{v}$, and $\mathbf{x}$ represent the resulting linear acceleration, linear velocity, and position of the branch, respectively.

Such a strong relation allows us to approximate underlying dynamics and synthesize motion directly. Instead of explicitly solving the dynamical equation, we directly combine the motion resulting function by carefully picking and superimposing frequency bands. An example of such a noise function, composed from the series of waves, is presented in Figure 6-2.

In Figure 6-2, segment A represents a tree leaning away from the strong wind. Segment B represents the combined effect of turbulence: a temporary decrease in the wind drag force leads to a strong response by the trunk due to internal elastic (spring) force. In other words, the tree springs back and "overshoots" its point of equilibrium. Higher frequency noise adds chaotic details, simulating the effect of the smaller branches.

We can simulate a tree with greater mass and lower elasticity by lowering the amplitude of the function and decreasing the frequency. Figure 6-3 shows an example of such a function.

The final animation of the trunk results from the combination of two noise functions, representing motion parallel and perpendicular to the wind direction. An additional

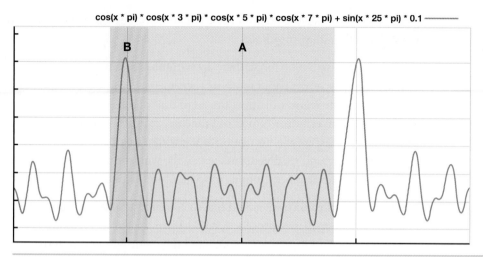

Figure 6-2. The Noise Function Used for Animating a Tree Trunk

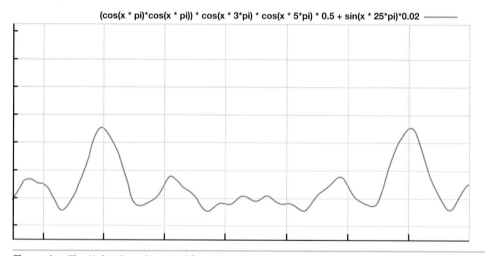

Figure 6-3. The Noise Function Used for Animating the Trunk of a Large, Stiff Tree

third noise function can be used to simulate a slight rotation around the trunk axis. As we already noted, the amplitudes of the perpendicular motion and the rotation are much lower compared with that of the parallel motion. Thus, much simpler noise functions can be used to simulate such motions while retaining the same visual quality.

Animating the Branches

Numerous methods of simulating tree motion suggest modeling the wind effect on the branches as pure drag force. However, such an approach does not completely suit trees

　　Chapter 6　GPU-Generated Procedural Wind Animations for Trees with relatively broad, flat leaves on stiff petioles, or evergreens with thick needles. We observe that branches of such trees exhibit more aerodynamic properties, and we suggest analyzing them as wings in the wind field. Such branches will produce a lift while being affected by the wind field. *Lift* in terms of aerodynamics is defined as the sum of all external forces on a body acting perpendicular to the direction of the flow.

Again, we do not calculate drag and lift forces for branches explicitly. Instead, we choose to approximate the behavior of the branch with a set of simple rules, keeping in mind how drag and lift forces would affect winglike objects with single-point constraints (such as branches connected to a trunk or to another branch).

We can distinguish three different cases of spatial relation between a branch and the main trunk:

- The branch is on the wind-facing side of the tree.
- The branch is on the opposite side of the tree.
- The branch is perpendicular to the wind direction.

If the branch is facing the wind, as depicted in Figure 6-4, the combination of lift and drag forces will press it toward the trunk, and thus the branch will exhibit less free swaying. For a branch on the back side of the tree, turbulence inside the tree and the lift force will dominate over the motion of the branch, as shown in Figure 6-5. Such a branch will exhibit high-amplitude motion, such as random swaying or flapping. Finally, for a branch perpendicular to wind direction, the strong drag force and the large attack angle will cause it to bend around the axis of the parent branch. Also, the lift force will twist it a little bit around its own main axis, as shown in Figure 6-6.

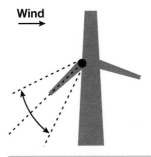

Figure 6-4. A Branch Facing the Wind
Dashed lines depict the amplitude of the swinging branch. Note that the branch is pressed toward the trunk by the wind.

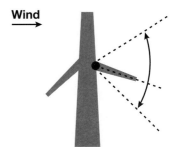

Figure 6-5. A Branch on the Back Side of the Trunk
The branch is flapping in the wind.

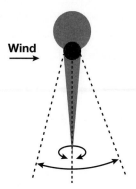

Figure 6-6. A Branch Perpendicular to the Wind Direction
In this view from above, the branch not only bends around the trunk, but also twists around its own main axis.

Even a simple periodic function results in a visually pleasant behavior of the branch once combined according to the previous rules. The actual motion simulation for a branch will be a weighted sum of the simulated cases. Because all cases are represented as periodic functions, there is no need to explicitly solve for branch suppression, bending, and twisting constraints. Such constraints are modeled as amplitude modifiers for periodic functions.

Because the resulting motion is a weighted sum of the described cases, shearing may appear on some branches. However, such a side effect is not visually unpleasant and can be neglected.

Improvements for Branch Animations

At this point, a monotonic wind field should produce convincing tree motion overall. However, branches might move in an unnatural, synchronous way. We choose to add some variations by introducing phase shifts to the previous functions representing branch motions. A phase shift value is assigned randomly for each branch as a preprocess step. A low correlation ratio among the phase shift values will lead to very chaotic tree branch behavior, and vice versa.

Inertia is another important visual property of the branch motion. We propose to simulate the effect of inertia by using information from the trunk simulation step to modify previously discussed suppression and bending constraints (or rather, representative amplitudes). The desired visual effect is that the branches pressed toward the trunk will be released while the tree swings in the direction opposite from the wind. Such and effect creates a notion of inertia.

If accurate stiffness parameters are required per branch, the following formula mentioned in Ota 2003 can be used to modify the amplitudes of parametric motions:

$$k = \frac{Ebt^3}{4l^3},$$

where E is an elastic modulus specific to each tree species and b, t, and l are the width, thickness, and length of the branch, respectively.

6.4 The Simulation Step

The proposed stochastic approach to animation of a tree can be done completely on the GPU. Our approach has the advantage of a simulation that doesn't require information from previous iterations; thus, all branches can be processed simultaneously, independent of their position in the hierarchy. Wind field state, bone hierarchy, and tree parameters are the only required input for each step of the simulation. Required parametric functions can be combined directly on the GPU by summing series of simple periodic functions (such as cosine and sine) or can be precomputed on the CPU and passed on to the GPU as an array of samples.

The wind field can either be sampled from a two-dimensional texture in the vertex shader or be retrieved as vectors representing wind direction and velocity from the additional vertex buffer as tree-instance-specific data (using D3DSTREAMSOURCE_INDEXEDDATA in DirectX 9). The first approach is most suitable when the wind field is simulated completely on the GPU as well. Other required input data, such as bone hierarchy, noise-related data, and miscellaneous tree parameters can be uploaded to the GPU as vertex shader constants.

The following data is associated with each branch and uploaded to the GPU in an array of vertex constants:

- The origin of the branch: the defining point around which the branch will rotate
- The main axis of the branch
- The tangent perpendicular to both the main axis of the given branch and that of its parent
- The stiffness factor of the branch
- The index specifying parent branch, or the terminating index, in case of a trunk

Along with the usual geometric information, each vertex also stores the following:

- A list of branch indices affecting a given vertex (starting from the branch to which the given vertex directly belongs and listing all parent branches until the root of the hierarchy is reached)
- A list of branch weights affecting a given vertex

The simulation step is executed for each vertex and is implemented as a part of custom vertex shader.

The list of branches affecting a given vertex is traversed during every simulation step. The list of branches is assigned for every vertex and includes branches starting from the one to which the given vertex directly to and listing all its parent branches until the root of the hierarchy is reached. Affecting branches are determined beforehand and are stored in the vertex attributes as an array of indices, as shown in Figure 6-7.

For each branch affecting the given vertex, a rotation angle around its axis is calculated by combining periodic functions according to the scenarios described earlier in the chapter. Branch rotation angles are converted into a quaternion representation, as shown in Figure 6-8. Final rotation is obtained by concatenating all rotational quaternions of traversed branches for a given vertex.

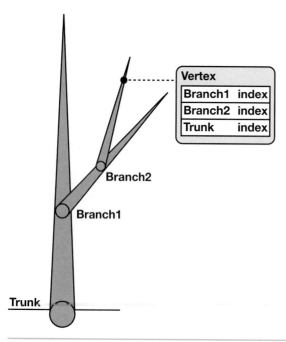

Figure 6-7. The List of Branch Indices Affecting the Given Vertex, Stored in the Vertex Attributes

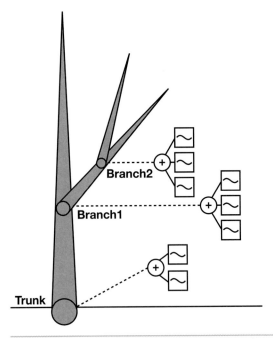

Figure 6-8. Angular Motion Is Synthesized for Each Branch

Our approach differs from conventional matrix-palette skinning (NVIDIA 2004) in two major ways: (1) we synthesize transformation matrices directly in the vertex shader, and (2) we use a concatenation operation, not linear interpolation, to obtain the final transformation. Listing 6-1 contains sample code implementing part of our method.

6.4.1 The Quaternion Library in HLSL

We chose quaternions for the simulation step implementation because they are convenient, compact, and fast while dealing with angular rotations. However, rotating vectors using a rotational matrix proved to be much faster in practice. Thus, our implementation uses quaternions only during synthesis of angular motion and then converts the result to a rotational matrix.

The following quaternion-related functions were implemented in HLSL to be used with the simulation step:

- Angle-axis-to-quaternion rotation conversions
- Quaternion concatenation
- Quaternion-to-rotation matrix conversion (Watt and Watt 1992)

Listing 6-1. An HLSL Function That Simulates a Bending Branch

```
float4 bendBranch(float3 pos,
                  float3 branchOrigin,
                  float3 branchUp,
                  float  branchNoise,
                  float3 windDir,
                  float  windPower)
{
  float3 posInBranchSpace = pos - branchOrigin.xyz;
  float towardsX = dot(normalize(float3(posInBranchSpace.x, 0,
                                        posInBranchSpace.z)),
                   float3(1, 0, 0));
  float facingWind = dot(normalize(float3(posInBranchSpace.x, 0,
                                          posInBranchSpace.z)),
                     windDir);

  float a = branchSwayPowerA * cos(time + branchNoise *
                                   branchMovementRandomization);
  float b = branchSwayPowerB * cos(timeWithDelay + branchNoise *
                                   branchMovementRandomization);

  float oldA = a;
  a = -0.5 * a + branchSuppressPower * branchSwayPowerA;
  b *= windPower;

  a = lerp(oldA * windPower, a * windPower, delayedWindPower *
           saturate(1 - facingWind));

  float3 windTangent = float3(-windDir.z, windDir.y, windDir.x);

  float4 rotation1 = quatAxisAngle(windTangent, a);
  float4 rotation2 = quatAroundY(b);

  return lerp(rotation1, rotation2, 1 - abs(facingWind));
}
```

HLSL source code containing the necessary quaternion operations can be found on this book's DVD.

6.5 Rendering the Tree

The motion composition step uses rigid segments to represent branches. We chose to blend between two bones to conceal the resulting unnatural visual stiffness of the tree during rendering. Thus, each vertex of the tree is affected by two transformations:

- The position and rotation of the branch to which the vertex belongs
- The position and rotation of the branch one step higher in the hierarchy

Identity is used as a second transformation in case the branch is the trunk, because it is the root of the hierarchy.

For each vertex, a weighted transformation is applied to its position and normal. The vertex's tangent and binormal, if present, should be transformed analogously. The ratio of influence between the local and parent branches can be determined offline and stored in the vertex data or can be calculated at runtime as a function of distance between the vertex position and the origin of the branch, modified according to the branch stiffness parameter.

To achieve the best rendering performance, geometric level of detail should be combined with the previously discussed simulation level of detail.

6.5.1 DirectX 10

Implementation of the approach presented here has unnecessary overhead under DirectX 9, as shown in Figure 6-9: the branch transformation must be recalculated for each vertex. DirectX 10's stream-out functionality enables us to store temporary results from the simulation step and reapply them during the rendering step, as depicted in Figure 6-10, thus saving a number of operations per vertex.

DirectX 10 implementation separates the simulation and skinning steps in two separate vertex shaders. First, information about branches and the hierarchy is stored in a vertex buffer instead of shader constants, as was necessary in the DirectX 9 implementation. A vertex buffer containing branch information is used as input to the vertex shader responsible for the simulation step. When the simulation is run for each branch, the vertex shader treats each branch as a separate vertex. The resulting branch transformations are stored in another temporary vertex buffer using DirectX 10 stream-out functionality.

Next, rendering of the actual geometry takes place. The temporary vertex buffer, filled during the simulation step, is bound as an instance data input to the skinning vertex shader. Branch transformations for each vertex are fetched accordingly for the temporary vertex buffer.

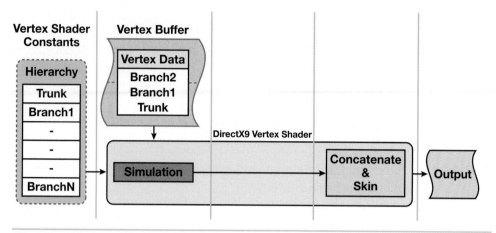

Figure 6-9. GPU Processes Under DirectX 9
All simulation and rendering steps are executed in the same vertex shader.

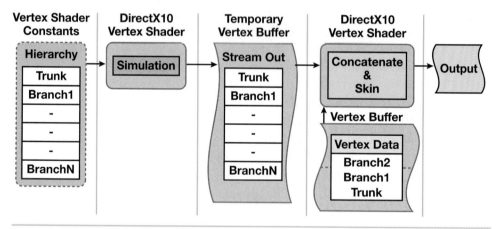

Figure 6-10. GPU Processes Under DirectX 10
Simulation and rendering steps are separated for better performance. Temporary simulation results are stored using stream-out functionality.

6.6 Analysis and Comparison

Our approach for procedural motion generation of trees in a wind field has the following advantages and disadvantages.

6.6.1 Pros

- Our method leverages GPU power by synthesizing animations in the vertex shaders. Also, it opens the possibility for better integration of GPU-based wind-field fluid simulation, completely bypassing otherwise required readbacks of wind-field information to host memory.
- This approach is fully compatible with GPU instancing—a significant benefit while rendering large numbers of trees.
- Various visually important phenomena can be simulated with this technique, creating believable motion of the trees. Additionally, our method handles local effects such as explosions with ease.
- The simulation step is highly parallelizable and doesn't force us to retain information from the previous frame. Thus, it can be easily adapted to different multiprocessor environments.

6.6.2 Cons

- The DirectX 9 implementation suffers from additional per-vertex overhead, because simulation, whose results otherwise would be shared by a group of vertices belonging to the same branch, must be repeated. However, DirectX 10 provides a way to significantly reduce the per-vertex cost of the approach.
- Simulation is not strictly physically correct, because the main goal of the approach is to satisfy only those applications that can accept merely visual resemblance to trees affected by a wind field.

6.6.3 Performance Results

The following hardware was used for performance testing:

CPU: Intel Xeon 2.33 GHz

GPU: NVIDIA GeForce 8800 GTX

Table 6-1 shows the results.

6.7 Summary

In this chapter we described an approach to synthesize the motion of trees while affected by external forces, such as a wind field. It is based on existing methods of modeling tree

Table 6-1. Performance of DirectX 9 and DirectX 10 Implementations of the Algorithm

4,617 Vertices per Instance		DirectX 9 Implementation (Milliseconds)		DirectX 10 Implementation (Milliseconds)	Two-Bone Skinning Without Branch Simulation (Milliseconds)
Instances	Branches	SLOD3	SLOD2		
30	2,400	1.46	1.34	0.86	1.39
100	8,000	3.90	3.82	2.32	2.22
256	20,480	9.81	9.68	5.82	5.59
1,000	80,000	38.21	37.61	22.48	21.61

motion as stochastic processes and extends them by adding simple rules, while simulating aerodynamical properties in branch behavior. We provide the means for combining GPU-based fluid simulation with our approach to improve the user's general feeling of the wind. We also presented detailed explanations of motion synthesis on the GPU along with implementations of our approach based on DirectX 9 and DirectX 10.

6.8 References

Di Giacomo, Thomas, Stéphane Capo, and François Faure. 2001. "An Interactive Forest." In *Proceedings of the Eurographic Workshop on Computer Animation and Simulation*, pp. 65–74.

Harker, George. 2002. "Animation of Trees in the Wind: Efficient and Believable Tree Motion." Submission for SIGGRAPH 2002.

Harris, Mark J. 2004. "Fast Fluid Dynamics Simulation on the GPU." In *GPU Gems*, edited by Randima Fernando, pp. 637–665. Addison-Wesley.

Kanda, Hitoshi, and Jun Ohya. 2003. "Efficient, Realistic Method for Animating Dynamic Behaviors of 3D Botanical Trees." In *Proceedings of the IEEE International Conference on Multimedia and Expo 2003*, vol. 2, pp. 89–92.

NVIDIA Corporation. 2004. "Matrix Palette Skinning" NVIDIA SDK White Paper. Available online at http://download.nvidia.com/developer/SDK/Individual_Samples/DEMOS/Direct3D9/src/HLSL_PaletteSkin/docs/HLSL_PaletteSkin.pdf.

Ota, Shin, et al. 2003. "1/fβ Noise-Based Real-Time Animation of Trees Swaying in Wind Fields." In *Proceedings of Computer Graphics International 2003*, pp. 52–60.

Stam, Jos. 1997. "Stochastic Dynamics: Simulating the Effects of Turbulence on Flexible Structures." *Computer Graphics Forum* 16(3), pp. 159–164.

Watt, Alan, and Mark Watt. 1992. *Advanced Animation and Rendering Techniques.* Addison-Wesley. See pp. 363–364.

Wejchert, Jakub, and David Haumann. 1991. "Animation Aerodynamics." In *Proceedings of the 18th Annual Conference on Computer Graphics and Interactive Techniques,* pp. 19–21.

Chapter 7

Point-Based Visualization of Metaballs on a GPU

Kees van Kooten
Playlogic Game Factory

Gino van den Bergen
Playlogic Game Factory

Alex Telea
Eindhoven University of Technology

In this chapter we present a technique for rendering metaballs on state-of-the-art graphics processors at interactive rates. Instead of employing the marching cubes algorithm to generate a list of polygons, our method samples the metaballs' implicit surface by constraining free-moving particles to this surface. Our goal is to visualize the metaballs as a smooth surface by rendering thousands of particles, with each particle covering a tiny surface area. To successfully apply this point-based technique on a GPU, we solve three basic problems. First, we need to evaluate the metaballs' implicit function and its gradient per rendered particle in order to constrain the particles to the surface. For this purpose, we devised a novel data structure for quickly evaluating the implicit functions in a fragment shader. Second, we need to spread the particles evenly across the surface. We present a fast method for performing a nearest-neighbors search on each particle that takes two rendering passes on a GPU. This method is used for computing the repulsion forces according to the method of smoothed particle hydrodynamics. Third, to further accelerate particle dispersion, we present a method for transferring particles from high-density areas to low-density areas on the surface.

7.1 Metaballs, Smoothed Particle Hydrodynamics, and Surface Particles

The visualization of deformable implicit surfaces is an interesting topic, as it is aimed at representing a whole range of nonrigid objects, ranging from soft bodies to water and gaseous phenomena. *Metaballs*, a widely used type of implicit surface invented by Blinn in the early 1980s (Blinn 1982), are often used for achieving fluid-like appearances.

The concept of metaballs is closely related to the concept of *smoothed particle hydrodynamics* (SPH) (Müller et al. 2003), a method used for simulating fluids as clouds of particles. Both concepts employ smooth scalar functions that map points in space to a mass density. These scalar functions, referred to as *smoothing kernels*, basically represent point masses that are smoothed out over a small volume of space, similar to Gaussian blur in 2D image processing. Furthermore, SPH-simulated fluids are visualized quite naturally as metaballs. This chapter does not focus on the dynamics of the metaballs themselves. We are interested only in the visualization of clouds of metaballs in order to create a fluid surface. Nevertheless, the proposed techniques for visualizing metaballs rely heavily on the SPH method. We assume that the metaballs, also referred to as *fluid atoms*, are animated on the CPU either by free-form animation techniques or by physics-based simulation. Furthermore, we assume that the dynamics of the fluid atoms are interactively determined, so preprocessing of the animation sequence of the fluid such as in Vrolijk et al. 2004 is not possible in our case.

The fluid atoms in SPH are basically a set of particles, defining the implicit metaball surface by its spatial configuration. To visualize this surface, we use a separate set of particles called *surface particles*, which move around in such a way that they remain on the implicit surface defined by the fluid atoms. These particles can then be rendered as billboards or oriented quads, as an approximation of the fluid surface.

7.1.1 A Comparison of Methods

The use of surface particles is not the most conventional way to visualize implicit surfaces. More common methodologies are to apply the marching cubes algorithm (Lorenson and Cline 1987) or employ ray tracing (Parker et al. 1998). Marching cubes discretizes the 3D volume into a grid of cells and calculates for every cell a set of primitives based on the implicit-function values of its corners. These primitives interpolate the intersection of the implicit surface with the grid cells. Ray tracing shoots rays from the viewer at the surface to determine the depth and color of the surface at every pixel. Figure 7-1 shows a comparison of the three methods.

Point-based methods (Witkin and Heckbert 1994) have been applied much less frequently for visualizing implicit surfaces. The most likely reason for this is the high computational cost of processing large numbers of particles for visualization. Other techniques such as ray tracing are computationally expensive as well but are often easier to implement on traditional CPU-based hardware and therefore a more obvious choice for offline rendering.

With the massive growth of GPU processing power, implicit-surface visualization seems like a good candidate to be offloaded to graphics hardware. Moreover, the parallel nature of today's GPUs allows for a much faster advancement in processing power over time, giving GPU-run methods an edge over CPU-run methods in the future. However, not every implicit-surface visualization technique is easily modified to work in a parallel environment. For instance, the marching cubes algorithm has a complexity in the order of the entire volume of a metaball object; all grid cells have to be visited to establish a surface (Pascucci 2004). An iterative optimization that walks over the surface by visiting neighboring grid cells is not suitable for parallelization. Its complexity is therefore worse than the point-based method, which has to update all surface particle positions; the number of particles is linearly related to the fluid surface area.

By their very nature, particle systems are ideal for exploiting temporal coherence. Once the positions of surface particles on a fluid surface are established at a particular moment in time, they have to be moved only a small amount to represent the fluid surface a fraction of time later. Marching cubes and ray tracing cannot make use of this characteristic. These techniques identify the fluid surface from scratch every time again.

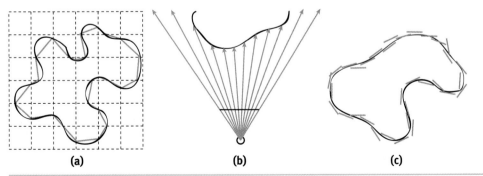

(a) (b) (c)

Figure 7-1. Methods of Visualizing Implicit Surfaces
(a) Marching cubes, (b) ray tracing, and (c) the point-based method.

7.1.2 Point-Based Surface Visualization on a GPU

We propose a method for the visualization of metaballs, using surface particles. Our primary goal is to cover as much of the fluid surface as possible with the surface particles, in the least amount of time. We do not focus on the actual rendering of the particles itself; we will only briefly treat blending of particles and shader effects that create a more convincing surface.

Our method runs almost entirely on a GPU. By doing so, we avoid a lot of work on the CPU, leaving it free to do other tasks. We still need the CPU for storing the positions and velocities of the fluid atoms in a form that can be processed efficiently by a fragment shader. All other visualization tasks are offloaded to the GPU. Figure 7-2 gives an overview of the process.

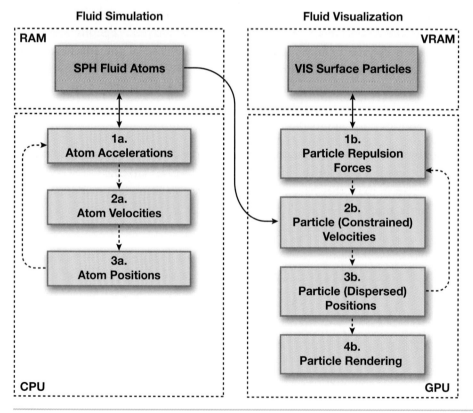

Figure 7-2. The Fluid Simulation Loop Performed on the CPU Together with the Fluid Visualization Loop Performed on the GPU
In essence, the visualization is a simulation in its own right.

Our approach is based on an existing method by Witkin and Heckbert (1994). Here, an implicit surface is sampled by constraining particles to the surface and spreading them evenly across the surface. To successfully implement this concept on GPUs with at least Shader Model 3.0 functionality, we need to solve three problems:

First, we need to efficiently evaluate the implicit function and its gradient in order to constrain the particles on the fluid surface. To solve this problem, we choose a data structure for quickly evaluating the implicit function in the fragment shader. This data structure also optionally minimizes the GPU workload in GPU-bound scenarios. We describe this solution in Section 7.2.

Second, we need to compute the repulsion forces between the particles in order to obtain a uniform distribution of surface particles. A uniform distribution of particles is of vital importance because on the one hand, the amount of overlap between particles should be minimized in order to improve the speed of rendering. On the other hand, to achieve a high visual quality, the particles should cover the complete surface and should not allow for holes or cracks. We solve this problem by computing repulsion forces acting on the surface particles according to the SPH method. The difficulty in performing SPH is querying the particle set for nearest neighbors. We provide a novel algorithm for determining the nearest neighbors of a particle in the fragment shader. We present the computation of repulsion forces in Section 7.3.

Finally, we add a second distribution algorithm, because the distribution due to the repulsion forces is rather slow, and it fails to distribute particles to disconnected regions. This global dispersion algorithm accelerates the distribution process and is explained in Section 7.4.

In essence, the behavior of the particles can be defined as a fluid simulation of particles moving across an implicit surface. GPUs have been successfully applied for similar physics-based simulations of large numbers of particles (Latta 2004). However, to our knowledge, GPU-based particle systems in which particles influence each other have not yet been published.

7.2 Constraining Particles

To constrain particles to an implicit surface generated by fluid atoms, we will restrict the velocity of all particles such that they will only move along with the change of the surface. For the moment, they will be free to move tangentially to the surface, as long as they do not move away from it. Before defining the velocity equation for surface particles, we will start with the definition of the function yielding our implicit surface.

7.2.1 Defining the Implicit Surface

For all of the following sections, we define a set of fluid atoms $\{j: 1 \leq j \leq m\}$—the metaballs—simulated on the CPU with positions $\mathbf{a}_j$, and a set of surface particles $\{i: 1 \leq i \leq n\}$ with positions $\mathbf{p}_i$. The fluid atoms define a fluid surface, which we are going to visualize using the fluid particles. The surface is computed as an isosurface of a fluid density function $F(\mathbf{x}, \bar{\mathbf{q}})$. The function depends on the evaluation position $\mathbf{x}$ and a state vector $\bar{\mathbf{q}}$ representing the concatenation of all fluid atom positions. Following the SPH model of Müller et al. 2003, the fluid density is given by

$$F(\mathbf{x}, \bar{\mathbf{q}}) = s_a \sum_{j=1}^{m} W_a\left(\mathbf{x} - \mathbf{a}_j,\ h_a\right), \tag{1}$$

using smoothing kernels $W_a(\mathbf{r}, h_a)$ to distribute density around every atom position by a scaling factor s_a. The smoothing kernel takes a vector $\mathbf{r}$ to its center, and a radius h_a in which it has a nonzero contribution to the density field. Equation 1 is the sum of these smoothing kernels with their centers placed at different positions. The actual smoothing kernel function can take different forms; the following is the one we chose, which is taken from Müller et al. 2003 and illustrated in Figure 7-3.

$$W_{poly6}(\mathbf{r},\ h) = \frac{315}{64\pi h^9} \begin{cases} \left(h^2 - |\mathbf{r}|^2\right)^3 & \text{if } |\mathbf{r}| < h \\ 0 & \text{otherwise} \end{cases}, \quad \text{with } h = 1.$$

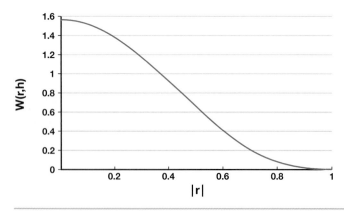

Figure 7-3. The Smoothing Kernel

7.2.2 The Velocity Constraint Equation

To visualize the fluid isosurface described in Section 7.2.1, we will use the point-based method of Witkin and Heckbert 1994. This method proposes both an equation for moving particles along with the surface and an equation for moving the surface along with the particles. We require only the former, shown here as Equation 2. This equation yields the constrained velocity of a surface particle; the velocity will always be tangent to the fluid surface as the surface changes.

$$\dot{\mathbf{p}}_i = \mathbf{D}_i - \frac{F_i^x \cdot \mathbf{D}_i + F_i^q \cdot \dot{\mathbf{q}} + \phi F_i}{F_i^x \cdot F_i^x} F_i^x, \tag{2}$$

where $\dot{\mathbf{p}}_i$ is the constrained velocity of particle i obtained by application of the equation; $\mathbf{D}_i$ is a desired velocity that we may choose; $\dot{\mathbf{q}}$ is the concatenation of all fluid atom velocities; F_i is the density field $F(\mathbf{x}, \bar{\mathbf{q}})$ evaluated at particle position $\mathbf{p}_i$; and F_i^x, F_i^q are the derivatives of the density field $F(\mathbf{x}, \bar{\mathbf{q}})$ with respect to $\mathbf{x}$ and $\bar{\mathbf{q}}$, respectively, evaluated at particle position $\mathbf{p}_i$ as well.

We choose the desired velocity $\mathbf{D}_i$ in such a way that particles stay at a fixed position on the fluid surface as much as possible. The direction and size of changes in the fluid surface at a certain position $\mathbf{x}$ depend on both the velocity of the fluid atoms influencing the density field at $\mathbf{x}$, as well as the gradient magnitude of their smoothing kernel at $\mathbf{x}$. This results in the definition of $\mathbf{D}_i$, shown in Equation 3. We denote this component of $\mathbf{D}_i$ by $\mathbf{D}_i^{env}$, because we will add another component to $\mathbf{D}_i$ in Section 7.3.

$$\mathbf{D}_i^{env} = \frac{\sum\limits_{j=0}^{m} w_j^i \dot{\mathbf{a}}_j}{\sum\limits_{j=0}^{m} w_j^i}, \tag{3}$$

with

$$w_j^i = \begin{cases} \left| F_i^{aj} \right| & \text{if } \left| \mathbf{p}_i - \mathbf{a}_j \right| < h \\ 0 & \text{otherwise} \end{cases}.$$

F_i^{aj} equals

$$\frac{\partial F(\mathbf{x}, \bar{\mathbf{q}})}{\partial \mathbf{a}_j}$$

evaluated at particle position $\mathbf{p}_i$, which equals

$$-\frac{\partial W_a(\mathbf{x} - \mathbf{a}_j, h_a)}{\partial \mathbf{x}}$$

evaluated at $\mathbf{p}_i$ (omitting s_a). This is simply the negative gradient of a single smoothing kernel centered at $\mathbf{a}_j$, evaluated at $\mathbf{p}_i$. Summarizing, $\mathbf{D}_i^{env}$ is a weighted sum of atom velocities $\dot{\mathbf{a}}_j$, with their weight determined by the length of F_i^{aj}.

To put the preceding result in perspective: In our simulation of particle movement, the velocity of the particles will be defined by Equation 2. The equation depends on the implicit function with its gradients at particle positions and a desired velocity $\mathbf{D}_i$, which in turn consists of a number of components, $\mathbf{D}_i^{env}$ and $\mathbf{D}_i^{rep}$. These components are influenced by fluid atom velocities and surface particle repulsion forces, respectively. The first component is defined by Equation 3; the second component is discussed in Section 7.3. The implementation of the algorithm appears in Listing 7-1.

Listing 7-1. Implementation Part 1: Pseudocode of a Fragment Program Simulating the Velocity of a Surface Particle

```
void mainvel()
{
  //Perform two lookups to find the particle position and velocity
  //in the corresponding textures.
  position = f3tex2D(pos_texture, particle_coord);
  velocity = f3tex2D(vel_texture, particle_coord);

  //Compute the terms of Equations 2 and 3.
  for each fluid atom  //See Listing 7-2.
  {
    fluid_atom_pos, fluid_atom_vel; //See Listing 7-2 for data lookup.
    r = position - fluid_atom_pos;
    if |r| within atomradius
    {
      //Compute density "F".
      density += NORM_SMOOTHING_NORM * (atomradius - |r|*|r|)^3;
      //The gradient "Fx"
      gradient_term = 6 * NORM_SMOOTHING_NORM * r *
                      (atomradius - |r|*|r|)^2;
      gradient -= gradient_term;
      //The dot product of atom velocity with
      //the gradient "dot(Fq,q')"
      atomvelgradient += dot(gradient_term, fluid_atom_vel);
      //The environment velocity "wj*aj"
      vel_env_weight += |gradient_term|;
      vel_environment += vel_env_weight * fluid_atom_vel,
    }
  }
```

Listing 7-1 (*continued*). Implementation Part 1

```
//Compute final environment velocity.
vel_environment /= vel_env_weight;

//Compute repulsion velocity (incorporates velocity).
//See Listing 7-4 for querying the repulsion force hash.

//Compute desired velocity.
vel_desired = vel_environment + vel_repulsion;

//Compute the velocity constraint from Equation 2.
terms = - dot(gradient, vel_desired)  //dot(Fx,D)
           - atomvelgradient              //dot(Fq,q')
           - 0.5f * density;              //phi * F
newvelocity = terms / dot(gradient, gradient) * gradient;

//Output the velocity, gradient, and density.
}
```

7.2.3 Computing the Density Field on the GPU

Now that we have established a velocity constraint on particles with Equation 2, we will discuss a way to calculate this equation efficiently on the GPU. First, note that the function can be reconstructed using only fluid atom positions and fluid atom velocities—the former applies to terms F_i, F_i^x, F_i^q, and D_i^{env}; the latter to $\dot{q}$ and D_i^{env}. Therefore, only atom positions and velocities have to be sent from the SPH simulation on the CPU to the GPU. Second, instead of evaluating every fluid atom position or velocity to compute Equation 1 and its derivatives—translating into expensive texture lookups on the GPU—we aim to exploit the fact that atoms contribute nothing to the density field outside their influence radius h_a.

For finding all neighboring atoms, we choose to use the spatial hash data structure described in Teschner et al. 2003. An advantage of a spatial hash over tree-based spatial data structures is the constant access time when querying the structure. A tree traversal requires visiting nodes possibly not adjacent in video memory, which would make the procedure unnecessarily expensive.

In the following, we present two enhancements of the hash structure of Teschner et al. 2003 in order to make it suitable for application on a GPU. We modify the hash function for use with floating-point arithmetic, and we adopt a different way of constructing and querying the hash.

7.2.4 Choosing the Hash Function

First, the spatial hash structure we use is different in the choice of the hash function. Because we have designed this technique to work on Shader Model 3.0 hardware, we cannot rely on real integer arithmetic, as in Shader Model 4.0. As a result, we are restricted to using the 23 bits of the floating-point mantissa. Therefore, we use the hash function from Equation 4.

$$H(x, y, z) = \left(p_1 \mathbf{B}_x(x, y, z) + p_2 \mathbf{B}_y(x, y, z) + p_3 \mathbf{B}_z(x, y, z) \right) \bmod hs, \qquad (4)$$

with

$$\mathbf{B}(x, y, z) = (\lfloor (x + c)/s \rfloor, \lfloor (y + c)/s \rfloor, \lfloor (z + c)/s \rfloor),$$

where the three-vector of integers $\mathbf{B}(x, y, z)$ is the discretization of the point (x, y, z) into *grid cells*, with B_x, B_y, and B_z its x, y, and z components, and s the *grid cell size*. We have added the constant term c to eliminate symmetry around the origin. The hash function $H(x, y, z)$ maps three-component vectors to an integer representing the index into an array of *hash buckets*, with hs being the *hash size* and p_1, p_2, and p_3 large primes. We choose primes 11,113, 12,979, and 13,513 to make sure that the world size could still be reasonably large without exceeding the 23 bits available while calculating the hash function.

7.2.5 Constructing and Querying the Hash

Before highlighting the second difference of our hash method, an overview of constructing and querying the hash is in order. We use the spatial hash to carry both the fluid atom positions and the velocities, which have to be sent from the fluid simulation on the CPU to the fluid visualization on the GPU. We therefore perform its construction on the CPU, while querying happens on the GPU.

The implementation of the spatial hash consists of two components: a hash index table and atom attribute pools. The hash index table of size hs indexes the atom attribute pools storing the fluid atoms' positions and velocities. Every entry e in the hash index table corresponds to hash bucket e, and the information in the hash index table points to the bucket's first attribute element in the atom attribute pools, together with the number of elements present in that bucket. Because the spatial hash is used to send atom positions and velocities from the CPU to the GPU, we perform construction on the CPU, while querying happens on the GPU. Figure 7-4 demonstrates the procedure of querying this data structure on the GPU.

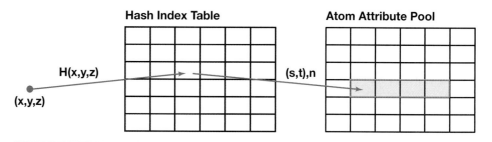

Figure 7-4. Querying the Hash Table
When the GPU wants to query the hash table on the basis of a surface particle position (x, y, z), it calculates a hash value H(x, y, z) used as an index into the hash index table. Because for every bucket the data in the atom attribute pool forms a contiguous block, it can then be read by the GPU with the obtained position (s, t) and number of elements n returned by the hash index table.

We will now describe the second difference compared to Teschner et al. 2003, relating to the method of hash construction. The traditional method of constructing a spatial hash adds every fluid atom to the hash table once, namely to the hash bucket to which its position maps. When the resulting structure is used to find neighbors, the traditional method would perform multiple queries per fluid atom: one for every grid cell intersecting a sphere around its position with the radius of the fluid atoms. This yields all fluid atoms influencing the density field at its position. However, we use an inverted hash method: the fluid atom is added to the hash multiple times, for every grid cell intersecting its influence area. Then, the GPU has to query a hash bucket only once to find all atoms intersecting or encapsulating the grid cell. The methods are illustrated in Figure 7-5. Listing 7-2 contains the pseudocode.

Performance-wise, the inverted hash method has the benefit of requiring only a single query on the GPU, independent of the chosen grid cell size. When decreasing the hash cell size, we can accomplish a better approximation of a grid cell with respect to the fluid atoms that influence the positions inside it. These two aspects combined minimize the number of data lookups a GPU has to perform in texture memory. However, construction time on the CPU increases with smaller grid cell sizes, because the more grid cells intersect a fluid atom's influence radius, the higher the number of additions of a single atom to the hash. The traditional hash method works the other way around: a decreasing grid cell size implies more queries for the GPU, while an atom will always be added to the hash only once by the CPU. Hardware configurations bottlenecked by the GPU should therefore opt for the inverted hash method, while configurations bottlenecked by the CPU should opt for the traditional hash method.

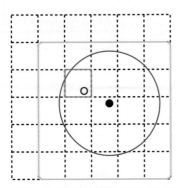 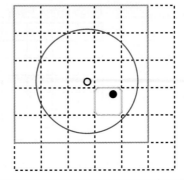

Figure 7-5. Comparing Hash Methods

Left: The traditional hash method. Right: The inverted hash method.

The white dot represents a fluid atom, the black dot a surface particle. The red squares and green rounded squares encapsulate the dashed grid cells that are visited for addition of the fluid atom and the surface particle's hash query, respectively. The area of these squares is determined by the size of the circular influence area around either a surface particle or a fluid atom, depending on the hash method. For example, the large square in the inverted method shows multiple additions of a fluid atom, while for the traditional method, it shows multiple queries of the surface particle.

Listing 7-2. Implementation Part 2: Pseudocode for Querying the Hash

```
float hash(float3 point)
{
    float3 discrete = (point + 100.0) * INV_CELL_SIZE;
    discrete = floor(discrete) * float3(11113.0f, 12979.0f, 13513.0f);
    float result = abs(discrete.x + discrete.y + discrete.z);
    return fmod(result, NUM_BUCKETS);
}

void mainvel(
    . . .
    const uniform float hashindex_dim, //Width of texRECT
    const uniform float hashdata_dim,
    const uniform samplerRECT hsh_idx_tex : TEXUNIT4,
    const uniform samplerRECT hsh_dta_tex_pos : TEXUNIT5,
    const uniform samplerRECT hsh_dta_tex_vel : TEXUNIT6,
    . . .
)
{
    //Other parts of this program discussed in Section 7.2.2
```

Listing 7-2 (*continued*). Implementation Part 2

```
//Compute density F, its gradient Fx, and dot(Fq,q').
//Calculate hashvalue; atomrange stores length and 1D index
//into data table.
float hashvalue = hash(position);
float2 hsh_idx_coords = float2(fmod(hashvalue, hashindex_dim),
                               hashvalue / hashindex_dim);
float4 atomrange = texRECT(hsh_idx_texture, hsh_idx_coords);
float2 hashdata = float2(fmod(atomrange.y, hashdata_dim),
                         atomrange.y / hashdata_dim);

//For each fluid atom
for(int i = 0; i < atomrange.x; i++)
{
  //Get the fluid atom position and velocity from the hash.
  float3 fluid_atom_pos = f3texRECT(hsh_dta_texture_pos, hashdata);
  float3 fluid_atom_vel = f3texRECT(hsh_dta_texture_vel, hashdata);

  //See Listing 7-1 for the contents of the loop.
}
}
```

7.3 Local Particle Repulsion

On top of constraining particles to the fluid surface, we require them to cover the entire surface area. To obtain a uniform distribution of particles over the fluid surface, we adopt the concept of repulsion forces proposed in Witkin and Heckbert 1994. The paper defines repulsion forces acting on two points in space by their distance; the larger the distance, the smaller the repulsion force. Particles on the fluid surface have to react to these repulsion forces. Thus they are not free to move to every position on the surface anymore.

7.3.1 The Repulsion Force Equation

We alter the repulsion function from Witkin and Heckbert 1994 slightly, for we would like particles to have a bounded region in which they influence other particles. To this end, we employ the smoothing kernels from SPH (Müller et al. 2003) once again, which have been used similarly for the fluid density field of Equation 1. Our new function is defined by Equation 5 and yields a density field that is the basis for the generation of repulsion forces.

$$\sigma(\mathbf{x}) = s_p \sum_{i=1}^{n} W_p(\mathbf{x} - \mathbf{p}_i, h_p), \tag{5}$$

where W_p is the smoothing kernel chosen for surface particles, h_p is the radius of the smoothing kernel in which it has a nonzero contribution to the density field, and s_p is a scaling factor for surface particles. Our choice for W_p is again taken from Müller et al. 2003 and presented in the equation below, and in Figure 7-6. We can use this smoothing kernel to calculate both densities and repulsion forces, because it has a nonnegative gradient as well.

$$W_{spiky}(\mathbf{r}, h) = \frac{15}{\pi h^6} \begin{cases} (h - |\mathbf{r}|)^3 & \text{if } |\mathbf{r}| < h \\ 0 & \text{otherwise} \end{cases}, \text{ with } h = 1.$$

The repulsion force $\mathbf{f}_i^{rep}$ at a particle position $\mathbf{p}_i$ is the negative gradient of the density field.

$$\mathbf{f}_i^{rep}(\mathbf{p}_i) = -\nabla\sigma(\mathbf{p}_i) = -s_p \sum_{j=1}^{n} \nabla W(\mathbf{p}_i - \mathbf{p}_j, h_p). \tag{6}$$

To combine the repulsion forces with our velocity constraint equation, the repulsion force is integrated over time to form a desired repulsion velocity $\mathbf{D}_i^{rep}$. We can use simple Euler integration:

$$\mathbf{D}_i^{rep}(t_{new}) = \mathbf{D}_i^{rep}(t_{old}) + \mathbf{f}_i^{rep} \cdot \Delta t, \tag{7}$$

where $\Delta t = t_{new} - t_{old}$.

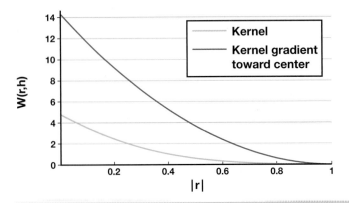

Figure 7-6. The Smoothing Kernel Used for Surface Particles
The green line shows the kernel, and the blue line shows its gradient in the direction toward the center.

The final velocity $\mathbf{D}_i$ is obtained by adding $\mathbf{D}_i^{env}$ and $\mathbf{D}_i^{rep}$:

$$\mathbf{D}_i = \mathbf{D}_i^{env} + \mathbf{D}_i^{rep}. \tag{8}$$

The total desired velocity $\mathbf{D}_i$ is calculated and used in Equation 2 every time the surface particle velocity is constrained on the GPU.

7.3.3 Nearest Neighbors on a GPU

Now that we have defined the repulsion forces acting on surface particles with Equation 6, we are once again facing the challenge of calculating them efficiently on the GPU. Just as we did with fluid atoms influencing a density field, we will exploit the fact that a particle influences the density field in only a small neighborhood around it. A global data structure will not be a practical solution in this case; construction would have to take place on the GPU, not on the CPU. The construction of such a structure would rely on sorting or similar kinds of interdependent output, which is detrimental to the execution time of the visualization. For example, the construction of a data structure like the spatial hash in Section 7.2.3 would consist of more than one pass on the GPU, because it requires variable-length hash buckets.

Our way around the limitation of having to construct a data structure is to use a render target on the video card itself. We use it to store floating-point data elements, with construction being performed by the transformation pipeline. By rendering certain primitives at specific positions while using shader programs, information from the render target can be queried and used during the calculation of repulsion forces.

The algorithm works in two steps:

First Pass

1. Set up a transformation matrix M representing an orthogonal projection, with a viewport encompassing every surface particle, and a `float4` render target.

2. Render surface particles to the single pixel to which their center maps.

3. Store their world-space coordinate at the pixel in the frame buffer.

4. Save the render target as texture "Image 1," as shown in Figure 7-7a.

Second Pass

1. Enable additive blending, and keep a `float4` render target.[1]

2. Render a quad around every surface particle encapsulating the projection of their influence area in image space, as shown in Figure 7-7b.

---

1. On many GPUs, 32-bit floating-point blending is not supported, so blending will be performed with 16-bit floating-point numbers. However, the GeForce 8800 can do either.

3. Execute the fragment program, which compares the world-space position of the particle stored at the center of the quad with the world-space position of a possible neighbor particle stored in Image 1 at the pixel of the processed fragment, and then outputs a repulsion force. See Figure 7-7c. The repulsion force is calculated according to Equation 6.

4. Save the render target as texture "Image 2," as shown in Figure 7-7d.

When two particles overlap during the first step, the frontmost particle is stored and the other one discarded. By choosing a sufficient viewport resolution, we can keep this

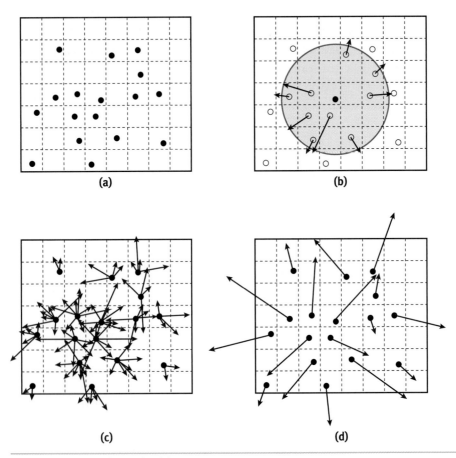

(a)

(b)

(c)

(d)

Figure 7-7. The Repulsion Algorithm
(a) The particles (in black) are mapped to the screen pixels (the dashed lines), and their world positions are stored. (b) A quad is drawn around a particle; for every pixel within a certain radius (the disk), a position is read and a repulsion force is calculated. (c) The collection of forces after all quads are rendered. (d) The forces that remain after additive blending.

loss of information to a minimum. However, losing a particle position does not harm our visualization; because the top particle moves away from the crowded area due to repulsion forces, the bottom particle will resurface.

The second step works because a particle's influence area is a sphere. This sphere becomes a disk whose bounding box can be represented by a quad. This quad then contains all projected particle positions within the sphere, and that is what we draw to perform the nearest-neighbor search on the data stored in the first step.

Querying the generated image of repulsion forces is performed with the same transformation matrix M as the one active during execution of the two-pass repulsion algorithm. To query the desired repulsion force for a certain particle, transform its world-space position by using the transformation matrix to obtain a pixel location, and read the image containing the repulsion forces at the obtained pixel.

We execute this algorithm, which results in an image of repulsion forces, separately from the particle simulation loop, as demonstrated in Listing 7-3. Its results will be queried before we determine a particle's velocity.

Listing 7-3. Fragment Shader of Pass 2 of the Nearest-Neighbor Algorithm

```
void pass2main(
  in float4 screenpos : WPOS,
  in float4 particle_pos,
  out float4 color : COLOR0,
  const uniform float rep_radius,
  const uniform samplerRECT neighbour_texture : TEXUNIT0
)
{
  //Read fragment position.
  float4 neighbour_pos = texRECT(neighbour_texture, screenpos.xy);

  //Calculate repulsion force.
  float3 posdiff = neighbour_pos.xyz - IN.particle_pos.xyz;
  float2 distsq_repsq = float2(dot(posdiff, posdiff), rep_radius *
                              rep_radius);
  if(distsq_repsq.x < 1.0e-3 || distsq_repsq.x > distsq_repsq.y)
    discard;

  float dist = sqrt(distsq_repsq.x);
  float e1 = rep_radius - dist;
```

```
    float resultdens = e1*e1/distsq_repsq.y;
    float3 resultforce = 5.0 * resultdens * posdiff / dist;

    //Output the repulsion force.
    color = float4(resultforce, resultdens);

}
```

7.4 Global Particle Dispersion

To accelerate the particle distribution process described in Section 7.3, we introduce a particle dispersion method. This method acts immediately on the position of the surface particles simulated by the GPU. We change the position of particles based on their particle density—defined in Equation 5—which can be calculated with the same nearest-neighbors algorithm used for calculation of repulsion forces. Particles from high-density areas are removed and placed at positions in areas with low density. To this end, we compare the densities of a base particle and a comparison particle to a certain threshold T. When the density of the comparison particle is lowest and the density difference is above the threshold, the position of the base particle will change in order to increase density at the comparison position and decrease it at the base position. The base particle will be moved to a random location on the edge of the influence area of the comparison particle, as shown in Figure 7-8, in order to minimize fluctuations in density at the position of the comparison particle. Such fluctuations would bring about even more particle relocations, which could make the fluid surface restless.

It is infeasible to have every particle search the whole pool of surface particles for places of low density on the fluid surface at every iteration of the surface particle simulation. Therefore, for each particle, the GPU randomly selects a comparison particle in the pool every t seconds, by using a texture with random values generated on the CPU. The value of t can be chosen arbitrarily. Here is the algorithm:

For each surface particle:
1. Determine if it is time for the particle to switch position.
2. If so, choose the comparison position and compare densities at the two positions.
3. If the density at this particle is higher than the density at the comparison particle, with a difference larger than threshold T, change the position to a random location at the comparison particle's influence border.

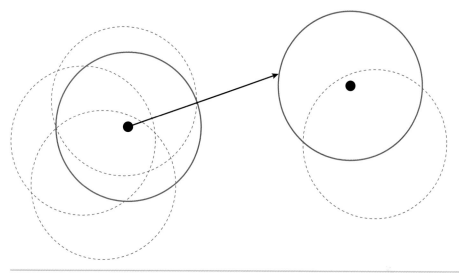

Figure 7-8. The Dispersion of Particles
The black dots are surface particles, and the circles represent their influence areas. Dashed circles are neighboring particles' influence areas. On the left is surface particle x, with its density higher than surface particle y on the right. Therefore x might move to the edge of y's influence area.

To determine the threshold T, we use a heuristic, minimizing the difference in densities between the two original particle positions. This heuristic takes as input the particle positions $\mathbf{p}$ and $\mathbf{q}$, with their densities before any position change σ_{p_0} and σ_{q_0}. It then determines if a position change of the particle originally at $\mathbf{p}$ increases the density difference between the input positions. The densities at the (fixed) positions $\mathbf{p}$ and $\mathbf{q}$ after the particle position change are σ_{p_1} and σ_{q_1}, respectively. Equation 9 is used by the heuristic to determine if there is a decrease in density difference after a position change, thereby yielding the decision for a change of position of the particle originally located at $\mathbf{p}$.

$$\left(\sigma_{p_1} - \sigma_{q_1}\right)^2 < \left(\sigma_{p_0} - \sigma_{q_0}\right)^2. \tag{9}$$

Because the original particle would move to the edge of influence of the comparison particle—as you can see in Figure 7-8—the following equations hold in the case of a position change.

$$\sigma_{p_1} = \sigma_{p_0} - k$$
$$\sigma_{q_1} = \sigma_{q_0}, \tag{10}$$

where k is the value at the center of the particle smoothing kernel, $s_p W_p(\mathbf{0}, h_p)$. Using Equation 9, substituting Equation 10, and solving for the initial density difference, we obtain Equation 11:

$$\left| \sigma_{p_0} - \sigma_{q_0} - k \right| < \left(\sigma_{p_0} - \sigma_{q_0} \right) = \left(\sigma_{p_0} - \sigma_{q_0} \right) > \tfrac{1}{2}k. \tag{11}$$

Equation 11 gives us the solution for our threshold T:

$$T = \tfrac{1}{2} s_p W_p \left(\mathbf{0},\ h_p \right). \tag{12}$$

Still, it depends on the application of the dispersion algorithm if this threshold is enough to keep the fluid surface steady. Especially in cases where all particles can decide at the same time to change their positions, a higher threshold might be desired to keep the particles from changing too much. The effect of our particle distribution methods is visible in Figure 7-9. Both sides of the figure show a fluid simulation based on SPH, but in the sequence on the left, only particle repulsion is enabled, and on the right, both repulsion and dispersion are enabled. The particles sample a cylindrical fluid surface during a three-second period, starting from a bad initial distribution. Figure 7-9 shows that our particle dispersion mechanism improves upon the standard repulsion behavior considerably. We can even adapt the particle size based on the particle density, to fill gaps even faster. (You'll see proof of this later, in Figure 7-11.)

No matter how optimally the particle distribution algorithm performs, it can be aided by selecting reasonable starting locations for the particles. Because we do not know where the surface will be located for an arbitrary collection of fluid atoms, we try to guess the surface by positioning fluid particles on a sphere around every fluid atom. If we use enough surface particles, the initial distribution will make the surface look like a blobby object already. We assign an equal amount of surface particles to every fluid atom at the start of our simulation, and distribute them by using polar coordinates (r, θ) for every particle, varying θ and the z coordinate of r linearly over the number of surface particles assigned to a single atom.

Because particle dispersion acts on the positions of particles, we should query particle densities and change positions based on those densities during the position calculation pass in Figure 7-2. Listing 7-4 demonstrates a query on the repulsion force texture to obtain the surface particle density at a certain position.

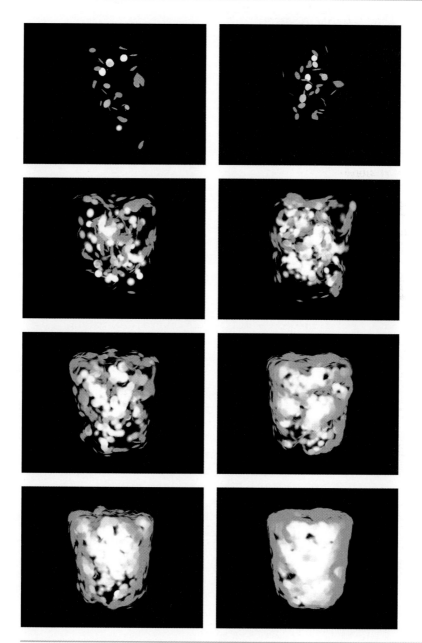

Figure 7-9. The Distribution Methods at Work: Surface Particles Spread over a Group of Fluid Atoms in the Form of a Cylinder

Every second a snapshot is taken. The left series uses only the repulsion mechanism, while the series on the right also uses distribution. Apart from the distribution speed, the dispersion method also has the advantage that surface particles do not move around violently due to extreme particle repulsion forces.

Listing 7-4. Excerpt from a Fragment Program Simulating the Position of a Surface Particle

```
void mainpos(
   . . .
   in float4 particle : TEXCOORD0,
   out float4 color : COLOR0,
   const uniform float time_step,
   const uniform samplerRECT rep_texture : TEXUNIT5,
   const uniform float4x4 ModelViewProj)
{
   //ModelViewProj is the same as during repulsion calculation
   //in Listing 7-3.

   //oldpos and velocity passed through via textures

   float3 newposition;
   float  normalintegration = 1.0;

   //Perform the query.
   float4 transformedpos = mul(ModelViewProj, oldpos);
   transformedpos /= transformedpos.w;
   transformedpos.xy = transformedpos.xy * 0.5 + 0.5;
   transformedpos.xy = float2(transformedpos.x * screen_width,
                              transformedpos.y * screen_height);
   float4 rep_density1 = texRECT(rep_texture, transformedpos.xy);

   //1. If it's time to compare particles (determine via a texture or
   //   uniform parameter)
   //2. Make a query to obtain rep_density2 for another
   //   particle (determine randomly via texture).
   //3. If the density difference is greater than our threshold,
   //   set newposition to edge of comparison particle boundary
   //   (normalintegration becomes false).

   if(normalintegration)
     newposition = oldpos + velocity*time_step;

   //Output the newposition.
   color.xyz = newposition;
   color.a = 1.0;
}
```

7.5 Performance

The performance of our final application is influenced by many different factors. Figure 7-2 shows three stages that could create a bottleneck on the GPU: the particle repulsion stage, the constrained particle velocity calculation, and the particle dispersion algorithm. We have taken the scenario of water in a glass from Figure 7-11 in order to analyze the performance of the three different parts.

We found that most of the calculation time of our application was spent in two areas. The first of these bottlenecks is the calculation of constrained particle velocities. To constrain particle velocities, each particle has to iterate over a hash structure of fluid atom positions, performing multiple texture lookups and distance calculations at each iteration. To maximize performance, we have minimized the number of hash collisions by increasing the number of hash buckets. We have also chosen smaller grid cell sizes to decrease the number of redundant neighbors visited by a surface particle; the grid cell size is a third to a fifth of a fluid atom's diameter.

The second bottleneck is the calculation of the repulsion forces. The performance of the algorithm is mainly determined by the query size around a surface particle. A smaller size will result in less overdraw and faster performance. However, choosing a small query size may decrease particle repulsion too much. The ideal size will therefore depend on the requirements of the application. To give a rough impression of the actual number of frames per second our algorithm can obtain, we have run our application a number of times on a GeForce 6800, choosing different query sizes for 16,384 surface particles. The query sizes are visualized by quads, as shown in Figure 7-10.

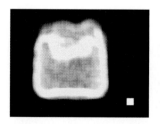 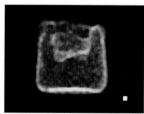 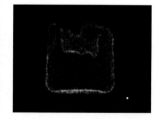

Figure 7-10. Surface Particle Query Area Visualized for a Glass of Water, Using 16,384 Particles
Blending is used to show the amount of overdraw, with a white pixel corresponding to 30 or more overlapping particles. The bright quads at the lower right corner represent the queried area for a single particle. The performance increases from 40 frames/sec in the leftmost scenario to 65 frames/sec in the middle, and 80 frames/sec on the right.

7.6 Rendering

To demonstrate the level of realism achievable with our visualization method, Figure 7-11 shows examples of a fluid surface rendered with lighting, blending, surface normal curvature, and reflection and refraction. To render a smooth transparent surface, we have used a blending method that keeps only the frontmost particles and discards the particles behind others. The challenge lies in separating the particles on another part of the surface that should be discarded, from overlapping particles on the same part of the surface that should be kept for blending.

To solve the problem of determining the frontmost particles, we perform a depth pass to render the particles as oriented quads, and calculate the projective-space position of the quad at every generated fragment. We store the minimum-depth fragment at every pixel in a depth texture. When rendering the fluid surface as oriented quads, we query the depth buffer only at the particle's position: the center of the quad. Using an offset equal to the fluid atom's radius, we determine if a particle can be considered frontmost or not. We render those particles that pass the test. This way, we allow multiple overlapping quads to be rendered at a single pixel.

We perform blending by first assigning an alpha value to every position on a quad, based on the distance to the center of the quad. We accumulate these alpha values in an alpha pass before the actual rendering takes place. During rendering, we can determine the contribution of a quad to the overall pixel color based on the alpha value of the fragment and the accumulated alpha value stored during the alpha pass.

Finally, we use a normal perturbation technique to increase detail and improve blending of the fluid surface. While rendering the surface as oriented quads, we perturb the normal at every fragment slightly. The normal perturbation is based on the curvature of the fluid density field at the particle position used for rendering the quad. The curvature of the density field can be calculated when we calculate the gradient and density field during the velocity constraint pass. Using the gradient, we can obtain a vector the size of our rendered quad, tangent to the fluid surface. This vector is multiplied by the curvature, a 3×3 matrix, to obtain the change in normal over the tangent vector. We only store the change in normal projected onto the tangent vector using a dot product, resulting in a scalar. This is the approximation of the divergence at the particle position (while in reality it constitutes only a part of the divergence). This scalar value is stored, and during surface rendering it is used together with the reconstructed tangent vector to form a perturbation vector for our quad's normal.

7.7 Conclusion

We have presented a solution for efficiently and effectively implementing the point-based implicit surface visualization method of Witkin and Heckbert 1994 on the GPU, to render metaballs while maintaining interactive frame rates. Our solution combines three components: calculating the constraint velocities, repulsion forces, and particle densities for achieving near-uniform particle distributions. The latter two components involve a novel algorithm for a GPU particle system in which particles influence each other. The last component of our solution also enhances the original method by accelerating the distribution of particles on the fluid surface and enabling distribution among disconnected surfaces in order to prevent gaps. Our solution has a clear performance advantage compared to marching cubes and ray-tracing methods, as its complexity depends on the fluid surface area, whereas the other two methods have a complexity depending on the fluid volume.

Still, not all problems have been solved by the presented method. Future adaptations of the algorithm could involve adaptive particle sizes, in order to fill temporarily originating gaps in the fluid surface more quickly. Also, newly created disconnected surface components do not always have particles on their surface, which means they are not likely to receive any as long as they remain disconnected. The biggest problem, however, lies in dealing with small parts of fluid that are located far apart. Because the repulsion algorithm requires a clip space encapsulating every particle, the limited resolution of the viewport will likely cause multiple particles to map to the same pixel, implying data loss. A final research direction involves rendering the surface particles to achieve various visual effects, of which Figure 7-11 is an example.

Figure 7-11. Per-Pixel Lit, Textured, and Blended Fluid Surfaces
Left: A blobby object in a zero-gravity environment. Right: Water in a glass.

7.8 References

Blinn, James F. 1982. "A Generalization of Algebraic Surface Drawing." In *ACM Transactions on Graphics* 1(3), pp. 235–256.

Latta, Lutz. 2004. "Building a Million Particle System." Presentation at Game Developers Conference 2004. Available online at http://www.2ld.de/gdc2004/.

Lorensen, William E., and Harvey E. Cline. 1987. "Marching Cubes: A High Resolution 3D Surface Construction Algorithm." In *Proceedings of the 14th Annual Conference on Computer Graphics and Interactive Techniques*, pp. 163–169.

Müller, Matthias, David Charypar, and Markus Gross. 2003. "Particle-Based Fluid Simulation for Interactive Applications." In *Proceedings of the 2003 ACM SIGGRAPH/Eurographics Symposium on Computer Animation*, pp. 154–159.

Parker, Steven, Peter Shirley, Yarden Livnat, Charles Hansen, and Peter-Pike Sloan. 1998. "Interactive Ray Tracing for Isosurface Rendering." In *Proceedings of the Conference on Visualization '98*, pp. 233–238.

Pascucci, V. 2004. "Isosurface Computation Made Simple: Hardware Acceleration, Adaptive Refinement and Tetrahedral Stripping." In *Proceedings of Joint EUROGRAPHICS3—IEEE TCVG Symposium on Visualization 2004*.

Teschner, M., B. Heidelberger, M. Mueller, D. Pomeranets, and M. Gross. 2003. "Optimized Spatial Hashing for Collision Detection of Deformable Objects." In *Proceedings of Vision, Modeling, Visualization 2003*.

Vrolijk, Benjamin, Charl P. Botha, and Frits H. Post. 2004. "Fast Time-Dependent Isosurface Extraction and Rendering." In *Proceedings of the 20th Spring Conference on Computer Graphics*, pp. 45–54.

Witkin, Andrew P., and Paul S. Heckbert. 1994. "Using Particles to Sample and Control Implicit Surfaces." In *Proceedings of the 21st Annual Conference on Computer Graphics and Interactive Techniques*, pp. 269–277.

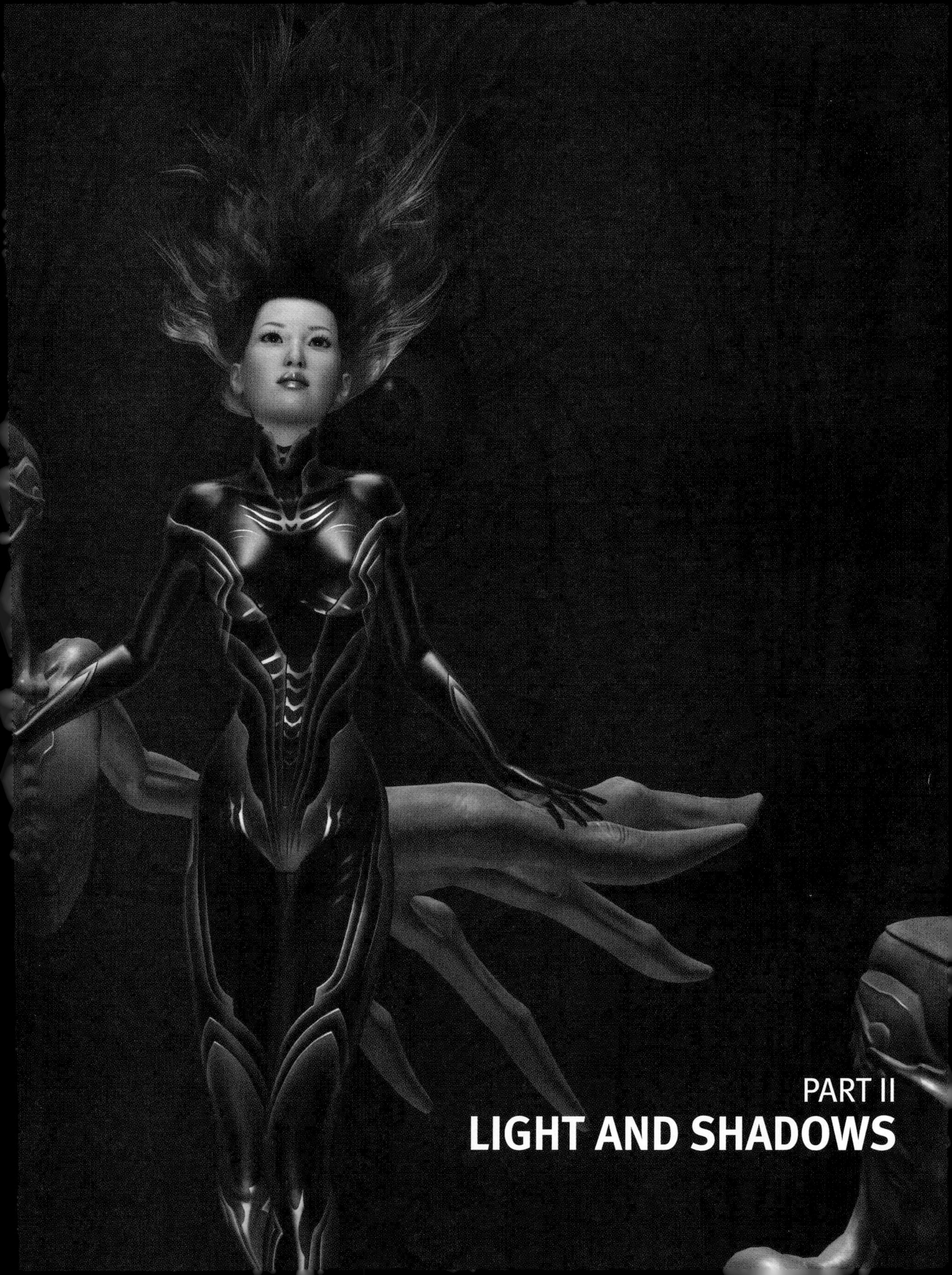

PART II
LIGHT AND SHADOWS

The subject of light and shadows may appear simplistic, but in reality it concisely represents what modern rendering is all about. Modeling light visibility is fundamental and sublime in the field of computer graphics. After all, it is the subtleties of reality that we strive most fervently to capture—the fine differences that allow the human eye to accept what is being presented as more than just a simulation. With the rise in popularity of programmable shading and the refinement of high-level shading languages, we have come a long way from static light maps and projected shadows, so this part of the book presents six chapters that are the state of the art in representing the interplay of light and shadow.

The shadow map is the primary light visibility tool currently used in real-time applications. The simplicity of the algorithm is what makes using shadow maps so attractive. At the same time, the latest applications require more than a pedestrian point light. Shadow-map filtering has long been used to mitigate shadow-map aliasing. Today filtering is used to simulate the effect of area lights. With some clever filtering, plausible soft shadows can be constructed from a shadow map using algorithms such as *percentage-closer soft shadows*. Large filter kernels needed for area light simulation are expensive because each shadow-map sample must be compared against the shaded fragment's distance from the light. One method for accelerating this, introduced in 2006, is *variance shadow maps* (VSMs), which can be prefiltered. In **Chapter 8, "Summed-Area Variance Shadow Maps," Andrew Lauritzen** of the University of Waterloo presents a detailed explanation of VSMs and introduces a method for changing the filtered kernel arbitrarily per pixel.

Offline rendering does not have the same time constraints as, say, a first-person shooter. Time is still important, though, and making full use of the computing resources at hand is critical as the complexity of the rendering algorithms and scenes increases. When artists need to iterate on scenes many times to achieve the desired effect, it is critical that each iteration have the highest possible performance. To meet this requirement, relighting engines have been developed that make assumptions about the scene, such as the camera position not changing, to accelerate each step of the lighting refinement. In **Chapter 9, "Interactive Cinematic Relighting with Global Illumination,"** **Fabio Pellacini** of Dartmouth College, **Miloš Hašan** of Cornell University, and **Kavita Bala**, also of Cornell, present how to use the GPU to achieve much faster relighting than was possible with a CPU.

An issue that haunts many shadow map implementations is the limited resolution of the shadow map. Because a shadow map discretizes a continuous function of depth, aliasing is inherent without infinite resolution. Compounding the problem is the lack of correlation between the distribution of samples in the shadow map and the distribution of fragments in the final scene. It is therefore imperative that the limited resolution of the shadow map be used properly. In **Chapter 10, "Parallel-Split Shadow Maps on Programmable GPUs,"** **Fan Zhang** and **Hanqiu Sun** of The Chinese University of Hong Kong and **Oskari Nyman** of Helsinki University of Technology present an intuitive approach to partitioning the resolution for shadow mapping to more correctly map to the actual usage.

Although shadow maps have received much attention, they are not perfect, and their limitations are unacceptable for some applications. The most widely accepted alternative for real-time dynamic shadows is *stencil shadow volumes* (SSVs). Like shadow maps, SSVs have been well studied and have been shown to be an elegant solution to the aliasing problems that plague shadow maps. Because the complexity of SSVs is tied to the complexity of the shadowing geometry, robust and fast SSVs have been a topic of much research. With **Chapter 11, "Efficient and Robust Shadow Volumes Using Hierarchical Occlusion Culling and Geometry Shaders,"** **Martin Stich** of mental images and **Carsten Wächter** and **Alexander Keller** of Ulm University show how to handle many of the SSV "gotchas" and detail a system that can even handle nonclosed meshes.

Beyond modeling local lighting with shadow maps or SSVs, current applications demand global illumination techniques that provide more immersive sensory feedback by taking into account the entire scene. Several techniques, from radiosity to precomputed radiance transfer, can achieve good results for static scenes but are difficult to adapt to the dynamic world of a game. Hybrid techniques that combine traditional real-time dynamic lighting models for local lights, along with some representation of the global lighting contribution, will be used more frequently to achieve greater realism without sacrificing too much performance. One such technique, which works well to simulate the contribution of a distant light such as the sun, is *ambient occlusion*. Real-time ambient occlusion is possible today, even for dynamic scenes, but it suffers from several artifacts caused by approximations assumed in Michael Bunnell's original approach (which appeared in *GPU Gems 2*). **Chapter 12, "High-Quality Ambient Occlusion"** by **Jared Hoberock** and **Yuntao Jia** of the University of Illinois at Urbana-Champaign, builds upon Bunnell's work and robustly and efficiently solves many of these artifacts.

Chapter 13, "Volumetric Light Scattering as a Post-Process" by Kenny Mitchell of Electronic Arts, tackles the topic of modeling light as it travels through more-complex mediums. Often called "god rays," this effect that the atmosphere has upon light transport adds more believability to outdoor scenes. This chapter presents a functional approach to estimating such scattering with a post-process shader, which properly handles occlusion by opaque objects such as large buildings.

Kevin Myers, NVIDIA Corporation

Chapter 8

Summed-Area Variance Shadow Maps

Andrew Lauritzen
University of Waterloo

In this chapter, we discuss shadow-map filtering and soft shadows. We review the variance shadow-mapping algorithm and explain how it can help solve many common shadow-mapping problems. We also present a simple but effective technique for significantly reducing the light-bleeding artifacts associated with variance shadow maps (VSMs).

Finally, we introduce a real-time shadowing algorithm based on VSMs and summed-area tables (SATs). We achieve efficient computation of shadow contributions for arbitrary rectangular filter regions, which makes summed-area variance shadow mapping (SAVSM) an ideal algorithm for soft shadows without aliasing.

8.1 Introduction

Shadow mapping (Williams 1978) is a popular shadowing algorithm that offers several important advantages over shadow volumes (Crow 1977). In particular, shadow maps can be queried at arbitrary locations and are less sensitive to geometric complexity. Unfortunately, standard shadow maps also suffer from several well-known texture-mapping artifacts.

Magnification artifacts occur when the projected shadow-map texels cover a large area in screen space. Conversely, *minification* artifacts occur when several shadow-map texels are mapped to the same screen-space pixel.

Solving these problems involves properly filtering the shadow map, which is the focus of this chapter. Figure 8-1 is a good example of efficient, soft-edged shadows using the techniques described in this chapter.

Figure 8-1. Efficient, Soft-Edged Shadows Using Our Techniques

8.2 Related Work

One method of reducing shadow-map aliasing is to alter the shadow-map projection so that areas of extreme magnification and minification are reduced. There has been a lot of research in this area, notably concerning perspective shadow maps (Stamminger and Drettakis 2002), light-space perspective shadow maps (Wimmer et al. 2004), and trapezoidal shadow maps (Martin and Tan 2004). Unless the scene contains only a single planar shadow receiver, however, it is impossible to achieve a perfect one-to-one, texel-to-pixel mapping by using a uniform affine projection.

Therefore, to properly handle minification cases, we require texture filtering. Unfortunately, hardware texture filtering—such as trilinear and anisotropic filtering—is inapplicable to standard shadow maps. The hardware will average the depth values contained in the shadow map, and the resulting filtered depth will still be subjected to a single binary depth comparison. Percentage-closer filtering (PCF) (Reeves et al. 1987) solves this problem, achieving a correct outcome by filtering the *results* of several depth comparisons rather than the depth values themselves.

Another solution is to use variance shadow maps (Donnelly and Lauritzen 2006). By treating each shadow map texel as a distribution of depth values rather than as a single depth, the shadow map can be represented in a manner that can be filtered linearly. Techniques such as mipmapping, anisotropic filtering, and summed-area tables are therefore applicable.

Note that shadow-map filtering is generally orthogonal to projection warping. In particular, filtering does little to address magnification artifacts, a problem that is the primary concern of projection-warping algorithms. Thus, both of these techniques should be used together in a robust shadow-mapping implementation.

In this chapter, we discuss percentage-closer filtering briefly, and then we focus on variance shadow maps because they have several beneficial performance and quality characteristics.

8.3 Percentage-Closer Filtering

Percentage-closer filtering works by projecting the current screen-space pixel extents onto the shadow map and sampling the resulting region, a process that is similar to standard texture filtering. Each sample is then compared to a reference depth, producing a binary result. Next, these depth comparisons are combined to compute the percentage of texels in the filter region that are closer than the reference depth. This percentage is used to attenuate the light.

Reeves et al. 1987 notes that increasing the size of the filter region softens the edges of the shadows, as shown in Figure 8-2. By clamping the minimum filter size, we can get arbitrarily soft edges while still avoiding minification aliasing. Large filter sizes, however, require high-resolution shadow maps in order to maintain detail.

A common variant of the algorithm is to sample a fixed region of neighboring shadow-map texels. This is easy to implement; however, it merely softens the shadow edge and doesn't address the aliasing artifacts we mentioned.

8.3.1 Problems with Percentage-Closer Filtering

Although the quality of PCF can be very good, achieving such high quality requires a large number of samples. As with standard texture filtering, surfaces at shallow angles require huge anisotropic filter regions. In the case of percentage-closer filtering, it is

Figure 8-2. Soft Shadow Edges via Percentage-Closer Filtering

impossible to use prefiltered mipmaps to accelerate the process, because of the per-sample depth comparison. Consequently, in the worst case, we must sample and compare every individual texel in the shadow map in order to compute the light attenuation for a single frame-buffer pixel! As expected, this process can be slow.

The situation deteriorates when we use PCF to achieve edge softening, because this approach is equivalent to placing a lower bound on the size of the filter region and, consequently, on the cost of shading a pixel.

Another problem with percentage-closer filtering is that it inherits, and indeed exacerbates, the classic nuisances of shadow mapping: "shadow acne" and biasing. The most difficult to solve biasing issues are caused by shadow-map texels that cover large ranges of depths. This scenario often results from polygons that are almost parallel to the light direction, as shown in Figure 8-3.

To prevent improper self-shadowing, we need to choose a constant depth bias that is proportional to the maximum depth range covered by any texel in the shadow map. Of course, this range can be arbitrarily large, and setting the bias accordingly will cause shadows to pull away from their casters (known as *Peter Panning*). Choosing a per-texel

Figure 8-3. A Difficult Case for Percentage-Closer Filtering
Both extremes of biasing artifacts are visible in this picture: improper self-shadowing (the vertical lines on the ground) and Peter Panning (the shadow does not connect with the front wheel of the car). No amount of bias tweaking can eliminate these problems.

depth bias proportional to the slope of the occluding polygon, as suggested by Kilgard 2001, can help, but this does not eliminate the problem.

Sampling neighboring texels for PCF makes this situation worse because it effectively requires the bias to be proportional to the depth range over the entire filter region. Because this region is computed dynamically in the shading pass, it is impossible to choose a good per-texel bias that works for all filter sizes.

8.4 Variance Shadow Maps

Another elegant solution to the problem of shadow-map filtering is to use variance shadow maps. The main idea is to represent the depth data in a manner that can be filtered linearly, so that we can use algorithms and hardware that work with color and other linear data.

The algorithm is similar to the algorithm for standard shadow maps, except that instead of simply writing depth to the shadow map, we write depth and depth squared to a two-component variance shadow map. By filtering over some region, we recover the *moments* M_1 and M_2 of the depth distribution in that region, where

$$M_1 = E(x) = \int_{-\infty}^{\infty} xp(x)\,dx$$

$$M_2 = E(x^2) = \int_{-\infty}^{\infty} x^2 p(x)\,dx.$$

From these we can compute the mean μ and variance σ^2 of the distribution:

$$\mu = E(x) = M_1$$

$$\sigma^2 = E(x^2) - E(x)^2 = M_2 - M_1^2.$$

Using the variance, we can apply Chebyshev's inequality to compute an upper bound on the probability that the currently shaded surface (at depth t) is occluded:

$$P(x \geq t) \leq p_{max}(t) = \frac{\sigma^2}{\sigma^2 + (t - \mu)^2}.$$

This "one-tailed" version of Chebyshev's inequality is valid for $t > \mu$. If $t \leq \mu$, $p_{max} = 1$ and the surface is fully lit.

The inequality gives an upper bound on the percentage-closer filtering result over an arbitrary filter region. An upper bound is advantageous to avoid self-shadowing in regions that should be fully lit. More important, Donnelly and Lauritzen 2006 show that this inequality becomes exact for a single planar occluder and single planar receiver, which is a reasonable approximation for many real scenes. In particular for a single occluder and single receiver, there is a small neighborhood in which they will be locally planar, and thus p_{max} computed over this region will be a good approximation of the true probability.

Therefore, we can use p_{max} directly in rendering. Listing 8-1 gives some sample code in HLSL.

Note that it is useful to clamp the minimum variance to a very small value, as we have done here, to avoid any numeric issues that may occur during filtering. Additionally, simply clamping the variance often eliminates shadow biasing issues (discussed in detail in Section 8.4.2).

8.4.1 Filtering the Variance Shadow Map

Now that the shadow map is linearly filterable, a host of techniques and algorithms are available to us. Most notably, we can simply enable mipmapping, trilinear and

Listing 8-1. Computing p_{max} During Scene Shading

```
float ChebyshevUpperBound(float2 Moments, float t)
{
  // One-tailed inequality valid if t > Moments.x
  float p = (t <= Moments.x);

  // Compute variance.
  float Variance = Moments.y - (Moments.x*Moments.x);
  Variance = max(Variance, g_MinVariance);

  // Compute probabilistic upper bound.
  float d = t - Moments.x;
  float p_max = Variance / (Variance + d*d);

  return max(p, p_max);
}

float ShadowContribution(float2 LightTexCoord, float DistanceToLight)
{
  // Read the moments from the variance shadow map.
  float2 Moments = texShadow.Sample(ShadowSampler, LightTexCoord).xy;

  // Compute the Chebyshev upper bound.
  return ChebyshevUpperBound(Moments, DistanceToLight);
}
```

anisotropic filtering, and even multisample antialiasing (while rendering the shadow map). This alone significantly improves the quality compared to using standard shadow maps and constant-filter percentage-closer filtering, as shown in Figure 8-4.

We can do much more, however. In particular, Donnelly and Lauritzen 2006 suggests blurring the variance shadow map before shading (a simple box filter is sufficient). This approach is equivalent to neighborhood-sampled percentage-closer filtering, but it is significantly cheaper because of the use of a separable blur convolution. As discussed earlier, effectively clamping the minimum filter width like this will soften the shadow edges, helping hide magnification artifacts.

An alternative to using hardware filtering is to use summed-area tables, which also require linearly filterable data. We discuss this option in more detail in Section 8.5.

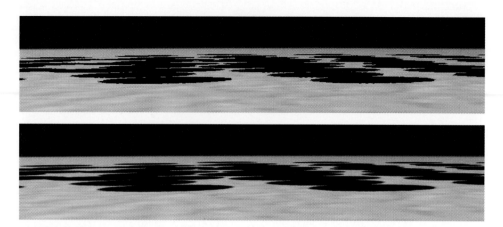

Figure 8-4. Hardware Filtering with Variance Shadow Maps
Shadow map aliasing (top) is eliminated by using anisotropic filtering with variance shadow maps (bottom).

8.4.2 Biasing

In addition to providing cheap, high-quality filtering, a variance shadow map offers an elegant solution to the problem of shadow biasing.

As we discussed for percentage-closer filtering, polygons that span large depth ranges are typically a problem for shadow-mapping algorithms. Variance shadow maps, however, give us a way to represent the depth extents of a pixel by using the second moment.

Instead of considering the entire extent of a shadow map texel to be at depth μ, we consider it to represent a locally planar distribution, given parametrically by

$$ f(x,y) = \mu + x \frac{\partial f}{\partial x} + y \frac{\partial f}{\partial y}. $$

We can then compute M_2, using the linearity of the expectation operator and the fact that $E(x) = E(y) = E(xy) = 0$:

$$ M_2 = E\left(f^2\right) = E\left(\mu^2\right) + E\left(x^2\right)\left[\frac{\partial f}{\partial x}\right]^2 + E\left(y^2\right)\left[\frac{\partial f}{\partial y}\right]^2. $$

Now, representing the pixel as a symmetric Gaussian distribution with a half-pixel standard deviation σ yields

$$E(\mu^2) = \mu^2$$

$$E(x^2) = E(y^2) = \sigma^2 = \left(\frac{1}{2}\right)^2 = \frac{1}{4}.$$

Therefore

$$M_2 = \mu^2 + \frac{1}{4}\left(\left[\frac{\partial f}{\partial x}\right]^2 + \left[\frac{\partial f}{\partial y}\right]^2\right).$$

Note that this formula reduces to simply the squared depth when the partial derivatives are both 0 (that is, when the surface is parallel to the light projection plane). Also note that no additional issues arise from increasing the filter width because the variance will automatically be computed over the entire region.

We can easily compute the moments during shadow-map rendering, using the HLSL partial derivative instructions shown in Listing 8-2.

One potential issue that remains is *numeric inaccuracy*. We can deal with this problem simply and entirely by clamping the minimum variance to a very small value before computing p_{max}, as in Listing 8-1. This value is independent of the scene geometry, so it can be set once without requiring incessant tweaking. Thus, biasing alone is a compelling reason to use variance shadow maps, as demonstrated in Figure 8-5.

Listing 8-2. Computing the Moments During Variance Shadow Map Rendering

```
float2 ComputeMoments(float Depth)
{
  float2 Moments;

  // First moment is the depth itself.
  Moments.x = Depth;

  // Compute partial derivatives of depth.
  float dx = ddx(Depth);
  float dy = ddy(Depth);

  // Compute second moment over the pixel extents.
  Moments.y = Depth*Depth + 0.25*(dx*dx + dy*dy);

  return Moments;
}
```

Figure 8-5. Variance Shadow Maps Resolve Biasing Issues
Note that there are no visible biasing artifacts when the scene from Figure 8-3 is rendered using variance shadow maps. Additionally, variance shadow maps do not require any bias tweaking.

Finally, it is usually beneficial to clamp the partial derivative portion of M_2 to avoid an excessively high variance if an occluder is almost parallel to the light direction. Hardware-generated partial derivatives become somewhat unstable in these cases and a correspondingly unstable variance can produce random, flashing pixels of light in regions that should be fully shadowed.

Many scenes can avoid this instability entirely by not using the partial derivative bias at all. If the shadow resolution is high enough, clamping the minimum variance may be all that is required to eliminate surface acne.

8.4.3 Light Bleeding

One known issue of variance shadow maps is the potential for *light bleeding* (light that occurs in areas that should be fully in shadow). This artifact is usually seen when the soft edge of a shadow is visible both on the first receiver (as it should be) and, to a lesser extent, on a second receiver (which should be fully occluded by the first), as shown in Figure 8-6. In Figure 8-7, the most objectionable light bleeding occurs when the ratio of Δa to Δb is large.

Figure 8-6. Light Bleeding
In this image, light bleeding is visible under the car when that area should be completely in shadow.

The bad news is that this problem cannot be completely solved without taking more samples (which degenerates into brute-force percentage-closer filtering). This is true for any algorithm because the occluder distribution, and thus the visibility over a filter region, is a step function.

Of course, we can frequently accelerate the common filtering cases (as variance shadow mapping does nicely), but it is always possible to construct a pathological case with N distinct occluders over a filter region of N items. Any algorithm that does not sample all N values cannot correctly reconstruct the visibility function, because the ideal function is a piecewise step function with N unique pieces. As a result, an efficient shadow-map sampling algorithm that computes an exact solution over arbitrary filter regions must be adaptive.

This requirement is certainly not convenient, but it's not crippling: variance shadow mapping is actually a good building block for both an exact and an approximate shadowing algorithm. We are primarily interested in maintaining high performance and are willing to accept some infrequent physical inaccuracy, so approximate algorithms are arguably the most promising approach.

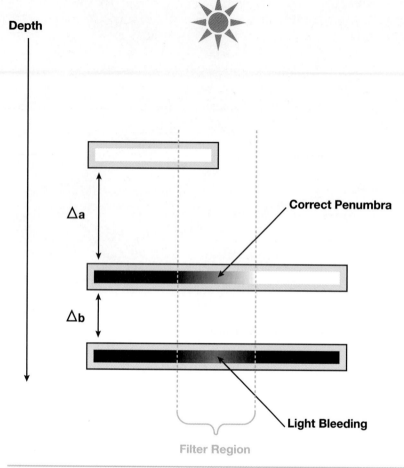

Figure 8-7. How Light Bleeding Occurs
In this example, the bottom object should be fully occluded (dark), yet a small amount of light from the top object's shadow penumbra is visible. The severity of this artifact is proportional to the ratio $\Delta a{:}\Delta b$.

To that end, a simple modification to p_{max} can greatly reduce the light bleeding, at the cost of somewhat darkening the penumbra regions.

An Approximate Algorithm (Light-Bleeding Reduction)

An important observation is that if a surface at depth t is fully occluded over some filter region with average depth μ, then $t > \mu$. Therefore $(t - \mu)^2 > 0$, and from Chebyshev's inequality, $p_{max} < 1$. Put simply, incorrect penumbrae on fully occluded surfaces will never reach full intensity.

We can remove these regions by modifying p_{max} so that any values below some minimum intensity are mapped to 0, and the remaining values are rescaled so that they map from 0 (at the minimum intensity) to 1.

This function can be implemented trivially in HLSL, as shown in Listing 8-3.

Listing 8-3. Applying a Light-Bleeding Reduction Function

```
float linstep(float min, float max, float v)
{
  return clamp((v - min) / (max - min), 0, 1);
}


float ReduceLightBleeding(float p_max, float Amount)
{
  // Remove the [0, Amount] tail and linearly rescale (Amount, 1].
  return linstep(Amount, 1, p_max);
}
```

Note that `linstep()` can be replaced with an arbitrary monotonically increasing continuous function over [0, 1]. For example, `smoothstep()` produces a nice cubic falloff function that may be desirable.

The `Amount` parameter is artist-editable and effectively sets the aggressiveness of the light-bleeding reduction. It is scene-scale independent, but scenes with more light bleeding will usually require a higher value. The optimal setting is related to the depth ratios of occluders and receivers in the scene. Some care should be taken with this parameter, because setting it too high will decrease shadow detail. It should therefore be set just high enough to eliminate the most objectionable light bleeding, while maintaining as much detail as possible.

In practice this solution is effectively free and works well for many scenes, as is evident in Figure 8-8. Light-bleeding reduction is therefore much more attractive than an exact adaptive algorithm for games and other performance-sensitive applications.

8.4.4 Numeric Stability

Another potential issue is *numeric stability*. In particular, the calculation of variance is known to be numerically unstable because of the differencing of two large, approximately equal values. Thankfully, an easy solution to the problem is to use 32-bit floating-point textures and filtering, which are supported on the GeForce 8 Series cards.

Figure 8-8. Results After Applying the Light-Bleeding Reduction Function
A simple modification to the approximation function eliminates the light bleeding in Figure 8-6, while slightly darkening the shadow penumbra.

We also highly recommend using a linear depth metric rather than the post-projection z value. The latter suffers from significant precision loss as the distance from the light increases. This loss may not be a huge issue for comparison-based shadow mapping such as percentage-closer filtering, but the precision loss quickly makes the variance computation unstable. A linear metric with more uniform precision, such as the distance to the light, is more appropriate and stable.

A sample implementation of the "distance to light" depth metric for a spotlight or point light is given in Listing 8-4.

Note that the depth metric can easily be normalized to [0, 1] if a fixed-point shadow-map format is used.

For a directional light, "distance to light plane" is a suitable metric and can be obtained from the z value of the fragment position in light space. Furthermore, this z value can be computed in the vertex shader and safely interpolated, whereas the nonlinear `length()` function in Listing 8-4 must be computed per pixel.

We have seen no numeric stability issues when we used a linear depth metric with 32-bit floating-point numbers.

Listing 8-4. Using a Linear Depth Metric for a Spotlight

```
// Render variance shadow map from the light's point of view.
DepthPSIn Depth_VS(DepthVSIn In)
{
  DepthPSIn Out;
  Out.Position = mul(float4(In.Position, 1), g_WorldViewProjMatrix);
  Out.PosView  = mul(float4(In.Position, 1), g_WorldViewMatrix);
  return Out;
}


float4 Depth_PS(DepthPSIn In) : SV_Target
{
  float DistToLight = length(In.PosView);
  return ComputeMoments(DistToLight);
}


// Render and shade the scene from the camera's point of view.
float4 Shading_PS(ShadingPSIn In) : SV_Target
{
  // Compute the distance from the light to the current fragment.
  float SurfaceDistToLight = length(g_LightPosition - In.PosWorld);
  . . .
}
```

8.4.5 Implementation Notes

At this point, variance shadow maps are already quite usable, providing efficient filtering, cheap edge softening, and a solution to the biasing problems of standard shadow maps. Indeed, the implementation so far is suitable for use in games and other real-time applications.

To summarize, we can implement hardware variance shadow maps as follows:

- Render to the variance shadow map by using a linear depth metric (Listing 8-4), outputting depth and depth squared (Listing 8-2). Use multisample antialiasing (MSAA) on the shadow map (if it's supported).
- Optionally blur the variance shadow map by using a separable box filter.
- Generate mipmaps for the variance shadow map.

- Render the scene, projecting the current fragment into light space as usual, but using a single, filtered (anisotropic and trilinear) texture lookup into the variance shadow map to retrieve the two moments.
- Use Chebyshev's inequality to compute p_{max} (Listing 8-1).
- Optionally, apply light-bleeding reduction to p_{max} (Listing 8-3).
- Use p_{max} to attenuate the light contribution caused by shadowing.

Using variance shadow maps is therefore similar to using normal shadow maps, except that blurring, multisampling, and hardware filtering can be utilized. Note, however, that some techniques used with standard shadow maps (such as the following) are inapplicable to variance shadow maps:

- Rendering "second depth" or "midpoints" into the variance shadow map will not work properly because the recovered depth distribution should represent the depths of the nearest shadow casters in light space. This is not a problem, however, because the second-depth rendering technique is used to avoid biasing issues, which can be addressed more directly with variance shadow maps (see Section 8.4.2).
- Rendering only casters (and not receivers) into the variance shadow map is incorrect! For the interpolation to work properly, the receiving surface must be represented in the depth distribution. If it is not, shadow penumbrae will be improperly sized and fail to fade smoothly from light to dark.

Projection-warping and frustum-partitioning techniques, however, are completely compatible with VSMs. Indeed, the two techniques complement one another. Variance shadow maps hide many of the artifacts introduced by warping or splitting the frustum, such as discontinuities between split points and swimming along shadow edges when the camera moves.

8.4.6 Variance Shadow Maps and Soft Shadows

Moving forward, we address a few issues with using hardware filtering. First, high-precision hardware filtering may not be available. More important, however, we want per-pixel control over the filter region.

As we have seen earlier, clamping the minimum filter width softens shadow edges. Several recent soft shadows algorithms have taken advantage of this capability by choosing the filter width dynamically, based on an estimation of the "blocker depth." This approach can produce convincing shadow penumbrae that increase in size as the distance between the blocker and receiver increases.

Unfortunately, we cannot use blurring to clamp the minimum filter width in this case, because that width changes per pixel, based on the result of the blocker search. We can certainly clamp the mipmap level that the hardware uses, but using mipmapping to blur in this manner produces extremely objectionable boxy artifacts, as shown in Figure 8-9. There is some potential for obtaining better results by using a high-order filter to manually generate the mipmap levels, which is a promising direction for future work.

In the best of circumstances, we would have a filtering scheme that allows us to choose the filter size dynamically per pixel, ideally at constant cost and without dynamic branching. This capability is exactly what summed-area tables give us.

Figure 8-9. Boxy Artifacts Caused by Mipmap Level-of-Detail Clamping
Using level-of-detail clamping to blur the shadow produces ugly boxy shadow edges that swim when the occluder or light moves.

8.5 Summed-Area Variance Shadow Maps

Summed-area tables were introduced by Crow 1984 to accelerate texture filtering. Using a source texture with elements $a[i, j]$, we can build a summed-area table $t[i, j]$ so that

$$t[i, j] = \sum_{x=0}^{i} \sum_{y=0}^{j} a[x, y].$$

In other words, each element in the SAT is the sum of all texture elements in the rectangle above and to the left of the element (or below, if you like your origin in the bottom left). Figure 8-10 shows an example of some arbitrary data and the associated summed-area table.

The sum of any rectangular region can then be determined in constant time:

$$s = t[x_{max}, y_{max}] - t[x_{max}, y_{min}] - t[x_{min}, y_{max}] + t[x_{min}, y_{min}].$$

We can easily compute the average over this region by dividing by the number of pixels in the region. Bilinear interpolation can be used when sampling the corners, producing a smooth gradient.

Note that this formula is inclusive on the "max" sides of the rectangle, but exclusive on the "min" sides. Subtracting 1 from the coordinates before lookup will produce the more common min-inclusive/max-exclusive policy.

In the example from Figure 8-10, we can compute the sum or average over the highlighted data rectangle by querying the highlighted values from the SAT (in this example, we're being inclusive on both sides for simplicity). This yields

$$s = 28 - 8 - 6 + 2 = 16,$$

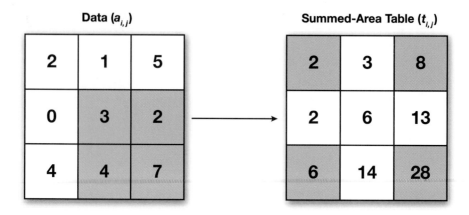

Figure 8-10. Sample Data and the Associated Summed-Area Table

which is the correct sum over the highlighted data region. Dividing by the number of elements in the region (4) gives the correct average of 4.

Summed-area tables give us the ability to sample arbitrary rectangular regions, which is sufficient for our purposes. They can, however, be extended to adaptively sample non-rectangular regions (Glassner 1986).

8.5.1 Generating Summed-Area Tables

We want to generate the summed-area table on the GPU to achieve better performance and to avoid excessive data movements. Two algorithms in particular are potentially suitable: *line-by-line* and *recursive doubling*.

The line-by-line approach is basically a running sum, performed one dimension at a time. On the GPU this algorithm can be implemented by working one line at a time, adding the current line to the previous sum. The disadvantage of this method is that it requires (*width* + *height*) passes.

An alternative approach to summed-area table generation on the GPU is recursive doubling, as proposed by Hensley et al. 2005. Refer to that publication for a complete description of the algorithm. An implementation is also available as part of the sample code accompanying this book.

8.5.2 Numeric Stability Revisited

Summed-area tables burn precision fairly quickly: log(*width* × *height*) bits. A 512×512 SAT, therefore, consumes 18 bits of precision (in the worst case), leaving only 5 bits of the 23-bit mantissa for the data itself! The average case is not this catastrophic, but using summed-area tables significantly decreases the effective precision of the underlying data.

Luckily, there are a few tricks we can use to increase the precision to an acceptable level. Hensley et al. 2005 gave a number of suggestions to improve precision for floating-point summed-area tables. One recommendation is to bias each of the elements by –0.5 before generating the SAT, and to unbias after averaging over a region. This approach effectively gains an extra bit of precision from the sign bit. For images (in our case, shadow maps) that contain a highly nonuniform distribution of data, biasing by the mean value of the data can produce even greater gains. Additionally, the authors suggest using an "origin-centered" SAT to save two more bits, at the cost of increased complexity. This is a particularly useful optimization for spotlights because it pushes the areas of low precision out to the four corners of the shadow projection so that any artifacts will be largely hidden by the circular spotlight attenuation cone.

A trick suggested by Donnelly and Lauritzen 2006 is also useful here: distributing precision into multiple components. Instead of storing a two-component variance shadow map, we store four components, distributing each of the first two moments into two components. This precision splitting cannot be done arbitrarily; to work properly with linear filtering, it must be a linear operation. Nevertheless, Listing 8-5 gives a sample implementation that works fairly well in practice.

Listing 8-5. Distributing Floating-Point Precision

```
// Where to split the value. 8 bits works well for most situations.
float g_DistributeFactor = 256;

float4 DistributePrecision(float2 Moments)
{
  float FactorInv = 1 / g_DistributeFactor;

  // Split precision
  float2 IntPart;
  float2 FracPart = modf(Value * g_DistributeFactor, IntPart);

  // Compose outputs to make reconstruction cheap.
  return float4(IntPart * FactorInv, FracPart);
}

float2 RecombinePrecision(float4 Value)
{
  float FactorInv = 1 / g_DistributeFactor;
  return (Value.zw * FactorInv + Value.xy);
}
```

This step, of course, doubles the storage and bandwidth requirements of summed-area variance shadow maps, but the resulting implementation can still outperform brute-force percentage-closer filtering in many situations, as we show in Section 8.5.3.

Another option, made available by the GeForce 8 Series hardware, is to use 32-bit integers to store the shadow map. Storing the shadow map this way saves several bits of precision that would otherwise be wasted on the exponent portion of the float (which we do not use).

When we use integers, overflow is a potential problem. To entirely avoid overflow, we must reserve $\log(width \times height)$ bits for accumulation. Fortunately, the overflow behavior in Direct3D 10 (wraparound) actually works to our advantage. In particular, if we know the maximum filter size that we will ever use is $M_x \times M_y$, we need only reserve $\log(M_x \times M_y)$ bits. Because a fairly conservative upper bound can often be put on filter sizes, plenty of bits are left for the data. In practice, this solution works extremely well even for large shadow maps and does not require any tricks such as distributing precision.

A final alternative, once hardware support is available, is to use double-precision floating-point numbers to store the moments. The vast precision improvement of double precision (52 bits versus 23 bits) will eliminate any issues that numeric stability causes.

8.5.3 Results

Figure 8-11 shows an image rendered using a 512×512 summed-area variance shadow map. Note the lack of any visible aliasing. Figure 8-12 shows hard and soft shadows obtained simply by varying the minimum filter width. The performance of the technique is independent of the filter width, so arbitrarily soft shadows can be achieved without affecting the frame rate.

Figure 8-11. Shadows Using Summed-Area Variance Shadow Maps

Figure 8-12. Hard-Edged and Soft-Edged Shadows Using Summed-Area Variance Shadow Maps

The technique is also very fast on modern hardware. Figure 8-13 compares the performance of PCF (with hardware acceleration), blurred VSMs (with and without shadow multisampling), and SAVSMs. We chose a simple test scene to evaluate relative performance, because all of these techniques operate in image space and are therefore largely independent of geometric complexity.

Clearly, standard blurred variance shadow maps are the best solution *for constant filter widths*. Even when multisampling is used, VSMs are faster than the competition. Note that the cost of blurring the variance shadow map is theoretically linear in the filter width, but because modern hardware can perform these separable blurs extremely quickly, the reduced performance is not visible unless extremely large filters are used.

For dynamic filter widths, summed-area variance shadow maps have a higher setup cost than percentage-closer filtering (generating the SAT). However, this cost is quickly negated by the higher sampling cost of PCF, particularly for larger minimum filter sizes (such as softer shadows). In our experience, a minimum filter width of at least four is required to eliminate the most objectionable aliasing artifacts of shadow maps, so SAVSM is the obvious winner. We expect that additional performance improvements can be realized with more aggressive optimization.

8.6 Percentage-Closer Soft Shadows

Now that we have an algorithm that can filter arbitrary regions at constant cost, we are ready to use SAVSMs to produce plausible soft shadows. Any algorithm that does a PCF-style sampling over the shadow map is a potential candidate for integration.

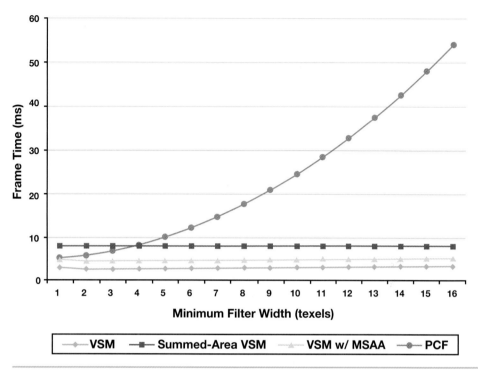

Figure 8-13. Relative Frame Times of PCF, VSM, and SAVSM
Performance results were obtained on a GeForce 8800 GTX in Direct3D 10 at 1600×1200, 4×MSAA, using a 512×512 shadow map. Note that VSM with shadow map MSAA yields the highest-quality shadows, and all other techniques have relatively comparable quality.

One such algorithm, proposed by Fernando 2005, is *percentage-closer soft shadows* (PCSS), which is particularly attractive because of its simplicity. PCSS works in three steps: (1) the blocker search, (2) penumbra size estimation, and (3) shadow filtering.

8.6.1 The Blocker Search

The blocker search samples a search region around the current shadow texel and finds the average depth of any blockers in that region. The search region size is proportional to both the light size and the distance to the light. A sample is considered a blocker if it is closer to the light than the current fragment (using the standard depth test).

One unfortunate consequence of this step is that it will reintroduce the biasing issues of PCF into our soft shadows algorithm, because of the depth test. Moreover, taking many samples over some region of the shadow map is disappointing after having worked so hard to get constant-time filtering.

8.6.2 Penumbra Size Estimation

This step of the algorithm uses the previously computed blocker depth to estimate the size of the penumbra, based on a parallel planes approximation. We list the formula here and refer the reader to Fernando 2005 for the derivation based on similar triangles:

$$w_{penumbra} = \frac{w_{light}\left(d_{receiver} - d_{blocker}\right)}{d_{blocker}}.$$

Here, w_{light} refers to the light size.

8.6.3 Shadow Filtering

During filtering, summed-area variance shadow maps can be used directly, improving the quality and performance of the algorithm over the uniform grid percentage-closer filtering that was used in the original implementation.

8.6.4 Results

Figure 8-14 shows a side-by-side comparison of PCSS using percentage-closer filtering (*left*) and summed-area variance shadow maps (*right*) for the filtering step. The sample scene is especially difficult, forcing both implementations to take many samples (64) during the blocker search step. Regardless of this equalizing bottleneck, the SAVSM

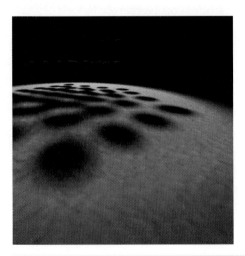 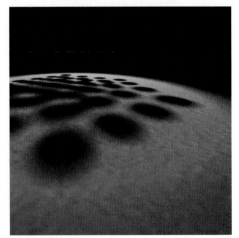

Figure 8-14. Plausible Soft Shadows Using PCSS
Left: A scene rendered using PCF for the filtering step. Right: The same scene rendered using SAVSM.

implementation outperformed the PCF implementation by a reasonable margin: 40 frames/sec versus 25 frames/sec at 1600×1200. Furthermore, the image quality of the PCF implementation was inferior because it sparsely sampled the filter region.

Although preliminary, these results imply that summed-area variance shadow maps are well suited to usage in a soft shadows algorithm. We are looking forward to further research in this area.

8.7 Conclusion

We have discussed the topic of shadow-map filtering in detail and have provided solutions to many associated problems, such as minification aliasing, biasing, and soft shadows.

We have shown that variance shadow maps are quite useful and are a promising direction for future research. That said, standard blurred variance shadow maps, combined with a light-bleeding reduction function, are extremely fast and robust, and they provide excellent quality. We highly recommend using this implementation for shadow filtering in most applications, which do not require per-pixel filter width control.

For plausible soft shadows, variance shadow maps have also proven useful. Combined with summed-area tables, they provide constant-time filtering of arbitrary rectangular regions.

In conclusion, we hope this chapter has offered useful solutions and that it will motivate future research into variance shadow maps and real-time shadow-filtering algorithms in general.

8.8 References

Crow, Franklin. 1977. "Shadow Algorithms for Computer Graphics." In *Computer Graphics (Proceedings of SIGGRAPH 1977)* 11(2), pp. 242–248.

Crow, Franklin. 1984. "Summed-Area Tables for Texture Mapping." In *Computer Graphics (Proceedings of SIGGRAPH 1984)* 18(3), pp. 207–212.

Donnelly, William, and Andrew Lauritzen. 2006. "Variance Shadow Maps." In *Proceedings of the Symposium on Interactive 3D Graphics and Games 2006*, pp. 161–165.

Fernando, Randima. 2005. "Percentage-Closer Soft Shadows." In *SIGGRAPH 2005 Sketches*.

Glassner, Andrew. 1986. "Adaptive Precision in Texture Mapping." In *Computer Graphics (Proceedings of SIGGRAPH 1986)* 20(4), pp. 297–306.

Hensley, Justin, Thorsten Scheuermann, Greg Coombe, Montek Singh, and Anselmo Lastra. 2005. "Fast Summed-Area Table Generation and Its Applications." *Computer Graphics Forum* 24(3), pp. 547–555.

Kilgard, Mark. 2001. "Shadow Mapping with Today's OpenGL Hardware." Presentation at CEDEC 2001.

Martin, Tobias, and Tiow-Seng Tan. 2004. "Anti-aliasing and Continuity with Trapezoidal Shadow Maps." In *Eurographics Symposium on Rendering Proceedings 2004*, pp. 153–160.

Reeves, William, David Salesin and Robert Cook. 1987. "Rendering Antialiased Shadows with Depth Maps." In *Computer Graphics (Proceedings of SIGGRAPH 1987)* 21(3), pp. 283–291.

Stamminger, Marc, and George Drettakis. 2002. "Perspective Shadow Maps." In *ACM Transactions on Graphics (Proceedings of SIGGRAPH 2002)* 21(3), pp. 557–562.

Williams, Lance. 1978. "Casting Curved Shadows on Curved Surfaces." In *Computer Graphics (Proceedings of SIGGRAPH 1978)* 12(3), pp. 270–274.

Wimmer, Michael, D. Scherzer, and Werner Purgathofer. 2004. "Light Space Perspective Shadow Maps." In *Proceedings of the Eurographics Symposium on Rendering 2004*, pp. 143–152.

Many people deserve thanks for providing helpful ideas, suggestions, and feedback, including William Donnelly (University of Waterloo), Michael McCool (RapidMind), Mandheerej Nandra (Caltech), Randy Fernando (NVIDIA), Kevin Myers (NVIDIA), and Hubert Nguyen (NVIDIA). Additional thanks go to Chris Iacobucci (Silicon Knights) for the car and commando 3D models and textures.

Chapter 9

Interactive Cinematic Relighting with Global Illumination

Fabio Pellacini
Dartmouth College

Miloš Hašan
Cornell University

Kavita Bala
Cornell University

9.1 Introduction

Cinematic lighting design is the process artists use for defining the look of each frame in a feature film by carefully setting all the parameters of the light shaders. Rendering high-quality images interactively for cinematic lighting is becoming a necessity, but it remains a challenge due to the complex data sets used in production rendering.

For faster user feedback, relighting engines were developed to take advantage of the fact that lighting artists are often interested in changing light parameters during lighting design—not the camera, objects, or materials. Relighting engines use a deep frame buffer to cache position, normals, and material parameters of all visible points and then recompute lighting on them interactively. This approach is similar to deferred shading techniques used in games, but it differs because the caches are computed offline. While deep frame buffers have been common in most relighting engines, the use of GPUs to interactively compute the final lighting was first introduced by Gershbein and Hanrahan 2000 and was extended to support a production scene's geometric and shading complexity in the Lpics system (Pellacini et al. 2005). Even though these systems show interactive relighting for cinematic scenes, they remain limited to direct illumination and cannot support indirect effects.

The *direct-to-indirect transfer algorithm* (Hašan et al. 2006) extends relighting engines to support cinematic relighting with multiple-bounce indirect illumination. The relighting is achieved by transferring the direct illumination of a set of gather samples to the visible samples, which can be computed using a large transfer matrix precomputed offline. Our implementation achieves high-quality multiple-bounce indirect illumination at 10 to 20 frames per second for scenes with up to two million polygons, with diffuse and glossy materials and arbitrary direct illumination shaders. Precomputation takes up to 3 hours. We review the principles behind this framework here, describe the details of the implementation, and discuss the trade-offs.

9.2 An Overview of the Algorithm

We would like to compute the direct and indirect illumination on a set of points visible from the current camera (the pixels in the deep frame buffer), which we call *view samples*. Computing the direct illumination component is straightforward. The deep frame buffer contains the positions, normals, and material parameters for each view sample. Shadows are computed using shadow mapping.

To compute indirect illumination, we will need a set of points distributed throughout the scene, called *gather samples*. Note that gather samples are everywhere, not just in the visible part of the scene, because indirect illumination can come from surfaces that are not directly visible.

The basic idea behind the algorithm is that indirect illumination on the view samples can be computed by a linear transformation from the direct illumination on the gather samples—thus the name *direct-to-indirect transfer*. If we arrange the view and gather samples into vectors, this linear transformation can be thought of as a large matrix, which can be precomputed offline and multiplied by the direct illumination every time the lighting changes. Figure 9-1 shows a high-level overview of the overall algorithm, which can be summarized with the following equation:

$$\mathbf{v}_f = \mathbf{v}_d + \mathbf{v}_i = \mathbf{v}_d + \mathbf{T} \cdot \mathbf{g}_d,$$

where $\mathbf{v}_f$ is the final solution, $\mathbf{v}_d$ is the direct illumination on view samples, $\mathbf{v}_i$ is the indirect illumination on view samples, $\mathbf{T}$ is the transfer matrix, and $\mathbf{g}_d$ is the direct illumination on the gather cloud. Note that the gather samples are diffuse-only, so this

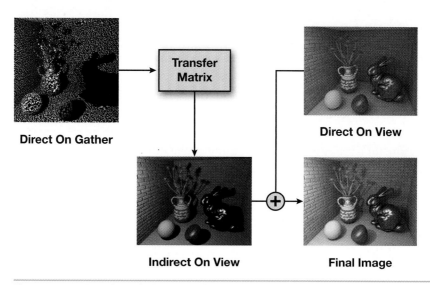

Figure 9-1. An Overview of Direct-to-Indirect Transfer

algorithm cannot handle caustics.

Unfortunately, the algorithm is not practical in this simplistic form. One reason is that the transfer matrix is very large. If we use a 640×480 image with 65,536 gather samples, it will produce a matrix with 19 billion elements, which is difficult to store and multiply with. Worse, every column of the matrix is essentially an image with one point light and full global illumination, so a naive approach to precomputation would take a long time. Therefore, we introduce several new ideas. First, we split the transfer $\mathbf{T}$ into a final gather component $\mathbf{F}$ and a multibounce component $\mathbf{M}$ so that the indirect illumination will be computed as

$$\mathbf{v}_i = \mathbf{F} \cdot (\mathbf{M} + \mathbf{I}) \cdot \mathbf{g}_d.$$

The advantage of using this equation is that elements of the final gather matrix $\mathbf{F}$ can be defined analytically and stored in high precision; the multibounce matrix $\mathbf{M}$ can be precomputed and stored with lower precision because it does not influence image quality as directly as the final gather. Next, we apply the Haar wavelet transform (Stollnitz et al. 1995) to the rows of the matrices and cull unimportant coefficients, achieving a sparse representation. Finally, we map the sparse matrix multiplications to the GPU, achieving a real-time update of indirect illumination as the direct lighting changes.

In the rest of this chapter, we explain in more detail how to implement these ideas.

9.3 Gather Samples

Here we discuss how to compute the gather samples and map them into a square texture. Each gather sample includes a position, a normal, and a diffuse color. The surface area it represents should also be stored, but we need it only for precomputation, so we don't have to send it to the GPU. It is advantageous to choose the number of gather samples as a power of four, because we will need to map them to a square power-of-two texture for wavelet projection. Our implementation uses 65,536 (256×256) samples; we found this to be the lowest number that gives enough quality.

A simple divide-and-conquer approach to creating the gather samples is presented in Listing 9-1. The idea is to distribute a budget of samples onto a set of mesh triangles by recursively splitting the budget and the set until there is only one sample or only one triangle left. The simple divide-and-conquer method works well for scenes such as rooms, but it becomes less efficient for large environments, where choosing gather samples in a nonuniform way can improve the accuracy of the overall algorithm. Hašan et al. 2006 presents a more complex importance-sampling variation of gather selection that is robust enough even for large environments.

Listing 9-1. Pseudocode for Divide-and-Conquer Gather Sample Computation

```
GatherSample[] createGather(Triangle[] triangles, int budget)
{
  if (triangles.length == 1)
  {
    // Pick all samples within one triangle.
    // Distribute the area across the samples.
    float area = triangles[0].area / budget;
    return sampleTriangle(triangles[0], budget, area);
  }
  else if (budget == 1)
  {
    // Pick a random triangle and pick one sample on it.
    Triangle t = pickRandomAreaWeighted(triangles);
    float area = getTotalArea(triangles);
    return sampleTriangle(t, 1, area);
  }
  else
  {
    // Split triangles (e.g., by some plane).
    (ts1, ts2) = split(triangles);
```

```
    // Split budget based on total areas.
    area1 = getTotalArea(ts1); area2 = getTotalArea(ts2);
    int b1 = (int)(budget * area1 / (area1 + area2));
    b1 = max(b1, 1); b1 = min(b1, budget - 1);
    int b2 = budget - b1;
    // Continue recursively.
    return union(createGather(ts1, b1), createGather(ts2, b2));
  }
}
```

We have created the set of gather samples, but we still have to "flatten" them—that is, define the mapping to the power-of-two texture. (In this mapping, sub-block samples that correspond to Haar wavelet basis functions should be similar to each other; this will become important later.) The solution is another divide-and-conquer algorithm. We will need a function, `splitSamples()` that takes a set of gather samples (of a size divisible by two) and splits it coherently into two subsets of equal size with respect to positions and normals of the samples. A sample implementation of this function, based on "k-means clustering," can be found in Hašan et al. 2006. However, a simpler technique should work fine, as long as it takes both positions and normals into account. Assuming we have such a function, we can implement the mapping easily, as shown in Listing 9-2.

Listing 9-2. Pseudocode for Flattening the Gather Samples into a Texture

```
float dist(GatherSample x, GatherSample y)
{
  // Distance should depend on both positions and normals.
  // The constant "sceneBoundingBoxDiagonal" should be precomputed.
  return 400 * length(x.pos - y.pos)^2 +
    sceneBoundingBoxDiagonal^2 * length(x.normal - y.normal)^2;
}

(Gathersample[], GatherSample[]) splitSamples(GatherSample[] samples)
{
  // Split into 2 clusters using the distance function above.
  // Use (for example) the k-means algorithm.
  return kMeans(samples, 2, dist);
}
```

```
SquareTexture flattenGather(GatherSample[] samples)
{
    int n = samples.length;
    assert isPowerOf4(n);   // Has to be power of 4
    SquareTexture result = new SquareTexture();
    map(samples, result, 0, 0, n);
    return result;
}

void map(GatherSample[] smp, SquareTexture t, int x, int y, int a)
{
    // Trivial case
    if (a == 1) { t(x, y) = smp[0]; return; }

    // Split into 4 subsets.
    (s1, s2) = splitSamples(smp);
    (s11, s12) = splitSamples(s1);
    (s21, s22) = splitSamples(s2);

    // Map recursively.
    map(s11, x, y, a/2);
    map(s12, x + a/2, y, a/2);
    map(s21, x, y + a/2, a/2);
    map(s22, x + a/2, y + a/2, a/2);
}
```

9.4 One-Bounce Indirect Illumination

As given, the matrix $\mathbf{T}$ contains multiple bounces of indirect illumination for each of its elements. However, such a matrix is very expensive to precompute directly. For simplicity, we first aim for one-bounce indirect, and later we show how to handle multiple bounces. For one bounce, precomputing the elements of $\mathbf{T}$ is relatively simple, as shown in Listing 9-3.

At this point we could try out the algorithm, using a 256×256 image and 1,024 gather samples. If we store each matrix element as three floats, the matrix size will be $256 \times 256 \times 1024 \times 3 \times 4 = 768$ MB—too heavyweight for real-time performance. However, for higher quality, we might want 65,536 gather samples and a 640×480 view resolution, which requires a transfer matrix of roughly 19 billion elements. Clearly, we need a good compression approach, which we discuss next.

Listing 9-3. Pseudocode for Matrix Element Evaluation

```
RgbColor evalElement(ViewSample v, GatherSample g, Vector3 cameraPos)
{
  Vector3 out = (cameraPos - v.position).normalize();
  Vector3 in = (g.position - v.position).normalize();

  // Evaluate the surface shader (or "brdf").
  // The cosine term is assumed to be included.
  RgbColor color = v.evalBrdfCosine(in, out);

  // The gather sample is treated as a cosine-emitting light.
  color *= max(dot(g.normal, -in), 0);
  color *= g.area;

  // The 1/r^2 distance falloff term
  color /= (g.position - v.position).lengthSquared();

  // Trace a shadow ray to check visibility.
  if (!color.isZero()) color *= visibility(v.position, g.position);
  // Clamping is needed to prevent blowup of 1/r^2 term in corners
  color.clamp(CLAMP_CONST);
  return color;
}
```

9.5 Wavelets for Compression

There are several approaches for compressing the large matrices that arise in lighting. For example, precomputed radiance transfer techniques have introduced spherical harmonics and wavelets to solve this problem, but they traditionally considered only distant illumination, not truly local lighting. Our algorithm extends these techniques to direct-to-indirect transfer matrices. We decided to use wavelets because they work well when sharp lighting details need to be maintained. In our case, these details may be sharp, secondary shadows or glossy reflections. We suggest that readers unfamiliar with wavelets consult Stollnitz et al. 1995.

As in Ng et al. 2003, we project the rows of **T** into 2D Haar wavelets, which results in many coefficients close to zero. This allows us to discard most of these coefficients, keeping only a few per row (let's say 100 per row), which makes the matrix sparse.

The question is which coefficients to keep. Should we preserve the ones with the largest absolute values? We found that this is not optimal, and we should instead weight the coefficients by the area of support of the corresponding wavelet basis function (the number of its nonzero elements). The wavelet transform code is presented in Listing 9-4.

Once a row of the matrix is computed and transformed, we need to preserve the most important coefficients and store the result as a sparse vector, as in Listing 9-5.

Now we have everything we need to precompute the whole sparse matrix for one-bounce indirect illumination. For each view sample, we compute the corresponding row of **T**, transform it, cull unimportant coefficients, and output the resulting sparse vector to a file (so that we do not have to store it in memory).

Listing 9-4. Pseudocode for the 2D Haar Wavelet Transform

```
SquareTexture waveletTransform(SquareTexture a)
{
    int n = a.size();   // Texture is n x n
    assert isPowerOf2(n);   // Only works for power-of-two textures
    SquareTexture b = new SquareTexture(n);

    for (int side = n; side >= 2; side /= 2)
      for (int i = 0; i < side; i += 2)
        for (int j = 0; j < side; j += 2)
        {
            b(i/2, j/2) = 0.5 *   // Box filter
                          (a(i,j) + a(i+1, j) + a(i, j+1) +
                           a(i+1, j+1));
            b(i/2, j/2 + side/2) = 0.5 *   // Horizontal
                          (a(i,j) - a(i+1, j) + a(i, j+1) -
                           a(i+1, j+1));
            b(i/2 + side/2, j/2) = 0.5 *   // Vertical
                          (a(i,j) + a(i+1, j) - a(i, j+1) -
                           a(i+1, j+1));
            b(i/2 + side/2, j/2 + side/2) = 0.5 *   // Diagonal
                                   (a(i,j) - a(i+1, j) -
                                    a(i, j+1) + a(i+1, j+1));
        }

    return b;
}
```

Listing 9-5. Pseudocode for Wavelet Coefficient Culling

```
struct WaveletCoefficient
{
  int index,
  RgbColor value;

  // Assuming 64k gather samples
  int getX() { return index % 256; }
  int getY() { return index / 256; }

  // You might want to use lookup tables instead.
  int getLevel() { return ceil(log(1 + max(getX(), getY())))); }
  int getArea() { return 4^(9 - getLevel()); }
}

type SparseVector = List<WaveletCoefficient>;

SparseVector keepImportantCoeffs(SquareTexture a)
{
  int n = a.size();  // Texture is n x n.
  SparseVector sv = new SparseVector();

  // Turn the 2D array into a list of coefficients.
  for (int i = 0; i < n; i++)
    for (int j = 0; j < n; j++)
    {
      WaveletCoefficient w = new WaveletCoefficient();
      w.index = i * 256 + j;
      w.value = a(i, j) * w.getArea();  // Weight by area
      sv.add(w);
    }

  sortDescendingByAbsoluteValue(sv);
  sv.keepSubList(0, 100);  // Keep 100 most important coefficients.

  // Undo the area weighting.
  for (WaveletCoefficient w: sv) w.value /= w.getArea();

  return result;
}
```

9.6 Adding Multiple Bounces

To make multiple bounces manageable, we split the transfer matrix into two components: a multibounce matrix to encode the direct-to-indirect transfer within the gather cloud, and a final gather matrix to encode the transfer from gather samples to view samples. The advantage of this split is that we can compute the multibounce matrix at lower accuracy. This split can be summarized by the following equation:

$$\mathbf{v}_i = \mathbf{F} \cdot (\mathbf{M} + \mathbf{I}) \cdot \mathbf{g}_d,$$

where $\mathbf{F}$ is the final gather matrix, $\mathbf{M}$ is the multiple-bounce matrix, and $\mathbf{I}$ is the identity matrix. If we denote by $\mathbf{g}_i$ the (multibounce) indirect illumination on the gather cloud, we can also write this equation as

$$\mathbf{g}_i = \mathbf{M} \cdot \mathbf{g}_d$$

$$\mathbf{v}_i = \mathbf{F} \cdot (\mathbf{g}_d + \mathbf{g}_i).$$

We can afford to compute the matrix $\mathbf{M}$ at lower accuracy because its contribution to the image is not often directly visible. We do so by using a modified version of the photon-mapping algorithm (Jensen 2001). We treat each gather sample as a small area light with Lambertian emission. We then shoot about one million photons from the gather samples (about 15 photons from each). A larger number of photons might improve accuracy at the price of longer precomputation time; however, as noted before, this matrix does not require very high accuracy. Each photon carries the ID of the gather sample from which it originated. In a second pass, a k-nearest-neighbor computation is done on each gather sample (k is about 1,000), and these k photons are treated as a sparse, k-element approximation to the corresponding row of the matrix $\mathbf{M}$. More details can be found in Hašan et al. 2006.

The multibounce matrix is already sparse, so we might choose not to compress it at all. However, we can improve performance by applying the same wavelet compression technique we used for the final gather matrix. We can use a smaller number of coefficients per row (we use 40, but again note that this number does not affect image quality much because the final gather will blur out errors). This means that each row of the matrix will have 40 nonzero elements instead of 1,000. The complete relighting algorithm, with multiple bounces and wavelet compression included, can be summarized as

$$\mathbf{v}_i = \mathbf{F} \cdot (\mathbf{M} + \mathbf{I}) \cdot \mathbf{g}_d = \mathbf{F}^w \cdot wt\big(\mathbf{M}^w \cdot wt(\mathbf{g}_d) + \mathbf{g}_d\big),$$

where $\mathbf{F}^w$ and $\mathbf{M}^w$ are the wavelet-projected final gather and multiple-bounce matrixes, respectively, and *wt* is the wavelet transform operator. Listing 9-6 shows the full relighting algorithm (for one light) summarized in pseudocode, and Figure 9-2 shows the algorithm applied.

Listing 9-6. Pseudocode for the Complete Relighting Algorithm

```
Texture computeLighting(light, viewSamples, gatherSamples)
{
  // Direct illumination on view and gather samples
  viewDirect = computeDirectIllumination(light, viewSamples);
  gatherDirect = computeDirectIllumination(light, gatherSamples);

  // Multibounce indirect illumination on gather samples
  gatherDirectWavelet = waveletTransform(gatherDirect);
  gatherIndirect =
    sparseMultiply(multiBounceWaveletMatrix, gatherDirectWavelet);
  gatherFull = gatherDirect + gatherIndirect;

  // Final bounce from gather to view samples
  gatherFullWavelet = waveletTransform(gatherFull);
  viewIndirect =
    sparseMultiply(finalGatherWaveletMatrix, gatherFullWavelet);

  // Combine into final image.
  viewFull = viewDirect + viewIndirect;
  return viewFull;
}
```

9.7 Packing Sparse Matrix Data

There are many ways to store a sparse matrix. The three most common methods are these:

1. **Row-based**—store a list of nonzero elements for each row

2. **Column-based**—store a list of nonzero elements for each column

3. **An unordered list of triples**—row, column, value

None of these methods is particularly efficient for GPU implementation, so the question is whether we can do better.

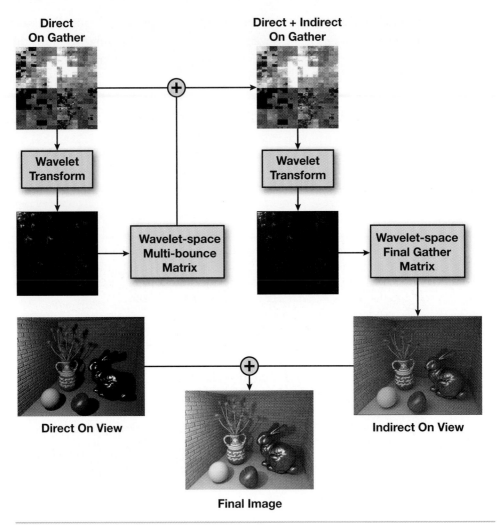

Figure 9-2. The Complete Relighting Algorithm

Figure 9-3 shows the columns of the compressed final gather matrix. You can think of these columns as images lit by "wavelet lights." We can see that many of these are zero, and that the nonzero elements tend to cluster together. This scenario suggests that we should use a simple image-based technique to store the data; that is, cut out the nonzero elements from each of these images into one or more rectangles. The easiest approach is to cut out a single rectangle that fits most tightly around the nonzero elements, but we can use more than one rectangle, to improve the storage efficiency.

Figure 9-3. Example Columns from the Transformed One-Bounce Matrix

Finally, we pack all these rectangular blocks into 4,096×4,096 texture atlases. This is much more efficient than using a separate texture for each block, because the number of state changes is much lower. Figure 9-4 illustrates this packing.

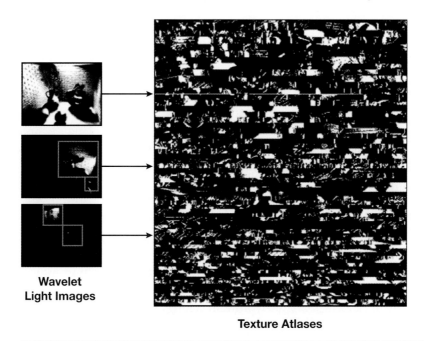

**Wavelet
Light Images**

Texture Atlases

Figure 9-4. Packing the Sparse Final Gather Matrix
Nonzero elements are shown as white; zero elements are shown as black.

9.8 A GPU-Based Relighting Engine

While we ran all the precomputation on the CPU, we implemented the interactive relighting engine entirely on the GPU, using the OpenGL API and GLSL running on a Shader Model 3 graphics card (a GeForce 7800, in our case). The complete algorithm for one light is summarized in pseudocode in Listing 9-7, in Section 9.8.2. The algorithm appears complex, but only three operations need to be implemented: direct illumination computation, wavelet transform of a square image, and sparse-matrix multiplication. In the rest of this chapter, we describe our implementation for each operation.

9.8.1 Direct Illumination

We evaluate direct illumination in the same way we did on the Lpics relighting engine (Pellacini et al. 2005). We use deferred shading of deep frame-buffer data that is stored using four texture rectangles encoding positions, normals, and diffuse and specular coefficients, respectively. We use two sets of textures for view and gather samples. To save GPU memory, we encode normals and diffuse components by using 8 bits per channels (bpc), while keeping positions and specular coefficients in floating point at 16 bpc.

We shade the deep frame buffer by drawing a quad that covers the required resolution. A GLSL shader is used to define the direct illumination model. In our implementation, we used Phong shading for surface reflection; alternatively, a more complex uber-shader can be used for material representation. We tested our algorithm with many different light models, including point and spotlights, a projector light, and a light inspired by the uber-light cinematic light shader (Pellacini and Vidimče 2004). To avoid code duplication, we include all possible light types by using preprocessor macros, and then we bind the proper shader variant for each light.

We support shadowing by using shadow mapping for sharp shadows. For spot and projector lights, we use a standard shadow map, and we use six maps for point lights. We have also implemented a slower method for area lights that samples their shadows uniformly with multiple shadow maps. We render shadow maps by using frame-buffer objects. For each object in the scene, we store triangles by using vertex-buffer objects directly in video memory. View-frustum culling of objects further speeds up rendering shadow maps. Although this implementation could be improved substantially, we found it sufficient in our case because most of the computation time remains in the multiplication.

To increase image quality, we antialias direct illumination by supersampling it at 2×2 samples per pixel. We compute indirect illumination per pixel and upsample it to the direct illumination's resolution, while trying to avoid light leaking across the edges. We do this by assigning the closest neighbor (based on normal and position) searched in a 3×3 region around each pixel. We finally sum the direct and indirect contributions and downsample using a 2×2 box filter.

9.8.2 Wavelet Transform

We perform the Haar 2D wavelet transform of square images by using a simple recursive algorithm. As shown earlier in Listing 9-4, the transform is essentially a sequence of filtering operations. To implement this on the GPU, we convert the outer for-loop to a multipass approach, and we use a fragment shader to implement the filtering operation in each pass. Listing 9-7 shows the pseudocode for the recursive algorithm, and Listing 9-8 shows the fragment shader code.

Listing 9-7. Pseudocode for the CPU-Side Wavelet Transform Loop

```
SquareTexture waveletTransform(SquareTexture source)
{
  int size = source.size();  // 256 in our implementation
  SquareTexture result = new SquareTexture(size);
  bindBuffer(result);

  while (size >= 2)
  {
    glViewport(0, 0, size, size);
    bindProgram(waveletFragmentShader, source);
    drawQuadWithTextureCoordinates(0, 0, size, size);
    unbindProgram();
    size /= 2;  // Size is halved in each pass
    copyToTexture(source);
  }

  unbindBuffer();
  return result;
}
```

Listing 9-8. The Wavelet Transform Fragment Shader

```
void main(uniform samplerRect source,
          uniform float size) {
  vec2 loc = 0;
  vec4 weights = 0;
  vec2 curLoc = floor(gl_TexCoord[0].xy);
  float halfSize = floor(size/2);
```

Listing 9-8 (*continued*). The Wavelet Transform Fragment Shader

```
// Determine which coefficient to compute
// and set appropriate weights.
if(curLoc.x >= halfSize) {
  if(curLoc.y >= halfSize) {
    loc = curLoc - vec2(halfSize, halfSize);
    weights = vec4(+1, -1, -1, +1);
  } else {
    loc = curLoc - vec2(halfSize, 0);
    weights = vec4(+1, -1, +1, -1);
  }
} else {
  if(curLoc.y >= halfSize) {
    loc = curLoc - vec2(0, halfSize);
    weights = vec4(+1, +1, -1, -1);
  } else {
    loc = curLoc;
    weights = vec4(+1, +1, +1, +1);
  }
}

// Look up source pixels.
vec4 s00 = textureRect(source, 2*loc + vec2(0, 0));
vec4 s01 = textureRect(source, 2*loc + vec2(0, 1));
vec4 s10 = textureRect(source, 2*loc + vec2(1, 0));
vec4 s11 = textureRect(source, 2*loc + vec2(1, 1));

// Compute the weighted average for the coefficient.
vec4 c = 0.5 * (weights.x * s00 + weights.y * s10 +
                weights.z * s01 + weights.w * s11);

gl_FragColor = c;
}
```

9.8.3 Sparse Matrix Multiplication

Sparse matrix multiplication is the most expensive component of the relighting algorithm in terms of speed and memory. As shown in the previous section, we store matrix coefficients by using rectangular image blocks packed in 4,096×4,096 texture atlases. To obtain maximum performance, we convert the multiplication to a (large) sequence of blending operations by interpreting the multiplication as column (image) accumulation. In particular, we accumulate the values in each block, multiplied by the intensity of the corresponding wavelet light in the final image. Furthermore, this image-based strategy lets us take advantage of the sparsity in the light vector by skipping all blocks whose light intensity is smaller than a threshold. We call this *on-the-fly culling*.

For each block, we construct a camera-aligned quad whose vertices are set to the block image coordinates. At each quad vertex, we store the atlas texture coordinates. Texture data is quantized using 8 bpc together with a scale and an offset value stored at the vertices of each quad. We store all quads in a vertex-buffer object to avoid transferring to the GPU during rendering. We evaluate the sparse matrix multiply by drawing all the quads and using shaders to multiply the wavelet light coefficients (constant per quad) by the matrix coefficients (after scaling and offsetting) stored in the texture atlases. Using frame-buffer blending, we accumulate the results by setting the source and destination weights to 1. Listing 9-9 lists the vertex and fragment shader code used for the multiply.

To support on-the-fly culling of wavelet lights, we store image norms in quad vertex data and multiply them by the wavelet light coefficient in the vertex shader. If such a product is smaller than a given epsilon, we cull the quad by sending it off-screen directly in the vertex shader. This allows us to speed up the operation considerably without requiring any CPU intervention.

Listing 9-9. Vertex and Fragment Shader Code for Sparse Matrix Multiplication

```
// Vertex Shader ---------------------------------------------
void main(uniform float waveletEpsilon, // For on-the-fly culling
          uniform sampler2D waveletLightCoefficients,
          uniform vec2 waveletLightCoefficientsSize) {
  gl_Position = gl_ModelViewProjectionMatrix * gl_Vertex;

  gl_TexCoord[0] = gl_MultiTexCoord0; // Block atlas texture coord
  gl_TexCoord[1] = gl_MultiTexCoord1; // Light coefficient coord
  gl_TexCoord[2] = gl_MultiTexCoord2; // Scale/offset of block

  float boxNorm = gl_MultiTexCoord2.y; // Column norm of the block
  vec3 waveletCoefficient = texture2D(sourceVertex,
        gl_MultiTexCoord1.xy / sourceVertexSize).xyz;
  float sourceNorm = dot(waveletCoefficient, waveletCoefficient);
  // Test the culling threshold against the product of
  // wavelet light coefficient times column norm
  if(boxNorm * sourceNorm < waveletEpsilon) {
    gl_Position = vec4(-10, 0, 0, 1); // Toss out the vertex
  }
}
```

```
// Fragment shader --------------------------------------
void main(uniform samplerRect waveletLightCoefficients,
          uniform samplerRect transferCoefficients) {
  // Read wavelet light intensity.
  vec3 l = textureRect(waveletLightCoefficients, gl_TexCoord[1].xy).xyz;
  // Read matrix coefficient.
  vec3 w = textureRect(transferCoefficients, gl_TexCoord[0].xy).xyz;
  // Scale and offset the matrix coefficient to support 8 bits compression.
  w = gl_TexCoord[2].z + (gl_TexCoord[2].w-gl_TexCoord[2].z) * w;

  // Scale the result and return.
  gl_FragColor = vec4(l*w,1);
}
```

9.9 Results

We tested our algorithm on a 3.2 GHz Pentium 4 with 2 GB of RAM and an NVIDIA GeForce 7800 graphics accelerator with 256 MB of RAM. We ran our tests at a video resolution of 640×480, with per-pixel indirect illumination computed from 65,536 gather samples and 2×2 supersampled direct illumination. Images of the scenes we tested, lit by omnilights and spotlights, are presented in Figure 9-5 and show large areas with pure indirect illumination. Figure 9-6 shows the same scenes lit using arbitrary direct lighting shaders, while still providing interactive feedback to light designers with global illumination.

For all tested scenes, ranging from roughly 60,000 to 2.1 million triangles, we were able to compute accurate indirect illumination at interactive rates of about 7 to 15 frames per second without on-the-fly wavelet culling, and about 9 to 25 frames per second with culling, with almost no perceptible difference. Because the algorithm runs entirely on the GPU, we found that the performance depends mostly on the GPU. Relighting times are dominated by the transfer computation and occasionally by the shadow-map rendering. The bottleneck of the CPU precomputation is the final gather matrix, which took at most 2.6 hours; all other precomputation phases combined should be well under 20 minutes. GPU memory requirements are dominated by the transfer matrices, which took about 100 MB (using 100 coefficients for final gather and 40 for the multi-bounce matrix) after quantization.

Figure 9-5. Scenes Rendered in Our Systems Using Point and Spot Lighting

Figure 9-6. Arbitrary Lighting Effects Can Be Supported by Our Algorithm
Textured lights (left), an uber-light-inspired shader (middle), and a sun-sky model (right).

9.10 Conclusion

In this chapter we presented a GPU relighting engine for cinematic lighting design, using an engine that extends traditional frame-buffer approaches. This engine supports multiple-bounce indirect illumination for scenes with high geometric complexity, glossy materials, and flexible direct lighting models expressed using procedural shaders.

9.11 References

Gershbein, Reid, and Patrick M. Hanrahan. 2000. "A Fast Relighting Engine for Interactive Cinematic Lighting Design." In *Proceedings of SIGGRAPH 2000*.

Hašan, Miloš, Fabio Pellacini, and Kavita Bala. 2006. "Direct-to-Indirect Transfer for Cinematic Relighting." In *ACM Transactions on Graphics (Proceedings of SIGGRAPH 2006)* 25(3).

Jensen, Henrik W. 2001. *Realistic Image Synthesis Using Photon Mapping.* AK Peters.

Ng, Ren, Ravi Ramamoorthi, and Pat Hanrahan. 2003. "All-Frequency Shadows Using Non-linear Wavelet Lighting Approximation." In ACM Transactions on Graphics (Proceedings of SIGGRAPH 2003) 22(3).

Pellacini, Fabio, and Kiril Vidimče. 2004. "Cinematic Lighting." In *GPU Gems*, edited by Randima Fernando, pp. 167–183. Addison-Wesley.

Pellacini, Fabio, Kiril Vidimče, Aaron Lefohn, Alex Mohr, Mark Leone, and John Warren. 2005. "Lpics: A Hybrid Hardware-Accelerated Relighting Engine for Computer Cinematography." In *ACM Transactions on Graphics (Proceedings of SIGGRAPH 2005)* 24(3).

Stollnitz, Eric, Tony DeRose, and David Salesin. 1995. "Wavelets for Computer Graphics: A Primer. Part 1." Available online at http://grail.cs.washington.edu/pub/stoll/wavelet1.pdf.

Chapter 10

Parallel-Split Shadow Maps on Programmable GPUs

Fan Zhang
The Chinese University of Hong Kong

Hanqiu Sun
The Chinese University of Hong Kong

Oskari Nyman
Helsinki University of Technology

Shadow mapping (Williams 1978) has been used extensively in 3D games and applications for producing shadowing effects. However, shadow mapping has inherent aliasing problems, so using standard shadow mapping is not enough to produce high-quality shadow rendering in complex and large-scale scenes. In this chapter we present an advanced shadow-mapping technique that produces antialiased and real-time shadows for large-scale environments. We also show the implementation details of our technique on modern programmable GPUs.

10.1 Introduction

The technique we present is called *parallel-split shadow maps* (PSSMs) (Zhang et al. 2007 and Zhang et al. 2006). In this technique the view frustum is split into multiple depth layers using clip planes parallel to the view plane, and an independent shadow map is rendered for each layer, as shown in Figure 10-1.

The split scheme is motivated by the observation that points at different distances from the viewer need different shadow-map sampling densities. By splitting the view frustum

Figure 10-1. Parallel-Split Shadow Maps in *Dawnspire: Prelude*

into parts, we allow each shadow map to sample a smaller area, so that the sampling frequency in texture space is increased. With a better matching of sampling frequencies in view space and texture space, shadow aliasing errors are significantly reduced.

In comparison with other popular shadow-mapping techniques, such as *perspective shadow maps* (PSMs) (Stamminger and Drettakis 2002), *light-space perspective shadow maps* (LiSPSMs) (Wimmer et al. 2004) and *trapezoidal shadow maps* (TSMs) (Martin and Tan 2004), PSSMs provide an intuitive way to discretely approximate the warped distribution of the shadow-map texels, but without mapping singularities and special treatments.

The idea of using multiple shadow maps was introduced in Tadamura et al. 2001. It was further studied in Lloyd et al. 2006 and implemented as cascaded shadow mapping in Futuremark's benchmark application 3DMark 2006.

The two major problems with all these algorithms, including our PSSMs, are the following:

- How do we determine the split positions?
- How do we alleviate the performance drop caused by multiple rendering passes when generating shadow maps and rendering the scene shadows?

These two problems are handled well in PSSMs. We use a fast and robust scene-independent split strategy to adapt the view-driven resolution requirement, and we show how to take advantage of DirectX 9-level and DirectX 10-level hardware to improve performance.

10.2 The Algorithm

In this chapter we use a directional light to illustrate the PSSMs technique for clarity, but the implementation details are valid for point lights as well. The notation PSSM(m, res) denotes the split scheme that splits the view frustum into m parts; res is the resolution for each shadow map. Figure 10-2 shows the general configuration for the split scheme with an overhead light, in which the view frustum V is split into $\{V_i \mid 0 \le i \le m - 1\}$ using clip planes at $\{C_i \mid 0 \le i \le m\}$ along the z axis. In particular, $C_0 = n$ (near plane position) and $C_m = f$ (far plane position).

We apply the split-scheme PSSM(m, res) in the following steps:

1. Split the view frustum V into m parts $\{V_i\}$ using split planes at $\{C_i\}$.

2. Calculate the light's view-projection transformation matrix for each split part V_i.

3. Generate PSSMs $\{T_i\}$ with the resolution res for all split parts $\{V_i\}$.

4. Synthesize shadows for the scene.

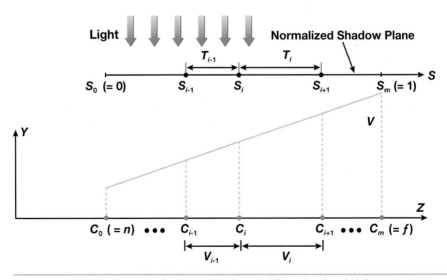

Figure 10-2. The Configuration for the Split Scheme with an Overhead Light

10.2.1 Step 1: Splitting the View Frustum

The main problem in step 1 is determining where the split planes are placed. Although users can adjust the split positions according to an application-specific requirement, our implementations use the *practical split scheme* proposed in Zhang et al. 2006.

Before we introduce this split scheme, we briefly review the aliasing problem in shadow mapping, which has been extensively discussed in Stamminger and Drettakis 2002, Wimmer et al. 2004, and Lloyd et al. 2006.

In Figure 10-3, the light beams passing through a texel (with the size ds) fall on a surface of the object with the length dz in world space. From the standard projection matrix in Direct3D, we know that the size of view beams dp (on the normalized screen) projected from the surface is $dy(z \tan \phi)^{-1}$, where 2ϕ is the field-of-view of the view frustum. From the local view of the surface in Figure 10-3, we get the approximation $dy \approx dz \cos \phi / \cos \theta$, where ϕ and θ stand for the angles between the surface normal and vector to the screen, and the shadow-map plane, respectively.

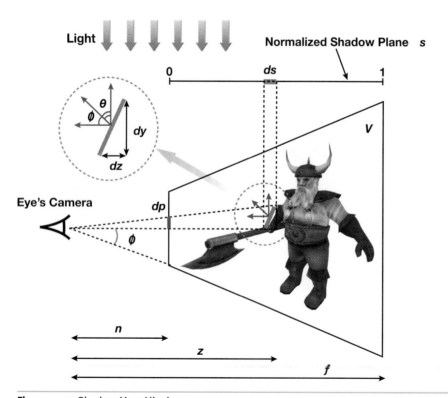

Figure 10-3. Shadow Map Aliasing

Shadow-Map Aliasing

The aliasing error for the small surface is then defined as

$$\frac{dp}{ds} = \frac{1}{\tan\phi}\frac{dz}{zds}\frac{\cos\phi}{\cos\theta}.$$

We usually decompose this aliasing representation dp/ds into two parts: *perspective aliasing* dz/zds and *projection aliasing* $\cos\phi/\cos\theta$ (note that ϕ is a constant for a given view matrix). Shadow-map undersampling can occur when perspective aliasing or projection aliasing becomes large.

Projection aliasing depends on local geometry details, so the reduction of this kind of aliasing requires an expensive scene analysis at each frame. On the other hand, perspective aliasing comes from the perspective foreshortening effect and can be reduced by warping the shadow plane, using a perspective projection transformation. More important, perspective aliasing is scene independent, so the reduction of perspective aliasing doesn't require complicated scene analysis.

The practical split scheme is based on the analysis of perspective aliasing.

The Practical Split Scheme

In the practical split scheme, the split positions are determined by this equation:

$$C_i = \lambda C_i^{\log} + (1-\lambda)C_i^{\text{uni}} \qquad 0 < \lambda < 1,$$

where $\{C_i^{\log}\}$ and $\{C_i^{\text{uni}}\}$ are the split positions in the *logarithmic split scheme* and the *uniform split scheme*, respectively. Theoretically, the logarithmic split scheme is designed to produce optimal distribution of perspective aliasing over the whole depth range. On the other hand, the aliasing distribution in the uniform split scheme is the same as in standard shadow maps. Figure 10-4 visualizes the three split schemes in the shadow-map space.

The theoretically optimal distribution of perspective aliasing makes dz/zds constant over the entire depth range. As shown in Wimmer et al. 2004, the following simple derivation gives the optimal shadow-map parameterization $s(z)$:

$$\frac{dz}{zds} = \rho \Rightarrow s(z) = \int_0^s ds = \frac{1}{\rho}\int_n^z \frac{1}{z}dz = \frac{1}{\rho}\ln\left(\frac{z}{n}\right),$$

where ρ is a constant. From $s(f) = 1$, we have $\rho = \ln(f/n)$. The only nonlinear transform supported by current hardware is the perspective-projection transformation ($s = A/z + B$),

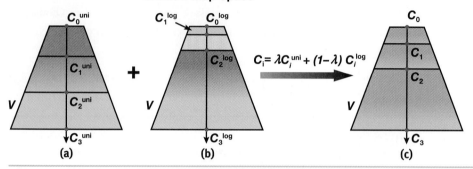

Figure 10-4. Visualization of the Practical Split Scheme in Shadow-Map Space
(a) The uniform split scheme. (b) The logarithmic split scheme. (c) The practical split scheme. Note that the brown color in the practical split scheme corresponds to "moderate sampling" in the color bar on the top.

so in order to approximate the previous logarithmic mapping from z to s, the logarithmic split scheme discretizes it at several depth layers $z = C_i^{\text{log}}$, as in the following equation:

$$s_i = s\left(C_i^{\text{log}}\right) = \frac{1}{\ln(f/n)} \ln\left(\frac{C_i^{\text{log}}}{n}\right).$$

Because the logarithmic split scheme is designed to produce the theoretically even distribution of perspective aliasing, the resolution allocated for each split should be $1/m$ of the overall texture resolution. Substituting $s_i = i/m$ into the preceding equation gives

$$C_i^{\text{log}} = n\left(\frac{f}{n}\right)^{i/m}.$$

The main drawback of the logarithmic split scheme is that, in practice, the lengths of split parts near the viewer are too small, so few objects can be included in these split parts. Imagine the situation in the split-scheme PSSM(3)—that is, the view frustum is split into three parts. With $f = 1000$ and $n = 1$, the first split V_0 and second split V_1 occupy only 1 percent and 10 percent of the view distance. Oversampling usually occurs for parts near the viewer, and undersampling occurs for parts farther from the viewer. As a result, in practice, the logarithmic split scheme is hard to use directly.

The uniform split scheme simply places the split planes evenly along the view direction:

$$C_i^{\text{uni}} = n + (f - n)\frac{i}{m}.$$

The aliasing distribution in the uniform split scheme is the same as that in standard shadow maps. Because $s = (z - n)/(f - n)$ in standard shadow maps, by ignoring the projection aliasing, we have

$$\frac{dp}{ds} \approx \frac{1}{\tan\phi}\frac{dz}{zds} = \frac{1}{\tan\phi}\frac{f - n}{z}.$$

This means the aliasing error in standard shadow maps increases hyperbolically as the object moves near the view plane. Like standard shadow mapping, the uniform split scheme results in undersampling for objects near the viewer and oversampling for distant objects.

Because the logarithmic and uniform split schemes can't produce appropriate sampling densities for the near and far depth layers simultaneously, the practical split scheme integrates logarithmic and uniform schemes to produce moderate sampling densities over the whole depth range. The weight λ adjusts the split positions according to practical requirements of the application. $\lambda = 0.5$ is the default setting in our current implementation. In Figure 10-4, the practical split scheme produces moderate sampling densities for the near and far split parts. An important note for Figure 10-4: the colorized sampling frequency in each split scheme is for schematic illustration only, not for precisely visualizing the aliasing distribution in theory. Readers interested in the (perspective) aliasing distributions in multiple depth layers can refer to Lloyd et al. 2006.

Preprocessing

Before splitting the view frustum, we might adjust the camera's near and far planes so that the view frustum contains the visible objects as tightly as possible. This will minimize the amount of empty space in the view frustum, increasing the available shadow-map resolution.

10.2.2 Step 2: Calculating Light's Transformation Matrices

As in standard shadow mapping, we need to know the light's view and projection matrices when generating the shadow map. As we split the light's frustum W into multiple subfrusta $\{W_i\}$, we will need to construct an independent projection matrix for each W_i separately.

We present two methods to calculate these matrices:

- The scene-independent method simply bounds the light's frustum W_i to the split frustum V_i, as seen in Figure 10-5. Because information about the scene is not used, the usage of shadow-map resolution might not be optimal.

- The scene-dependent method increases the available texture resolution by focusing the light's frustum W_i on the objects that potentially cast shadows to the split frustum V_i, as seen later in Figure 10-6.

Scene-Independent Projection

Before calculating the projection matrix for the subfrustum W_i, we must find the *axis-aligned bounding box* (AABB) of the split frustum V_i with respect to the light's coordinates frame. The class BoundingBox is represented in Figure 10-5 using two vectors—a minimum vector and a maximum vector—to store the smallest and largest coordinates, respectively.

To simplify the computations, we determine the axis-aligned bounding box of the split frustum in the light's clip space, using the function CreateAABB(). Note that we set the bounding box's minimum z-value to 0 because we want the near plane position to remain unchanged. We want this position unchanged because we might have shadow casters between the near plane of the split's bounding box and the light's near plane. This case is illustrated by the "caster" object in Figure 10-5.

Afterward, we build a *crop* matrix to effectively "zoom in" the light's frustum W_i to the bounding box computed by CreateAABB(). The crop matrix is an off-center orthogonal projection matrix, computed as shown in Listing 10-1.

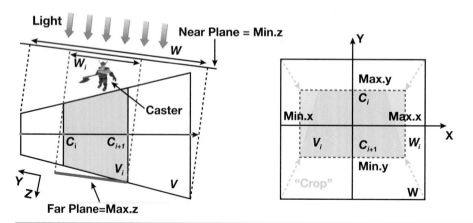

Figure 10-5. Calculation of the Light's Projection Matrix for the Split Part V_i.
Left: Side view. Right: Light's view.

Listing 10-1. Pseudocode for Constructing a Crop Matrix from Clip-Space Bounding Values

```
// Build a matrix for cropping light's projection
// Given vectors are in light's clip space
Matrix Light::CalculateCropMatrix(Frustum splitFrustum)
{
  Matrix lightViewProjMatrix = viewMatrix * projMatrix;

  // Find boundaries in light's clip space
  BoundingBox cropBB = CreateAABB(splitFrustum.AABB,
                                  lightViewProjMatrix);
  // Use default near-plane value
  cropBB.min.z = 0.0f;

  // Create the crop matrix
  float scaleX, scaleY, scaleZ;
  float offsetX, offsetY, offsetZ;
  scaleX = 2.0f / (cropBB.max.x - cropBB.min.x);
  scaleY = 2.0f / (cropBB.max.y - cropBB.min.y);
  offsetX = -0.5f * (cropBB.max.x + cropBB.min.x) * scaleX;
  offsetY = -0.5f * (cropBB.max.y + cropBB.min.y) * scaleY;
  scaleZ = 1.0f / (cropBB.max.z - cropBB.min.z);
  offsetZ = -cropBB.min.z * scaleZ;
  return Matrix( scaleX,      0.0f,      0.0f,   0.0f,
                   0.0f,    scaleY,      0.0f,   0.0f,
                   0.0f,      0.0f,    scaleZ,   0.0f,
                offsetX,   offsetY,   offsetZ,   1.0f);
}
```

Finally, we use the light's view-projection transformation `lightViewMatrix *`
`lightProjMatrix * cropMatrix` when generating the shadow map texture T_i.

Note that instead of computing a crop matrix in the light's clip space, we can calculate
the split-specific projection matrix in other spaces, such as the light's view space. However, because both point and directional lights are converted into directional lights in
the light's clip space, our method works the same way for directional and point lights.
Furthermore, calculating the bounding box in the light's clip space is more intuitive.

Scene-Dependent Projection

Although using a scene-independent projection works well in most cases, we can further optimize the usage of the texture resolution by taking the scene geometries into
account.

As we can see in Figure 10-6, a scene-independent W_i may contain a large amount of empty space. Each W_i only needs to contain the objects potentially casting shadows into V_i, termed *shadow casters*, exemplified by B_C. Because the invisible parts of objects don't need to be rendered into the final image, we separately store the shadow-related objects inside (or partially inside) V_i as *shadow receivers*, exemplified by B_R. When synthesizing the shadowed image of the whole scene, we render only shadow receivers to improve rendering performance. Note that objects that never cast shadows (such as the terrain) should be included in receivers only.

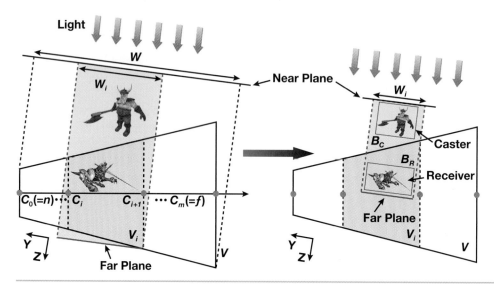

Figure 10-6. Comparing Projection Methods
Left: Scene-independent projection. Right: Scene-dependent projection.

In the scene-dependent method, the near plane of W_i is moved to bound either V_i or any shadow caster, and the far plane of W_i is moved to touch either V_i or any shadow receiver. The optimized near and far planes improve the precision of discrete depth quantization. Furthermore, because only shadow receivers need to do depth comparison during shadow determination, we adjust the x- and y-boundaries of W_i to bound V_i or any shadow receiver. The pseudocode for the scene-dependent method is shown in Listing 10-2. Pay special attention to how the depth boundaries (`min.z` and `max.z`) are chosen.

The final light's view-projection transformation matrix for the current split is still `lightViewMatrix * lightProjMatrix * cropMatrix`.

Listing 10-2. Pseudocode for Computing Scene-Dependent Bounds

```
Matrix Light::CalculateCropMatrix(ObjectList casters,
                                  ObjectList receivers,
                                  Frustum frustum)
{
  // Bounding boxes
  BoundingBox receiverBB, casterBB, splitBB;
  Matrix lightViewProjMatrix = viewMatrix * projMatrix;
  // Merge all bounding boxes of casters into a bigger "casterBB".
  for(int i = 0; i < casters.size(); i++){
    BoundingBox bb = CreateAABB(casters[i]->AABB,
                                lightViewProjMatrix);
    casterBB.Union(bb);
  }
  // Merge all bounding boxes of receivers into a bigger "receiverBB".
  for(int i = 0; i < receivers.size(); i++){
      bb = CreateAABB(receivers[i]->AABB,
                      lightViewProjMatrix);
    receiverBB.Union(bb);
  }
  // Find the bounding box of the current split
  // in the light's clip space.
  splitBB = CreateAABB(splitFrustum.AABB, lightViewProjMatrix);
  // Scene-dependent bounding volume
  BoundingBox cropBB;
  cropBB.min.x = Max(Max(casterBB.min.x, receiverBB.min.x),
                     splitBB.min.x);
  cropBB.max.x = Min(Min(casterBB.max.x, receiverBB.max.x),
                     splitBB.max.x);
  cropBB.min.y = Max(Max(casterBB.min.y, receiverBB.min.y),
                     splitBB.min.y);
  cropBB.max.y = Min(Min(casterBB.max.y, receiverBB.max.y),
                     splitBB.max.y);
  cropBB.min.z = Min(casterBB.min.z, splitBB.min.z);
  cropBB.max.z = Min(receiverBB.max.z, splitBB.max.z);
  // Create the crop matrix.
  float scaleX, scaleY, scaleZ;
  float offsetX, offsetY, offsetZ;
  scaleX = 2.0f / (cropBB.max.x - cropBB.min.x);
  scaleY = 2.0f / (cropBB.max.y - cropBB.min.y);
```

```
    offsetX = -0.5f * (cropBB.max.x + cropBB.min.x) * scaleX;
    offsetY = -0.5f * (cropBB.max.y + cropBB.min.y) * scaleY;
    scaleZ = 1.0f / (cropBB.max.z - cropBB.min.z);
    offsetZ = -cropBB.min.z * scaleZ;
    return Matrix(scaleX, 0.0f, 0.0f, 0.0f,
                  0.0f, scaleY, 0.0f, 0.0f,
                  0.0f, 0.0f, scaleZ, 0.0f,
                  offsetX, offsetY, offsetZ, 1.0f);
}
```

10.2.3 Steps 3 and 4: Generating PSSMs and Synthesizing Shadows

Steps 3 and 4 can be implemented differently, depending on your system hardware. Because we use multiple shadow maps in PSSMs, extra rendering passes may be needed when we generate shadow maps and synthesize shadows.

To reduce this burden on rendering performance, we could use a hardware-specific approach. In the next section we present three hardware-specific methods for generating PSSMs and synthesizing shadows:

- The multipass method (without hardware acceleration): This method doesn't use hardware acceleration; multiple rendering passes are required for generating shadow maps (step 3) and for synthesizing shadows (step 4).

- Partially accelerated on DirectX 9-level hardware (for example, Windows XP and an NVIDIA GeForce 6800 GPU): In this method, we remove extra rendering passes for synthesizing scene shadows.

- Fully accelerated on DirectX 10-level hardware (for example, Windows Vista and a GeForce 8800 GPU): Here we alleviate the burden of extra rendering passes for generating shadow maps. To achieve this goal, we describe two different approaches: geometry shader cloning and instancing.

In all three methods, the implementations for splitting the view frustum and calculating the light's transformation matrices are the same as described earlier.

10.3 Hardware-Specific Implementations

To make it easier to understand our three hardware-specific implementations, we visualize the rendering pipelines of different implementations, as in Figure 10-7.

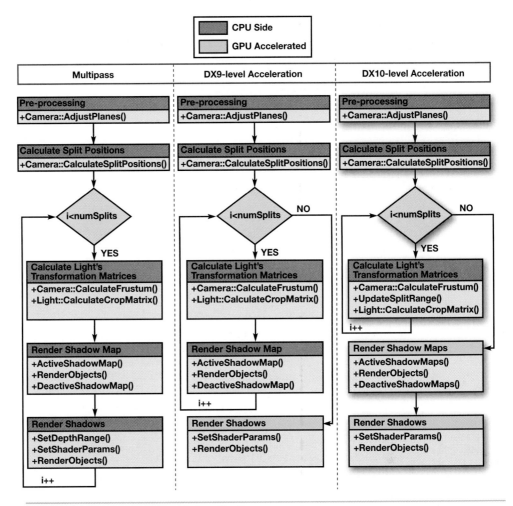

Figure 10-7. Visualization of Rendering Pipelines
Left: The multipass method. Middle: The DirectX 9 method. Right: The DirectX 10 method. For the split scheme PSSM(m), the number of rendering passes for the three implementations is 2m, m+1, and 2, respectively.

10.3.1 The Multipass Method

In the first implementation of PSSMs, we simply render each shadow map, with shadows in each split part, sequentially.

Generating Shadow Maps

Once we have the light's view-projection transformation matrix `lightViewMatrix * lightProjMatrix * cropMatrix` for the current split part, we can render the associated shadow-map texture. The procedure is the same as for standard shadow mapping: we render all shadow casters to the depth buffer. Our implementation uses a 32-bit floating-point (R32F) texture format.

In our multipass implementation, instead of storing PSSMs in several independent shadow-map textures, we reuse a single shadow-map texture in each rendering pass, as shown in Listing 10-3.

Listing 10-3. Pseudocode for the Rendering Pipeline of the Multipass Method

```
for(int i = 0; i < numSplits; i++)
{
  // Compute frustum of current split part.
  splitFrustum = camera->CalculateFrustum(splitPos[i], splitPos[i+1]);
  casters = light->FindCasters(splitFrustum);
  // Compute light's transformation matrix for current split part.
  cropMatrix = light->CalculateCropMatrix(receivers, casters,
                                          splitFrustum);
  splitViewProjMatrix = light->viewMatrix * light->projMatrix *
                          cropMatrix;
  // Texture matrix for current split part
  textureMatrix = splitViewProjMatrix * texScaleBiasMatrix;
  // Render current shadow map.
  ActivateShadowMap();
  RenderObjects(casters, splitViewProjMatrix);
  DeactivateShadowMap();
  // Render shadows for current split part.
  SetDepthRange(splitPos[i], splitPos[i+1]);
  SetShaderParam(textureMatrix);
  RenderObjects(receivers, camera->viewMatrix * camera->projMatrix);
}
```

Synthesizing Shadows

With PSSMs generated in the preceding step, shadows can now be synthesized into the scene. In the multipass method, we need to synthesize the shadows immediately after rendering the shadow map.

For optimal performance, we should render the splits from front to back. However, some special considerations are needed. We need to adjust the camera's near and far planes to the respective split positions to provide clipping, because the objects in one split may also overlap other splits. However, as we modify the near and far planes, we are also changing the range of values written to the depth buffer. This would make the depth tests function incorrectly, but we can avoid this problem by using a different depth range in the viewport. Simply convert the split-plane positions from view space to clip space and use them as the new depth minimum and maximum.

After this we can render the shadow receivers of the scene while sampling the shadow map in the standard manner. This means that implementing the multipass method doesn't require the use of shaders. Figure 10-8 compares SSM(2K×2K) and multipass PSSM(3; 1K×1K). However, as the method's name implies, multiple rendering passes will always be performed for both generating shadow maps and rendering scene shadows.

10.3.2 DirectX 9-Level Acceleration

When implementing the simple multipass method as presented, we need to use multiple rendering passes to synthesize shadows in the scene. However, with programmable GPUs, we can perform this step in a single rendering pass.

We can create a pixel shader to find and sample the correct shadow map for each fragment. The operation for determining which split a fragment is contained in is simple because the split planes are parallel to the view plane. We can simply use the depth value—or, as in our implementation, use the view space z coordinate of a fragment—to determine the correct shadow map.

The Setup

Because we render the scene shadows in a single pass, we need to have access to all the shadow maps simultaneously. Unlike our previous implementation, this method requires that shadow maps be stored separately, so we create an independent texture for each shadow map.

Note that the number of texture samplers supported by the hardware will limit the number of shadow maps we can use. We could, alternatively, pack multiple shadow maps in a single texture; however, most DirectX 9-level hardware supports eight texture samplers, which should be more than enough.

Also note that we need to use the "border color" texture address mode, because sometimes shadow maps are sampled outside the texture-coordinate range. This could occur when we use a scene-dependent projection, because the light's subfrustum W_i does not necessarily cover all the receivers.

Synthesizing Shadows

When we render the scene shadows, we use a custom vertex and pixel shader, as shown in Listing 10-4. In the vertex shader, we transform each vertex as usual. However, we

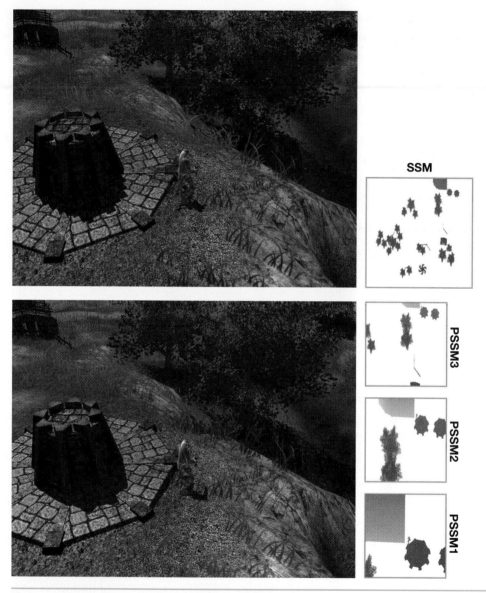

Figure 10-8. Comparison of SSM and Multipass PSSM
Top: Shadows rendered with SSM (2K×2K). Bottom: Shadows rendered with PSSM (3; 1K×1K).
The associated shadow maps are shown to the right of each rendering.

also calculate (1) the view-space position of the vertex, because we will use it for determining the shadow maps associated with fragments; and (2) the position of the vertex in the texture space of each shadow map. We determine the position of the vertex by multiplying the vertex with a textureMatrix. It is the same approach we use for standard shadow mapping, only now we use it for all shadow maps. We output all the transformed coordinates into texture-coordinate registers for the pixel shader to use.

In the pixel shader, we loop through all splits and test whether the view-space distance of the fragment is less than the end position of the split. After determining the split index, we sample the associated shadow map with the associated texture coordinates and perform a standard shadow-map depth test.

Listing 10-4. Vertex and Pixel Shaders for Synthesizing Shadows in DirectX 9

```
sampler2D shadowMapSampler[numSplits];

void VS_RenderShadows(
  in float4 pos : POSITION, // Object-space coordinates
  out float4 posOut : POSITION, // Clip-space coordinates
  out float4 texCoord[numSplits+1] : TEXCOORD) // Texture coordinates
{
  // Calculate world position.
  float4 posWorld = mul(pos, worldMatrix);

  // Transform vertex.
  posOut = mul(posWorld, viewProjMatrix);

  // Store view-space position in the first texture
  // coordinate register.
  texCoord[0] = mul(posWorld, viewMatrix)

  // Store shadow-map coordinates in the remaining
  // texture coordinate registers.
  for(int i = 0; i < numSplits; i++)
  {
    texCoord[i+1] = mul(posWorld, textureMatrix[i]);
  }
}

float4 PS_RenderShadows(
  float4 texCoord[numSplits+1] : TEXCOORD): COLOR
{
  float light = 1.0f;
```

```
// Fetch view-space distance from first texture coordinate register.
float distance = texCoord[0].z;
for(int i = 0; i < numSplits; i++)
{
  if(distance < splitPlane[i])
  {
    float depth = texCoord[i+1].z/ texCoord[i+1].w;
    float depthSM = tex2Dproj(shadowMapSampler[i], texCoord[i+1]);
    // Standard depth comparison
    light = (depth < depthSM) ? 1.0f : 0.0f;
    break;
  }
}
return light;
}
```

Performance

We implemented this partially accelerated method in both DirectX 9 and OpenGL. In DirectX 9, we implemented *percentage-closer filtering* (PCF) (Reeves et al. 1987) in the pixel shader (approximately 25 instructions), and in OpenGL we used hardware-accelerated PCF (one instruction). We compared the performance to the multipass method when we increased the number of objects in the scene. In all tests, the number of splits was four.

From the results shown in Figure 10-9, we can see that the DirectX 9-level acceleration increases performance. But when PCF is implemented in the pixel shader, the shaders become more complex. This increase in the shader complexity causes performance to decrease, but this becomes less significant as the scene complexity increases.

10.3.3 DirectX 10-Level Acceleration

Although rendering scene shadows is accelerated on DirectX 9-level hardware, multiple rendering passes are still required for generating PSSMs. In other words, DirectX 9 provides us a partial acceleration of PSSMs. On the other hand, we can accelerate both generating PSSMs and rendering scene shadows on DirectX 10-level hardware.

Features in Direct3D 10

The Direct3D 10 pipeline introduces the *geometry shader* (GS) as a new shader stage between vertex and pixel shaders. Geometry shaders are executed once for each primi-

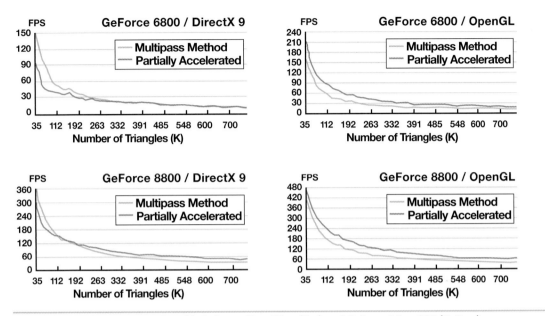

Figure 10-9. Performance Results with GeForce 6800 Ultra (*Top*) and GeForce 8800 GTS (*Bottom*)
Left: Using DirectX 9 with PCF implemented in the pixel shader. Right: Using OpenGL with hardware-accelerated PCF.

tive, taking the vertices of the primitive as input and outputting a number of new primitives. They also provide access to primitive adjacency information and have an instruction set similar to that of vertex shaders (including support for texture sampling).

Another new feature in Direct3D 10 is the render target array, which is similar to Direct3D 9's multiple render targets (MRTs). But while MRTs only enable separate pixel shader output for each render target, the render target arrays (with the help of geometry shaders) can output entirely different geometries to each render target. This is done in the GS output, where we can specify a render target index for each primitive separately.

These features enable us to dynamically "clone" the geometry into different render targets with different transformations. We can now improve the performance of generating PSSMs because each shadow caster needs to be submitted only once.

The Setup
First we need to create a texture array for the shadow maps. As shown in Listing 10-5, we use a 32-bit floating-point texel format as usual, but we define it as "typeless" because it will need to work both as a depth buffer and as a texture. The `ArraySize` parameter is set to the number of splits, so we have one texture for each. Also, we must

set the `BindFlags` to allow us to bind the texture array to both a depth-stencil view and a shader resource view.

Resource views, another new feature in Direct3D 10, allow a single resource to be interpreted in different ways. In our case, we need to access the texture array both as a renderable depth-stencil surface and as a shader-accessible texture, so we must create views for both.

As shown in Listing 10-6, creating the shader resource view is simple. We set the view dimension to a texture 2D array and set the texel format to a single-channel floating-point color. Otherwise, we use the same settings as when we create the texture array.

The depth-stencil view is created in a similar manner, but the texel format must be set to a depth-buffer-compatible format, as shown in Listing 10-7.

Now we have an array of shadow maps that we can set as depth-stencil targets and bind as sampleable textures. Note that we don't need to create a render target, because we are interested in rendering only depth values, not color information.

We still have to create the needed shaders, which will be explained in the next two subsections.

Listing 10-5. Creating a Texture Array

```
D3D10_TEXTURE2D_DESC DescTex = {};
DescTex.Width = shadowMapSize;
DescTex.Height = shadowMapSize;
DescTex.ArraySize = numSplits;
DescTex.Format = DXGI_FORMAT_R32_TYPELESS;
DescTex.Usage = D3D10_USAGE_DEFAULT;
DescTex.BindFlags = D3D10_BIND_DEPTH_STENCIL |
D3D10_BIND_SHADER_RESOURCE;
DescTex.MipLevels = 1;
DescTex.SampleDesc.Count = 1;
device->CreateTexture2D(...)
```

Listing 10-6. Creating a Shader Resource View

```
D3D10_SHADER_RESOURCE_VIEW_DESC DescSRV = {};
DescSRV.Format = DXGI_FORMAT_R32_FLOAT;
DescSRV.ViewDimension = D3D10_SRV_DIMENSION_TEXTURE2DARRAY;
DescSRV.Texture2DArray.ArraySize = numSplits;
DescSRV.Texture2DArray.MipLevels = 1;
device->CreateShaderResourceView(...)
```

Listing 10-7. Creating a Depth-Stencil Resource View

```
D3D10_DEPTH_STENCIL_VIEW_DESC DescDSV = {};
DescDSV.Format = DXGI_FORMAT_D32_FLOAT;
DescDSV.ViewDimension = D3D10_DSV_DIMENSION_TEXTURE2DARRAY;
DescDSV.Texture2DArray.ArraySize = numSplits;
device->CreateDepthStencilView(...);
```

Generating Shadow Maps

The rendering pipeline looks similar to the DirectX 9 version. The major difference is that we render shadow maps only once. Also, we now need to store the crop matrices of each split into an array, because we will need them all in the shaders.

More important, after finding the potential shadow casters for a split, we need each caster to keep track of two variables: `firstSplit` and `lastSplit`. These variables determine the range of the split indices into which the shadow caster needs to be rendered, as shown in Figure 10-10. Note that we need to store only the first and last indices, because a continuous bounding shape will always overlap a continuous range of split parts.

As we begin rendering the shadow maps, we need to set a new viewport and change the render targets. This is shown in Listing 10-8, where the variable pDSV points to the previously created depth-stencil view. Because we will only render depth information, we must set the number of render targets to 0 and the render target pointer to NULL.

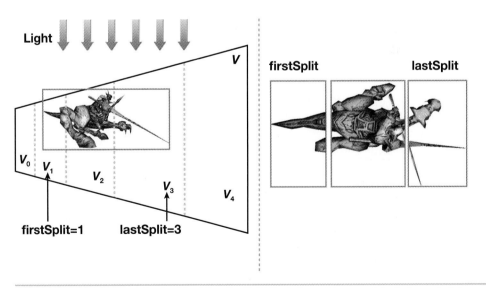

Figure 10-10. The Shadow Caster Straddles the Split Parts from `firstSplit` to `lastSplit`
Left: Side view. Right: Light's view.

Listing 10-8. Activating Shadow-Map Rendering

```
D3D10_VIEWPORT vp;
vp.Width = shadowMapSize;
vp.Height = shadowMapSize;
vp.MinDepth = 0; vp.MaxDepth = 1;
vp.TopLeftX = 0; vp.TopLeftY = 0;
device->RSSetViewports(1, &vp);
device->OMSetRenderTargets(0, NULL, pDSV);
```

Then we draw each shadow caster once, but in a special rendering loop. In this loop, we must update the shader constants `firstSplit` and `lastSplit` with corresponding values from the shadow caster. Because these variables are "per-instance" data, they should be handled like, for example, an object's world matrix.

In the following, we present two different approaches for dynamically cloning the geometry for different splits.

Using Geometry Shader Cloning

In this first method, we use the geometry shader to clone submitted triangles into different render targets. This technique is similar to the single-pass cube map technique presented in the Microsoft DirectX SDK. We first explain the details here, and then we discuss the performance advantages.

With this technique, the vertex shader simply transforms each vertex with the world matrix, the light's view matrix, and the light's projection matrix. This transformation is common for all shadow casters, regardless of which shadow maps they must be rendered into. The split-specific transformations will be applied in the geometry shader instead, as visualized in Figure 10-11.

In other words, we now use the geometry shader to clone triangles into the split-specific render targets and then transform these triangles with the corresponding crop matrices as well.

The geometry shader code is shown in Listing 10-9, where we loop through each split to be rendered—that is, from `firstSplit` to `lastSplit`. Inside this loop, we transform each vertex with the split's corresponding crop matrix. We also set a render target index, and then finally we output the transformed vertices as a new triangle. Note that the render target index is in fact specified per vertex, but only the value in the leading (first) vertex is relevant.

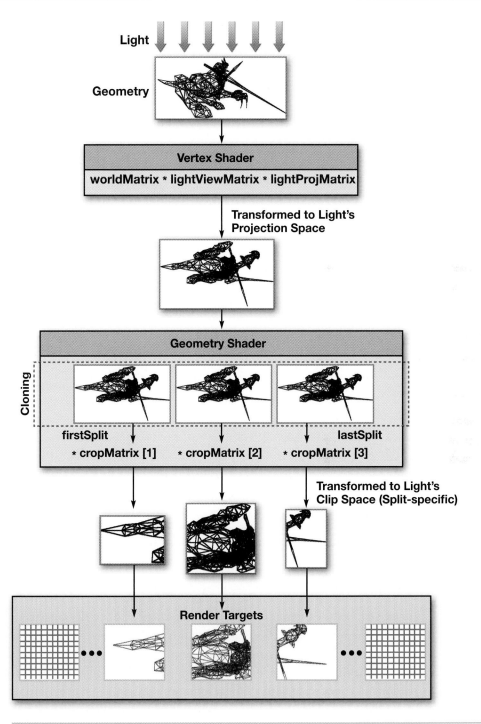

Figure 10-11. The GPU Rendering Pipeline in the Geometry Shader Cloning Method

Listing 10-9. Geometry Shader Code for Rendering Shadow Maps

```
// Geometry shader output structure
struct GS_OUT
{
    float4 pos : SV_POSITION;
    uint RTIndex : SV_RenderTargetArrayIndex;
};

// Geometry shader
[maxvertexcount(NUMSPLITS * 3)]
void GS_RenderShadowMap(triangle VS_OUT In[3],
                        inout TriangleStream<GS_OUT> triStream)
{
    // For each split to render
    for(int split = firstSplit; split <= lastSplit; split++)
    {
        GS_OUT Out;
        // Set render target index.
        Out.RTIndex = split;
        // For each vertex of triangle
        for(int vertex = 0; vertex < 3; vertex++)
        {
            // Transform vertex with split-specific crop matrix.
            Out.pos = mul(In[vertex].pos, cropMatrix[split]);
            // Append vertex to stream
            triStream.Append(Out);
        }
        // Mark end of triangle
        triStream.RestartStrip();
    }
}
```

A pixel shader is not needed at this stage because we aren't interested in drawing color information. So, it can simply be set to NULL.

For the sake of clarity, the implementation we presented uses separate transformations for all matrices. By premultiplying view/projection/crop matrices together, we can implement the split-scheme PSSM(m) using this method such that the number of transformations is $(1 + m)$ per vertex. That is, every vertex is transformed with the world matrix (one time) and then with the view/projection/crop matrices (m times). Standard shadow-map rendering with a similar setup would use ($m + m$) transformations. However, if we premultiply the world matrices as well, the number of transformations is the same (*m*) for both methods. The advantage of the geometry shader cloning method is that it reduces the API overhead—the overhead of extra draw calls, render target switches, and so on is removed because we submit each shadow caster only once.

Using Instancing

The second approach for generating shadow maps is possible with the improved instancing support in Direct3D 10. Vertex shaders can now acquire the index of an instance being rendered through the semantic `SV_InstanceID`.

This means we can use instancing to clone our geometry for each split, and determine the split index from the instance index. We can then perform the crop matrix transformation in the vertex shader, so that the only task left for the geometry shader is setting the render target index, as shown in Listing 10-10 and visualized in Figure 10-12.

To render with instancing, we need to call the function `DrawIndexedInstanced()` with the number of instances set to `lastSplit − firstSplit + 1`. This is the only change needed on the CPU side; it is not necessary to set up any extra vertex streams.

Listing 10-10. Vertex and Geometry Shaders for Generating Shadow Maps with Instancing

```
struct VS_IN
{
  float4 pos : POSITION;
  uint instance : SV_InstanceID;
};

struct VS_OUT
{
  float4 pos : POSITION;
  uint split : TEXTURE0;
};

VS_OUT VS_RenderShadowMap(VS_IN In)
{
  VS_OUT Out;
  // Transform with world/view/projection.
  Out.pos = mul(In.pos, ...);
  // Determine split index from instance ID.
  Out.split = firstSplit + In.instance;
  // Transform with split-specific crop matrix.
  Out.pos = mul(Out.pos, cropMatrix[Out.split]);
  return Out;
}
```

```
[maxvertexcount(3)]
void GS_RenderShadowMap(triangle VS_OUT In[3],
                        inout TriangleStream<GS_OUT> triStream)
{
  GS_OUT Out;
  // Set render target index.
  Out.RTIndex = In[0].split;
  // Pass triangle through.
  Out.pos = In[0].pos;
  triStream.Append(Out);
  Out.pos = In[1].pos;
  triStream.Append(Out);
  Out.pos = In[2].pos;
  triStream.Append(Out);
  triStream.RestartStrip();
}
```

Using this method, we again remove the extra API overhead. However, the number of transformations is the same as with standard shadow-map rendering. Still, the instancing method may be faster than using geometry shader cloning because expanding large amounts of data with the geometry shader may be expensive.

We can also use the cloning and instancing methods together, so that both are used to generate geometry for a portion of the splits. For example, in the split-scheme PSSM(4), instancing could be used for two splits and geometry shader cloning for another two splits.

Synthesizing Shadows

The process of rendering shadows is nearly the same as in DirectX 9. The main difference is in the sampling of the texture array. To do things the traditional way, we can use the function `SampleLevel()` to sample from a given texture of the array.

Using this function is straightforward, but note that the second parameter is a `float3`, where the first two floats are for the UV coordinates and the third float is for the texture index. The mipmap level is defined in the function's third parameter.

After sampling the correct texture with this function, we would perform the depth comparison as usual. However, this is not the optimal method, especially if we wish to use PCF. We present a better approach next, which uses cube maps.

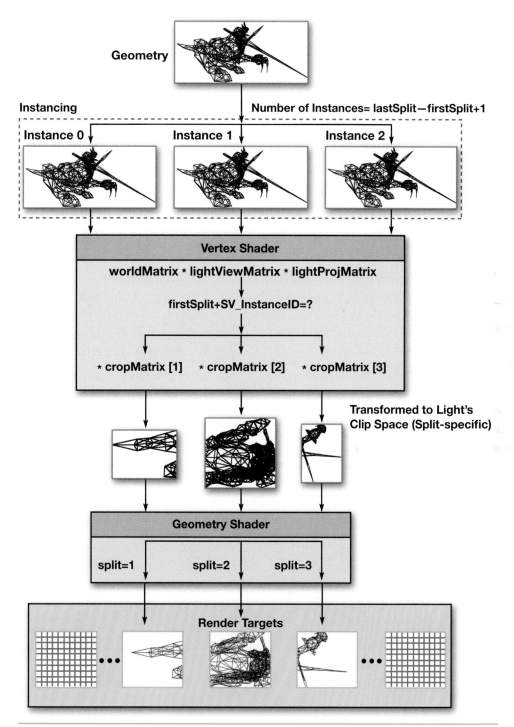

Figure 10-12. The GPU Rendering Pipeline in the Instancing Method

Using Cube Maps

HLSL 4 introduces a new function called `SampleCmpLevelZero()`, which performs sampling and comparison simultaneously. It can also be used with a linear comparison filter to get PCF, which means the function will take four samples, compare each separately, and then bilinearly filter the results.

Unfortunately, `SampleCmpLevelZero()` cannot currently be used with Texture2DArrays. It can, however, be used with TextureCubes. TextureCubes are normally used for cube maps, but they are essentially a texture array with six textures, one for each face of the cube.

This means we can use a TextureCube for up to six splits. Using a TextureCube requires only a few changes in the setup, as shown in Listing 10-11. Rendering shadow maps works the same way as before.

Sampling is slightly complicated by the fact that a cube map is not accessed with standard texture coordinates, but instead with a vector pointing to a face of the cube. This cube is a unit cube, and it is centered in the origin. The faces are ordered so that from array index 0 to 5, the faces are located at $+x$, $-x$, $+y$, $-y$, $+z$, and $-z$, respectively. From this we can determine the correct direction vector for accessing each face, as shown in Listing 10-12.

However, the approach shown in Listing 10-12 is not necessary, because we can separate the different cases into three lookup arrays, as shown in Listing 10-13, which slightly increases the pixel shader's performance.

Another issue is that border color addressing mode cannot be used, because the borders are simply mapped onto another face of the cube map. However, we can simulate the border color addressing mode by avoiding sampling altogether if the coordinates are outside the valid range of texture coordinates. This is also shown in Listing 10-13.

In our tests, using `SampleCmpLevelZero()` with a TextureCube slightly improved our performance compared to using a Texture2DArray with four-tap PCF implemented in the pixel shader (approximately 25 instructions). However, with a TextureCube, six textures will always be allocated even if fewer are needed, often resulting in wasted memory.

Listing 10-11. Changes Needed for Creating a TextureCube

```
// When creating the texture array
DescTex.ArraySize = 6;
DescTex.MiscFlags = D3D10_RESOURCE_MISC_TEXTURECUBE;
. . .
// When creating the shader resource view
DescSRV.ViewDimension = D3D10_SRV_DIMENSION_TEXTURECUBE;
DescSRV.TextureCube.MipLevels = 1;
```

Listing 10-12. Choosing Faces from a TextureCube

```
float3 cubeCoord;
if(split == 0)
  cubeCoord = float3(0.5, 0.5 - pos.y, 0.5 - pos.x);
else if(split == 1)
  cubeCoord = float3(-0.5, 0.5 - pos.y, pos.x - 0.5);
else if(split == 2)
  cubeCoord = float3(pos.x - 0.5, 0.5, pos.y - 0.5);
else if(split == 3)
  cubeCoord = float3(pos.x - 0.5, -0.5, 0.5 - pos.y);
else if(split == 4)
  cubeCoord = float3(pos.x - 0.5, 0.5 - pos.y, 0.5);
else if(split == 5)
  cubeCoord = float3(0.5 - pos.x, 0.5 - pos.y, -0.5);
```

Listing 10-13. Pixel Shader Code for Synthesizing Shadows with a TextureCube

```
static const float3 offset[6] = {
  float3(0.5, 0.5, 0.5), float3(-0.5, 0.5, -0.5),
  float3(-0.5, 0.5, -0.5), float3(-0.5, -0.5, 0.5),
  float3(-0.5, 0.5, 0.5), float3(0.5, 0.5, -0.5)};

static const float3 mulX[6] = {
  float3(0, 0, -1), float3(0, 0, 1), float3(1, 0, 0),
  float3(1, 0, 0), float3(1, 0, 0), float3(-1, 0, 0)};

static const float3 mulY[6] = {
  float3(0, -1, 0), float3(0, -1, 0), float3(0, 0, 1),
  float3(0, 0, -1), float3(0, -1, 0), float3(0, -1, 0)};

SamplerComparisonState shadowMapSampler
{
  ComparisonFunc = Less;
  Filter = COMPARISON_MIN_MAG_LINEAR_MIP_POINT;
};
```

```
float4 PS_RenderShadows(PS_INPUT In)  : SV_Target
{
  float light = 1.0f;
  for(int split = 0; split < numSplits; split++)
  {
    if(In.distance > splitEnd[split])
    {
      float4 texpos = In.texturePos[split];
      texpos.xyz /= texpos.w;
      // Cube map vector lookup
      float3 cubeCoord = offset[split] +
                         mulX[split] * texpos.x +
                         mulY[split] * texpos.y;
      // Don't sample outside the border.
      if(min(pos.x, pos.y) > 0 && max(pos.x, pos.y) < 1)
      {
        light = shadowMapCube.SampleCmpLevelZero(shadowMapSampler,
                                      cubeCoord, texpos.z);
      }
      break;
    }
  }
  return light;
}
```

10.4 Further Optimizations

To improve the shadow quality with PSSMs, use the following optimizations:

- **Filtering Techniques.** *Percentage-closer filtering* (PCF) helps antialiasing in shadow mapping by performing multiple depth tests for each pixel, which makes the shadow boundaries look considerably smoother. *Variance shadow maps* (VSMs) (Donnelly and Lauritzen 2006) treat shadow map texels as a distribution of depths and represent this distribution in a way that can be linearly filtered. Chebyshev's inequality is used to approximate the occlusion over an arbitrary filter region.

- **Packing of Textures.** Instead of storing PSSMs into multiple textures in hardware-accelerated implementations, users may pack them into a single texture. This is a possible solution when few texture samplers are available. In DirectX 10, texture arrays can be utilized instead.

- **Warping Algorithms.** An interesting application of the split scheme is applying warping algorithms (for example, PSMs, LiSPSMs, and TSMs) separately in split parts.
- **Varying Texture Resolution.** All shadow maps in our current implementation of PSSMs have the same resolution. To reduce the required consumption of textures, users can adjust the size of each shadow map at different split layers.
- **Linearized Depth Distribution** (Brabec et al. 2002). Using a linear depth metric instead of standard projected z increases the precision of discrete depth quantization for point lights.

10.5 Results

The screen shots in Figures 10-13 through 10-16 from *Dawnspire: Prelude*—displayed throughout the remainder of the chapter—were rendered using the PSSM(3; 1K×1K) scheme (multipass method) at an image size of 1280×1024. The performance is measured on a PC configured with an AMD Athlon64 X2 3800 CPU, 1 GB DDR RAM, and a GeForce 7800 GTX GPU. The number of visible triangles processed in these figures ranges from 165 K to 319 K. In our experiments, both PSSM(3) and PSSM(4) achieve a good trade-off between the performance and visual qualities (more than 31 frames/sec and 27 frames/sec in the two schemes, respectively).

In many applications, especially for complex and large-scale scenes, rendering high-quality shadows is crucial for the users' perception of realism. Even without hardware acceleration, it is worth the cost of multipass rendering to dramatically improve shadow quality.

10.6 Conclusion

The basic idea of parallel-split shadow maps is intuitive and simple to implement, as with our multipass method. We can quickly determine the split positions using the practical split scheme without complicated scene analysis. However, without using hardware acceleration, the performance drop caused by multiple rendering passes prevents this technique from being extensively used in mass-market applications.

In this chapter, we present two hardware-accelerated methods: partially accelerated implementation on DirectX 9-level GPUs and fully accelerated implementation on

Figure 10-13. Screen Shot from *Dawnspire: Prelude*

DirectX 10-level GPUs. The extra rendering passes required for synthesizing shadows are avoided in the partially accelerated implementation. In the DirectX 10 rendering pipeline, our fully accelerated implementation reduces the cost of extra rendering passes for rendering both shadow maps and scene shadows.

There are many other ways to improve performance and shadow quality in our PSSMs technique, but one thing is certain: With the rapid evolution of GPUs, PSSMs are a promising approach for high-quality shadow rendering.

Demos with full source code can be found on the book's accompanying DVD. All three implementation methods presented in this chapter are included.

Figure 10-14. From *Dawnspire: Prelude*

10.7 References

Brabec, Stefan, Thomas Annen, and Hans-Peter Seidel. 2002. "Practical Shadow Mapping." *Journal of Graphical Tools* 7(4), pp. 9–18.

Donnelly, William, and Andrew Lauritzen. 2006. "Variance Shadow Maps." In *Proceedings of the Symposium on Interactive 3D Graphics and Games 2006*, pp. 161–165.

Lloyd, Brandon, David Tuft, Sung-Eui Yoon, and Dinesh Manocha. 2006. "Warping and Partitioning for Low Error Shadow Maps." In *Proceedings of the Eurographics Symposium on Rendering 2006*, pp. 215–226.

Martin, Tobias, and Tiow-Seng Tan. 2004. "Anti-aliasing and Continuity with Trapezoidal Shadow Maps." In *Proceedings of the Eurographics Symposium on Rendering 2004*, pp. 153–160.

Figure 10-15. From *Dawnspire: Prelude*

Reeves, William, David Salesin, and Robert Cook. 1987. "Rendering Antialiased Shadows with Depth Maps." In *Computer Graphics (Proceedings of SIGGRAPH 1987)* 21(3), pp. 283–291.

Stamminger, Marc, and George Drettakis. 2002. "Perspective Shadow Maps." In *ACM Transactions on Graphics (Proceedings of SIGGRAPH 2002)* 21(3), pp. 557–562.

Tadamura, Katsumi, Xueying Qin, Guofang Jiao, and Eihachiro Nakamae. 2001. "Rendering Optimal Solar Shadows with Plural Sunlight Depth Buffers." *The Visual Computer* 17(2), pp. 76–90.

Williams, Lance. 1978. "Casting Curved Shadows on Curved Surfaces." In *Computer Graphics (Proceedings of SIGGRAPH 1978)* 12(3), pp. 270–274.

Wimmer, Michael, Daniel Scherzer, and Werner Purgathofer. 2004. "Light Space Perspective Shadow Maps." In *Proceedings of the Eurographics Symposium on Rendering 2004*, pp. 143–152.

Figure 10-16. From *Dawnspire: Prelude*

Zhang, Fan, Hanqiu Sun, Leilei Xu, and Kit-Lun Lee. 2006. "Parallel-Split Shadow Maps for Large-Scale Virtual Environments." In *Proceedings of ACM International Conference on Virtual Reality Continuum and Its Applications 2006*, pp. 311–318.

Zhang, Fan, Hanqiu Sun, Leilei Xu, and Kit-Lun Lee. 2007. "Hardware-Accelerated Parallel-Split Shadow Maps." *International Journal of Image and Graphics*. In press.

All screen shots are from Dawnspire: Prelude *(http://www.dawnspire.com), courtesy of Silent Grove Studios. Thanks to Anders Hammervald (anders@hammervald.com) for his sincere help with preparing the images. The models used in the illustrative figures are downloaded from http://www.planetquake.com.*

Chapter 11

Efficient and Robust Shadow Volumes Using Hierarchical Occlusion Culling and Geometry Shaders

Martin Stich
mental images

Carsten Wächter
Ulm University

Alexander Keller
Ulm University

11.1 Introduction

RealityServer is a mental images platform for creating and deploying 3D Web services and other applications (mental images 2007). The hardware renderer in RealityServer needs to be able to display a large variety of scenes with high performance and quality. An important aspect of achieving these kinds of convincing images is realistic shadow rendering.

RealityServer supports the two most common shadow-rendering techniques: *shadow mapping* and *shadow volumes*. Each method has its own advantages and drawbacks. It's relatively easy to create soft shadows when we use shadow maps, but the shadows suffer from aliasing problems, especially in large scenes. On the other hand, shadow volumes are rendered with pixel accuracy, but they have more difficulty handling light sources that are not perfect point lights or directional lights.

In this chapter, we explain how robust stencil shadow rendering is implemented in Reality-Server and how state-of-the-art hardware features are used to accelerate the technique.

11.2 An Overview of Shadow Volumes

The idea of rendering shadows with shadow volumes has been around for quite some time, but it became practical only relatively recently with the development of robust algorithms and enhanced graphics hardware support. We briefly explain the basic principles of the approach here; refer to McGuire et al. 2003, McGuire 2004, and Everitt and Kilgard 2002 for more-detailed descriptions.

11.2.1 Z-Pass and Z-Fail

Figure 11-1 shows the main idea behind shadow volumes. The actual shadow volume corresponds to the green area (all points behind the occluder that are not visible from the light source). Obviously, we would like to render all geometry that intersects the shadow volume without (or only with ambient) lighting, while everything outside the volume would receive the full contribution of the light source. Consider a ray with its origin at the camera cast toward the scene geometry, as shown in Figure 11-1a. We count the ray's intersections with the shadow volume, so that at each entry into the volume, a counter is increased and at each exit the counter is decreased. For the geometry parts in shadow (only), we end up with a value different from zero. That simple fact is the most important principle behind shadow volumes. If the counter value is available for each pixel, we have separated shadowed from nonshadowed areas and can easily use multipass rendering to exploit that information.

To obtain the counter values, we don't have to perform "real" ray tracing but can rely on the stencil functionality in any modern graphics hardware. First, we clear the stencil buffer by setting it to zero. Then, we render the boundary of the shadow volume into the stencil buffer (not into the color and depth buffer). We set up the hardware so that the value in the stencil buffer is increased on front-facing polygons and decreased on back-facing polygons. The increasing and the decreasing operations are both set to "wrap around," so decreasing zero and increasing the maximum stencil value do not result in saturation.

As a result of this pass, the stencil buffer will contain the intersection counter value for each pixel (which is zero for all nonshadowed pixels). On current graphics cards, volume rendering can be performed in a single render pass by using two-sided stencil writing, which is controlled in OpenGL with the `glStencilOpSeparate()` function. Before the shadow volumes are drawn, the z-buffer must be filled with the scene's depth values, which is usually the case because an ambient pass has to be rendered anyway.

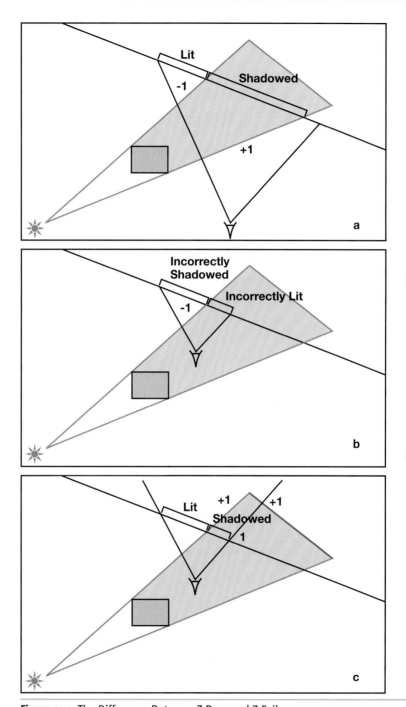

Figure 11-1. The Difference Between Z-Pass and Z-Fail
(a) Z-pass works well for the camera outside the shadow volume. (b) Z-pass fails with the camera inside the volume. (c) Z-fail yields correct results for all cases but requires volume caps to be rendered.

Note that the stencil writes must be performed for every fragment for which the depth test *passes*. Hence, the method just described is called *z-pass*.

Z-pass is easy, but there is a problem with it. Take a look at Figure 11-1b. When the camera is inside a shadow volume, the algorithm yields the wrong results. Fortunately, a simple solution exists: Instead of counting the ray-volume intersections *in front of* the actual geometry, we can count the intersections *behind* it, as shown in Figure 11-1c. All we need to do is set up the graphics hardware to write to the stencil buffer if the depth test *fails*, and invert the increasing and decreasing operations. This method was discovered by John Carmack (2000) and is usually referred to as *z-fail* (or *Carmack's reverse*). Z-fail works for any case, but unlike z-pass, it must be assured that the volume caps are correctly rendered; that is, the volume must be closed both at its front end and at its back end. You can see in Figure 11-1c that a missing back cap would give the wrong results. For z-pass, the front cap does not need to be drawn because the depth test would fail, resulting in no stencil write anyway. The back cap can be omitted because it is placed at infinity behind all objects, so it would fail any depth test as well.

11.2.2 Volume Generation

The following approach is the most common way to generate shadow volumes. Note, however, that it works correctly only for closed two-manifold polygon meshes, meaning that objects cannot have holes, cracks, or self-intersections. We present a method that removes these restrictions in Section 11.3.

Rendering Steps

The actual rendering of the shadow volumes breaks down into these three steps:

1. Rendering the front cap
2. Rendering the back cap
3. Rendering the object's extruded silhouette (the *sides* of the volume)

For the front cap, we loop over all the polygons in the model and render the ones that face the light. Whether a polygon faces the light or not can be checked efficiently by testing the sign of the dot product between the face normal and the direction to the light. For the back cap, we render the same polygons again, with all the vertices projected to infinity in the direction of the light. This projection method is also used for the volume sides, where we draw the possible silhouette edges extruded to infinity, resulting in quads. The possible silhouette edges (the edges that may be part of the actual occluder silhouette) are found by comparing the signs of the dot products between the surface normal and the direction to the light with those of the neighboring faces. If the signs differ, the edge is extruded. For nonconvex objects, this extrusion can result in nested silhouettes, which do not break shadow rendering. Yet it is important that in all cases, the generated faces are oriented so that their normal points outside the shadow volume; otherwise, the values in the stencil buffer will get out of balance.

Rendering at Infinity

How are all these vertices at infinity actually handled? *Rendering at infinity* is intrinsic to homogeneous coordinates in OpenGL (and Direct3D as well). A vertex can be rendered as if it were projected onto an infinitely large sphere by passing a direction instead of a position. In our case, this direction is the vector from the light position toward the vertex. In homogeneous coordinates, directions are specified by setting the w component to zero, whereas positions usually have w set to one.

When rendering at infinity, we run into the problem that primitives will be clipped against the far plane. A convenient way to counteract this clipping is to use *depth clamping*, which is supported by the `NV_depth_clamp` extension in OpenGL. When enabled, geometry is rendered even behind the far plane and produces the maximum possible depth value there. If the extension is not available, a special projection matrix can be used to achieve the same effect, as described in Everitt and Kilgard 2002.

11.2.3 Performance and Optimizations

For reasonably complex scenes, shadow volumes can cost a lot of performance. Thus, many optimizations have been developed, some of which we discuss briefly here. The first important observation is that z-pass usually performs faster than z-fail, mainly because we don't have to render the volume caps. In addition, the occluded part of the shadow volume is usually larger on screen than the unoccluded part, which makes z-fail consume more fill rate. It therefore makes sense to use z-pass whenever possible and switch to z-fail only when necessary (when the camera is inside the shadow volume).

Z-pass and z-fail can be used simultaneously in a render pass, and it pays off to dynamically switch between the two, requiring only a (conservative) test whether the camera is inside a volume. Fill rate is often the main bottleneck for shadow volumes, so further optimizations that have been proposed include volume culling, limiting volumes using the scissor test, and depth bounds (see McGuire et al. 2003 for more information on these methods).

11.3 Our Implementation

Now that we have discussed the basics of shadow volumes, let's take a look at some methods to improve robustness and performance. This section shows you some of the approaches we have taken at mental images to make shadow volumes meet the requirements of RealityServer.

11.3.1 Robust Shadows for Low-Quality Meshes

Traditionally, shadow volume algorithms are used in applications such as games, where the artist has full control over the meshes the game engine has to process. Hence, it is often possible to constrain occluders to be two-manifold meshes, which simplifies shadow volume generation. However, RealityServer needs to be able to correctly handle meshes of low quality, such as meshes that are not closed or that have intersecting geometry. These kinds of meshes are often generated by CAD software or conversion tools. We would therefore like to lower the constraints on meshes for which artifact-free shadows are rendered, without sacrificing too much performance.

A Modified Volume Generation Algorithm

The method we implemented is a small modification to the volume generation algorithm described in Section 11.2.2. In that approach, in addition to drawing the caps, we simply extruded an edge of a polygon facing the light whenever its corresponding neighbor polygon did not face the light.

Now, to work robustly for non-two-manifolds, the algorithm needs to be extended in two ways:

- First, we also extrude edges that do not have any neighbor polygons at all. This is an obvious extension needed for nonclosed meshes (imagine just a single triangle as an occluder, for example).

- Second, we take into account all the polygons in a mesh, not only the ones facing the light, to extrude possible silhouette edges and to draw the caps. This means that all silhouette edges that have a neighbor polygon are actually extruded *twice*, once for each connected polygon.

Now why does this make sense? Take a look at Figure 11-2. The shadow volume for this open mesh is rendered correctly, because the two highlighted edges are extruded twice. The resulting sides close the shadow volumes of both the light-facing and the nonlight-facing polygon sets.

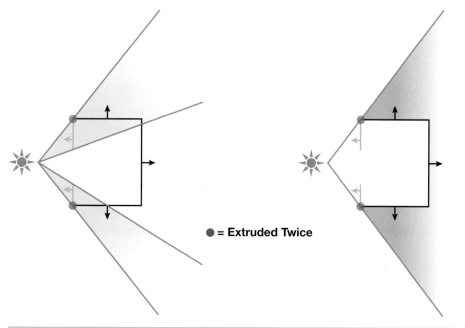

Figure 11-2. Dividing an Object into Multiple Parts
The robust algorithm can be seen as dividing the mesh into multiple parts, with light-facing polygons (green) and non-light-facing polygons (black) each casting their own shadow volumes. The combination of both gives a correct shadow volume for the entire mesh.

In fact, the algorithm can now be seen as a method that divides an object into multiple parts, with each part consisting of only front-facing or back-facing polygons with respect to the light source. Then for each part, the corresponding shadow volume is rendered, similar to multiple separate objects behind each other. This technique even works for self-intersecting objects. As before, we have to pay careful attention that all shadow volume geometry is oriented correctly (with the normal pointing out of the volume). Now that we also consider polygons not facing the light, we have to invert all the generated volume faces on these polygons.

Performance Costs

The new approach is simple and effective, but it comes at a cost. If, for example, we are rendering a two-manifold mesh, we are doing twice the work of the nonrobust algorithm. For z-fail, the caps are rendered twice instead of once (for the front and the back faces), and all the possible silhouette edges are extruded twice as well. However, the caps are not too much of a problem, because for most scenes, only a few occluders will need to be handled with z-fail. Remember that for z-pass, we don't have to draw any caps at all.

A bigger issue is that there is twice the number of extruded silhouette edges. One simple solution would be to extrude and render edges connected to two faces only once, and increase or decrease the value in the stencil buffer by 2 instead of 1. For z-pass, this would bring down the cost of the algorithm to be the same as for the nonrobust method! However, this functionality is not supported in graphics hardware, so we cannot get around rendering those edges twice. To minimize the unavoidable performance loss, our implementation detects if a mesh is two-manifold in a preprocessing step and employs the robust volume generation only if necessary.

Also, note that there are still cases that are not handled by our implementation: in particular, more than two polygons sharing an edge, and polygons that share an edge but have different vertex winding order. This, as well, is handled during preprocessing, where such cases are converted into single, disconnected polygons.

Even though dealing with difficult meshes in combination with shadow volumes sounds tricky at first, it should be extremely easy to integrate the presented method into any existing stencil shadow system. For RealityServer, robust shadows are a must—even if they come at the cost of some performance—because it's usually impossible to correct the meshes the application has to handle.

11.3.2 Dynamic Volume Generation with Geometry Shaders

NVIDIA's GeForce 8 class hardware enables programmable primitive creation on the GPU in a new pipeline stage called the *geometry shader* (GS). Geometry shaders operate on primitives and are logically placed between the vertex shader (VS) and the fragment shader (FS). The vertices of an entire primitive are available as input parameters. A detailed description can be found in NVIDIA Corporation 2007.

It is obvious that this new capability is ideally suited for the dynamic creation of shadow volumes. Silhouette determination is not a cheap task and must be redone every frame for animated scenes, so it is preferable to move the computational load from the CPU to the GPU. Previous approaches to creating shadow volumes entirely on the GPU required fancy tricks with vertex and fragment shaders (Brabec and Seidel 2003). Now, geometry shaders provide a "natural" solution to this problem. A trivial GS reproducing the fixed-function pipeline would just take the input primitive and emit it again, in our case generating the front cap of a shadow volume. We will be creating additional primitives for the back cap and extruded silhouette edges, as needed. The exact same robust algorithm as described in Section 11.3.1 can be implemented entirely on the GPU, leading to a very elegant way of creating dynamic shadows.

To compute the silhouette edges of a mesh, the geometry shader has to have access to adjacency information of triangles. In OpenGL, we can pass in additional vertices per triangle using the new `GL_TRIANGLES_ADJACENCY_EXT` mode for `glBegin`. In this mode we need six, instead of three, vertices to complete a triangle, three of which specify the neighbor vertices of the edges. Figure 11-3 illustrates the vertex layout of a triangle with neighbors.

In addition to specifying the input primitive type, we need to specify the type of primitives a GS will create. We choose triangle strips, which lets us efficiently render single triangles (for the caps), as well as quads (for the extruded silhouette edges). The maximum allowed number of emitted vertices will be set to 18 (3 + 3 for the two caps plus 4 × 3 for the sides).

Listing 11-1 shows the GLSL implementation of the geometry shader. The code assumes that `gl_PositionIn` contains the coordinates of the vertices transformed to eye space. This transformation is done in the VS simply by multiplying the input vertex with `gl_ModelViewMatrix` and writing it to `gl_Position`. All the vertices of a primitive will then show up in the `gl_PositionIn` array. If an edge does not have a neighbor triangle, we encode this by setting w to zero for the corresponding adjacency vertex.

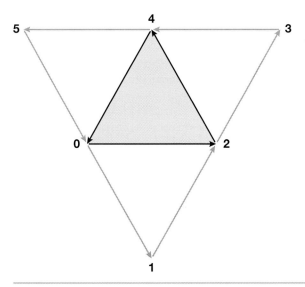

Figure 11-3. Input Vertices for a Geometry Shader
The main triangle is composed of the vertices 0, 2, and 4. The vertices 1, 3, and 5 specify the neighbors of the first, second, and third edge of the main triangle, respectively.

Listing 11-1. A GLSL Implementation of the Volume Generation Geometry Shader

```
#version 120
#extension GL_EXT_geometry_shader4: enable

uniform vec4 l_pos;   // Light position (eye space)
uniform int robust;   // Robust generation needed?
uniform int zpass;    // Is it safe to do z-pass?

void main()
{
  vec3 ns[3];   // Normals
  vec3 d[3];    // Directions toward light
  vec4 v[4];    // Temporary vertices

  vec4 or_pos[3] = {   // Triangle oriented toward light source
    gl_PositionIn[0],
    gl_PositionIn[2],
    gl_PositionIn[4]
  };

  // Compute normal at each vertex.
  ns[0] = cross(
    gl_PositionIn[2].xyz - gl_PositionIn[0].xyz,
    gl_PositionIn[4].xyz - gl_PositionIn[0].xyz );
  ns[1] = cross(
    gl_PositionIn[4].xyz - gl_PositionIn[2].xyz,
    gl_PositionIn[0].xyz - gl_PositionIn[2].xyz );
  ns[2] = cross(
    gl_PositionIn[0].xyz - gl_PositionIn[4].xyz,
    gl_PositionIn[2].xyz - gl_PositionIn[4].xyz );

  // Compute direction from vertices to light.
  d[0] = l_pos.xyz-l_pos.w*gl_PositionIn[0].xyz;
  d[1] = l_pos.xyz-l_pos.w*gl_PositionIn[2].xyz;
  d[2] = l_pos.xyz-l_pos.w*gl_PositionIn[4].xyz;

  // Check if the main triangle faces the light.
  bool faces_light = true;
  if ( !(dot(ns[0],d[0])>0 || dot(ns[1],d[1])>0 ||
         dot(ns[2],d[2])>0) ) {
    // Not facing the light and not robust, ignore.
    if ( robust == 0 ) return;
```

```
  // Flip vertex winding order in or_pos.
  or_pos[1] = gl_PositionIn[4];
  or_pos[2] = gl_PositionIn[2];
  faces_light = false;
}

// Render caps. This is only needed for z-fail.
if ( zpass == 0 ) {
  // Near cap: simply render triangle.
  gl_Position = gl_ProjectionMatrix*or_pos[0];
  EmitVertex();
  gl_Position = gl_ProjectionMatrix*or_pos[1];
  EmitVertex();
  gl_Position = gl_ProjectionMatrix*or_pos[2];
  EmitVertex(); EndPrimitive();

  // Far cap: extrude positions to infinity.
  v[0] =vec4(l_pos.w*or_pos[0].xyz-l_pos.xyz,0);
  v[1] =vec4(l_pos.w*or_pos[2].xyz-l_pos.xyz,0);
  v[2] =vec4(l_pos.w*or_pos[1].xyz-l_pos.xyz,0);
  gl_Position = gl_ProjectionMatrix*v[0];
  EmitVertex();
  gl_Position = gl_ProjectionMatrix*v[1];
  EmitVertex();
  gl_Position = gl_ProjectionMatrix*v[2];
  EmitVertex(); EndPrimitive();
}

// Loop over all edges and extrude if needed.
for ( int i=0; i<3; i++ ) {
  // Compute indices of neighbor triangle.
  int v0 = i*2;
  int nb = (i*2+1);
  int v1 = (i*2+2) % 6;

  // Compute normals at vertices, the *exact*
  // same way as done above!
  ns[0] = cross(
    gl_PositionIn[nb].xyz-gl_PositionIn[v0].xyz,
    gl_PositionIn[v1].xyz-gl_PositionIn[v0].xyz);
```

```glsl
  ns[1] = cross(
    gl_PositionIn[v1].xyz-gl_PositionIn[nb].xyz,
    gl_PositionIn[v0].xyz-gl_PositionIn[nb].xyz);
  ns[2] = cross(
    gl_PositionIn[v0].xyz-gl_PositionIn[v1].xyz,
    gl_PositionIn[nb].xyz-gl_PositionIn[v1].xyz);

  // Compute direction to light, again as above.
  d[0] =l_pos.xyz-l_pos.w*gl_PositionIn[v0].xyz;
  d[1] =l_pos.xyz-l_pos.w*gl_PositionIn[nb].xyz;
  d[2] =l_pos.xyz-l_pos.w*gl_PositionIn[v1].xyz;

  // Extrude the edge if it does not have a
  // neighbor, or if it's a possible silhouette.
  if ( gl_PositionIn[nb].w < 1e-3  ||
       ( faces_light != (dot(ns[0],d[0])>0 ||
                         dot(ns[1],d[1])>0 ||
                         dot(ns[2],d[2])>0) ))
  {
    // Make sure sides are oriented correctly.
    int i0 = faces_light ? v0 : v1;
    int i1 = faces_light ? v1 : v0;

    v[0] = gl_PositionIn[i0];
    v[1] = vec4(l_pos.w*gl_PositionIn[i0].xyz - l_pos.xyz, 0);
    v[2] = gl_PositionIn[i1];
    v[3] = vec4(l_pos.w*gl_PositionIn[i1].xyz - l_pos.xyz, 0);
    // Emit a quad as a triangle strip.
    gl_Position = gl_ProjectionMatrix*v[0];
    EmitVertex();
    gl_Position = gl_ProjectionMatrix*v[1];
    EmitVertex();
    gl_Position = gl_ProjectionMatrix*v[2];
    EmitVertex();
    gl_Position = gl_ProjectionMatrix*v[3];
    EmitVertex(); EndPrimitive();
  }
  }
}
```

One thing to take care of at this point is to transform the actual rendered scene geometry exactly like the geometry in the shadow volume shader. That is, if you use `ftransform` or the fixed-function pipeline for rendering, you will probably have to adjust the implementation so that at least the front caps use coordinates transformed with `ftransform` as well. Otherwise, you are likely to get shadow artifacts ("shadow acne") caused by z-fighting. The parameter `l_pos` contains the light position in eye space, in 4D homogeneous coordinates. This makes it easy to pass in point lights and directional lights without having to handle each case separately.

The uniform variable `robust` controls whether or not we need to generate volumes with the algorithm from Section 11.3.1. If we know a mesh is a two-manifold, `robust` can be set to false, in which case the shader simply ignores all polygons not facing the light. This means we effectively switch to the well-known volume generation method described in Section 11.2.2. The `zpass` flag specifies whether we can safely use the z-pass method. This decision is determined at runtime by checking if the camera is inside the shadow volume. (In fact, we check conservatively by using a coarser bounding volume than the exact shadow volume.) If so, z-fail needs to be used; otherwise, the shader can skip rendering the front and back caps.

Note that the code also takes care of an issue that we have not discussed yet, but frequently arises with low-quality meshes: degenerate triangles. A triangle can either be degenerate from the beginning or become degenerate when being transformed to eye space, due to numerical inaccuracies in the computations. Often, this happens with meshes that have been tessellated to polygons and contain very small or very thin triangles. Degenerate (or nearly degenerate) triangles are an ugly problem in shadow volume generation because the artifacts they cause are typically not only visible in the shadow itself, but also show up as shadow streaks "leaking" out of the occluder.

The main difficulty with degenerate triangles is to decide whether or not they face the light. Depending on how we compute the normal that is later compared to the light direction, we may come to different conclusions. We then run into trouble if, as in a geometry shader, we need to look at the same triangle multiple times (what is our "main" triangle at one point can be a "neighbor" triangle at another point). If two such runs don't yield the same result, we may have one extruded silhouette too many, or one too few, which causes the artifacts.

To handle this problem, we make sure we perform exactly the same computations whenever we need to decide whether a triangle faces the light or not. Unfortunately, this solution leads to computing three normals per triangle and comparing them to three different light direction vectors. This operation, of course, costs some precious performance, so you might go back to a less solid implementation if you know you will be handling only meshes without "difficult" triangles.

11.3.3 Improving Performance with Hierarchical Occlusion Culling

Shadow volumes were integrated into RealityServer mainly for use in large scenes, such as city models, where shadow maps typically do not perform well. In such scenes, we can increase rendering performance dramatically by using a hierarchical occlusion culling method, such as the one presented in Wimmer and Bittner 2005. A description of this approach is also available online (Bittner et al. 2004).

The idea is to organize all objects in the scene in a hierarchical tree structure. During rendering, the tree is recursively traversed in a front-to-back order, and the objects contained in the leaf nodes are rendered. Before a tree node is traversed, however, it is tested for visibility using the occlusion culling feature provided by the graphics hardware. If the node is found to be invisible, the entire subtree can be pruned. The simplest hierarchical structure to use in this case is a binary bounding-volume hierarchy (BVH) of axis-aligned bounding boxes (AABBs). This kind of hierarchy is extremely fast to generate, which is important for animated scenes, where the BVH (or parts of it) needs to be rebuilt every frame.

To check whether a node is visible, we can first test it against intersection with the viewing frustum and then perform an occlusion query simply by rendering the AABB. Only if it is actually visible do we continue tree traversal or render the leaf content, respectively.

To optimally exploit the hierarchical occlusion culling technique, we should make use of asynchronous occlusion queries and temporal coherence, as described by Wimmer and Bittner 2005. Because occlusion queries require a readback from the GPU, they have a relatively large overhead. Thus, we can issue an asynchronous occlusion query and continue traversal at some other point in the tree until the query result is available. Storing information about whether or not a node was visible in the previous frame helps estimate whether an occlusion query is required at all, or whether it may be faster to just traverse the node without a query.

We now extend this idea to shadow volumes as well. We would like to find out if we can skip a certain node in the tree because we know that no object in this part of the hierarchy will cast a visible shadow. Instead of testing the bounding box of the node with an occlusion query, we test the bounding box extruded in the light direction, as if the AABB itself would cast a shadow. In other words, we effectively perform *occlusion culling on the shadow volumes of the node bounding boxes*. If this extruded box is not visible, it means that any shadow cast by an object inside the bounding box cannot be visible, and the node can be disregarded. The principle is shown in Figure 11-4. Two occluders, for which shadow volume rendering is potentially expensive, are contained in a BVH. The shadow volume of the AABB of the blue object is occluded by the orange object and thus is not visible to the camera, so we can safely skip generating and rendering the actual shadow volume of the blue object.

This conclusion is, of course, also true if the occluded node holds an entire subtree of the scene instead of just one object. When the tree traversal reaches a *visible* leaf node, its shadow volume is rendered using the methods described earlier in this chapter. Note that we need to give special attention to cases of the light source being inside the currently processed AABB or of the camera being inside the extruded AABB. It is, however, quite simple to detect these cases, and we can then just traverse the node without performing an occlusion query.

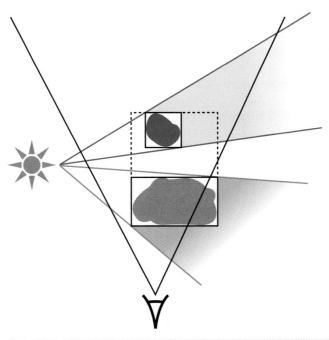

Figure 11-4. Two Occluders in a BVH
The shadow volume of the AABB of the blue object is not visible to the camera. Thus, the blue object can be ignored during shadow rendering.

Obviously, the same optimizations as used for conventional hierarchical occlusion culling can also be used for the extended method. Asynchronous occlusion queries and temporal coherence work as expected. The only difference is that, in order to take into account temporal coherence, we must include the coherency information *per light source* in each BVH node. That is, for each light and node, we store a visibility flag (whether or not a node's shadow volume was visible the last time it was checked), along with a frame ID (describing when the visibility information was last updated).

The hierarchical culling method described here does not increase performance in all cases. In fact, in some situations, rendering may even be slightly slower compared to simply drawing all the objects in the scene. However, for the majority of our scenes, hierarchical culling (both the original and the shadow volume variant) improves performance considerably. In cases such as a city walkthrough, this speedup is often dramatic.

11.4 Conclusion

We achieve very robust rendering of shadows, even for difficult meshes, by employing a nonstandard method for generating shadow volume geometry. By using this method in combination with hierarchical hardware occlusion queries and geometry shaders, we also achieve high performance for situations that previously did not work well with stencil shadows. Examples can be seen in Figures 11-5 and 11-6. All the presented techniques are relatively straightforward to implement.

In the future, we will investigate additional performance optimizations, especially for handling scenes with extremely high geometric complexity.

11.5 References

Bittner, J., M. Wimmer, H. Piringer, and W. Purgathofer. 2004. "Coherent Hierarchical Culling: Hardware Occlusion Queries Made Useful." In *Computer Graphics Forum (Proceedings of Eurographics 2004)* 23(3), pp. 615–624.

Brabec, S., and H. Seidel. 2003. "Shadow Volumes on Programmable Graphics Hardware." In *Computer Graphics Forum (Proceedings of Eurographics 2003)* 25(3).

Carmack, John. 2000. Personal communication. Available online at http://developer.nvidia.com/object/robust_shadow_volumes.html.

Figure 11-5. A City Scene Close-up Containing a Complex Tree Mesh with Roughly Half a Million Polygons

The robust algorithm correctly handles shadowing between the tree leaves. None of the meshes in this scene is a two-manifold.

Everitt, Cass, and Mark Kilgard. 2002. "Practical and Robust Stenciled Shadow Volumes for Hardware-Accelerated Rendering." Available online at http://developer.nvidia.com/object/robust_shadow_volumes.html.

McGuire, Morgan. 2004. "Efficient Shadow Volume Rendering." In *GPU Gems*, edited by Randima Fernando, pp. 137–166. Addison-Wesley.

McGuire, Morgan, John F. Hughes, Kevin Egan, Mark Kilgard, and Cass Everitt. 2003. "Fast, Practical and Robust Shadows." *Brown Univ. Tech. Report* CS03-19. Oct. 27, 2003. Available online at http://developer.nvidia.com/object/fast_shadow_volumes.html.

mental images. 2007. "RealityServer Functional Overview." White paper. Available online at http://www.mentalimages.com/2_3_realityserver/index.html.

Figure 11-6. The Same Model as in Figure 11-5, Zoomed Out
Both views render at interactive rates with dynamic shadow volume generation turned on.

NVIDIA Corporation. 2007. "NVIDIA OpenGL Extension Specifications." Available online at http://developer.nvidia.com/object/nvidia_opengl_specs.html.

Wimmer, Michael, and Jiri Bittner. 2005. "Hardware Occlusion Queries Made Useful." In *GPU Gems 2*, edited by Matt Pharr, pp. 91–108. Addison-Wesley.

Chapter 12

High-Quality Ambient Occlusion

Jared Hoberock
University of Illinois at Urbana-Champaign

Yuntao Jia
University of Illinois at Urbana-Champaign

Ambient occlusion is a technique used in production to approximate the effect of environment lighting. Unlike the dull, flat look of local lighting models, ambient occlusion can add realism to a scene by accentuating small surface details and adding soft shadows. Bunnell 2005 demonstrated a novel technique for approximating this effect by integrating occlusion with an adaptive traversal of the hierarchical approximation of a model. While this technique does a good job of approximating smoothly varying shadows, it makes assumptions about the input model that make it not robust for general high-quality applications.

In this chapter, we demonstrate the problems that arise with this technique in practice. Additionally, we show how a few small changes to the algorithm extend its usefulness and improve its robustness for more general models that exist in production. The end result is a fast, GPU-accelerated, high-quality ambient occlusion algorithm that can produce convincing, smooth soft shadows and realistic, sharp local details.

12.1 Review

The original technique represents a polygonal mesh with a set of approximating disks. A disk is associated with each vertex of the mesh to approximate its adjacent polygons. The algorithm computes occlusion at a vertex by summing shadow contributions from every other individual disk. It does so by computing the *form factor*—a geometric quantity that is proportional to the disk's area and inversely proportional to the distance to it squared.

However, this technique ignores visibility: disks that are obscured by others should not contribute any shadow. The algorithm deals with this issue in the following way. First, it computes the occlusion at each disk from others and stores it with that disk. However, when the shadow contribution from each disk is evaluated, it is multiplied by that disk's occlusion. In this way, the algorithm approximates visibility with occlusion. If we iterate with a few passes of this technique, the solution converges to a result that remarkably resembles ambient occlusion—all without casting a single ray.

Summing each pair of disk-to-disk interactions can be quite expensive. In fact, a straightforward implementation of this algorithm is $O(n^2)$, which is prohibitive in practice. Instead, Bunnell observed that the contribution from distant surfaces can be approximated, while nearby surfaces require a more precise computation. We can achieve this by grouping disks near each other into a single aggregate disk that approximates them. We can group these aggregate disks into bigger aggregates, and so on, until finally we have a single disk that approximates the entire model.

In this way, the algorithm creates a hierarchical tree of disks, which coarsely approximates the model near the top and finely approximates it at the bottom. When we need to evaluate the occlusion at any given disk, we traverse the tree starting at the top. Depending on the distance between the disk and our current level in the tree, we may decide that we are far enough away to use the current approximation. If so, we replace the shadow computations of many descendant disks with a single one at their ancestor. If not, we descend deeper into the tree, summing the contributions from its children. This adaptive traversal transforms what would ordinarily be an $O(n^2)$ computation into an efficient $O(n \log n)$. In fact, the technique is so efficient that it can be performed in real time for deforming geometry on a GeForce 6800 GPU. For a detailed description of the technique, we refer the reader to Bunnell 2005.

12.2 Problems

The original technique is quite useful for computing smoothly varying per-vertex occlusion that may be linearly interpolated across triangles. However, it would be nice if we could evaluate this occlusion function at any arbitrary point. For example, a high quality renderer may wish to evaluate ambient occlusion on a per-fragment basis to avoid the linear interpolation artifacts that arise from vertex interpolation. Additionally, some ambient occlusion features are not smooth at all. For instance, contact shadows are sharp features that occur where two surfaces come together; they are an important ingredient in establishing realism. These shadows are too high frequency to be accurately reconstructed by an interpolated result. The left side of Figure 12-1 shows both linear interpolation artifacts and missing shadows due to applying this method at per-vertex rates.

We might try to avoid these interpolation artifacts and capture high-frequency details by increasing the tessellation density of the mesh—that is, by simply adding more triangles. This is not satisfying because it places an unnecessary demand on the mesh author and increases our storage requirements. But more important, increasing the sampling rate in this manner exposes the first of our artifacts. These are the disk-shaped regions occurring on the back of the bunny in Figure 12-2.

Instead of increasing the tessellation density of the mesh, we could alternatively increase the sampling density in screen space. That is, we could apply the occlusion shader on a per-fragment basis. Unfortunately, the straightforward application of this shader yields the second of our problems that render this method unusable as-is. The right sides of Figures 12-1 and 12-2 illustrate these artifacts. Notice the high-frequency "pinching" features occurring near vertices of the mesh. Additionally, the increase in sampling density brings the disk-shaped artifacts into full clarity.

Figure 12-1. Artifacts on a Sparsely Tessellated Mesh
Left: Per-vertex artifacts. Right: Per-fragment artifacts.

Figure 12-2. Artifacts on a Densely Tessellated Mesh
Left: Per-vertex artifacts. Right: Per-fragment artifacts.

12.2.1 Disk-Shaped Artifacts

Before we demonstrate how to fix these problems, it is useful to understand their origin. First, consider the disk-shaped artifacts. These appear as a boundary separating a light region and a dark region of the surface. Suppose we are computing occlusion from some disk at a point on one side of the boundary. As we shade points closer and closer to the boundary, the distance to the disk shrinks smaller and smaller. Finally, we reach a point on the boundary where our distance criterion decides that the disk is too close to provide a good approximation to the mesh. At this point, we descend one level deeper into the tree and sum occlusion from the disk's children.

Here, we have made a discrete transition in the approximation, but we expect the shadow to remain smooth. In reality, there is no guarantee that the occlusion value computed from the disk on one side of the boundary will be exactly equal to the sum of its children on the other side. What we are left with is a discontinuity in the shadow. Because parents deeper in the tree are more likely to approximate their children well, we can make these discontinuities arbitrarily faint by traversing deeper and deeper into the tree. Of course, traversing into finer levels of the tree in this manner increases our workload. We would prefer a solution that is more efficient.

12.2.2 High-Frequency Pinching Artifacts

Next, we examine the pinching artifacts. Suppose we are shading a point that is very near a disk at the bottom level of the hierarchy. When we compute occlusion from this disk, its contribution will overpower those of all other disks. Because the form factor is inversely proportional to the square of the distance, the problem worsens as we shade closer. In effect, we are dividing by a number that becomes arbitrarily small at points around the disk.

One solution might ignore disks that are too close to the point that we are shading. Unfortunately, there is no general way to know how close is too close. This strategy also introduces a discontinuity around these ignored disks. Additionally, nearby geometry is crucial for rendering sharp details such as contact shadows and creases. We would like a robust solution that "just works" in all cases.

12.3 A Robust Solution

In this section, we describe a robust solution to the artifacts encountered in the original version of this algorithm. The basic skeleton of the algorithm remains intact—we adaptively sum occlusion from a coarse occlusion solution stored in a tree—but a few key changes significantly improve the robustness of the result.

12.3.1 Smoothing Discontinuities

First, we describe our solution to the disk-shaped shadow discontinuities. Recall that there is no guarantee that any given point will receive shadow from a parent disk that is exactly equal to the sum of its children. However, we can force the transition to be a smooth blend between the shadows on either side of the boundary. To do this, we define a zone around the transition boundary where the occlusion will be smoothly interpolated between a disk's contribution and its children's. Figure 12-3 illustrates the geometry of the transition zone.

Inside this zone, when we compute occlusion from a disk, we also consider the occlusion from its parent. The code snippet of Listing 12-1 shows the details. First, when our distance criterion tells us we must descend into the hierarchy, we note the occlusion contribution at the current level of approximation. We also note the area of the disk, which the weighted blend we apply later will depend on. Finally, we compute a weight

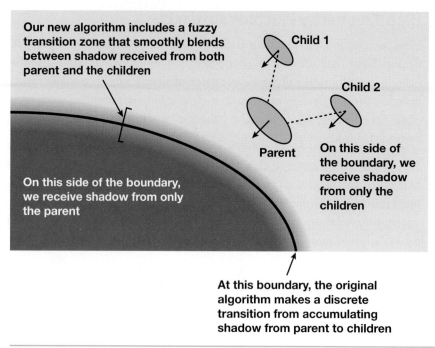

Our new algorithm includes a fuzzy transition zone that smoothly blends between shadow received from both parent and the children

Child 1

Child 2

Parent

On this side of the boundary, we receive shadow from only the parent

On this side of the boundary, we receive shadow from only the children

At this boundary, the original algorithm makes a discrete transition from accumulating shadow from parent to children

Figure 12-3. The Geometry of the Transition Zone

for this parent disk that depends on our position inside the transition zone. You can see that when d2 is at the outer boundary of the zone, at `tooClose * (1.0 + r)`, the parent's weight is one. On the inner boundary, at `tooClose * (1.0 - r)`, the parent's weight is zero. Inside the zone, the weight is a simple linear blend between parent and children. However, a more sophisticated implementation involving a higher order polynomial that takes into account grandparents could be even smoother.

Later, we finish our descent into the tree and sum the occlusion contribution from a disk. At this step, we apply the blend. Additionally, the contribution from the parent is modulated by the ratio of the area of the child to its parent's. To understand why this step is necessary, recall that the area of the parent disk is equal to the sum of its children's. Because we will sum the occlusion contributed from each of the parent's children, we ensure that we do not "overcount" the parent's contribution by multiplying by this ratio.

Note that in applying this blend, we assume that we have descended to the same depth for each of the parent's children. In general, it is possible that the traversal depths for a disk's children may not be the same. A more correct implementation of this blend could account for this. In our experiments, we have compensated for this assumption by increasing the traversal depth.

Listing 12-1. Smoothing Out Discontinuities

```
// Compute shadow contribution from the current disk.
float contribution = . . .

// Stop or descend?
if(d2 < tooClose * (1.0 + r))
{
  // Remember the parent's contribution.
  parentContribution = contribution;

  // Remember the parent's area.
  parentArea = area;

  // Compute parent's weight: a simple linear blend.
  parentWeight = (d2 - (1.0 - r) * tooClose)/(2.0 * r * tooClose);

  // Traverse deeper into hierarchy.
  . . .
}
else
{
  // Compute the children's weight.
  childrenWeight = 1.0 - parentWeight;

  // Blend contribution:
  // Parent's contribution is modulated by the ratio of the child's
  // area to its own.
  occlusion += childrenWeight * contribution;
  occlusion += parentWeight * parentContribution * (area/parentArea);
}
```

12.3.2 Removing Pinches and Adding Detail

Our solution to the pinching artifacts has two components. We begin with the placement of the finest level of disks. The original version of this algorithm associated a disk with each vertex of the mesh that approximated the vertex's neighboring faces. Recall that for points near these vertices, these disks are a very poor approximation of the actual surface. For points around areas of high curvature, the result is large, erroneous shadow values.

Instead of associating the finest level of disks at vertices, our solution places them at the centroid of each mesh face. This is a much better approximation to the surface of the mesh, and it removes a large portion of the pinching artifacts.

These disks represent the finest level of surface approximation, but they cannot represent the true mesh. As a result, sharp shadow features in areas of high detail are noticeably absent. To attain this last level of missing detail, we go one step further than the disk-based approximation. At the lowest level in the hierarchy, rather than consider approximating disks, we evaluate analytic form factors from actual mesh triangles.

This turns out to be easier than it sounds. For a general polygon, we can analytically evaluate its form factor with respect to a point via the following equation:

$$F_{pA} = \frac{1}{2\pi}\Sigma_i \mathbf{n} \cdot \mathbf{\Gamma}_i.$$

This equation, found in standard global illumination texts (such as Sillion and Puech 1994), computes the form factor from a polygonal source A to a point p with normal $\mathbf{n}$. With each edge e_i of A, we associate a unit vector, $\mathbf{\Gamma}_i$. $\mathbf{\Gamma}_i$ is formed by taking the cross product of a vector pointing along e_i with a vector pointing from p to e_i's start vertex. For each edge of A, we dot $\mathbf{\Gamma}_i$ with $\mathbf{n}$, and sum. Figure 12-4 illustrates the approach.

This equation assumes that the entire polygon is visible. For our application, we need to determine the visible portion of the polygon by clipping it to our shading point's plane of support. This is simply the plane passing through the point to be shaded facing in a direction equal to the shading normal. Not performing this clipping will overestimate the true form factor and produce disturbing artifacts. Figure 12-5 shows the geometry of the clip.

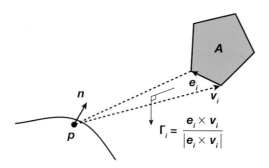

Figure 12-4. Point to Polygon Form Factor

Chapter 12   High-Quality Ambient Occlusion

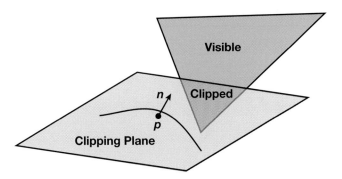

Figure 12-5. Clipping a Triangle to a Visible Quadrilateral

Clipping a triangle by a plane results in one of three cases:

- The entire triangle lies under the plane and is not visible.
- The triangle lies partially under the plane and is partially visible. In this case, we clip the triangle to produce a quadrilateral.
- The triangle lies completely above the plane and is completely visible.

Our clipping algorithm works by inspecting the triangle's three vertices with respect to the clipping plane. A point may lie above or under a plane, but for robustness issues, we also allow a point to lie on the plane. For three vertices with three possible configurations, there are $3^3 = 27$ possible configurations in all. Fortunately, the GeForce 8800's powerful branch performance quickly determines the configuration and tests only five branch conditions in the worst case.

Listing 12-2 shows our function that computes the visible portion of a triangle. The function accepts the clipping plane described by a point and normal, and the three vertices of the triangle to be clipped as input. It outputs the four vertices of the visible quad of the triangle. Note that a degenerate quad with two equal vertices may describe a fully visible triangle. Similarly, a degenerate quad with four equal vertices may describe an invisible triangle.

We begin by specifying an epsilon value that will control the robustness of the clip. Vertices that are closer to the plane than this value will be considered to lie on the plane. Next, we evaluate the plane equation for each vertex. This results in a signed distance from each vertex to the plane. Points above the plane have a positive distance; points below, a negative distance. Points that are too close to the plane have their distance clamped to zero.

Listing 12-2. Finding the Visible Quadrilateral Portion of a Triangle

```
void visibleQuad(float3 p,
                 float3 n,
                 float3 v0,
                 float3 v1,
                 float3 v2,

             out float3 q0,
             out float3 q1,
             out float3 q2,
             out float3 q3)
{
  const float epsilon = 1e-6;
  float d = dot(n, p);

  // Compute the signed distances from the vertices to the plane.
  float sd[3];
  sd[0] = dot(n, v0) - d;
  if(abs(sd[0]) <= epsilon) sd[0] = 0.0;
  sd[1] = dot(n, v1) - d;
  if(abs(sd[1]) <= epsilon) sd[1] = 0.0;
  sd[2] = dot(n, v2) - d;
  if(abs(sd[2]) <= epsilon) sd[2] = 0.0;

  // Determine case.
  if(sd[0] > 0.0)
  {
    if(sd[1] > 0.0)
    {
      if(sd[2] < 0.0)
      {
        // v0, v1 above, v2 under
        q0 = v0;
        q1 = v1;

        // Evaluate ray-plane equations:
        q2 = v1 + (sd[1]/(sd[1] - sd[2])) * (v2 - v1);
        q3 = v0 + (sd[0]/(sd[0] - sd[2])) * (v2 - v0);
      }
```

```
        else
        {
            // v0, v1, v2 all above
            q0 = v0;
            q1 = v1;
            q2 = v2;
            q3 = q3;
        }
    }
}

// Other cases similarly
. . .
```

We clip the triangle by inspecting the signs of these distances. When two signs match but the other does not, we must clip. In this case, two of the triangle's edges intersect the plane. The intersection points define two vertices of the visible quad. Depending on which edges intersect the plane, we evaluate two ray-plane intersection equations. With the visible portion of the triangle computed, we can compute its form factor with a straightforward implementation of the form factor equation applied to quadrilaterals.

12.4 Results

Next, we compare the results of our improved algorithm to those of the original. We chose two tests, the bunny and a car, to demonstrate the effectiveness of the new solution over a range of input. The bunny is a smooth, well-tessellated mesh with fairly equilateral triangles. In contrast, the car has heterogeneous detail with sharp angles and triangles with a wide range of aspect ratios. Figures 12-6 and 12-7 show the results.

You can see that the original per-vertex algorithm is well suited to the bunny due to its dense and regular tessellation. However, both disk-shaped and linear interpolation artifacts are apparent. The new algorithm removes these artifacts.

However, the original algorithm performs worse on the car. The sparse tessellation reveals linear interpolation artifacts on the per-vertex result. Applying the original shader at per-fragment rates smooths out this interpolation but adds both disk-shaped discontinuities and pinching near vertices. Our new algorithm is robust for both of these kinds of artifacts and produces a realistic result.

Figure 12-6. Ambient Occlusion Comparison on the Bunny
Left: The original algorithm applied per vertex. Right: Our new algorithm applied per fragment.

Figure 12-7. Ambient Occlusion Comparison on the Car
Upper left: The original algorithm applied per vertex. Lower left: The original algorithm applied per fragment. Upper right: Our new algorithm applied to flat normals. Lower right: Our new algorithm applied to smooth shading normals.

12.5 Performance

Here we include a short discussion of performance. In all experiments, we set epsilon, which controls traversal depth, to 8. First, we measured the performance of the initial iterative steps that shade the disks of the coarse occlusion hierarchy. Our implementation of this step is no different from the original algorithm and serves as a comparison. Next, we measured the performance of our new shader with and without triangle clipping and form factors. We used a deferred shading method to ensure that only visible fragments were shaded. Finally, we counted the number of total fragments shaded to measure the shading rate. Table 12-1 and Figure 12-8 show our performance measurements.

We found the performance of shading disks in the hierarchy to be roughly comparable to shading fragments with the high-quality form factor computations. We observed that the disk shading rate tended to be much lower than per-fragment shading. We believe this is due to a smaller batch size than the total number of fragments to be shaded. Including the high-quality form factor computation in the shader requires extensive branching and results in a lower shading rate. However, this addition ensures a robust result.

Table 12-1. Performance Results

Model	Size in Triangles	Total Fragments Shaded	Total Disks Shaded
Bunny	69,451	381,046	138,901
Car	29,304	395,613	58,607

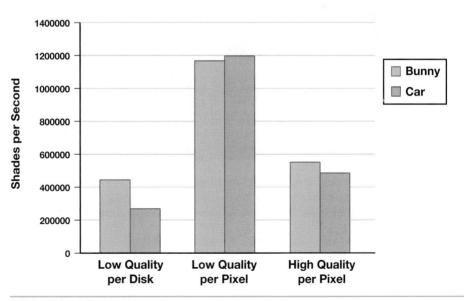

Figure 12-8. Performance Results

12.6 Caveats

We continue with some notes on applying our algorithm in practice. First, as we previously mentioned, our smoothing solution may not completely eliminate all discontinuities. However, in all cases we have been able to make them arbitrarily faint by increasing the traversal depth. Additionally, because this algorithm can only approximate visibility, the results are often biased on the side of exaggerated shadows and may not match a reference computed by a ray tracer. To control the depth of occlusion, we introduce some tunable parameters that are useful in controlling error or achieving a desired artistic result.

12.6.1 Forcing Convergence

Recall that this method approximates visibility by applying the occlusion algorithm to disks iteratively over several passes. In our experiments, we have found that this algorithm tends not to converge to a unique solution on general scenes. In particular, architectural scenes with high occlusion usually oscillate between two solutions. To deal with this, we iteratively apply the original occlusion algorithm to compute disk-to-disk occlusion for a few passes as before. Then, we force convergence by setting each disk's occlusion to a weighted minimum of the last two results. Figure 12-9 presents the results achieved with this adjustment; Listing 12-3 shows the code.

Figure 12-9. The Benefits of Using a Weighted Minimum
Left and middle: The original algorithm's iterative method tends to oscillate between two solutions that are clearly incorrect. Right: Our new algorithm takes a weighted minimum of the two solutions, which produces a plausible result.

Listing 12-3. Forcing Convergence

```
float o0 = texture2DRect(occlusion0, diskLocation).x;
float o1 = texture2DRect(occlusion1, diskLocation).x;

float m = min(o0, o1);
float M = max(o0, o1);

// weighted blend
occlusion = minScale * m + maxScale * M;
```

Here, occlusion0 and occlusion1 contain the results of the last two iterations of the occlusion solution. We set the result to be a blend of the two. Because this algorithm overestimates occlusion in general, we bias the final result toward the smaller value. We have found 0.7 and 0.3 to be good values for minScale and maxScale, respectively.

12.6.2 Tunable Parameters

We have noted that our method in general tends to overestimate ambient occlusion. In fact, a completely enclosed environment produces a black scene! In general, ambient occlusion may not necessarily be exactly the quantity we are interested in computing. More generally, we might be interested in a function that resembles ambient occlusion for nearby shadow casters but falls off smoothly with distance. Such a function will produce deep contrast in local details but will not completely shadow a closed environment. We introduce two tunable parameters to control this effect.

Distance Attenuation

First, we allow the occlusion contribution of an element (whether it is a disk or a triangle) to be attenuated inversely proportional to the distance to it squared. Adjusting this parameter tends to brighten the overall result, as Figure 12-10 illustrates. Listing 12-4 shows the details.

Listing 12-4. Attenuating Occlusion by Distance

```
// Compute the occlusion contribution from an element
contribution = solidAngle(. . .);

// Attenuate by distance
contribution /= (1.0 + distanceAttenuation * e2);
```

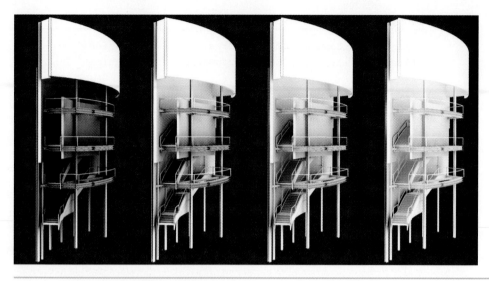

Figure 12-10. Parameters' Effect on Result

          Left: `distanceAttenuation = 0,`   `trianglePower = 1`
 Middle left: `distanceAttenuation = 0.5,` `trianglePower = 1`
Middle right: `distanceAttenuation = 0.5,` `trianglePower = 1.5`
     Right: `distanceAttenuation = 1,`   `trianglePower = 2`

Staircase model courtesy of Tony Kaap.

Triangle Attenuation

We also attenuate the occlusion contribution from triangles at the finest level of the hierarchy. Recall that we account for point-to-triangle visibility with two factors: we clip each triangle to a plane and we modulate the form factor by the triangle's occlusion. The combination of both of these factors can underestimate the true visibility, because the form factor of the clipped triangle is further dampened by modulation. We can compensate for this by raising the triangle's occlusion to a power before it is multiplied by its form factor and added to the sum. Low values for this parameter emphasize small features such as creases and cracks, which would otherwise be lost. High values lessen the influence of large, distant triangles that are probably not visible. In particular, you can see this parameter's influence on the stairs' shading in Figure 12-10. Listing 12-5 shows the details.

Listing 12-5. Triangle Attenuation

```
// Get the triangle's occlusion.
float elementOcclusion = . . .

// Compute the point-to-triangle form factor.
contribution = computeFormFactor(. . .);

// Modulate by its occlusion raised to a power.
contribution *= pow(elementOcclusion, triangleAttenuation);
```

12.7 Future Work

We have presented a robust, GPU-accelerated algorithm for computing high-quality ambient occlusion. By adaptively traversing the approximation of a shadow caster, we both quickly produce smooth soft shadows and reconstruct sharp local details.

We conclude by noting that this adaptive integration scheme is not limited to computing ambient occlusion. Bunnell 2005 showed how the same scheme could be used to compute indirect lighting. We also point out that subsurface scattering may be computed with the same hierarchical integration method. As shown in Figure 12-11, we can implement a multiple scattering technique (Jensen and Buhler 2002) in our framework simply by computing irradiance at each disk and then replacing calls to `solidAngle()` with `multipleScattering()`. Listing 12-6 shows the details.

Figure 12-11. Multiple Scattering Implemented via Hierarchical Integration

Listing 12-6. Implementing Multiple Scattering

```
float3 multipleScattering(float d2,
                          float3 zr,      // Scattering parameters
                          float3 zv,      // defined in
                          float3 sig_tr)  // Jensen and Buhler 2002
{
  float3 r2   = float3(d2, d2, d2);
  float3 dr1  = rsqrt(r2 + (zr * zr));
  float3 dv1  = rsqrt(r2 + (zv * zv));
  float3 C1   = zr * (sig_tr + dr1);
  float3 C2   = zv * (sig_tr + dv1);
  float3 dL   = C1 * exp(-sig_tr/dr1) * dr1 * dr1;
         dL  += C2 * exp(-sig_tr/dv1) * dv1 * dv1;
  return dL;
}
```

We include this effect alongside our ambient occlusion implementation on this book's accompanying DVD. Because many illumination effects may be defined as an integral over scene surfaces, we encourage the reader to generalize this technique to quickly generate other dazzling effects.

12.8 References

Bunnell, Michael. 2005. "Dynamic Ambient Occlusion and Indirect Lighting." In *GPU Gems 2*, edited by Matt Pharr, pp. 223–233. Addison-Wesley.

Jensen, Henrik Wann, and Juan Buhler. 2002. "A Rapid Hierarchical Rendering Technique for Translucent Materials." In *ACM Transactions on Graphics (Proceedings of SIGGRAPH 2002)* 21(3).

Sillion, François X., and Claude Puech. 1994. *Radiosity and Global Illumination.* Morgan Kaufmann.

Chapter 13

Volumetric Light Scattering as a Post-Process

Kenny Mitchell
Electronic Arts

In this chapter, we present a simple post-process method that produces the effect of volumetric light scattering due to shadows in the atmosphere. We improve an existing analytic model of daylight scattering to include the effect of volumetric occlusion, and we present its implementation in a pixel shader. The demo, which is included on the DVD accompanying this book, shows the technique can be applied to any animating image of arbitrary scene complexity. A screenshot from the demo appears in Figure 13-1.

13.1 Introduction

In the real world, we rarely see things in a vacuum, where nothing exists between an object and its observer. In real-time rendering, the effect of participating media on light transport is often subject to low-complexity homogeneous assumptions. This is due to the intractable nature of the radiative transport equation (Jensen and Christensen 1998), accounting for emission, absorption, and scattering, in a complex interactive animated environment. In this chapter, we consider the effect of volumetric shadows in the atmosphere on light scattering, and we show how this effect can be computed in real time with a GPU pixel shader post-process applied to one or more image light sources.

Figure 13-1. Volumetric Light Scattering on a Highly Animated Scene in Real Time

13.2 Crepuscular Rays

Under the right conditions, when a space contains a sufficiently dense mixture of light-scattering media such as gas molecules and aerosols, light occluding objects will cast volumes of shadow and appear to create rays of light radiating from the light source. These phenomena are variously known as crepuscular rays, sunbeams, sunbursts, star flare, god rays, or light shafts. In sunlight, such volumes are effectively parallel but appear to spread out from the sun in perspective.

Rendering crepuscular rays was first tackled in non-real-time rendering using a modified shadow volume algorithm (Max 1986) and shortly after that, an approach was developed for multiple light sources (Nishita et al. 1987). This topic was revisited in real-time rendering, using a slice-based volume-rendering technique (Dobashi et al. 2002) and more recently applied using hardware shadow maps (Mitchell 2004). However, slice-based volume-rendering methods can exhibit sampling artifacts, demand high fill rate, and require extra scene setup. While a shadow-map method increases efficiency, here it also has the slice-based detractors and requires further video memory resources and rendering synchronization. Another real-time method, based on the work of Radomir Mech (2001), uses polygonal volumes (James 2003), in which overlapping volumes are accumulated using frame-buffer blending with depth peeling. A similar method (James 2004) removes the need for depth peeling using accumulated volume thickness. In our approach, we apply a per-pixel post-processing operation that requires no preprocessing or other scene setup, and which allows for detailed light shafts in animating scenes of arbitrary complexity.

In previous work (Hoffman and Preetham 2003), a GPU shader for light scattering in homogeneous media is implemented. We extend this with a post-processing step to account for volumetric shadows. The basic manifestation of this post-process can be traced to an image-processing operation, *radial blur*, which appears in many CG demo productions (Karras 1997). Although such demos used software rasterization to apply a post-processing effect, we use hardware-accelerated shader post-processing to permit more sophisticated sampling based on an analytic model of daylight.

13.3 Volumetric Light Scattering

To calculate the illumination at each pixel, we must account for scattering from the light source to that pixel and whether or not the scattering media is occluded. In the case of sunlight, we begin with our analytic model of daylight scattering (Hoffman and Preetham 2003). Recall the following:

$$L(s, \theta) = L_0 e^{-\beta_{ex}s} + \frac{1}{\beta_{ex}} E_{sun} \beta_{sc}(\theta)\left(1 - e^{-\beta_{ex}s}\right), \tag{1}$$

where s is the distance traveled through the media and θ is the angle between the ray and the sun. E_{sun} is the source illumination from the sun, β_{ex} is the extinction constant composed of light absorption and out-scattering properties, and β_{sc} is the angular scattering term composed of Rayleigh and Mie scattering properties. The important aspect of this equation is that the first term calculates the amount of light absorbed from the point of emission to the viewpoint and the second term calculates the additive amount due to light scattering into the path of the view ray. As in Hoffman and Mitchell 2002, the effect due to occluding matter such as clouds, buildings, and other objects is modeled here simply as an attenuation of the source illumination,

$$L(s, \theta, \phi) = (1 - D(\phi))L(s, \theta), \tag{2}$$

where $D(\phi)$ is the combined attenuated sun-occluding objects' opacity for the view location ϕ.

This consideration introduces the complication of determining the occlusion of the light source for every point in the image. In screen space, we don't have full volumetric information to determine occlusion. However, we can estimate the probability of occlusion at each pixel by summing samples along a ray to the light source in image space. The proportion of samples that hit the emissive region versus those that strike occluders gives us the desired percentage of occlusion, $D(\phi)$. This estimate works best where the emissive region is brighter than the occluding objects. In Section 13.5, we describe methods for dealing with scenes in which this contrast is not present.

If we divide the sample illumination by the number of samples, n, the post-process simply resolves to an additive sampling of the image:

$$L(s, \theta, \phi) = \sum_{i=0}^{n} \frac{L(s_i, \theta_i)}{n}. \tag{3}$$

13.3.1 Controlling the Summation

In addition, we introduce attenuation coefficients to parameterize control of the summation:

$$L(s, \theta, \phi) = exposure \times \sum_{i=0}^{n} decay^i \times weight \times \frac{L(s_i, \theta_i)}{n}, \tag{4}$$

where *exposure* controls the overall intensity of the post-process, *weight* controls the intensity of each sample, and *decay^i* (for the range [0, 1]) dissipates each sample's contribution as the ray progresses away from the light source. This exponential decay factor practically allows each light shaft to fall off smoothly away from the light source.

The exposure and weight factors are simply scale factors. Increasing either of these increases the overall brightness of the result. In the demo, the sample weight is adjusted with fine-grain control and the exposure is adjusted with coarse-grain control.

Because samples are derived purely from the source image, semitransparent objects are handled with no additional effort. Multiple light sources can be applied through successive additive screen-space passes for each ray-casting light source. Although in this explanation we have used our analytic daylight model, in fact, any image source may be used.

For the sun location, α, and each screen-space image location, ϕ, we implement the summation with successive samples from the source image at regular intervals along the ray vector, $\Delta\phi = (\phi - \alpha)/n(density)$. Here we introduce *density* to permit control over the separation between samples for cases in which we wish to reduce the overall number of sample iterations while retaining a sufficiently alias-free sampling density. If we increase the density factor, we decrease the separation between samples, resulting in brighter light shafts covering a shorter range.

In Figure 13-2, no samples from ϕ_1 are occluded, resulting in maximum scattering illumination under regular evaluation of $L(s, \theta)$. At ϕ_2, a proportion of samples along the ray hit the building, and so less scattering illumination is accumulated. By summing over cast rays for each pixel in the image, we generate volumes containing occluded light scattering.

We may reduce the bandwidth requirements by downsampling the source image. With filtering, this reduces sampling artifacts and consequently introduces a local scattering contribution by neighborhood sampling due to the filter kernel. In the demo, a basic bilinear filter is sufficient.

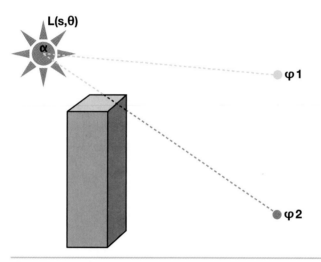

Figure 13-2. Ray Casting in Screen Space

13.4 The Post-Process Pixel Shader

The core of this technique is the post-process pixel shader, given in Listing 13-1, which implements the simple summation of Equation 4.

Given the initial image, sample coordinates are generated along a ray cast from the pixel location to the screen-space light position.[1] The light position in screen space is computed by the standard world-view-project transform and is scaled and biased to obtain coordinates in the range $[-1, 1]$. Successive samples $L(s, \theta, \phi_i)$ in the summation of Equation 4 are scaled by both the *weight* constant and the exponential *decay* attenuation

---

1. When facing away from the light source, the sample ray is consequently inverted to create the appearance of anti-crepuscular rays.

coefficients for the purpose of parameterizing control of the effect. The separation between samples' *density* may be adjusted and as a final control factor, the resulting combined color is scaled by a constant attenuation coefficient *exposure*.

Listing 13-1. Post-Process Shader Implementation of Additive Sampling

```
float4 main(float2 texCoord : TEXCOORD0) : COLOR0
{
    // Calculate vector from pixel to light source in screen space.
    half2 deltaTexCoord = (texCoord - ScreenLightPos.xy);

    // Divide by number of samples and scale by control factor.
    deltaTexCoord *= 1.0f / NUM_SAMPLES * Density;

    // Store initial sample.
    half3 color = tex2D(frameSampler, texCoord);

    // Set up illumination decay factor.
    half illuminationDecay = 1.0f;

    // Evaluate summation from Equation 3 NUM_SAMPLES iterations.
    for (int i = 0; i < NUM_SAMPLES; i++)
    {
        // Step sample location along ray.
        texCoord -= deltaTexCoord;

        // Retrieve sample at new location.
        half3 sample = tex2D(frameSampler, texCoord);

        // Apply sample attenuation scale/decay factors.
        sample *= illuminationDecay * Weight;

        // Accumulate combined color.
        color += sample;

        // Update exponential decay factor.
        illuminationDecay *= Decay;
    }

    // Output final color with a further scale control factor.
    return float4( color * Exposure, 1);
}
```

13.5 Screen-Space Occlusion Methods

As stated, sampling in screen space is not a pure occlusion sampling. Undesirable streaks may occur due to surface texture variations. Fortunately, we can use the following measures to deal with these undesirable effects.

13.5.1 The Occlusion Pre-Pass Method

If we render the occluding objects black and untextured into the source frame buffer, image processing to generate light rays is performed on this image. Then the occluding scene objects are rendered with regular shading, and the post-processing result is additively blended into the scene. This approach goes hand in hand with the common technique of rendering an unshaded depth pre-pass to limit the depth complexity of fully shaded pixels. Figure 13-3 shows the steps involved.

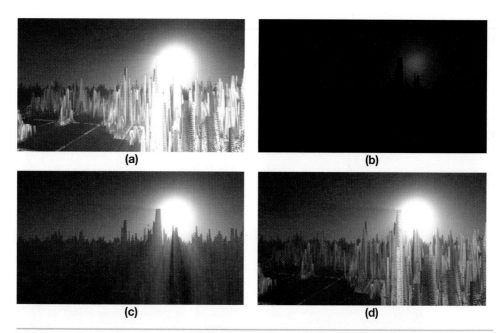

Figure 13-3. The Effect of the Occlusion Pre-Pass
Without an occlusion pre-pass, we may see streaks (a), so we render objects black (b) and perform the post-process (c) additively to get the fully shadowed scene (d).

13.5.2 The Occlusion Stencil Method

On earlier graphics hardware the same results can be achieved without a pre-pass by using a stencil buffer or alpha buffer. The primary emissive elements of the image (such as the sky) are rendered as normal while simultaneously setting a stencil bit. Then the occluding scene objects are rendered with no stencil bit. When it comes to applying the post-process, only those samples with the stencil bit set contribute to the additive blend.

13.5.3 The Occlusion Contrast Method

Equally though, this problem may be managed by reducing texture contrast through the texture's content, fog, aerial perspective, or light adaption as the intensity of the effect increases when facing the light source. Anything that reduces the illumination frequency and contrast of the occluding objects diminishes streaking artifacts.

13.6 Caveats

Although compelling results can be achieved, this method is not without limitations. Light shafts from background objects can appear in front of foreground objects, when dealing with relatively near light sources, as shown in Figure 13-4. In a full radiative transfer solution, the foreground object would correctly obscure the background shaft. One reason this is less noticeable than expected is that it can be perceived as the manifestation of a camera lens effect, in which light scattering occurs in a layer in front of the scene. This artifact can also be reduced in the presence of high-frequency textured objects.

Figure 13-4. Dealing with One Limitation
Shadows appear to pass in front of foreground objects (left) only if the light source is finitely distant. Otherwise, the effect is less perceivable if these objects are textured (right).

As occluding objects cross the image's boundary, the shafts will flicker, because they are beyond the range of visible samples. This artifact may be reduced by rendering an extended region around the screen to increase the range of addressable samples.

Finally, when facing perpendicular to the source, the light's screen-space location can tend toward infinity and therefore lead to large separation between samples. This can be diminished by clamping the screen-space location to an appropriate guard-band region. Alternatively, the effect can be faded toward the perpendicular and is further decreased when using an occlusion method.

13.7 The Demo

The demo on this book's DVD uses Shader Model 3.0 to apply the post-process, because the number of texture samples needed exceeds the limits of Shader Model 2.0. However, the effect has been implemented almost as efficiently with earlier graphics hardware by using additive frame-buffer blending over multiple passes with a stencil occlusion method, as shown in Figure 13-5.

Figure 13-5. Crepuscular Rays with Multiple Additive Frame-Buffer Passes on Fixed-Function Hardware

13.8 Extensions

Sampling may occur at a lower resolution to reduce texture bandwidth requirements. A further enhancement is to vary the sample pattern with stochastic sampling, thus reducing regular pattern artifacts where sampling density is reduced.

Our method performs the post-process in a single-pass execution of a shader. In one multipass approach, the pixel shader summation may be performed where the results of concentric rectangular bands emanating from the light source may be accumulated into successive outer bands, where $L(s, \theta, \phi) = L_{i-1}(s, \theta, \phi) + L_i(s, \theta, \phi)$. While this may not be most suited to current hardware design, this approach is the minimal required sampling and computation limit.

Creating a balance between light shaft intensity and avoiding oversaturation requires adjustments of the attenuation coefficients. An analytic formula that performs light adaption to a consistent image tone balance may yield an automatic method for obtaining a consistently perceived image. For example, perhaps we can evaluate a combination of average, minimum, and maximum illumination across the image and then apply a corrective color ramp, thus avoiding excessive image bloom or gloominess.

13.9 Summary

We have shown a simple post-process method that produces the effect of volumetric light scattering due to shadows in the atmosphere. We have expanded an existing analytic model of daylight scattering to include the contribution of volumetric occlusion, and we have described its implementation in a pixel shader. The demo shows that this is a practical technique that can be applied to any animating image of arbitrary scene complexity.

13.10 References

Dobashi, Y., T. Yamamoto, and T. Nishita. 2002. "Interactive Rendering of Atmospheric Scattering Effects Using Graphics Hardware." *Graphics Hardware.*

Hoffman, N., and K. Mitchell. 2002. "Methods for Dynamic, Photorealistic Terrain Lighting." In *Game Programming Gems 3*, edited by D. Treglia, pp. 433–443. Charles River Media.

Hoffman, N., and A. Preetham. 2003. "Real-Time Light-Atmosphere Interactions for Outdoor Scenes." In *Graphics Programming Methods*, edited by Jeff Lander, pp. 337–352. Charles River Media.

James, R. 2003. "True Volumetric Shadows." In *Graphics Programming Methods*, edited by Jeff Lander, pp. 353–366. Charles River Media.

Jensen, H. W., and P. H. Christensen. 1998. "Efficient Simulation of Light Transport in Scenes with Participating Media Using Photon Maps." In *Proceedings of SIGGRAPH 98*, pp. 311–320.

Karras, T. 1997. Drain by Vista. *Abduction'97.* Available online at http://www.pouet.net/prod.php?which=418&page=0.

Max, N. 1986. "Atmospheric Illumination and Shadows." In *Computer Graphics (Proceedings of SIGGRAPH 86)* 20(4), pp. 117–124.

Mech, R. 2001. "Hardware-Accelerated Real-Time Rendering of Gaseous Phenomena." *Journal of Graphics Tools* 6(3), pp. 1–16.

Mitchell, J. 2004. "Light Shafts: Rendering Shadows in Participating Media." Presentation at Game Developers Conference 2004.

Nishita, T., Y. Miyawaki, and E. Nakamae. 1987. "A Shading Model for Atmospheric Scattering Considering Luminous Intensity Distribution of Light Sources." In *Computer Graphics (Proceedings of SIGGRAPH 87)* 21(4), pp. 303–310.

PART III
RENDERING

Programmable hardware and high-level shading languages have enabled an unlimited number of rendering effects. Developers are using GPUs in new, interesting, and unexpected ways, taking advantage of their horsepower to create unprecedented, real-time effects. Much of the inspiration for these effects comes from the movie industry. Many of the chapters in this section borrow ideas from techniques employed in high-quality, final-frame renders and are able to achieve realism previously obtained only in offline rendering.

A good example is the impressive face rendering depicted on our book cover. Employing physically accurate models, **Eugene d'Eon** and **David Luebke** demonstrate how to adapt them to the GPU to produce highly realistic, real-time images of human skin. In **Chapter 14, "Advanced Techniques for Realistic Real-Time Skin Rendering,"** our contributors show how to achieve these images by combining physically based BRDFs, translucent shadow maps, and subsurface scattering via a variant of texture-space diffusion.

To create believable characters, it's not enough to accurately render skin surfaces—it's also necessary to realistically animate facial expressions. A major problem of most geometry animation systems is that they don't capture the infinite complexity of the human face. Eyebrow movements, lip stretches, skin wrinkles, and subtle lighting changes are usually not modeled by these systems. Yet **George Borshukov, Jefferson Montgomery**, and **John Hable** achieve realism by capturing details from real characters and storing them as animated diffuse maps. Their solution is a real-time implementation of Universal Capture, a technique used in noninteractive films such as *The Matrix*. In **Chapter 15, "Playable Universal Capture,"** the authors describe how this technique is also practical for video games by using principal component analysis to compress the large data sets that result from the motion capture.

Crysis has already become a synonym for gorgeous islands, lush jungles, and stunning visuals. Proud of constantly pushing the envelope, **Tiago Sousa** reveals where his inspiration comes from: the techniques employed in DreamWorks' animated movie *Madagascar*. In **Chapter 16, "Vegetation Procedural**

Animation and Shading in *Crysis*,**" Tiago gives us an overview of the procedural animation techniques and shading methods that enable rendering these immersive and densely populated environments.

Although they are standard in the domain of offline rendering, complex refractions and reflections are hard to render in real time. However, in **Chapter 17, "Robust Multiple Specular Reflections and Refractions," Tamás Umenhoffer**, **Gustavo Patow**, and **László Szirmay-Kalos** challenge common knowledge and show us how to use the power of modern GPUs to convincingly simulate these ray tracing effects, bringing them into the realm of real-time rendering.

Relief mapping is becoming a more attractive approach for adding geometric details to object surfaces. Still, popular implementations are neither powerful nor effective enough for use in real game scenarios. In **Chapter 18, "Relaxed Cone Stepping for Relief Mapping," Fabio Policarpo** and **Manuel Oliveira** present a robust and efficient technique that increases the performance of previous approaches and eliminates their distracting artifacts. After reading this chapter, developers won't have an excuse not to enable relief mapping as an integral effect of their rendering pipelines.

Chapter 19, "Deferred Shading in *Tabula Rasa*," revisits and expands upon a topic from the second volume in our series. Since *GPU Gems 2*, deferred shading became very popular, but many developers realized that the road to successfully implementing it was challenging. **Rusty Koonce** was kind enough to share his experiences writing the deferred shading engine for the game *Tabula Rasa*, NCsoft's latest MMO. His chapter is full of chewy ideas and interesting tidbits, and I'm sure many readers will appreciate the author for taking the time and effort to present it in a readable format.

Finally, in **Chapter 20, "GPU-Based Importance Sampling," Mark Colbert** and **Jaroslav Křivánek** borrow techniques from high-quality renders to evaluate realistic BRDFs in a way that requires minimal precomputation. As a result, these BRDFs are suitable for use in dynamic environments with varying lighting conditions, making them appealing for use in real-time game environments.

The chapters in this part of the book demonstrate that real-time rendering is still an exciting area of exploration, and I'm sure they will open your imagination and inspire you to create realistic, real-time characters and environments never seen before.

I'd like to thank all the authors for their great work and effort, and the peer reviewers for spending their valuable time to make this book even better. With their help it has been very rewarding to assemble this section. I hope you will have as much fun reading it as I had editing it.

Ignacio Castaño Aguado, NVIDIA Corporation

Chapter 14

Advanced Techniques for Realistic Real-Time Skin Rendering

Eugene d'Eon
NVIDIA Corporation

David Luebke
NVIDIA Corporation

The shading performance of modern GPUs, coupled with advances in 3D scanning technology, research in rendering of subsurface scattering effects, and a detailed understanding of the physical composition of skin, has made it possible to generate incredibly realistic real-time images of human skin and faces. Figure 14-1 shows one example. In this chapter, we present advanced techniques for generating such images. Our goal throughout is to employ the most physically accurate models available that exhibit a tractable real-time implementation. Such physically based models provide flexibility by supporting realistic rendering across different lighting scenarios and requiring the least amount of tweaking to get great results.

14.1 The Appearance of Skin

Skin has always been difficult to render: it has many subtle visual characteristics, and human viewers are acutely sensitive to the appearance of skin in general and faces in particular. The sheer amount of detail in human skin presents one barrier. A realistic model of skin must include wrinkles, pores, freckles, hair follicles, scars, and so on. Fortunately, modern 3D scanning technology allows us to capture even this extreme

Figure 14-1. Real-Time Rendering of Realistic Human Skin
The techniques discussed in this chapter require no preprocessing, enabling deformable or animated models, and support distant and local dynamic lighting with both high- and low-frequency content.

level of detail. However, naively rendering the resulting model gives an unrealistic, hard, dry-looking appearance, as you can see in Figure 14-2a. What's missing? The difficulties arise mainly due to *subsurface scattering*, the process whereby light goes beneath the skin surface, scatters and gets partially absorbed, and then exits somewhere else. Skin is in fact slightly translucent; this subtle but crucial effect gives skin its soft appearance and is absolutely vital for realistic rendering, as shown in Figure 14-2b.

For most materials, the reflectance of light is usually separated into two components that are handled independently: (1) surface reflectance, typically approximated with a simple specular calculation; and (2) subsurface scattering, typically approximated with a simple diffuse calculation. However, both of these components require more advanced models to generate realistic imagery for skin. Even the highly detailed diffuse, specular, and normal maps available with modern scanning techniques will not make skin look real without accurate specular reflection and subsurface scattering.

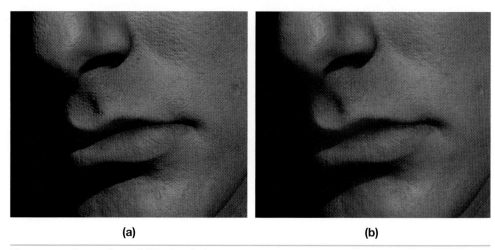

(a)   (b)

Figure 14-2. Comparison of Skin Rendering
(a) The rendering ignores subsurface scattering, creating a hard, dry appearance. (b) The rendering accounts for subsurface scattering, creating soft, believable skin.

14.1.1 Skin Surface Reflectance

A small fraction of the light incident on a skin surface (roughly 6 percent over the entire spectrum (Tuchin 2000)) reflects directly, without being colored. This is due to a Fresnel interaction with the topmost layer of the skin, which is rough and oily, and we can model it using a specular reflection function. We illustrate this process in Figure 14-3 in relation to a multilayer skin model that works well for skin rendering (Donner and Jensen 2006). The light reflects directly off of the oily layer and the epidermis without entering and without being scattered or colored. The reflection is not a perfect mirror-like reflection because the surface of skin has a very fine-scale roughness, causing a single incident angle to reflect into a range of exitant angles. We can describe the effect of this roughness with a specular *bidirectional reflectance distribution function*, or BRDF.

Simple empirical specular calculations, such as the familiar Blinn-Phong model long supported by OpenGL and Direct3D, do not accurately approximate the specular reflectance of skin. Physically based specular models provide more accurate-looking results, leading to more realistic images. In Section 14.3, we explore one such model (used to compute all the images shown in this chapter) and show how to implement it efficiently on the GPU.

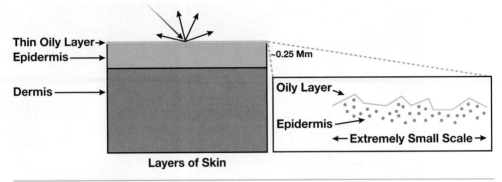

Figure 14-3. A Multilayer Skin Model
Light reflecting directly off the topmost, rough, oily layer of skin does not enter the tissue layers and is not colored by them. We simulate this process using a physically based, specular reflection term.

14.1.2 Skin Subsurface Reflectance

Any light not directly reflected at the skin surface enters the subsurface layers. The scattering and absorption of light in subsurface tissue layers give skin its color and soft appearance. Light enters these layers, where it is partially absorbed (acquiring color) and scattered often, returning and exiting the surface in a 3D neighborhood surrounding the point of entry. Sometimes light travels completely through thin regions such as ears. A realistic skin shader must model this scattering process; Figure 14-2a appears hard and dry precisely because this process is ignored and because light can reflect only from the location where it first touches the surface.

Complicating the process further, multiple layers within the skin actually absorb and scatter light differently, as shown in Figure 14-4. Graphics researchers have produced very detailed models that describe optical scattering in skin using as many as five separate layers (Krishnaswamy and Baranoski 2004). Real skin is even more complex; medically, the epidermis alone is considered to contain five distinct layers (Poirer 2004). Simulating scattering at this complexity is probably excessive, but realistic rendering requires modeling at least two distinct layers below the oily layer responsible for specular reflection. Donner and Jensen 2005 demonstrate that a single-layer model is insufficient and show the improvement obtained from using a three-layer model. We show a similar comparison in Figure 14-11, in Section 14.4.3, using our real-time system, which is capable of modeling this multilayer scattering. Donner and Jensen 2006 later introduce a two-layer model that still gives convincing results.

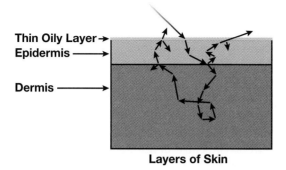

Thin Oily Layer →
Epidermis ——————→

Dermis ——————→

Layers of Skin

Figure 14-4. Scattering and Absorption in Multiple Tissue Layers
The reflectance of light from skin is complicated by such physical phenomena. Maximum realism requires modeling at least two distinct scattering layers.

To simulate this process for the purpose of image synthesis, researchers have borrowed (and improved upon) scattering models from the physics community. A certain class of scattering models has proven very successful for skin rendering. Beneath the skin surface, the incoming light quickly becomes diffuse as it scatters: photons scatter often in the tissue layers, and after only a few scattering events, even a completely coherent beam of light will be flowing equally in all directions. This simplifies the general scattering problem greatly, leading to what are called *diffusion models*. However, diffusion models remain mathematically sophisticated and the literature can be challenging to read. In Section 14.5, we discuss shading operations, many as simple as blurring an image, that serve to accurately and efficiently simulate the core effects of these models, allowing easy-to-program GPU algorithms that produce realistic, real-time images.

14.2 An Overview of the Skin-Rendering System

The following sections present the details of our real-time skin-rendering system, which is the sum of a specular reflection component and a subsurface scattering component. The GPU implementation of both components is described in detail, including a review of diffuse scattering theory and presentation of a new formulation for scattering profiles.

Section 14.3 addresses the topmost interaction of light and skin, specular surface reflectance, and discusses an efficient implementation of the Kelemen and Szirmay-Kalos 2001 analytic BRDF. This model closely approximates the Torrance/Sparrow model, which has been shown to produce realistic images of faces (Donner and Jensen 2005,

Donner and Jensen 2006, Weyrich et al. 2006) but is significantly cheaper to evaluate and gives much of the same appearance. Measured parameters from Weyrich et al. 2006 work well for tuning both models for rendering faces.

In Section 14.4 we review existing scattering theory, with a focus on diffusion profiles, how they are used to render images with subsurface scattering, and in particular how their exact shape is important for producing a realistic skin appearance. We present a new sum-of-Gaussians formulation of diffusion profiles that has many advantages, including new rendering algorithms presented in Section 14.5. The new formulation can closely approximate the popular dipole (Jensen et al. 2001) and multipole (Donner and Jensen 2005) analytic diffusion profiles, and we discuss how to accurately fit Gaussian sums to known profiles (with a brief error analysis). The sum-of-Gaussians profiles for the three-layer skin model used to render all images in this chapter are given as a starting point for the reader.

In Section 14.5, we begin by modifying texture-space diffusion (Borshukov and Lewis 2003) to take advantage of the sum-of-Gaussians diffusion profiles by convolving irradiance separably and hierarchically, similar to Green 2004. However, a series of intermediate Gaussian convolution textures are retained and combined in the final render pass to quickly and accurately approximate the scattering predicted by a multilayered model. Distortions that arise when convolving in texture space are corrected similar to Gosselin 2004 by using a stretch texture that locally corrects convolution kernels. However, our stretch-correction texture corrects for distortions in both the U and V directions independently and is quickly computed using a simple fragment shader (allowing considerable deformations of the mesh and eliminating the need for precomputation and artist input).

Transmission through thin surface regions such as ears is accomplished by modifying *translucent shadow maps* (Dachsbacher and Stamminger 2004) to compute depth through the surface and to connect shadowed regions to locations on the light-facing surface, where multiple convolutions of irradiance are available by accessing the same textures computed for local scattering. The separability of Gaussians in the third dimension is exploited to reuse 2D convolutions of irradiance when computing the desired 3D convolution.

Finally, in Section 14.6, the same separable and hierarchical techniques used to accelerate subsurface scattering are used to accelerate 2D convolution with a wide, nonseparable bloom filter by approximating it as a sum of two Gaussians.

14.3 Specular Surface Reflectance

The Phong specular model is almost ubiquitous in real-time computer graphics, but using a more accurate physically based surface reflectance model can easily improve image quality at a cost of a few extra shader instructions. The Phong model fails to capture increased specularity at grazing angles and is not physically plausible (it can output more energy than it receives, for example). Figure 14-5 demonstrates the limitations of the Phong model compared to a physically based specular BRDF.

This section discusses the implementation of physically based specular BRDFs in general, as well as specific details pertaining to skin rendering. We present an efficient implementation of the Kelemen/Szirmay-Kalos model and discuss all of the model parameters and how they are adjusted for rendering skin.

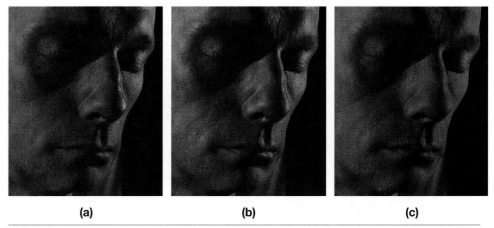

| (a) | (b) | (c) |

Figure 14-5. Comparing the Kelemen/Szirmay-Kalos Specular BRDF to the Phong Model
The popular Phong model provides a reasonable approximation of specular reflectance for a fixed light and view direction, but it fails to capture increased brightness at grazing angles seen in skin and other materials. In (b) we show a Phong specular term adjusted to match the bright specular highlights on the right side of the physically based image (a); the result is overly specular on the left, resulting in an oily appearance. In (c) we adjust a Phong specular term to match the subtle specular highlights on the left of (a), losing the bright specular on the right and producing a flat, dry appearance.

14.3.1 Implementing a Physically Based Specular Reflectance Model for Skin

Many physically based specular BRDFs from computer graphics literature can be used to improve the realism of skin rendering. We first discuss implementation details common to all BRDF models and then give the specifics of the Kelemen/Szirmay-Kalos model that we chose for its efficient evaluation.

Rendering with a BRDF

Most specular BRDF models describe reflectance with analytic functions that are straightforward to evaluate in a fragment shader. Such models are typically the product of several terms, such as Fresnel and geometric attenuation terms, and have several parameters.

These analytic BRDFs typically have a constant `rho_s` term that scales their intensity. The other common inputs are surface normal `N`, view vector `V`, light vector `L`, index of refraction `eta` (needed for the Fresnel term), and a roughness parameter `m`. The total specular reflectance for each light is then:

```
specularLight += lightColor[i] * lightShadow[i] * rho_s *
        specBRDF( N, V, L[i], eta, m) * saturate( dot( N, L[i] ) );
```

Because of the definition of a BRDF, the `dot(N, L[i])` term is required in addition to computing the BRDF itself. A distance attenuation term may also be added per light to reduce intensity as a function of the distance to the light source. This code works for point, directional, or spotlights, for which an `L` vector and a shadow term can be computed. Specular reflections from rough surfaces due to environment map light sources or area lights—called glossy reflections—are complicated and computationally quite costly and we do not incorporate them into our skin rendering system. The interested reader should see Kautz and McCool 2000 for a real-time technique that uses prefiltered environment maps.

Fresnel Reflectance for Rendering Skin

All physically based specular BRDF models contain a Fresnel term, which is typically not explained in detail. This should be an unpolarized, dielectric Fresnel reflectance function with an F_0 (or R_0) parameter (reflectance at normal incidence) of 0.028. This comes from Beer's Law and assumes an index of refraction for skin of 1.4 (Donner and Jensen 2006). Pharr and Humphreys 2004 provide an excellent presentation of Fresnel reflectance and Beer's Law, and we will not repeat the formulae here. When computing a Fresnel term for a rough surface like skin, all θ terms should be measured from the half-angle vector, **H**, and not from **N**. Schlick's Fresnel approximation (Schlick 1993) works well for skin, as shown in Figure 14-6. Listing 14-1 gives the function for computing the Schlick Fresnel reflectance.

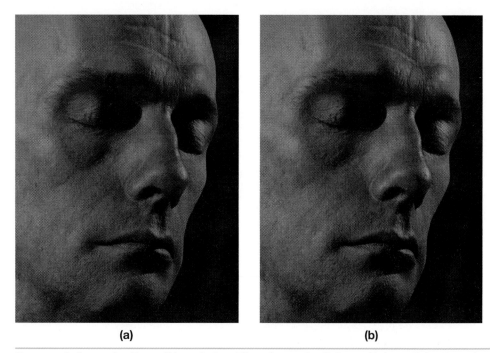

| (a) | (b) |

Figure 14-6. Comparing Fresnel Formulations When Computing Kelemen/Szirmay-Kalos Specular Reflectance
(a) Using the textbook Fresnel formula. (b) Using Schlick's Fresnel approximation. The approximation in (b) looks very similar to (a) but saves 37 shader instructions.

Listing 14-1. A Function for Computing the Fresnel Reflectance in Specular BRDFs

H is the standard half-angle vector. F0 is reflectance at normal incidence (for skin use 0.028).

```
float fresnelReflectance( float3 H, float3 V, float F0 )
{
  float base = 1.0 - dot( V, H );
  float exponential = pow( base, 5.0 );
  return exponential + F0 * ( 1.0 - exponential );
}
```

Factoring BRDFs for Efficient Evaluation

Heidrich and Seidel 1999 describe a precomputation strategy useful for efficiently evaluating BRDF models, based on factoring the BRDF into multiple precomputed 2D textures. We employ a similar approach to efficiently compute the Kelemen/Szirmay-Kalos specular BRDF, but instead we precompute a single texture (the Beckmann distribution function) and use the Schlick Fresnel approximation for a fairly efficient specular reflectance calculation that allows m, the roughness parameter, to vary over the object.

We first render a screen-aligned quad with the fragment shader shown in Listing 14-2, which precomputes the Beckmann distribution texture. Figure 14-7c shows the resulting texture. This step can be done once when the application starts or simply saved to a texture file for later use. We use an exponential scale and halve the resulting value to map the function into a range we can store in an 8-bit texture and then we invert this mapping during the specular computation. (Alternatively, we could use a floating-point texture to reduce computation at the cost of texture bandwidth.) Listing 14-3 gives the final specular function used to render with the precomputed texture. Figure 14-7 compares the full specular computation to the fast version for a range of roughness values. Only the specular reflection is shown. It is difficult to distinguish the approximation from the full BRDF evaluation.

Listing 14-2. Code to Precompute the Beckmann Texture

```
float PHBeckmann( float ndoth, float m )
{
  float alpha = acos( ndoth );
  float ta = tan( alpha );
  float val = 1.0/(m*m*pow(ndoth,4.0))*exp(-(ta*ta)/(m*m));
  return val;
}
// Render a screen-aligned quad to precompute a 512x512 texture.
float KSTextureCompute(float2 tex : TEXCOORD0)
{
  // Scale the value to fit within [0,1] - invert upon lookup.
  return 0.5 * pow( PHBeckmann( tex.x, tex.y ), 0.1 );
}
```

Listing 14-3. Computing Kelemen/Szirmay-Kalos Specular Using a Precomputed Beckmann Texture

```
float KS_Skin_Specular( float3 N, // Bumped surface normal
                        float3 L, // Points to light
                        float3 V, // Points to eye
                        float m,  // Roughness
                        float rho_s, // Specular brightness
                        uniform texobj2D beckmannTex )
{
  float result = 0.0;
  float ndotl = dot( N, L );
```

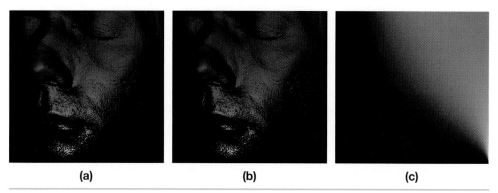

(a)   **(b)**   **(c)**

Figure 14-7. Comparing Direct Computation of the Specular Model to the Fast Version
*(a) Directly evaluating the analytic Kelemen/Szirmay-Kalos specular BRDF model. (b) The
optimized version uses a precomputed texture for the Beckmann distribution. The roughness
parameter* m *varies from 0.05 at the chin to 0.6 at the top to illustrate that the optimization
approximates the analytic model well for a wide range of roughness values. (c) The precomputed
texture generated by Listing 14-2. The horizontal axis represents* dot (N, H) *from 0 (left) to 1
(right), and the vertical axis represents roughness parameter* m *from 0 (bottom) to 1 (top).*

Listing 14-3 (*continued*). Computing Kelemen/Szirmay-Kalos Specular Using a Precomputed
Beckmann Texture

```
if( ndotl > 0.0 )
{
    float3 h = L + V; // Unnormalized half-way vector
    float3 H = normalize( h );
    float ndoth = dot( N, H );
    float PH = pow( 2.0*f1tex2D(beckmannTex,float2(ndoth,m)), 10.0 );
    float F = fresnelReflectance( H, V, 0.028 );
    float frSpec = max( PH * F / dot( h, h ), 0 );
    result = ndotl * rho_s * frSpec; // BRDF * dot(N,L) * rho_s
}
return result;
}
```

Specular Reflectance from Skin Is White

The tissue cells and oil in the outermost layer of skin are dielectric materials that reflect
light without coloring it (whereas metals such as gold color the light that is reflected due
to highly varying indices of refraction over visible wavelengths of light.) Thus, a physically
based skin shader should use a white specular color. In other words, the specular reflection
of a white light from skin will be white, and the specular reflection of a colored light will

be the same color as that light—regardless of the color of the underlying skin. A common problem encountered when rendering skin without proper gamma correction (see Chapter 24 of this book, "The Importance of Being Linear") is an overly yellow color when adding white specular reflectance to the diffuse subsurface scattering term. If all rendering is done in a linear color space and displayed correctly, the specular color should not need to be adjusted to something other than white.

Varying Specular Parameters over the Face

A survey of human faces presented by Weyrich et al. 2006 provides measured parameters for the Torrance/Sparrow specular BRDF model with the Beckmann microfacet distribution function. They assume such a model is valid for skin surface reflectance and measure roughness m and intensity rho_s for ten regions of the face across 149 faces. The results, available in their SIGGRAPH 2006 paper, provide a great starting point for tuning a specular BRDF for rendering faces. The Torrance/Sparrow model is approximated closely by the Kelemen/Szirmay-Kalos model, and the measured parameters work well for either. Their data can be easily painted onto a face using a low-resolution two-channel map that specifies m and rho_s for each facial region. Figure 14-8 compares rendering with the measured values of Weyrich et al. versus constant values for m and rho_s over the entire face. The difference is subtle but apparent, adding some nice variation (for example, by making the lips and nose shinier).

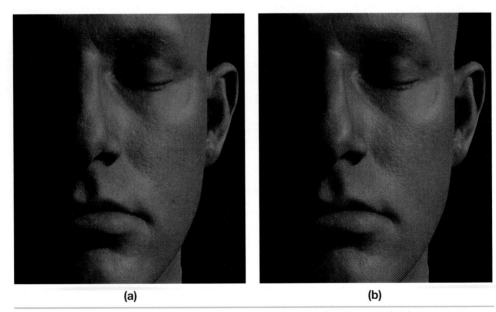

| (a) | (b) |

Figure 14-8. Comparing Constant Values for m and rho_s to Using Measured Values
(a) Using constant specular roughness (m = 0.3) and intensity (rho_s = 0.18) across the face.
(b) Using the measured parameters from Weyrich et al. 2006.

Using a clever application of light polarization, Ma et al. 2007 rapidly capture reflectance from faces, which they separate into specular and diffuse components. This is used to produce high-resolution normal, color, and specular intensity (`rho_s`) maps, as well as high-resolution geometry of the face. The resulting data yields realistic renderings (see d'Eon et al. 2007), and the specular map provides specular variation at a much higher resolution than the Weyrich et al. parameters (but assumes a fixed roughness).

14.4 Scattering Theory

We now turn from specular surface reflectance to diffuse subsurface scattering. Before tackling realistic skin-rendering algorithms, we must first introduce the concept of a *diffusion profile*. This key concept from subsurface scattering theory, derived from a fairly complex mathematical analysis of the physics of propagation and scattering of light in translucent materials, is nonetheless intuitive and easy to explain.

We should note that the techniques described in this chapter apply only to diffusion models. In particular, we do not handle single scattering effects, where each light ray scatters beneath the surface exactly once. Ignoring single scattering when rendering skin generally proves acceptable (however, see Section 14.7.1), but for some materials (such as marble, jade, and smoke), single scattering will significantly impact appearance. Realistic rendering of these materials must incorporate single scattering, with methods that to date are far more expensive or restrictive than the techniques we present (Jensen et al. 2001, Wang et al. 2005). Fortunately, a diffusion approximation alone works very well for skin.

14.4.1 Diffusion Profiles

A diffusion profile provides an approximation for the manner in which light scatters underneath the surface of a highly scattering translucent material. Specifically, it describes the outcome of the following simple experiment (which is sometimes used to measure diffusion profiles). Consider a flat surface in a dark room with a very thin, white laser beam illuminating it. We will see a glow around the center point where the laser beam is striking the surface, because some light is going beneath the surface and returning nearby, as shown in Figure 14-9a. The diffusion profile tells us how much light emerges as a function of the angle and distance from the laser center. If we consider only uniform materials, the scattering is the same in all directions and the angle is irrelevant. Each color has its own profile, which we can plot as a 1D curve, as illustrated in Figure 14-9b.[1]

Notice that the profiles are strongly color dependent: red light scatters much farther than green and blue. The absorption properties of skin are very sensitive to changes in frequency; in fact, researchers have implemented spectral models that simulate scattering in 150 color bands separately (Donner and Jensen 2006), and thus compute 150 diffusion profiles! Though we could in principle implement a similar spectral model on the GPU, the resulting improvement probably would not justify the many extra render passes and textures required. All images in this chapter were rendered using RGB light transport.

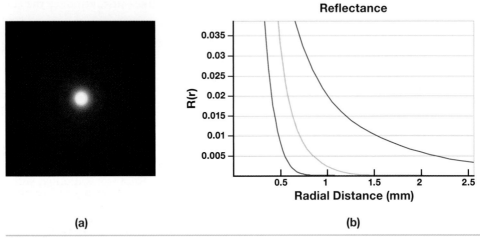

(a)   (b)

Figure 14-9. Visualizing a Diffusion Profile
(a) A narrow beam of white light scattered and reflected back from a translucent material. (b) We can plot the red, green, and blue profiles describing the amount of light scattered at a given distance from the illuminating beam. Both images illustrate the diffusion profiles of the three-layer skin model used to render all images in this chapter.

14.4.2 Rendering with Diffusion Profiles

Given the appropriate diffusion profiles, simulating subsurface scattering within skin reduces to the process of collecting all incoming light for each location on the surface and then spreading it around into neighboring locations based on the exact shapes of

---

1. Because of the enormous number of photons involved at the observable scale we see smooth falloffs. However, this is actually the contribution of many random paths such as those shown in Figure 14-4, and this random photon-path concept is at the heart of all mathematical scattering models.

the profiles. We can think of each tiny region on a surface as simulating the laser dot experiment shown in Figure 14-9a. A very narrow patch of incoming light creates a larger, colored patch of outgoing light. Every region on the surface needs to do this and all the overlapping, colored patches sum to give a translucent appearance.

Because incoming light becomes diffuse so quickly in skin, we can sum all incident light at each point on the surface and ignore its direction, except for an $\mathbf{N} \cdot \mathbf{L}$ term for each light and optional Fresnel transmittance terms we discuss later (in Section 14.5.2). The directionality of incoming light is lost almost immediately, so only the total amount of light is important. This diffuse light then scatters into neighboring regions (the exact amount is determined by the diffusion profiles) and is assumed to exit the surface flowing equally in all directions (again, for maximum realism a Fresnel transmittance term is required as the diffuse light exits the surface). This allows fairly simple rendering algorithms, which we present shortly. But first we need to know the exact diffusion profiles that describe scattering in skin.

The widely used scattering model of Jensen et al. 2001 introduces an analytic formula for diffusion profiles based on several material properties. Given these properties, the profiles are computed using a *dipole* equation. A later paper (Donner and Jensen 2005) introduces a *multipole* theory for handling multilayered materials. They also present a three-layer skin model and we use the profiles predicted by this model for our skin rendering system.

Along with the dipole model, Jensen et al. 2001 also presents an efficient technique for rendering curved surfaces using diffusion profiles. The idea is to simply use the spatial separation, *r*, between two points on the surface to evaluate the diffusion profiles. This determines diffuse scattering between any two locations, regardless of the geometry between them, as shown in Figure 14-10. Although not physically accurate, the typical curvatures encountered in skin surfaces are fairly low compared to the effective radius of scattering, and the approximation works well in practice.

14.4.3 The Shape of Diffusion Profiles

Accurate rendering requires knowing the exact shapes of the diffusion profiles for the material we want to simulate, which the dipole (Jensen et al. 2001) or multipole (Donner and Jensen 2005) diffusion models compute based on measured scattering parameters. The simpler dipole model suffices for many materials. To render milk, marble, or ketchup, we can look up measured scattering coefficients and use a dipole model to compute diffusion profiles for them.

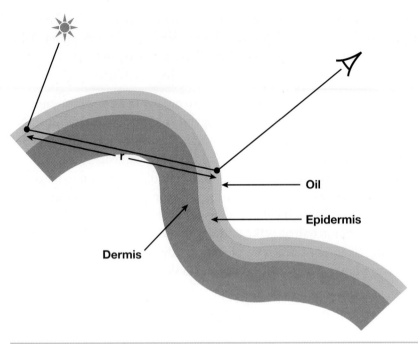

Figure 14-10. An Efficient Estimation of Diffuse Scattering in Curved Surfaces
The spatial separation between two points, regardless of geometry in between, is used to evaluate the diffusion profile when computing diffuse scattering. Though not strictly physically accurate, this approximation generally works well.

However, for materials composed of several layers, each with different scattering properties, the shapes of the profiles become more complicated than a dipole can represent. Using the more complicated multipole model can significantly improve the visual appearance of multilayered materials such as skin. Figure 14-11 compares skin renderings with single-layer versus three-layer subsurface scattering. Note that the specular light, the normals, and the diffuse color are exactly the same in each rendering. The key difference is in the shape of the diffusion profiles used. The simple shape of the dipole, derived for scattering in a single, infinitely thick layer, leads to a waxy look. The dipole cannot capture the combined reflectance of a thin, narrowly scattering epidermis layer on top of a widely scattering dermis layer.

14.4.4 A Sum-of-Gaussians Diffusion Profile

The profiles plotted in Figure 14-9b resemble the well-known Gaussian function e^{-r^2}. Although a single Gaussian doesn't accurately fit any diffusion profile, we have found

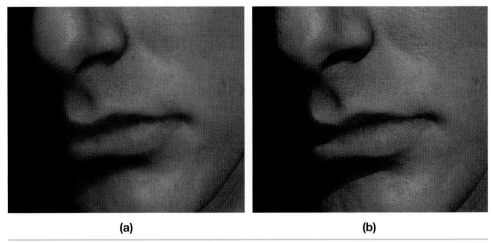

(a)   (b)

Figure 14-11. The Exact Shape of Diffusion Profiles Matters
A comparison of skin rendering with (a) subsurface scattering that assumes a single layer of uniform material, leading to a waxy appearance, and (b) subsurface scattering that simulates reflectance from a three-layer skin model.

that multiple Gaussians summed together can provide an excellent approximation. This proves enormously useful in practice. Gaussians have some nice properties that let us evaluate subsurface scattering very efficiently when we express diffusion profiles as sums of Gaussians. Gaussians are unique in that they are simultaneously separable and radially symmetric, and they convolve with each other to produce new Gaussians.

The rendering techniques presented in this chapter use a sum-of-Gaussians formulation. This requires a mapping from a dipole or multipole-based profile to a Gaussian sum. For each diffusion profile $R(r)$, we find k Gaussians with weights w_i and variances v_i such that

$$R(r) \approx \sum_{i=1}^{k} w_i G(v_i, r),$$

where we choose the following definition for the Gaussian of variance v:

$$G(v, r) := \frac{1}{2\pi v} e^{-r^2/(2v)}.$$

The constant $1/(2\pi v)$ is chosen such that $G(v, r)$, when used for a radial 2D blur, does not darken or brighten the input image (it has unit impulse response).

Figure 14-12 shows a diffusion profile (for the scattering of green light in marble) and approximations of the profile using two and four Gaussian sums. We use the scattering parameters from Jensen et al. 2001:

$$\sigma_a = 0.0041 \text{ mm}^{-1},$$

$$\sigma_s' = 2.62 \text{ mm}^{-1},$$

$$\eta = 1.5.$$

The four-Gaussian sum is

$$R(r) = 0.070G\left(0.036,\ r\right) + 0.18G\left(0.14,\ r\right) + 0.21G\left(0.91,\ r\right) + 0.29G\left(7.0,\ r\right).$$

Rendering with the true dipole versus the four-Gaussian sum (using an octree structure following Jensen and Buhler 2002 to ensure accuracy) produces indistinguishable results.

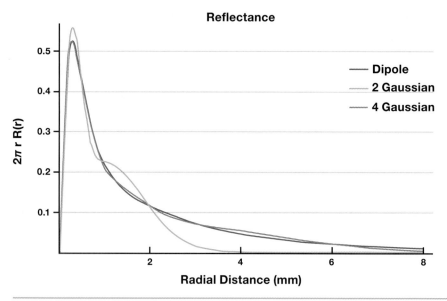

Figure 14-12. Approximating Dipole Profiles with Sums of Gaussians
The diffusion profile for describing the scattering of green light in marble (based on values from Jensen et al. 2001) is compared to several Gaussian sums which approximate it. One or two Gaussians are not sufficient to accurately approximate subsurface scattering, but four Gaussians can match the dipole extremely closely.

14.4.5 Fitting Predicted or Measured Profiles

This section discusses techniques for approximating a known diffusion profile with a sum of Gaussians. This is not essential to implementing the rendering techniques presented later on, but this section may be useful to readers wishing to accurately approximate subsurface scattering for a material for which they have measured scattering coefficients. Other readers will simply wish to implement the skin shader and interactively experiment with a small number of intuitive parameters (the individual Gaussian weights) to explore the softness of the material, instead of using the parameters computed from scattering theory. We also provide the exact Gaussians used to render all images in this chapter, which should provide a good starting point for rendering Caucasian skin.

The dipole and multipole functions mentioned already can be used to compute diffusion profiles for any material with known scattering coefficients.[2] Alternatively, diffusion profiles can be measured from a real-world object by analyzing scattering of laser or structured light patterns (Jensen et al. 2001, Tariq et al. 2006). Once we know exact profiles for the desired material, we must find several Gaussians whose sum matches these profiles closely. We can find these by discretizing the known profile and then using optimization tools (such as those available in Mathematica and MATLAB) that perform the fitting for us. These fitting functions are based on minimizing an error term. If we know a target diffusion profile $R(r)$ with which we want to render, we find k Gaussians that minimize the following:

$$\int_0^\infty r \left[R(r) - \sum_{i=1}^k w_i G(v_i, r) \right]^2 dr.$$

This computes an error function, where a squared error between $R(r)$ and the sum of Gaussians at radial distance r is weighted by r, because the profile at position r gathers light from a circle with circumference proportional to r. Both w_i and v_i for each Gaussian are allowed to vary.

Four Gaussians are sufficient to model most single-layer materials. As an experiment, we have fit four Gaussians to every material profile listed in Jensen et al. 2001, which

---

2. When computing dipoles, note the accidental extra σ_t' term in Jensen et al. 2001 (see Jensen and Buhler 2002 for the correct formula) and be careful of the sign when summing or subtracting the two poles. In some papers, the z coordinates are signed and in others they are not. Plot dipoles to check; they should never be negative.

gives measured parameters for many materials such as milk, marble, ketchup, skin, and more. For each material, we measured error with the following metric

$$E = \frac{\sqrt{\int_0^\infty r \left(R(r) - G_{sum}(r) \right)^2 dr}}{\sqrt{\int_0^\infty r \left(R(r) \right)^2 dr}},$$

which gives a root-mean-square ratio between the error in fitting $R(r)$ with a sum of Gaussians, $G_{sum}(r)$, and the target profile itself. The errors ranged from 1.52 percent (for Spectralon, blue wavelength) to 0.0323 percent (for ketchup, green wavelength). Of course, additional Gaussians can be used for increased accuracy and for approximating multilayer materials, which have more complex profiles.

14.4.6 Plotting Diffusion Profiles

Plotting the 1D radial profile and the Gaussian sum that approximates it can help visualize the quality of the fit. We recommend a radially-weighted visualization that plots $r \times R(r)$ versus distance, r, as shown previously in Figure 14-12; this weights the importance of a value at radius r based on the circle proportional to radius r to which it is applied during rendering. This has the nice property that the area under the curve is proportional to the total diffuse response (the color reflected when unit white light reflects off the surface). If the fit is poor for r in the range $[r_1, r_2]$ but the area under the curve in $[r_1, r_2]$ relative to the total area under the curve for all $r > 0$ is negligible, then errors in the profile at distances $[r_1, r_2]$ are also negligible in all but certain contrived lighting scenarios. We can then quickly see whether errors in the fit really matter or not, which is hard to see with standard or logarithmic plots of $R(r)$.

14.4.7 A Sum-of-Gaussians Fit for Skin

Multilayer diffusion profiles can have more complex shapes than dipole profiles, and we found six Gaussians were needed to accurately match the three-layer model for skin given in Donner and Jensen 2005. We use the Gaussian parameters described in Figure 14-13 to match their skin model. The resulting diffusion profiles are shown in Figure 14-14.

Notice here that the Gaussian weights for each profile sum to 1.0. This is because we let a diffuse color map define the color of the skin rather than have the diffusion profiles embed it. By normalizing these profiles to have a diffuse color of white, we ensure that the result, after scattering incoming light, remains white on average. We then multiply this result by a photo-based color map to get a skin tone. We also describe alternative methods for incorporating diffuse color in Section 14.5.2.

	Variance (mm^2)	Red	Blur Weights Green	Blue
	0.0064	0.233	0.455	0.649
	0.0484	0.100	0.336	0.344
	0.187	0.118	0.198	0
	0.567	0.113	0.007	0.007
	1.99	0.358	0.004	0
	7.41	0.078	0	0

Figure 14-13. Our Sum-of-Gaussians Parameters for a Three-Layer Skin Model
A visual representation of each Gaussian blur kernel used in the sum is given on the left.

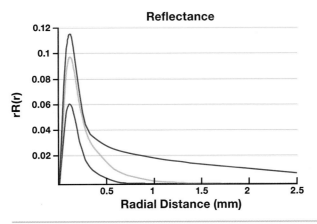

Figure 14-14. Plot of the Sum-of-Gaussians Fit for a Three-Layer Skin Model

Also note that we used the same six Gaussians with the same six variances, and each profile weights them differently. This reduces the amount of shader work required to render with these profiles, and we found that this still produces very good results. However, letting green and blue each fit their own set of six Gaussians would provide more accurate diffusion profiles for green and blue.

With the Gaussian sums that fit our red, green, and blue diffusion profiles, we are ready to render using the new methods presented next. We use the relative weighting of the Gaussians in each sum, as well as the exact variance of each Gaussian in the sum, in our shading system.

14.5 Advanced Subsurface Scattering

This section presents the details of the subsurface scattering component of our skin-rendering system, including our extensions to texture-space diffusion and translucent shadow maps. We compute several blurred irradiance textures and combine them all in the final render pass. One texture is computed for each Gaussian function used in the diffusion profiles. A simple stretch-correction texture enables more accurate separable convolution in the warped UV texture space. We modify the translucent shadow maps technique (Dachsbacher and Stamminger 2004) and combine it with the blurred irradiance textures to allow convincing scattering through thin regions, such as ears.

Using six off-screen blur textures allows accurate rendering with the three-layer skin model as used in Donner and Jensen 2005. We replicate one of their renderings as closely as possible, and show the real-time result in Figure 14-15. The skin color does not match exactly, since the average color of their diffuse map was not specified and their shadow edges are softer due to an area-light source. The real-time result is otherwise very similar to the offline rendering, which required several minutes to compute.

14.5.1 Texture-Space Diffusion

The *texture-space diffusion* technique introduced by Borshukov and Lewis 2003 for rendering faces in *The Matrix* sequels can be used to accurately simulate subsurface scattering. Their simple yet powerful insight was to exploit the local nature of scattering in skin and simulate it efficiently in a 2D texture by unwrapping the 3D mesh using texture coordinates as render coordinates. They then model the scattering of light by applying a convolution operation (blur) to the texture, which can be performed very efficiently. The desired shape of the blur is exactly the diffusion profiles of the material (thus requiring different blurs in red, green, and blue). They use a sum of two simple, analytic diffusion profiles: a broad base and a sharp spike (details in Borshukov and Lewis 2005). These two terms approximate the narrow scattering of the epidermis on top of the broadly scattering dermis, but introduce parameters not directly based on any physical model. Adjustment of these parameters is left to an artist and must be tuned by hand. Our sum-of-Gaussians diffusion profile approximations enable faster rendering and produce more accurate scattering since they are derived from physically based models.

Texture-space diffusion extends nicely to GPUs, as shown by Green 2004. We extend Green's implementation in several ways to incorporate transmission through thin regions such as ears (where Borshukov and Lewis used ray tracing) and to improve the accuracy of the results by using stretch correction and better kernels. Previous real-time

Figure 14-15. A Real-Time Result (After Donner and Jensen)
This image closely matches a rendering from Donner and Jensen 2005 but requires an order of magnitude less time to generate.

implementations of texture-space diffusion (Green 2004, Gosselin 2004) use only a single Gaussian kernel (or Poisson-disk sampling), which is only a very rough approximation of true scattering.

14.5.2 Improved Texture-Space Diffusion

We modify texture-space diffusion to provide a more accurate approximation to subsurface scattering. The new algorithm, executed every frame—illustrated in Figure 14-16—is as follows:

1. Render any shadow maps.
2. Render stretch correction map (optional: it may be precomputed).
3. Render irradiance into off-screen texture.
4. For each Gaussian kernel used in the diffusion profile approximation:
   a. Perform a separable blur pass in U (temporary buffer).
   b. Perform a separable blur pass in V (keep all of these for final pass).
5. Render mesh in 3D:
   a. Access each Gaussian convolution texture and combine linearly.
   b. Add specular for each light source.

Many Blurs

Our first extension of standard texture-space diffusion is to perform many convolution operations to the irradiance texture and to store the results (discarding the temporary buffers used during separable convolutions). We start with the same modified vertex shader in Green 2004 to unwrap the mesh using the texture coordinates as render coordinates. A fragment shader then computes the incoming light from all light sources (excluding specular) to produce the irradiance texture. Figure 14-17 shows an irradiance texture, and also the same texture convolved by the largest Gaussian in our scattering profiles.

Because we fit our diffusion profiles to a sum of six Gaussians, we compute six irradiance textures. The initial, non-blurred irradiance texture is treated as the narrowest Gaussian convolution (because the kernel is so narrow it wouldn't noticeably blur into neighboring pixels), and then we convolve it five times to produce five textures similar to the one in Figure 14-17b. These textures may or may not include diffuse color information, depending on the manner in which diffuse color gets integrated (see upcoming discussion).

As Figure 14-18 shows, none of the six convolved irradiance textures will generate realistic skin if used alone as an approximation of subsurface scattering. But when blended using the exact same linear combination as was used to fit the six Gaussians to the diffusion profiles of the skin model, they produce the desired appearance. This comes

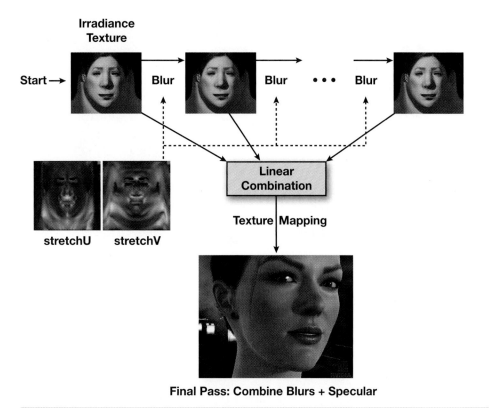

Irradiance Texture

Start → | Blur → | Blur • • • | Blur

stretchU   stretchV

Linear Combination

Texture Mapping

Final Pass: Combine Blurs + Specular

Figure 14-16. Overview of the Improved Texture-Space Diffusion Algorithm
We compute many blurred irradiance textures and combine them during the final render pass according to the sum-of-Gaussians diffusion profile. We perform blurs separably, modulated at each step by the stretch textures.

from a convenient property of convolution: the convolution of an image by a kernel that is a weighted sum of functions is the same as a weighted sum of images, each of which is the original image convolved by each of the functions:

$$I * \left(\sum_{i=1}^{k} w_i G(v_i, r) \right) = \sum_{i=1}^{k} w_i I * G(v_i, r).$$

Figure 14-19 shows the result of diffusing white light over the face using improved texture-space diffusion with six irradiance textures. No diffuse color texture is used, no specular light is added, and the diffusion profiles are normalized to a white color and then displayed separately in grayscale for red, green, and blue to show the difference in scattering for different wavelengths of light.

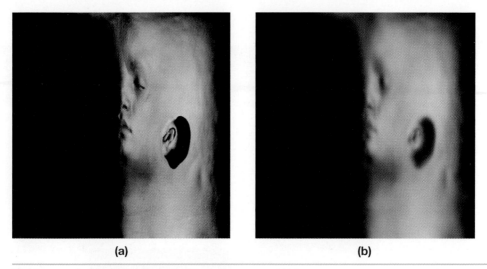

Figure 14-17. An Irradiance Texture
(a) The irradiance texture. (b) The irradiance texture convolved with the widest Gaussian from Figure 14-13.

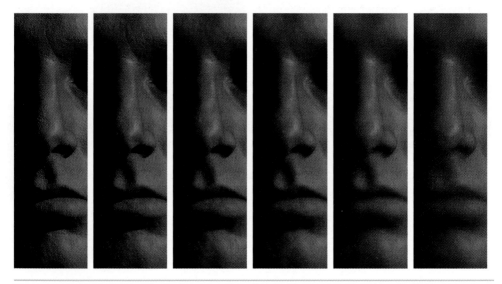

Figure 14-18. Using Only a Single Gaussian Does Not Generate a Realistic Image of Skin
Each of the six Gaussian kernels from the skin model is used to individually approximate diffuse scattering. No single Gaussian kernel produces a realistic result, but the correct linear combination of them (independently in red, green, and blue) creates the desired look.

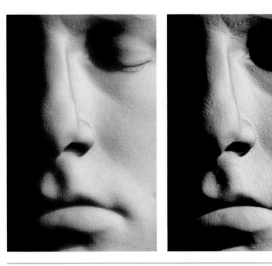

Figure 14-19. Visualizing Diffusion in Skin for Red, Green, and Blue Light
Comparison of the different diffusion in the red channel (left), green channel (center), and blue channel (right) when the six Gaussians and weights in Figure 14-13 are used to diffuse white light using improved texture-space diffusion. Each color is displayed in grayscale and the profiles have been normalized to white (the weights sum to 1.0) for easier visual comparison of the different shapes of diffusion. Note the highly different scattering between the various colors. It is helpful to view color channels separately as grayscale when tuning subsurface scattering to any kind of reference image.

Advantages of a Sum-of-Gaussians Diffusion Profile

We could directly convolve the irradiance texture by a diffusion profile using a one-pass 2D convolution operation (as is done by Borshukov and Lewis 2003). However, this would be quite expensive: we store an average of 4 samples (texels) per millimeter on the face in the irradiance texture, and the width of the diffusion profile for red light would be about 16 mm, or 64 texels. Thus, we would need a 64×64 or 4,096-tap blur shader. If the diffusion profile was separable we could reduce this to only a $64 + 64$ or 128-tap blur. But diffusion profiles are radially symmetric because we assume a homogeneous material that scatters light equally in all directions, and therefore they are not separable, for Gaussians are the only simultaneously separable and radially symmetric functions and we have seen that diffusion profiles are not Gaussians.

However, each Gaussian convolution texture *can* be computed separably and, provided our fit is accurate, the weighted sum of these textures will accurately approximate the lengthy 2D convolution by the original, nonseparable function. This provides a nice way to accelerate general convolutions by nonseparable functions: approximate a non-separable convolution with a sum of separable convolutions. We use this same idea to accelerate a high-dynamic-range (HDR) bloom filter in Section 14.6.

Another nice property of Gaussians is that the convolution of two Gaussians is also a Gaussian. This allows us to generate each irradiance texture by convolving the result of the previous one, in effect allowing us to convolve the original image by wider and wider Gaussians without increasing the number of taps at each step. Two radial Gaussians with variances v_1 and v_2 convolve into the following

$$G(v_1, r) * G(v_2, r) = \int_0^\infty \int_0^\infty G\left(v_1, \sqrt{x'^2 + y'^2}\right) G\left(v_2, \sqrt{(x - x')^2 + (y - y')^2}\right) dx'dy'$$
$$= G(v_1 + v_2, r),$$

where G is the Gaussian defined on page 309 and $r = \sqrt{x^2 + y^2}$. Thus, if the previous irradiance texture contains $I * G(v_1, r)$ (where I is irradiance) and we wish to compute $I * G(v_2, r)$, we simply convolve with $G(v_2 - v_1, r)$.

We use a seven-tap, separable convolution shader and store the intermediate result of convolution in the U direction to a temporary buffer before convolving in V. The seven Gaussian taps are {0.006, 0.061, 0.242, 0.383, 0.242, 0.061, 0.006}. This represents a Gaussian with a standard deviation of 1.0, assuming the coordinates of the taps are {−3.0, −2.0, −1.0, 0.0, 1.0, 2.0, 3.0}. This seven-tap kernel is used for all convolution steps, and the taps are linearly scaled about the center tap to convolve by any desired Gaussian. (The spacing should be scaled by the square root of the variance—the standard deviation—of the desired Gaussian.) Successive kernel widths in a sum-of-Gaussians fit should never be more than about twice the previous width. Doing so would increase the error from the use of stretch-correction values (presented in the next section) and would require more than seven samples in later convolution steps to prevent under-sampling. In our experience, fitting several Gaussians to a diffusion profile invariably gives a set of widths in which each is roughly double the last (variance changes by roughly 4×), and thus using seven taps at every step works well.

To summarize, we perform six 7-tap separable convolutions, for a total of $6 \times 2 \times 7 = 84$ texture accesses per output texel instead of the 4,096 required to convolve with the original diffusion profile in one step.

Correcting for UV Distortion

If the surface is flat and the convolution kernels used to blur the irradiance are exactly the diffusion profiles of the material, then texture-space diffusion is very accurate. However, some issues arise when this technique is applied to curved surfaces.

On curved surfaces, distances between locations in the texture do not correspond directly to distances on the mesh due to UV distortion. We need to address UV distortion to more accurately handle convolution over curved surfaces. Using simple stretch values that can be computed quickly every frame we have found it possible to correct for this (to a large degree), and the results look very good, especially for surfaces like faces which do not have extreme curvature. Ignoring UV distortion can cause a red glow around shadows and can produce waxy-looking diffusion in regions such as ears, which are typically more compressed in texture space compared to other surface regions.

We compute a stretch-correction texture that modulates the spacing of convolution taps for each location in texture space, as shown in Figure 14-20. The resulting width of convolution is roughly the same everywhere on the mesh (and therefore varies across different regions of the texture). We compute stretching in both the U and V texture-space directions, since horizontal and vertical stretching usually differ significantly.

We compute the stretch-correction texture using a simple fragment shader, presented in Listing 14-4. We reuse the same vertex shader used to unwrap the head into texture

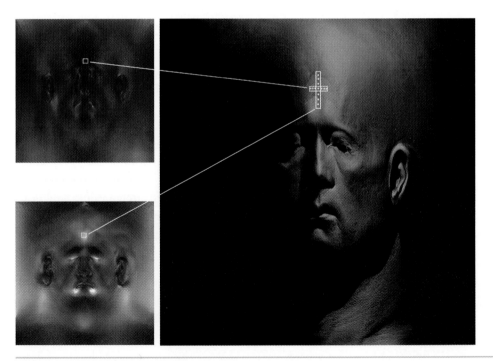

Figure 14-20. Using a Stretch Texture
Top left: The U-stretch correction texture. Bottom left: The V-stretch correction texture. Right: The U-stretch value determines the width of horizontal convolutions for each location in the texture. The V-stretch determines the width of vertical convolutions.

space for computing the irradiance texture, and store the world-space coordinates of the mesh in a texture coordinate. Screen-space derivatives of these coordinates give efficient estimates of the stretching, which we invert and store in the stretch-correction texture. The same values are accessed later in the convolution shaders (Listing 14-5) for directly scaling the spread of convolution taps.

Listing 14-4. Computing a Two-Component Stretch Texture

The stretch texture is computed very efficiently and can be computed per frame for highly deforming meshes. Texture-space derivatives of world-space coordinates give an accurate estimate of local stretching, which is inverted and directly multiplied by blur widths later. A constant may be needed to scale the values into the [0,1] range.

```
float2 computeStretchMap( float3 worldCoord : TEXCOORD0 )
{
    float3 derivu = ddx( worldCoord );
    float3 derivv = ddy( worldCoord );
    float stretchU = 1.0 / length( derivu );
    float stretchV = 1.0 / length( derivv );
    return float2( stretchU, stretchV ); // A two-component texture
}
```

The Convolution Shader

Listing 14-5 is used to convolve each texture in the U direction. An analogous convolveV() shader is used for the second half of a separable convolution step.

Optional: Multiscale Stretching

The stretch maps will have a constant value across each triangle in the mesh and thus will be discontinuous across some triangle edges. This should not be a problem for very small convolutions, but high-frequency changes in stretch values could cause high-frequency artifacts for very large convolutions. The derivatives used to compute stretching consider two neighboring texels, and thus the values may be poor estimates of the average stretching over a width of, say, 64 texels.

A more general approach is to duplicate the convolution passes used to convolve irradiance and convolve the stretch maps as well. Then use the kth convolution of the stretch map to convolve the kth irradiance texture. The idea here is to select a stretch map that has locally averaged the stretching using the same radius you are about to convolve with, and use that average value to correct the current convolution of irradiance.

Listing 14-5. A Separable Convolution Shader (in the U Texture Direction)

The final spacing of the seven taps is determined by both the stretch value and the width of the desired Gaussian being convolved with.

```
float4 convolveU( float2 texCoord : TEXCOORD0,
  // Scale - Used to widen Gaussian taps.
  // GaussWidth should be the standard deviation.
  uniform float GaussWidth,
  // inputTex - Texture being convolved
  uniform texobj2D inputTex,
  // stretchTex - Two-component stretch texture
  uniform texobj2D stretchTex
)
{
  float scaleConv = 1.0 / 1024.0;
  float2 stretch = f2tex2D( stretchTex, texCoord );
  float netFilterWidth = scaleConv * GaussWidth * stretch.x;

  // Gaussian curve - standard deviation of 1.0
  float curve[7] = {0.006,0.061,0.242,0.383,0.242,0.061,0.006};

  float2 coords = texCoord - float2( netFilterWidth * 3.0, 0.0 );
  float4 sum = 0;
  for( int i = 0; i < 7; i++ )
  {
    float4 tap = f4tex2D( inputTex, coords );
    sum += curve[i] * tap;
    coords += float2( netFilterWidth, 0.0 );
  }
  return sum;
}
```

The Accuracy of Stretch-Corrected Texture-Space Diffusion

Figure 14-21 shows artifacts that arise from convolving in texture space without correcting for stretching, and the degree to which they are corrected using static and multiscale stretch maps. A spatially uniform pattern of squares is projected onto a head model and convolved over the surface in texture space. We show convolution by three Gaussians of varying widths. The left images use no stretching information and exhibit considerable artifacts, especially for the wide convolutions. In the center images, the results are greatly improved by using a single, static stretch map (used for all convolutions of any size).

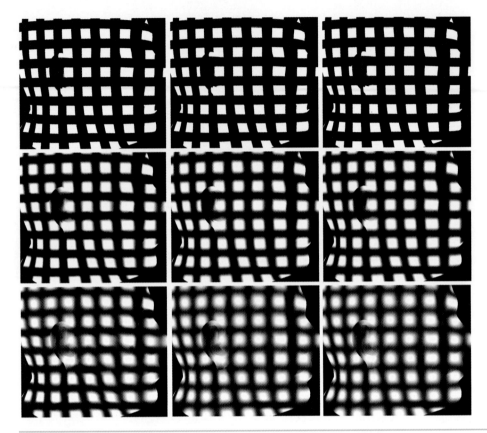

Figure 14-21. A Regular Pattern Projected onto a Head Model and Convolved in Texture Space by Three Different Gaussians (Top, Middle, Bottom)
The left images use no stretch correction and exhibit considerable distortion artifacts, which are mostly eliminated by using a single, static stretch map (center). Multiscale stretch correction (right) requires extra render passes and additional texture memory, and for this model it does not improve substantially over using a single, static stretch map.

Multiscale stretch correction (right) does not improve the results dramatically for the face model, and a single, static map is probably sufficient. However, when we render more complicated surfaces with very high distortions in texture space, multiscale stretch correction may prove noticeably beneficial. Further accuracy may be achieved by using the most conformal mapping possible (and possibly even locally correcting convolution directions to be nonorthogonal in texture space to ensure orthogonality on the mesh).

Incorporating Diffuse Color Variation

Diffusion profiles implicitly determine the net diffuse color of a material. Consider, again, the laser dot experiment. If a focused white laser light illuminates a surface and the total amount of light reflected back (considering every point on the surface) is less than (1, 1, 1) (that is, unit white light), then some of the light is absorbed by the surface. The total reflected amount, (r, g, b), is the diffuse color of the material (or the total diffuse reflectance R_d). This can be computed for known diffusion profiles by integrating over all distances $r > 0$. Each distance r corresponds to light reflected at a circle of radius $2\pi r$, giving the following:

$$R_d = \int_0^\infty 2\pi r R(r)\, dr.$$

This is trivial to compute for a profile expressed as a sum of Gaussians: R_d is simply the sum of the weights in the Gaussian sum (the constant factor in our Gaussian definition was chosen to achieve this result):

$$\int_0^\infty 2\pi r \sum_{i=1}^k w_i G(v_i, r)\, dr = \sum_{i=1}^k w_i.$$

Dipole and multipole theories assume a homogeneous material, perfectly uniform over the plane, and thus predict a perfectly constant skin color everywhere, R_d. However, skin has both high-frequency and low-frequency variation in color, which we would like to model. Physically this corresponds to nonuniformities in the different layers of skin that cause the scattering and absorption properties to vary within the tissue layers. This is currently impractical to simulate in real time (and it's not even clear how to measure these variations, especially within living tissue), so we resort to using textures to simulate the effects of this much more complicated process.

Diffuse color maps can be generated from photographs or painted by an artist and are an obvious way to control color variation across the skin surface. The color maps used in this chapter were made directly from photographs of a real person under diffuse illumination (white light arriving equally from all directions). Multiple photos were projected onto a single mesh and combined into a single texture.

We can choose among several ways to incorporate diffuse color maps into our scattering model. Since the model was derived assuming a perfectly uniform material, none of these techniques is completely physically based, and each may prove useful in different scenarios.

Post-Scatter Texturing

One option is to first perform all scattering computations without any coloring producing a value that everywhere averages to white, and then multiply by the diffuse color map to get the desired skin tone. The diffusion profile is normalized to white by using the code in Listing 14-6, which divides each Gaussian weight by the sum of all weights. Diffuse color is not used in the irradiance texture computation. The resulting scattered light is thus white on average (or, to be more exact, the color of the incoming light), and the final linear combination of all irradiance textures looks like Figure 14-22 (top right). The diffuse color texture is multiplied after scattering: the result is shown in Figure 14-22 (bottom right) (specular was also added). All the high-frequency texture detail is maintained because it is not blurred by the convolution passes, but no color bleeding of the skin tones occurs, which may make this option undesirable. However, if the diffuse map came from photographs of real skin, natural color bleeding has already occurred, and performing extra blurring may not be appropriate, so this *post-scatter texturing* may be the best alternative. The images in this chapter of the Adrian data set from XYZ RGB, Inc. (shown previously in Figure 14-15) are rendered with post-scatter texturing.

Donner and Jensen 2005 suggest also convolving the diffuse color map using the exact same profiles with which irradiance is convolved, to achieve proper color bleeding, and then multiplying this convolved color value by the convolved irradiance (which is convolved separately). This is slightly different from the next option, *pre-scatter texturing*. One is the convolution of a product; the other, a product of convolutions, and either may look better, depending on the diffuse map used.

Pre-Scatter Texturing

Another way to incorporate diffuse color variation is pre-scatter texturing. The lighting is multiplied by the diffuse color when computing the irradiance texture and then not used in the final pass. This scatters the diffuse color the same way the light is scattered, blurring it and softening it, as shown in Figure 14-22 (bottom left).

A possible drawback to this method is that it may lose too much of the high-frequency detail such as stubble, which sits at the top of the skin layers and absorbs light just as it is exiting. However, a combination of the two techniques is easy to implement and offers some color bleeding while retaining some of the high-frequency details in the color map.

Combining Pre-Scatter and Post-Scatter Texturing

A portion of the diffuse color can be applied pre-scatter and the rest applied post-scatter. This allows some of the color detail to soften due to scattering, yet it allows

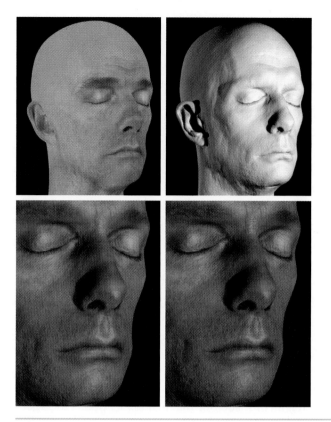

Figure 14-22. Comparing Pre- and Post-Scatter Texturing Techniques
Top left: The diffuse color map. Top right: Total subsurface scattering with no diffuse color (where the profiles are normalized to white). Bottom left: Pre-scatter texturing. Bottom right: Post-scatter texturing.

some portion to remain sharp. Because the diffuse color map contains the final desired skin tone, we can't multiply by `diffuseColor` twice. Instead, we can multiply the lighting by `pow(diffuseColor, mix)` before blurring and multiply the final combined results of all blurred textures by `pow(diffuseColor, 1 - mix)`. The `mix` value determines how much coloring applies pre-scattering and post-scattering, and the final skin tone will be the desired `diffuseColor` value. A `mix` value of 0.5 corresponds to an infinitesimal absorption layer on the very top of the skin surface that absorbs light exactly twice: once as it enters before scattering, and once as it leaves. This is probably the most physically plausible of all of these methods and is the technique used in Weyrich et al. 2006.

The images of Doug Jones in this chapter (such as Figure 14-1) use a `mix` value of 0.5. However, other values may look better, depending on the diffuse color texture and how it was generated. When using a `mix` value of exactly 0.5, replace the `pow(diffuse-Color, 0.5)` instructions with `sqrt(diffuseColor)` for better performance.

Compute Specular and Diffuse Light with the Same Normals

One approximation to subsurface scattering mimics the softening of diffuse lighting by using different normal maps (or bump height/displacement maps) for computing specular versus diffuse lighting (or even separate maps for each of red, green, and blue diffuse lighting, as described in Ma et al. 2007). Specular lighting reflects directly off the surface and isn't diffused at all, so it shows the most dramatic, high-frequency changes in the skin surface. The remaining (nonspecular) lighting is diffused through the skin, softening the high-frequency changes in lighting due to surface detail—bumps, pores, wrinkles, and so on—with red light diffusing farthest through the skin's subsurface layers and softening the most. However, simply blurring normal maps does not correctly diffuse the skin tones or the actual lighting itself. Because the methods we present in this chapter directly model the subsurface scattering responsible for the softening of surface details, the true normal information should be used for both specular and diffuse computations.

The Final Shader

Listing 14-6 gives the fragment shader for the final render pass. The mesh is rendered in 3D using a standard vertex shader. Gaussian weights that define the diffusion profiles are input as float3 constants (x for red, y for green, and z for blue). These should be the values listed in Figure 14-13 so that the mixing of the blurred textures matches the diffusion profiles. The Gaussian weights are renormalized in the shader allowing them to be mapped to sliders for interactive adjustment. Raising any Gaussian weight automatically lowers the other five to keep the total at 1.0. Thus the final diffuse light is not brightened or darkened, but the ratio of broad blur to narrow blur is changed; this will change the softness of the skin and is a convenient way to interactively edit the final appearance. This may be necessary for achieving skin types for which exact scattering parameters are not know, or for which the game or application demands a particular "look" rather than photorealism, but we have found that the three-layer model in Donner and Jensen 2005 works well for realistic Caucasian skin and we do not modify the weights at all.

Listing 14-6. The Final Skin Shader

```
float4 finalSkinShader(float3 position : POSITION,
  float2 texCoord : TEXCOORD0,
  float3 normal : TEXCOORD1,

  // Shadow map coords for the modified translucent shadow map
  float4 TSM_coord : TEXCOORD2,

  // Blurred irradiance textures
  uniform texobj2D irrad1Tex,
  . . .
  uniform texobj2D irrad6Tex,

  // RGB Gaussian weights that define skin profiles
  uniform float3 gauss1w,
  . . .
  uniform float3 gauss6w,

  uniform float mix, // Determines pre-/post-scatter texturing

  uniform texobj2D TSMTex,
  uniform texobj2D rhodTex )
{
  // The total diffuse light exiting the surface
  float3 diffuseLight = 0;

  float4 irrad1tap = f4tex2D( irrad1Tex, texCoord );
  . . .
  float4 irrad6tap = f4tex2D( irrad6Tex, texCoord );

  diffuseLight += gauss1w * irrad1tap.xyz;
  . . .
  diffuseLight += gauss6w * irrad6tap.xyz;

  // Renormalize diffusion profiles to white
  float3 normConst = gauss1w + guass2w + . . . + gauss6w;
  diffuseLight /= normConst; // Renormalize to white diffuse light

  // Compute global scatter from modified TSM
  // TSMtap = (distance to light, u, v)
  float3 TSMtap = f3tex2D( TSMTex, TSM_coord.xy / TSM_coord.w );
```

Listing 14-6 (*continued*). The Final Skin Shader

```
// Four average thicknesses through the object (in mm)
float4 thickness_mm = 1.0 * -(1.0 / 0.2) *
                      log( float4( irrad2tap.w, irrad3tap.w,
                                   irrad4tap.w, irrad5tap.w ));

float2 stretchTap = f2tex2D( stretch32Tex, texCoord );
float stretchval = 0.5 * ( stretchTap.x + stretchTap.y );

float4 a_values = float4( 0.433, 0.753, 1.412, 2.722 );
float4 inv_a = -1.0 / ( 2.0 * a_values * a_values );
float4 fades = exp( thickness_mm * thickness_mm * inv_a );

float textureScale = 1024.0 * 0.1 / stretchval;
float blendFactor4 = saturate(textureScale *
                              length( v2f.c_texCoord.xy - TSMtap.yz ) /
                              ( a_values.y * 6.0 ) );
float blendFactor5 = saturate(textureScale *
                              length( v2f.c_texCoord.xy - TSMtap.yz ) /
                              ( a_values.z * 6.0 ) );
float blendFactor6 = saturate(textureScale *
                              length( v2f.c_texCoord.xy - TSMtap.yz ) /
                              ( a_values.w * 6.0 ) );

diffuseLight += gauss4w / normConst * fades.y * blendFactor4 *
                f3tex2D( irrad4Tex, TSMtap.yz ).xyz;
diffuseLight += gauss5w / normConst * fades.z * blendFactor5 *
                f3tex2D( irrad5Tex, TSMtap.yz ).xyz;
diffuseLight += gauss6w / normConst * fades.w * blendFactor6 *
                f3tex2D( irrad6Tex, TSMtap.yz ).xyz;

// Determine skin color from a diffuseColor map
diffuseLight *= pow(f3tex2D( diffuseColorTex, texCoord ), 1.0-mix);

// Energy conservation (optional) - rho_s and m can be painted
// in a texture
float finalScale = 1 - rho_s*f1tex2D(rhodTex, float2(dot(N, V), m);
diffuseLight *= finalScale;

float3 specularLight = 0;
```

Listing 14-6 (*continued*). The Final Skin Shader

```
// Compute specular for each light
for (each light)
  specularLight += lightColor[i] * lightShadow[i] *
            KS_Skin_Specular( N, L[i], V, m, rho_s, beckmannTex );

return float4( diffuseLight + specularLight, 1.0 );
}
```

Dealing with Seams

Texture seams can create problems for texture-space diffusion, because connected regions on the mesh are disconnected in texture space and cannot easily diffuse light between them. Empty regions of texture space will blur onto the mesh along each seam edge, causing artifacts when the convolved irradiance textures are applied back onto the mesh during rendering.

An easy solution is to use a map or alpha value to detect when the irradiance textures are being accessed in a region near a seam (or even in empty space). When this is detected, the subsurface scattering is turned off and the diffuse reflectance is replaced with an equivalent local-light calculation. A `lerp` makes this transition smooth by blending between scattered diffuse light and nonscattered diffuse light (the alpha map is pre-blurred to get a smooth `lerp` value). Also, painting the stretch textures to be black along all seam edges causes the convolution kernels to not blur at all in those regions, reducing the distance from the seam edges at which the scattering needs to be turned off. This solution creates hard, dry-looking skin everywhere the object contains a seam, and may be noticeable, but it worked well for the NVIDIA "Froggy" and "Adrianne" demos. For the head models shown in this chapter the UV mappings fill the entire texture space, so none of these techniques are required. Objectionable seams are visible only under very specific lighting setups.

A more complicated solution involves duplicating certain polygons of the mesh for the irradiance texture computation. If there is sufficient space, all polygons that lie against seam-edges are duplicated and placed to fill up the empty texture space along seam edges. If light never scatters farther than the thickness of these extra polygons, then empty space will never diffuse onto accessed texels and light will properly scatter across seam edges. These extra polygons are rendered only in the irradiance texture pass and not in the final render pass. The duplicated polygons may need to overlap in a small number of places in the texture, but this should not create significant artifacts. We expect this technique would provide a good solution for many meshes, but have not tried it ourselves.

A more general solution is to find many overlapping parameterizations of the surface such that every point is a safe distance away from seam edges in at least one texture. The irradiance texture computation and convolution passes are duplicated for each parameterization (or many parameterizations are stored in the same texture) and a *partition of unity*—a set of weights, one for each parameterization—blends between the different sets of textures at every location on the surface. This "turns off" bad texture coordinates in locations where seam edges are near and "turns on" good ones. These weights should sum to 1.0 everywhere and vary smoothly over the surface. For each surface location, all weights that are nonzero should correspond to texture parameterizations that are a safe distance away from seam edges. Techniques for computing such parameterizations and their respective partitions of unity can be found in Piponi and Borshukov 2000. Given a partition of unity, the entire texture-space diffusion algorithm is run for each parameterization and the results are blended using the partition weights. This requires a considerable amount of extra shading and texture memory and is comparatively expensive, but probably still outperforms other subsurface-scattering implementations.

Exact Energy Conservation

Specular reflectance and diffuse reflectance are often treated completely independently, regardless of incoming and outgoing angles. This approach ignores a subtle interplay between the two from an energy standpoint, for if the specular reflections (not just for a single view direction, but over the entire hemisphere of possible view directions) consume, say, 20 percent of all incoming light, no more than 80 percent is left for diffuse. This seems fine, because shading is often computed as `Ks * specular + Kd * diffuse`, where `Ks` and `Kd` are constants. But the total amount of energy consumed by specular reflectance is highly dependent on the angle between **N** and **L**, and a constant mix of the two does not conserve energy. This topic has been addressed in coupled reflection models such as Ashikmin and Shirley 2000 and Kelemen and Szirmay-Kalos 2001, and it has also been addressed for subsurface scattering in Donner and Jensen 2005. The non-Lambertian diffuse lighting that results is easy to compute on GPUs. Because we are rendering skin we discuss only the subsurface-scattering version here.

The energy available for subsurface scattering is exactly all energy not reflected directly by the specular BRDF. A single specular calculation gives the portion of total input energy reflecting in a single outgoing direction (one **L** direction, one **V** direction). To sum the total energy used by specular reflection, all **V** directions must be considered. Thus, before storing light in the irradiance texture, we need to integrate specular reflectance over all directions on the hemisphere and multiply diffuse light by the fraction of energy that remains. If f_r is the specular BRDF and **L** is the light vector at position x on the surface, then we attenuate diffuse lighting for each light by the following

$$\rho_{dt}(x,\mathbf{L}) = 1 - \int_{2\pi} f_r(x,\boldsymbol{\omega}_o,\mathbf{L})(\boldsymbol{\omega}_o \cdot \mathbf{N})d\boldsymbol{\omega}_o, \tag{1}$$

where $\boldsymbol{\omega}_o$ are vectors in the hemisphere about **N**.

Using spherical coordinates, the integral in Equation 1 is computed as

$$\int_0^{2\pi} \int_0^{\pi/2} f_r(x,\boldsymbol{\omega}_o,\mathbf{L})(\boldsymbol{\omega}_o \cdot \mathbf{N})\sin(\theta)\,d\theta d\phi. \tag{2}$$

This value will change depending on roughness m at position x, and on $\mathbf{N} \cdot \mathbf{L}$. We remove the ρ_s constant from the specular BRDF (because it can be applied as a constant factor later) and precompute the integral in Equation 2. We precompute it for all combinations of roughness values and angles and store it in a 2D texture to be accessed based on m and $\mathbf{N} \cdot \mathbf{L}$. This precomputation is easily performed in the fragment shader given in Listing 14-7. This is only a rough estimate of the 2D integral, because of the uniform sampling, and better numerical integration techniques could also be used on the CPU or GPU to compute this texture. The uniform sample integration is especially poor for low roughness values, as seen in Figure 14-23, but such low values are not used by our skin shader.

Listing 14-7. A Fragment Shader for Preintegrating a Specular BRDF over the Hemisphere

The resulting scalar texture is used to retrieve ρ_{dt} terms when computing accurate subsurface scattering within rough surfaces.

```
float computeRhodtTex( float2 tex : TEXCOORD0 )
{
    // Integrate the specular BRDF component over the hemisphere
    float costheta = tex.x;
    float pi = 3.14159265358979324;
    float m = tex.y;
    float sum = 0.0;
    // More terms can be used for more accuracy
    int numterms = 80;
    float3 N = float3( 0.0, 0.0, 1.0 );
    float3 V = float3(0.0, sqrt( 1.0 - costheta*costheta ), costheta);
```

```
for( int i = 0; i < numterms; i++ )
{
   float phip = float(i) / float( numterms - 1 ) * 2.0 * pi;
   float localsum = 0.0f;
   float cosp = cos( phip );
   float sinp = sin( phip );
   for( int j = 0; j < numterms; j++ )
   {
      float thetap = float(j) / float( numterms - 1 ) * pi / 2.0;
      float sint = sin( thetap );
      float cost = cos( thetap );
      float3 L = float3( sinp * sint, cosp * sint, cost );
      localsum += KS_Skin_Specular( V, N, L, m, 0.0277778 ) * sint;
   }
   sum += localsum * (pi / 2.0) / float( numterms );
}
return sum * (2.0 * pi) / ( float( numterms ) );
}
```

Figure 14-23. A Precomputed ρ_{dt} Attenuation Texture
N · L *varies from zero (left) to one (right). m varies from zero (bottom) to one (top).*

This ρ_{dt} texture can then be used to modify diffuse lighting calculations using the code in Listing 14-8. This is executed for each point or spotlight when generating the irradiance texture. Environment lights have no **L** direction and should technically be multiplied by a constant that is based on a hemispherical integral of ρ_{dt}, but because this is just a constant (except for variation based on m) and probably close to 1.0, we don't bother computing this. The correct solution would be to convolve the original cube map using the ρ_{dt} directional dependence instead of just with **N** · **L**.

Listing 14-8. Computing Diffuse Irradiance for a Point Light

```
float ndotL[i] = dot( N, L[i] );
float3 finalLightColor[i] = LColor[i] * LShadow[i];
float3 Ldiffuse[i] = saturate( ndotL[i] ) * finalLightColor[i];
float3 rho_dt_L[i] = 1.0 - rho_s*f1tex2D(rhodTex, float2(ndotL[i], m));

irradiance += Ldiffuse[i] * rho_dt_L[i];
```

After light has scattered beneath the surface, it must pass through the same rough interface that is governed by a BRDF, and directional effects will come into play again. Based on the direction from which we view the surface (based on **N** · **V**), a different amount of the diffuse light will escape. Because we use a diffusion approximation, we can consider the exiting light to be flowing equally in all directions as it reaches the surface. Thus another integral term must consider a hemisphere of incoming directions (from below the surface) and a single outgoing **V** direction. Because the physically based BRDF is reciprocal (that is, the light and camera can be swapped and the reflectance will be the same) we can reuse the same ρ_{dt} term, this time indexed based on **V** instead of **L**. The end of Listing 14-6 shows how this attenuation is computed.

Failing to account for energy conservation in the scattering computation can lead to overly bright silhouette edges. The effect is subtle but noticeable, especially for skin portrayed against a dark background where it appears to "glow" slightly (see Figure 14-24). Adding energy conservation using our precomputed `rho_dt` texture provides more realistic silhouettes, but the same effect can unnaturally darken regions such as the edge of the nose in Figure 14-24. Again, the effect is subtle but perceptible. In fact, this darkening represents another failure to conserve energy, this time in a different guise: since we do not account for interreflection, our model misses the light that should be bouncing off the cheekbone region to illuminate the edge of the nose. Precomputed radiance transfer (PRT) techniques can capture such interreflections, but do not support animated or deformable models and thus don't easily apply to human characters. Since the "glow" artifact tends to cancel out the "darkening" effect, but produces its own artifacts, you should evaluate the visual impact of these effects in your application and decide whether to implement energy conservation in the scattering computation.

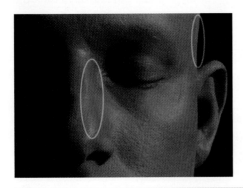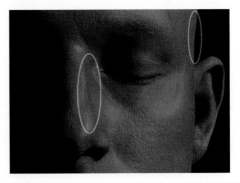

Figure 14-24. Skin Rendering and Energy Conservation
Left: Rendering using no energy conservation. Right: Using energy conservation.

14.5.3 Modified Translucent Shadow Maps

Texture-space diffusion will not capture light transmitting completely through thin regions such as ears and nostrils, where two surface locations can be very close in three-dimensional space but quite distant in texture space. We modify translucent shadow maps (TSMs) (Dachsbacher and Stamminger 2004) in a way that allows a very efficient estimate of diffusion through thin regions by reusing the convolved irradiance textures.

Instead of rendering z, normal, and irradiance for each point on the surface nearest the light (the *light-facing surface*), as in a traditional translucent shadow map, we render z and the (u, v) coordinates of the light-facing surface. This allows each point in shadow to compute a thickness through the object and to access the convolved irradiance textures on the opposite side of the surface, as shown in Figure 14-25.

We analyze the simple scenario depicted in Figure 14-26 to see how to compute global scattering. A shadowed point C being rendered needs to sum the scattered light from all points in a neighborhood of point A on the other side of the object. This is typically

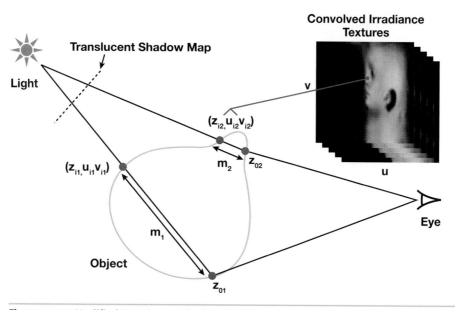

Figure 14-25. Modified Translucent Shadow Maps
We store z and the (u, v) coordinates of the light-facing surface in a three-component shadow map. This enables regions in shadow to compute depth through the surface, and to access blurred versions of lighting on the other side.

computed by sampling points around A (on the 2D light-facing surface) and computing the reflectance[3] profile $R(m)$, where m is the true distance from C to each point near A.

We can use a modified TSM and the convolved irradiance textures to estimate this global transmitted light. At any shadowed location C, the TSM provides the distance m and the UV coordinates of point A on the light-facing surface. We want to estimate the scattered light exiting at C, which is the convolution of the light-facing points by the profile R, where distances from C to each sample are computed individually. Computing this for B, however, turns out to be much easier, and for small angles θ, B will be close to C. For large θ, Fresnel and $\mathbf{N} \cdot \mathbf{L}$ terms will cause the contribution to be small and hide most of the error. Computing the correct value at C is probably not worth the considerable cost.

---

3. The multipole theory (Donner and Jensen 2005) computes transmission profiles as well as reflectance profiles, but transmission profiles are typically not used for rendering, except for uniformly thin surfaces such as leaves and paper. For thin regions of skin, rendering with a transmission profile would require two epidermis layers on each side of a finitely thick dermis layer, but this requires fixing the dermis thickness at some average. This would not show the proper variation in transmission over varying regions of the ear. A more correct solution would compute a new transmission profile for every sample, depending on each sample's thickness through the object. This computation would be prohibitively expensive, so reflectance profiles are used instead. Donner and Jensen 2007 presents an offline technique for more accurately estimating the correct scattering in this scenario.

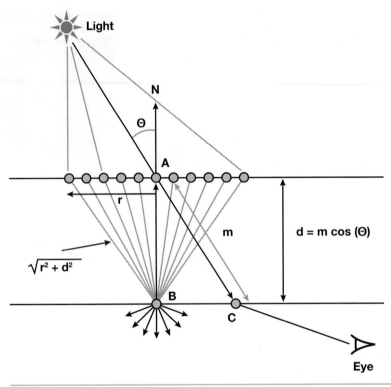

Figure 14-26. A Region in Shadow (*C*) Computes Transmitted Light at Position *B*
This can be done very quickly using only two or three texture lookups at A into the same blurred textures used for local scattering.

Computing scattering at *B*, any sample at distance *r* away from *A* on the light-facing surface needs to be convolved by the following

$$R\left(\sqrt{r^2 + d^2}\right) = \sum_{i=1}^{k} w_i G\left(v_i, \sqrt{r^2 + d^2}\right)$$

$$= \sum_{i=1}^{k} w_i e^{-d^2/v_i} G\left(v_i, r\right),$$

where we have used the separability of Gaussians in the third dimension to transform a function of $\sqrt{r^2 + d^2}$ into a function of *r*. This is convenient since the light-facing points have already been convolved by $G(v_i, r)$ at *A* (this is what we store in each of the convolved irradiance textures). Thus the total diffuse light exiting at location *C* (estimated at *B* instead) is a sum of *k* texture lookups (using the (*u*, *v*) for location *A* stored in the TSM), each weighted by w_i and an exponential term based on v_i and d. This transformation works because each Gaussian in the sum-of-Gaussians diffusion profile is separable. A single 2D convolution of light-facing points by the diffusion profile $R(r)$ could not be used for computing scattering at B or C (only at A).

Depths, m, computed by the shadow map are corrected by $\cos(\theta)$ because a diffusion approximation is being used and the most direct thickness is more applicable. Surface normals at A and C are compared, and this correction is applied only when the normals face opposite directions. A simple `lerp` blends this correction back to the original distance m as the two normals approach perpendicular. Although derived in a planar setting, this technique tends to work fairly well when applied to nonplanar surfaces such as ears (as shown in Figure 14-27).

So far we have considered only one path of light through the object, which can lead to some problems. High-frequency changes in depth computed from the TSM can lead to high-frequency artifacts in the output. This is undesirable for highly scattering translucence, which blurs all transmitted light and should have no sharp features. A useful trick to mask this problem is to store depth through the surface in the alpha channel of the irradiance texture and blur it over the surface along with irradiance. Each Gaussian, when computing global scattering, uses a corresponding blurred version of depth. (We use the alpha of texture $i - 1$ for the depth when computing Gaussian i.) This allows each ray through the object to consider the average of a number of different paths, and each Gaussian can choose an average that is appropriate. To pack the distance value into an 8-bit alpha, we store `exp(-const * d)` for some constant, d, convolve this exponential of depth over the surface, and reverse after lookup. See Listing 14-9.

Listing 14-9. Computing the Irradiance Texture

Depth through the surface is stored in the alpha channel and is convolved over the surface.

```
float4 computeIrradianceTexture()
{
  float distanceToLight = length( worldPointLight0Pos - worldCoord );
  float4 TSMTap = f4tex2D( TSMTex, TSMCoord.xy / TSMCoord.w );
  // Find normal on back side of object, Ni
  float3 Ni = f3tex2D( normalTex, TSMTap.yz ) * float3( 2.0, 2.0, 2.0 ) -
              float3( 1.0, 1.0, 1.0 );
  float backFacingEst = saturate( -dot( Ni, N ) );
  float thicknessToLight = distanceToLight - TSMTap.x;
```

Listing 14-9 (*continued*). Computing the Irradiance Texture

```
   // Set a large distance for surface points facing the light
   if( ndotL1 > 0.0 )
   {
      thicknessToLight = 50.0;
   }

   float correctedThickness = saturate( -ndotL1 ) * thicknessToLight;
   float finalThickness = lerp( thicknessToLight, correctedThickness,
                                backFacingEst );

   // Exponentiate thickness value for storage as 8-bit alpha
   float alpha = exp( finalThickness * -20.0 );
   return float4( irradiance, alpha );
}
```

Double contribution can occur when the (*u*, *v*) of the point being rendered approaches the (*u*, *v*) of the point in the TSM. We lerp the TSM contribution to 0 for each Gaussian term as the two (*u*, *v*) coordinates approach each other. This is done using the blendFactor terms in Listing 14-6.

Figure 14-27 shows two renders using this technique, one where the distance correction is not used, and another where it is. Figure 14-28 shows the local scattering and then each individual Gaussian global scatter term separately. When summed, these four images give the final image in Figure 14-27 (right).

Multiple Lights and Environment Lighting

The extended TSM technique was derived assuming a single point light with a single TSM. Using many TSMs requires creating convolved irradiance textures for each light and storing them separately. (Each TSM needs an associated set of convolved irradiance textures for that light only.) This requires many extra blur passes and extra texture memory. A possible way around this is to compute the minimum of all depths through the surface (using multiple TSMs) and convolve that over the surface. In the final shader, each TSM can be accessed, and the (*u*, *v*) corresponding to the smallest of all computed thicknesses can be used to do a single TSM global scatter computation. This is certainly an approximation, but it avoids scaling the entire texture-space diffusion algorithm by the number of point light sources.

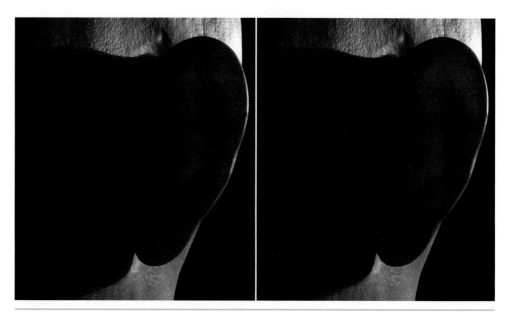

Figure 14-27. The Benefits of Distance Correction
Left: No distance correction. Right: Distance correction.

Figure 14-28. Local Scattering and the Individual Gaussian Terms Used for Global Scattering
Left to right: Local scatter only, transmittance convolution by G(0.567), transmittance convolution by G(1.99), and transmittance convolution by G(7.41). Each Gaussian in the sum-of-Gaussians diffusion profile is used to separately transmit scattered light through the ear (however, only the widest three have significant contributions), exploiting the 3D separability of Gaussians. The sum of all four images gives the final image in Figure 14-27 (right).

In general, we have found modified translucent shadow maps to work well for dramatic lighting (Figure 14-27), but it still leaves ears looking somewhat opaque with bright environment lighting. This is a common phenomenon for offline rendering as well and has been addressed in Donner and Jensen 2007. The solution is rather expensive, and no real-time approximation is immediately obvious.

14.6 A Fast Bloom Filter

The same techniques used to accelerate convolutions for subsurface scattering apply in general to other nonseparable convolutions, such as bloom filters. Pharr and Humphreys 2004 recommend a bloom filter of $(1 - r/d)^4$ for adding bloom to a final rendered image (especially nice for HDR images). This filter is not separable and must be computed brute-force in 2D. However, it is well approximated by a sum of two Gaussians, and the same separable, hierarchical convolution techniques used for improved texture-space diffusion (excluding the stretch textures) can be used to efficiently evaluate it. For $d = 1$, $(1 - r)^4$ is well approximated by $0.0174\, G(0.008, r) + 0.192\, G(0.0576, r)$. Figure 14-29 shows an image with skin rendering and an HDR bloom filter computed using this two-Gaussian kernel.

14.7 Conclusion

Our new sum-of-Gaussians formulation of diffusion profiles makes possible new algorithms based on texture-space diffusion and translucent shadow maps that produce highly realistic real-time images of human skin. Physically based multilayer skin models map directly to these new algorithms, enabling us to demonstrate real-time renderings with a level of realism attained previously only in offline rendering. See Figure 14-29 for a final example.

Real-time imagery such as Figure 14-29 will consume most of the resources of an entire GeForce 8800 Ultra GPU. However, the techniques presented in this chapter are somewhat scalable and the texture resolutions can be greatly reduced for characters that do not fill the entire screen. Using fewer than six Gaussians to approximate diffusion profiles will likely suffice for most characters. Subsurface scattering becomes less noticeable in very far away characters, and a level-of-detail system should be able to move between multiple levels of diffusion accuracy without noticeable popping.

We were greatly inspired by the groundbreaking work of Craig Donner and Henrik Wann Jensen in 2005, and hopefully, like us, readers will be inspired to approximate

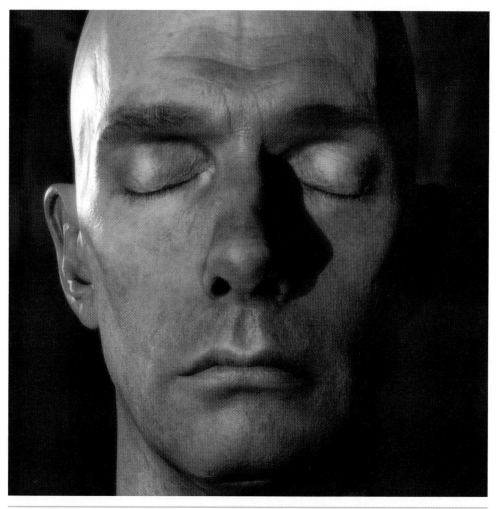

Figure 14-29. Real-Time Skin Rendering with a Two-Gaussian HDR Bloom Filter

these and future results as closely as they can—as their applications permit—and create the most realistic real-time characters possible.

14.7.1 Future Work

Although this chapter focuses on real-time face rendering, many of the techniques apply to a wide variety of materials with highly scattering translucence. We expect that the subsurface-scattering algorithms we have developed for efficient GPU rendering may also prove useful in an offline rendering pipeline.

The skin-rendering techniques we presented work wonderfully for faces, but texture seams pose difficulties for rendering general surfaces, especially hands and feet. The solutions discussed for addressing seams need to be explored in more detail to determine to what extent they can be addressed automatically with no user input (which might make the texture-space diffusion idea more viable for general-purpose rendering), and to test the applicability of improved texture-space diffusion to more general rendering of translucent materials.

Correcting texture-space convolution kernels based on multiscale normal curvature proved negligible for face rendering, but improvements such as this and multiscale stretch correction should be explored further to determine the degree to which texture-space diffusion can generate realistic images of subsurface scattering as the surface curvatures become comparable to the effective radius of scattering. Donner and Jensen 2007 presents a more accurate solution for diffuse scattering in curved surfaces and their results should be considered when improving real-time scattering techniques.

For skin rendering in general, the spectral bidirectional surface-scattering reflectance distribution function (BSSRDF) model by Donner and Jensen 2006 and the five-layer BioSpec model (Krishnaswamy and Baranoski 2004) should provide more accurate images, but exact comparisons between these models and the three-layer skin model in Donner and Jensen 2005 have not been generated. It is not clear what visual impact these more physically accurate models have. In particular, a study comparing spectral skin rendering with varying numbers of color bands in the range of 3–150 would be telling. An exact-as-possible comparison of the Donner and Jensen diffusion models to a full Monte-Carlo, ground-truth simulation based on the BioSpec model should also reveal the impact of the simplification of using two or three layers instead of five, as well as what is lost in assuming a diffusion approximation.

Single scattering is often ignored for subsurface-scattering simulations and in particular for skin rendering. Methods from Hanrahan and Krueger 1993 are not directly applicable due to the rough surface layer, which turns a single-scattering process into a triple-scattering process. The extent to which this directional component of subsurface scattering matters could be studied using Monte Carlo methods. If significant at grazing angles, this component could potentially be modeled as a BRDF or BSSRDF by decoupling subsurface irradiance into diffuse and single-scattering. A physically based bidirectional transmittance distribution function (BTDF) (Stam 2001) for the epidermis based on a model of the cells in the *stratum corneum*—the outermost layer of the epidermis—should provide the best data.

Incorporating variation in skin color still remains a rather ad hoc process. Future work for capturing, incorporating, and editing skin color variation with predictably good results would be very beneficial. Anisotropy and varying scattering coefficients over different facial regions were noted in Weyrich et al. 2006 and Tariq et al. 2006. A fast-capture system for capturing spatially varying diffusion profiles with multilayered fidelity over a face could also potentially improve images.

Asperity scattering (Koenderink and Pont 2003) has not been modeled and should be incorporated to simulate scattering from hairs on the face.

The Torrance/Sparrow specular BRDF might be improved by using a model fit to real-world measurements of real skin reflectance or to a simulation of surface scattering based on a physically based model of the cells in the stratum corneum. One such BTDF model is used in BioSpec. The polarization techniques from Debevec et al. 2000 should allow direct measurement of the exact specular-only BRDF for real skin.

14.8 References

Ashikmin, Michael, and Peter Shirley. 2000. "An Anisotropic Phong Light Reflection Model." Technical report UUCS-00-014, University of Utah.

Borshukov, George, and J. P. Lewis. 2003. "Realistic Human Face Rendering for *The Matrix Reloaded.*" In *ACM SIGGRAPH 2003 Sketches and Applications*.

Borshukov, George, and J. P. Lewis. 2005. "Fast Subsurface Scattering." In *ACM SIGGRAPH 2005 Course on Digital Face Cloning*.

d'Eon, Eugene. 2007. "NVIDIA Demo Team Secrets–Advanced Skin Rendering." Presentation at Game Developer Conference 2007. Available online at http://developer.download.nvidia.com/presentations/2007/gdc/Advanced_Skin.pdf.

d'Eon, Eugene, David Luebke, and Eric Enderton. 2007. "Efficient Rendering of Human Skin." In *Rendering Techniques 2007 (Proceedings of the Eurographics Symposium on Rendering)*, Grenoble, France.

Dachsbacher, Carsten, and Marc Stamminger. 2004. "Translucent Shadow Maps." In *Proceedings of the 13th Eurographics Workshop on Rendering*, pp. 197–201.

Debevec, Paul, Tim Hawkins, Chris Tchou, Haarm-Pieter Duiker, Westley Sarokin, and Mark Sagar. 2000. "Acquiring the Reflectance Field of a Human Face." In *Proceedings of ACM SIGGRAPH 2000*, pp. 145–156.

Donner, Craig, and Henrik Wann Jensen. 2005. "Light Diffusion in Multi-Layered Translucent Materials." In *ACM Transactions on Graphics (Proceedings of SIGGRAPH 2005)* 24(3).

Donner, Craig, and Henrik Wann Jensen. 2006. "A Spectral BSSRDF for Shading Human Skin." In *Rendering Techniques (Proceedings of the Eurographics Symposium on Rendering 2006)*, pp. 409–417.

Donner, Craig, and Henrik Wann Jensen. 2007. "Rendering Translucent Materials Using Photon Diffusion." In *Rendering Techniques (Proceedings of the Eurographics Symposium on Rendering 2007)*.

Gosselin, David. 2004. "Real-Time Skin Rendering." Presentation at Game Developers Conference 2004. Available online at http://ati.de/developer/gdc/Gosselin_skin.pdf.

Green, Simon. 2004. "Real-Time Approximations to Subsurface Scattering." In *GPU Gems*, edited by Randima Fernando, pp. 263–278. Addison-Wesley.

Hanrahan, Pat, and Wolfgang Krueger. 1993. "Reflection from Layered Surfaces due to Subsurface Scattering." In *Computer Graphics (SIGGRAPH '93 Proceedings)*, pp. 165–174.

Heidrich, Wolfgang, and Hans-Peter Seidel. 1999. "Realistic, Hardware-accelerated Shading and Lighting." In *Proceedings of SIGGRAPH 99*, pp. 171–178. Available online at http://www.cs.ubc.ca/~heidrich/Papers/Siggraph.99.pdf.

Jensen, Henrik Wann, Stephen R. Marschner, Marc Levoy, and Pat Hanrahan. 2001. "A Practical Model for Subsurface Light Transport." In *Proceedings of SIGGRAPH 2001*.

Jensen, Henrik Wann, and Juan Buhler. 2002. "A Rapid Hierarchical Rendering Technique for Translucent Materials." In *ACM Transactions on Graphics (Proceedings of SIGGRAPH 2002)* 21(3).

Kautz, Jan, and Michael McCool. 2000. "Approximation of Glossy Reflection with Prefiltered Environment Maps." In *Proceedings of Graphics Interface 2000*.

Kelemen, Csaba, and László Szirmay-Kalos. 2001. "A Microfacet Based Coupled Specular-Matte BRDF Model with Importance Sampling." Presentation at Eurographics 2001.

Koenderink, Jan, and Sylvia Pont. 2003. "The Secret of Velvety Skin." In *Machine Vision and Applications* 14(4), pp. 260–268.

Krishnaswamy, Aravind, and Gladimir V. G. Baranoski. 2004. "A Biophysically-Based Spectral Model of Light Interaction with Human Skin." In *Computer Graphics Forum (Proceedings of Eurographics 2004)* 23(3).

Ma, Wan-Chun, Tim Hawkins, Pieter Peers, Charles-Felix Chabert, Malte Weiss, and Paul Debevec. 2007. "Rapid Acquisition of Specular and Diffuse Normal Maps from Polarized Spherical Gradient Illumination." In *Rendering Techniques 2007: Eurographics Symposium on Rendering*.

Pharr, Matt, and Greg Humphreys. 2004. *Physically Based Rendering: From Theory to Implementation*. Morgan Kaufmann.

Piponi, Dan, and George Borshukov. 2000. "Seamless Texture Mapping of Subdivision Surfaces by Model Pelting and Texture Blending." In *Proceedings of SIGGRAPH 2000*, pp. 471–478.

Poirer, Guillaume. 2004. "Human Skin Modeling and Rendering." Technical Report CS-2004-05, University of Waterloo, January 2004.

Schlick, Christophe. 1993. "A Customizable Reflectance Model for Everyday Rendering." In *Fourth Eurographics Workshop on Rendering*, Paris, France, pp. 73–84.

Shirley, Peter. 2005. *Fundamentals of Computer Graphics*. 2nd ed. A K Peters.

Stam, Jos. 2001. "An Illumination Model for a Skin Layer Bounded by Rough Surfaces." In *Rendering Techniques 2001: 12th Eurographics Workshop on Rendering*, pp. 39–52.

Tariq, Sarah, Andrew Gardner, Ignacio Llamas, Andrew Jones, Paul Debevec, and Greg Turk. 2006. "Efficient Estimation of Spatially Varying Subsurface Scattering Parameters." USC ICT Technical Report ICT-TR-01-2006.

Tuchin, Valery. 2000. *Tissue Optics: Light Scattering Methods and Instruments for Medical Diagnosis*. SPIE Tutorial Texts in Optical Engineering Vol. TT38. The International Society for Optical Engineering.

Wang, Rui, John Tran, and David Luebke. 2005. "All-Frequency Interactive Relighting of Translucent Objects with Single and Multiple Scattering". In *ACM Transactions on Graphics (Proceedings of SIGGRAPH 2005)* 24(3), pp. 1202–1207.

Weyrich, Tim, W. Matusik, H. Pfister, B. Bickel, C. Donner, C. Tu, J. McAndless, J. Lee, A. Ngan, H. W. Jensen, and M. Gross. 2006. "Analysis of Human Faces Using a Measurement-Based Skin Reflectance Model." In *ACM Transactions on Graphics (Proceedings of SIGGRAPH 2006)* 25(3), pp. 1013–1024.

Thanks to XYZ RGB, Inc., for the high-quality head scans. Special thanks to Doug Jones for allowing us to use his likeness. Thanks to George Borshukov, Paul Debevec, Craig Donner, Henrik Wann Jensen, and Sarah Tariq for answering many questions about their work. Chris Cowan and Cam de Leon were instrumental in preparing the models and textures for real-time rendering and deserve plenty of credit for the images in this book. Thanks also to Craig Duttweiler, Eric Enderton, Larry Gritz, John Tran, and Dan Wexler for proofreading, suggestions, and helpful discussions regarding the material.

Chapter 15

Playable Universal Capture

George Borshukov
Electronic Arts

Jefferson Montgomery
Electronic Arts

John Hable
Electronic Arts

In this chapter, we discuss a real-time implementation of Universal Capture, abbreviated UCap. The technique has progressed from its noninteractive film applications (in *The Matrix* movies) through real-time playback (E3 2005 Fight Night Round 3 Concept Demo) to fully interactive (E3 2006 Tiger Woods demo), ultimately being used for animating high-fidelity facial performances in the video game titles *Tiger Woods PGA Tour 07* and *Need for Speed: Carbon*. Based on what we learned from those projects, the system described here is what we believe is the best trade-off that we would advocate for future games and interactive applications.

15.1 Introduction

Digital reproduction of realistic, animated faces is a hard problem for two main reasons:

- There are a vast number of factors involved in reproducing realistic facial animation. If one considers the color of a single pixel, there is near-infinite complexity: the bone structure of the face, blood vessels, muscles, and fat (and their dynamic constriction, excitation, and density); the structure and condition of the layers of skin, makeup, sweat, oil, and dirt affecting reflections and refractions, and so on and so on.

- Despite the subtle nature of some of these factors, many if not all are extremely important because human observers are ultimate experts at watching faces. This is perhaps best described using the Uncanny Valley hypothesis originally posited about humans' response to robots by Dr. Moshiro Mori (Mori 1982). In a nutshell, the Uncanny Valley describes the steep descent toward an unintentionally creepy appearance as the level of realism *increases*.

The implication of these two factors makes it extremely difficult for an animator or a computer simulation to achieve genuinely realistic results. We simply don't have sufficient models for the important characteristics and subtle dynamics of facial expressions. That is why the techniques in this chapter are based on a philosophy of performance capture. Essentially, we let real-world physics handle the complexity and merely try to capture and reproduce the end result (as pixel values on the face).

Most faces in video games use a diffuse map (which is painted or derived from a photograph) on skinned geometry that is captured through motion capture (a.k.a. *mocap*). We show how to use three high-resolution video cameras to create an animated diffuse map. This diffuse map captures details that are virtually impossible to animate by hand, including subtle eyebrow movements, subtle lighting changes and self-shadowing effects, stretching of the lips, and wrinkles that move around. We then compress the textures using a variant of *principal component analysis* (PCA) and entropy-encode both the animated PCA weights and geometry. The textures are then decompressed in a pixel shader on the GPU.

The techniques we present are a direct attempt to avoid the Uncanny Valley in the most challenging applications of all for digital humans: those requiring real-time interactivity. Ultimately, we hope that our collection of techniques will help human characters in video games and other real-time applications to approach the believability and emotional impact offered by their film counterparts.

15.2 The Data Acquisition Pipeline

We have developed a more robust production-level version of the Universal Capture system (Borshukov et al. 2003). To guarantee robustness, we deploy a state-of-the-art facial motion capture system consisting of eight infrared cameras plus three synchronized, high-definition, color cameras framed on the actor's face in an ambient lighting setup. Around 70 small retroreflective markers are placed on the actor's face. The reconstructed 3D motion path of the face markers is then used as the direct source of deformation for the static scanned and surfaced head geometry. We achieve the deformation with a facial bone rig. The number of bones is equal to the number of markers on the face. Figure 15-1 illustrates the process. This deformation approach achieves excellent results in accurately reconstructing the facial shape and motion in all areas of the face—except for the interior contour of the lips, because obviously we cannot place markers there. We solve the lip contour problem with a small set of additional bones that control the lip interior and are quickly keyed by an animator using the background images as a reference. See Figure 15-2. Once we have achieved successful reconstruction of the facial deformations, we can re-project and blend in UV space the input image sequences from each camera for every frame to produce animated diffuse texture maps. The presence of facial markers is not a problem, as our motion capture system needs retroreflective markers only 1.5 mm in diameter, which can easily be keyed out and removed in the final textures, as shown in Figure 15-3. Figure 15-4 shows the final results.

Our technique enables a straightforward solution to good dynamic lighting of the face: the performances are captured in ambient lighting and a high-detail normal map extracted from a head scan or constructed by an artist can be used for lighting and shading.[1] We treat the diffuse color textures captured by our system as diffuse albedo maps that already contain baked-in ambient occlusion. Subsurface scattering approximation

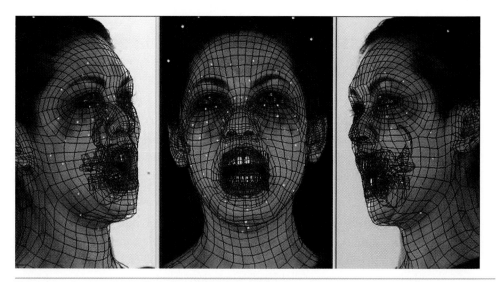

Figure 15-1. Images from All Three of the Camera Views

1. Animated normal maps for the medium-scale wrinkles not present in the deforming geometry can be extracted using image processing from the animated color maps, overlaid over the high-detail normal map and then compressed using the approach described in this chapter.

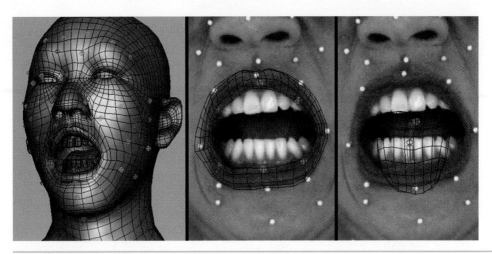

Figure 15-2. Mocap Markers, Lips, and Tongue Are Tracked

is crucial for close-ups of realistic skin, and we recommend use of the texture space diffusion approach suggested by Borshukov and Lewis 2003 with its most recent real-time implementation by d'Eon 2007. For specular reflectance, we rely on the highly detailed normal map in combination with specular intensity and roughness maps perturbing an analytical model based on findings of Weyrich et al. 2006.

15.3 Compression and Decompression of the Animated Textures

The compression scheme we will use is based on a very simple assumption that can be demonstrated by considering the two-dimensional data set shown in Figure 15-5. We assume in this case that the variance along the x axis is more important than the variance along y. If it is sufficiently more important (enough to disregard the deltas in y as noise), then we can project the data onto this one important dimension and store it in half of the size.

It turns out that for animated facial textures, a large number of dimensions can be deemed unimportant just as y was, and a reasonable compression ratio can be achieved. Further, decompression of this representation involves a simple algorithm that is particularly amenable to parallel implementation on a GPU.

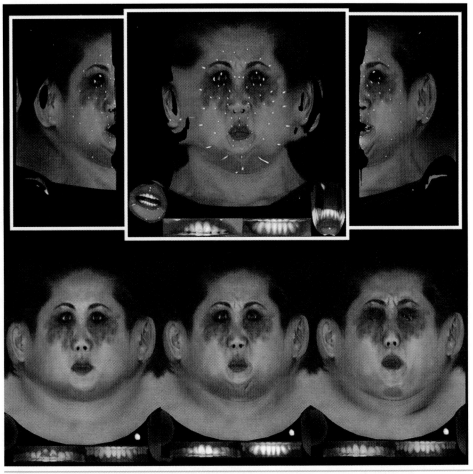

Figure 15-3. The Three Camera Views Are Merged and the Markers Are Removed to Create the Final Animated Diffuse Textures

15.3.1 Principal Component Analysis

Animated facial textures are not simple two-dimensional data sets, so we need a technique such as principal component analysis to help us determine which multidimensional axes are the most important. These axes, which are called *principal components*, are orthogonal and are aligned with the directions of maximal variance, as shown in Figure 15-6. The way that PCA determines these components is by assuming that each data point represents a

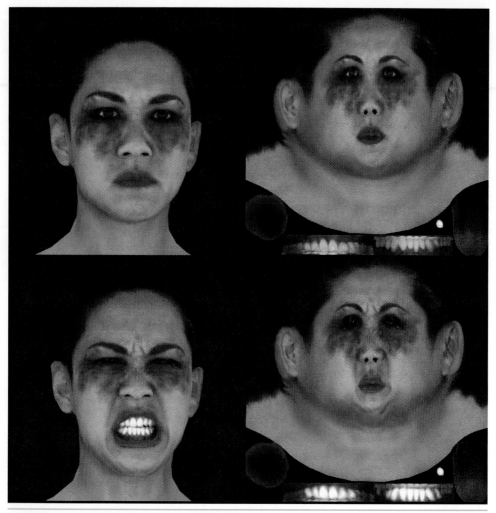

Figure 15-4. The Final Unshaded "Leanne" Character
Demonstrating the ability of an animated diffuse map applied to skinned geometry to capture details of the performance.

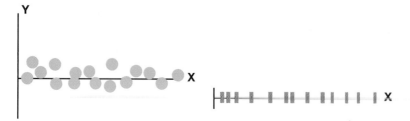

Figure 15-5. A 2D Data Set Demonstrating Our Assumption about Variance
Left: More horizontal variance than vertical. Right: The same data projected onto the x axis.

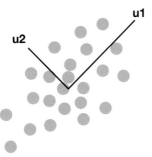

Figure 15-6. A Distribution of Data Points Showing Two Principal Components

sample from a multivariate normal distribution.[2] This means that the entire set can be parameterized by a mean vector and a covariance matrix; finding the directions of maximal variance is equivalent to finding a projection that diagonalizes the covariance matrix. For animated facial textures, such an assumption is not entirely dubious, primarily because features are spatially stationary in the UV representation.

The first step in this analysis is to map the texture data into a matrix where rows represent random variables and columns represent samples from a multivariate normal distribution. As shown in Figure 15-7, we treat each texture frame as three samples (corresponding to the red, green, and blue channels) drawn from the same distribution. While this may seem like a strange choice, we have found that this structure allows us to capitalize on correlations between the color channels and ultimately enables better compression.

The next step is to compute the underlying parameters of the distribution. First, we compute the mean vector and subtract it from each column of the data matrix, thereby "centering" the data:

$$a_i = \frac{1}{3F} \sum_{j=1}^{3F} A_{i,j}$$

$$B_{i,j} = A_{i,j} - a_i$$

We then want to compute the covariance matrix of **B** and diagonalize it. Both of these steps can be performed at once by determining the singular value decomposition (SVD) of the matrix **B**:

$$\mathbf{B} = \mathbf{U}\mathbf{\Sigma}\mathbf{V}^T$$

---

2. Although such an assumption is dubious, PCA tends to work well and is popular because of its efficiency and ease of use.

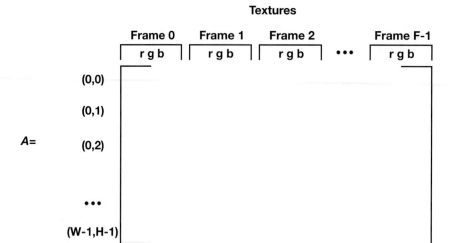

Figure 15-7. The Matrix Structure of an Animated Diffuse Map Used in Principal Component Analysis
The structure contains f frames of W×H texture data.

The result of this operation is the following:

- The columns of **U** contain the principal components of **A**. Each component is a vector of length $W \times H$, and there are *rank*(**B**) of them.

- Σ is a diagonal matrix whose values are a direct measure of the corresponding component's importance.

- The rows of **V** are weights that describe how to linearly combine the principal components to reconstruct **B**.

15.3.2 Compression

After PCA, the components that make up the animation are ranked in terms of importance. The relative importance of each component can be viewed by plotting the diagonal terms of Σ, as was done in Figure 15-8. Although for this data very few components are truly redundant (indicated by an importance of zero), a large number of them contribute relatively little to the final result.

The idea behind PCA compression is to simply exclude those components that contribute the least. This effectively projects the data onto a lower-dimensional representation, thereby compressing the data set. For our Leanne example, we may choose to use only 16 out of the 10,644 components to represent the animation. Although this is a significant amount of compression, it is important to note that it introduces errors, because the excluded components (all but the top row in Figure 15-9) contain relevant structure that is lost.

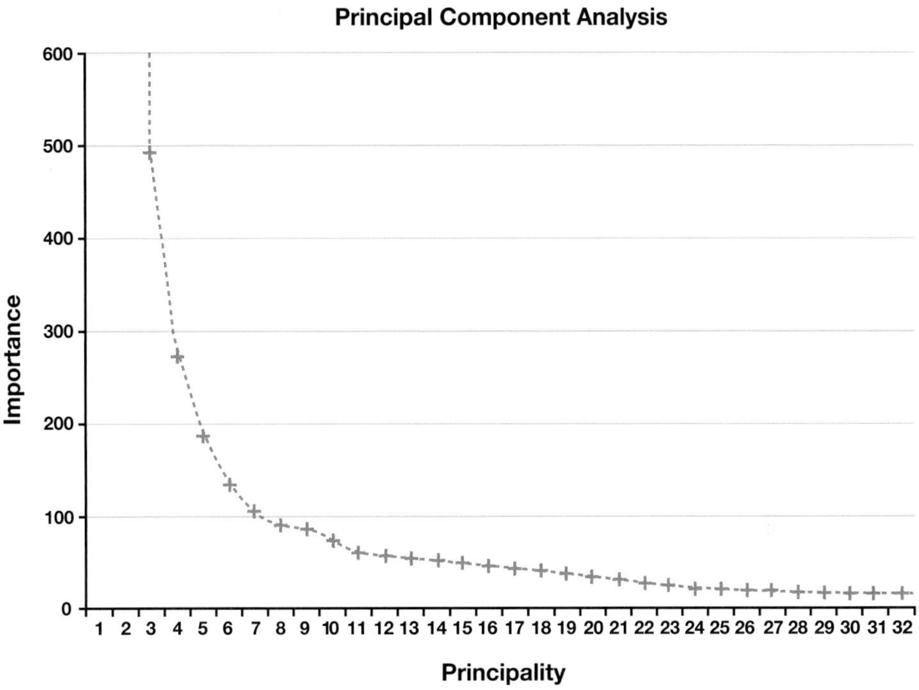

Principal Component Analysis
600
500
400
300
200
100
0
Importance
1 2 3 4 5 6 7 8 9 10 11 12 13 14 15 16 17 18 19 20 21 22 23 24 25 26 27 28 29 30 31 32
Principality

Figure 15-8. The First 32 Diagonal Values of Σ for a Particular Leanne Performance
These values denote the amount of information each component contributes to the data set (as well as the amount of error introduced by excluding it).

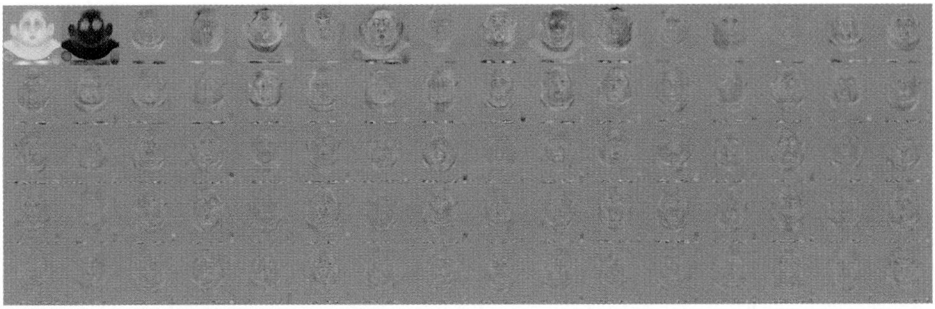

Figure 15-9. The 80 Most Principal Components of a Leanne Performance Ordered from Left to Right, Top to Bottom
These texture tiles represent the first 80 columns of the matrix ***U****, and a weighted sum of them can produce the original performance.*

15.3.3 Decompression

The decompression algorithm is simply the matrix arithmetic required to recombine $\mathbf{U}$, Σ, $\mathbf{V}$, and a into $\mathbf{A}$ based on the equations in Section 15.3.1. For notational simplicity, consider the matrices $\mathbf{L}$ and $\mathbf{R}$ such that $\mathbf{A} = \mathbf{LR}$. See Figure 15-10.

$$\mathbf{L} = [a \mid \mathbf{U}\Sigma]$$

$$\mathbf{R} = \begin{bmatrix} 1...1 \\ \mathbf{V}^T \end{bmatrix}$$

To reconstruct frame f from this representation using C components, the following equations are used (as shown in Figure 15-11).

$$red(x, y) = \sum_{k=1}^{C} L_{xy,k} R_{k,3f+0}$$

$$green(x, y) = \sum_{k=1}^{C} L_{xy,k} R_{k,3f+1}$$

$$blue(x, y) = \sum_{k=1}^{C} L_{xy,k} R_{k,3f+2}$$

PCA ensures that this is the optimal linear combination of any C components. Further, because the decompression algorithm is simply a matrix-matrix multiplication, it can be easily implemented by a GPU shader. Listing 15-1, where the C columns of $\mathbf{L}$ are stored in textures and the frame's corresponding three columns of $\mathbf{R}$ are passed in as uniform parameters, shows just such a shader.

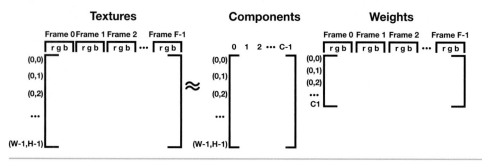

Figure 15-10. Matrix Dimensions for the Decompression Algorithm, $\mathbf{A} = \mathbf{LR}$

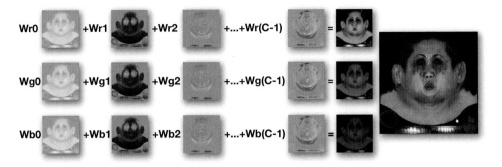

Figure 15-11. Graphical Representation of the Frame Decompression Algorithm

Listing 15-1. GPU Implementation of PCA Decompression of 16 Components

*The first 16 columns of **U** are packed into four textures by translating the values into the range [0, 255].*

```
// Decompress a pixel color using 16 components.
float4 PcaDecompress16(
  uniform float2 uv,
  uniform sampler2D componentTexture[4],
  uniform float4 rFrameWeights[4],
  uniform float4 gFrameWeights[4],
  uniform float4 bFrameWeights[4])
{
  // components[0] holds the first four components; the values must be
  // mapped from [0, 1] to [-1, 1], which is the original range of the
  // columns of U
  float4 components[4];
  components[0] = 2 * tex2D(componentTexture[0], uv.xy) - 1;
  components[1] = 2 * tex2D(componentTexture[1], uv.xy) - 1;
  components[2] = 2 * tex2D(componentTexture[2], uv.xy) - 1;
  components[3] = 2 * tex2D(componentTexture[3], uv.xy) - 1;

  // Matrix multiply LxR
  float4 color;
  color.r = dot(components[0], rFrameWeights[0]) +
            dot(components[1], rFrameWeights[1]) +
            dot(components[2], rFrameWeights[2]) +
            dot(components[3], rFrameWeights[3]);
  color.g = dot(components[0], gFrameWeights[0]) +
            dot(components[1], gFrameWeights[1]) +
            dot(components[2], gFrameWeights[2]) +
            dot(components[3], gFrameWeights[3]);
```

```
color.b = dot(components[0], bFrameWeights[0]) +
          dot(components[1], bFrameWeights[1]) +
          dot(components[2], bFrameWeights[2]) +
          dot(components[3], bFrameWeights[3]);
color.a = 1.0;

return color;
}
```

15.3.4 Variable PCA

The optimality of PCA is based on the preceding assumptions as well as one that mean-squared error is an appropriate measure of quality. This is unfortunately not the case for animated facial diffuse maps, where certain pixels have a higher qualitative importance and therefore should suffer less error. The prototypical example is to compare the eyes with the back of the head—although PCA treats each pixel with equivalent importance, a human observer would be more offended by an error in the eyes than in the hair.

We have devised a technique designed to retain the benefits of PCA while relaxing the orthonormal constraint on **U**, allowing us to be selective about how much data is retained per pixel. With variable PCA, the standard compression step of retaining only the most-principal C components is replaced with a step in which each pixel is assigned a distinct number of most-principal components. Pixel i gets C_i components and pixel j gets C_j components, but C_i does not necessarily equal C_j. This way, we can affect the quality of the image on a pixel-by-pixel basis. For example, hair pixels can use 4 components while eye pixels can use 88.

The component assignment can also be performed on a region-by-region basis, which greatly simplifies the decompression algorithm because the handling of each region can be hard-coded. For example, Figure 15-12 shows one particular region specification along with the number of components used in each region. This particular specification allows the use of 88 components in the eye regions and greatly increases perceived quality while still fitting all of the component data into the same texture size used by the standard 16-component PCA representation.

15.3.5 Practical Considerations

As the length of an animation increases, the matrix **A** can easily become too large to fit into memory on many machines. There are various solutions to this problem, either by

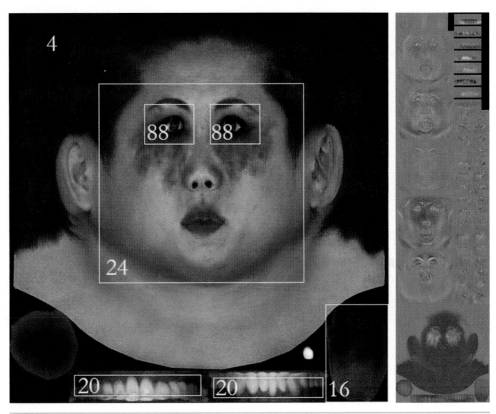

Figure 15-12. A Region Specification
Left: The number of components to use in each region, which implies the region's qualitative importance. Right: The nonzero elements of the first 88 Leanne components used by variable PCA packed into a single texture.

using an out-of-core SVD implementation that is able to operate on subsets of **A** at a time, or by simply analyzing a subset of the frames and then projecting the unanalyzed frames into the basis obtained.

Final quality, memory usage, and required computation are factors that need to be balanced on a per-application basis. Should further compression be required, it can be achieved by compressing the PCA weight streams using a technique such as entropy encoding. The loss in quality is typically worth the memory savings. The weight decompression does require CPU time, but the CPU cost is relatively small because each frame's PCA weights and bone animation involve only a few hundred floats. Ultimately, the majority of the decompression cost is performed on the GPU in the pixel shader, which is beneficial because only visible pixels need be decompressed.

The achieved data size and decompression speed allow us to render multiple, high-quality character performances simultaneously in real time. For example, using the variable PCA region layout in Figure 15-12, the components for a 512×512 texture can be stored inside a 512×2048 texture requiring 4MB of RAM. The largest performance set we tested containing 5,672 frames required 803KB of PCA weights and 601KB of bone animation[3]—a total size less than 6MB. Figure 15-13 shows the resulting performance.

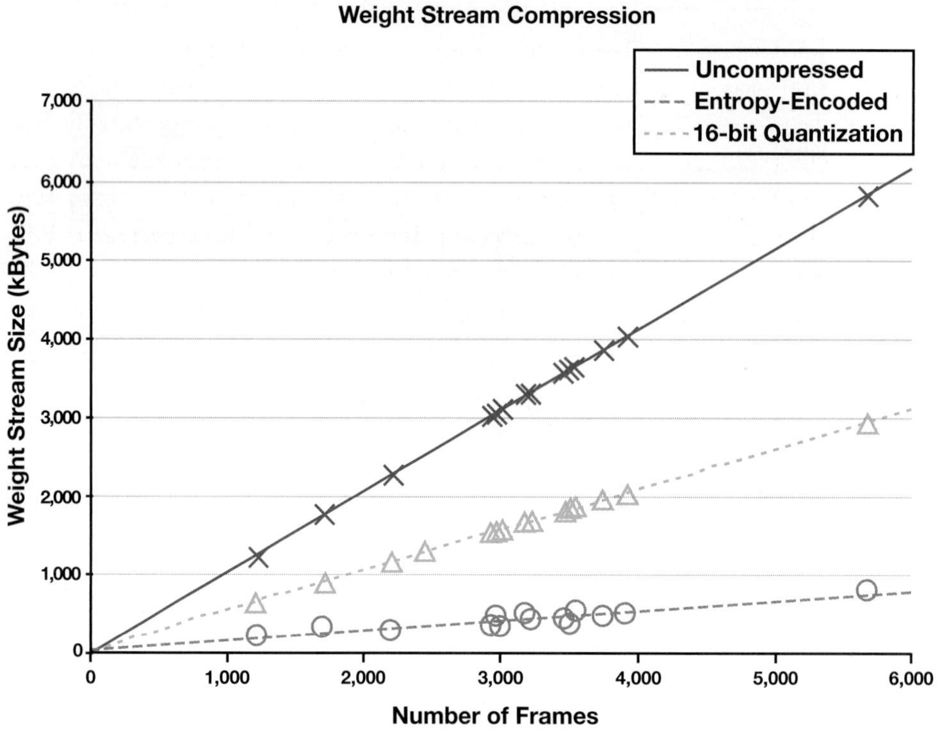

Weight Stream Compression

Figure 15-13. Typical Compression Ratios for PCA Weight Streams
Each data point represents the results from a particular performance we have captured and analyzed.

---

3. Geometry animation represents considerably less data than the texture animation. Nonetheless, it too can be compressed. If the geometry is treated as an animated vertex cloud, the vertex streams can be compressed using PCA exactly the same way that the textures are described earlier, yielding significant compression along with GPU decompression. Other compression techniques (such as discrete cosine transform and entropy encoding) can operate on the bone animations. These techniques decompress the bone animations on the CPU and skin the geometry on the GPU. We have found that these techniques produce better quality, more stable, and more flexible results than the PCA-compressed geometry.

15.4 Sequencing Performances

Not only does this compression technique allow us to encode large libraries of performance clips, but it also allows random access as well as any linear operation to be done in compressed space. For example, blending the PCA weights representing two frames prior to decompression is equivalent to pixel-wise blending of the entire frames but requires much less computation. We use these advantages to sequence multiple performances dynamically, blending across transitions.

The fact that this technique preserves the captured subtlety and variety of a performance allows us to apply *motion graphs* to facial animation. Using motion graphs (a.k.a *move trees*) is a common practice in video game development, and they have been applied successfully to produce rich and realistic body movement from both captured and hand-animated clips. To apply the motion graph approach to facial animation, a library of facial expression clips, fundamental to a certain context, are captured. A motion graph is designed to connect the expressions, and the graph can be traversed, rendering the clips and interpolating both textures and geometry across the transitions. Performances can be triggered either by an AI subsystem or directly by the user through a game controller.

15.5 Conclusion

We have demonstrated a powerful approach for realistic human character animation and rendering. Figures 15-14 through 15-17 show some examples of the results. Listing 15-2 has the code for the shader. Our approach is based on the application of PCA for compression and GPU decompression of animated diffuse texture maps acquired by a state-of-the-art facial performance capture system. The results have been applied and tested in high-fidelity real-time prototypes as well as in real video game production.

Listing 15-2. The Variable PCA Shader for the Regions from Figure 15-12

```
struct tPcaTex
{
  uniform float faceHeight;
  uniform float eyesHeight;
  uniform sampler2D Tex0;
  uniform float4 TexWeightR[32];
  uniform float4 TexWeightG[32];
  uniform float4 TexWeightB[32];
};
```

```
float PcaDec(
  float4 weights[],
  float4 components[],
  const int num,
  const int w_start,
  const int c_start)
{
  int i;
  float ret;
```

Figure 15-14. The Final Shaded "Leanne" Character

```
  ret = 0;
  for(int i = 0; i < num; i++)
    ret += dot(weights[i+w_start], components[i+c_start]);
  return ret;
}

struct UcapWindow
{
  float x, y, width, height;

  void Set(float f1, float f2, float f3, float f4)
  {
    x = f1/512.0;
    y = f2/512.0;
    width = f3/512.0;
    height = f4/512.0;
  }

  float2 GetCorner()
  {
    return float2(x, y);
  }

};

bool InWindow(UcapWindow win, float2 uv)
{
  if(win.x < uv.x && uv.x < win.x + win.width &&
     win.y < uv.y && uv.y < win.y + win.height)
    return true;
  else
    return false;
}

float3 DecompressPcaColor(float2 tex, tPcaTex pcaTex)
{
  float4 comp_all[1];
  float4 comp_face[5];
  float4 comp_eyes[16];
  float4 comp_upper_tongue[3];
  float4 comp_lower_teeth[4];
  float4 comp_upper_teeth[4];
```

```
float3 color;
comp_all[ 0 ] = tex2D(pcaTex.Tex0, tex.xy * float2(1, .25))*2 - 1;

color.r = PcaDec(pcaTex.TexWeightR, comp_all, 1, 0, 0);
color.g = PcaDec(pcaTex.TexWeightG, comp_all, 1, 0, 0);
color.b = PcaDec(pcaTex.TexWeightB, comp_all, 1, 0, 0);

UcapWindow faceWindow, eyesWindow, upperTongueWindow, upperTeethWindow,
    lowerTeethWindow;

faceWindow.Set(96, pcaTex.faceHeight, 320, 288);
eyesWindow.Set(160, pcaTex.eyesHeight, 192, 64);
upperTeethWindow.Set(106, 2, 150, 56);
lowerTeethWindow.Set(256, 2, 150, 56);
upperTongueWindow.Set(414, 2, 96, 96);
```

Figure 15-15. A Frame from the E3 2006 Tiger Woods Demo Showing Faithful Reproduction of Tiger's Signature Smile

Figure 15-16. More Frames from the Tiger Woods Demo

```
if(InWindow(faceWindow, tex.xy))
{
  for(int i = 0; i < 5; i++)
  {
    comp_face[ i ] = tex2D(pcaTex.Tex0,
        ((tex.xy - faceWindow.GetCorner()) * float2(1, .25)) +
        float2(0, .25 + i * (288.0/2048.0))) * 2 - 1;
  }

  color.r += PcaDec(pcaTex.TexWeightR, comp_face, 5, 1, 0);
  color.g += PcaDec(pcaTex.TexWeightG, comp_face, 5, 1, 0);
  color.b += PcaDec(pcaTex.TexWeightB, comp_face, 5, 1, 0);

  if(InWindow(eyesWindow, tex.xy))
  {
    for(int i = 0; i < 16; i++)
    {
      comp_eyes[i] = tex2D(pcaTex.Tex0,
          ((tex.xy - eyesWindow.GetCorner()) *  float2(1, .25)) +
          float2(320.0/512.0, .25 +  i * (64.0/2048.0))) * 2 - 1;
    }

    color.r += PcaDec(pcaTex.TexWeightR, comp_eyes, 16, 6, 0);
    color.g += PcaDec(pcaTex.TexWeightG, comp_eyes, 16, 6, 0);
    color.b += PcaDec(pcaTex.TexWeightB, comp_eyes, 16, 6, 0);
  }
}
else
{
  if(InWindow(upperTeethWindow, tex.xy))
  {
    for(int i = 0; i < 4; i++)
    {
      comp_upper_teeth[ i ] = tex2D(pcaTex.Tex0,
          ((tex.xy - upperTeethWindow.GetCorner()) *
          float2(1, .25)) +  float2(320.0/512.0, .75 + i *
          (128.0/2048.0))) * 2 - 1;
    }
```

Figure 15-17. A Frame from *Need for Speed: Carbon*

Listing 15-2 (*continued*). The Variable PCA Shader for the Regions from Figure 15-12

```
      color.r += PcaDec(pcaTex.TexWeightR, comp_upper_teeth, 4, 1, 0);
      color.g += PcaDec(pcaTex.TexWeightG, comp_upper_teeth, 4, 1, 0);
      color.b += PcaDec(pcaTex.TexWeightB, comp_upper_teeth, 4, 1, 0);
  }

  if(InWindow(lowerTeethWindow, tex.xy))
  {
    for(int i = 0; i < 4; i++)
    {
      comp_lower_teeth[ i ] = tex2D(pcaTex.Tex0,
          ((tex.xy - lowerTeethWindow.GetCorner()) *
          float2(1, .25)) +  float2(320.0/512.0, .75 +
          (64 + i * 128.0)/2048.0)) * 2 - 1;
    }

    color.r += PcaDec(pcaTex.TexWeightR, comp_lower_teeth, 4, 1, 0);
    color.g += PcaDec(pcaTex.TexWeightG, comp_lower_teeth, 4, 1, 0);
    color.b += PcaDec(pcaTex.TexWeightB, comp_lower_teeth, 4, 1, 0);
  }
```

```
    if(InWindow(upperTongueWindow, tex.xy))
    {
      for(int i = 0; i < 3; i++)
      {
        comp_upper_tongue[ i ] = tex2D(pcaTex.Tex0,
            ((tex.xy - upperTongueWindow.GetCorner()) *
            float2(1, .25)) +  float2(i * (96 / 512.0),
            1952.0/2048.0)) * 2 - 1;
      }

      color.r += PcaDec(pcaTex.TexWeightR, comp_upper_tongue, 3, 1, 0);
      color.g += PcaDec(pcaTex.TexWeightG, comp_upper_tongue, 3, 1, 0);
      color.b += PcaDec(pcaTex.TexWeightB, comp_upper_tongue, 3, 1, 0);
    }
  }

  color.rgb /= 255;

  return color;
}

float4 mainf(PsInput IN, tPcaTex pcaTex) : COLOR
{
  float4 out_color;
  out_color.rgb = 0;

  out_color.rgb = DecompressPcaColor(IN.tex.xy, pcaTex);
  out_color.a = 1;
  return out_color;
}
```

15.6 References

Borshukov, George, and J. P. Lewis. 2003. "Realistic Human Face Rendering for *The Matrix Reloaded.*" In *ACM SIGGRAPH 2003 Sketches and Applications.*

Borshukov, George, Dan Piponi, Oystein Larsen, J. P. Lewis, and Christina Tempelaar-Lietz. 2003. "Universal Capture: Image-Based Facial Animation for *The Matrix Reloaded.*" Sketch presented at SIGGRAPH 2003.

d'Eon, Eugene. 2007. "NVIDIA Demo Team Secrets–Advanced Skin Rendering." Presentation at Game Developers Conference 2007. Available online at http://developer.download.nvidia.com/presentations/2007/gdc/Advanced_Skin.pdf.

Mori, M. 1982. *The Buddha in the Robot*. Tuttle.

Shlens, Jonathon. 2005. "A Tutorial on Principal Component Analysis." Available online at http://www.cs.cmu.edu/~elaw/papers/pca.pdf.

Strang, G. 1998. *Introduction to Linear Algebra*. Wellesley-Cambridge Press.

Weyrich, Tim, W. Matusik, H. Pfister, B. Bickel, C. Donner, C. Tu, J. McAndless, J. Lee, A. Ngan, H. W. Jensen, and M. Gross. 2006. "Analysis of Human Faces Using a Measurement-Based Skin Reflectance Model." In *ACM Transactions on Graphics (Proceedings of SIGGRAPH 2006)* 25(3), pp. 1013–1024.

Chapter 16

Vegetation Procedural Animation and Shading in *Crysis*

Tiago Sousa
Crytek

At Crytek, one of our primary goals for *Crysis* was to define a new standard for computer game graphics. For our latest game, we have developed several new technologies that together comprise CryENGINE 2. A key feature of *Crysis* among these technologies is *vegetation rendering*, which is composed of several parts, including procedural breaking and physics interaction, shading, procedural animation, and distant sprite generation, among others.

Vegetation in games has always been mainly static, with some sort of simple bending to give the illusion of wind. Our game scenes can have thousands of different vegetations, but still we pushed the envelope further by making vegetation react to global and local wind sources, and we bend not only the vegetation but also the leaves, in detail, with all computations procedurally and efficiently done on the GPU.

In this chapter, we describe how we handle shading and procedural vegetation animation in an efficient and realistic way.

16.1 Procedural Animation

In our approach, we divide animation into two parts: (1) the main bending, which animates the entire vegetation along the wind direction; and (2) the detail bending, which animates the leaves. A wind vector is computed per-instance, in world space, by summing up the wind forces affecting the instance. A wind area can be a directional or an omni-directional wind source. In our case, we compute this sum in a very similar way to light sources affecting a single point, taking direction and attenuation into account. Also, each instance has its own stiffness, and the wind strength gets dampened over time when the instance stops being affected by any wind sources. Figure 16-1 shows an example.

Figure 16-1. Visualization of Increasing Main Bending Strength
Left: No wind. Middle: Mild wind. Right: Strong wind.

Designers can place wind sources at specific locations, attach them to an entity (for example, helicopters), and attach then to particle systems as well. With this approach, we can theoretically afford a large number of wind sources while keeping the per-vertex cost constant, although with some extra linear per-instance CPU cost.

We generate the main bending by using the *xy* components of the wind vector, which gives us the wind direction and its strength, using the vegetation mesh height as a scale to apply a directional vertex deformation. Note that care must be taken to limit the amount of deformation; otherwise, the results will not look believable.

For leaves' detail bending, we approach things in a similar fashion, but in this case only wind strength is taken into account. Artists paint one RGB color per-vertex, using a common 3D modeling software. This color gives us extra information about the detail bending. As shown in Figure 16-2, the red channel is used for the stiffness of leaves' edges, the green channel for per-leaf phase variation, and the blue channel for the overall stiffness of the leaves. The alpha channel is used for precomputed ambient occlusion. For more details on this shading, see Section 16.2.

16.1.1 Implementation Details

One of our main objectives was to achieve an intuitive system, as simple as possible for an artist or designer to use. Therefore, designers' main inputs are wind direction and

Figure 16-2. Using Vertex Color
Left: The stiffness of the leaves' edges. Middle: The per-leaf phase variation. Right: The overall stiffness of the leaves.

speed. If required in particular cases, artists can still override default settings, for leaves' wind speed (frequency), edges, and per-leaf amplitude, to make the vegetation animation more visually pleasing.

Approximating Sine Waves

The traditional approach for procedural vertex animation relies on using sine waves. We can approximate similar results in a cheaper way by using *triangle waves*.[1] More specifically, for our detail bending case, we use a total of four vectorized triangle waves: two for the leaves' edges and two for the leaves' bending. After computing these waves, we smooth them using cubic interpolation (Bourke 1999), as shown in Listing 16-1. Figure 16-3 illustrates the process.

Listing 16-1. Functions Used for Wave Generation

```
float4 SmoothCurve( float4 x ) {
  return x * x *( 3.0 - 2.0 * x );
}

float4 TriangleWave( float4 x ) {
  return abs( frac( x + 0.5 ) * 2.0 - 1.0 );
}

float4 SmoothTriangleWave( float4 x ) {
  return SmoothCurve( TriangleWave( x ) );
}
```

1. For general information on sine waves and triangle waves, see the following articles on Wikipedia: http://en.wikipedia.org/wiki/Sine_wave and http://en.wikipedia.org/wiki/Triangle_wave.

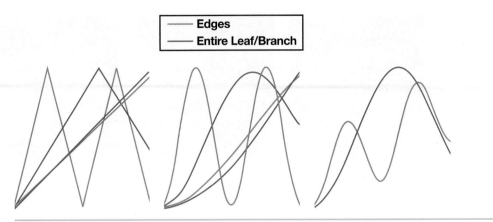

Figure 16-3. Wave Composition
Left: Vectorized triangle waves. Middle: Smoothed waves. Right: Composed waves. Orange represents edges; blue represents entire leaves or branches.

Detail Bending

Leaves' bending, as we have mentioned, is done by deforming the edges, using the vertex color's red channel for controlling edge stiffness control. This deformation is done along the world-space vertex normal xy direction.

Finally, we come to per-leaf bending, which we produce simply by deforming up and down along the z-axis, using the blue channel for leaf stiffness.

The vertex color's green channel contains a per-leaf phase variation, which we use to give each individual leaf its own phase, so that every leaf moves differently. Listing 16-2 shows the code for our detail-bending approach.

Leaves' shape and the number of vertices can vary depending on the vegetation type. For example, we model an entire leaf for a palm tree, which gives us the ability to nicely animate it in a very controllable way. For bigger trees, however, we model the leaves as several planes; we accept that total control is not possible, because several leaves can be on a relatively low-polygon-count plane placed as a texture. Still, we use the same approach for all different cases with good results.

Main Bending

We accomplish the main vegetation bending by displacing vertices' xy positions along the wind direction, using normalized height to scale the amount of deformation. Performing a simple displace is not enough, because we need to restrict vertex movement to minimize deformation artifacts. We achieve this by computing the vertex's distance to the mesh center and using this distance for rescaling the new displaced normalized position.

This process results in a spherical limited movement, which is enough for our vegetation case, because it is a single vegetation object. The amount of bending deformation needs to be carefully tweaked as well: too much bending will ruin the illusion. Listing 16-3 shows our implementation. Figure 16-4 shows some examples produced using this main bending technique.

Listing 16-2. The Implementation of Our Detail-Bending Approach

```
// Phases (object, vertex, branch)
float fObjPhase = dot(worldPos.xyz, 1);
fBranchPhase += fObjPhase;
float fVtxPhase = dot(vPos.xyz, fDetailPhase + fBranchPhase);

// x is used for edges; y is used for branches
float2 vWavesIn = fTime + float2(fVtxPhase, fBranchPhase );
// 1.975, 0.793, 0.375, 0.193 are good frequencies
float4 vWaves = (frac( vWavesIn.xxyy *
                        float4(1.975, 0.793, 0.375,  0.193) ) *
                        2.0 - 1.0 ) * fSpeed * fDetailFreq;
vWaves = SmoothTriangleWave( vWaves );

float2 vWavesSum = vWaves.xz + vWaves.yw;
// Edge (xy) and branch bending (z)
vPos.xyz += vWavesSum.xxy * float3(fEdgeAtten * fDetailAmp *
                        vNormal.xy, fBranchAtten * fBranchAmp);
```

Listing 16-3. The Main Bending Implementation

```
// Bend factor - Wind variation is done on the CPU.
float fBF = vPos.z * fBendScale;
// Smooth bending factor and increase its nearby height limit.
fBF += 1.0;
fBF *= fBF;
fBF = fBF * fBF - fBF;
// Displace position
float3 vNewPos = vPos;
vNewPos.xy += vWind.xy * fBF;
// Rescale
vPos.xyz = normalize(vNewPos.xyz)* fLength;
```

Figure 16-4. Bending on Different Types of Vegetation

16.2 Vegetation Shading

We have thousands of different vegetation objects in *Crysis*, often covering the entire screen. So we needed to keep in mind a quality/efficiency ratio.

For this reason, we combined per-pixel shading with vertex shading, and in the case of grass, it's handled the exact same way. The only difference is that we do all shading per-vertex due to grass's heavy fill-rate requirements.

Trunk shading is handled using standard Lambert and Phong shading models.

Foliage is approached in a different way. We render it as double-sided, and leaves use alpha test while grass uses alpha blending. We tried different approaches at the beginning of our project, such as a two-pass alpha test/blending, but for our case, the quality/efficiency ratio was not worth it.

In reality, foliage can have different thicknesses (for our foliage, that is the assumption we always make) and lets variable amounts of light pass through in different areas. Therefore, we needed a subsurface-scattering approximation.

We approximate this term by using an artist-made subsurface texture map, as shown in Figure 16-5, which is created using a regular image-editing software package. This map can have internal depth leaves' details such as veins and internal branches, and it can be relatively low-res (for example, 128×128), depending on the detail required. Listing 16-4 in Section 16.2.4 provides implementation details.

Because performance and quality for vegetation were crucial, for this case we decided to use a cheap and artist-friendly subsurface-scattering approximation that is computed per-vertex, simply using $-\mathbf{N} \cdot \mathbf{L}$ multiplied with light position visibility, $\mathbf{E} \cdot \mathbf{L}$ (the eye vector dot product with the light vector), both multiplied by subsurface texture for thickness variation. Figure 16-6 shows some examples.

Figure 16-5. Examples of the Subsurface Texture Map

Figure 16-6. Visualization of the Subsurface-Scattering Approximation
Left: Using only front shading. Middle: With the subsurface-scattering term added. Right: Using the subsurface texture map for thickness variation.

It is worth mentioning also that all shading in CryENGINE 2 is done in world space, which in our particular solution, helped to work around hardware limits for the attribute-based instancing case and minimized shading discontinuities in some specific cases.

16.2.1 Ambient Lighting

Traditional constant ambient color looks very boring and has become outdated. At the beginning of development, we had two different vegetation shaders. One ended up being the implementation we describe in this chapter; the other was more complex, using spherical harmonics for indirect lighting, which was used mainly for big trees. To decrease the number of shader permutations and because of the complexity of spherical harmonics, we unfortunately had to drop this latter approach in favor of a unified and cheaper outdoor ambient-lighting solution.

Ambient lighting in our engine now has three variations: outdoor, indoor, and a simple solution for low-spec hardware. The way we handle outdoor and indoor ambient lighting is quite complex and would require two more chapters to explain; therefore, it's outside this chapter's scope.

All three variations try to give an interesting look to unlit surfaces, and for this chapter, we'll assume the low-spec hardware solution, which is implemented using hemisphere lighting (Taylor 2001) to break the flat look on shadowed areas.

Finally we also use a precomputed ambient occlusion term stored in the vertex's alpha channel, which is painted by artists or computed using standard 3D modeling software.

16.2.2 Edge Smoothing

One big issue when using alpha testing is the hard edges. At the time we developed vegetation main shading, there was no alpha-to-coverage support in any hardware (we do now support it as well). So we came up with a special solution to smooth out the edges through post-processing.

In CryENGINE 2, we use a deferred rendering approach, by first rendering a z-pass and writing depth into a floating-point texture.

This technique enables a wide range of effects (Wenzel 2007), which require depth information. Edge smoothing is one such effect; it works by doing edge detection using the depth texture and then using rotated triangle samples for dependent texture lookups using bilinear filtering. Edge smoothing works only on opaque geometry, however, because nonopaque geometry doesn't write depth into the z-target. Figure 16-7 shows how beneficial edge smoothing can be.

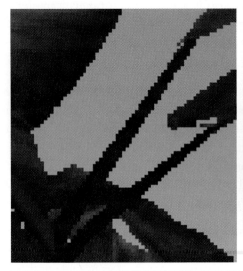 

Figure 16-7. The Benefits of Edge Smoothing
Left: No edge smoothing. Right: Edge smoothing.

16.2.3 Putting It All Together

The final results are achieved with the help of high-quality shadows together with an exponential tone mapper and various post-processing methods, such as bloom (Kawase 2004) and sun shafts, among others. Thanks to the combination of all these techniques, we achieve the final, in-game image quality we desire, as shown in Figure 16-8.

Figure 16-8. The Final Result
Left: No high dynamic range or shadows or post-processing applied. Right: With all techniques applied.

16.2.4 Implementation Details

Before showing the shader implementation, we would point out that a unified shader library solution was developed for CryENGINE 2 that not only simplified shaders, but also made them more readable and easier to maintain. It also added the extra benefit of enforcing naming conventions and minimizing code duplication.

The idea was simply to share as much as possible and minimize users' interaction with the shading kernel. As a result, all lights management, ambient computation, and other important computations (such as parallax occlusion mapping or decals) are hidden from shader writers.

Users have access to four custom functions, which allow them to initialize custom data, do per-light computations, ambient lighting, and shading finalization. Everything else is handled as a black box, which gives users important data for each of the four functions through a unified data structure. This data structure contains important shareable data, such as eye vector, normal vector, diffuse map color, bump map color, alpha, and so on.

Listings 16-4 and 16-5 show the final shader implementations. The functions in Listing 16-5 are the user custom functions, where we do the per-light source shading computation and apply light properties such as light diffuse and specular color. The ambient function is where we do the hemisphere lighting approximation. At the end of the listing, the shading final composition is where material properties such as diffuse texture, diffuse color, and specular color are applied.

Listing 16-4. Functions Used for Shading Leaves' Back and Front Sides

```
half3 LeafShadingBack( half3 vEye,
                       half3 vLight,
                       half3 vNormal,
                       half3 cDiffBackK,
                       half fBackViewDep )
{
   half fEdotL = saturate(dot(vEye.xyz, -vLight.xyz));
   half fPowEdotL = fEdotL * fEdotL;
   fPowEdotL *= fPowEdotL;

   // Back diffuse shading, wrapped slightly
   half fLdotNBack = saturate(dot(-vNormal.xyz, vLight.xyz)*0.6+0.4);

   // Allow artists to tweak view dependency.
   half3 vBackShading = lerp(fPowEdotL, fLdotNBack, fBackViewDep);

   // Apply material back diffuse color.
   return vBackShading * cDiffBackK.xyz;
}

void LeafShadingFront(half3 vEye,
                      half3 vLight,
                      half3 vNormal,
                      half3 cDifK,
                      half4 cSpecK,
                      out half3 outDif,
                      out half3 outSpec)
{
   half fLdotN = saturate(dot(vNormal.xyz, vLight.xyz));

   outDif = fLdotN * cDifK.xyz;
   outSpec = Phong(vEye, vLight, cSpecK.w) * cSpecK.xyz;
}
```

Listing 16-5. Pixel Shader Code for Vegetation

```
void frag_custom_per_light( inout fragPass pPass,
                            inout fragLightPass pLight ) {
  half3 cDiffuse = 0, cSpecular = 0;
  LeafShadingFront( pPass.vReflVec, pLight.vLight, pPass.vNormal.xyz,
                    pLight.cDiffuse.xyz, pLight.cSpecular,
                    cDiffuse, cSpecular );
  // Shadows * light falloff * light projected texture
  half3 cK = pLight.fOcclShadow * pLight.fFallOff * pLight.cFilter;
  // Accumulate results.
  pPass.cDiffuseAcc += cDiffuse * cK;
  pPass.cSpecularAcc += cSpecular * cK;
  pPass.pCustom.fOcclShadowAcc += pLight.fOcclShadow;
}
void frag_custom_ambient(inout fragPass pPass, inout half3 cAmbient)
{
  // Hemisphere lighting approximation
  cAmbient.xyz = lerp(cAmbient*0.5f, cAmbient,
                      saturate(pPass.vNormal.z*0.5f+0.5f));
  pPass.cAmbientAcc.xyz = cAmbient;
}

void frag_custom_end(inout fragPass pPass, inout half3 cFinal) {
  if( pPass.nlightCount && pPass.pCustom.bLeaves ) {
    // Normalize shadow accumulation.
    half fOccFactor = pPass.pCustom.fOcclShadowAcc/pPass.nlightCount;
    // Apply subsurface map.
    pPass.pCustom.cShadingBack.xyz *= pPass.pCustom.cBackDiffuseMap;
    // Apply shadows and light projected texture.
    pPass.pCustom.cShadingBack.xyz *= fOccFactor *
                                      pPass.pCustom.cFilterColor;
  }
  // Apply diffuse texture and material diffuse color to
  // ambient/diffuse/sss terms.
  cFinal.xyz = (pPass.cAmbientAcc.xyz + pPass.cDiffuseAcc.xyz +
               pPass.pCustom.cShadingBack.xyz) *
               pPass.cDiffuseMap.xyz * MatDifColor.xyz;
  // Apply gloss map and material specular color, add to result.
  cFinal.xyz += pPass.cSpecularAcc.xyz * pPass.cGlossMap.xyz *
               MatSpecColor.xyz;
  // Apply prebaked ambient occlusion term.
  cFinal.xyz *= pPass.pCustom.fAmbientOcclusion;
}
```

16.3 Conclusion

In this chapter, we have presented a snapshot of how the vegetation shading and procedural animation in *Crysis* is done, at the time this chapter was written. CryENGINE 2 evolves at such rapid pace that improvements might be added before *Crysis* is finished.

The presented procedural animation technique was implemented in a general way, so it is possible to apply wind forces even to nonvegetation objects, such as cloth and hair; the only difference is that no main bending is used for these cases.

We can have helicopters, grenade explosions, and even weapon fire affecting vegetation, cloth, and hair, all in an extremely efficient way.

As much as we pushed the envelope on vegetation rendering, there's still a lot of room for improvement as hardware gets faster. For example, shading could be improved, the leaves' specular lighting in most cases is not isotropic, and we could also use a more accurate subsurface-scattering approximation computed per-pixel. Finally, using more waves for bending would expand the range of the animation variation.

16.4 References

Baer, M. 2005. "Effects in *Madagascar*: Escape from Realism." Presentation at Eurographics 2005. More information available online at http://isg.cs.tcd.ie/eg2005/IS1.html.

Bourke, P. 1999. "Interpolation Methods." Available online at http://local.wasp.uwa.edu.au/~pbourke/other/interpolation/index.html.

Green, Simon. 2004. "Real-Time Approximations to Subsurface Scattering" In *GPU Gems*, edited by Randima Fernando, pp. 263–278. Addison-Wesley.

Kawase, M. 2004. "Practical Implementation of High Dynamic Range Rendering." Presentation at Game Developers Conference 2004. Available online at http://www.daionet.gr.jp/~masa/column/2004-04-04.html.

NVIDIA Corporation. 2005. "GPU Programming Exposed: The Naked Truth Behind NVIDIA's Demos." Presentation at SIGGRAPH 2005. Available online at http://http.download.nvidia.com/developer/presentations/2005/SIGGRAPH/Truth_About_NVIDIA_Demos_Med.pdf.

Taylor, P. 2001. "Per-Pixel Lighting." Online article available at
http://msdn2.microsoft.com/en-us/library/ms810494.aspx.

Wenzel, C. 2007. "Real-Time Atmospheric Effects in Games Revisited." Presentation at
Game Developers Conference 2007. Available online at http://ati.amd.com/
developer/gdc/2007/D3DTutorial_Crytek.pdf.

The wind technique presented was partially inspired by the movie Madagascar *and the
artist-oriented presentation done by Matt Baer of DreamWorks Animation SKG at Eurographics 2005 (Baer 2005). Unfortunately, Baer 2005 seems not to be available anywhere
online.*

*A special thanks to Marco Corbetta and Martin Mittring for helping me review and im-
prove this chapter, and to everyone on Crytek's R&D team involved in vegetation rendering.*

Chapter 17

Robust Multiple Specular Reflections and Refractions

Tamás Umenhoffer
Budapest University of Technology and Economics

Gustavo Patow
University of Girona

László Szirmay-Kalos
Budapest University of Technology and Economics

In this chapter, we present a robust algorithm to compute single and multiple reflections and refractions on the GPU. To allow the fragment shader to access the geometric description of the whole scene when looking for the hit points of secondary rays, we first render the scene into a *layered distance map*. Each layer is stored as a cube map in the texture memory. The texels of these cube maps contain not only color information, but also the distance from a reference point and the surface normal, so the texels can be interpreted as sampled representations of the scene. The algorithm searches this representation to trace secondary rays. The search process starts with *ray marching*, which makes sure that no ray surface intersection is missed, and continues with a *secant search*, which provides accuracy.

After we introduce the general machinery for tracing secondary rays, we present the applications, including single and multiple reflections and refractions on curved surfaces. To compute multiple reflections and refractions, the normal vector stored at the distance maps is read and used to generate the reflected/refracted rays. These higher-order rays are traced similar to how the first reflection ray was traced by the fragment shader. The intensity of the reflected ray is calculated according to a simplified Fresnel formula that is also appropriate for metals. The resulting algorithm is simple to implement, runs in real time, and is accurate enough to render self-reflections. The implementation of our proposed method requires dynamic branching support.

17.1 Introduction

Image synthesis computes the radiance of points that are visible through the pixels of the virtual camera. Local illumination models compute the radiance from local properties—such as the position, normal vector, and material data—in addition to global light source parameters. Each point is shaded independently, which opens up a lot of possibilities for parallel computation. This independent and parallel shading concept is heavily exploited in current GPUs, owing its appealing performance to the parallel architecture made possible by the local illumination model. However, for ideal reflectors and refractors, the radiance of a point depends also on the illumination of other points; thus, points cannot be shaded independently. This condition means that the radiance computation of a point recursively generates new visibility and color computation tasks to determine the intensity of the indirect illumination.

The basic operation for solving the visibility problem of a point at a direction is to trace a ray. To obtain a complete path, we should continue ray tracing at the hit point to get a second point and further scattering points. GPUs trace rays of the same origin very efficiently, taking a "photo" from the shared ray origin and using the fragment shader unit to compute the radiance of the visible points. The photographic process involves rasterizing the scene geometry and exploiting the z-buffer to find the first hits of the rays passing through the pixels.

This approach is ideal for primary rays, but not for the secondary rays needed for the specular reflection and refraction terms of the radiance, because these rays do not share the same origin. To trace these rays, the fragment shader should have access to the scene. Because fragment shaders may access global (that is, uniform) parameters and textures, this requirement can be met if the scene geometry is stored in uniform parameters or in textures.

Scene objects can be encoded as the set of parameters of the surface equation, similar to classical ray tracing (Havran 2001, Purcell et al. 2002, and Purcell et al. 2003). If the scene geometry is too complex, simple proxy geometries can be used that allow fast approximate intersections (Bjorke 2004 and Popescu et al. 2006).

On the other hand, the scene geometry can also be stored in a sampled form. The oldest application of this idea is the *depth map* used by shadow algorithms (Williams 1978), which stores light-space z coordinates for the part of the geometry that is seen from the light position through a window.

To consider all directions, we should use a cube map instead of a single depth image. If we store world-space Euclidean distance in texels, the cube map becomes similar to a *sphere map* (Patow 1995 and Szirmay-Kalos et al. 2005). Thus, a pair of direction and distance values specifies the point visible at this direction, without knowing the orientation of the cube-map faces. This property is particularly important when we interpolate between two directions, because it relieves us from taking care of cube-map face boundaries. These cube maps that store distance values are called *distance maps*.

A depth or distance cube map represents only the surfaces directly visible from the eye position that was used to generate this map. The used eye position is called the *reference point* of the map. To also include surfaces that are occluded from the reference point, we should generate and store several layers of the distance map (in a texel we store not only the closest point, but all points that are in this direction).

In this chapter, we present a simple and robust ray-tracing algorithm that computes intersections with the geometry stored in layered distance maps. Note that this map is the sampled representation of the scene geometry. Thus, when a ray is traced, the intersection calculation can use this information instead of the triangular meshes. Fragment shaders can look up texture maps but cannot directly access meshes, so this replacement is crucial for the GPU implementation. In our approach, ray tracing may support searches for the second and third (and so on) hit points of the path, while the first point is identified by rasterization. Our approach can be considered an extension to *environment mapping* because it puts distance information into texels in order to obtain more-accurate ray environment intersections.

This robust machinery for tracing secondary rays can be used to compute real-time, multiple reflections and refractions.

17.2 Tracing Secondary Rays

The proposed ray tracing algorithm works on geometry stored in layered distance maps. A single layer of these layered distance maps is a cube map, where a texel contains the material properties, the distance, and the normal vector of the point that is in the direction of the texel. The *material property* is the reflected radiance for diffuse surfaces and the Fresnel factor at perpendicular illumination for specular reflectors. For refractors, the index of refraction is also stored as a material property. The distance is measured from the center of the cube map (that is, from the reference point).

17.2.1 Generation of Layered Distance Maps

Computing distance maps is similar to computing classical environment maps. We render the scene six times, taking the reference point as the eye and the faces of a cube as the window rectangles. The difference is that not only is the color calculated and stored in additional cube maps, but also the distance and the normal vector. We can generate the texture storing the color, plus the texture encoding the normal vector and the distance, in a single rendering pass, using the *multiple render target* feature.

The set of layers representing the scene could be obtained by *depth peeling* (Everitt 2001 and Liu et al. 2006) in the general case. To control the number of layers, we can limit the number of peeling passes, so we put far objects into a single layer whether or not they occlude each other, as shown in Figure 17-1. If the distance of far objects is significantly larger than the size of the reflective object, this approximation is acceptable.

For simpler reflective objects that are not too close to the environment, the layer generation can be further simplified. The reference point is put at the center of the reflective object, and the front and back faces of the reflective object are rendered separately into two layers. Note that this method may not fill all texels of a layer, so some texels may represent no visible point. If we clear the render target with a negative distance value

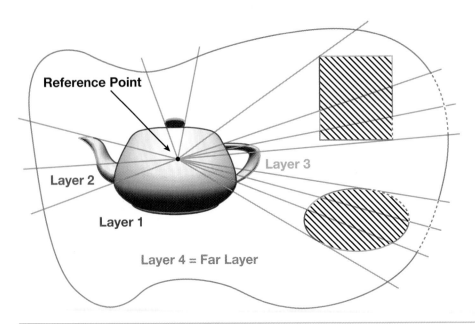

Figure 17-1. A Layered Distance Map with 3 + 1 Layers
The first three layers are identified with depth peeling and the rest are assigned to the fourth layer.

Chapter 17   Robust Multiple Specular Reflections and Refractions before rendering, then invalid texels containing no visible point can be recognized later by checking the sign of the distance.

When scene objects are moving, distance maps should be updated.

17.2.2 Ray Tracing Layered Distance Maps

The basic idea is discussed using the notations of Figure 17-2. The *place vectors* of points are represented by lowercase letters and the *direction vectors* are indicated by uppercase letters. Let us assume that center $\mathbf{o}$ of our coordinate system is the reference point and that we are interested in the illumination of point $\mathbf{x}$ from direction $\mathbf{R}$.

The illuminating point is thus on the ray of equation $\mathbf{x} + \mathbf{R} \cdot d$, where d is the parameter of the ray that needs to be determined. We can check the accuracy of an arbitrary approximation of d by reading the distance of the environment surface stored with the direction of $\mathbf{l} = \mathbf{x} + \mathbf{R} \cdot d$ in the cube map ($|\mathbf{l}'|$) and comparing it with the distance of approximating point $\mathbf{l}$ on the ray $|\mathbf{l}|$. If $|\mathbf{l}| \approx |\mathbf{l}'|$, then we have found the intersection. If the point on the ray is in front of the surface, that is $|\mathbf{l}| < |\mathbf{l}'|$, the current approximation is *undershooting*. On the other hand, when point $|\mathbf{l}|$ is behind the surface ($|\mathbf{l}| > |\mathbf{l}'|$), the approximation is *overshooting*.

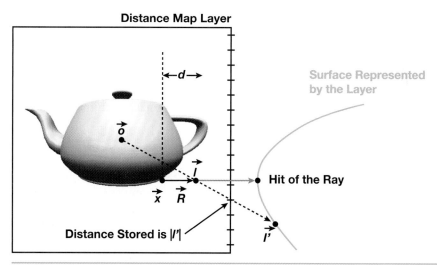

Figure 17-2. Tracing a Ray from **x** at Direction **R**
The current approximation of the ray parameter is d, which corresponds to point l on the ray. Looking up the distance map in the direction of l, we can obtain the parameters of surface point l'.

Ray parameter d can be found by using an iterative process. The process starts with ray marching (that is, a *linear search*) and continues with a secant search. The robust linear search computes a rough overshooting guess and an undershooting approximation that enclose the first intersection of the ray. Starting with these approximations, the secant search quickly obtains an accurate intersection.

Linear Search

The possible intersection points are on the ray. Thus, the intersection can be found by marching on the ray (that is, checking points $\mathbf{r}(d) = \mathbf{x} + \mathbf{R} \cdot d$ generated with an increasing sequence of positive parameter d, and detecting the first pair of subsequent points where one point is overshooting while the other is undershooting). The real intersection, then, lies between these two guesses and is found by using a secant search (discussed in the following subsection).

The definition of the increments of ray parameter d needs special consideration because now the geometry is sampled, and it is not worth checking the same sample many times while ignoring other samples. Unfortunately, making uniform steps on the ray does not guarantee that the texture space is uniformly sampled. As we get farther from the reference point, unit-length steps on the ray correspond to smaller steps in texture space. This problem can be solved by marching on a line segment that looks identical to the ray from the reference point, except that its two end points are at the same distance. The end points of such a line segment can be obtained by projecting the start of the ray, $\mathbf{r}(0)$ and the end of the ray, $\mathbf{r}(\infty)$ onto a unit sphere, resulting in new start $\mathbf{s} = \mathbf{x}/|\mathbf{x}|$ and end point $\mathbf{e} = \mathbf{R}/|\mathbf{R}|$, respectively. The intersection must be found at the texels that are seen at a direction between $\mathbf{s}$ and $\mathbf{e}$, as shown in Figure 17-3.

The intersection algorithm searches these texels, making uniform steps on the line segment of $\mathbf{s}$ and $\mathbf{e}$:

$$\mathbf{r}'(t) = \mathbf{s} \cdot (1 - t) + \mathbf{e} \cdot t, \qquad t = 0, \Delta t, 2\Delta t, \dots, 1.$$

The correspondence between ray parameter d and parameter t can be found by projecting $\mathbf{r}'$ onto the ray, which leads to the following formula:

$$d(t) = \frac{|\mathbf{x}|}{|\mathbf{R}|} \cdot \frac{t}{1 - t}.$$

A fragment shader implementation should take inputs of the ray of origin x and direction R—as well as cube map map of type samplerCUBE passed as a uniform parameter—and sequentially generate ray parameters d and points on the ray r, and return an undershooting ray parameter dl and an overshooting ray parameter dp. Ratios $|\mathbf{l}|/|\mathbf{l}'|$

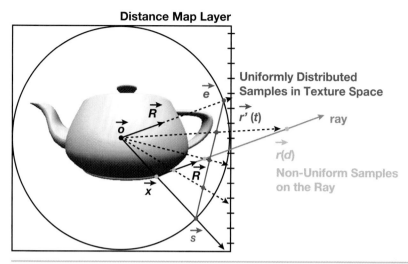

Distance Map Layer

Uniformly Distributed Samples in Texture Space

$\vec{e}$
$\vec{r'}(t)$ ray

$\vec{r}(d)$

Non-Uniform Samples on the Ray

Figure 17-3. Marching on the Ray, Making Uniform Steps in Texture Space

and $|\mathbf{p}|/|\mathbf{p'}|$ are represented by variables `llp` and `ppp`, respectively. The distance values are stored in the alpha channel of the cube map. Listing 17-1 shows the algorithm for the fragment shader executing a linear search.

This algorithm finds a pair of subsequent undershooting and overshooting points in a single layer, advancing on the ray making uniform steps `Dt` in texture space. Step size `Dt` is set proportionally to the length of line segment of **s** and **e** and to the resolution of the cube map. By setting texel step `Dt` to be greater than the distance of two neighboring texels, we speed up the algorithm but also increase the probability of missing the reflection of a thin object. At a texel, the distance value is obtained from the alpha channel of the cube map. Note that we use function `texCUBElod()`—setting the mipmap level explicitly to 0—instead of `texCUBE()`, because `texCUBE()`, like `tex2D()`, would force the DirectX 9 HLSL compiler to unroll the dynamic loop (Sander 2005).

Linear search should be run for each layer. The layer where the ray parameter (`dp`) is minimal contains the first hit of the ray.

Acceleration with Min-Max Distance Values

To speed up the intersection search in a layer, we compute a minimum and a maximum distance value for each distance map. When a ray is traced, the ray is intersected with the spheres centered at the reference point and having radii equal to the minimum and maximum values. The two intersection points significantly reduce the ray space that needs to be marched. This process moves the start point **s** and end point **e** closer, so fewer marching steps would provide the same accuracy. See Figure 17-4.

Listing 17-1. The Fragment Shader Executing a Linear Search in HLSL

```
float a = length(x) / length(R);
bool undershoot = false, overshoot = false;
float dl, llp;  // Ray parameter and |l|/|l'| of last undershooting
float dp, ppp;  // Ray parameter and |p|/|p'| of last overshooting

float t = 0.0001f;
while( t < 1 && !(overshoot && undershoot) ) {   // Iteration
  float d = a * t / (1-t);  // Ray parameter corresponding to t
  float3 r = x + R * d;  // r(d): point on the ray
  float ra = texCUBElod(map, float4(r,0)).a; // |r'|
  if (ra > 0) {  // Valid texel, i.e. anything is visible
    float rrp = length(r)/ra;  //|r|/|r'|
    if (rrp < 1) {  // Undershooting
      dl = d;  // Store last undershooting in dl
      llp = rrp;
      undershoot = true;
    } else {  // Overshooting
      dp = d;  // Store last overshooting as dp
      ppp = rrp;
      overshoot = true;
    }
  } else {  // Nothing is visible: restart search
    undershoot = false;
    overshoot = false;
  }
  t += Dt;  // Next texel
}
```

Refinement by Secant Search

A linear search provides the first undershooting and overshooting pair of subsequent samples, so the real intersection must lie between these points. Let us denote the undershooting and overshooting ray parameters by d_p and d_l, respectively. The corresponding two points on the ray are **p** and **l** and the two points on the surface are **p'** and **l'**, respectively, as shown in Figure 17-5.

Assuming that the surface is planar between points **p'** and **l'**, we observe that it is intersected by the ray at point $\mathbf{r} = \mathbf{x} + \mathbf{R} \cdot d_{new}$, where

$$d_{new} = d_l + (d_p - d_l) \cdot \frac{1 - |\mathbf{l}|/|\mathbf{l'}|}{|\mathbf{p}|/|\mathbf{p'}| - |\mathbf{l}|/|\mathbf{l'}|}.$$

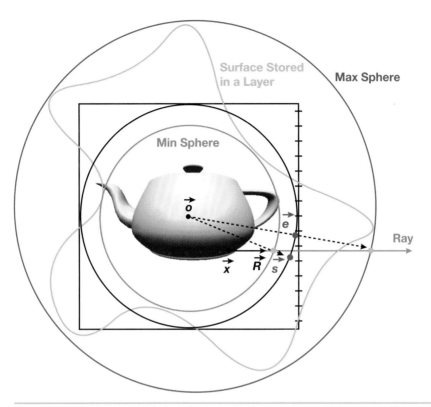

Figure 17-4. Min-Max Acceleration

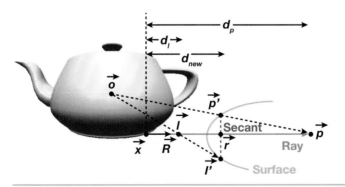

Figure 17-5. Refinement by a Secant Step
We have an undershooting approximation defined by ray parameter d_l, point on the ray l, and point on the surface l', as well as an overshooting approximation of ray parameter d_p, point on the ray p, and point on the surface p'. The new approximation of ray parameter d_{new} is obtained by intersecting the ray with the line of p' and l'.

If a single secant step does not provide accurate enough results, then d_{new} can replace one of the previous approximations d_l or d_p (always keeping one overshooting and one undershooting approximation) and we can proceed with the same iteration step. Note that a secant search obtains exact results for planar surfaces in a single iteration step and requires just finite steps for planar meshes. Listing 17-2 shows the fragment shader implementation of the secant search.

Listing 17-2. The Fragment Shader Implementation of the Secant Search in HLSL

```
for(int i = 0; i < NITER; i++) {
  // Ray parameter of the new intersection
  dnew = dl + (dp-dl) * (1-llp)/(ppp-llp);
  float3 r = x + R * dnew;   // New point on the ray
  float rrp = length(r)/ texCUBElod(map, float4(r,0)).a; // |r|/|r'|
  if (rrp < 0.9999) {  // Undershooting
    llp = rrp;   // Store as last undershooting
    dl = dnew;
  } else if (rrp > 1.0001) {   // Overshooting
    ppp = rrp;   // Store as last overshooting
    dp = dnew;
  } else i = NITER;
}
```

We put the linear search executed for every layer, plus the secant search that processes a single layer, together in a Hit() function. We now have a general tool to trace an arbitrary ray in the scene. This function finds the first hit l. Reading the cube maps in this direction, we can obtain the material properties and the normal vector associated with this point.

17.3 Reflections and Refractions

Let us first consider specular reflections. Having generated the layered distance map, we render the reflective objects and activate custom vertex and fragment shader programs. The vertex shader transforms the reflective object to clipping space—and also to the coordinate system of the cube map—by first applying the modeling transform, then translating to the reference point. View vector V and normal N are also obtained in this space. Listing 17-3 shows the vertex shader of reflections and refractions.

Listing 17-3. The Vertex Shader of Reflections and Refractions in HLSL

```
void SpecularReflectionVS(
    in  float4 Pos  : POSITION,    // Vertex in modeling space
    in  float3 Norm : NORMAL,      // Normal in modeling space
    out float4 hPos : POSITION,    // Vertex in clip space
    out float3 x    : TEXCOORD1,   // Vertex in cube-map space
    out float3 N    : TEXCOORD2,   // Normal in cube-map space
    out float3 V    : TEXCOORD3,   // View direction
    uniform float4x4 WorldViewProj,  // Modeling to clip space
    uniform float4x4 World,          // Modeling to world space
    uniform float4x4 WorldIT,        // Inverse-transpose of World
    uniform float3   RefPoint,       // Reference point in world space
    uniform float3   EyePos          // Eye in world space
) {
    hPos = mul(Pos, WorldViewProj);
    float3 wPos = mul(Pos, World).xyz;  // World space
    N = mul(Norm, WorldIT);
    V = wPos - EyePos;
    x = wPos - RefPoint;  // Translate to cube-map space
}
```

The fragment shader calls the function `Hit()` that returns the first hit `l`, its radiance `Il`, and normal vector `Nl`. If the surface is an ideal mirror, the incoming radiance should be multiplied by the Fresnel term evaluated for the angle between surface normal **N** and reflection direction **R**. We apply an approximation of the Fresnel function (Schlick 1993), which takes into account not only *refraction index n*, but also *extinction coefficient k* (which is essential for realistic metals) (Bjorke 2004; Lazányi and Szirmay-Kalos 2005):

$$F(\mathbf{N}, \mathbf{R}) = F_p + \left(1 - F_p\right) \cdot (1 - \mathbf{N} \cdot \mathbf{R})^5,$$

where

$$F_p = \frac{(n-1)^2 + k^2}{(n+1)^2 + k^2}$$

is the Fresnel function (that is, the probability that the photon is reflected) at perpendicular illumination. Note that F_p is constant for a given material. Thus, this value can be computed on the CPU from the refraction index and the extinction coefficient and passed to the GPU as a global variable. Listing 17-4 shows the fragment shader of single reflection.

Listing 17-4. The Fragment Shader of Single Reflection in HLSL

```
float4 SingleReflectionPS(
  float3 x : TEXCOORD1,   // Shaded point in cube-map space
  float3 N : TEXCOORD2,   // Normal vector
  float3 V : TEXCOORD3,   // View direction
  uniform float3 Fp0      // Fresnel at perpendicular direction
) : COLOR
{
  V = normalize(V);
  N = normalize(N);
  float3 R = reflect(V, N);   // Reflection direction
  float3 N1;   // Normal vector at the hit point
  float3 I1;   // Radiance at the hit point

  // Trace ray x+R*d and obtain hit 1, radiance I1, normal N1
  float3 l = Hit(x, R, I1, N1);

  // Fresnel reflection
  float3 F = Fp0 + pow(1-dot(N, -V), 5) * (1-Fp0);
  return float4(F * I1, 1);
}
```

The shader of single refraction is similar, but the direction computation should use the law of refraction instead of the law of reflection. In other words, the `reflect` operation should be replaced by the `refract` operation, and the incoming radiance should be multiplied by $1-F$ instead of F.

Light may get reflected or refracted on ideal reflectors or refractors several times before it arrives at a diffuse surface. If the hit point is on a specular surface, then a reflected or a refracted ray needs to be computed and ray tracing should be continued, repeating the same algorithm for the secondary, ternary, and additional rays. When the reflected or refracted ray is computed, we need the normal vector at the hit surface, the Fresnel function, and the index of refraction (in case of refractions). This information can be stored in two cube maps for each layer. The first cube map includes the material properties (the reflected color for diffuse surfaces or the Fresnel term at perpendicular illumination for specular surfaces) and the index of refraction. The second cube map stores the normal vectors and the distance values.

To distinguish reflectors, refractors, and diffuse surfaces, we check the sign of the index of refraction. Negative, zero, and positive values indicate a reflector, a diffuse surface, and a refractor, respectively. Listing 17-5 shows the code for computing multiple specular reflection/refraction.

Listing 17-5. The HLSL Fragment Shader Computing Multiple Specular Reflection/Refraction

This shader organizes the ray tracing process in a dynamic loop.

```
float4 MultipleReflectionPS(
  float3 x : TEXCOORD1,  // Shaded point in cube-map space
  float3 N : TEXCOORD2,  // Normal vector
  float3 V : TEXCOORD3,  // View direction
  uniform float3 Fp0,    // Fresnel at perpendicular direction
  uniform float3 n0      // Index of refraction
) : COLOR
{
  V = normalize(V); N = normalize(N);
  float3 I = float3(1, 1, 1);  // Radiance of the path
  float3 Fp = Fp0;  // Fresnel at 90 degrees at first hit
  float n = n0;  // Index of refraction of the first hit
  int depth = 0;  // Length of the path
  while (depth < MAXDEPTH) {
    float3 R;  // Reflection or refraction dir
    float3 F = Fp + pow(1-abs(dot(N, -V)), 5) * (1-Fp);
    if (n <= 0) {
      R = reflect(V, N);  // Reflection
      I *= F;  // Fresnel reflection
    } else {  // Refraction
      if (dot(V, N) > 0) {  // Coming from inside
        n = 1 / n;
        N = -N;
      }
      R = refract(V, N, 1/n);
      if (dot(R, R) == 0)  // No refraction direction exists
          R = reflect(V, N);  // Total reflection
      else  I *= (1-F);  // Fresnel refraction
    }
    float3 Nl;  // Normal vector at the hit point
    float4 Il;  // Radiance at the hit point
    // Trace ray x+R*d and obtain hit l, radiance Il, normal Nl
    float3 l = Hit(x, R, Il, Nl);
    n = Il.a;
```

```
    if (n != 0) {  // Hit point is on specular surface
      Fp = Il.rgb;  // Fresnel at 90 degrees
      depth += 1;
    } else {  // Hit point is on diffuse surface
      I *= Il.rgb;  // Multiply with the radiance
      depth = MAXDEPTH;  // terminate
    }
    N = Nl; V = R; x = 1; // Hit point is the next shaded point
  }
  return float4(I, 1);
}
```

17.4 Results

Our algorithm was implemented in a DirectX 9 HLSL environment and tested on an NVIDIA GeForce 8800 GTX graphics card. To simplify the implementation, we represented the reflective objects by two layers (containing the front and the back faces, respectively) and rasterized all diffuse surfaces to the third layer. This simplification relieved us from implementing the depth-peeling process and maximized the number of layers to three. To handle more-complex reflective objects, we need to integrate the depth-peeling algorithm.

All images were rendered at 800×600 resolution. The cube maps had 6×512×512 resolution and were updated in every frame. We should carefully select the step size of the linear search and the iteration number of the secant search because they can significantly influence the image quality and the rendering speed. If we set the step size of the linear search greater than the distance of two neighboring texels of the distance map, we can speed up the algorithm but also increase the probability of missing the reflection of a thin object. If the geometry rendered into a layer is smooth (that is, it consists of larger polygonal faces), the linear search can take larger steps and the secant search is able to find exact solutions with just a few iterations. However, when the distance value in a layer varies abruptly, the linear search should take fine steps to avoid missing spikes of the distance map, which correspond to thin reflected objects.

Another source of undersampling artifacts is the limitation of the number of layers and of the resolution of the distance map. In reflections we may see parts of the scene that are coarsely, or not at all, represented in the distance maps because of occlusions and their grazing angle orientation for the center of the cube map. Figure 17-6 shows these artifacts and demonstrates how they can be reduced by appropriately setting the step size of the linear search and the iteration number of the secant search.

Note how the stair-stepping artifacts are generally eliminated by adding secant steps. The thin objects zoomed-in on in the green and red frames require fine linear steps because, if they are missed, the later secant search is not always able to quickly correct the error. Note that in Figure 17-6b, the secant search was more successful for the table object than for the mirror frame because the table occupies more texels in the distance maps. The aliasing of the reflection of the shadowed area below the table in the left mirror of Figures 17-6a and 17-6c, which is zoomed-in on in the blue frame, is caused by the limitation of distance map layers to three. This area is not represented in the layers, so not even the secant search can compute accurate reflections (Figures 17-6b and 17-6d). We can address these types of problems by increasing the number of layers.

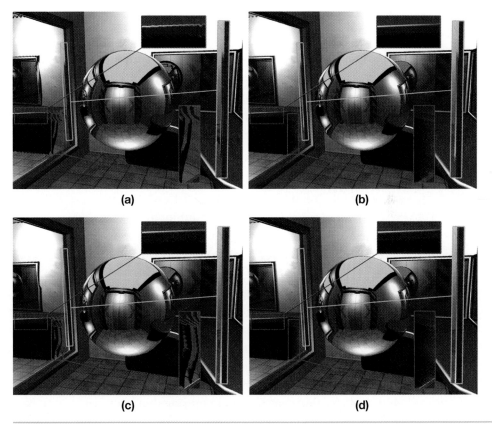

(a) (b)

(c) (d)

Figure 17-6. Aliasing Artifacts When the Numbers of Linear/Secant Steps Are Maximized to 15/1, 15/10, 80/1, and 80/10, Respectively
(a) Max 15 linear and 1 secant steps. (b) Max 15 linear and 10 secant steps. (c) Max 80 linear and 1 secant steps. (d) Max 80 linear and 10 secant steps.

Figure 17-7 shows images of a reflective teapot in a box, rendered with the proposed method and with Maya (for comparison), limiting the maximum number of reflections in a path to one, two, and three, respectively.

Note the high similarity between the GPU-rendered and software-rendered images. It is also worth mentioning that the frame rate decreases very little when the maximum number of reflections increases. This scenario indicates the excellent dynamic branching performance of the latest NVIDIA cards and also shows that early ray termination can improve performance, even in GPU solutions.

Figure 17-8 shows images of a more complex scene containing a reflective sphere and a mirror, when the maximum ray depth variable is incremented from one to eight. The assignment of all diffuse surfaces to a single layer causes minor blurring artifacts where view-dependent occlusions occur (for example, in the reflection of the handle of the lamp on the mirroring sphere). We could eliminate these artifacts by using more layers, but at the cost of a more complex implementation and lower rendering speed.

Figure 17-9 shows a sphere that both reflects and refracts light. Finally, Figure 17-10 contains snapshots of a video about a reflective teapot in a complex environment. The video is rendered at 25 fps without using min-max acceleration. When a min-max pair is computed for each layer, the speed increases to 50 fps. The maximum number of reflections is set to two.

17.5 Conclusion

In this chapter, we presented a robust algorithm to trace rays in scenes represented by layered distance maps. The method is used to compute single and multiple reflections and refractions on the GPU. An important advantage of tracing rays in rasterized geometric representations instead of directly implementing classic ray tracing is that these methods can be integrated into game engines, benefit from visibility algorithms developed for games (Wimmer and Bittner 2005), and use the full potential of the latest graphics cards. This method is particularly effective if the geometry rendered into a layer is smooth (that is, consists of larger polygonal faces). In this case, the linear search can take larger steps and the secant search is able to find exact solutions, taking just a few iterations. However, when the distance value in a layer varies abruptly, the linear search should take fine steps to prevent missing thin, reflected objects. Note that a similar problem also arises in relief mapping, and multiple solutions have been developed (Donnelly 2005; Policarpo and Oliveira 2007—Chapter 18 of this book). In the future, we would consider integrating similar solutions into our technique.

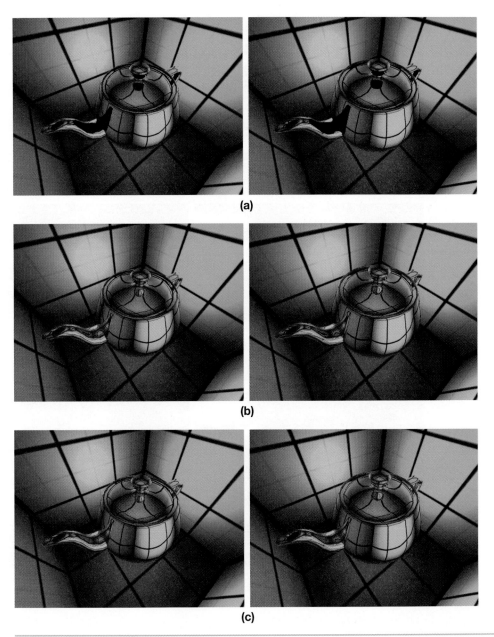

(a)

(b)

(c)

Figure 17-7. Single and Multiple Reflections on a Teapot (*Left Column*) and Comparisons with the Software Ray Tracer of the Maya 7 Renderer (*Right Column*)

(a) GPU: Max one reflection, 50/100 fps. (b) GPU: Max two reflections, 36/80 fps. (c) GPU: Max three reflections, 30/60 fps. Note: The fps data refer to the cases without and with acceleration, using min-max values per layers.

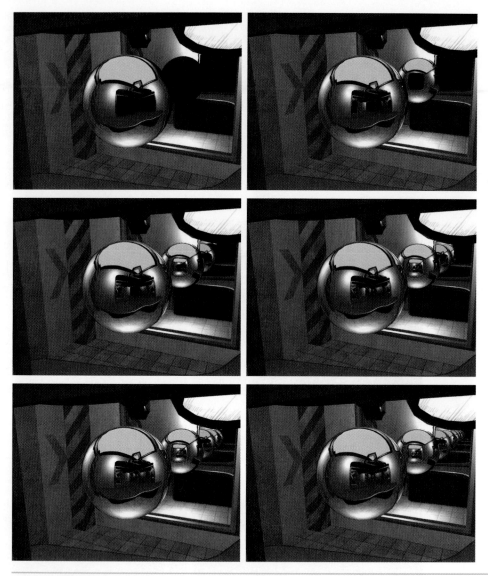

Figure 17-8. Multiple Reflections Incrementing the Maximum Depth Variable from One up to Eight

Figure 17-9. A Sphere That Is Both Reflective and Refractive

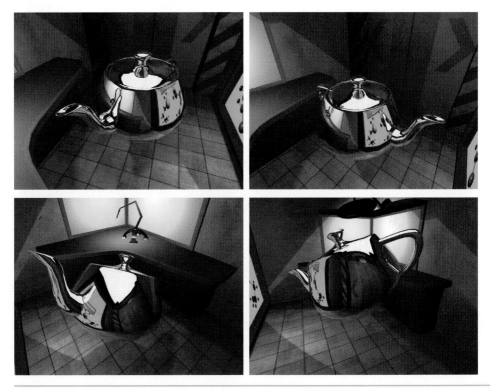

Figure 17-10. Snapshots of the Video Rendered at 25/50 FPS

17.6 References

Bjorke, Kevin. 2004. "Image-Based Lighting." In *GPU Gems,* edited by Randima Fernando, pp. 307–321. Addison-Wesley.

Donnelly, William. 2005. "Per-Pixel Displacement Mapping with Distance Functions." In *GPU Gems 2*, edited by Matt Pharr, pp. 123–136. Addison-Wesley.

Everitt, Cass. 2001. "Interactive Order-Independent Transparency." NVIDIA technical report. Available online at http://developer.nvidia.com/object/Interactive_Order_Transparency.html.

Havran, Vlastimil. 2001. "Heuristic Ray Shooting Algorithms." Czech Technical University, Ph.D. dissertation. Available online at http://www.cgg.cvut.cz/~havran/phdthesis.html.

Krüger, Jens, Kai Burger, and Rüdiger Westermann. 2006. "Interactive Screen-Space Accurate Photon Tracing on GPUs." In *Eurographics Symposium on Rendering 2006*, pp. 319–329.

Lazányi, István, and László Szirmay-Kalos. 2005. "Fresnel Term Approximations for Metals." In *Short Paper Proceedings of WSCG*, pp. 77–80.

Liu, Baoquan, Li-Yi Wei, and Ying-Qing Xu. 2006. "Multi-Layer Depth Peeling via Fragment Sort." Technical report. MSR-TR-2006-81, Microsoft Research.

Patow, Gustavo. 1995. "Accurate Reflections through a z-buffered Environment Map." In *Proceedings of Sociedad Chilena de Ciencias de la Computacion.*

Policarpo, Fabio, and Manuel Oliveira. 2007. "Relaxed Cone Stepping for Relief Mapping." In *GPU Gems 3*, edited by Hubert Nguyen. Addison-Wesley. (Chapter 18 of this book)

Popescu, Voicu, Chunhui Mei, Jordan Dauble, and Elisha Sacks. 2006. "Reflected-Scene Impostors for Realistic Reflections at Interactive Rates." In *Computer Graphics Forum (Proceedings of Eurographics 2006)* 25(3), pp. 313–322.

Purcell, Timothy J., Ian Buck, William R. Mark, and Pat Hanrahan. 2002. "Ray Tracing on Programmable Graphics Hardware." In *ACM Transactions on Graphics (Proceedings of SIGGRAPH 2002)* 21(3), pp. 703–712. Available online at http://graphics.stanford.edu/papers/rtongfx/.

Purcell, Tim, Craig Donner, Mike Cammarano, Henrik-Wann Jensen, and Pat Hanrahan. 2003. "Photon Mapping on Programmable Graphics Hardware." In *Proceedings of the SIGGRAPH/Eurographics Workshop on Graphics Hardware 2003*, pp. 41–50.

Sander, Pedro. 2005. "DirectX9 High Level Shading Language." SIGGRAPH 2005 tutorial. Available online at http://ati.amd.com/developer/SIGGRAPH05/ShadingCourse_HLSL.pdf.

Schlick, Christophe. 1993. "A Customizable Reflectance Model for Everyday Rendering." In *Fourth Eurographics Workshop on Rendering*, pp. 73–83.

Szirmay-Kalos, László, Barnabás Aszódi, István Lazányi, and Mátyás Premecz. 2005. "Approximate Ray-Tracing on the GPU with Distance Impostors." In *Computer Graphics Forum (Proceedings of Eurographics 2005)* 24(3), pp. 695–704.

Williams, Lance. 1978. "Casting Curved Shadows on Curved Surfaces." In *Computer Graphics (Proceedings of SIGGRAPH 1978)* 12(3), pp. 270–274.

Wimmer, Michael, and Jiri Bittner. 2005. "Hardware Occlusion Queries Made Useful." In *GPU Gems 2*, edited by Matt Pharr, pp. 91–108. Addison-Wesley.

Chapter 18

Relaxed Cone Stepping for Relief Mapping

Fabio Policarpo
Perpetual Entertainment

Manuel M. Oliveira
Instituto de Informática—UFRGS

18.1 Introduction

The presence of geometric details on object surfaces dramatically changes the way light interacts with these surfaces. Although synthesizing realistic pictures requires simulating this interaction as faithfully as possible, explicitly modeling all the small details tends to be impractical. To address these issues, an image-based technique called *relief mapping* has recently been introduced for adding per-fragment details onto arbitrary polygonal models (Policarpo et al. 2005). The technique has been further extended to render correct silhouettes (Oliveira and Policarpo 2005) and to handle non-height-field surface details (Policarpo and Oliveira 2006). In all its variations, the ray-height-field intersection is performed using a binary search, which refines the result produced by some linear search procedure. While the binary search converges very fast, the linear search (required to avoid missing large structures) is prone to aliasing, by possibly missing some thin structures, as is evident in Figure 18-1a. Several space-leaping techniques have since been proposed to accelerate the ray-height-field intersection and to minimize the occurrence of aliasing (Donnelly 2005, Dummer 2006, Baboud and Décoret 2006). *Cone step mapping* (CSM) (Dummer 2006) provides a clever solution to accelerate the intersection calculation for the average case and avoids skipping height-field structures by using some precomputed data (a cone map). However, because CSM uses a conservative approach, the rays tend to stop before the actual surface, which introduces different kinds of artifacts, highlighted in Figure 18-1b. Using an extension to CSM that consists of employing four different radii for each fragment (in the directions north, south, east, and west), one can just slightly reduce the occurrence of these artifacts. We call this approach *quad-directional cone step mapping* (QDCSM). Its results are shown in Figure 18-1c, which also highlights the technique's artifacts.

(a) Linear + binary search   (b) Cone step mapping

(c) Quad-directional cone step mapping   (d) Relaxed cone stepping + binary search

Figure 18-1. Comparison of Four Different Ray-Height-Field Intersection Techniques Used to Render a Relief-Mapped Surface from a 256×256 Relief Texture
(a) Fifteen steps of linear search followed by six steps of binary search. Note the highlighted aliasing artifacts due to the step size used for the linear search. (b) Fifteen steps of the cone step mapping technique. Note the many artifacts caused by the fact that the technique is conservative and many rays will never hit the surface. (c) Fifteen steps of the quad-directional cone step mapping technique. The artifacts in (b) have been reduced but not eliminated. (d) Fifteen steps of the relaxed cone stepping followed by six steps of binary search. Note that the artifacts have been essentially eliminated.

In this chapter, we describe a new ray-height-field intersection strategy for per-fragment displacement mapping that combines the strengths of both cone step mapping and binary search. We call the new space-leaping algorithm *relaxed cone stepping* (RCS), as it relaxes the restriction used to define the radii of the cones in CSM. The idea for the ray-height-field intersection is to replace the linear search with an aggressive space-leaping approach, which is immediately followed by a binary search. While CSM conservatively defines the radii of the cones in such a way that a ray never pierces the surface, RCS allows the rays to pierce the surface at most once. This produces much wider cones, accelerating convergence. Once we know a ray is inside the surface, we can safely apply a binary search to refine the position of the intersection. The combination of RCS and binary search produces renderings of significantly higher quality, as shown in Figure 18-1d. Note that both the aliasing visible in Figure 18-1a and the distortions noticeable in Figures 18-1b and 18-1c have been removed. As a space-leaping technique, RCS can be used with other strategies for refining ray-height-field intersections, such as the one used by *interval mapping* (Risser et al. 2005).

18.2 A Brief Review of Relief Mapping

Relief mapping (Policarpo et al. 2005) simulates the appearance of geometric surface details by shading individual fragments in accordance to some depth and surface normal information that is mapped onto polygonal models. A depth map[1] (scaled to the [0,1] range) represents geometric details assumed to be under the polygonal surface. Depth and normal maps can be stored as a single RGBA texture (32-bit per texel) called a *relief texture* (Oliveira et al. 2000). For better results, we recommend separating the depth and normal components into two different textures. This way texture compression will work better, because a specialized normal compression can be used independent of the depth map compression, resulting in higher compression ratios and fewer artifacts. It also provides better performance because during the relief-mapping iterations, only the depth information is needed and a one-channel texture will be more cache friendly (the normal information will be needed only at the end for lighting). Figure 18-2 shows the normal and depth maps of a relief texture whose cross section is shown in Figure 18-3. The mapping of relief details to a polygonal model is done in the conventional way, by assigning a pair of texture coordinates to each vertex of the model. During rendering, the depth map can be dynamically rescaled to achieve different effects, and correct occlusion is achieved by properly updating the depth buffer.

---

1. We use the term *depth map* instead of *height map* because the stored values represent depth measured under a reference plane, as opposed to height (measured above it). The reader should not confuse the expression "depth map" used here with shadow buffers.

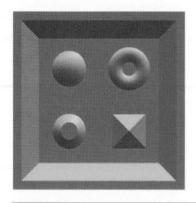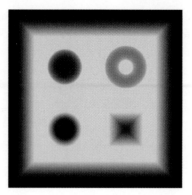

Figure 18-2. Example of a Relief Texture
Left: The normal map is stored in the RGB channels of the texture. Right: The depth map is stored in the alpha channel. Brighter pixels represent deeper geometry.

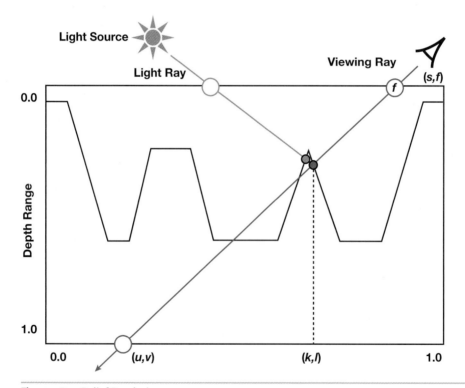

Figure 18-3. Relief Rendering
The viewing ray is transformed to the tangent space of fragment f and then intersected with the relief at point P, with texture coordinates (k, l). Shading is performed using the normal and color stored at the corresponding textures at (k, l). Self-shadowing is computed by checking if the light ray hits P before any other surface point.

Relief rendering is performed entirely on the GPU and can be conceptually divided into three steps. For each fragment *f* with texture coordinates (s, t), first transform the view direction V to the tangent space of *f*. Then, find the intersection P of the transformed viewing ray against the depth map. Let (k, l) be the texture coordinates of such intersection point (see Figure 18-3). Finally, use the corresponding position of P, expressed in camera space, and the normal stored at (k, l) to shade *f*. Self-shadowing can be applied by checking whether the light ray reaches P before reaching any other point on the relief. Figure 18-3 illustrates the entire process. Proper occlusion among relief-mapped and other scene objects is achieved simply by updating the z-buffer with the *z* coordinate of P (expressed in camera space and after projection and division by *w*). This updated z-buffer also supports the combined use of shadow mapping (Williams 1978) with relief-mapped surfaces.

In practice, finding the intersection point P can be entirely performed in 2D texture space. Thus, let (u, v) be the 2D texture coordinates corresponding to the point where the viewing ray reaches depth = 1.0 (Figure 18-3). We compute (u, v) based on (s, t), on the transformed viewing direction and on the scaling factor applied to the depth map. We then perform the search for P by sampling the depth map, stepping from (s, t) to (u, v), and checking if the viewing ray has pierced the relief (that is, whether the depth along the viewing ray is bigger than the stored depth) before reaching (u, v). If we have found a place where the viewing ray is under the relief, the intersection P is refined using a binary search.

Although the binary search quickly converges to the intersection point and takes advantage of texture filtering, it could not be used in the beginning of the search process because it may miss some large structures. This situation is depicted in Figure 18-4a, where the depth value stored at the texture coordinates halfway from (s, t) and (u, v) is bigger than the depth value along the viewing ray at point 1, even though the ray has already pierced the surface. In this case, the binary search would incorrectly converge to point Q. To minimize such aliasing artifacts, Policarpo et al. (2005) used a linear search to restrict the binary search space. This is illustrated in Figure 18-4b, where the use of small steps leads to finding point 3 under the surface. Subsequently, points 2 and 3 are used as input to find the desired intersection using a binary search refinement. The linear search itself, however, is also prone to aliasing in the presence of thin structures, as can be seen in Figure 18-1a. This has motivated some researchers to propose the use of additional preprocessed data to avoid missing such thin structures (Donnelly 2005, Dummer 2006, Baboud and Décoret 2006). The technique described in this chapter was inspired by the cone step mapping work of Dummer, which is briefly described next.

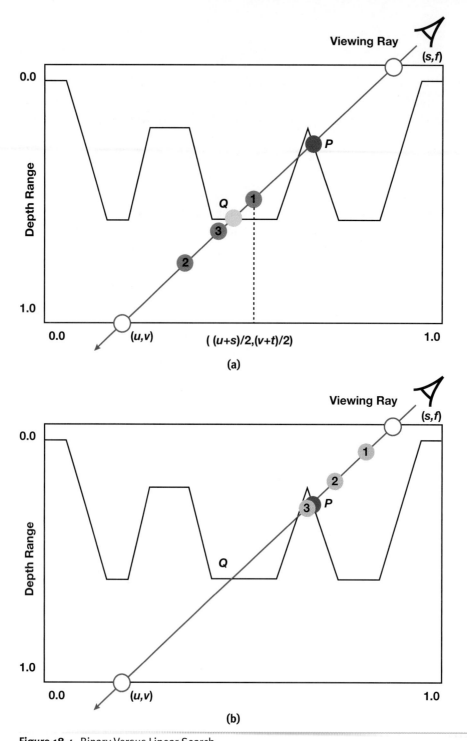

Figure 18-4. Binary Versus Linear Search
(a) A binary search may skip some large structures, missing the first ray-surface intersection (P) and returning a wrong intersection (Q). The numbers inside the circles indicate the order in which the points are visited along the viewing ray. (b) By using smaller steps, the linear search is less prone to aliasing, but not immune to it.

18.3 Cone Step Mapping

Dummer's algorithm for computing the intersection between a ray and a height field avoids missing height-field details by using cone maps (Dummer 2006). A cone map associates a circular cone to each texel of the depth texture. The angle of each cone is the maximum angle that would not cause the cone to intersect the height field. This situation is illustrated in Figure 18-5 for the case of three texels at coordinates (s, t), (a, b), and (c, d), whose cones are shown in yellow, blue, and green, respectively.

Starting at fragment f, along the transformed viewing direction, the search for an intersection proceeds as follows: intersect the ray with the cone stored at (s, t), obtaining point 1 with texture coordinates (a, b). Then advance the ray by intersecting it with the

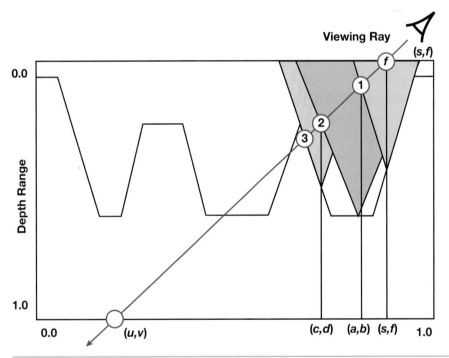

Figure 18-5. Cone Step Mapping
At each pass of the iteration, the ray advances to its intersection with the cone centered at the current texel.

cone stored at (a, b), thus obtaining point 2 at texture coordinates (c, d). Next, intersect the ray with the cone stored at (c, d), obtaining point 3, and so on. In the case of this simple example, point 3 coincides with the desired intersection. Although cone step mapping is guaranteed never to miss the first intersection of a ray with a height field, it may require too many steps to converge to the actual intersection. For performance reasons, however, one is often required to specify a maximum number of iterations. As a result, the ray tends to stop before the actual intersection, implying that the returned texture coordinates used to sample the normal and color maps are, in fact, incorrect. Moreover, the 3D position of the returned intersection, P', in camera space, is also incorrect. These errors present themselves as distortion artifacts in the rendered images, as can be seen in Figures 18-1b and 18-1c.

18.4 Relaxed Cone Stepping

Cone step mapping, as proposed by Dummer, replaces both the linear and binary search steps described in Policarpo et al. 2005 with a single search based on a cone map. A better and more efficient ray-height-field intersection algorithm is achieved by combining the strengths of both approaches: the space-leaping properties of cone step mapping followed by the better accuracy of the binary search. Because the binary search requires one input point to be under and another point to be over the relief surface, we can relax the constraint that the cones in a cone map cannot pierce the surface. In our new algorithm, instead, we force the cones to actually intersect the surface whenever possible. The idea is to make the radius of each cone as large as possible, observing the following constraint: *As a viewing ray travels inside a cone, it cannot pierce the relief more than once.* We call the resulting space-leaping algorithm *relaxed cone stepping*. Figure 18-7a (in the next subsection) compares the radii of the cones used by the conservative cone stepping (blue) and by relaxed cone stepping (green) for a given fragment in a height field. Note that the radius used by RCS is considerably larger, making the technique converge to the intersection using a smaller number of steps. The use of wider relaxed cones eliminates the need for the linear search and, consequently, its associated artifacts. As the ray pierces the surface once, it is safe to proceed with the fast and more accurate binary search.

18.4.1 Computing Relaxed Cone Maps

As in CSM, our approach requires that we assign a cone to each texel of the depth map. Each cone is represented by its *width/height* ratio (ratio w/h, in Figure 18-7c). Because a cone ratio can be stored in a single texture channel, both a depth and a cone map can be stored using a single luminance-alpha texture. Alternatively, the cone map could be stored in the blue channel of a relief texture (with the first two components of the normal stored in the red and green channels only).

For each reference texel t_i on a relaxed cone map, the angle of cone C_i centered at t_i is set so that no viewing ray can possibly hit the height field more than once while traveling inside C_i. Figure 18-7b illustrates this situation for a set of viewing rays and a given cone shown in green. Note that cone maps can also be used to accelerate the intersection of shadow rays with the height field. Figure 18-6 illustrates the rendering of self-shadowing, comparing the results obtained with three different approaches for rendering per-fragment displacement mapping: (a) relief mapping using linear search, (b) cone step mapping, and (c) relief mapping using relaxed cone stepping. Note the shadow artifacts resulting from the linear search (a) and from the early stop of CSM (b).

Relaxed cones allow rays to enter a relief surface but never leave it. We create relaxed cone maps offline using an $O(n^2)$ algorithm described by the pseudocode shown in Listing 18-1. The idea is, for each source texel `ti`, trace a ray through each destination texel `tj`, such that this ray starts at (`ti.texCoord.s`, `ti.texCoord.t`, `0.0`) and points to (`tj.texCoord.s`, `tj.texCoord.t`, `tj.depth`). For each such ray, compute its next (second) intersection with the height field and use this intersection point to compute the cone ratio `cone_ratio(i,j)`. Figure 18-7c illustrates the situation for a given pair of (`ti`, `tj`) of source and destination texels. C_i's final ratio is given by the smallest of all cone ratios computed for t_i, which is shown in Figure 18-7b. The relaxed cone map is obtained after all texels have been processed as source texels.

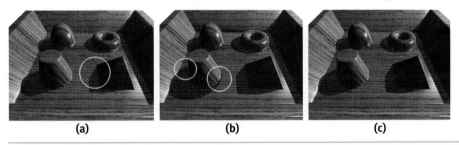

(a) (b) (c)

Figure 18-6. Rendering Self-Shadowing Using Different Approaches
(a) Relief mapping with linear search. Note the aliasing on the pyramid shadow. (b) Cone step mapping using cone maps to check the intersection of shadow rays. Note the incorrect shadow cast by the truncated cone on the bottom left. (c) Relief mapping with relaxed cone stepping. Images a, b, and c were generated using the same number of steps shown in Figure 18-1. The intersection with shadow rays used 15 steps/iterations for all images.

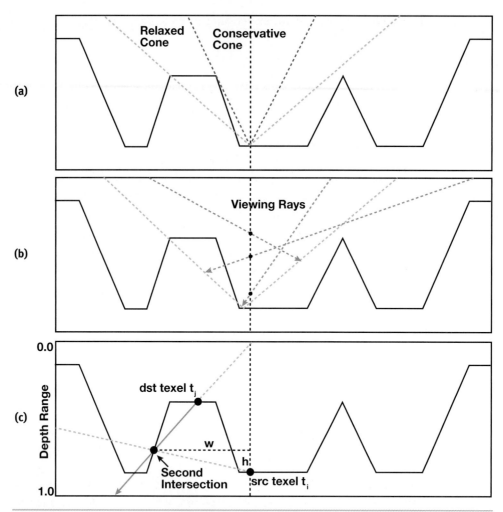

Figure 18-7. Computing Relaxed Cone Maps
(a) Conservative (blue) and relaxed (green) cones for a given texel in the depth map. Notice how the relaxed cone is much wider. (b) No viewing ray can pierce a relief surface more than once while traveling inside a relaxed cone. (c) An intermediate step during computation of the cone ratio for the relaxed cone shown in b.

Listing 18-1. Pseudocode for Computing Relaxed Cone Maps

```
for each reference texel ti do
  radius_cone_C(i) = 1;
  source.xyz = (ti.texCoord.s, ti.texCoord.t, 0.0);
  for each destination texel tj do
    destination.xyz = (tj.texCoord.s, tj.texCoord.t, tj.depth);
    ray.origin = destination;
```

Listing 18-1 (**continued**). Pseudocode for Computing Relaxed Cone Maps

```
ray.direction = destination - source;
(k,w) = text_cords_next_intersection(tj, ray, depth_map);
d = depth_stored_at(k,w);
if ((d - ti.depth) > 0.0)  // dst has to be above the src
  cone_ratio(i,j) = length(source.xy - destination.xy) /
                     (d - tj.depth);
  if (radius_cone_C(i) > cone_ratio(i,j))
    radius_cone_C(i) = cone_ratio(i,j);
```

Note that in the pseudocode shown in Listing 18-1, as well as in the actual code shown in Listing 18-2, we have clamped the maximum cone ratio values to 1.0. This is done to store the cone maps using integer textures. Although the use of floating-point textures would allow us to represent larger cone ratios with possible gains in space leaping, in practice we have observed that usually only a small subset of the texels in a cone map would be able to take advantage of that. This is illustrated in the relaxed cone map shown in Figure 18-8c. Only the saturated (white) texels would be candidates for having cone ratios bigger than 1.0.

Listing 18-2 presents a shader for generating relaxed cone maps. Figure 18-8 compares three different kinds of cone maps for the depth map associated with the relief texture shown in Figure 18-2. In Figure 18-8a, one sees a conventional cone map (Dummer 2006) stored using a single texture channel. In Figure 18-8b, we have a quad-directional cone map, which stores cone ratios for the four major directions into separate texture channels. Notice how different areas in the texture are assigned wider cones for different directions. Red texels indicate cones that are wider to the right, while green ones are wider to the left. Blue texels identify cones that are wider to the bottom, and black ones are wider to the top. Figure 18-8c shows the corresponding relaxed cone map, also stored using a single texture channel. Note that its texels are much brighter than the corresponding ones in the conventional cone map in Figure 18-8a, revealing its wider cones.

Listing 18-2. A Preprocess Shader for Generating Relaxed Cone Maps

```
float4 depth2relaxedcone(
  in float2 TexCoord : TEXCOORD0,
  in Sampler2D ReliefSampler,
  in float3 Offset ) : COLOR
{
  const int search_steps = 128;
  float3 src = float3(TexCoord,0);  // Source texel
  float3 dst = src + Offset;  // Destination texel
  dst.z = tex2D(ReliefSampler,dst.xy).w;  // Set dest. depth
```

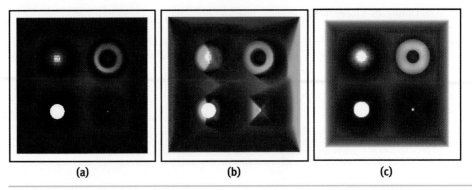

(a)	**(b)**	**(c)**

Figure 18-8. A Comparison of Different Kinds of Cone Maps Computed for the Depth Map Shown in Figure 18-2

(a) A conventional cone map (Dummer 2006) (one channel). (b) A quad-directional cone map. The cone ratio values for each of the major four directions are stored in the different channels of the texture. (c) The corresponding relaxed cone map (one channel).

Listing 18-2 (*continued*). A Preprocess Shader for Generating Relaxed Cone Maps

```
float3 vec = dst - src; // Ray direction
vec /= vec.z;   // Scale ray direction so that vec.z = 1.0
vec *= 1.0 - dst.z;  // Scale again
float3 step_fwd = vec/search_steps;  // Length of a forward step

// Search until a new point outside the surface
float3 ray_pos = dst + step_fwd;
for( int i=1; i<search_steps; i++ )
{
  float current_depth = tex2D(ReliefSampler, ray_pos.xy).w;
  if ( current_depth <= ray_pos.z )
    ray_pos += step_fwd;
}

// Original texel depth
float src_texel_depth = tex2D(ReliefSampler,TexCoord).w;
// Compute the cone ratio
float cone_ratio = (ray_pos.z >= src_texel_depth) ? 1.0 :
                   length(ray_pos.xy - TexCoord) /
                   (src_texel_depth - ray_pos.z);
```

```
// Check for minimum value with previous pass result
float best_ratio = tex2D(ResultSampler, TexCoord).x;
if ( cone_ratio > best_ratio )
  cone_ratio = best_ratio;

return float4(cone_ratio, cone_ratio, cone_ratio, cone_ratio);
}
```

18.4.2 Rendering with Relaxed Cone Maps

To shade a fragment, we step along the viewing ray as it travels through the depth texture, using the relaxed cone map for space leaping. We proceed along the ray until we reach a point inside the relief surface. The process is similar to what we described in Section 18.3 for conventional cone maps. Figure 18-9 illustrates how to find the intersection between a transformed viewing ray and a cone. First, we scale the vector representing the ray direction by dividing it by its *z* component (*ray.direction.z*), after which, according to Figure 18-9, one can write

$$scaled\_ray.direction.xyz = \frac{ray.direction.xyz}{ray.direction.z} \tag{1}$$

$$m = d \times length(scaled\_ray.direction.xy) = d \times ray\_ratio$$

Likewise:

$$m = g \times cone\_ratio \tag{2}$$

$$m = ((current\_texel.depth - ray\_current\_depth) - d) \times (cone\_ratio)$$

Solving Equations 1 and 2 for *d* gives the following:

$$d = \frac{(current\_texel.depth - ray\_current\_depth) \times cone\_ratio}{ray\_ratio + cone\_ratio}. \tag{3}$$

From Equation 3, we compute the intersection point *I* as this:

$$I = ray\_current\_position + d \times scaled\_ray.direction.xyz. \tag{4}$$

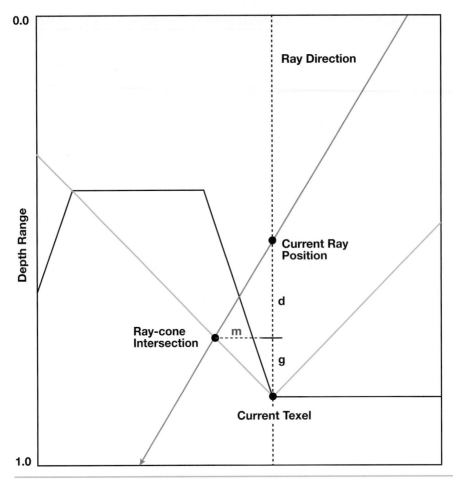

Figure 18-9. Intersecting the Viewing Ray with a Cone
m is the distance, measured in 2D, between the current texel coordinates and the texel coordinates of the intersection point. The difference between the depth at the current ray position and the depth of the current texel is d + g.

The code in Listing 18-3 shows the ray-intersection function for relaxed cone stepping. For performance reasons, the first loop iterates through the relaxed cones for a fixed number of steps. Note the use of the `saturate()` function when calculating the distance to move. This guarantees that we stop on the first visited texel for which the viewing ray is under the relief surface. At the end of this process, we assume the ray has pierced the surface once and then start the binary search for refining the coordinates of the intersection point. Given such coordinates, we then shade the fragment as described in Section 18.2.

Listing 18-3. Ray Intersect with Relaxed Cone

```
// Ray intersect depth map using relaxed cone stepping.
// Depth value stored in alpha channel (black at object surface)
// and relaxed cone ratio stored in blue channel.
void ray_intersect_relaxedcone(
  sampler2D relief_map,  // Relaxed cone map
  inout float3 ray_pos,  // Ray position
  inout float3 ray_dir)  // Ray direction
{
  const int cone_steps = 15;
  const int binary_steps = 6;

  ray_dir /= ray_dir.z;  // Scale ray_dir

  float ray_ratio = length(ray_dir.xy);

  float3 pos = ray_pos;
  for( int i=0; i<cone_steps; i++)
  {
    float4 tex = tex2D(relief_map, pos.xy);
    float cone_ratio = tex.z;
    float height = saturate(tex.w - pos.z);
    float d = cone_ratio*height/(ray_ratio + cone_ratio);
    pos += ray_dir * d;
  }
  // Binary search initial range and initial position
  float3 bs_range = 0.5 * ray_dir * pos.z;
  float3 bs_position = ray_pos + bs_range;

  for( int i=0; i<binary_steps; i++ )
  {
    float4 tex = tex2D(relief_map, bs_position.xy);
    bs_range *= 0.5;
    if (bs_position.z < tex.w)  // If outside
      bs_position += bs_range;  // Move forward
    else
      bs_position -= bs_range;  // Move backward
  }
}
```

Let f be the fragment to be shaded and let K be the point where the viewing ray has stopped (that is, just before performing the binary search), as illustrated in Figure 18-10. If too few steps were used, the ray may have stopped before reaching the surface. Thus, to avoid skipping even thin height-field structures (see the example shown in Figure 18-4a), we use K as the end point for the binary search. In this case, if the ray has not pierced the surface, the search will converge to point K.

Let (m, n) be the texture coordinates associated to K and let d_K be the depth value stored at (m, n) (see Figure 18-10). The binary search will then look for an intersection along the line segment ranging from points H to K, which corresponds to texture coordinates $((s + m)/2, (t + n)/2)$ to (m, n), where (s, t) are the texture coordinates of fragment f (Figure 18-10). Along this segment, the depth of the viewing ray varies linearly from $(d_K/2)$ to d_K. Note that, instead, one could use (m, n) and (q, r) (the texture coordinates of point J, the previously visited point along the ray) as the limits for starting the binary search refinement. However, because we are using a fixed number of iterations for stepping over the relaxed cone map, saving (q, r) would require a conditional statement in the code. According to our experience, this tends to increase the number of registers used in the fragment shader. The graphics hardware has a fixed number of registers and it runs as many threads as it can fit in its register pool. The fewer registers we use, the more threads we will have running at the same time. The latency imposed by the large number of dependent texture reads in relief mapping is hidden when multiple threads are running simultaneously. More-complex code in the loops will increase

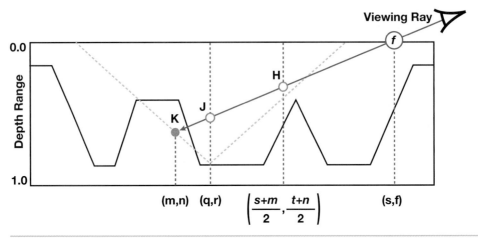

Figure 18-10. The Viewing Ray Through Fragment f, with Texture Coordinates (s, t)
H is the point halfway between f and K, the point where the ray stopped. J is the last visited point along the viewing ray before reaching K.

the number of registers used and thus reduce the number of parallel threads, exposing the latency from the dependent texture reads and reducing the frame rate considerably. So, to keep the shader code shorter, we start the binary search using H and K as limits. Note that after only two iterations of the binary search, one can expect to have reached a search range no bigger than the one defined by the points J and K.

It should be clear that the use of relaxed cone maps could still potentially lead to some distortion artifacts similar to the ones produced by regular (conservative) cone maps (Figure 18-1b). In practice, they tend to be significantly less pronounced for the same number of steps, due to the use of wider cones. According to our experience, the use of 15 relaxed cone steps seems to be sufficient to avoid such artifacts in typical height fields.

18.5 Conclusion

The combined use of relaxed cone stepping and binary search for computing ray-height-field intersection significantly reduces the occurrence of artifacts in images generated with per-fragment displacement mapping. The wider cones lead to more-efficient space leaping, whereas the binary search accounts for more accuracy. If too few cone stepping iterations are used, the final image might present artifacts similar to the ones found in cone step mapping (Dummer 2006). In practice, however, our technique tends to produce significantly better results for the same number of iterations or texture accesses. This is an advantage, especially for the new generations of GPUs, because although both texture sampling and computation performance have been consistently improved, computation performance is scaling faster than bandwidth.

Relaxed cone stepping integrates itself with relief mapping in a very natural way, preserving all of its original features. Figure 18-11 illustrates the use of RCS in renderings involving depth scaling (Figures 18-11b and 18-11d) and changes in tiling factors (Figures 18-11c and 18-11d). Note that these effects are obtained by appropriately adjusting the directions of the viewing rays (Policarpo et al. 2005) and, therefore, not affecting the cone ratios.

Mipmapping can be safely applied to color and normal maps. Unfortunately, conventional mipmapping should not be applied to cone maps, because the filtered values would lead to incorrect intersections. Instead, one should compute the mipmaps manually, by conservatively taking the minimum value for each group of pixels. Alternatively, one can sample the cone maps using a nearest-neighbors strategy. In this case, when an

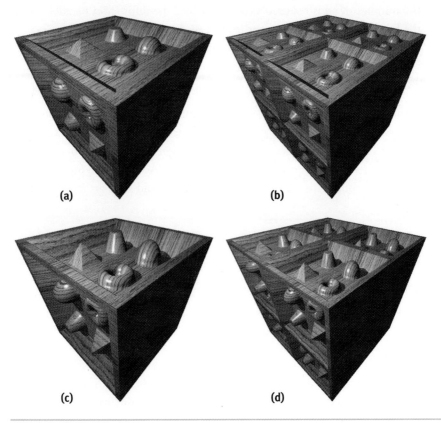

(a)

(b)

(c)

(d)

Figure 18-11. Images Showing Changes in Apparent Depth and Tiling Factors
The same relaxed cone map is used for all variations.

object is seen from a distance, the properly sampled color texture tends to hide the aliasing artifacts resulting from the sampling of a high-resolution cone map. Thus, in practice, the only drawback of not applying mipmapping to the cone map is the performance penalty for not taking advantage of sampling smaller textures.

18.5.1 Further Reading

Relief texture mapping was introduced in Oliveira et al. 2000 using a two-pass approach consisting of a prewarp followed by conventional texture mapping. The prewarp, based on the depth map, was implemented on the CPU and the resulting texture sent to the graphics hardware for the final mapping. With the introduction of fragment processors, Policarpo et al. (2005) generalized the technique for arbitrary polygonal models and showed how to efficiently implement it on a GPU. This was achieved by performing the ray-height-field intersection in 2D texture space. Oliveira and Policarpo (2005) also described how to render curved silhouettes by fitting a quadric surface at each vertex of the model. Later, they showed how to render relief details in preexisting applications using a minimally invasive approach (Policarpo and Oliveira 2006a). They have also generalized the technique to map non-height-field structures onto polygonal models and introduced a new class of impostors (Policarpo and Oliveira 2006b). More recently, Oliveira and Brauwers (2007) have shown how to use a 2D texture approach to intersect rays against depth maps generated under perspective projection and how to use these results to render real-time refractions of distant environments through deforming objects.

18.6 References

Baboud, Lionel, and Xavier Décoret. 2006. "Rendering Geometry with Relief Textures." In *Proceedings of Graphics Interface 2006.*

Donnelly, William. 2005. "Per-Pixel Displacement Mapping with Distance Functions." In *GPU Gems 2*, edited by Matt Pharr, pp. 123–136. Addison-Wesley.

Dummer, Jonathan. 2006. "Cone Step Mapping: An Iterative Ray-Heightfield Intersection Algorithm." Available online at http://www.lonesock.net/files/ConeStepMapping.pdf.

Oliveira, Manuel M., Gary Bishop, and David McAllister. 2000. "Relief Texture Mapping." In *Proceedings of SIGGRAPH 2000*, pp. 359–368.

Oliveira, Manuel M., and Fabio Policarpo. 2005. "An Efficient Representation for Surface Details." UFRGS Technical Report RP-351. Available online at http://www.inf.ufrgs.br/~oliveira/pubs_files/Oliveira_Policarpo_RP-351_Jan_2005.pdf.

Oliveira, Manuel M., and Maicon Brauwers. 2007. "Real-Time Refraction Through Deformable Objects." In *Proceedings of the 2007 Symposium on Interactive 3D Graphics and Games*, pp. 89–96.

Policarpo, Fabio, Manuel M. Oliveira, and João Comba. 2005. "Real-Time Relief Mapping on Arbitrary Polygonal Surfaces." In *Proceedings of the 2005 Symposium on Interactive 3D Graphics and Games*, pp. 155–162.

Policarpo, Fabio, and Manuel M. Oliveira. 2006a. "Rendering Surface Details in Games with Relief Mapping Using a Minimally Invasive Approach." In *SHADER X4: Advance Rendering Techniques*, edited by Wolfgang Engel, pp. 109–119. Charles River Media, Inc.

Policarpo, Fabio, and Manuel M. Oliveira. 2006b. "Relief Mapping of Non-Height-Field Surface Details." In *Proceedings of the 2006 Symposium on Interactive 3D Graphics and Games*, pp. 55–62.

Risser, Eric, Musawir Shah, and Sumanta Pattanaik. 2005. "Interval Mapping." University of Central Florida Technical Report. Available online at http://graphics.cs.ucf.edu/IntervalMapping/images/IntervalMapping.pdf.

Williams, Lance. 1978. "Casting Curved Shadows on Curved Surfaces." In *Computer Graphics (Proceedings of SIGGRAPH 1978)* 12(3), pp. 270–274.

Chapter 19

Deferred Shading in
Tabula Rasa

Rusty Koonce
NCsoft Corporation

This chapter is meant to be a natural extension of "Deferred Shading in *S.T.A.L.K.E.R.*" by Oles Shishkovtsov in *GPU Gems 2* (Shishkovtsov 2005). It is based on two years of work on the rendering engine for the game *Tabula Rasa*, a massively multiplayer online video game (MMO) designed by Richard Garriott. While Shishkovtsov 2005 covers the fundamentals of implementing deferred shading, this chapter emphasizes higher-level issues, techniques, and solutions encountered while working with a deferred shading based engine.

19.1 Introduction

In computer graphics, the term *shading* refers to the process of rendering a lit object. This process includes the following steps:

1. Computing geometry shape (that is, the triangle mesh)
2. Determining surface material characteristics, such as the normal, the bidirectional reflectance distribution function, and so on
3. Calculating incident light
4. Computing surface/light interaction, yielding the final visual

Typical rendering engines perform all four of these steps at one time when rendering an object in the scene. Deferred shading is a technique that separates the first two steps from the last two, performing each at separate discrete stages of the render pipeline.

In this chapter, we assume the reader has a basic understanding of deferred shading. For an introduction to deferred shading, refer to Shishkovtsov 2005, Policarpo and Fonseca 2005, Hargreaves and Harris 2004, or another such resource.

In this chapter, the term *forward shading* refers to the traditional shading method in which all four steps in the shading process are performed together. The term *effect* refers to a Direct3D D3DX effect. The terms *technique, annotation,* and *pass* are used in the context of a D3DX effect.

The term *material shader* refers to an effect used for rendering geometry (that is, in the first two steps of the shading process) and *light shader* refers to an effect used for rendering visible light (part of the last two steps in the shading process). A *body* is a geometric object in the scene being rendered.

We have avoided GPU-specific optimizations or implementations in this chapter; all solutions are generic, targeting either Shader Model 2.0 or Shader Model 3.0 hardware. In this way, we hope to emphasize the technique and not the implementation.

19.2 Some Background

In *Tabula Rasa*, our original rendering engine was a traditional forward shading engine built on top of DirectX 9, using shaders built on HLSL D3DX effects. Our effects used pass annotations within the techniques that described the lighting supported by that particular pass. The engine on the CPU side would determine what lights affected each body. This information, along with the lighting data in the effect pass annotations, was used to set light parameters and invoke each pass the appropriate number of times.

This forward shading approach has several issues:

- Computing which lights affect each body consumes CPU time, and in the worst case, it becomes an $O(n \times m)$ operation.
- Shaders often require more than one render pass to perform lighting, with complicated shaders requiring worst-case $O(n)$ render passes for n lights.
- Adding new lighting models or light types requires changing all effect source files.
- Shaders quickly encounter the instruction count limit of Shader Model 2.0.

Working on an MMO, we do not have tight control over the game environment. We can't control how many players are visible at once or how many visual effects or lights may be active at once. Given our lack of control of the environment and the poor scalability of lighting costs within a forward renderer, we chose to pursue a deferred-shading renderer. We felt this could give us visuals that could match any top game engine while making our lighting costs independent of scene geometric complexity.

The deferred shading approach offers the following benefits:

- Lighting costs are independent of scene complexity; there is no overhead of determining what lights affect what body.
- There are no additional render passes on geometry for lighting, resulting in fewer draw calls and fewer state changes required to render the scene.
- New light types or lighting models can be added without requiring any modification to material shaders.
- Material shaders do not perform lighting, freeing up instructions for additional geometry processing.

Deferred shading requires multiple render target (MRT) support and utilizes increased memory bandwidth, making the hardware requirements for deferred shading higher than what we wanted our minimum specification to be. Because of this, we chose to support both forward and deferred shading. We leveraged our existing forward shading renderer and built on top of it our deferred rendering pipeline.

With a full forward shading render pipeline as a fallback, we were able to raise our hardware requirements for our deferred shading pipeline. We settled on requiring Shader Model 2.0 hardware for our minimum specification and forward rendering pipeline, but we chose to require Shader Model 3.0 hardware for our deferred shading pipeline. This made development of the deferred pipeline much easier, because we were no longer limited in instruction counts and could rely on dynamic branching support.

19.3 Forward Shading Support

Even with a deferred shading-based engine, forward shading is still required for translucent geometry (see Section 19.8 for details). We retained support for a fully forward shaded pipeline within our renderer. Our forward renderer is used for translucent geometry as well as a fallback pipeline for all geometry on lower-end hardware.

This section describes methods we used to make simultaneous support for both forward and deferred shading pipelines more manageable.

19.3.1 A Limited Feature Set

We chose to limit the lighting features of our forward shading pipeline to a very small subset of the features supported by the deferred shading pipeline. Some features could not be supported for technical reasons, some were not supported due to time constraints, but many were not supported purely to make development easier.

Our forward renderer supports only hemispheric, directional, and point lights, with point lights being optional. No other type of light is supported (such as spotlights and box lights, both of which are supported by our deferred renderer). Shadows and other features found in the deferred pipeline were not supported in our forward pipeline.

Finally, the shader in the forward renderer could do per-vertex or per-pixel lighting. In the deferred pipeline, all lighting is per-pixel.

19.3.2 One Effect, Multiple Techniques

We have techniques in our effects for forward shading, deferred shading, shadow-map rendering, and more. We use an annotation on the technique to specify which type of rendering the technique was written for. This allows us to put all shader code in a single effect file that handles all variations of a shader used by the rendering engine. See Listing 19-1. This includes techniques for forward shading static and skinned geometry, techniques for "material shading" static and skinned geometry in our deferred pipeline, as well as techniques for shadow mapping.

Having all shader code for one effect in a single place allows us to share as much of that code as possible across all of the different techniques. Rather than using a single, monolithic effect file, we broke it down into multiple shader libraries, source files that contain shared vertex and pixel programs and generic functions, that are used by many effects. This approach minimized shader code duplication, making maintenance easier, decreasing the number of bugs, and improving consistency across shaders.

19.3.3 Light Prioritization

Our forward renderer quickly generates additional render passes as more lights become active on a piece of geometry. This generates not only more draw calls, but also more state changes and more overdraw. We found that our forward renderer with just a fraction of the lights enabled could be slower than our deferred renderer with many lights enabled. So to maximize performance, we severely limited how many lights could be active on a single piece of geometry in the forward shading pipeline.

Listing 19-1. Sample Material Shader Source

```
// These are defined in a common header, or definitions
// can be passed in to the effect compiler.
#define RM_FORWARD 1
#define RM_DEFERRED 2
#define TM_STATIC 1
#define TM_SKINNED 2

// Various techniques are defined, each using annotations to describe
// the render mode and the transform mode supported by the technique.
technique ExampleForwardStatic
<
  int render_mode = RM_FORWARD;
  int transform_mode = TM_STATIC;
>
{ . . . }

technique ExampleForwardSkinned
<
  int render_mode = RM_FORWARD;
  int transform_mode = TM_SKINNED;
>
{ . . . }

technique ExampleDeferredStatic
<
  int render_mode = RM_DEFERRED;
  int transform_mode = TM_STATIC;
>
{ . . . }

technique ExampleDeferredSkinned
<
  int render_mode = RM_DEFERRED;
  int transform_mode = TM_SKINNED;
>
{ . . . }
```

Our deferred rendering pipeline can handle thirty, forty, fifty, or more active dynamic lights in a single frame, with the costs being independent of the geometry that is affected. However, our forward renderer quickly bogs down when just a couple of point lights start affecting a large amount of geometry. With such a performance discrepancy between the two pipelines, using the same lights in both pipelines was not possible.

We gave artists and designers the ability to assign priorities to lights and specify if a light was to be used by the forward shading pipeline, the deferred shading pipeline, or both. A light's priority is used in both the forward and the deferred shading pipelines whenever the engine needs to scale back lighting for performance. With the forward shading pipeline, scaling back a light simply means dropping it from the scene; however, in the deferred shading pipeline, a light could have shadows disabled or other expensive properties scaled back based on performance, quality settings, and the light's priority.

In general, maps were lit targeting the deferred shading pipeline. A quick second pass was made to ensure that the lighting in the forward shading pipeline was acceptable. Generally, the only additional work was to increase ambient lighting in the forward pipeline to make up for having fewer lights than in the deferred pipeline.

19.4 Advanced Lighting Features

All of the following techniques are possible in a forward or deferred shading engine. We use all of these in our deferred shading pipeline. Even though deferred shading is not required, it made implementation much cleaner. With deferred shading, we kept the implementation of such features separate from the material shaders. This meant we could add new lighting models and light types without having to modify material shaders. Likewise, we could add material shaders without any dependency on lighting models or light types.

19.4.1 Bidirectional Lighting

Traditional hemispheric lighting as described in the DirectX documentation is fairly common. This lighting model uses two colors, traditionally labeled as *top* and *bottom*, and then linearly interpolates between these two colors based on the surface normal. Typically hemispheric lighting interpolates the colors as the surface normal moves from pointing directly up to directly down (hence the terms top and bottom). In *Tabula Rasa*, we support this traditional hemispheric model, but we also added a *back* color to directional lights.

With deferred lighting, artists are able to easily add multiple directional lights. We found them adding a second directional light that was aimed in nearly the opposite direction of the first, to simulate bounce or radiant light from the environment. They really liked the look and the control this gave them, so the natural optimization was to combine the two opposing directional lights into a single, new type of directional light—one with a forward color and a back color. This gave them the same control at half of the cost.

As a further optimization, the back color is just a simple $N \cdot L$, or a simple Lambertian light model. We do not perform any specular, shadowing, occlusion, or other advanced lighting calculation on it. This back color is essentially a cheap approximation of radiant or ambient light in the scene. We save $N \cdot L$ computed from the front light and just negate it for the back color.

19.4.2 Globe Mapping

A globe map is a texture used to color light, like a glass globe placed around a light source in real life. As a ray of light is emitted from the light source, it must pass through this globe, where it becomes colored or blocked. For point lights, we use a cube map for this effect. For spotlights, we use 2D texture. These can be applied to cheaply mimic stained-glass effects or block light in specific patterns. We also give artists the ability to rotate or animate these globe maps.

Artists use globe maps to cheaply imitate shadow maps when possible, to imitate stained-glass effects, disco ball reflection effects, and more. All lights in our engine support them. See Figures 19-1 through 19-3 for an example of a globe map applied to a light.

19.4.3 Box Lights

In *Tabula Rasa*, directional lights are global lights that affect the entire scene and are used to simulate sunlight or moonlight. We found artists wanting to light a small area with a directional light, but they did not want the light to affect the entire scene. What they needed were localized directional lights.

Our solution for a localized directional light was a *box light*. These lights use our basic directional lighting model, but they are confined within a rectangular volume. They support falloff like spotlights, so their intensity can fade out as they near the edge of their light volume. Box lights also support shadow maps, globe maps, back color, and all of the other features of our lighting engine.

19.4.4 Shadow Maps

There is no precomputed lighting in *Tabula Rasa*. We exclusively use shadow maps, not stencil shadows or light maps. Artists can enable shadow casting on any light (except hemispheric). We use cube maps for point light shadow maps and 2D textures for everything else.

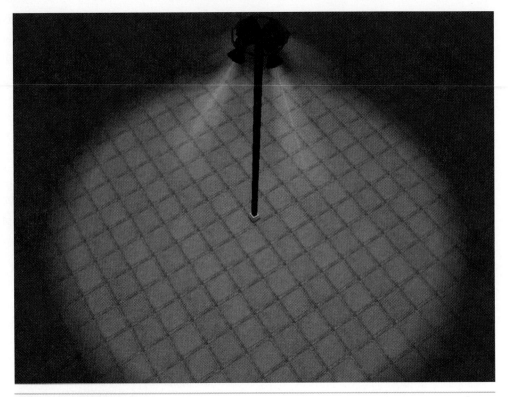

Figure 19-1. A Basic Spotlight

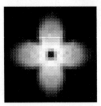

Figure 19-2. A Simple Globe Map

All shadow maps currently in *Tabula Rasa* are floating-point textures and utilize jitter sampling to smooth out the shadows. Artists can control the spread of the jitter sampling, giving control over how soft the shadow appears. This approach allowed us to write a single solution that worked and looked the same on all hardware; however, hardware-specific texture formats can be used as well for shadow maps. Hardware-specific formats can provide benefits such as better precision and hardware filtering.

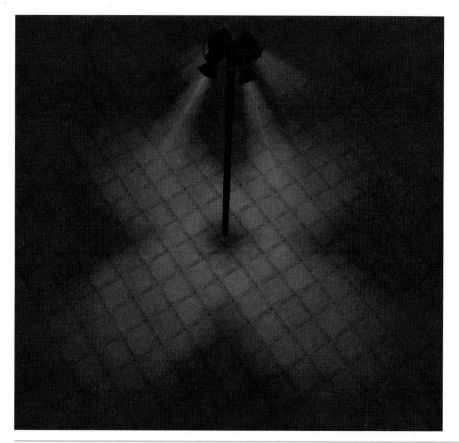

Figure 19-3. A Spotlight with Globe Map

Global Shadow Maps

Many papers exist on global shadow mapping, or shadow mapping the entire scene from the perspective of a single directional light. We spent a couple of weeks researching and playing with perspective shadow maps (Stamminger and Drettakis 2002) and trapezoidal shadow maps (Martin and Tan 2004). The downfall of these techniques is that the final result depends on the angle between the light direction and the eye direction. In both methods, as the camera moves, the shadow quality varies, with the worst case reducing to the standard orthographic projection.

In *Tabula Rasa*, there is a day and night cycle, with the sun and moon constantly moving across the sky. Dusk and dawn are tricky because the light direction comes close to being parallel to the ground, which largely increases the chance of the eye direction becoming parallel to the light direction. This is the worst-case scenario for perspective and trapezoidal shadow maps.

Due to the inconsistent shadow quality as the camera or light source moved, we ended up using a single large 2048×2048 shadow map with normal orthographic projection. This gave us consistent results that were independent of the camera or light direction. However, new techniques that we have not tried may work better, such as cascaded shadow maps.

We used multisample jitter sampling to soften shadow edges, we quantized the position of the light transform so it always pointed to a consistent location within a subpixel of the shadow map, and we quantized the direction of the light so the values going into the shadow map were not minutely changing every frame. This gave us a stable shadow with a free-moving camera. See Listing 19-2.

Listing 19-2. C++ Code That Quantizes Light Position for Building the Shadow Map Projection Matrix

```cpp
// Assumes a square shadow map and square shadow view volume.
// Compute how "wide" a pixel in the shadow map is in world space.
const float pixelSize = viewSize / shadowMapWidth;

// How much has our light position changed since last frame?
vector3 delta(lightPos - lastLightPos);

// Project the delta onto the basis vectors of the light matrix.
float xProj = dot(delta, lightRight);
float yProj = dot(delta, lightUp);
float zProj = dot(delta, lightDir);

// Quantize the projection to the nearest integral value.
// (How many "pixels" across and up has the light moved?)
const int numStepsX = static_cast<int>(xProj / pixelSize);
const int numStepsY = static_cast<int>(yProj / pixelSize);

// Go ahead and quantize "z" or the light direction.
// This value affects the depth components going into the shadowmap.
// This will stabilize the shadow depth values and minimize
// shadow bias aliasing.
const float zQuantization = 0.5f;
const int numStepsZ = static_cast<int>(zProj / zQuantization);

// Compute the new light position that retains the same subpixel
// location as the last light position.
lightPos = lastLightPos + (pixelSize * numStepsX) * lgtRight +
                          (pixelSize * numStepsY) * lgtUp +
                          (zQuantization * numStepsZ) * lgtDir;
```

Local Shadow Maps

Because any light can cast shadows in our engine, with maps having hundreds of lights, the engine must manage the creation and use of many shadow maps. All shadow maps are generated on the fly as they are needed. However, most shadow maps are static and do not need to be regenerated each frame. We gave artists control over this by letting them set a flag on each shadow-casting light if they wanted to use a static shadow map or a dynamic shadow map. Static shadow maps are built only once and reused each frame; dynamic shadow maps are rebuilt each frame.

We flag geometry as static or dynamic as well, indicating if the geometry moves or not at runtime. This allows us to cull geometry based on this flag. When building static shadow maps, we cull out dynamic geometry. This prevents a shadow from a dynamic object, such as an avatar, from getting "baked" into a static shadow map. However, dynamic geometry is shadowed just like static geometry by these static shadow maps. For example, an avatar walking under a staircase will have the shadows from the staircase fall across it.

A lot of this work can be automated and optimized. We chose not to prebuild static shadow maps; instead, we generate them on the fly as we determine they are needed. This means we do not have to ship and patch shadow map files, and it reduces the amount of data we have to load from disk when loading or running around a map. To combat video memory usage and texture creation overhead, we use a shadow map pool. We give more details on this later in the chapter.

Dynamic shadow-casting lights are the most expensive, because they have to constantly regenerate their shadow maps. If a dynamic shadow-casting light doesn't move, or doesn't move often, several techniques can be used to help improve its performance. The easiest is to not regenerate one of these dynamic shadow maps unless a dynamic piece of geometry is within its volume. The other option is to render the static geometry into a separate static shadow map that is generated only once. Each frame it is required, render just the dynamic geometry to a separate dynamic shadow map. Composite these two shadow maps together by comparing values from each and taking the lowest, or nearest, value. The final result will be a shadow map equivalent to rendering all geometry into it, but only dynamic geometry is actually rendered.

19.4.5 Future Expansion

With all lighting functionality cleanly separated from geometry rendering, modifying or adding lighting features is extremely easy with a deferred shading-based engine. In fact, box lights went from a proposal on a whiteboard to fully functional with complete integration into our map editor in just three days.

High dynamic range, bloom, and other effects are equally just as easy to add to a deferred shading-based engine as to a forward-based one. The architecture of a deferred shading pipeline lends itself well to expansion in most ways. Typically, adding features to a deferred engine is easier or not any harder than it would be for a forward shading-based engine. The issue that is most likely to constrain the feature set of a deferred shading engine is the limited number of material properties that can be stored per pixel, available video memory, and video memory bandwidth.

19.5 Benefits of a Readable Depth and Normal Buffer

A requirement of deferred shading is building textures that hold depth and normal information. These are used for lighting the scene; however, they can be used outside of the scope of lighting for various visual effects such as fog, depth blur, volumetric particles, and removing hard edges where alpha-blended geometry intersects opaque geometry.

19.5.1 Advanced Water and Refraction

In *Tabula Rasa*, if using the deferred shading pipeline, our water shader takes into account water depth (in eye space). As each pixel of the water is rendered, the shader samples the depth saved from the deferred shading pipeline and compares it to the depth of the water pixel. This means our water can auto-shoreline, the water can change color and transparency with eye-space depth, and pixels beneath the water refract whereas pixels above the water do not. It also means that we can do all of these things in a single pass, unlike traditional forward renderers.

Our forward renderer supports only our basic refraction feature, and it requires an additional render pass to initialize the alpha channel of the refraction texture in order to not refract pixels that are not underneath the water. This basic procedure is outlined in Sousa 2005.

In our deferred renderer, we can sample the eye depth of the current pixel and the eye depth of the neighboring refracted pixel. By comparing these depths, we can determine if the refracted pixel is indeed behind the target pixel. If it is, we proceed with the refraction effect; otherwise we do not. See Figures 19-4 and 19-5.

Figure 19-4. Water Using Forward Shading Only
Refraction occurs only to pixels below the water surface; however, there is no depth access. Multiple passes are required and no eye-depth-dependent effects are possible.

Figure 19-5. Water Using Forward Shading, but with Access to the Depth Buffer from Deferred Shading Opaque Geometry
Notice the subtle color and transparency changes based on the eye depth of the water, removing hard edges along the water's edge. Only a single pass is required.

To give the artist control over color and transparency with depth, we actually use a volume texture as well as a 1D texture. The 1D texture is just a lookup table for transparency with the normalized water depth being used for the texture coordinate. This technique allowed artists to easily simulate a nonlinear relationship between water depth and its transparency. The volume texture was actually used for the water surface color. This could be a flat volume texture (becoming a regular 2D texture) or it could have two or four W layers. Again, the normalized depth was used for the W texture coordinate with the UV coordinates being specified by the artists. The surface normal of the water was driven by two independently UV-animated normal maps.

19.5.2 Resolution-Independent Edge Detection

Shishkovtsov 2005 presented a method for edge detection that was used for faking an antialiasing pass on the frame. The implementation relied on some magic numbers that varied based on resolution. We needed edge detection for antialiasing as well; however, we modified the algorithm to make the implementation resolution independent.

We looked at changes in depth gradients and changes in normal angles by sampling all eight neighbors surrounding a pixel. This is basically the same as Shishkovtsov's method. We diverge at this point and compare the maximum change in depth to the minimum change in depth to determine how much of an edge is present. This depth gradient between pixels is resolution dependent. By comparing relative changes in this gradient instead of comparing the gradient to fixed values, we are able to make the logic resolution independent.

Our normal processing is very similar to Shishkovtsov's method. We compare the changes in the cosine of the angle between the center pixel and its neighboring pixels along the same edges at which we test depth gradients. We use our own constant number here; however, the change in normals across pixels is not resolution dependent. This keeps the logic resolution independent.

We do not put any logic in the algorithm to limit the selection to "top right" or "front" edges; consequently, many edges become a couple of pixels wide. However, this works out well with our filtering method to help smooth those edges.

The output of the edge detection is a per-pixel weight between zero and one. The weight reflects how much of an edge the pixel is on. We use this weight to do four bilinear samples when computing the final pixel color. The four samples we take are at the pixel center for a weight of zero and at the four corners of the pixel for a weight of one. This results in a weighted average of the target pixel with all eight of its neighbors. The more of an edge a pixel is, the more it is blended with its neighbors. See Listing 19-3.

Listing 19-3. Shader Source for Edge Detection

```
///////////////////////////
// Neighbor offset table
///////////////////////////
const static float2 offsets[9] = {
  float2( 0.0,  0.0), //Center        0
  float2(-1.0, -1.0), //Top Left      1
  float1( 0.0, -1.0), //Top           2
  float1( 1.0, -1.0), //Top Right     3
  float1( 1.0,  0.0), //Right         4
  float1( 1.0,  1.0), //Bottom Right  5
  float1( 0.0,  1.0), //Bottom        6
  float1(-1.0,  1.0), //Bottom Left   7
  float1(-1.0,  0.0)  //Left          8
};

float DL_GetEdgeWeight(in float2 screenPos)
{
  float Depth[9];
  float3 Normal[9];

  //Retrieve normal and depth data for all neighbors.
  for (int i=0; i<9; ++i)
  {
    float2 uv = screenPos + offsets[i] * PixelSize;
    Depth[i] = DL_GetDepth(uv);   //Retrieves depth from MRTs
    Normal[i]= DL_GetNormal(uv); //Retrieves normal from MRTs
  }

  //Compute Deltas in Depth.
  float4 Deltas1;
  float4 Deltas2;
  Deltas1.x = Depth[1];
  Deltas1.y = Depth[2];
  Deltas1.z = Depth[3];
  Deltas1.w = Depth[4];

  Deltas2.x = Depth[5];
  Deltas2.y = Depth[6];
  Deltas2.z = Depth[7];
  Deltas2.w = Depth[8];
```

Listing 19-3 (*continued*). Shader Source for Edge Detection

```
//Compute absolute gradients from center.
Deltas1   = abs(Deltas1 - Depth[0]);
Deltas2   = abs(Depth[0] - Deltas2);

//Find min and max gradient, ensuring min != 0
float4 maxDeltas = max(Deltas1, Deltas2);
float4 minDeltas = max(min(Deltas1, Deltas2), 0.00001);

// Compare change in gradients, flagging ones that change
// significantly.
// How severe the change must be to get flagged is a function of the
// minimum gradient. It is not resolution dependent. The constant
// number here would change based on how the depth values are stored
// and how sensitive the edge detection should be.
float4 depthResults = step(minDeltas * 25.0, maxDeltas);

//Compute change in the cosine of the angle between normals.
Deltas1.x = dot(Normal[1], Normal[0]);
Deltas1.y = dot(Normal[2], Normal[0]);
Deltas1.z = dot(Normal[3], Normal[0]);
Deltas1.w = dot(Normal[4], Normal[0]);

Deltas2.x = dot(Normal[5], Normal[0]);
Deltas2.y = dot(Normal[6], Normal[0]);
Deltas2.z = dot(Normal[7], Normal[0]);
Deltas2.w = dot(Normal[8], Normal[0]);

Deltas1 = abs(Deltas1 - Deltas2);

// Compare change in the cosine of the angles, flagging changes
// above some constant threshold. The cosine of the angle is not a
// linear function of the angle, so to have the flagging be
// independent of the angles involved, an arccos function would be
// required.
float4 normalResults = step(0.4, Deltas1);

normalResults = max(normalResults, depthResults);
return (normalResults.x + normalResults.y +
        normalResults.z + normalResults.w) * 0.25;
}
```

19.6 Caveats

19.6.1 Material Properties

Choose Properties Wisely

In *Tabula Rasa* we target DirectX 9, Shader Model 3.0-class hardware for our deferred shading pipeline. This gives us a large potential user base, but at the same time there are constraints that DirectX 10, Shader Model 4.0-class hardware can alleviate. First and foremost is that most Shader Model 3.0-class hardware is limited to a maximum of four simultaneous render targets without support for independent render target bit depths. This restricts us to a very limited number of data channels available for storing material attributes.

Assuming a typical DirectX 9 32-bit multiple render target setup with four render targets, one exclusively for depth, there are 13 channels available to store pixel properties: 3 four-channel RGBA textures, and one 32-bit high-precision channel for depth. Going with 64-bit over 32-bit render targets adds precision, but not necessarily any additional data channels.

Even though most channels are stored as an ordinal value in a texture, in Shader Model 3.0, all access to that data is via floating-point registers. That means using bit masking or similar means of compressing or storing more data into a single channel is really not feasible under Shader Model 3.0. Shader Model 4.0 does support true integer operations, however.

It is important that these channels hold generic material data that maximizes how well the engine can light each pixel from any type of light. Try to avoid data that is specific to a particular type of light. With such a limited number of channels, each should be considered a very valuable resource and utilized accordingly.

There are some common techniques to help compress or reduce the number of data channels required for material attributes. Storing pixel normals in view space will allow storing the normal in two channels instead of three. In view space, the z component of the normals will all have the same sign (all visible pixels face the camera). Utilizing this information, along with the knowledge that every normal is a unit vector, we can reconstruct the z component from the x and y components of the normal. Another technique is to store material attributes in a texture lookup table, and then store the appropriate texture coordinate(s) in the MRT data channels.

These material attributes are the "glue" that connects material shaders to light shaders. They are the output of material shaders and are part of the input into the light shaders.

As such, these are the only shared dependency of material and light shaders. As a result, changing material attribute data can necessitate changing all shaders, material and light alike.

Encapsulate and Hide MRT Data

We do not expose the data channel or the data format of a material attribute to the material or light shaders. Functions are used for setting and retrieving all material attribute data. This allows any data location or format to change, and the material and light shaders only need to be rebuilt, not modified.

We also use a function to initialize all MRT data in every material shader. This does possibly add unnecessary instructions, but it also allows us to add new data channels in the future, and it saves us from having to modify existing material shaders. The material shader would only need to be modified if it needed to change the default value for the newly added material attribute. See Listing 19-4.

Listing 19-4. Encapsulate and Hide MRT Layout from Material Shaders

```
// Put all of the material attribute layout information in its own
// header file and include this header from material and light
// shaders. Provide accessor and mutator functions for each
// material attribute and use those functions exclusively for
// accessing the material attribute data in the MRTs.

// Deferred lighting material shader output
struct DL_PixelOutput
{
  float4 mrt_0 : COLOR0;
  float4 mrt_1 : COLOR1;
  float4 mrt_2 : COLOR2;
  float4 mrt_3 : COLOR3;
};

// Function to initialize material output to default values
void DL_Reset(out DL_PixelOutput frag)
{
  // Set all material attributes to suitable default values
  frag.mrt_0 = 0;
  frag.mrt_1 = 0;
  frag.mrt_2 = 0;
  frag.mrt_3 = 0;
}
```

```
// Mutator/Accessor - Any data conversion/compression should be done
// here to keep it and the exact storage specifics abstracted and
// hidden from shaders
void DL_SetDiffuse(inout DL_PixelOutput frag, in float3 diffuse)
{
  frag.mrt_0.rgb = diffuse;
}
float3 DL_GetDiffuse(in float2 coord)
{
  return tex2D(MRT_Sampler_0, coord).rgb;
}


. . .


// Example material shader
DL_PixelOutput psProgram(INPUT input)
{
  DL_PixelOutput output;

  // Initialize output with default values
  DL_Reset(output);

  // Override default values with properties
  // specific to this shader.
  DL_SetDiffuse(output, input.diffuse);
  DL_SetDepth(output, input.pos);
  DL_SetNormal(output, input.normal);

  return output;
}
```

19.6.2 Precision

With deferred shading, it is easy to run into issues that result from a loss of data preci-sion. The most obvious place for loss of precision is with the storing of material attrib-utes in the MRT data channels. In *Tabula Rasa*, most data channels are 8-bit or 16-bit, depending on whether 32-bit or 64-bit render targets are being used, respectively (four channels per render target). The internal hardware registers have different precisions and internal formats from the render target channel, requiring conversion upon read and write from that channel. For example, our normals are computed with the hardware's full precision per component, but then they get saved with only 8-bit or 16-bit precision per component. With 8-bit precision, our normals do not yield smooth specular highlights and aliasing is clearly visible in the specular lighting.

19.7 Optimizations

With deferred shading, the performance of lighting is directly proportional to the number of pixels on which the lighting shaders must execute. The following techniques are designed to reduce the number of pixels on which lighting calculations must be performed, and hence increase performance.

Early z-rejection, stencil masking, and dynamic branching optimizations all have something in common: dependency on locality of data. This really does depend on the hardware architecture, but it is true of most hardware. Generally, for early z-rejection, stencil masking, and dynamic branching to execute as efficiently as possible, all pixels within a small screen area need to behave homogeneously with respect to the given feature. That is, they all need to be z-rejected, stenciled out, or taken down the same dynamic branch together for maximum performance.

19.7.1 Efficient Light Volumes

We use light volume geometry that tightly bounds the actual light volume. Technically, a full screen quad could be rendered for each light and the final image would look the same. However, performance would be dramatically reduced. The fewer pixels the light volume geometry overlaps in screen space, the less often the pixel shader is executed. We use a cone-shaped geometry for spotlights, a sphere for point lights, a box for box lights, and full screen quads only for global lights such as directional lights.

Another approach documented in most deferred shading papers is to adjust the depth test and cull mode based on the locations of the light volume and the camera. This adjustment maximizes early z-rejection. This technique requires using the CPU to determine which depth test and cull mode would most likely yield the most early-z-rejected pixels.

We settled on using a "greater" depth test and "clockwise" winding (that is, inverted winding), which works in every case for us (our light volumes never get clipped by the far clip plane). Educated guesses can quickly pick the most likely best choice of culling mode and depth test. However, our bottlenecks were elsewhere, so we decided not to use any CPU resources trying to optimize performance via this technique.

19.7.2 Stencil Masking

Using the stencil to mask off pixels is another common technique to speed up lighting in a deferred renderer. The basic technique is to use the stencil buffer to mark pixels that a light cannot affect. When rendering the light's volume geometry, one simply sets the stencil test to reject the marked pixels.

We tried several variations of this technique. We found that on average, the performance gains from this method were not great enough to compensate for any additional draw call overhead the technique may generate. We tried performing "cheap" passes prior to the lighting pass to mark the stencil for pixels facing away from the light or out of range of the light. This variation did increase the number of pixels later discarded by the final lighting pass. However, the draw call overhead of DirectX 9.0 along with the execution of the cheap pass seemed to cancel out or even cost more than any performance savings achieved during the final lighting pass (on average).

We do utilize the stencil technique as we render the opaque geometry in the scene to mark pixels that deferred shading will be used to light later. This approach excludes pixels belonging to the sky box or any pixel that we know up front will not or should not have lighting calculations performed on it. This does not require any additional draw calls, so it is essentially free. The lighting pass then discards these marked pixels using stencil testing. This technique can generate significant savings when the sky is predominant across the screen, and just as important, it has no adverse effects on performance, even in the worst case.

The draw call overhead is reduced with DirectX 10. For those readers targeting that platform, it may be worthwhile to explore using cheap passes to discard more pixels. However, using dynamic branches instead of additional passes is probably the better option if targeting Shader Model 3.0 or later.

19.7.3 Dynamic Branching

One of the key features of Shader Model 3.0 hardware is dynamic branching support. Dynamic branching not only increases the programmability of the GPU but, in the right circumstances, can also function as an optimization tool as well.

To use dynamic branching for optimization purposes, follow these two rules:

1. Create only one or maybe two dynamic branches that maximize both the amount of skipped code and the frequency at which they are taken.
2. Keep locality of data in mind. If a pixel takes a particular branch, be sure the chances of its neighbors taking the same branch are maximized.

With lighting, the best opportunities for using dynamic branching for optimization are to reject a pixel based on its distance from the light source and perhaps its surface normal. If normal maps are in use, the surface normal will be less homogeneous across a surface, which makes it a poor choice for optimization.

19.8 Issues

Deferred shading is not without caveats. From limited channels for storing material attribute information to constraints on hardware memory bandwidth, deferred shading has several problematic issues that must be addressed to utilize the technique.

19.8.1 Alpha-Blended Geometry

The single largest drawback of deferred shading is its inability to handle alpha-blended geometry. Alpha blending is not supported partly because of hardware limitations, but it is also fundamentally not supported by the technique itself as long as we limit ourselves to keeping track of the material attributes of only the nearest pixel. In *Tabula Rasa*, we solve this the same way everyone to date has: we render translucent geometry using our forward renderer after our deferred renderer has finished rendering the opaque geometry.

To support true alpha blending within a deferred renderer, some sort of deep frame buffer would be needed to keep track of every material fragment that overlapped a given pixel. This is the same mechanism required to solve order-independent transparency. This type of deep buffer is not currently supported by our target hardware.

However, our target hardware can support additive blending (a form of alpha blending) as well as alpha testing while MRTs are active, assuming the render targets use a compatible format. If alpha testing while MRTs are active, the alpha value of color 0 is used for the test. If the fragment fails, none of the render targets gets updated. We do not use alpha testing. Instead, we use the clip command to kill a pixel while our deferred shading MRTs are active. We do this because the alpha channel of render target 0 is used to store other material attribute data and not diffuse alpha. Every pixel rendered within the deferred pipeline is fully opaque, so we choose not to use one of our data channels to store a useless alpha value.

Using the forward renderer for translucent geometry mostly solves the problem. We use our forward renderer for our water and all translucent geometry. The water shader uses our depth texture from our deferred pipeline as an input. However, the actual lighting on the water is done by traditional forward shading techniques. This solution is problematic, however, because it is nearly impossible to match the lighting on the translucent geometry with that on the opaque geometry. Also, many light types and lighting features supported by our deferred renderer are not supported by our forward renderer. This makes matching lighting between the two impossible with our engine.

In *Tabula Rasa*, there are two main cases in which the discrepancy in lighting really became an issue: hair and flora (ground cover). Both hair and flora look best when rendered using alpha blending. However, it was not acceptable for an avatar to walk into shadow and not have his hair darken. Likewise, it was not acceptable for a field of grass to lack shadows when all other geometry around it had them.

We settled on using alpha testing for hair and flora and not alpha blending. This allowed hair and flora to be lit using deferred shading. The lighting was then consistent across hair and flora. To help minimize the popping of flora, we played around with several techniques. We considered some sort of screen-door transparency, and we even tried actual transparency by rendering the fading in flora with our forward renderer, then switching to the deferred renderer once it became fully opaque. Neither of these was acceptable. We currently are scaling flora up and down to simulate fading in and out.

19.8.2 Memory Bandwidth

Deferred shading significantly increases memory bandwidth utilization on hardware. Instead of writing to a single render target, we render to four of them. This quadruples the number of bytes written. During the lighting pass, we then sample from all of these buffers, increasing the bytes read. Memory bandwidth, or fill rate, is the single largest factor that determines the performance of a deferred shading engine on a given piece of hardware.

The single largest factor under our control to mitigate the memory bandwidth issue is screen resolution. Memory bandwidth is directly proportional to the number of pixels rendered, so 1280×1024 can be as much as 66 percent slower than 1024×768. Performance of deferred shading-based engines is largely tied to the resolution at which they are being rendered.

Checking for independent bit depth support and utilizing reduced bit depth render targets for data that does not need extra precision can help reduce overall memory bandwidth. This was not an option for us, however, because our target hardware does not support that feature. We try to minimize what material attribute data we need to save in render targets and minimize writes and fetches from those targets when possible.

When rendering our lights, we actually are using multiple render targets. We have two MRTs active and use an additive blend. These render targets are accumulation buffers for diffuse and specular light, respectively. At first this might seem to be an odd choice for minimizing bandwidth, because we are writing to two render targets as light shaders execute instead of one. However, overall this choice can actually be more efficient.

The general lighting equation that combines diffuse and specular light for the final fragment color looks like this:

$$Frag_{lit} = Frag_{unlit} \times Light_{diffuse} + Light_{specular}.$$

This equation is separable with respect to diffuse light and specular light. By keeping diffuse and specular light in separate render targets, we do not have to fetch the unlit fragment color inside of our light shaders. The light shaders compute and output only two colors: diffuse light and specular light; they do not compute anything other than the light interaction with the surface.

If we did not keep the specular light component separate from the diffuse light, the light shaders would have to actually compute the final lit fragment color. This computation requires a fetch of the unlit fragment color and a fetch of any other material attribute that affects its final lit fragment color. Computing this final color in the light shader would also mean we would lose what the actual diffuse and specular light components were; that is, we could not decompose the result of the shader back into the original light components. Having access to the diffuse and specular components in render targets lends itself perfectly to high dynamic range (HDR) or any other post-process that needs access to "light" within the scene.

After all light shaders have executed, we perform a final full-screen pass that computes the final fragment color. This final post-processing pass is where we compute fog, edge detection and smoothing, and the final fragment color. This approach ensures that each of these operations is performed only once per pixel, minimizing fetches and maximizing texture cache coherency as we fetch material attribute data from our MRTs. Fetching material data from MRTs can be expensive, especially if it is done excessively and the texture cache in hardware is getting thrashed.

Using these light accumulation buffers also lets us easily disable the specular accumulation render target if specular lighting is disabled, saving unnecessary bandwidth. These light accumulation buffers are also great for running post-processing on lighting to increase contrast, compute HDR, or any other similar effect.

19.8.3 Memory Management

In *Tabula Rasa*, even at a modest 1024×768 resolution, we can consume well over 50 MB of video memory just for render targets used by deferred shading and refraction. This does not include the primary back buffer, vertex buffers, index buffers, or textures. A resolution of 1600×1200 at highest quality settings requires over 100 MB of video memory just for render targets alone.

We utilize four screen-size render targets for our material attribute data when rendering geometry with our material shaders. Our light shaders utilize two screen-size render targets. These render targets can be 32 bits per pixel or 64, depending on quality and graphics settings. Add to this a 2048×2048 32-bit shadow map for the global directional light, plus additional shadow maps that have been created for other lights.

One possible suggestion is to use render targets that are at a lower resolution, and then scale the results up at the end. This has lots of benefits, but we found the image quality poor. We did not pursue this option very far, but perhaps it could be utilized successfully for specific applications.

The amount of video memory used by render targets is only part of the issue. The lifetime and placement of these render targets in video memory have significant impact on performance as well. Even though the actual placement of these textures in video memory is out of our control, we do a couple of things to help the driver out.

We allocate our primary MRT textures back to back and before any other texture. The idea is to allocate these while the most video memory is available so the driver can place them in video memory with minimal fragmentation. We are still at the mercy of the driver, but we try to help it as much as we can.

We use a shadow-map pool and have lights share them. We limit the number of shadow maps available to the engine. Based on light priority, light location, and desired shadow-map size, we dole out the shadow maps to the lights. These shadow maps are not released but kept and reused. This minimizes fragmentation of video memory and reduces driver overhead associated with creating and releasing resources.

Related to this, we also throttle how many shadow maps get rendered (or regenerated) in any one frame. If multiple lights all require their shadow maps to be rebuilt on the same frame, the engine may only rebuild one or two of them that frame, amortizing the cost of rebuilding all of them across multiple frames.

19.9 Results

In *Tabula Rasa*, we achieved our goals using a deferred shading renderer. We found the scalability and performance of deferred shading acceptable. Some early Shader 3.0 hardware, such as the NVIDIA GeForce 6800 Ultra, is able to hold close to 30 fps with basic settings and medium resolutions. We found that the latest DirectX 10 class hardware, such as the NVIDIA GeForce 8800 and ATI Radeon 2900, is able to run *Tabula Rasa* extremely well at high resolutions with all settings maxed out.

Figures 19-6 through 19-10 show the results we obtained with our approach.

19.10 Conclusion

Deferred shading has progressed from theoretical to practical. Many times new techniques are too expensive, too abstract, or just too impractical to be used outside of a tightly scoped demo. Deferred shading has proven to be a versatile, powerful, and manageable technique that can work in a real game environment.

The main drawbacks of deferred shading include the following:

- High memory bandwidth usage
- No hardware antialiasing
- Lack of proper alpha-blending support

Figure 19-6. An Outdoor Scene with a Global Shadow Map

Figure 19-7. An Indoor Scene with Numerous Static Shadow-Casting Lights
Shown are box, spot, and point lights.

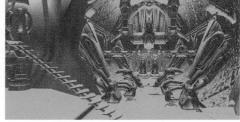

Figure 19-8. Fragment Colors and Normals
Left: Unlit diffuse fragment color. Right: Normals

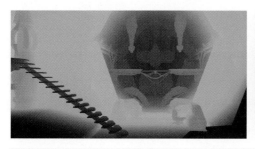

Figure 19-9. Depth and Edge Weight Visualization
Left: The depth of pixels. Right: Edge detection.

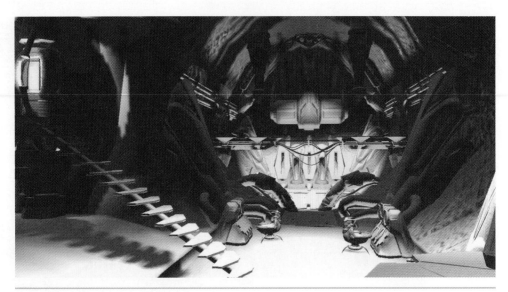

Figure 19-10. Light Accumulation

We have found that current midrange hardware is able to handle the memory bandwidth requirements at modest resolution, with current high-end hardware able to handle higher resolutions with all features enabled. With DirectX 10 hardware, MRT performance has been improved significantly by both ATI and NVIDIA. DirectX 10 and Shader Model 4.0 also provide integer operations in pixel shaders as well as read access to the depth buffer, both of which can be used to reduce memory bandwidth usage. Performance should only continue to improve as new hardware and new features become available.

Reliable edge detection combined with proper filtering can significantly minimize aliasing artifacts around geometry edges. Although these techniques are not as accurate as the subsampling found in hardware full-scene antialiasing, the method still produces results that trick the eye into smoothing hard edges.

The primary outstanding issue with deferred shading is the lack of alpha-blending support. We consciously sacrificed some visual quality related to no transparency support while in the deferred pipeline. However, we felt overall the gains from using deferred shading outweighed the issues.

The primary benefits of deferred shading include the following:

- Lighting cost is independent of scene complexity.
- Shaders have access to depth and other pixel information.

- Each pixel is lit only once per light. That is, no lighting is computed on pixels that later become occluded by other opaque geometry.
- Clean separation of shader code: material rendering is separated from lighting computations.

Every day, new techniques and new hardware come out, and with them, the desirability of deferred shading may go up or down. The future is hard to predict, but we are happy with our choice to use deferred shading in the context of today's hardware.

19.11 References

Hargreaves, Shawn, and Mark Harris. 2004. "6800 Leagues Under the Sea: Deferred Shading." Available online at http://developer.nvidia.com/object/6800_leagues_deferred_shading.html.

Kozlov, Simon. 2004. "Perspective Shadow Maps: Care and Feeding." In *GPU Gems*, edited by Randima Fernando, pp. 217–244.

Martin, Tobias, and Tiow-Seng Tan. 2004. "Anti-aliasing and Continuity with Trapezoidal Shadow Maps." In *Eurographics Symposium on Rendering Proceedings 2004*, pp. 153–160.

Policarpo, Fabio, and Francisco Fonseca. 2005. "Deferred Shading Tutorial." Available online at http://fabio.policarpo.nom.br/docs/Deferred_Shading_Tutorial_SBGAMES2005.pdf.

Shishkovtsov, Oles. 2005. "Deferred Shading in *S.T.A.L.K.E.R.*" In *GPU Gems 2*, edited by Matt Pharr, pp.143–166. Addison-Wesley.

Sousa, Tiago. 2005. "Generic Refraction Simulation." In *GPU Gems 2*, edited by Matt Pharr, pp. 295–306. Addison-Wesley.

Stamminger, Marc, and George Drettakis. 2002. "Perspective Shadow Maps." In *ACM Transactions on Graphics (Proceedings of SIGGRAPH 2002)* 21(3), pp. 557–562.

I would like to thank all of the contributors to this chapter, including a few at NCsoft Austin who also have helped make our rendering engine possible: Sean Barton, Tom Gambill, Aaron Otstott, John Styes, and Quoc Tran.

Chapter 20

GPU-Based Importance Sampling

Mark Colbert
University of Central Florida

Jaroslav Křivánek
Czech Technical University in Prague

20.1 Introduction

High-fidelity real-time visualization of surfaces under high-dynamic-range (HDR) image-based illumination provides an invaluable resource for various computer graphics applications. Material design, lighting design, architectural previsualization, and gaming are just a few such applications. Environment map prefiltering techniques (Kautz et al. 2000)—plus other frequency space solutions using wavelets (Wang et al. 2006) or spherical harmonics (Ramamoorthi and Hanrahan 2002)—provide real-time visualizations. However, their use may be too cumbersome because they require a hefty amount of precomputation or a sizable code base for glossy surface reflections.

As an alternative, we present a technique for image-based lighting of glossy objects using a *Monte Carlo quadrature* that requires minimal precomputation and operates within a single GPU shader, thereby fitting easily into almost any production pipeline requiring real-time dynamically changing materials or lighting. Figure 20-1 shows an example of our results.

20.2 Rendering Formulation

The goal in rendering is to compute, for each pixel, how much light from the surrounding environment is reflected toward the virtual camera at a given surface point, as shown in Figure 20-2. To convert the incoming light from one particular direction, $L_i(\mathbf{u})$, into

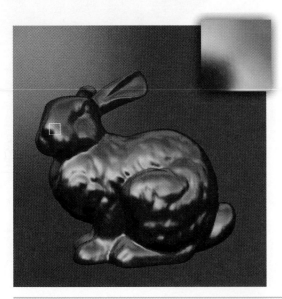

Figure 20-1. Real-Time Rendering of the Stanford Bunny with 40 Samples per Pixel
The inset is a close-up on the bunny's nose, showing the smooth shading variation over the surface. Material and illumination can be changed in real time.

reflected light toward the direction of the camera, **v**, we use the material function f, known as the *bidirectional reflectance distribution function* (BRDF). One common BRDF is the classic Phong reflection model. To compute the total reflected light, $L_o(\mathbf{v})$, the contributions from every incident direction, **u**, must be summed (or integrated, in the limit) together over the hemisphere H:

$$L_o(\mathbf{v}) = \int_H L_i(\mathbf{u}) f(\mathbf{u}, \mathbf{v}) \cos\theta_{\mathbf{u}} \, d\mathbf{u}. \qquad (1)$$

This equation is referred to as the *reflectance equation* or the *illumination integral*. Here, $\theta_{\mathbf{u}}$ is the angle between the surface normal and the incoming light's direction **u**.

In image-based lighting, the incoming light L_i is approximated by an environment map, where each texel corresponds to an incoming direction **u** and occlusion is ignored. However, even with this approximation, the numerical integration of the illumination integral for one pixel in the image requires thousands of texels in the environment map to be multiplied with the BRDF and summed. This operation is clearly too computationally expensive for real-time rendering.

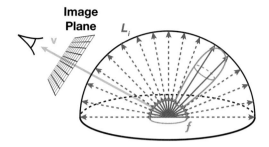

Figure 20-2. Illumination Integral Illustration
Incoming light along rays from the hemisphere (blue) are multiplied with the BRDF, f, and summed to produce the amount of light reflected toward the camera (green).

20.2.1 Monte Carlo Quadrature

We cannot afford evaluating the illumination integral for all incident directions, so we randomly choose a number of directions and evaluate the integrated function, $L_i(\mathbf{u})f(\mathbf{u}, \mathbf{v})\cos\theta_\mathbf{u}$, at these directions to obtain *samples*, or estimates of the integral. The average of these samples produces an approximation of the integral, which is the essence of Monte Carlo quadrature. In fact, if we had an infinite set of samples, the average of the samples would equal the true value of the integral. However, when we use only a practical, finite set of samples, the average value varies from the actual solution and introduces noise into the image, as shown in Figure 20-5b (in Section 20.4). One way to reduce this noise is to choose the most important samples that best approximate the integral.

20.2.2 Importance Sampling

Generating uniform random directions is not the best method for approximating the integral if we have a rough idea about the behavior of the integrated function. For instance, if we are integrating a glossy material with the environment, it makes the most sense to sample directions around the specular direction (in other words, the mirror reflection direction), because much of the reflected light originates from these directions. To represent this mathematically, a *probability density function* (PDF) is used to define the optimal directions for sampling. The PDF is a normalized function, where the integral over the entire domain of the function is 1 and the peaks represent important regions for sampling.

However, when we skew sample directions, not all estimates of the integral are equal, and thus we must weight them accordingly when averaging all the samples. For instance, one sample in a low-value region of the PDF is representative of what would be many samples if uniform sampling were used. Similarly, one sample in a high-value PDF region represents only a few samples with uniform sampling. To compensate for this property of the PDF-proportional sampling, we multiply each sample by the inverse of the PDF. This yields a *Monte Carlo estimator* that uses the weighted average of all the samples:

$$L_o(\mathbf{v}) \approx \frac{1}{N} \sum_{k=1}^{N} \frac{L_i(\mathbf{u}_k) f(\mathbf{u}_k, \mathbf{v}) \cos\theta_{\mathbf{u}_k}}{p(\mathbf{u}_k, \mathbf{v})}. \tag{2}$$

To define the optimal PDF for the illumination integral, we need an accurate approximation of the product between the material BRDF and the incident lighting. However, generating samples according to this product is quite involved (Clarberg et al. 2005). Fortunately, creating samples according to the BRDF alone is straightforward, and when we use it in combination with sample filtering—described in Section 20.1.4—it provides good results.

20.2.3 Sampling Material Functions

Because BRDFs are a part of the integration, they serve as a good measure to guide the sampling to produce directions that best approximate the integral. Here, we use a normalized BRDF as the PDF for sampling. To sample this PDF, we convert a random number pair into an important direction for the BRDF. For example, Equations 7 and 8, later in this section, perform such a conversion for the specular lobe of the Phong BRDF. If you are interested in how such sampling formulas are derived, keep reading.

We find the sample directions by converting the PDF into a *cumulative distribution function* (CDF). Intuitively, think of a CDF as a mapping between a PDF-proportional distribution and a uniform distribution. In the discrete case, where there are only a finite number of samples, we can define the CDF by stacking each sample. For instance, if we divide all possible sampling directions for rendering into four discrete directions, where one of the sample directions, S2, is known *a priori* to be more important, then the probabilities of the four samples can be stacked together as depicted in Figure 20-3.

In this case, if we choose a random number, where there exists an equal likelihood that any value between 0 and 1 will be produced, then more numbers will map to the important sample, S2, and thus we will sample that direction more often.

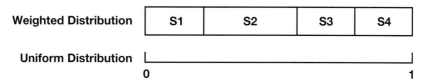

Weighted Distribution	S1	S2	S3	S4

Uniform Distribution		
0		1

Figure 20-3. Discrete Cumulative Distribution Function

For continuous one-dimensional PDFs, we must map an infinite number of the PDF-weighted samples to a uniform distribution of numbers. This way, we can generate a random number from a uniform distribution and be more likely to obtain an important sample direction, just as more random values would map to the important sample S2. The mapping is performed by the same stacking operation, which is represented as the integral of the infinite sample directions. We can obtain the position of a sample s within the uniform distribution by stacking all the previous weighted samples, $p(\theta)\,d\theta$, before s on top of each other via integration:

$$P(s) = \int_0^s p(\theta)\,d\theta. \tag{3}$$

To obtain the PDF-proportional sample from a random number, we set $P(s)$ equal to a random value ξ and solve for s. In general, we denote the mapping from the random value to the sample direction distributed according to the PDF as $P^{-1}(\xi)$.

As an example, let us sample the glossy component of the Phong BRDF (Lewis 1994). The glossy component assumes light is reflected based upon a cosine falloff from the specular reflection direction computed as the mirror reflection of the viewing direction $\mathbf{v}$ with respect to the normal of the surface. We can represent the glossy component mathematically as $\cos^n \theta_s$, where θ_s is the angle between the sample direction and the specular direction, and n is the shininess of the surface. To convert this material function into a PDF, $p(\theta_s, \phi_s)$, we must first normalize the cosine lobe to integrate to one:

$$p(\theta_s, \phi_s) = \frac{\cos^n \theta_s \, \sin \theta_s}{\displaystyle\int_0^{2\pi}\int_0^{\pi/2} \cos^n \theta \, \sin \theta \, d\theta \, d\phi} = \frac{(n+1)}{2\pi}\cos^n \theta_s \, \sin \theta_s. \tag{4}$$

Here, θ_s and ϕ_s are the spherical coordinates of the sample direction in a coordinate frame where the specular direction is the z-axis, as shown in Figure 20-4. The extra sine appears because we work with spherical coordinates instead of the intrinsic parameterization of directions by differential solid angles.

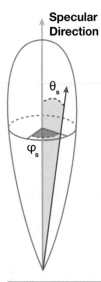

Figure 20-4. Coordinate Frame for Sample Generation in the Phong BRDF Model

To generate the two-dimensional importance sample direction (θ_s, ϕ_s) according to this PDF, it is best if we find each dimension of the sample direction separately. Therefore, we need a PDF for each dimension so we can apply Equation 3 to convert the PDF into a CDF and create a partial sample direction. To accomplish this, the *marginal probability* of the θ_s direction, $p(\theta_s)$, can be separated from $p(\theta_s, \phi_s)$ by integrating the PDF across the entire domain of ϕ_s:

$$p(\theta_s) = \int_0^{2\pi} p(\theta_s, \phi_s)\, d\phi_s = (n+1)\cos^n \theta_s \sin \theta_s. \tag{5}$$

This one-dimensional PDF can now be used to generate θ_s. Given the value of θ_s, we find the PDF for ϕ_s using the *conditional probability* $p(\phi_s \mid \theta_s)$ defined as

$$p(\phi_s \mid \theta_s) = \frac{p(\theta_s, \phi_s)}{p(\theta_s)} = \frac{1}{2\pi}. \tag{6}$$

The two probability functions are converted into CDFs by Equation 3 and inverted to map a pair of independent uniform random variables (ξ_1, ξ_2) to a sample direction (θ_s, ϕ_s)[1]:

$$\theta_s = \cos^{-1}\left(\xi_1^{\frac{1}{n+1}}\right), \tag{7}$$

---

1. The integration for $p(\theta_s)$ is actually $(1-\xi_1)^{1/(n+1)}$, but because ξ_1 is a uniformly distributed random variable between 0 and 1, $(1-\xi_1)$ is also uniformly distributed between 0 and 1.

$$\phi_s = 2\pi\xi_2. \tag{8}$$

To operate in a Cartesian space, the spherical coordinates are simply mapped to their Cartesian counterparts:

$$x_s = \cos\phi_s \sin\theta_s$$
$$y_s = \sin\phi_s \sin\theta_s \tag{9}$$
$$z_s = \cos\theta_s$$

Remember, x_s, y_s, and z_s are defined in a coordinate frame where the specular direction is the z-axis (see Figure 20-4). To sample the surrounding environment, the sample direction must be transformed to world space. This rotation is done by applying two linear transformations: tangent-space to world-space and specular-space to tangent-space. Tangent-space to world-space is derived from the local tangent, binormal, and normal at the surface point. The specular-space to tangent-space transformation is underconstrained because only the specular direction defines the space. Thus, we introduce an arbitrary axis-aligned vector to generate the transformation.

Similar importance sampling methods can be used for other material models, such as the Lafortune BRDF (Lafortune et al. 1997) or Ward's anisotropic BRDF (Walter 2005). Pharr and Humphreys 2004 gives more details on deriving sampling formulas for various BRDFs.

20.3 Quasirandom Low-Discrepancy Sequences

The problem with generating random sample directions using pseudorandom numbers is that the directions are not well distributed, which leads to poor accuracy of the estimator in Equation 2. We can improve accuracy by replacing pseudorandom numbers with quasirandom low-discrepancy sequences, which intrinsically guarantee well-distributed directions. One such sequence is known as the *Hammersley sequence*. A random pair x_i in the two-dimensional Hammersley sequence with N values is defined as

$$x_i = \left(\frac{i}{N}, \Phi_2(i)\right), \tag{10}$$

where the radical inverse function, $\Phi_2(i)$ returns the number obtained by reflecting the digits of the binary representation of i around the decimal point, as illustrated in Table 20-1.

Table 20-1. Radical Inverse Sequence

	Binary	Inverse Binary	Value
1	1	0.1	0.5
2	10	0.01	0.25
3	11	0.11	0.75
4	100	0.001	0.125

Another problem, pertaining both to pseudorandom numbers and the low-discrepancy series, is that it is computationally expensive to generate random sample directions on the GPU. Instead, we precompute the numbers on the CPU and store them as literals in the shader or upload them into the constant registers to optimize the algorithm. As a consequence, the same sequence of quasirandom numbers is used for integration when computing the color of each pixel. The use of such deterministic number sequences, in combination with a relatively low sample count, produces an aliasing effect, as shown in Figure 20-5a, that we suppress by filtering the samples, as detailed in the next section.

20.4 Mipmap Filtered Samples

As shown in Figure 20-5a, deterministic importance sampling causes sharp aliasing artifacts that look like duplicate specular reflections. In standard Monte Carlo quadrature, this problem is combated by introducing randomness, which changes aliasing into more visually acceptable noise, as is evident in Figure 20-5b. However, keeping the noise level low requires using hundreds or even thousands of samples for each pixel—which is clearly not suitable for real-time rendering on the GPU. We use a different approach—filtering with mipmaps—to reduce aliasing caused by the low sample count, as shown in Figure 20-5c.

The idea is as follows: if the PDF of a sample direction is small (that is, if the sample is not very probable), it is unlikely that other samples will be generated in a similar direction. In such a case, we want the sample to bring illumination from the environment map averaged over a large area, thereby providing a better approximation of the overall integration. On the other hand, if the PDF of a direction is very high, many samples are likely to be generated in similar directions. Thus, multiple samples will help average out the error in the integral estimation from this region. In this case, the sample should only average a small area of the environment map, as shown in Figure 20-6a.

(a)   **(b)**   **(c)**

Figure 20-5. Importance Sampling with 40 Samples per Pixel
*(a) Deterministic importance sampling without filtering. (b) Random importance sampling.
(c) Deterministic importance sampling with filtering.*

In short, the lower the PDF, the more pixels of the environment should be averaged for that sample. We define this relationship in terms of the solid angle associated with a sample, computed as the inverse of the product between the PDF and the total number of samples, N:

$$\Omega_s = \frac{1}{N \cdot p(\mathbf{u}, \mathbf{v})}. \tag{11}$$

Here, we should average all pixels of the environment map within the solid angle Ω_s around a sample direction. To make the averaging efficient, we use the mipmap data structure available on the GPU. Remember, the mipmap is a pyramidal structure over a texture, where each pixel of level l is the average of the four corresponding pixels of level $l - 1$, as shown in Figure 20-6b, and level zero is the original texture. Therefore, averaging all the pixels within the solid angle Ω_s can be approximated by choosing an appropriate level of the mipmap.

Here is how we proceed. First, we need to compute the number of environment map pixels in Ω_s. This number is given by the ratio of Ω_s to the solid angle subtended by one pixel of the zeroth mipmap level Ω_p, which in turn, is given by the texture resolution, $w \cdot h$, and the mapping distortion factor $d(\mathbf{u})$:

$$\Omega_p = \frac{d(\mathbf{u})}{w \cdot h}. \tag{12}$$

Let us assume for a while that the distortion $d(\mathbf{u})$ is known (we will get back to it in Section 20.4.1).

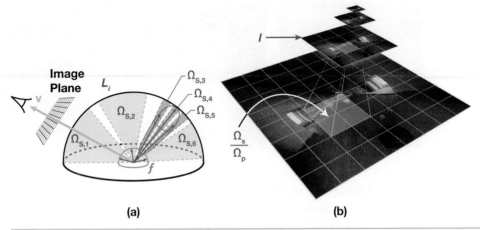

Figure 20-6. Illustration of Filtered Importance Sampling
(a) Various samples and their associated solid angle Ω_s, as defined in Equation 12, for the illumination integral. (b) A visualization of a mipmapped environment texture, where Ω_s/Ω_p is shown on the zeroth level of the environment map and the corresponding filtered sample is highlighted on level l.

As a reminder, we want the environment map lookup to correspond to averaging Ω_s/Ω_p pixels, which yields a simple formula for the mipmap level:

$$l = \max\left[\frac{1}{2}\log_2 \frac{\Omega_s}{\Omega_p}, 0\right] = \max\left[\frac{1}{2}\log_2\left(\frac{w \cdot h}{N}\right) - \frac{1}{2}\log_2\left(p\left(\mathbf{u}, \mathbf{v}\right) d\left(\mathbf{u}\right)\right), 0\right]. \quad \text{(13)}$$

Notice that all solid angles are gone from the final formula! In addition, the $\frac{1}{2}\log_2\left[(w \cdot h)/N\right]$ expression can be precomputed with minimal computational cost. Now all we need to do for each sample direction is to evaluate the PDF $p(\mathbf{u}, \mathbf{v})$ and the distortion $d(\mathbf{u})$, plug these numbers into the preceding formula, and feed the result to `tex2Dlod()` as the level-of-detail (LOD) parameter when we look up the environment map.

In practice, we found that introducing small amounts of overlap between samples (for example, biasing Ω_s/Ω_p by a constant) produces smoother, more visually acceptable results. Specifically, we perform the bias by adding 1 to the calculated mipmap level defined by Equation 13.

20.4.1 Mapping and Distortion

Cube maps are typically used for environment mapping. However, although cube maps have very low distortion (which is good), they also have a serious flaw—the mipmap generation is performed on each face separately. Unfortunately, our filtering operation assumes that the mipmap is generated by averaging pixels from the *entire* environment map. Therefore, we need a way to introduce as much surrounding information of the environment map as possible into a single image, which will reduce seamlike artifacts from the mipmaps without modifying the hardware-accelerated mipmap generation.

Thus, instead of using cube maps, we use *dual-paraboloid environment maps* (Heidrich and Seidel 1998, Kilgard 1999). The environment is stored in two textures: one represents directions from the upper hemisphere ($z \geq 0$) and the other represents directions from the lower hemisphere ($z < 0$). Although the mipmap for the two textures is computed separately, artifacts rarely appear in rendered images. Why? Because the texture corresponding to each hemisphere contains some information from the opposite hemisphere.

Still, some occasional seams in the rendered images might correspond to the sampling from the environment map at a location where the circle in Figure 20-7a touches the edge of the texture. To remedy this situation, we adjust the usual paraboloid mapping by adding a scaling factor b of 1.2, which adds even more information from the opposite hemisphere, as shown in Figure 20-7b.

Given a direction, $\mathbf{u} = (x, y, z)$, the (s, t) texture coordinates for this scaled mapping are computed as follows in Table 20-2.

By computing the inverse of the Jacobian determinant of this mapping, we can model the rate of change from a unit of area on the hemisphere to a unit of area on the texture (in other words, the distortion for the mapping, $d(\mathbf{u})$):

$$d(\mathbf{u}) = 4b^2 \left(|z| + 1 \right)^2 . \tag{14}$$

Table 20-2. Equations for Scaled Dual-Paraboloid Mapping

Lower Hemisphere ($z < 0$)	Upper Hemisphere ($z \geq 0$)
$s = \dfrac{1}{2b}\dfrac{x}{1-z} + \dfrac{1}{2}$	$s = -\dfrac{1}{2b}\dfrac{x}{1+z} + \dfrac{1}{2}$
$t = \dfrac{1}{2b}\dfrac{y}{1-z} + \dfrac{1}{2}$	$t = -\dfrac{1}{2b}\dfrac{y}{1+z} + \dfrac{1}{2}$

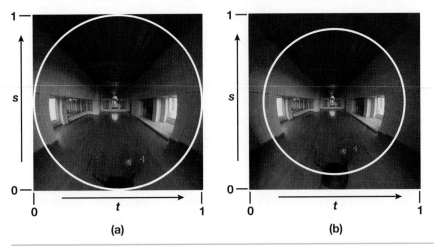

Figure 20-7. Scaled Dual-Paraboloid Environment Mapping
(a) The texture corresponding to a hemisphere in dual-paraboloid mapping contains some information from the opposite hemisphere (the region outside the circle). (b) Scaling the (s, t) texture coordinates introduces even more information from the opposite hemisphere.

20.5 Performance

As seen in Listing 20-1, the implementation of the algorithm follows straight from the Monte Carlo estimator (Equation 2) and the computation of the mipmap level (Equation 13). To optimize image quality and performance, we use a spherical harmonics representation for the diffuse component of the material (Ramamoorthi 2001). Spherical harmonics work well for low-frequency diffuse shading and, together with our sampling approach for glossy shading, provide an ideal hybrid solution.

Figure 20-8a plots the error of the approximation with respect to a reference solution, demonstrating that the fidelity of the rendering directly correlates to the number of samples used. In practice, only 24 or fewer samples are needed for surfaces with complex geometry. Smooth surfaces, such as the spheres in Figure 20-8b, often need more samples, but 40 samples are sufficient for visually acceptable solutions. Thus, much like the wavelet-based approaches, the filtered importance sampling does not require many samples to produce accurate, glossy surface reflection. In addition, Figure 20-9 shows that our technique performs well on a variety of GPUs and that the performance varies almost linearly with the number of samples.

Listing 20-1. Pseudocode for Our Sampling Algorithm

The actual implementation of the shader looks slightly different from this pseudocode, but it is indeed just an optimized version. The most important optimizations are these: (1) Four directions are generated in parallel. (2) The BRDF is not explicitly evaluated, because it only appears divided by the PDF, which cancels out most of the terms of the BRDF. (3) The trigonometric functions associated with generating a sample direction using the Hammersley sequence (Equation 10) are precomputed.

```
float4 GPUImportanceSampling(
  float3 viewing : TEXCOORD1
  uniform sampler2D env) : COLOR
{
  float4 c = 0;

  // Sample loop
  for (int k=0; k < N; k++) {
    float2 xi = hammersley_seq(k);
    float3 u = sample_material(xi);
    float pdf = p(u, viewing);
    float lod = compute_lod(u, pdf);
    float3 L = tex2Dlod(env, float4(texcoord, lod.xy));
    c += L*f(u,viewing)/pdf;
  }

  return c/N;
}
```

20.6 Conclusion

Our GPU-based importance sampling is a real-time rendering algorithm for various parameterized material models illuminated by an environment map. Performing Monte Carlo integration with mipmap-based filtering sufficiently reduces the computational complexity associated with importance sampling to a process executable within a single GPU shader. This combination also shows that non-BRDF-specific filters (such as mipmaps) are sufficient for approximating the illumination integral. Consequently, BRDFs and environments can be changed in real time.

Given that the BRDF and environment can be completely dynamic, visualizations for applications such as material or lighting design become trivial and afford new user

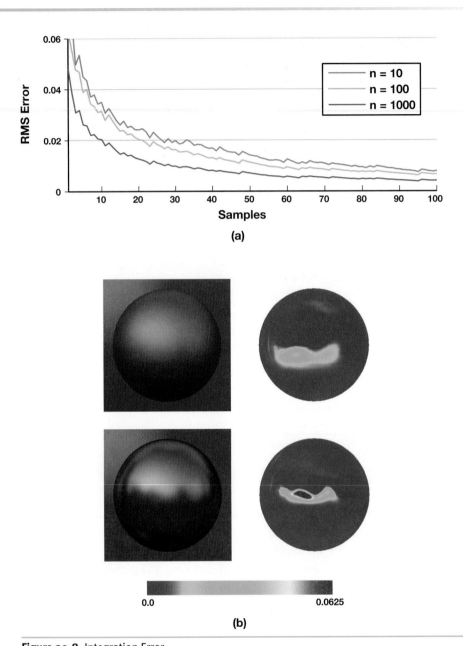

Figure 20-8. Integration Error
(a) The root mean square error with respect to the number of samples per pixel. (b) Left: Our solution for a sphere rendered under the Pisa light probe with 40 samples per pixel. Right: The false color difference image between our method and the reference solution.

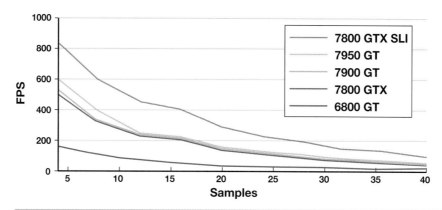

Figure 20-9. Algorithm Performance
When rendering a sphere, in frames per second, at a resolution of 512×512 for various numbers of samples and on different NVIDIA GPUs.

interfaces. In Figure 20-10, we show such an interface for a spatially varying BRDF painting program, in which the user can choose a parameterization of a BRDF and paint it onto the mesh in real time. In general, our technique provides a rendering solution that is easy to integrate into existing production pipelines by using a single shader that harnesses the computational power of the GPU.

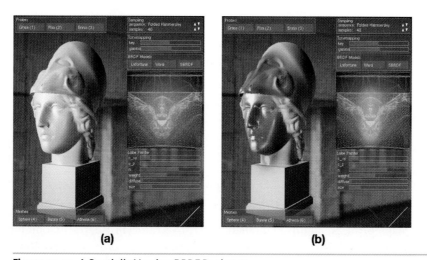

(a)   (b)

Figure 20-10. A Spatially Varying BRDF Designer
(a) The starting condition for the designer. (b) The result of painting glossy reflection onto the spatially varying BRDF map.

20.7 Further Reading and References

For a more in-depth introduction into Monte Carlo and its uses in rendering, we suggest reading *Physically Based Rendering: From Theory to Implementation* (Pharr and Humphreys 2004). Additionally, Alexander Keller's report, "Strictly Deterministic Sampling Methods in Computer Graphics" (Keller 2003), provides detailed information on using quasirandom low-discrepancy sequences and other random number sequences for rendering.

Clarberg, P., W. Jarosz, T. Akenine-Möller, and H. W. Jensen. 2005. "Wavelet Importance Sampling: Efficiently Evaluating Products of Complex Functions." In *ACM Transactions on Graphics (Proceedings of ACM SIGGRAPH 2005)* 24(3), pp. 1166–1175.

Heidrich, W., and H.-P. Seidel. 1998. "View-Independent Environment Maps." In *Proceedings of the ACM SIGGRAPH/Eurographics Workshop on Graphics Hardware 1998*, pp. 39–45.

Kautz, J., P.-P. Vázquez, W. Heidrich, and H.-P. Seidel. 2000. "A Unified Approach to Prefiltered Environment Maps." In *Proceedings of the Eurographics Workshop on Rendering Techniques 2000*, pp. 185–196.

Keller, A. 2003. "Strictly Deterministic Sampling Methods in Computer Graphics." In "Monte Carlo Ray Tracing," ACM SIGGRAPH 2003 Course No. 44, July 2003.

Kilgard, M. 1999. "View Independent Environment Mapping with Dual Paraboloid Maps." Presentation at Game Developers Conference 1999.

Lafortune, E. P., S. Foo, K. E. Torrance, and D. P. Greenberg. 1997. "Non-linear Approximation of Reflectance Functions." In *Proceedings of SIGGRAPH 97*, pp. 117–126.

Lewis, R. R. 1994. "Making Shaders More Physically Plausible." *Computer Graphics Forum* 13(2), pp. 109–120.

Pharr, Matt, and Greg Humphreys. 2004. *Physically Based Rendering: From Theory to Implementation*. Morgan Kaufmann.

Ramamoorthi, R., and P. Hanrahan. 2001. "An Efficient Representation for Irradiance Environment Maps." In *Proceedings of SIGGRAPH 2001*, pp. 497–500.

Ramamoorthi, R., and P. Hanrahan. 2002. "Frequency Space Environment Map Rendering." In *ACM Transactions on Graphics (Proceedings of SIGGRAPH 2002)* 21(3), pp. 517–526.

Walter, B. 2005. "Notes on the Ward BRDF." Technical Report PCG-05-06, Cornell Program of Computer Graphics.

Wang, R., J. Tran, and D. Luebke. 2006. "All-Frequency Relighting of Glossy Objects." *ACM Transactions on Graphics* 25(2), pp. 293–318.

PART IV
IMAGE EFFECTS

In preparing this section of *GPU Gems 3*, I revisited the matching sections of the previous volumes. It's exciting to see that the ideas presented in our first two books have already become *de rigeur* throughout the game and entertainment industries. Standards like HDR and OpenEXR (*GPU Gems*) and techniques like high-quality GPU color transformations (*GPU Gems 2*) are already widely accepted and in use everywhere. Some of the informative chapters ahead, from my vantage point, look to be equally influential over the coming years. As of 2007, with more emphasis than ever on high-quality 2D and 3D imaging—not just in games but even on the basic desktop views of the newest operating systems—this is especially promising.

Alongside the rapid growth in GPU power over the past few years, we've seen surprising quality improvements and a drop in prices for large displays. Some gamers and other high-end computer users are already using resolutions as high as 2560×1600—on a single monitor—on a daily basis. Many are spreading their screen real estate even further by attaching additional monitors. Truly pocketable still cameras of 10 megapixels or higher are already common in discount stores, and consumer HD video can be seen at every neighborhood-league soccer game. The demand for great-looking ways to fill these newly available pixels—more than a 5× increase over the 1024×768 screens that are still expected by many games—helps drive new improvements and ideas in imaging.

Traditional TV and movie makers have been industrious in picking up on these new technologies, offering comprehensive broadcast content at HD sizes and seizing on the capabilities of interactive imaging to push the boundaries of their craft. Interactive computer imaging is forging ahead, not just in the new generations of special effects, but as a core part of the entire film and video production pipeline, providing greater interaction, higher productivity, and better, more sophisticated pictures. Even scientific visualizations and the interactive graphics of the evening TV weather report have surged ahead both in gloss and resolution, offering not just prettier numbers but more informative ones. This flood of new imagery is seen daily by every consumer, and in turn it drives their expectations ever higher.

For game makers, the new changes in resolution provide challenges in design. How can they make games (especially multiplayer games) that are approachable by players using not only the newest, high-performance computers but also older, low-capability computers—giving all players great experiences while still respecting the advancing trends in consumer choices and engaging the leading edge of what the new hardware permits? What strategies can game designers take so that their games look terrific today and also in the future?

Image effects provide a great way to layer new and increasingly sophisticated looks onto existing graphics frameworks. They can create images using vector-style graphics that will scale beautifully to any resolution, use 2D/3D-hybrid particle systems for environmental richness, and apply effects that can be tuned in complexity according to the capabilities of the player's computer and the demands of their display device. At a minimum, they can ensure that the experience of color is nuanced and true to the art department's vision.

Image effects, more than any other specialty, deal directly with human visual perception—whether the images are real-world pictures and videos, or completely synthetic inventions. The chapters in this part of the book address the elements of perception: issues of color, of perceived detail, and of the use of visual tools like motion blur and depth of field to enrich and direct the user's gaze and their game-playing experience.

These ideas are not theoretical—the chapters here all come from ideas being incorporated into real software for today's PCs, and tomorrow's.

Kevin Bjorke, NVIDIA Corporation

Chapter 21

True Impostors

Eric Risser
University of Central Florida

In this chapter we present the *true impostors* method, an efficient technique for adding a large number of simple models to any scene without rendering a large number of polygons. The technique utilizes modern shading hardware to perform ray casting into texture-defined volumes. With this method, multiple depth layers representing non-height-field surface data are associated with quads.

Like traditional impostors, the true impostors approach rotates the quad around its center so that it always faces the camera. Unlike the traditional impostors technique, which displays a static texture, the true impostors technique uses the pixel shader to ray-cast a view ray through the quad in texture-coordinate space to intersect the 3D model and compute the color at the intersection point. The texture-coordinate space is defined by a frame with the center of the quad as the origin.

True impostors supports self-shadowing on models, reflections, and refractions, and it is an efficient method for finding distances through volumes.

21.1 Introduction

Most interesting environments, both natural as well as synthetic ones, tend to be densely populated with many highly detailed objects. Rendering this kind of environment typically requires a huge set of polygons, as well as a sophisticated scene graph and the overhead to run it.

As an alternative, image-based techniques have been explored to offer practical remedies to these limitations. Among current image-based techniques is *impostors*, a powerful technique that has been used widely for many years in the graphics community. An impostor is a two-dimensional image texture that is mapped onto a rectangular card or *billboard*, producing the illusion of highly detailed geometry. Impostors can be created on the fly or precomputed and stored in memory. In both cases, the impostor is accurate only for a specific viewing direction. As the view deviates from this ideal condition, the impostor loses accuracy. The same impostor is reused until its visual error surpasses a given arbitrary threshold and it is replaced with a more accurate impostor.

The true impostors method takes advantage of the latest graphics hardware to achieve an accurate geometric representation that is updated every frame for any arbitrary viewing angle. True impostors builds off previous per-pixel displacement mapping techniques. It also extends the goal of adding visually accurate subsurface features to any arbitrary surface by generating whole 3D objects on a billboard. The true impostors method distinguishes itself from previous per-pixel displacement mapping impostor methods because it does not restrict viewing, yet it provides performance optimizations and true multiple refraction.

21.2 Algorithm and Implementation Details

A single four-channel texture can hold four height fields, which can represent many volumes. More texture data can be added to extend this to any shape. We generate a billboard (that is, a quad that always faces the camera) for use as a window to view our height fields from any given direction, as illustrated in Figure 21-1.

The image in Figure 21-1b shows a representation of our billboard's texture coordinates after they have been transformed into a 3D plane and rotated around our functions (model) in the center (represented by the asteroid). Figure 21-1a shows the perspective of our function that would be displayed on our billboard, and Figure 21-1c shows the function (in bitmap form) that represents our asteroid.

To expand on this concept, see Figure 21-2. In Figure 21-2a, we see the component of this method that operates on geometry in world space. The camera is viewing a quad that is rotated so that its normal is the vector produced between the camera and the center of the quad. As shown, texture coordinates are assigned to each vertex. Figure 21-2b reveals texture space, traditionally a two-dimensional space, where we add a third dimension, W, and shift the UV coordinates by -0.5. In Figure 21-2c, we simply set the W component of our texture coordinates to 1.

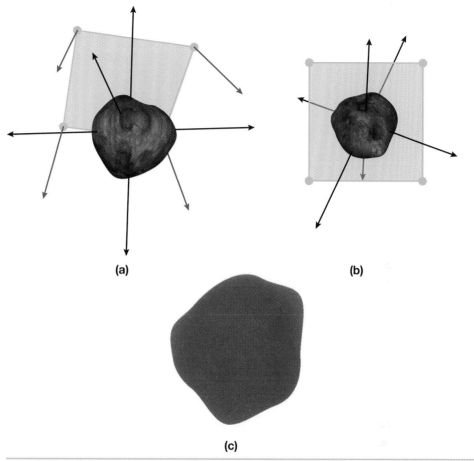

(a)

(b)

(c)

Figure 21-1. Generating a Billboard
(a) The quad's texture coordinates transformed into a 3D plane and rotated around the origin.
(b) The corresponding image it produces. (c) An asteroid.

Keep in mind that the texture map only has UV components, so it is bound to two dimensions and therefore can only be translated along the UV plane, where any value of W will reference the same point. Although bound to the UV plane, the texture map can represent volume data by treating each of the four variables that makes up a pixel as points on the W axis. In Figure 21-3, we can see the projection of the texture volume into three-dimensional space. The texture coordinates of each vertex are rotated around the origin—the same way our original quad was rotated around its origin—to produce the billboard.

Now we introduce the *view ray* into our concept. The view ray is produced by casting a ray from the camera to each vertex. During rasterization, both the texture coordinates and the view rays stored in each vertex are interpolated across the fragmented surface of

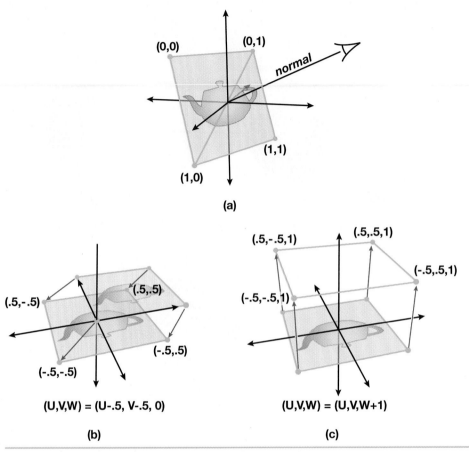

Figure 21-2. The Geometry of True Impostors Projections

our quad. This is conceptually similar to ray casting or ray tracing because we now have a viewing screen of origin points, where each point has a corresponding vector to define a ray. It should also be noted that each individual ray projects as a straight line onto our texture map plane and therefore takes a 2D slice out of the 3D volume to evaluate for collisions. This is shown in detail in Figure 21-3.

At this point two separate options exist, depending on the desired material type. For opaque objects, ray casting is the fastest and most accurate option available. A streamlined approach to this option is presented in Policarpo and Oliveira 2006, using a ray march followed by a binary search, as shown in Figure 21-4. Figure 21-4a shows a linear search in action. The view ray is tested at regular intervals to see whether it has intersected with a volume. Once the first intersection is found, it and the previous point

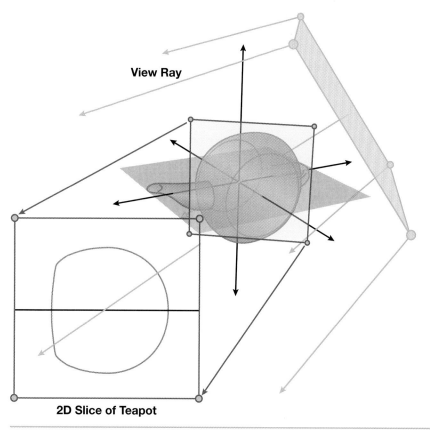

View Ray

2D Slice of Teapot

Figure 21-3. Projecting View Rays to Take a 2D Slice

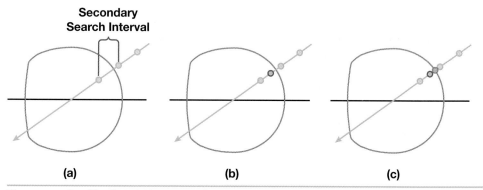

**Secondary
Search Interval**

(a)   (b)   (c)

Figure 21-4. Ray March and Binary Search to Determine Volume Intersection

are used as the beginning and ending points of a binary search space. This space is then repeatedly divided in half until the exact point of intersection into the volume is found.

Because of the nature of GPU design, it is impractical from an efficiency standpoint to exit out of a loop early; therefore, the maximum number of ray marches and texture reads must be performed no matter how early in the search the first collision is found. Rather than ignore this "free" data, we propose a method for adding rendering support for translucent material types through using a localized approximation. Instead of performing a binary search along the viewing ray, we use the points along the W axis to define a linear equation for each height field. We then test these linear equations for intersection with the view ray in a similar fashion as shown in Tatarchuk 2006.

As shown in Figure 21-5, the intersection that falls between the upper and lower bounding points is kept as the final intersection point. Because the material is translucent, the normal is checked for this point. Plus, the view ray is refracted according to a refractive index either held constant for the shader or stored in an extra color channel

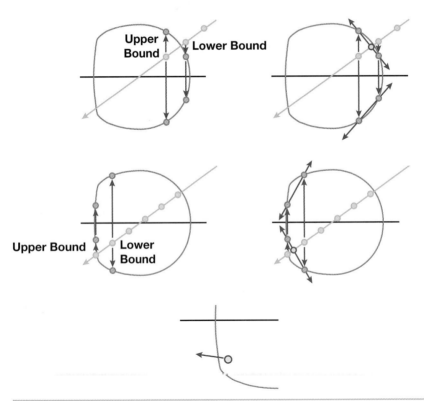

Figure 21-5. Expanding Intersection Tests to Support Translucence

in one of the texture maps. Once the new view direction is discovered, the ray march continues and the process is repeated for any additional surfaces that are penetrated. By summing the distances traveled through any volume, we determine the total distance traveled through our model and use it to compute the translucency for that pixel.

21.3 Results

The true impostors method performs similarly to other per-pixel displacement mapping techniques. However, there are concerns that are unique to this method: for example, performance is fill-rate dependent. Plus, billboards can occlude neighbors, so it is crucial to perform depth sorting on the CPU to avoid overdraw.

On the other hand, because the true impostors method is fill-rate dependent, the level of detail is intrinsic, which is a great asset.

With the true impostors method, you can represent more geometry on screen at once than you could using standard polygonal means. Figure 21-6 shows a model of Jupiter rendered using a quarter-of-a-million asteroids to constitute its ring. This technique was implemented in C++ using DirectX 9. All benchmarks were taken using an NVIDIA GeForce 6800 Go GPU and two GeForce 7800 GPUs run in SLI.

Although the vertex processor is crucial for this method, the resulting operations do not overload the vertex processing unit or noticeably reduce performance. The performance of this technique is primarily determined by the fragment processing unit speed, the number of pixels on the screen, the number of search steps for each pixel, and the choice of rendering technique. When ray casting was done, the performance mirrored that of Policarpo and Oliveira 2006 because of the similar ray casting technique used in both methods. Table 21-1 reports the performance of this technique as "ray casting."

Table 21-1. Performance Comparison of Both Methods
A model of Jupiter consisting of a quarter-of-a-million impostors was used for the ray casting results. A single impostor with true multiple refraction was used for the ray tracing results.

	Video Card	Resolution	Loops	Frame Rate
Ray casting	GeForce Go 6800	1024×768	10/8	10–12
	GeForce 7800 SLI	1024×768	10/8	35–40
Ray tracing	GeForce Go 6800	800×600	20	7–8
	GeForce 7800 SLI	800×600	20	25–30

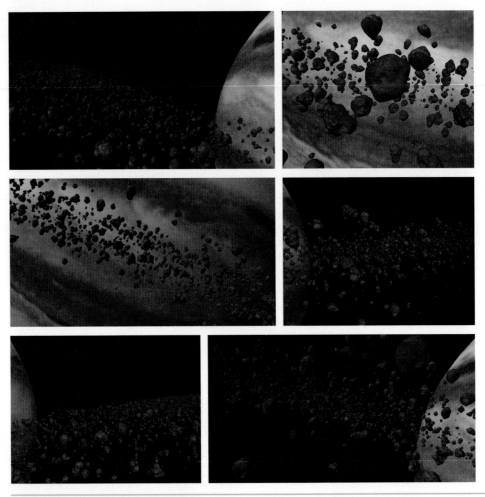

Figure 21-6. A Model of Jupiter Consisting of a Quarter Million Impostors

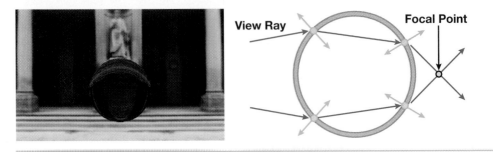

Figure 21-7. A Translucent True Impostor

No comparisons were made between the performances of the two techniques because of the fundamentally different rendering solutions they both offer. The only generalized performance statement we can make about the two techniques is that they both have been shown to achieve real-time frame rates on modern graphics hardware.

21.4 Conclusion

True impostors is a quick, efficient method for rendering large numbers of animated, opaque, reflective, or refractive objects on the GPU. It generates impostors with little rendering error and offers an inherent per-pixel level of detail. By representing volume data as multiple height fields stored in traditional texture maps, the vector processing nature of modern GPUs is exploited and a high frame rate is achieved, but with a low memory requirement.

By abandoning the restrictions that inherently keep per-pixel displacement mapping a subsurface detail technique, we achieved a new method for rendering staggering amounts of faux geometry. We accomplished this not by blurring the line between rasterization and ray tracing, but by using a hybrid approach that takes advantage of the best each has to offer.

21.5 References

Blinn, James F. 1978. "Simulation of Wrinkled Surfaces." In *Proceedings of SIGGRAPH '78*, pp. 286–292.

Cook, Robert L. 1984. "Shade Trees." In *Computer Graphics (Proceedings of SIGGRAPH 84)* 18(3), pp. 223–231.

Hart, John C. 1996. "Sphere Tracing: A Geometric Method for the Antialiased Ray Tracing of Implicit Surfaces." *The Visual Computer* 12(10), pp. 527–545.

Hirche, Johannes, Alexander Ehlert, Stefan Guthe, and Michael Doggett. 2004. "Hardware-Accelerated Per-Pixel Displacement Mapping." In *Proceedings of the 2004 Conference on Graphics Interface*, pp. 153–158.

Kaneko, Tomomichi, Toshiyuki Takahei, Masahiko Inami, Naoki Kawakami, Yasuyuki Yanagida, Taro Maeda, and Susumu Tachi. 2001. "Detailed Shape Representation with Parallax Mapping." In *Proceedings of the ICAT 2001 (The 11th International Conference on Artificial Reality and Telexistence)*, pp. 205–208.

Kautz, Jan, and H. P. Seidel. 2001. "Hardware-Accelerated Displacement Mapping for Image Based Rendering." In *Proceedings of Graphics Interface 2001*, pp. 61–70.

Kolb, Andreas, and Christof Rezk-Salama. 2005. "Efficient Empty Space Skipping for Per-Pixel Displacement Mapping." In *Proceedings of the Vision, Modeling and Visualization Conference 2005*, pp. 359–368.

Patterson, J. W., S. G. Hoggar, and J. R. Logie. 1991. "Inverse Displacement Mapping." *Computer Graphics Forum* 10(2), pp. 129–139.

Policarpo, Fabio, Manuel M. Oliveira, and João L. D. Comba. 2005. "Real-Time Relief Mapping on Arbitrary Polygonal Surfaces." In *Proceedings of the 2005 Symposium on Interactive 3D Graphics and Games*, pp. 155–162.

Policarpo, Fabio, and Manuel M. Oliveira. 2006. "Relief Mapping of Non-Height-Field Surface Details." In *Proceedings of the 2006 Symposium on Interactive 3D Graphics and Games*, pp. 55–62.

Sloan, Peter-Pike, and Michael F. Cohen. 2000. "Interactive Horizon Mapping." In *Proceedings of the Eurographics Workshop on Rendering Techniques 2000*, pp. 281–286.

Tatarchuk, N. 2006. "Dynamic Parallax Occlusion Mapping with Approximate Soft Shadows." In *Proceedings of ACM SIGGRAPH Symposium on Interactive 3D Graphics and Games 2006*, pp. 63–69.

Welsh, Terry. 2004. "Parallax Mapping with Offset Limiting: A Per-Pixel Approximation of Uneven Surfaces." Infiscape Technical Report. Available online at http://www.cs.cmu.edu/afs/cs/academic/class/15462/web.06s/asst/project3/parallax_mapping.pdf.

Chapter 22

Baking Normal Maps on the GPU

Diogo Teixeira
Move Interactive

Ever since normal mapping (Heidrich and Seidel 1999) became a standard technique in modern real-time rendering, it has raised productivity issues for artists as they strive to meet the demands of higher visual standards within their usual time constraints. The use of adequate tools, however, helps reduce production time—as in the case of normal-map baking, where minutes can add up to hours and inflate production costs. The limiting factor, though, has been the computing power required to make baking time a trivial issue.

The modern GPU is an extremely valuable resource for scientific computing and visualization. It has yet, however, to be fully tapped as a viable computing alternative for artistic asset production. Sometimes production costs can be considerably reduced without investing in additional hardware resources. The goal in this chapter is to prove that any midrange Shader Model 3.0 graphics card released in the last two years can be used to generate normal maps faster than most CPU-based tools. This is possible because the type of computation required is highly parallel and independent, therefore ideal for a stream processor.

In this chapter we start by analyzing how the traditional ray-cast-based normal-map projection technique can be successfully implemented on a graphics processor. We also address common problems such as memory limitations and antialiasing.

22.1 The Traditional Implementation

The traditional algorithm for baking a normal map consists of projecting points at the surface of a low-polygon mesh (the *working model*) in the direction of a high-polygon mesh (the *reference model*). For simplification purposes, we will assume that both meshes are triangulated.

In this implementation, the working model needs a texture coordinate set that we will use to rasterize the working model into texture space. The reference model, however, does not need texture coordinates. This is probably one of the best advantages of this implementation, because building decent texture coordinates for really dense polygon meshes can be troublesome.

Additionally, the working model also includes information about the position of the *boundary cage* at each vertex.

22.1.1 Projection

The projection is done first by rasterizing the working model's triangles into texture space, as shown in Figure 22-1, and using the hardware interpolators to interpolate the surface position, tangent basis, and texture coordinate at each pixel from the triangles' corners.

The next step is to trace a ray from the interpolated boundary cage position in the direction of the reference model. This may result in more than one hit along the direction of the ray, and from each hit we will derive a candidate normal. We then select the most appropriate normal, which in our case will be the closest to the boundary cage.

22.1.2 The Boundary Cage

The boundary cage (or *projection cage*) usually consists of a mesh extruded from the working model. The artist may visually modify the cage to provide finer control over the way the rays are cast and to avoid complications in certain regions of the mesh.

The cage surface will serve as a starting point for the rays being cast onto the reference model. The vector from each vertex in the cage to the matching vertex on the working model is also interpolated during rasterization and used as the ray direction.

Usually the cage is built so that it encloses both the reference model and the working model. As you can see from the sample in Figure 22-2, if a ray is cast as previously described, we can assume that the hit closest to the cage can be used to extract the normal for the current pixel.

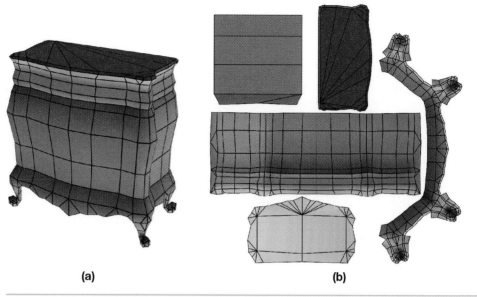

(a)   (b)

Figure 22-1. A Sample Model
(a) Rendered in world space.(b) Rendered in texture space.

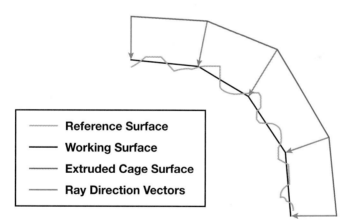

Figure 22-2. A Boundary Cage

22.2 Acceleration Structures

This implementation relies heavily on the ray tracing of high-polygon meshes, which can be extremely computational intensive without the use of proper acceleration structures. This is obviously also an issue when dealing with ray-tracing algorithms on the

GPU (Purcell et al. 2002, Christen 2005). In this case, the choice of an acceleration structure is less trivial because we are dealing with an architecture designed for highly parallel vertex and fragment shading (Lindholm et al. 2001).

We need a structure that maps well to GPU memory using texture resources. We also need to take advantage of the fact that the working and reference meshes are mostly spatially coherent (in other words, they roughly share the same space).

22.2.1 The Uniform Grid

The *uniform grid*, as shown in Figure 22-3, is a spatial subdivision scheme that partitions the mesh into constant-size voxels or cells, as described in Fujimoto and Iwata 1985.

To date, most publications on GPU ray tracing use a uniform grid for spatial subdivision and 3D digital differential analyzer (3D-DDA) for grid traversal. The structure maps well to GPU memory and the traversal algorithm is simple enough to be implemented in a pixel shader.

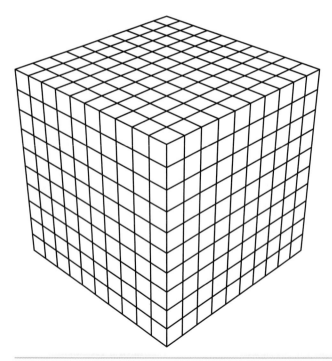

Figure 22-3. A Perspective View of a Uniform Grid

For general-purpose ray-tracing computations, the uniform grid may not be the best option (Havran 2001). In our specific case, however, it is a very good candidate. As you can see in Figure 22-4, where the grid overlays both models, the working model's surface is always very close to that of the reference model. This coherence can be exploited efficiently using a 3D-DDA traversal algorithm.

22.2.2 The 3D Digital Differential Analyzer

First introduced by Amanatides and Woo 1987, the 3D-DDA algorithm allows a fast voxel traversal between two voxels in a uniform grid.

The 3D-DDA algorithm requires only a small number of steps to correctly guide the ray as it travels between neighboring cells. The cost of traversal is linear to the number of voxels visited. In most cases, however, the path is very short, which reduces the average traversal cost. Also note that the voxels, and therefore the geometry, are visited in the correct order, meaning that a valid hit will occlude any hits in the remaining cells. Figure 22-5 illustrates this approach.

This algorithm, along with the uniform grid scheme, is a key component in exploring the spatial coherency between the meshes involved in the projection.

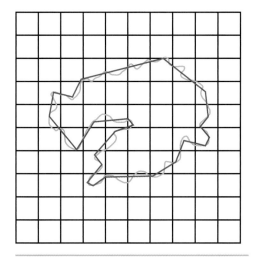

Figure 22-4. Both Models and the Grid Overlaid

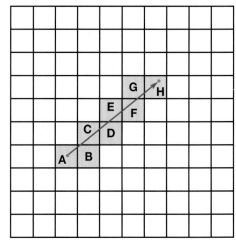

Figure 22-5. A Ray Traversing Grid Cells Using 3D-DDA
The cells are visited in the correct order.

22.3 Feeding the GPU

Mapping the uniform grid and reference geometry data to hardware has been presented almost the same way in most publications about GPU ray tracing. The data structure used in this chapter is mostly based on previous publications on GPU ray tracing, with the exception of using indexed triangle lists to save video memory. See Figure 22-6 for a representation of the data structure.

The uniform grid is stored as a 3D texture with the same size. Each voxel contains a pointer to the triangle list of the respective grid cell. Addressing the uniform grid consists simply of using normalized cubic coordinates when fetching data from the 3D texture. We will be referring to cubic coordinates as values between zero and the size of the grid. Helper functions to convert between grid coordinates are shown in Listing 22-1.

The triangle lists for each cell are stored in a separate 2D texture. Each entry on the triangle list contains a triplet of pointers to the respective triangle vertices in the geometry textures. The list is terminated by a null pointer. If the first pointer is null, it means the cell is empty. Addressing the 2D textures as a linear array requires a simple conversion, as you can see in Listing 22-2.

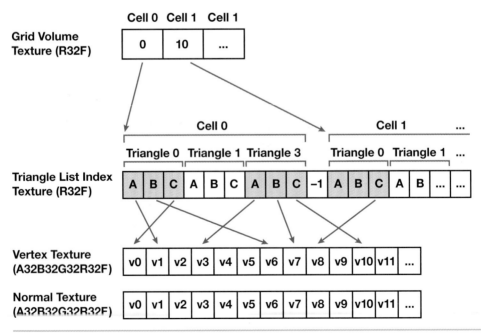

Figure 22-6. A Visual Representation of Data Mapped to the GPU

Listing 22-1. Helper Functions That Convert Between Grid Coordinates

```
float3 CoordCubicToSpatial(float3 cubic)
{
  float3 normCubic = cubic * g_invGridCubicSize;
  return g_gridSpatialMinPoint + (normCubic * g_gridSpatialSize);
}

float3 CoordSpatialToCubicNorm(float3 spatial)
{
  return (spatial - g_gridSpatialMinPoint) * g_invGridSpatialSize;
}
```

Listing 22-2. A Function That Maps a Linear Array Coordinate to a 2D Texture Coordinate

```
float2 Coord1Dto2D(float index, float2 invTexSize)
{
  float offset = index * invTexSize.x;
  float x = frac(offset);
  float y = (offset - x) * invTexSize.y;
  return float2(x, y);
}
```

The reference mesh is stored as a set of 2D textures. We keep the vertex positions and the normals separated because they won't need full 32-bit precision.

22.3.1 Indexing Limitations

For simplification purposes, we use 32-bit float indices, which provide us with an effective indexing range of 24 bits. This is probably enough because we are using only one texture for each data type and dealing with graphics cards that have a maximum texture size of 4,096.

To build a robust implementation and support reference meshes with millions of triangles, we could go beyond 24-bit indexing by using a packed 32-bit (RGBA) integer format. This way we could store the mesh across a maximum of 256 textures, using one of the packed elements to index the texture and the remaining element to index the data within the texture. However, directly addressing multiple textures in DirectX 9.0-class cards might involve emulating texture arrays with a 3D texture. This type of addressing could also be used on pointers stored in the grid texture.

22.3.2 Memory and Architectural Limitations

The base hardware specification used to test the solution presented in this chapter consisted of a Shader Model 3.0 medium-range ATI graphics card with 256 MB. This specific card is limited to power-of-two volumes, so the highest resolution volume we can safely allocate on this card is 256×256×256. However, when working with dense reference meshes with millions of polygons, we need to use a higher-resolution uniform grid to reduce the cost of visiting a cell containing geometry. Some NVIDIA cards already support non-power-of-two volumes.

Table 22-1 provides the memory usage statistics for a sample reference mesh with 700,000 triangles. Note that all textures used are power-of-two.

Although the vertex and normal textures consume only a small portion of the memory footprint required, they can be packed tighter, trading off accuracy for memory. The vertex texture could be reduced by half by using a 16-bit floating-point texture format (for example, A16B16G16R16F), which would be precise enough for some models. The normals could also be stored in a low-precision texture using a 32-bit packed format such as A8R8G8B8, which would also halve the memory costs.

Table 22-1. Memory Usage Statistics for a Sample Reference Mesh

Description	Dimensions	Format	Size
Grid Texture	256×256×256	R32F	64 MB
Triangle List Texture	4096×2048	R32F	32 MB
Vertex Texture	1024×1024	A32B32G32R32F	8 MB
Normal Texture	1024×1024	A16B16G16R16F	4 MB
		Total Size:	**108 MB**

22.4 Implementation

In this chapter we analyze only a basic implementation of the typical projection using the pixel shader. This version requires only a single rendering pass of the working model. It has, however, a few limitations related to static flow control on Shader Model 3.0 hardware, where the maximum number of iterations for each loop must not exceed 256.

Later we discuss possible workarounds for this limitation, including an implementation that involves multipass and tiled rendering. And at the end of this section, we cover antialiasing.

22.4.1 Setup and Preprocessing

The first step in implementing the projection is to load both meshes and generate a uniform grid based on the high-polygon reference model. The grid and geometry data are then mapped to textures in video memory so they can be used by the pixel shader.

The working model, however, should be mapped to hardware vertex buffers and include a tangent basis, which will be used to transform the world-space normal (extracted from the reference model) into tangent space. A cage position and a texture coordinate set for each vertex are also required.

Texture samplers—which include the grid volume, the triangle list, and the geometry textures—must be set before rendering. Sampling filters must be disabled because we are using integer indexing. Clamp addressing should also be set.

Listing 22-3 shows a few common data structures declared in the beginning of the shader. These define a grid cell, an axial-aligned bounding box, a ray, and a triangle. Also listed are a few utility functions to access the grid cells, and a few to access geometry texture data.

Please note that the functions RayAABBIntersect() and RayTriangleIntersect() are not included in the listing, but they can be found in the complete shader provided on this book's accompanying DVD.

Listing 22-3. Common Data Structures

```
struct Cell
{
  float3 cubicNormPos;       // Current cubic position in the grid
  float3 cubicPos;           // Current spatial position in the grid
  float triListStartIndex;   // Pointer to the start of the tri-list
};

struct AABB
{
  float3 center;
  float3 extents;
};
```

Listing 22-3 (*continued*). Common Data Structures

```
struct Ray
{
  float3 origin;
  float3 dir;
};

struct Triangle
{
  float3 p0;
  float3 p1;
  float3 p2;
};

bool GetCellAtPoint(out Cell cell, in float3 spatialPos)
{
  // Convert spatial to normalized cubic coordinates.
  cell.cubicNormPos = CoordSpatialToCubicNorm(spatialPos);

  // Compute unnormalized cubic coordinates.
  cell.cubicPos = cell.cubicNormPos * g_gridCubicSize;

  // Fetch the grid volume texture and find the pointer to the
  // beginning of this cell's triangle list.
  const float4 coord = float4(cell.cubicNormPos, 0);
  cell.triListStartIndex = tex3Dlod(gridSampler, coord).r;

  // Check if we are inside the grid.
  return (cell.cubicNormPos >= 0) && (cell.cubicNormPos <= 1);
}

float3 GetCellMinPoint(in Cell cell)
{
  return g_gridSpatialMinPoint + int3(cell.cubicPos) * g_cellSpatialSize;
}

float3 GetCellMaxPoint(in Cell cell)
{
  return g_gridSpatialMinPoint + (int3(cell.cubicPos) + 1) *
         g_cellSpatialSize;
}
```

Listing 22-3 (*continued*). Common Data Structures

```
float GetTriangleListIndex(float index)
{
    float4 tc = float4(Coord1Dto2D(index, g_invIndexTexSize), 0, 0);
    return tex2Dlod(indexSampler, tc).x;
}

float3 GetVertex(float index)
{
    float4 tc = float4(Coord1Dto2D(index, g_invVertexTexSize), 0, 0);
    return tex2Dlod(vertexSampler, tc).xyz;
}

float3 GetNormal(float index)
{
    float4 tc = float4(Coord1Dto2D(index, g_invNormalTexSize), 0, 0);
    return tex2Dlod(normalSampler, tc).xyz;
}
```

22.4.2   The Single-Pass Implementation

In this version of the algorithm, we render the working model directly to the normal-map render target only once. Following is a description of the steps taken inside the pixel shader.

Step 1

As shown in Listing 22-4, we start by using the interpolated vertex position and cage vector, both sent by the vertex shader, to set up the ray for the current pixel. We may need to adjust the origin of the ray if the cage falls outside the grid, as shown in Figure 22-7. We do this by intersecting the ray with the uniform grid's box to compute the first position along the ray that falls inside the grid. We use the adjusted origin of the ray to find the cell where we will begin the traversal.

Listing 22-4. Setting Up the Ray

```
// Set up the ray using interpolated position and cage vector.
Ray ray;
ray.dir = -Input.cageDir.xyz;
ray.origin = Input.position + Input.cageDir.xyz;
```

Listing 22-4 (*continued*). Setting Up the Ray

```
// Check if we are currently outside the grid.
Cell cell;
if (GetCellAtPoint(cell, ray.origin))
{

    // Compute the grid's min and max points.
    const float3 gridMin = g_gridSpatialMinPoint;
    const float3 gridMax = g_gridSpatialMinPoint + g_gridSpatialSize;

    // Compute intersection between the grid and the ray to find a
    // starting point within the boundaries of the grid.
    float t = 0;
    RayAABBIntersect(ray, gridMin, gridMax, t);

    // Adjust the ray origin to start inside the grid.
    ray.origin += ray.dir * t;

    // Find the first cell to begin traversal.
    GetCellAtPoint(cell, ray.origin);
}
```

Figure 22-7. The Cage May Fall Outside the Grid at Some Points
Adjusted ray origins are shown in red.

Step 2

The next step is to compute the vectors step, tmax, and delta, as described in Amanatides and Woo 1987, where step indicates whether the current position should be incremented or decremented as the ray crosses voxel boundaries. The vector tmax stores the value of t at which the ray crosses the voxel boundary in each axis. Delta indicates how far along the ray we must move (in units of t) along each direction to match the dimensions of the voxel. Listing 22-5 shows how to initialize step, tmax, and delta.

Listing 22-5. Preparing for 3D-DDA

```
// Compute tmax
float3 cellMin = GetCellMinPoint(cell);
float3 cellMax = GetCellMaxPoint(cell);
float3 tmaxNeg = (cellMin - ray.origin) / ray.dir;
float3 tmaxPos = (cellMax - ray.origin) / ray.dir;
float3 tmax = (ray.dir < 0) ? tmaxNeg : tmaxPos;

// Compute traversal steps based on ray direction and cell dimensions.
float3 step = (ray.dir < 0) ? float3(-1,-1,-1) : float3(1,1,1);
float3 tdelta = abs(g_cellSpatialSize / ray.dir);
```

Step 3

We are now ready to begin traversing the grid. As you can see, the traversal code requires only a few instructions, which can be further optimized using vectorized static branching. The main loop is used to traverse the grid to the next cell, while the nested secondary loop is used to test the ray against all triangles in the current cell. See Listings 22-6 and 22-7.

Listing 22-6. The Function Containing the Secondary Loop

This function checks all triangles in the cell and returns the normal closest to the ray origin (in the cage).

```
float3 FindNormalAtCell(in Cell cell, in Ray ray)
{
  // Prepare temporary vars:
  // - last_indices holds the vertex indices for the winning triangle
  // - last_ret holds the barycentric coords for the winning normal
  float3 indices, ret;
  float3 last_indices = 0;
  float3 last_ret = float3(0, 0, FLT_MAX);

  // Get the first vertex index; might be a terminator index (-1).
  float index = cell.triListStartIndex;
  float nextIndex = GetTriangleIndex(index++);
```

Listing 22-6 (*continued*). The Function Containing the Secondary Loop

```
// Loop until we find a terminator index.
while (nextIndex >= 0)
{
  // Get remaining vertex indices.
  indices.x = nextIndex;
  indices.y = GetTriangleListIndex(index++);
  indices.z = GetTriangleListIndex(index++);

  // Get triangle vertex positions.
  tri.p0 = GetVertex(indices.x);
  tri.p1 = GetVertex(indices.y);
  tri.p2 = GetVertex(indices.z);

  if (RayTriangleIntersect(ray, tri, ret) > 0)
  {
    // Use the current hit if closer to the ray origin.
    bool closest = (ret.z < last_ret.z);
    last_indices = closest ? indices : last_indices;
    last_ret = closest ? ret : last_ret;
  }

  // Get next index; might be a terminator index (-1).
  nextIndex = GetTriangleListIndex(index++);
}

// Check if we have a valid normal.
float3 normal = 0;
if (last_indices.x * last_indices.y > 0)
{
  // Get normals from the winning triangle.
  float3 n0 = GetNormal(last_indices.x);
  float3 n1 = GetNormal(last_indices.y);
  float3 n2 = GetNormal(last_indices.z);

  // Interpolate normal using barycentric coordinates.
  float u = last_ret.x;
  float v = last_ret.y;
  float t = 1 - (u + v);
  normal = n0 * t + n1 * u + n2 * v;
}
return normal;
}
```

Listing 22-7. The Main Loop in the Pixel Shader

Traversing the grid searching for a valid normal.

```
float3 normal = 0;
float done = 0;

while (!done)
{
  // Find a valid normal in the current cell.
  normal = FindNormalAtCell(cell, ray);

  // Advance to the next cell along the ray using 3D-DDA.
  float3 nextCubicPos = cell.cubicPos;

  if (tmax.x < tmax.y)
  {
    if (tmax.x < tmax.z)
    {
      nextCubicPos.x += step.x;
      tmax.x += tdelta.x;
    }
    else
    {
      nextCubicPos.z += step.z;
      tmax.z += tdelta.z;
    }
  }
  else
  {
    if (tmax.y < tmax.z)
    {
      nextCubicPos.y += step.y;
      tmax.y += tdelta.y;
    }
    else
    {
      nextCubicPos.z += step.z;
      tmax.z += tdelta.z;
    }
  }

  // Get the cell at the current point.
  bool insideGrid = GetCellAtCubicPos(cell, nextCubicPos);
```

Listing 22-7 (*continued*). The Main Loop in the Pixel Shader

```
   // We are done traversing when:
   // - We found a valid normal. Success.
   // - We fell outside the grid. Failure.
   done = (dot(normal, normal) > 0) || !insideGrid;
}
```

Step 4

To complete the pixel shader, we just need to convert the normal into the working model's tangent space and scale it to the 0..255 range to be stored in a bitmap, as shown in Listing 22-8.

Listing 22-8. Converting the Normal to Tangent Space

```
float3 normalTS;
normalTS.x = dot(normal, Input.binormal);
normalTS.y = dot(normal, Input.tangent);
normalTS.z = dot(normal, Input.normal);
normalTS = normalize(normalTS);
return float4(normalTS * 0.5 + 0.5, 1);
```

Limitation

As we discussed earlier, these loops in ps_3_0 are limited to 256 iterations. A possible workaround is to use two nested loops instead of a single loop, as shown in Listing 22-9, to theoretically achieve a total of 65,536 iterations for each nested pair. The DirectX 9.0 documentation does not address this specific case, though it does mention that the maximum nested loop depth is 4 and the maximum number of instructions executed by a pixel shader must be at least 65,536. This limit can be reached quite easily with a sufficiently complex reference model and a denser grid. You might have to revert to a multipass approach (described in Section 22.4.3) if the host GPU has such instruction limits.

Listing 22-9. An Example of Using Two Nested Loops to Work Around the Limitation

```
// Nested pair for the main loop
while (!done)
{
  while (!done)
  {
    . . .
```

```
// Nested pair inside the FindNormalAtCell function
while (nextIndex >= 0)
{
  while (nextIndex >= 0)
  {
    . . .
  }
}
. . .
}
}
```

22.4.3 The Multipass Implementation

To avoid having four nested loops inside the pixel shader, we could move some work to the CPU and perform the projection in multiple passes. To achieve this, we would need to split the pixel shader.

- The first pass would perform the same computations as described in the single-pass implementation (steps 1 and 2). Then we would store packed information about the cell and the ray, and store the variables step, tmax, and delta on a render texture to be accessed during the following traversal passes.

- The second pass and the next N passes would perform a single traversal step along the grid at each pixel. To avoid processing empty areas, this pass could use queries to track the rendered pixels and the stencil buffer.

- The last pass would convert all the pixels in the normal map to tangent space.

Limitation

The single and most obvious limitation of this implementation is the memory require-ment to store all the temporary variables in texture memory; however, tiled rendering solves this problem.

Tiled Rendering

As described in Purcell et al. 2002, the memory requirement limitation can be over-come by splitting the rendering into pieces or tiles. One tile would be rendered at a time and copied to a texture in system memory, allowing the render textures to be reused. The size of the tiles could be defined according to the available resources.

22.4.4 Antialiasing

The technique presented in this chapter can be extended to support antialiasing in at least two ways:

- Expanding the pixel shader to trace more rays, each one with a different path deviation. The results would be used as samples to compute an alias-free normal.

- Rendering the normal map multiple times and jittering the working model's vertex and cage position each time. The samples would then be weighted and accumulated in the render target. The cost of using this method is linear with the number of passes. If a normal map takes around 1 second to render, a 16-sample antialiased normal map will take about 16 seconds.

22.5 Results

The reference model for our test sample has around 560,000 triangles. The working model, on the other hand, has only 868 triangles. Figures 22-8 and 22-9 show the models.

Preparing the reference model for projection takes only 5.2 seconds: 3.6 seconds to load the file, 1.0 second to generate the uniform grid, and 0.6 seconds to feed the data to the GPU. Please keep in mind that the CPU part of the implementation is not yet fully optimized and is using only a single core.

These timings were recorded on a notebook with a T2400 Core Duo processor, 1 GB DDR2 memory at 667 MHz, and a 5400 rpm hard drive. The graphics processor is an ATI X1600 with 256 MB of dedicated video memory.

The charts in Figure 22-10 compare the GPU implementation described in this chapter with two popular CPU-based implementations, NVIDIA Melody and xNormal. The boundary cage used is similar in all tests and the settings are the simplest possible, with no antialiasing, padding, or dilation.

The resulting normal map shows minor precision issues that can be solved by improving the numerical robustness of the algorithm in the pixel shader. See Figure 22-11.

The normal map was rendered against a black background for illustration purposes only. Creating the map against a midblue background (rather than black) will ameliorate mipmapping issues.

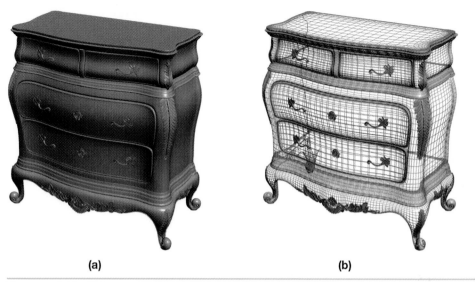

(a)   (b)

Figure 22-8. The Reference Model
(a) Shaded. (b) Wireframe. Ugo Volt sample model courtesy of Move Interactive.

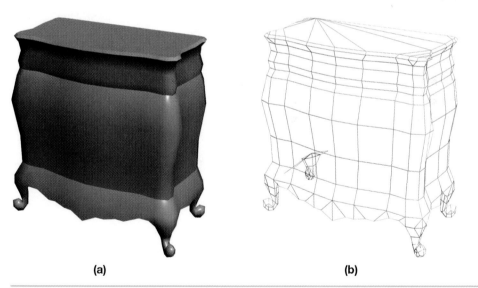

(a)   (b)

Figure 22-9. The Working Model
(a) Shaded. (b) Wireframe.

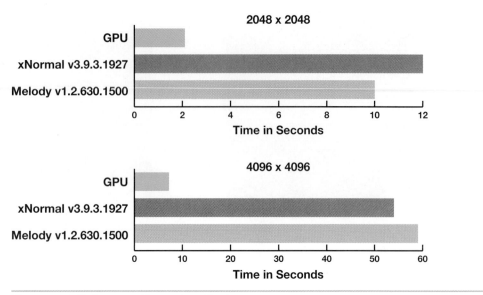

Figure 22-10. Performance Comparison Charts

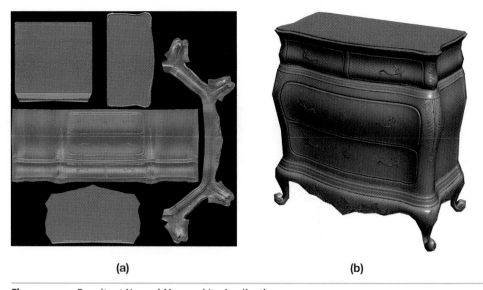

(a)   (b)

Figure 22-11. Resultant Normal Map and Its Application
(a) The normal map generated on the GPU. (b) The working model with normal mapping.

Possible Improvements

The reference mesh could be stored using triangle strips instead of lists: this would save texture memory by storing fewer triangle indices. It would also improve the performance in the pixel processor by reducing texture fetches.

The preprocessing part of this implementation, which runs on the CPU, could be optimized by using Streaming SIMD Extensions and OpenMP.

22.6 Conclusion

With minor modifications, this technique could be used to generate displacement maps, which can also be used for parallax and relief mapping. With a more complex shader, we could also generate local ambient occlusion or cavity maps.

One advantage of this technique is that it's fast enough to permit (and encourage) individually rendering all the mip levels explicitly, improving shading quality in mipmapped areas.

Because of the nature of the computations required for this technique, it scales very well with multithread-based architectures, which the latest generation of GPUs features.

In this chapter we have shown that the graphics processor can generate normal maps very efficiently, which allows fast, high-resolution previews.

22.7 References

Amanatides, John, and Andrew Woo. 1987. "A Fast Voxel Traversal Algorithm for Ray-tracing." In *Proceedings of Eurographics '87*, pp. 3–10. Available online at http://www.cse.yorku.ca/~amana/research/.

Christen, Martin. 2005. "Ray Tracing on GPU." University of Applied Sciences Basel, diploma thesis. Available online at http://www.clockworkcoders.com/oglsl/rt/.

Cohen, Jonathan, Marc Olano, and Dinesh Manocha. 1998. "Appearance-Preserving Simplification." In *Proceedings of the 25th Annual Conference on Computer Graphics and Interactive Techniques*, pp. 115–122. Available online at http://www.cs.unc.edu/~geom/APS/.

Fujimoto, A., and K. Iwata. 1985. "Accelerated Ray Tracing." In *Computer Graphics: Visual Technology and Art (Proceedings of Computer Graphics, Tokyo '85)*, pp. 41–65.

Havran, Vlastimil. 2001. "Heuristic Ray Shooting Algorithms." Czech Technical University, Ph.D. dissertation. Available online at http://www.cgg.cvut.cz/~havran/phdthesis.html.

Heidrich, Wolfgang, and Hans-Peter Seidel. 1999. "Realistic, Hardware-accelerated Shading and Lighting." In *Proceedings of SIGGRAPH 99*, pp. 171–178. Available online at http://www.cs.ubc.ca/~heidrich/Papers/Siggraph.99.pdf.

Krishnamurthy, Venkat, and Marc Levoy. 1996. "Fitting Smooth Surfaces to Dense Polygon Meshes." In *Proceedings of the 23rd Annual Conference on Computer Graphics and Interactive Techniques*, pp. 313–324. Available online at http://graphics.stanford.edu/papers/surfacefitting/.

Lindholm, Erik, Mark Kilgard, and Henry Moreton. 2001. "A User Programmable Vertex Engine." Presentation at SIGGRAPH 2001. Available online at http://developer.nvidia.com/object/SIGGRAPH_2001.html.

Purcell, Timothy J., Ian Buck, William R. Mark, and Pat Hanrahan. 2002. "Ray Tracing on Programmable Graphics Hardware." In *ACM Transactions on Graphics (Proceedings of SIGGRAPH 2002)* 21(3), pp. 703–712. Available online at http://graphics.stanford.edu/papers/rtongfx/.

Chapter 23

High-Speed, Off-Screen Particles

Iain Cantlay
NVIDIA Corporation

Particle effects are ubiquitous in games. Large particle systems are common for smoke, fire, explosions, dust, and fog. However, if these effects fill the screen, overdraw can be almost unbounded and frame rate problems are common, even in technically accomplished triple-A titles.

Our solution renders expensive particles to an off-screen render target whose size is a fraction of the frame-buffer size. This can produce huge savings in overdraw, at the expense of some image processing overhead.

23.1 Motivation

Particle systems often consume large amounts of overdraw and fill rate, leading to performance issues. There are several common scenarios and associated hazards.

Particle systems may model systems with complex animated behavior—for example, a mushroom cloud or an explosion. Such effects can require many polygons, maybe hundreds or thousands.

Particles are often used to model volumetric phenomena, such as clouds of fog or dust. A single, translucent polygon is not a good model for a volumetric effect. Several *layers* of particles are often used to provide visual depth complexity.

Many game engines have highly configurable particle systems. It can be trivial to add lots of particles, leading to a conflict with performance constraints.

Worse, the camera view is often centered on the most interesting, intense effects. For first-person and third-person games, weapon and explosion effects are usually directed *at* the player character. Such effects tend to fill the screen and even a single-particle polygon can easily consume an entire screen's worth of overdraw.

Fortunately, many of the effects modeled with particles are nebulous and soft. Put more technically, images of smoke and fog have only low frequencies, without sharp edges. They can be represented with a small number of samples, without loss of visual quality. So a low-resolution frame buffer can suffice.

Conversely, our technique is less well suited to particles with high image frequencies, such as flying rock debris.

23.2 Off-Screen Rendering

Particles are rendered to an off-screen render target whose size is a fraction of the main frame buffer's size. We do not require a particular ratio of sizes. It can be chosen by the application, depending on the speed-quality trade-off required. Our sample application provides scales of one, two, four, and eight times. Scales are not restricted to powers of two.

23.2.1 Off-Screen Depth Testing

To correctly occlude the particles against other items in the scene requires depth testing and a depth buffer whose size matches our off-screen render target. We acquire this by downsampling the main z-buffer. The basic algorithm is this:

1. Render all solid objects in the scene as normal, with depth-writes.
2. Downsample the resulting depth buffer.
3. Render the particles to the off-screen render target, testing against the small depth buffer.
4. Composite the particle render target back onto the main frame buffer, upsampling.

Figure 23-1 shows the first, third, and fourth stages. (It is not easy to show a meaningful representation of the depth buffer.) The orange arrow shows how the depth test creates a silhouette of the solid objects in the off-screen render target.

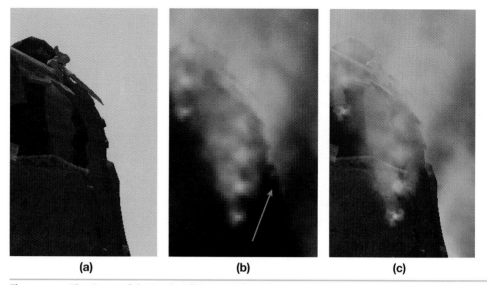

Figure 23-1. The Steps of the Basic Off-Screen Algorithm
(a) Solid objects only. (b) Particles only in the low-resolution, off-screen render target. (c) The composite scene.

23.2.2 Acquiring Depth

Conceptually, the preceding algorithm is straightforward. The devil is in the details.

Acquiring Depth in DirectX 9

Under DirectX 9, it is not possible to directly access the main z-buffer. Depth must be explicitly created using one of three methods.

Multiple render targets (MRTs) can be used: Color information is written to the first target; depth is written to the second. There are a couple of disadvantages to this approach. All targets must have equal bit depths. The back buffer will be 32-bit (or more), but less might suffice for depth. More seriously, MRTs are not compatible with multisample antialiasing (MSAA) in DirectX 9.

Alternatively, depth can be created by writing to a single render target in a separate pass. This has the obvious disadvantage of requiring an extra pass over most of the scene's geometry, or at least that part which intersects the particle effect. On the plus side, depth can be written directly at the required off-screen resolution, without a downsampling operation.

Depth can also be written to the alpha channel of an RGBA target, if alpha is not already in use. A8R8G8B8 might not have sufficient precision. It is quite limited, but it might work, if the application has a small range of depths. A16B16G16R16F is almost ideal. It has the same memory footprint of the MRT option. But again, MSAA is not supported on GeForce 6 and GeForce 7 Series cards.

None of these options is ideal. Depending on the target application, the issues may be too constraining. The lack of MSAA is a major stumbling block for games in which MSAA is an expected feature.

This is all rather frustrating, given that the graphics card *has* the required depth information in its depth buffer. On a console platform, you can simply help yourself to depth data. Perennially, at presentations on DirectX, someone asks, "When will we be able to access the z-buffer?"

DirectX 10 finally provides this feature—sort of.

Acquiring Depth in DirectX 10

DirectX 10 allows direct access to the values in the depth buffer. Specifically, you can bind a *shader resource view* (SRV) for the depth surface. Unsurprisingly, you must unbind it as a render target first. Otherwise, it is fairly straightforward.

There is still a catch. It is not possible to bind an SRV for a multisampled depth buffer. The reason is fairly deep. How should an MSAA resolve operation be applied to depth values? Unlike resolving color values, an average is incorrect; point sampling is also wrong. There is actually *no* correct answer. For our application to particles, point sampling might be acceptable. As will be discussed later, we prefer a highly application-specific function. And that's the point: it needs to be application specific, which is not supported in DirectX 10. However, support is planned for DirectX 10.1 (Boyd 2007).

Fortunately, most of the restrictions that applied to the DirectX 9 options have been lifted in DirectX 10. MRTs work with MSAA, and MRT targets can have different bit depths. There are also no restrictions on the use of MSAA with floating-point surface formats.

Our sample code demonstrates two options in DirectX 10: In the absence of MSAA, it binds the depth buffer as an SRV; when MSAA is used, it switches to the MRT method.

23.3 Downsampling Depth

Regardless of how we acquire depth values, the depth surface needs to be downsampled to the smaller size of the off-screen render target. (Actually, this is not true of rendering depth only in a separate pass. However, this method is equivalent to point-sampling minification.) As discussed previously for the MSAA resolve, there is no universally correct way to downsample depth.

23.3.1 Point Sampling Depth

Simply point sampling depth can produce obvious artifacts. In Figure 23-2, the green triangle is a foreground object, close to the view point, with a low depth value. The white background areas have maximum depth. The 16 pixels represented by the dotted lines are downsampled to 1 off-screen pixel. Point A is where we take the depth sample. It is not representative of most of the 16 input pixels; only pixel B has a similar depth.

If the green triangle is a foreground object with a particle behind, the depth test will occlude the particle for the low-resolution pixel and for all 16 high-resolution pixels. The result can be a halo around foreground objects. The center image of Figure 23-3 shows such a halo. (The parameters of Figure 23-3 are chosen to highly exaggerate the errors. The scaling is extreme: 8×8 frame-buffer pixels are downsampled to 1×1 off-screen pixels. The colors are chosen for maximum contrast: yellow background and red parti-

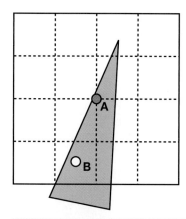

Figure 23-2. Point Sampling from 16 Pixels to 1
Point A is the depth sample that is taken. It is only representative of the depth of pixel B. No other pixel centers intersect the green triangle.

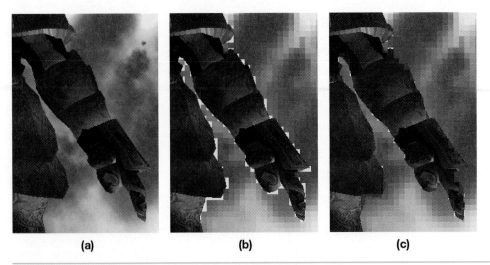

(a)　　　　　(b)　　　　　(c)

Figure 23-3. The Effects of Downsampled Depth Exaggerated
(a) High-resolution particles. (b) One-eighth resolution particles with point-sampled depth.
(c) One-eighth resolution particles with maximum depth.

cles. And linear magnification filtering is disabled to show individual low-resolution pixels.)

In some cases, the halos may be acceptable. For example, on a very fast moving effect such as an explosion, you may not notice the detail. Figure 23-4 shows a more realistic example, with more natural colors, a 2×2 to 1×1 downsample, and linear filtering.

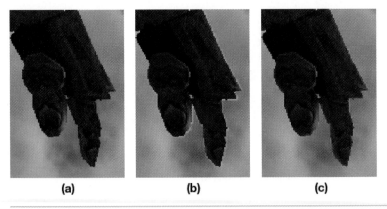

(a)　　　　　(b)　　　　　(c)

Figure 23-4. The Effects of Downsampled Depth on a Natural Scene
(a) High-resolution particles. (b) One-half resolution particles with point-sampled depth.
(c) One-half resolution particles with maximum of depth samples.

23.3.2 Maximum of Depth Samples

The halos can be improved by doing more than a single point sample. The right-hand images in Figures 23-3 and 23-4 show the result of applying a maximum function when downsampling. We sample a spread of four depth values from the full-resolution depth data and take the maximum one. This has the effect of shrinking the object silhouettes in the off-screen image of the particles. The particles encroach into the solid objects. There is absolutely no physical or theoretical basis for this. It just looks better than halos. It's an expedient hack. This is why depth downsampling functions have to be application defined.

Only four samples are taken. This completely eliminates the halos in Figure 23-4 because the four samples fully represent the high-resolution data. In Figure 23-3 however, four depth samples do not completely represent the 8×8 high-resolution pixels that are downsampled. So there are still minor halo artifacts. These are small enough that they are largely hidden by linear blending when the low-resolution particle image is added back to the main frame buffer.

23.4 Depth Testing and Soft Particles

Depth testing is implemented with a comparison in the pixel shader. The downsampled depth buffer is bound as a texture (an SRV in DirectX 10). The depth of the particle being rendered is computed in the vertex shader and passed down to the pixel shader. Listing 23-1 shows how the pixel is discarded when occluded.

Listing 23-1. The Depth Test Implemented in the Pixel Shader

```
float4 particlePS(VS_OUT vIn): COLOR
{
  float myDepth = vIn.depth;
  float sceneDepth = tex2D(depthSampler, vIn.screenUV).x;

  if (myDepth > sceneDepth)
    discard;
  // Compute color, etc.
  . . .
}
```

Given that we have access to the particle and scene depth in the pixel shader, it is trivial to additionally implement *soft particles*. The soft particles effect fades the particle alpha where it approaches an intersection with solid scene objects. Harsh, sharp intersections are thus avoided. The visual benefits are significant. Listing 23-2 shows the required pixel shader code. Note that the zFade value replaces the comparison and discard; zFade is zero where the particle is entirely occluded.

Listing 23-2. Soft Particles Are Better Than a Binary Depth Test

```
float4 particlePS(VS_OUT vIn) : COLOR
{
  float myDepth = vIn.depth;
  float sceneDepth = tex2D(depthSampler, vIn.screenUV).x;
  float zFade = saturate(scale * (myDepth - sceneDepth));
  // Compute (r,g,b,a), etc.

  . . .

  return float4(r,g,b, a * zFade);
}
```

We will not discuss soft particles further here. They are only a nice side effect, not the main focus. The technique is thoroughly explored in NVIDIA's DirectX 10 SDK (Lorach 2007).

23.5 Alpha Blending

Partly transparent particle effects are typically blended into the frame buffer. Alpha-blending render states are set to create the blending equation:

$$\mathbf{p}_1 = \mathbf{d}(1 - \alpha_1) + \mathbf{s}_1\alpha_1,$$

where $\mathbf{p}_1$ is the final color, $\mathbf{d}$ is the destination color already in the frame buffer, and $\mathbf{s}_1$ and α_1 are the incoming source color and alpha that have been output by the pixel shader. If more particles are subsequently blended over $\mathbf{p}_1$, the result becomes

$$\mathbf{p}_2 = (\mathbf{p}_1)(1 - \alpha_2) + \mathbf{s}_2\alpha_2 = (\mathbf{d}(1 - \alpha_1) + \mathbf{s}_1\alpha_1)(1 - \alpha_2) + \mathbf{s}_2\alpha_2,$$

$$\mathbf{p}_3 = (\mathbf{p}_2)(1 - \alpha_3) + \mathbf{s}_3\alpha_3 = ((\mathbf{d}(1 - \alpha_1) + \mathbf{s}_1\alpha_1)(1 - \alpha_2) + \mathbf{s}_2\alpha_2)(1 - \alpha_3) + \mathbf{s}_3\alpha_3,$$

and so on for further blended terms. Rearranging the equation for $\mathbf{p}_3$ to group $\mathbf{d}$ and $\mathbf{s}$ terms gives

$$\mathbf{p}_3 = \mathbf{d}(1 - \alpha_1)(1 - \alpha_2)(1 - \alpha_3) + \mathbf{s}_1\alpha_1(1 - \alpha_2)(1 - \alpha_3) + \mathbf{s}_2\alpha_2(1 - \alpha_3) + \mathbf{s}_3\alpha_3.$$

We have to store everything except the frame-buffer $\mathbf{d}$ term in our off-screen render target. The final compose operation then needs to produce $\mathbf{p}_3$, or more generally $\mathbf{p}_n$.

Take the $\mathbf{d}$ term first—that is simpler. It is multiplied by the inverse of every alpha value blended. So we multiplicatively accumulate these in the alpha channel of the render target.

Next, examine the $\mathbf{s}$ terms contributing to $\mathbf{p}_3$. Note that they take the same form as the conventional alpha-blending equations for $\mathbf{p}_2$, $\mathbf{p}_3$, etc., *if* the target is initialized to zero:

$$0(1 - \alpha_1) + \mathbf{s}_1 \alpha_1$$

$$0(1 - \alpha_1)(1 - \alpha_2) + \mathbf{s}_1 \alpha_1 (1 - \alpha_2) + \mathbf{s}_2 \alpha_2$$

$$0(1 - \alpha_1)(1 - \alpha_2)(1 - \alpha_3) + \mathbf{s}_1 \alpha_1 (1 - \alpha_2)(1 - \alpha_3) + \mathbf{s}_2 \alpha_2 (1 - \alpha_3) + \mathbf{s}_3 \alpha_3$$

So we accumulate the $\mathbf{s}$ terms in the RGB channels with conventional alpha blending. The blending equations are different for the color channels and the alpha channel. The SeparateAlphaBlendEnable flag is required. Listing 23-3 shows the DirectX 9 blending states required. Additionally, we *must* clear the render target to black before rendering any particles.

Listing 23-3. Alpha-Blending States for Rendering Off-Screen Particles

```
AlphaBlendEnable = true;
SrcBlend = SrcAlpha;
DestBlend = InvSrcAlpha;

SeparateAlphaBlendEnable = true;
SrcBlendAlpha  = Zero;
DestBlendAlpha = InvSrcAlpha;
```

It is also common to additively blend particles into the frame buffer for emissive effects such as fire. Handling this case is much simpler than the preceding alpha-blended case. Values are additively accumulated in the off-screen target and then added to the frame buffer.

Using both blended and additive particles is common in games. We have not tried this, but we believe that it would not be possible to combine both in a single off-screen buffer. Supporting both might require a separate off-screen pass for each.

23.6 Mixed-Resolution Rendering

Downsampling depth using the maximum of depth values reduces halos. However, the off-screen particle images can still be unacceptably blocky. Figure 23-5 shows an example. When the image is animated, these artifacts scintillate and pop. This might not be obvious in a fast-moving animation. However, our sample moves slowly and continuously, in an attempt to simulate the worst case.

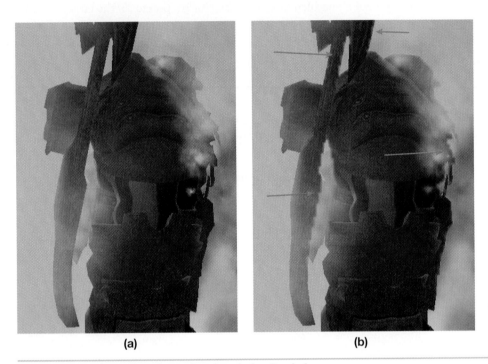

(a)   (b)

Figure 23-5. Blocky Artifacts Due to Low-Resolution Rendering
(a) High-resolution particles. (b) Upsampling from 1×1 to 4×4 can cause blocky pixelation artifacts.

23.6.1 Edge Detection

Examine the off-screen color and alpha channels in the render target, shown in Figure 23-6. (The alpha image is inverted. Recall that we store a product of inverse particle alphas.) The blocky problem areas in the final image of Figure 23-5 are due to sharp edges in the small, off-screen buffer.

The strong edges suggest that the artifacts can be fixed if we first extract the edges. Edge detection is easily achieved with a standard Sobel filter. The result is stored in another off-screen render target.

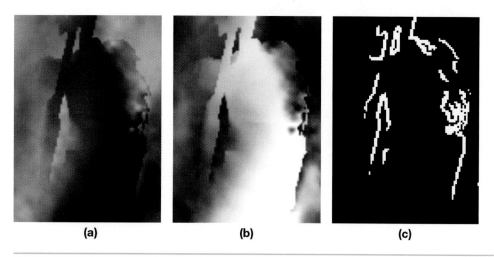

| (a) | (b) | (c) |

Figure 23-6. The Off-Screen Surfaces Corresponding to Figure 23-5
(a) Artifacts in the RGB off-screen surface. (b) Similarly for alpha. (c) The result of an edge detection.

23.6.2 Composing with Stenciling

The edge-detection filter selects a small minority of pixels that are blocky. (In Figures 23-5 and 23-6, large parts of the images are cropped; on the left and right, not shown, there are large entirely black areas with no edges. But these areas of both figures still contain particles.) The pixelated areas can be fixed by rendering the particles at the full frame-buffer resolution only where edges occur.

The stencil buffer is used to efficiently mask areas of the frame buffer. When the low-resolution, off-screen particles are composed back into the main frame buffer, we simultaneously write to the stencil buffer. The stencil value cannot explicitly be set by the pixel shader. However, stencil write can be enabled for all pixels, and then the pixel shader can invoke the `discard` keyword to abort further output. This prevents the stencil write for that pixel, and the pixel shader effectively controls the stencil value, creating a mask. See Listing 23-4.

At this stage, the low-resolution particles have been composed into the frame buffer, and it looks like the left-hand image in Figure 23-7.

The particles are then rendered a second time. The stencil states are set such that pixels are written only in the areas that were not touched by the previous compose pass—the magenta areas in Figure 23-7. The result is shown in Figure 23-8 on the right, in the next section. For comparison, the image on the left in Figure 23-8 shows the particle system rendered entirely at the full resolution.

```
float4 composePS(VS_OUT2 vIn): COLOR
{
  float4 edge = tex2D(edgesSampler, vIn.UV0.xy);

  if (edge.r == 0.0)
  {
    float4 col = tex2D(particlesRTSampler, vIn.UV1.xy);
    return rgba;
  }
  else
  {
    // Where we have an edge, abort to cause no stencil write.
    discard;
  }
}
```

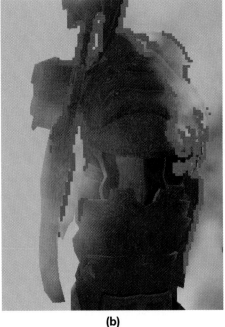

(a)   (b)

Figure 23-7. Intermediate Stages of Mixed-Resolution Rendering
(a) Low-resolution particles composed into non-edge areas of the frame buffer. (b) Magenta denotes pixels that do not have their stencil value set.

23.7 Results

23.7.1 Image Quality

Figure 23-8 compares the full-resolution particles with a mixed-resolution result, where the off-screen surfaces are scaled by 4×4. The mixed-resolution result is very close to the high-resolution version. There are a few minor artifacts. On the character's ax, on the left-hand side of the image, there are a few small spots of the beige color. These are due to linear filtering "leaking" pixelated areas out of the edge-detected mask.

There is a detailed spike on the very rightmost edge of the high-resolution image that has been obscured by particles. Note how the edge filter missed this detail in Figure 23-7. This is a pure subsampling issue: The low-resolution surface fails to adequately represent this detail.

Finally, some high frequencies have inevitably been lost in the low-resolution image. Note the gray particles on the rightmost edge of the images. Also, there is a clump of particles on top of the character's head. Both are slightly fuzzier in the mixed-resolution image.

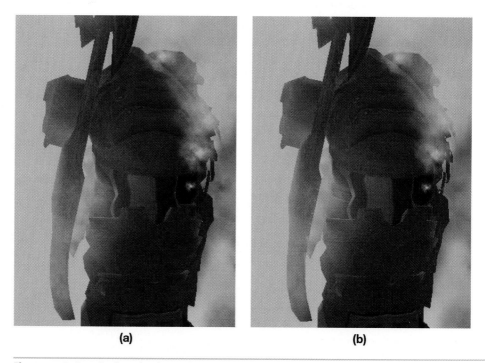

(a) **(b)**

Figure 23-8. Results for Mixed-Resolution Rendering
(a) High-resolution particles. (b) The final, mixed-resolution composite image.

We thought that it would be necessary to alter the high-resolution pass to match the loss of high frequencies in the low-resolution image. A mipmap level-of-detail bias of one or two levels would reduce the high frequencies. As it is, there are no obvious discontinuities where the two resolutions meet in the final image.

23.7.2 Performance

The following tables show some results for the scene shown in all the figures. The particle system is implemented with one draw call and 560 triangles. All results were taken on a GeForce 8800 GTX at a frame-buffer resolution of 1600×1200.

To amplify the differences between the techniques, we measured these results with artificially high numbers of pixels and also for quite large pixel shaders. By contrast, for a game currently in development, we recorded 20 million particle pixels with a 16-instruction shader.

Table 23-1 shows the effect of the various techniques and the effect of the scaling factor between the main frame buffer and the off-screen buffers. High-resolution particles are always the slowest, and simple, low-resolution particles are the fastest. The more complex mixed-resolution technique is somewhat slower, due to the higher image-processing cost and increased number of operations. Note however, much higher complexity of the mixed-resolution technique does not produce a huge increase in cost over the low-resolution technique. This is because the extra image-processing passes—edge detection, stencil writes, and so on—are performed at the low resolution.

Table 23-1 shows the cost for a pixel shader of 73 Shader Model 3.0 instructions. We artificially padded our shaders with an unrolled loop of mad instructions to simulate a complex, in-game shader. Table 23-2 shows the result of varying the number of instructions with a 2×2 scale factor.

Table 23-1. The Effect of Varying Technique and Scale Factor

Technique	FPS	Particle Pixels (Millions)	Image-Processing Pixels (Millions)
High resolution	25	46.9	0
Mixed resolution, 4×4 scale	51	3.5	2.0
Low resolution, max z, 4×4 scale	61	2.9	1.9
Mixed resolution, 2×2 scale	44	12.0	2.8
Low resolution, max z, 2×2 scale	46	11.7	2.3

Table 23-2. The Effect of Varying Particle Pixel Shader Cost

Technique	73-Instruction FPS	41-Instruction FPS	9-Instruction FPS
High resolution	25	36	44
Mixed resolution	44	47.6	50
Low resolution	46	53.5	57

Table 23-3 shows the result of varying the number of particle pixels shaded and blended. This was achieved by moving progressively away from the scene, so that it shrank with perspective. As the particle system becomes arbitrarily small on screen, there comes a point at which the cost of the image-processing operations outweighs the cost of the original, high-resolution particles. The scale factor is 2×2 for Table 23-3, and the number of particle pixel shader instructions is 41.

Table 23-3. The Effect of Varying Particle System Size on Screen

High-Resolution Pixels (Millions)	High-Resolution FPS	Mixed-Resolution FPS
47	36	47
32	43	52
12	55	60
3.5	64.4	63.3

23.8 Conclusion

The results show that our low-resolution, off-screen rendering can produce significant performance gains. It helps to make the cost of particles more scalable, so that frame rate does not plummet in the worst case for overdraw: where a particle system fills the screen. In a real game, this would translate to a more consistent frame rate experience.

Visually, the results can never be entirely free of artifacts, because there is no perfect way to downsample depth values. So there will always be some undersampling issues. However, in a game, particles such as explosions are often fast moving, so small artifacts may be acceptable. Our mixed-resolution technique often fixes many artifacts.

23.9 References

Boyd, Chas. 2007. "The Future of DirectX." Presentation at Game Developers Conference 2007. Available online at http://download.microsoft.com/download/e/5/5/e5594812-cdaa-4e25-9cc0-c02096093ceb/the%20future%20of%20directx.zip

Lorach, Tristan. 2007. "Soft Particles." In the NVIDIA DirectX 10 SDK. Available online at http://developer.download.nvidia.com/SDK/10/direct3d/Source/SoftParticles/doc/SoftParticles_hi.pdf.

Chapter 24

The Importance of Being Linear

Larry Gritz
NVIDIA Corporation

Eugene d'Eon
NVIDIA Corporation

24.1 Introduction

The performance and programmability of modern GPUs allow highly realistic lighting and shading to be achieved in real time. However, a subtle nonlinear property of almost every device that captures or displays digital images necessitates careful processing of textures and frame buffers to ensure that all this lighting and shading is computed and displayed correctly. Proper gamma correction is probably the easiest, most inexpensive, and most widely applicable technique for improving image quality in real-time applications.

24.2 Light, Displays, and Color Spaces

24.2.1 Problems with Digital Image Capture, Creation, and Display

If you are interested in high-quality rendering, you might wonder if the images displayed on your CRT, LCD, film, or paper will result in light patterns that are similar enough to the "real world" situation so that your eye will perceive them as realistic. You may be surprised to learn that there are several steps in the digital image creation pipeline where things can go awry. In particular:

- Does the capture of the light (by a camera, scanner, and so on) result in a digital image whose numerical values accurately represent the relative light levels that were present? If twice as many photons hit the sensor, will its numerical value be twice as high?
- Does a producer of synthetic images, such as a renderer, create digital images whose pixel values are proportional to what light would really do in the situation they are simulating?
- Does the display accurately turn the digital image back into light? If a pixel's numerical value is doubled, will the CRT, LCD, or other similar device display an image that appears twice as bright?

The answer to these questions is, surprisingly, *probably not.* In particular, both the capture (scanning, painting, and digital photography) and the display (CRT, LCD, or other) are likely not linear processes, and this can lead to incorrect and unrealistic images if care is not taken at these two steps of the pipeline.

The nonlinearity is subtle enough that it is often unintentionally or intentionally ignored, particularly in real-time graphics. However, its effects on rendering, particularly in scenes with plenty of dynamic range like Figure 24-1, are quite noticeable, and the simple steps needed to correct it are well worth the effort.

24.2.2 Digression: What Is *Linear*?

In the mathematical sense, a *linear* transformation is one in which the relationship between inputs and outputs is such that:

- The output of the sum of inputs is equal to the sum of the outputs of the individual inputs. That is, $f(x + y) = f(x) + f(y)$.
- The output scales by the same factor as a scale of the input (for a scalar k): $f(k \times x) = k \times f(x)$.

Light transport is linear. The illumination contributions from two light sources in a scene will *sum*. They will not multiply, subtract, or interfere with each other in unobvious ways.[1]

---

1. For certain fairly contrived situations, such as those involving interference or diffraction, the simple linear photon model is not quite adequate. But let's sweep that under the rug for now.

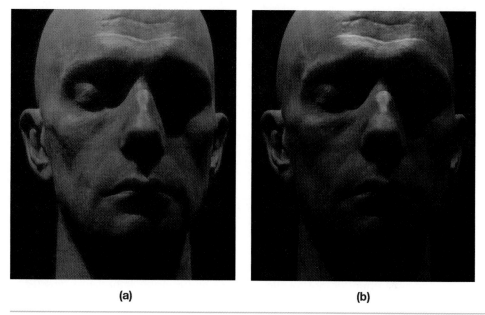

(a)   (b)

Figure 24-1. The Benefit of Proper Gamma Correction
Both images are rendered using the same textures, shaders, and lights. The image on the left, however, linearizes input color textures before shading and corrects the final pixel values for display on nonlinear display devices. The image on the right is generated without regard to linear color spaces, and as a result, a number of artifacts are present.

24.2.3 Monitors Are Nonlinear, Renderers Are Linear

CRTs do not behave linearly in their conversion of voltages into light intensities. And LCDs, although they do not inherently have this property, are usually constructed to mimic the response of CRTs.

A monitor's response is closer to an exponential curve, as shown in Figure 24-2, and the exponent is called *gamma*. A typical gamma of 2.2 means that a pixel at 50 percent intensity emits less than a quarter of the light as a pixel at 100 percent intensity—not half, as you would expect! Gamma is different for every individual display device,[2] but typically it is in the range of 2.0 to 2.4. Adjusting for the effects of this nonlinear characteristic is called *gamma correction*.

Note that regardless of the exponent applied, the values of *black* (zero) and *white* (one) will always be the same. It's the intermediate, midtone values that will be corrected or distorted.

---

2. Gamma can be slightly different for each component: red, green, and blue. And if you really want to be precise, monitor response is never exactly an exponential; it's somewhat more complex than that.

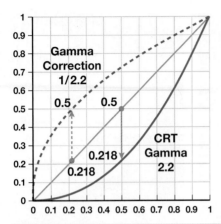

Figure 24-2. Typical Response Curve of a Monitor

Renderers, shaders, and compositors like to operate with linear data. They *sum* the contributions of multiple light sources and multiply light values by reflectances (such as a constant value or a lookup from a texture that represents diffuse reflectivity).

But there are hidden assumptions—such as, that a texture map that indicates how reflectivity varies over the surface also has a linear scale. Or that, upon display, the light intensities seen by the viewer will be indeed proportional to the values the renderer stored in the frame buffer.

The point is, if you have nonlinear inputs, then a renderer, shader, or compositor will "do the math wrong." This is an impediment to achieving realistic results.

Consider a digital painting. If you weren't viewing with "proper gamma correction" while you were creating the painting, the painting will contain "hidden" nonlinearities. The painting may look okay on *your* monitor, but it may appear different on other monitors and may not appear as you expected if it's used in a 3D rendering. The renderer will not actually use the values correctly if it assumes the image is linear. Also, if you take the implicitly linear output of a renderer and display it without gamma correction, the result will look too dark—but not uniformly too dark, so it's not enough to just make it brighter.

If you err on both ends of the imaging pipeline—you paint or capture images in gamma (nonlinear) space, render linear, and then fail to correct when displaying the rendered images—the results *might* look okay at first glance. Why? Because the nonlinear painting/capture and the nonlinear display may cancel each other out to some degree. But there will be subtle artifacts riddled through the rendering and display process, including colors that change if a nonlinear input is brightened or darkened by lighting, and alpha-channel values that are wrong (compositing artifacts), and so your mipmaps were made wrong (texture artifacts). Plus, any attempts at realistic lighting—such as high dynamic range (HDR) and imaged-based lighting—are not really doing what you expect.

Also, your results will tend to look different for everybody who displays them because the paintings and the output have both, in some sense, a built-in reference to a particular monitor—and not necessarily the same monitors will be used for creating the paintings and 3D lighting!

24.3 The Symptoms

If you ignore the problem—paint or light in monitor space and display in monitor space—you may encounter the following symptoms.

24.3.1 Nonlinear Input Textures

The average user doesn't have a calibrated monitor and has never heard of gamma correction; therefore, many visual materials are precorrected for them. For example, by convention, all JPEG files are precorrected for a gamma of 2.2. That's not exact for any monitor, but it's in the ballpark, so the image will probably look acceptable on most monitors. This means that JPEG images (including scans and photos taken with a digital camera) are not linear, so they should not be used as texture maps by shaders that assume linear input.

This precorrected format is convenient for directly displaying images on the average LCD or CRT display. And for storage of 8-bit images, it affords more "color resolution" in the darks, where the eye is more sensitive to small gradations of intensity. However, this format requires that these images be processed before they are used in any kind of rendering or compositing operation.

24.3.2 Mipmaps

When creating a mipmap, the obvious way to downsize at each level is for each lower-mip texel to be one-fourth the sum of the four texels "above" it at the higher resolution. Suppose at the high-resolution level you have an edge: two pixels at 1.0 and two at 0.0. The low-resolution pixel ought to be 0.5, right? Half as bright, because it's half fully bright and half fully dark? And that's surely how you're computing the mipmap. Aha, but that's *linear math.* If you are in a nonlinear color space with a gamma, say of 2.0, then that coarse-level texel with a value of 0.5 will be displayed at only 25 percent of the brightness. So you will see not-so-subtle errors in low-resolution mipmap levels, where the intensities simply aren't the correctly filtered results of the high-resolution levels. The brightness of rendered objects will change along contour edges and with distance from the 3D camera.

Furthermore, there is a subtle problem with texture-filtering nonlinear textures on the GPU (or even CPU renderers), even if you've tried to correct for nonlinearities when creating the mipmaps. The GPU uses the texture lookup filter extents to choose a texture level of detail (LOD), or "mipmap level," and will blend between two adjacent mipmap levels if necessary. We hope by now you've gotten the gist of our argument and understand that if the render-time blend itself is also done assuming linear math—and if the two texture inputs are nonlinear—the results won't quite give the right color intensities. This situation will lead to textures subtly pulsating in intensity during transitions between mipmap levels.

24.3.3 Illumination

Consider the illumination of a simple Lambertian sphere, as shown in Figure 24-3.[3] If the reflected light is proportional to $\mathbf{N} \cdot \mathbf{L}$, then a spot A on the sphere where $\mathbf{N}$ and $\mathbf{L}$ form a 60-degree angle should reflect half the light toward the camera. Thus, it appears half as bright as a spot B on the sphere, where $\mathbf{N}$ points straight to the light source. If these image values were converted to light linearly, when you view the image it should look like a real object with those reflective properties. But if you display the image on a monitor with a gamma of 2.0, A will actually only be 0.5^{gamma}, or one-fourth as bright as B.

In other words, computer-generated (CG) materials and lights will simply not match the appearance of real materials and lights if you render assuming linear properties of light but display on a nonlinear monitor. Overall, the scene will appear dimmer than an accurate simulation. However, merely brightening it by a constant factor is not good enough: The brights will be more correct than the midrange intensities. Shadow terminators and intensity transitions will be sharper—for example, the transition from light to dark will be faster—than in the real world. Corners will look too dark. And the more "advanced" lighting techniques that you use (such as HDR, global illumination of any kind, and subsurface scattering), the more critical it will become to stick to a linear color space to match the linear calculations of your sophisticated lighting.

---

3. You may notice that the image on the right looks like what you typically get when rendering a sphere in Maya, Max, XSI, or other 3D rendering packages. By default, these applications typically output linear pixel data and gamma controls must be explicitly set in the application to correct them for proper display.

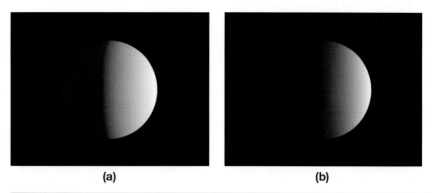

(a)   (b)

Figure 24-3. A Linear Image Gamma-Corrected (*Left*) and Uncorrected (*Right*)
The more physically correct, desired result is on the left. You can see that the light falloff, especially near the shadow terminator, is very different.

24.3.4 Two Wrongs Don't Make a Right

The most common gamma mistake made in rendering is using nonlinear color textures for shading and then not applying gamma correction to the final image. This double error is much less noticeable than making just one of these mistakes, because the corrections required for each are roughly opposites. However, this situation creates many problems that can be easily avoided.

Figure 24-4 shows a comparison between two real-time renderings using a realistic skin shader. (For more information on skin shaders, see Chapter 14 of this book, "Advanced Techniques for Realistic Real-Time Skin Rendering.") The left image converted the diffuse color texture into a linear space because the texture came from several JPEG photographs. Lighting (including subsurface scattering) and shading were performed correctly in a linear space and then the final image was gamma-corrected for display on average nonlinear display devices.

The image on the right made neither of these corrections and exhibits several problems. The skin tone from the color photographs is changed because the lighting was performed in a nonlinear space, and as the light brightened and darkened the color values, the colors were inadvertently changed. (The red levels of the skin tones are higher than the green and blue levels and thus receive a different boost when brightened or darkened by light and shadow.) The white specular light, when added to the diffuse lighting, becomes yellow. The shadowed regions become too dark, and the subsurface scattering (particularly the subtle red diffusion into shadowed regions) is almost totally missing because it is squashed by the gamma curve when it's displayed.

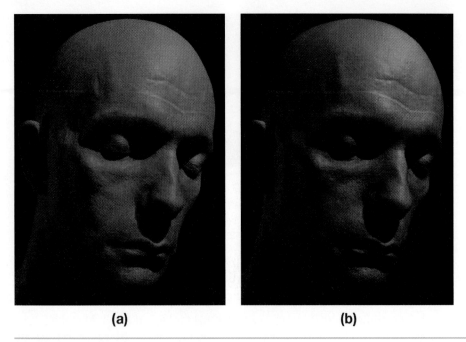

(a)   (b)

Figure 24-4. Rendering with Proper Gamma Correction (*Left*) and Rendering Ignoring Gamma (*Right*)
When rendering the image on the right, the diffuse color was not converted into a linear space before it was used in shading, and the final shaded pixels are not gamma-corrected for display. The two effects do not, however, cancel out. The tone of the skin is changed, the bright specular becomes yellow, the shadows become dark too quickly, and the subsurface scattering is almost lost.

Adjusting lighting becomes problematic in a nonlinear space. If we take the same scenes in Figure 24-4 and render them now with the light intensities increased, the problems in the nonlinear version become worse, as you can see in Figure 24-5. As a rule, if color tones change as the same object is brightened or darkened, then most likely nonlinear lighting is taking place and gamma correction is needed.

A common problem encountered when subsurface scattering is used for skin rendering (when gamma correction is ignored) is the appearance of a blue-green glow around the shadow edges and an overly waxy-looking skin, as shown in Figure 24-6. These problems arise when the scattering parameters are adjusted to give shadow edges the desired amount of red bleeding (as seen in Figure 24-5). This effect is hard to achieve in a nonlinear color space and requires a heavily weighted broad blur of irradiance in the red channel. The result causes far too much diffusion in the bright regions of the face (giving a waxy look) and causes the red to darken too much as it approaches a shadow edge (leaving a blue-green glow).

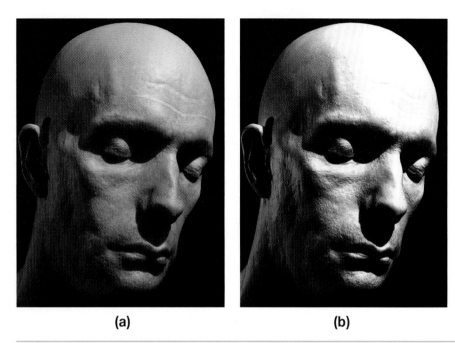

(a)   (b)

Figure 24-5. Rendering with Proper Gamma Correction (*Left*) and Rendering Incorrect Gamma (*Right*)
Comparing the same rendering setup in Figure 24-4 and boosting the light intensities to relight our character, which shows even more dramatic problems in the gamma-ignorant version.

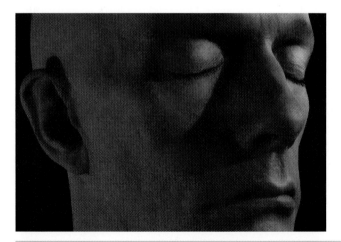

Figure 24-6. Tweaking Subsurface Scattering When Rendering Without Gamma Correction Is Problematic
Plenty of red bleeding into dark shadow edges requires diffusion profiles that look overly waxy and leave a strange blue-green tinge around shadow edges.

24.4 The Cure

Gamma correction is the practice of applying the *inverse* of the monitor transformation to the image pixels before they're displayed. That is, if we raise pixel values to the power 1/*gamma* before display, then the display implicitly raising to the power *gamma* will exactly cancel it out, resulting, overall, in a linear response (see Figure 24-2).

The usual implementation is to have your windowing systems apply color-correction *lookup tables* (LUTs) that incorporate gamma correction. This adjustment allows all rendering, compositing, or other image manipulation to use linear math and for any linear-scanned images, paintings, or rendered images to be displayed correctly.

Animation and visual effects studios, as well as commercial publishers, are very careful with this process. Often it's the exclusive job of a staff person to understand color management for their monitors, compositing pipeline, film and video scanning, and final outputs. In fact, for high-end applications, simple gamma correction is not enough. Often compositors use a much more sophisticated 3D color LUT derived from careful measurements of the individual displays or film stocks' color-response curves.[4] In contrast to visual effects and animation for film, game developers often get this process wrong, which leads to the artifacts discussed in this chapter. This is one reason why most (but not all) CG for film looks much better than games—a reason that has nothing to do with the polygon counts, shading, or artistic skills of game creators. (It's also sometimes a reason why otherwise well-made film CG looks poor—because the color palettes and gammas have been mismatched by a careless compositor.)

Joe GamePlayer doesn't have a calibrated monitor. We don't know the right LUTs to apply for his display, and in any case, he doesn't want to apply gamma-correcting LUTs to his entire display. Why? Because then the ordinary JPEG files viewed with Web browsers and the like will look washed out and he won't understand why. (Film studios don't care if random images on the Internet look wrong on an artist's workstation, as long as their actual work product—the film itself—looks perfect in the theatre, where they have complete control.) But simple gamma correction for the "average" monitor can get us most of the way there. The remainder of this chapter will present the easiest solutions to improve and avoid these artifacts in games you are developing.

---

4. For an excellent reference on this process, see the *GPU Gems 2* chapter "Using Lookup Tables to Accelerate Color Transformations," written by Jeremy Selan of Sony Pictures Imageworks.

24.4.1 Input Images (Scans, Paintings, and Digital Photos)

Most images you capture with scanning or digital photography are likely already gamma-corrected (especially if they are JPEGs by the time they get to you), and therefore are in a nonlinear color space. (Digital camera JPEGs are usually sharpened by the camera as well for capturing textures; try to use a RAW file format to avoid being surprised.) If you painted textures without using a gamma LUT, those paintings will also be in monitor color space. If an image looks right on your monitor in a Web browser, chances are it has been gamma-corrected and is nonlinear.

Any input textures that are already gamma-corrected need to be brought back to a linear color space before they can be used for shading or compositing. You want to make this adjustment for texture values that are used for (linear) lighting calculations. Color values (such as light intensities and diffuse reflectance colors) should always be uncorrected to a linear space before they're used in shading. Alpha channels, normal maps, displacement values (and so on) are almost certainly already linear and should not be corrected further, nor should any textures that you were careful to paint or capture in a linear fashion.

All modern GPUs support sRGB texture formats. These formats allow binding gamma-corrected pixel data directly as a texture with proper gamma applied by the hardware before the results of texture fetches are used for shading. On NVIDIA GeForce 8-class (and future) hardware, all samples used in a texture filtering operation are linearized before filtering to ensure the proper filtering is performed (older GPUs apply the gamma post-filtering). The correction applied is an IEC standard (IEC 61966-2-1) that corresponds to a gamma of roughly 2.2 and is a safe choice for nonlinear color data where the exact gamma curve is not known. Alpha values, if present, are not corrected.

Appropriate sRGB formats are defined for all 8-bit texture formats (RGB, RGBA, luminance, luminance alpha, and DXT compressed), both in OpenGL and in DirectX. Passing GL_SRGB_EXT instead of GL_RGB to glTexImage2D, for example, ensures that any shader accesses to the specified texture return linear pixel values.

The automatic sRGB corrections are free and are preferred to performing the corrections manually in a shader after each texture access, as shown in Listing 24-1, because each pow instruction is scalar and expanded to two instructions. Also, manual correction happens after filtering, which is incorrectly performed in a nonlinear space. The sRGB formats may also be preferred to preconverting textures to linear versions before they are loaded. Storing linear pixels back into an 8-bit image is effectively a loss of precision in low light levels and can cause banding when the pixels are converted back to monitor space or used in further shading.

Listing 24-1. Manually Converting Color Values to a Linear Space

Texture lookups can apply inverse gamma correction so that the rest of your shader is working with linear values. However, using an sRGB texture is faster, allows proper linear texture filtering (GeForce 8 and later), and requires no extra shader code.

```
float3 diffuseCol = pow( f3tex2D( diffTex, texCoord ), 2.2 );

// Or (cheaper, but assuming gamma of 2.0 rather than 2.2)
float3 diffuseCol = f3tex2D( diffTex, texCoord );
diffuseCol = diffuseCol * diffuseCol;
```

Managing shaders that need to mix linear and nonlinear inputs can be an ugly logistical chore for the engine programmers and artists who provide textures. The simplest solution, in many cases, is to simply require all textures to be precorrected to linear space before they're delivered for use in rendering.

24.4.2 Output Images (Final Renders)

The *last* step before display is to gamma-correct the final pixel values so that when they're displayed on a monitor with nonlinear response, the image looks "correct." Specifying an sRGB frame buffer leaves the correction to the GPU, and no changes to shaders are required. Any value returned in the shader is gamma-corrected before storage in the frame buffer (or render-to-texture buffer). Furthermore, on GeForce 8-class and later hardware, if blending is enabled, the previously stored value is converted back to linear before blending and the result of the blend is gamma-corrected. Alpha values are not gamma-corrected when sRGB buffers are enabled. If sRGB buffers are not available, you can use the more costly solution of custom shader code, as shown in Listing 24-2; however, any blending, if enabled, will be computed incorrectly.

Listing 24-2. Last-Stage-Output Gamma Correction

If sRGB frame buffers are not available (or if a user-defined gamma value is exposed), the following code will perform gamma correction.

```
float3 finalCol = do_all_lighting_and_shading();
float pixelAlpha = compute_pixel_alpha();

return float4(pow(finalCol, 1.0 / 2.2), pixelAlpha);

// Or (cheaper, but assuming gamma of 2.0 rather than 2.2)
return float4( sqrt( finalCol ), pixelAlpha );
```

24.4.3 Intermediate Color Buffers

A few subtle points should be kept in mind. If you are doing any kind of post-processing pass on your images, you should be doing the gamma correction as the *last step* of the last post-processing pass. Don't render, correct, and then do further math on the result as if it were a linear image.

Also, if you are rendering to create a texture, you need to either (a) gamma-correct, and then treat the texture as a nonlinear input when performing any further processing of it, or (b) not gamma-correct, and treat the texture as linear input for any further processing. Intermediate color buffers may lose precision in the darks if stored as 8-bit linear images, compared to the precision they would have as gamma-corrected images. Thus, it may be beneficial to use 16-bit floating-point or sRGB frame-buffer and sRGB texture formats for rendering and accessing intermediate color buffers.

24.5 Conclusion

OpenGL, DirectX, and any shaders you write are probably performing math as if all texture inputs, light/material interactions, and outputs are *linear* (that is, light intensities sum; diffuse reflectivities multiply). But it is very likely that your texture inputs may be nonlinear, and it's almost certain that your user's uncalibrated and uncorrected monitor applies a nonlinear color-space transformation. This scenario leads to all sorts of artifacts and inaccuracies, some subtle (such as mipmap filtering errors) and some grossly wrong (such as very incorrect light falloff).

We strongly suggest that developers take the following simple steps:

1. Assume that most game players are using uncalibrated, uncorrected monitors that can roughly be characterized by an exponential response with gamma = 2.2. (For an even higher-quality end-user experience: Have your game setup display a gamma calibration chart and let the user choose a good gamma value.)

2. When performing lookups from nonlinear textures (those that look "right" on uncorrected monitors) that represent light or color values, raise the results to the power *gamma* to yield a linear value that can be used by your shader. Do *not* make this adjustment for values already in a linear color space, such as certain high-dynamic-range light maps or images containing normals, bump heights, or other noncolor data. Use sRGB texture formats, if possible, for increased performance and correct texture filtering on GeForce 8 GPUs (and later).

3. Apply a gamma correction (that is, raise to power 1/*gamma*) to the final pixel values as *the very last step* before displaying them. Use sRGB frame-buffer extensions for efficient automatic gamma correction with proper blending.

Carefully following these steps is crucial to improving the look of your game and especially to increasing the accuracy of any lighting or material calculations you are performing in your shaders.

24.6 Further Reading

In this chapter, we've tried to keep the descriptions and advice simple, with the intent of making a fairly nontechnical argument for why you should use linear color spaces. In the process, we've oversimplified. For those of you who crave the gory details, an excellent treatment of the gamma problem can be found on Charles Poynton's Web page: http://www.poynton.com/GammaFAQ.html.

The Wikipedia entry on gamma correction is surprisingly good:

- http://en.wikipedia.org/wiki/Gamma_correction.

For details regarding sRGB hardware formats in OpenGL and DirectX, see these resources:

- http://www.nvidia.com/dev_content/nvopenglspecs/GL_EXT_texture_sRGB.txt
- http://www.opengl.org/registry/specs/EXT/framebuffer_sRGB.txt
- http://msdn2.microsoft.com/en-us/library/bb173460.aspx

Thanks to Gary King and Mark Kilgard for their expertise on sRGB and their helpful comments regarding this chapter. Special thanks to actor Doug Jones for kindly allowing us to use his likeness. And finally, Figure 24-2 was highly inspired by a very similar version we found on Wikipedia.

Chapter 25

Rendering Vector Art on the GPU

Charles Loop
Microsoft Research

Jim Blinn
Microsoft Research

25.1 Introduction

Vector representations are a resolution-independent means of specifying shape. They have the advantage that at any scale, content can be displayed without tessellation or sampling artifacts. This is in stark contrast to a raster representation consisting of an array of color values. Raster images quickly show artifacts under scale or perspective mappings. Our goal in this chapter is to present a method for accelerating the rendering of vector representations on the GPU.

Modern graphics processing units excel at rendering triangles and triangular approximations to smooth objects. It is somewhat surprising to realize that the same architecture is ideally suited to rendering smooth vector-based objects as well. A vector object contains layers of closed paths and curves. These paths and curves are generally quadratic and cubic Bézier spline curves, emitted by a drawing program. We present algorithms for rendering these spline curves directly in terms of their mathematical descriptions, so that they are resolution independent and have a minimal geometric representation.

The main ingredient of our algorithm is the notion of *implicitization*: the transformation from a parametric $[x(t)\ y(t)]$ to implicit $f(x, y) = 0$ plane curve. We render the convex hull of the Bézier control points as polygons, and a pixel shader program determines pixel inclusion by evaluating the curve's implicit form. This process becomes highly efficient by leveraging GPU interpolation functionality and choosing just the right implicit form. In addition to resolving in/out queries at pixels, we demonstrate a mechanism for performing antialiasing on these curves using hardware gradients. Much of this work originally appeared in Loop and Blinn 2005.

25.2 Quadratic Splines

The best way to understand our algorithm is to show how it works with a simple example. Consider the letter "e" shown in Figure 25-1. Figure 25-1a shows the TrueType data used to describe this font glyph. TrueType uses a combination of quadratic B-splines and line segments to specify an oriented vector outline. The region on the right-hand side of the curve is considered inside by convention. The hollow dots are B-spline control points that define curves; the solid dots are points on the curve that can define discontinuities such as sharp corners. As a preprocess, we convert the B-spline representation to Bézier form by inserting new points at the midpoint of adjacent B-spline control points. Each B-spline control point will correspond to a quadratic Bézier curve. Next, we triangulate the interior of the closed path and form a triangle for each quadratic Bézier curve. After triangulation, we will have interior triangles (shown in green) and boundary triangles that contain curves (shown in red and blue), as you can see in Figure 25-1b.

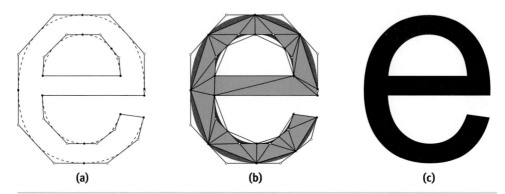

(a)   (b)   (c)

Figure 25-1. Rendering Quadratic Splines
(a) Oriented multicontour spline curves are input. (b) Each quadratic Bézier curve segment forms a triangle, and the remaining interior region is triangulated. (c) Interior triangles are filled and curve segments are rendered with a special pixel shader program.

The interior triangles are filled and rendered normally. Triangles that contain curves are either convex or concave, depending on which side of the curve is inside the closed region. See the red and blue curves in Figure 25-1b.

We use a shader program to determine if pixels are on the inside or outside of a closed region. Before getting to this shader, we must assign $[u\ v]$ coordinates to the vertices of the triangles that contain curves. An example is shown in Figure 25-2. When these triangles are rendered under an arbitrary 3D projective transform, the GPU will perform perspective-correct interpolation of these coordinates and provide the resulting $[u\ v]$ values to a pixel shader program. Instead of looking up a color value as in texture mapping, we use the $[u\ v]$ coordinate to evaluate a procedural texture. The pixel shader computes the expression

$$u^2 - v,$$

using the sign of the result to determine pixel inclusion. For convex curves, a positive result means the pixel is outside the curve; otherwise it is inside. For concave curves, this test is reversed.

The size of the resulting representation is proportional to the size of the boundary curve description. The resulting image is free of any artifacts caused by tessellation or undersampling because all the pixel centers that lie under the curved region are colored and no more.

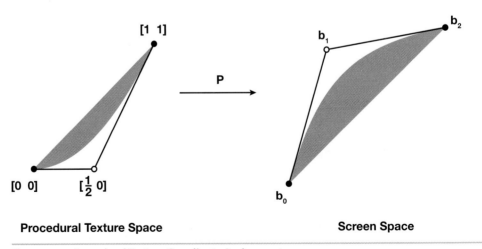

Procedural Texture Space   Screen Space

Figure 25-2. Procedural Texture Coordinate Assignment
*The screen space image of any quadratic curve segment is a projection **P** of a single proto-curve in procedural texture space.*

The intuition behind why this algorithm works is as follows. The procedural texture coordinates [0 0], [½ 0], and [1 1] (as shown in Figure 25-2) are themselves Bézier control points of the curve

$$u(t) = t, \qquad v(t) = t^2.$$

This is clearly a parameterization for the algebraic (implicit) curve $u^2 - v = 0$. Suppose **P** is the composite transform from u, v space to curve design (glyph) space to viewing and perspective space to screen space. Ultimately this will be a projective mapping from 2D onto 2D. Any quadratic curve segment projected to screen space will have such a **P**. When the GPU interpolates the texture coordinates, it is in effect computing the value of P^{-1} for each pixel. Therefore, we can resolve the inside/outside test in u, v space where the implicit equation is simple, needing only one multiply and one add.

As an alternative, we could find the algebraic equation of each curve segment in screen space. However, this would require dozens of arithmetic operations to compute the general second-order algebraic curve coefficients and require many operations to evaluate in the corresponding pixel shader. Furthermore, the coefficients of this curve will change as the viewing transform changes, requiring recomputation. Our approach requires no such per-frame processing, other than the interpolation of [u v] procedural texture coordinates done by the GPU.

Quadratic curves turn out to be a very simple special case. Assignment of the procedural texture coordinates is the same for all (integral) quadratic curves, and the shader equation is simple and compact. However, drawing packages that produce vector artwork often use more-flexible and smooth cubic splines. Next, we extend our rendering algorithm to handle cubic curves. The good news is that the runtime shader equation is also simple and compact. The bad news is that the preprocessing—assignment of procedural texture coordinates—is nontrivial.

25.3 Cubic Splines

Our algorithm for rendering cubic spline curves is similar in spirit to the one for rendering quadratic curves. An oriented closed path is defined by cubic Bézier curve segments, each consisting of four control points. See Figure 25-3a. We assume the right-hand side of the curve to be considered inside. The convex hull of these control points forms either a quadrilateral consisting of two triangles, or a single triangle. As before, we triangulate the interior of the path, as shown in Figure 25-3b. The interior triangles are filled and rendered normally. The interesting part is how to generalize the procedural texture technique we used for quadratics.

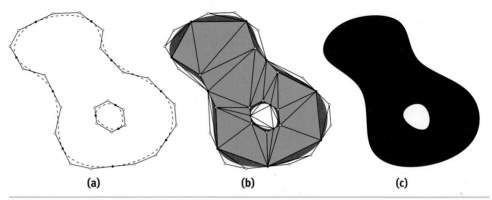

| (a) | (b) | (c) |

Figure 25-3. Rendering Cubic Splines
(a) Oriented multicontour cubic spline input. (b) Each Bézier convex hull is locally triangulated; the interior region is globally triangulated. (c) Interior triangles are filled and curve segments are rendered with a special pixel shader program.

Unlike parametric quadratic curves, parametric cubic plane curves are not all projectively equivalent. That is, there is no single proto-curve that all others can be projected from. It is well known that all rational parametric plane curves have a corresponding algebraic curve of the same degree. It turns out that the algebraic form of a parametric cubic belongs to one of three projective types (Blinn 2003), as shown in Figure 25-4. Any arbitrary cubic curve can be classified as a serpentine, cusp, or loop. Furthermore, a projective mapping exists that will transform an arbitrary parametric cubic curve onto one of these three curves. If we map the Bézier control points of the curve under this transform, we will get a Bézier parameterization of some segment of one of these three curves.

A very old result (Salmon 1852) on cubic curves states that all three types of cubic curves will have an algebraic representation that can be written

$$k^3 - lmn = 0,$$

where k, l, m, and n are linear functionals corresponding to lines $\mathbf{k}$, $\mathbf{l}$, $\mathbf{m}$, and $\mathbf{n}$ as in Figure 25-4. (The reason line $\mathbf{n}$ does not appear in Figure 25-4 will be made clear shortly.) More specifically, $k = au + bv + cw$, where $[u\ v\ w]$ are the homogeneous coordinates of a point in the plane, and $\mathbf{k} = [a\ b\ c]^T$ are the coordinates of a line; and similarly for l, m, and n. The relationship of the lines $\mathbf{k}$, $\mathbf{l}$, $\mathbf{m}$, and $\mathbf{n}$ to the curve $\mathbf{C}(s, t)$ has important geometric significance. A serpentine curve has inflection points at $\mathbf{k} \cap \mathbf{l}$, $\mathbf{k} \cap \mathbf{m}$, and $\mathbf{k} \cap \mathbf{n}$ and is tangent to lines $\mathbf{l}$, $\mathbf{m}$, and $\mathbf{n}$, respectively. A loop curve has a double point at $\mathbf{k} \cap \mathbf{l}$ and $\mathbf{k} \cap \mathbf{m}$ and is tangent to lines $\mathbf{l}$ and $\mathbf{m}$ at this point; $\mathbf{k} \cap \mathbf{n}$ corresponds to an inflection point. A cusp curve has a cusp at the point where coincident lines $\mathbf{l}$ and $\mathbf{m}$ intersect $\mathbf{k}$, and it is tangent to line $\mathbf{l} = \mathbf{m}$ at this point; and $\mathbf{k} \cap \mathbf{n}$ corresponds to an inflection point.

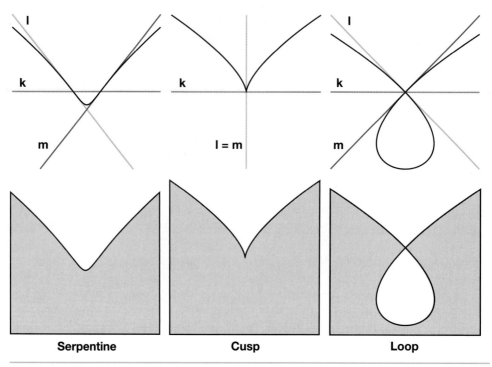

Figure 25-4. All Parametric Cubic Plane Curves Can Be Classified as the Parameterization of Some Segment of One of These Three Curve Types
*Top: Parametric curves together with lines **k**, **l**, and **m**. Bottom: Positive regions (in gray) determined by the corresponding implicit equation.*

The procedural texture coordinates are the values of the k, l, m, and n functionals at each cubic Bézier control point. When the (triangulated) Bézier convex hull is rendered, these coordinates are interpolated by the GPU and a pixel shader program is called that evaluates the shader equation $k^3 - lmn$. This will determine if a pixel is inside or outside the curve based on the sign of the result.

We work in homogeneous coordinates where points in the plane are represented by 3-tuples $[x \ y \ w]$; the 2D Cartesian coordinates are x/w and y/w. We also work with a homogeneous curve parameterization where the parameter value is represented by the pair $[s \ t]$; the 1D scalar parameter is s/t. We use homogeneous representations because the projective geometric notion of points at infinity is captured by $w = 0$; similarly, an infinite parameter value occurs when $t = 0$.

In principle, we can render any planar cubic Bézier curve defined this way; however, we make some simplifying assumptions to ease the derivation and implementation of our algorithm. The first is that the Bézier control points are affine, so $w = 1$. This means that curves must be integral as opposed to rational. This is not a severe limitation, because most drawing tools support only integral curves. We will still be able to render the correct projected image of an integral cubic plane curve, but in the plane where the curve is defined it cannot be rational. For integral curves the line $\mathbf{n} = [0 \ 0 \ 1]$; that is, the line at infinity. All three cubic proto-curves in Figure 25-4 have integral representations, so line $\mathbf{n}$ does not appear. The linear functional corresponding to the line at infinity is $n = 1$, so the shader equation simplifies to

$$k^3 - lm.$$

Although this saves only one multiply in the shader, it removes an entire texture coordinate from a vertex, leading to potentially more-efficient code. The primary reason for assuming integral curves, however, is to simplify curve classification. Our second assumption is that the control point coordinates are exact floating-point numbers. This assumption is not strictly necessary, but we can avoid floating-point round-off errors that might crop up in tests for equality. This corresponds to an interactive drawing scenario where control points lie on a regular grid.

A cubic Bézier curve in homogeneous parametric form is written

$$\mathbf{C}(s, t) = \begin{bmatrix} (s - t)^3 & 3(s - t)^2 s & 3(s - t)s^2 & s^3 \end{bmatrix} \cdot \begin{bmatrix} \mathbf{b}_0 \\ \mathbf{b}_1 \\ \mathbf{b}_2 \\ \mathbf{b}_3 \end{bmatrix},$$

where the $\mathbf{b}_i$ are cubic Bézier control points.

The first step is to compute the coefficients of the function $I(s, t)$ whose roots correspond to inflection points of $\mathbf{C}(s, t)$. An inflection point is where the curve changes its bending direction, defined mathematically as parameter values where the first and second derivatives of $\mathbf{C}(s, t)$ are linearly dependent. The derivation of the function I is not needed for our current purposes; see Blinn 2003 for a thorough discussion. For integral cubic curves,

$$I(s, t) = t\left(3d_1 s^2 - 3d_2 st + d_3 t^2\right),$$

where

$$d_1 = a_1 - 2a_2 + 3a_3, \quad d_2 = -a_2 + 3a_3, \quad d_3 = 3a_3$$

and

$$a_1 = \mathbf{b}_0 \cdot (\mathbf{b}_3 \times \mathbf{b}_2), \quad a_2 = \mathbf{b}_1 \cdot (\mathbf{b}_0 \times \mathbf{b}_3), \quad a_3 = \mathbf{b}_2 \cdot (\mathbf{b}_1 \times \mathbf{b}_0).$$

The function I is a cubic with three roots, not all necessarily real. It is the number of distinct real roots of $I(s, t)$ that determines the type of the cubic curve. For integral cubic curves, $[s \; t] = [1 \; 0]$ is always a root of $I(s, t)$. This means that the remaining roots of $I(s, t)$ can be found using the quadratic formula, rather than by the more general solution of a cubic—a significant simplification over the general rational curve algorithm.

Our cubic curve classification reduces to knowing the sign of the discriminant of $I(s, t)$, defined as

$$discr(I) = d_1^2 \left(3d_2^2 - 4d_1 d_3\right).$$

If $discr(I)$ is positive, the curve is a serpentine; if negative, it is a loop; and if zero, a cusp. Although it is true that all *cubic* curves are one of these three types, not all configurations of four Bézier control points result in cubic curves. It is possible to represent quadratic curves, lines, or even single points in cubic Bézier form. Our procedure will detect these cases, and our rendering algorithm can handle them. We don't need to consider (or render) lines or points, because the convex hull of the Bézier control points in these cases has zero area and, therefore, no pixel coverage. The general classification of cubic Bézier curves is given by Table 25-1.

If our Bézier control points have exact floating-point coordinates, the classification given in Table 25-1 can be done exactly. That is, there is no ambiguity between cases, because $discr(I)$ and all intermediate variables can be derived from exact floating representations.

Table 25-1. Cubic Curve Classification

Serpentine	$discr(I) > 0$
Cusp	$discr(I) = 0$
Loop	$discr(I) < 0$
Quadratic	$d_1 = d_2 = 0$
Line	$d_1 = d_2 = d_3 = 0$
Point	$\mathbf{b}_0 = \mathbf{b}_1 = \mathbf{b}_2 = \mathbf{b}_3$

Once a curve has been classified, we must find the texture coordinates $[k_i \ l_i \ m_i]$ corresponding to each Bézier control point $\mathbf{b}_i$, $i = 0, 1, 2, 3$. Our approach is to find scalar-valued cubic functions

$$k(s, t) = \mathbf{k} \cdot \mathbf{C}(s, t), \quad l(s, t) = \mathbf{l} \cdot \mathbf{C}(s, t), \quad m(s, t) = \mathbf{m} \cdot \mathbf{C}(s, t),$$

in Bézier form; the coefficients of these functions will correspond to our procedural texture coordinates. Because we know the geometry of the lines $\mathbf{k}$, $\mathbf{l}$, and $\mathbf{m}$ in Figure 25-4, we could find points and tangent vectors of $\mathbf{C}(s, t)$ and from these construct the needed lines. But lines are homogeneous, scale-invariant objects; what we need are the corresponding linear functionals, where (relative) scale matters.

Our strategy will be to construct $k(s, t)$, $l(s, t)$, and $m(s, t)$ by taking products of their linear factors. These linear factors are found by solving for the roots of $I(s, t)$ and a related polynomial called the *Hessian* of $I(s, t)$. For each curve type, we find the parameter values $[l_s \ l_t]$ and $[m_s \ m_t]$ of $I(s, t)$ where $\mathbf{k} \cap \mathbf{l}$ and $\mathbf{k} \cap \mathbf{m}$. We denote these linear factors by the following:

$$L \leftarrow (sl_t - tl_s), \qquad M \leftarrow (sm_t - tm_s).$$

We can reason about how to construct $k(s, t)$, $l(s, t)$, and $m(s, t)$ from L and M by studying the geometric relationship of $\mathbf{C}(s, t)$ to lines $\mathbf{k}$, $\mathbf{l}$, and $\mathbf{m}$. For example, $\mathbf{k}(s, t)$ will have roots at $[l_s \ l_t]$, $[m_s \ m_t]$, and a root at infinity $[1 \ 0]$. Therefore, for all cubic curves:

$$k(s, t) = LM.$$

Finding the cubic functions $l(s, t)$ and $m(s, t)$ for each of the three curve types has its own reasoning, to be described shortly.

Once the functions $k(s, t)$, $l(s, t)$, and $m(s, t)$ are known, we convert them to cubic Bézier form to obtain

$$\mathbf{M} = \begin{bmatrix} k_0 & l_0 & m_0 \\ k_1 & l_1 & m_1 \\ k_2 & l_2 & m_2 \\ k_3 & l_3 & m_3 \end{bmatrix},$$

where $[k_i \ l_i \ m_i]$ are the procedural texture coordinates associated with $\mathbf{b}_i$, $i = 0, 1, 2, 3$.

Finally, to make sure that the curve has the correct orientation—to the right is inside—we may need to reverse orientation by multiplying the implicit equation by -1. This is equivalent to setting $\mathbf{M} \leftarrow \mathbf{M} \cdot \mathbf{O}$, where

$$\mathbf{O} = \begin{bmatrix} -1 & 0 & 0 \\ 0 & -1 & 0 \\ 0 & 0 & 1 \end{bmatrix}.$$

The conditions for correcting orientation depend on curve type, described next.

25.3.1 Serpentine

For a serpentine curve, $\mathbf{C}(s, t)$ is tangent to line $\mathbf{l}$ at the inflection point where $\mathbf{k} \cap \mathbf{l}$. The scalar-valued function $l(s, t)$ will also have an inflection point at this parameter value; meaning that $l(s, t)$ will have a triple root there. A similar analysis applies for $m(s, t)$. We form products of the linear factors to get

$$k(s, t) = LM, \quad l(s, t) = L^3, \quad m(s, t) = M^3.$$

To find the parameter value of these linear factors, we compute the roots of $I(s, t)$:

$$\begin{bmatrix} l_s & l_t \end{bmatrix} = \begin{bmatrix} 3d_2 - \sqrt{9d_2^2 - 12d_1d_3} & 6d_1 \end{bmatrix},$$

$$\begin{bmatrix} m_s & m_t \end{bmatrix} = \begin{bmatrix} 3d_2 + \sqrt{9d_2^2 - 12d_1d_3} & 6d_1 \end{bmatrix}.$$

We convert $k(s, t)$, $l(s, t)$, and $m(s, t)$ to cubic Bézier form and form the coefficient matrix

$$\mathbf{M} = \begin{bmatrix} l_s m_s & l_s^3 & m_s^3 \\ \frac{1}{3}(3l_s m_s - l_s m_t - l_t m_s) & l_s^2(l_s - l_t) & m_s^2(m_s - m_t) \\ \frac{1}{3}(l_t(m_t - 2m_s) + l_s(3m_s - 2m_t)) & (l_t - l_s)^2 l_s & (m_t - m_s)^2 m_s \\ (l_t - l_s)(m_t - m_s) & -(l_t - l_s)^3 & -(m_t - m_s)^3 \end{bmatrix}.$$

Each row of the $\mathbf{M}$ matrix corresponds to the procedural texture coordinate associated with the Bézier curve control points. If $d_1 < 0$, then we must reverse orientation by setting $\mathbf{M} \leftarrow \mathbf{M} \cdot \mathbf{O}$.

25.3.2 Loop

For a loop curve, $\mathbf{C}(s, t)$ is tangent to line $\mathbf{l}$ and crosses line $\mathbf{m}$ at one of the double point parameters. This means that $l(s, t)$ will have a double root at $[l_s\ l_t]$ and a single root at $[m_s\ m_t]$. A similar analysis holds for $m(s, t)$. We then take products of the linear factors to get

$$k(s, t) = LM, \quad l(s, t) = L^2M, \quad m(s, t) = LM^2.$$

The parameter values of the double point are found as roots of the Hessian of $I(s, t)$, defined as

$$H(s, t) = \det \begin{vmatrix} \dfrac{\partial I(s,t)}{\partial s^2} & \dfrac{\partial I(s,t)}{\partial s \partial t} \\[2mm] \dfrac{\partial I(s,t)}{\partial t \partial s} & \dfrac{\partial I(s,t)}{\partial t^2} \end{vmatrix}$$

$$= -36\left(d_1^2 s^2 - d_1 d_2 st + \left(d_2^2 - d_1 d_3\right)t^2\right).$$

Because $H(s, t)$ is quadratic, we use the quadratic formula to find the roots:

$$[l_s\quad l_t] = \left[d_2 - \sqrt{4d_1 d_3 - 3d_2^2}\quad 2d_1\right],$$

$$[m_s\quad m_t] = \left[d_2 + \sqrt{4d_1 d_3 - 3d_2^2}\quad 2d_1\right].$$

We convert $k(s, t)$, $l(s, t)$, and $m(s, t)$ to cubic Bézier form to get

$$\mathbf{M} = \begin{bmatrix} l_s m_s & l_s^2 m_s & l_s m_s^2 \\[1mm] \tfrac{1}{3}(-l_s m_t - l_t m_s + l_s m_s) & -\tfrac{1}{3}l_s(l_s(m_t - 3m_s) + 2l_t m_s) & -\tfrac{1}{3}m_s(l_s(2m_t - 3m_s) + l_t m_s) \\[1mm] \tfrac{1}{3}(l_t(m_t - 2m_s) + l_s(3m_s - 2m_t)) & \tfrac{1}{3}(l_t - l_s)(l_s(2m_t - 3m_s) + l_t m_s) & \tfrac{1}{3}(m_t - m_s)(l_s(m_t - 3m_s) + 2l_t m_s) \\[1mm] (l_t - l_s)(m_t - m_s) & -(l_t - l_s)^2(m_t - m_s) & -(l_t - l_s)(m_t - m_s)^2 \end{bmatrix}.$$

A rendering artifact will occur if one of the double point parameters lies in the interval $[0/1, 1/1]$. To solve this problem, we subdivide the curve at the double point parameter—see Figure 25-5—and reverse the orientation of one of the subcurves. Note that the procedural texture coordinates of the subcurves can be found by subdividing the procedural texture coordinates of the original curve. Once a loop curve has been subdivided at its double point, the procedural texture coordinates k_i, $i = 0, \ldots, 3$ will have the same sign. Orientation reversal ($\mathbf{M} \leftarrow \mathbf{M} \cdot \mathbf{O}$) is needed if $(d_1 > 0$ and sign$(k_1) < 0)$ or $(d_1 < 0$ and sign$(k_1) > 0)$.

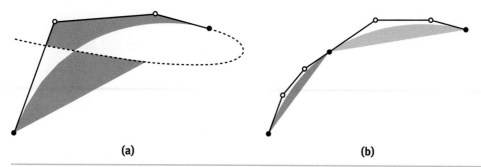

(a)   (b)

Figure 25-5. Cubic Curve with a Double Point
(a) A cubic Bézier loop curve with double point parameter in [0 1] and resulting rendering artifact.
(b) The curve after subdivision and reorientation of one subcurve.

25.3.3 Cusp

A cusp occurs when $discr(I) = 0$. This is the boundary between the serpentine and loop cases. Geometrically, the lines **l** and **m** are coincident; therefore $[l_s\ l_t] = [m_s\ m_t]$. We could use the procedure for either the loop or the serpentine case, because the texture coordinate matrices will turn out to be the same.

There is an exception: when $d_1 = 0$. In the serpentine and loop cases, it must be that $d_1 \neq 0$; otherwise $discr(I) = 0$ and we would have a cusp. The case where $d_1 = 0$ and $d_2 \neq 0$ corresponds to a cubic curve that has a cusp at the parametric value $[1\ 0]$—that is, homogeneous infinity. In this case, the inflection point polynomial reduces to

$$I(s, t) - t^2 (d_3 t - 3d_2 s),$$

which has a double root at infinity and a single root $[l_s\ l_t] = [d_3\ 3d_2]$. We find

$$k(s, t) = L, \quad l(s, t) = L^3, \quad m(s, t) = 1.$$

Converting these to Bézier form gives us the columns of the matrix:

$$\mathbf{M} = \begin{vmatrix} l_s & l_s^3 & 1 \\ l_s - \frac{1}{3}l_t & l_s^2(l_s - l_t) & 1 \\ l_s - \frac{2}{3}l_t & (l_s - l_t)^2 l_s & 1 \\ l_s - l_t & (l_s - l_t)^3 & 1 \end{vmatrix}.$$

The orientation will never need to be reversed in this case. An example of a cubic curve whose inflection point polynomial has a cusp at infinity is $[t\ t^3]$.

25.3.4 Quadratic

We showed earlier that quadratic curves could be rendered by a pixel shader that evaluated the expression $u^2 - v$. Switching away from the cubic shader would be inefficient for the GPU, and therefore undesirable. However, if we equate the cubic function $k(s, t) \equiv m(s, t)$, our cubic shader expression can be written as

$$k^3 - kl = k(k^2 - l).$$

We see that the part inside the parentheses is the quadratic shader expression with u and v replaced with k and l. The sign of this expression will agree with the quadratic shader, provided the value of k does not change sign inside the convex hull of the curve. We can degree-elevate the quadratic procedural texture coordinates to get

$$\mathbf{M} = \begin{bmatrix} 0 & 0 & 0 \\ \frac{1}{3} & 0 & \frac{1}{3} \\ \frac{2}{3} & \frac{1}{3} & \frac{2}{3} \\ 1 & 1 & 1 \end{bmatrix}.$$

Interpolation will not change the sign of k in this case. Finally, we reverse orientation if $d_3 < 0$.

25.4 Triangulation

Our triangulation procedure was only briefly discussed in Sections 25.2 and 25.3 in the interest of simplicity. An important detail not previously mentioned is that Bézier convex hulls cannot overlap. There are two reasons for this: one is that overlapping triangles cause problems for triangulation code; the other is that unwanted portions of one filled region might show through to the other, resulting in a visual artifact. This problem can be resolved by subdividing one of the offending curves so that Bézier curve convex hulls no longer overlap, as shown in Figure 25-6.

We locally triangulate all non-overlapping Bézier convex hulls. For quadratics, the Bézier convex hull is uniquely a triangle. For cubics, the Bézier convex hull may be a quad or a triangle. If it is a quad, we triangulate by choosing either diagonal. Next, the interior of the entire boundary is triangulated. The details of this procedure are beyond the scope of this chapter. Any triangulation procedure for a multicontour polygon will work.

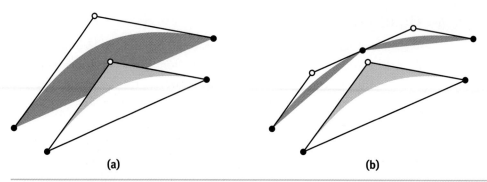

Figure 25-6. Handling Overlapping Triangles
(a) Overlapping triangles are not allowed. (b) One of the curves is subdivided to remove the overlap.

Recently, Kokojima et al. 2006 presented a variant on our approach for quadratic splines that used the stencil buffer to avoid triangulation. Their idea is to connect all points on the curve path and draw them as a triangle fan into the stencil buffer with the invert operator. Only pixels drawn an odd number of times will be nonzero, thus giving the correct image of concavities and holes. Next, they draw the curve segments, treating them all as convex quadratic elements. This will either add to or carve away a curved portion of the shape. A quad large enough to cover the extent of the stencil buffer is then drawn to the frame buffer with a stencil test. The result is the same as ours without triangulation or subdivision, and needing only one quadratic curve orientation. Furthermore, eliminating the triangulation steps makes high-performance rendering of dynamic curves possible. The disadvantage of their approach is that two passes over the curve data are needed. For static curves, they are trading performance for implementation overhead.

25.5 Antialiasing

We present an approach to antialiasing in the pixel shader based on a signed distance approximation to a curve boundary. By reducing pixel opacity within a narrow band that contains the boundary, we can approximate convolution with a filter kernel. However, this works only when pixel samples lie on both sides of a boundary, such as points well inside the Bézier convex hull of a curve. For points near triangle edges, or when the edge of a triangle is the boundary, this scheme breaks down. Fortunately, this is exactly the case that is handled by hardware *multisample antialiasing* (MSAA). MSAA uses a coverage mask derived as the percentage of samples (from a hardware-dependent sample pattern) covered by a triangle. Only one pixel shader call is initiated, and this is optionally located at the centroid of the covered samples, as opposed to the pixel center, to avoid sampling outside the triangle's image in texture space. In our case, out-of-gamut sampling is not a problem, because we use a procedural definition of a texture (an algebraic equation). Therefore, centroid sampling is not recommended.

For antialiasing of curved boundaries on the interior of the Bézier convex hull, we need to know the screen-space signed distance from the current pixel to the boundary. If this distance is ±½ a pixel (an empirically determined choice; this could be less or more), then the opacity of the pixel color is changed relative to the pixel's distance to the curved boundary. Computing the true distance to a degree d polynomial curve requires the solution to a degree $2d - 1$ equation. This is impractical on today's hardware, for performance reasons.

Instead, we use an approximate signed distance based on gradients. For a function $f(x, y)$, the gradient of f is a vector operator $\nabla f = [\partial f / \partial x \ \partial f / \partial y]$. The GPU has hardware support for taking gradients of variables in pixel shader programs via the ddx() and ddy() functions. We define the signed distance function to the screen-space curve $f(x, y) = 0$ to be

$$sd(x, y) = \frac{f(x, y)}{\|\nabla f(x, y)\|}.$$

In our case, the implicit function is not defined in screen (pixel) space. However, the process of interpolating procedural texture coordinates in screen space is, in effect, mapping screen $[x \ y]$ space to procedural texture coordinate space ($[u \ v]$ for quadratics, $[k \ l \ m]$ for cubics). In other words, we can think of the interpolated procedural texture coordinates as vector functions

$$[u(x, y) \quad v(x, y)] \quad \text{or} \quad [k(x, y) \quad l(x, y) \quad m(x, y)].$$

Each of these coordinate functions is actually the ratio of linear functionals whose quotient is taken in hardware (that is, perspective correction). An implicit function of these coordinate functions is a composition, defining a screen-space implicit function. Therefore, our signed distance function correctly measures approximate distance in pixel units.

Hardware gradients are based on differences between values of adjacent pixels, so they can only approximate the derivatives of higher-order functions. Although this rarely (if ever) results in artifacts, with only a few additional math operations, we can get exact derivatives by applying the chain rule to our shader equations. Let the following,

$$q(x, y) = u(x, y)^2 - v(x, y) = 0 \text{ and}$$

$$c(x, y) = k(x, y)^3 - l(x, y)m(x, y) = 0,$$

be our quadratic and cubic shader equations, respectively. Applying the chain rule, we get

$$\begin{bmatrix} \dfrac{\partial q}{\partial x} \\ \dfrac{\partial q}{\partial y} \end{bmatrix} = \begin{bmatrix} \dfrac{\partial u}{\partial x} & \dfrac{\partial v}{\partial x} \\ \dfrac{\partial u}{\partial y} & \dfrac{\partial v}{\partial y} \end{bmatrix} \cdot \begin{bmatrix} 2u \\ -1 \end{bmatrix} \text{ and}$$

$$\begin{bmatrix} \dfrac{\partial c}{\partial x} \\ \dfrac{\partial c}{\partial y} \end{bmatrix} = \begin{bmatrix} \dfrac{\partial k}{\partial x} & \dfrac{\partial l}{\partial x} & \dfrac{\partial m}{\partial x} \\ \dfrac{\partial k}{\partial y} & \dfrac{\partial l}{\partial y} & \dfrac{\partial m}{\partial y} \end{bmatrix} \cdot \begin{bmatrix} 3k^2 \\ -m \\ -l \end{bmatrix}.$$

We can write our signed distance function as

$$sd = \frac{f}{\sqrt{\left(\dfrac{\partial f}{\partial x}\right)^2 + \left(\dfrac{\partial f}{\partial y}\right)^2}},$$

where $f \leftarrow q$ for quadratics and $f \leftarrow c$ for cubics. For a boundary interval of $\pm\frac{1}{2}$ pixel, we map signed distance to opacity by $\alpha = \frac{1}{2} - sd$. This is based on a linear ramp blending; higher-order blending could be used at higher cost. If $\alpha > 1$, we set $\alpha \leftarrow 1$; if $\alpha < 0$, we abort the pixel.

25.6 Code

Listing 25-1 is HLSL code for our quadratic shader. The code for the cubic shader is similar.

Listing 25-1. Quadratic Curve Pixel Shader

```
float4 QuadraticPS(float2 p : TEXCOORD0,
  float4 color : COLOR0) : COLOR
{
  // Gradients
  float2 px = ddx(p);
  float2 py = ddy(p);

  // Chain rule
  float fx = (2*p.x)*px.x - px.y;
  float fy = (2*p.x)*py.x - py.y;

  // Signed distance
  float sd = (p.x*p.x - p.y)/sqrt(fx*fx + fy*fy);

  // Linear alpha
  float alpha = 0.5 - sd;

  if (alpha > 1)        // Inside
    color.a = 1;
  else if (alpha < 0)   // Outside
    clip(-1);
  else                  // Near boundary
    color.a = alpha;

  return color;
}
```

25.7 Conclusion

We have presented an algorithm for rendering vector art defined by closed paths containing quadratic and cubic Bézier curves. We locally triangulate each Bézier convex hull and globally triangulate the interior (right-hand side) of each path. We assign procedural texture coordinates to the vertices of each Bézier convex hull. These coordinates encode linear functionals and are interpolated by the hardware during rasterization. The process of interpolation maps the procedural texture coordinates to a space where the implicit equation of the curve has a simple form: $u^2 - v = 0$ for quadratics and $k^3 - lm = 0$ for cubics. A pixel shader program evaluates the implicit equation. The sign of the result will determine if a pixel is inside (negative) or outside (positive). We use hardware gradients to approximate a screen-space signed distance to the curve boundary. This signed distance is used for antialiasing the curved boundaries. We can apply an arbitrary projective transform to view our plane curves in 3D. The result has a small and static memory footprint, and the resulting image is resolution independent. Figure 25-7 shows an example of some text rendered in perspective using our technique.

In the future, we would like to extend this rendering paradigm to curves of degree 4 and higher. This would allow us to apply freeform deformations to low-order shapes (such as font glyphs) and have the resulting higher-order curve be resolution independent. The work of Kokojima et al. 2006 showed how to render dynamic quadratic curves; we would like to extend their approach to handle cubic curves as well. This is significantly more complicated than the quadratic case, because of the procedural texture-coordinate-assignment phase. However, it should be possible to do this entirely on the GPU using DirectX 10-class hardware equipped with a geometry shader (Blythe 2006).

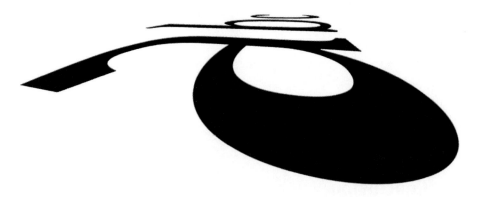

Figure 25-7. Our Algorithm Is Used to Render 2D Text with Antialiasing Under a 3D Perspective Transform

25.8 References

Blinn, Jim. 2003. *Jim Blinn's Corner: Notation, Notation, Notation.* Morgan Kaufmann.

Blythe, David. 2006. "The Direct3D 10 System." In *ACM Transactions on Graphics (Proceedings of SIGGRAPH 2006)* 25(3), pp. 724–734.

Kokojima, Yoshiyuki, Kaoru Sugita, Takahiro Saito, and Takashi Takemoto. 2006. "Resolution Independent Rendering of Deformable Vector Objects using Graphics Hardware." In *ACM SIGGRAPH 2006 Sketches*.

Loop, Charles, and Jim Blinn. 2005. "Resolution Independent Curve Rendering using Programmable Graphics Hardware." In *ACM Transactions on Graphics (Proceedings of SIGGRAPH 2005)* 24(3), pp. 1000–1008.

Salmon, George. 1852. *A Treatise on the Higher Order Plane Curves*. Hodges & Smith.

Chapter 26

Object Detection by Color: Using the GPU for Real-Time Video Image Processing

Ralph Brunner
Apple

Frank Doepke
Apple

Bunny Laden
Apple

In this chapter, we describe a GPU-based technique for finding the location of a uniquely colored object in a scene and then utilizing that position information for video effects. The technique uses a pixel shader in an atypical manner: to calculate a centroid and area rather than a per-pixel effect.

Object detection and tracking have applications in robotics, surveillance, and other fields. As the number of consumers who own computers equipped with video cameras increases, so do the possibilities of using the GPU for tracking objects for games and to enable new user-interaction models. In this chapter, we discuss one use of object detection: overlaying a tracked object with an image. As you'll see, the computational requirements of this implementation are so low that we can process the entire image area every video frame; we don't need to use any sophisticated region-of-interest tracking methods. By using the GPU for centroid computation, we leave the CPU free for other tasks, such as video decoding and encoding.

Because our program uses the Core Image image-processing framework on Mac OS X, we begin the chapter with a brief description of Core Image, why we use it, and how it works. Next we provide an overview of tracking objects using color, and then we describe the computations and kernel routines that process the video image.

26.1 Image Processing Abstracted

Core Image is an image-processing framework built into Mac OS X. It uses the GPU to perform real-time, pixel-accurate image processing. We chose to use Core Image to tackle the object detection and tracking problem rather than a kernel-level technology because Core Image does the following:

- **Abstracts the low-level work performed by the GPU in an easy-to-use, high-level programming interface.** You can easily follow and adapt the technique described in this chapter without needing to learn the low-level implementation details of specific hardware. Core Image takes care of all hardware-specific optimizations for you. It also converts image formats when necessary.

- **Processes only when necessary.** Because Core Image is predicated upon laziness, it is extremely efficient. It does not process data unless it must, and when it does, it takes the easiest route possible. When you apply a filter to an image, Core Image processes the pixels only when you need to paint the pixels to a destination. If you apply several filters in sequence, Core Image may change the order of processing or merge operations to perform the processing as optimally as possible.

We use Core Image to build several custom filters for the object-tracking problem. Before you read the specifics, you'll want to get an overall idea of the processing path, the components of a Core Image filter, and the terminology.

The custom Core Image filters that we use for object tracking have an Objective-C portion and a C portion. The Objective-C portion of a Core Image filter performs all the high-level tasks needed for image processing and calls the low-level routines that operate on pixels. A filter produces an output image by carrying out these steps:

- Setting up one or more objects, called *samplers*, to fetch pixels from the source image. If necessary, a sampler can apply a transform to the pixel prior to handing off the pixel for processing.

- Applying *kernel routines* to operate on the pixels supplied by the sampler. A kernel routine performs per-pixel processing. It always produces a four-element vector as output. Usually the vector represents RGBA (red, green, blue, alpha), but as you'll see in this chapter, that's not always the case. A filter can apply one or more kernel routines in sequence, or it can repeatedly apply the same kernel. Filters that apply more than one kernel routine are *multipass filters*.

- Writing the resulting image to a destination, most typically the screen.

The C portion of a Core Image filter includes the kernel routines that perform per-pixel processing on the GPU. The kernel routines use the Core Image kernel language, which is an extension to OpenGL Shading Language. This extension defines functions, data types, and keywords that make it easy to specify image-processing operations. You can use Core Image kernel language symbols together with the subset of the OpenGL Shading Language routines that Core Image supports.

You won't see the code for the Objective-C portion in this chapter; it's in the sample on the DVD that accompanies this book. What you will see in this chapter is code for most of the kernel routines that make up the C portion of the Core Image filter.

Now that you know a bit about what makes up a Core Image filter, let's take a look at how Core Image processes an image. See Figure 26-1 for an illustration of the process. The filter assembles the source image (or images) and then sets up a sampler for each source, defining any transformation that the sampler might need to perform after it fetches a pixel from a source. Setting up the sampler is straightforward; most of the time it involves creating and naming a sampler object and attaching it to an image source. Next the filter calls a routine to apply a kernel, passing the following:

- The name of the kernel routine to apply.
- The sampler (or samplers) needed by the kernel.
- A list of the arguments needed by the kernel.
- A dictionary (key-value pairs) of options that controls how Core Image evaluates the kernel. For example, you might want to specify the size of the output image.

When applying a kernel, Core Image sets up a calculation path that begins at the destination and works its way back to the source. Although this might seem a bit backward, this looking-ahead behavior is quite efficient because it allows Core Image to limit the processing to those pixels that are required to compute the final result. Take a look at Figure 26-1, and you'll see that the only pixels that need processing are those that overlap in the two source images. By looking ahead, Core Image figures a domain of definition: the area outside of which all pixels are transparent. There is no need to process any pixel that won't be seen. The alternative to looking ahead is to process every pixel and then, at the end, eliminate those that aren't needed.

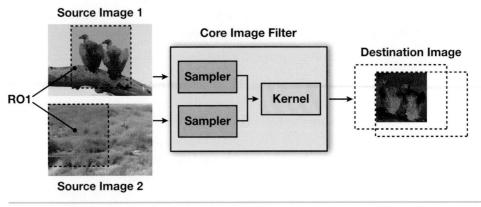

Figure 26-1. The Pixel Processing Path in Core Image

The shaded area in each of the source images in Figure 26-1 is the *region of interest* (ROI). The ROI defines the area in the source image from which a sampler takes pixel information to provide to the kernel for processing. The way the ROI and the domain of definition relate to each other determines whether the filter needs to perform additional setup work prior to applying a kernel. The ROI and the domain of definition can relate in these ways:

- They can *coincide exactly*: there is a 1:1 mapping between source and destination. For example, a hue filter processes a pixel from the working-space coordinate (r, s) in the ROI to produce a pixel at the working-space coordinate (r, s) in the domain of definition.

- They can *depend on each other*, but be modulated in some way. Some of the most interesting filters—blur and distortion, for example—use many source pixels in the calculation of one destination pixel. For example, a distortion filter might use a pixel (r, s) and its neighbors from the working coordinate space in the ROI to produce a single pixel (r, s) in the domain of definition.

- They can *be independent*. In this case, the domain of definition is calculated from values in a lookup table that are provided by the sampler. The locations of values in the map or table are unrelated to the working-space coordinates in the source image and the destination. A value located at (r, s) in a shading image does not need to be the value that produces a pixel at the working-space coordinate (r, s) in the domain of definition. Many filters use values provided in a shading image or lookup table in combination with an image source. For example, a color ramp or a table that approximates a function, such as the `arcsin()` function, provides values that are unrelated to the notion of working coordinates.

Core Image assumes that the ROI and domain of definition coincide unless you tell it otherwise. The object-tracking problem requires some filters for which we need to define a region of interest.

26.2 Object Detection by Color

If you've ever watched the audience at a tennis match, you know exactly what color tracking is. As the green tennis ball flies from side to side of the court, the heads of the onlookers move side to side. In this section, you'll see how to process video input of a moving ball and overlay the ball with an image of a duck, as shown in Figure 26-2. We process 1280×720 video in real time (30 frames per second) on a Macintosh computer equipped with an NVIDIA GeForce 7300 GT graphics card.

As illustrated in Figure 26-3, these are the tasks needed to detect an object using color and then track it:

1. Create a masking image by comparing each pixel with a target color value. Convert pixels that fall within the range to white, and convert those that fall outside the range to black.

2. Find the centroid of the target color. The centroid of the tracked color defines the center position for the overlay image. We use a multipass pixel-processing kernel to compute a location. The output of this phase is a 1×1-pixel image, containing the coordinate of the centroid in the first two components (`pixel.rg`) and the area in the third component (`pixel.b`). We use the area later to estimate the distance of the object from the camera.

3. Composite an image over the detected object. Assuming the shape of the object does not change with respect to the frame, then the change in area of the tracked color is proportional to the square of the distance of the object from the viewer. We use this information to scale the overlay image, so that the overlay image increases or decreases in size appropriately. (The assumption doesn't hold for objects such as an expanding balloon or an expanding pool of liquid, but it works well for the spherical ball in our sample.)

We discuss each task in more detail in the following sections.

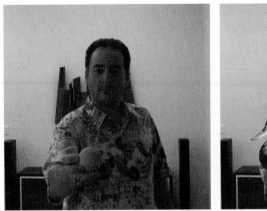

Figure 26-2. From Ball Tossing to Duck Tossing
No ducks were harmed in the making of this video.

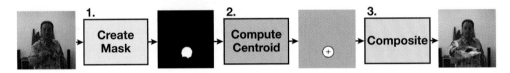

Figure 26-3. The Tasks Needed to Track Color

26.2.1 Creating the Mask

We create the mask using a Mask from Color filter that has two input parameters: an input color and an input threshold. The input color defines the color to track. The input threshold defines the range of color values around the input color that are included in the calculations for tracking, as shown in Figure 26-4. Choosing the threshold is a bit of an art. You'll want to make sure it is small enough to avoid extraneous noise (as you'll see in Figure 26-5, upcoming) but large enough to allow for lighting variations in the color of the object that you want to track. Recall that a Core Image filter (in this case, Mask from Color) performs the high-level tasks of setting up samplers and applying a kernel routine.

The Mask from Color filter calls the `maskFromColor()` kernel routine shown in Listing 26-1 to compute the mask. Before we get into describing this kernel routine in more detail, let's review the keywords in the Core Image kernel language that we use in Listing 26-1, starting with two data types: `sampler` and `color`. We described samplers earlier; the `sampler` keyword specifies an object that fetches samples from a source image (or, if appropriate, a lookup table.) The `__color` data type specifies a vector of color values that Core Image must match to the current working color space.

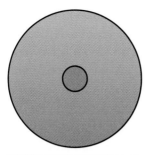

Figure 26-4. Targeting the Colors
The small circle shows a target color and the larger circle shows colors that fall within a threshold.

The `kernel` keyword tags a kernel routine; it is placed before the return type, which is always a `vec4` data type. All parameters to a kernel routine are implicitly marked `uniform`. You cannot mark parameters `out` and `inout`; it's not allowed.

The listing contains several functions that are specific to the Core Image kernel language. The `samplerCoord()` function returns the position (a two-element vector) in sampler space of the current pixel. It takes care of all the coordinate mapping from the source to the working coordinate space (such as rotating and scaling). The `sample()` function returns the pixel value produced from the sampler at the given position, where the position is given in sampler space.

Listing 26-1. Routines Used by the Color Masking Filter

```
vec3 normalizeColor(vec3 color )
{
  return color / max(dot(color, vec3(1.0/3.0)), 0.001);
}


kernel vec4 maskFromColor(sampler image, __color color,
                          float threshold)
{
  float d;
  vec4 p;
  // Compute distance between current pixel color and reference color.
  p = sample(image, samplerCoord(image));
  d = distance(normalizeColor(p.rgb), normalizeColor(color.rgb));

  // If color difference is larger than threshold, return black.
  return (d > threshold) ? vec4(0.0) : vec4(1.0);
}
```

Prior to calling the maskFromColor() kernel routine shown in Listing 26-1, the Mask from Color filter creates and sets up a sampler object to fetch pixels from the video input image. Then it passes the sampler object, the target color, and a threshold value to the maskFromColor() kernel routine. The kernel routine normalizes the color values to compensate for variations in the shading of the object due to lighting conditions. The kernel then calculates the distance between the color of the current pixel and the target color. If the color value is less than the threshold, the kernel routine returns (1.0, 1.0, 1.0, 1.0). Otherwise, it returns (0.0, 0.0, 0.0, 0.0). The mask returned for the input image shown in Figure 26-2 is shown in Figure 26-5.

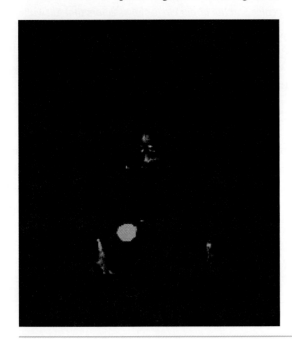

Figure 26-5. The Masked Image

26.2.2 Finding the Centroid

We compute the centroid of the masked area as a weighted average of all the coordinates in the mask image. If $m(x, y)$ is the value of the mask image at coordinate (x, y), the equation to compute the centroid is

$$\begin{pmatrix} c_x \\ c_y \end{pmatrix} = \frac{\sum_{x,y} m(x, y) \begin{pmatrix} x \\ y \end{pmatrix}}{\sum_{x,y} m(x, y)}. \tag{1}$$

Our implementation, the `coordinateMask()` kernel routine shown in Listing 26-2, first creates an image that contains these three components:

$$(x \cdot m(x, y), \quad y \cdot m(x, y), \quad m(x, y)).$$

The routine uses the Core Image kernel language function `destCoord()`, which returns the position, in working-space coordinates, of the pixel we are currently computing.

Listing 26-2. A Routine That Creates a Mask

```
kernel vec4 coordinateMask(sampler mask, vec2 invSize)
{
  vec4 d;

  // Create a vector with (x,y, 1,1), normalizing the coordinates
  // to 0-1 range.
  d = vec4(destCoord()*invSize, vec2(1.0));
  // Return this vector weighted by the mask value
  return sample(mask, samplerCoord(mask))*d;
}
```

Note that if we were to sum the values of all the pixel values computed by the `coordinateMask()` kernel routine, the first two components of the result would correspond to the numerator of Equation 1, while the third component would correspond to the denominator of that equation. Instead of computing the sum, our implementation computes the mean value over all those pixels and then multiplies (scales) by the number of pixels to get the sum.

We compute the average value of the image by repeatedly downsampling the image, from one that is $n \times n$ pixels to one that is 1×1 pixel, as shown in Figure 26-6.

We downsample by a factor of four, both horizontally and vertically, in a single pass, using the `scaleXY4()` kernel routine shown in Listing 26-3. Note that there are only

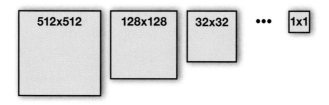

Figure 26-6. Downsampling an Image to Compute the Mean Pixel Value

four sample instructions in this routine to gather the values for 16 pixels. Requesting the texel between the sample locations leverages the linear interpolation hardware, which fetches the average of a 2×2-pixel block in a single operation.

Listing 26-3. A Routine That Downsamples by a Factor of Four

```
kernel vec4 scaleXY4(sampler image)
{
  vec4 p0,p1,p2,p3;
  vec2 d;
  // Fetch the position of the coordinate we want to compute,
  // scale it by 4.
  d   = 4.0*destCoord();
  // Fetch the pixels that surround the current pixel.
  p0 = sample(image, samplerTransform(image, d + vec2(-1.0,-1.0)));
  p1 = sample(image, samplerTransform(image, d + vec2(+1.0,-1.0)));
  p2 = sample(image, samplerTransform(image, d + vec2(-1.0,+1.0)));
  p3 = sample(image, samplerTransform(image, d + vec2(+1.0,+1.0)));
  // Sum the fetched pixels, scale by 0.25.
  return 0.25*(p0 + p1 + p2 + p3);
}
```

The `samplerTransform()` function is another Core Image kernel language function. It returns the position in the coordinate space of the source (the first argument) that is associated with the position defined in working-space coordinates (the second argument).

If the image is not square, you won't end up with a 1×1 image. If that's the case, you will need to downsample by a factor of two in the horizontal or vertical direction until the result is reduced to a single pixel.

If the width or height of the image is not a power of two, this method computes the mean over an area larger than the actual image. Because the image is zero outside its domain of definition, the result is simply off by a constant factor: the image area divided by the downsampled area. The implementation we provide uses the Core Image built-in filter `CIColorMatrix` filter to scale the result appropriately, so that the filter works correctly for any image size.

At the end of the downsampling passes, we use the `centroid()` kernel routine shown in Listing 26-4 to perform a division operation to get the centroid. The output of this phase is a 1×1-pixel image that contains the coordinate of the centroid in the first two components (`pixel.rg`) and the area in the third component (`pixel.b`).

```
kernel vec4 centroid(sampler image)
{
  vec4 p;

  p = sample(image, samplerCoord(image));
  p.xy = p.xy / max(p.z, 0.001);
  return p;

}
```

26.2.3 Compositing an Image over the Input Signal

To illustrate the result of the centroid calculation, we composite an image (in this case, a duck) on top of the video signal, using the duckComposite kernel routine shown in Listing 26-5. We also scale the composited image according to a distance estimate, which is simply the square root of the area from the previous phase. Note that Core Image, by default, stores image data with premultiplied alpha. That makes the compositing in this case simple (see the last line in Listing 26-5).

Listing 26-5. A Kernel Routine That Overlays an Image

```
kernel vec4 duckComposite(sampler image, sampler duck,
                          sampler location, vec2 size,
                          vec2 offset, float scale)
{
  vec4 p, d, l;
  vec2 v;

  p = sample(image, samplerCoord(image));
  // Fetch centroid location.
  l = sample(location, samplerTransform(location, vec2(0.5, 0.5)));

  // Translate to the centroid location, and scale image by
  // the distance estimate, which in this case is the square root
  // of the area.
  v = scale * (destCoord() - l.xy * size) / sqrt(l.z) + offset;

  // Get the corresponding pixel from the duck image, and composite
  // on top of the video.
  d = sample(duck, samplerTransform(duck,v));
  return (1.0 - d.a)*p + d*p.a;
}
```

26.3 Conclusion

In this chapter we presented a technique for detecting and tracking objects using color. We used the Core Image image-processing framework because, as a high-level framework, it allows the technique presented here to work on a variety of graphics hardware without the need to make hardware-specific changes. This technique performs well; it processes high-definition video in real time on Macintosh computers equipped with an NVIDIA GeForce 7300 GT graphics card.

There are two situations that can limit the effectiveness of the technique: interlaced video and a low degree of floating-point precision. Interlaced video signals display the odd lines of a frame and then display the even lines. Video cameras connected to a computer typically deinterlace the signal prior to displaying it. Deinterlacing degrades the signal and, as a result, can interfere with object tracking. You can improve the success of detection and tracking by using progressive-scan video, in which lines are displayed sequentially. If you don't have equipment that's capable of progressive scan, you can use just the odd or even field to perform the centroid and area calculations.

Although most modern graphics cards boast a high degree of floating-point precision, those with less precision can cause the median filter to produce banded results that can result in jerky motion of the overlay image or any effects that you apply. To achieve smooth results, you'll want to use a graphics card that has full 32-bit IEEE floating-point precision.

26.4 Further Reading

Apple, Inc. 2006. "Core Image Kernel Language Reference." Available online at http://developer.apple.com/documentation/GraphicsImaging/Reference/CIKernelLangRef/.

Apple, Inc. 2007. "Core Image Programming Guide." Available online at http://developer.apple.com/documentation/GraphicsImaging/Conceptual/CoreImaging/

Chapter 27

Motion Blur as a Post-Processing Effect

Gilberto Rosado
Rainbow Studios

27.1 Introduction

One of the best ways to simulate speed in a video game is to use motion blur. Motion blur can be one of the most important effects to add to games, especially racing games, because it increases realism and a sense of speed. Motion blur also helps smooth out a game's appearance, especially for games that render at 30 frames per second or less. However, adding support for motion blur to an existing engine can be challenging because most motion blur techniques require the scene to be rendered in a separate pass in order to generate a per-pixel velocity buffer. Such a multipass approach can be limiting: Many applications cannot afford to send the scene through the entire graphics pipeline more than once and still manage to reach the application's target frame rate.

Other ways to generate a per-pixel velocity map include using multiple render targets and outputting the velocity information to one of the render targets. A major disadvantage of this strategy is that it requires modifying all the scene's shaders to add code that will calculate velocity and output it to the second render target. Another disadvantage is that rendering to multiple render targets may decrease performance on some platforms. Additionally, some platforms have limited rendering memory and require a tiling mechanism in order to use multiple render targets on frame buffers that are 1280×720 or larger.

In this chapter, we introduce a technique that uses the depth buffer as a texture input to a pixel shader program in order to generate the scene's velocity map. The pixel shader program computes the world-space positions for each pixel by using the depth value—

which is stored in the depth buffer—in conjunction with the current frame's view-projection matrix. Once we determine the world-space position at that pixel, we can transform it by using the previous frame's view-projection matrix. Then we can compute the difference in the viewport position between the current frame and the previous frame in order to generate the per-pixel velocity values. A motion blur effect can then be achieved by using this velocity vector as a direction to gather multiple samples across the frame buffer, averaging them out along the way to generate a blur.

The benefit of our technique is that it can be performed as a post-processing step. This ability allows it to be easily integrated into existing engines targeting hardware that allows sampling from a depth buffer as a texture.

Figures 27-1 and 27-2 show how different a scene can look with and without motion blur. Notice how Figure 27-1 gives a strong illusion of motion.

27.2 Extracting Object Positions from the Depth Buffer

When an object is rendered and its depth values are written to the depth buffer, the values stored in the depth buffer are the interpolated z coordinates of the triangle divided by the interpolated w coordinates of the triangle after the three vertices of the triangles are transformed by the world-view-projection matrices. Using the depth buffer as a texture, we can extract the world-space positions of the objects that were rendered to the depth buffer by transforming the viewport position at that pixel by the inverse of the current view-projection matrix and then multiplying the result by the w component. We define the viewport position as the position of the pixel in viewport space— that is, the x and y components are in the range of -1 to 1 with the origin $(0, 0)$ at the center of the screen; the depth stored at the depth buffer for that pixel becomes the z component, and the w component is set to 1.

We can show how this is achieved by defining the viewport-space position at a given pixel as H. Let M be the world-view-projection matrix and W be the world-space position at that pixel.

$$H = \left(\frac{x}{w}, \frac{y}{w}, \frac{z}{w}, 1\right)$$

$$H \times M^{-1} = \frac{wX}{wW}, \frac{wY}{wW}, \frac{wZ}{wW}, wW = D$$

$$W = \frac{D}{D.w}$$

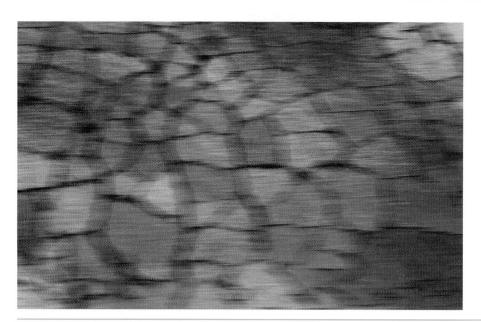

Figure 27-1. A Scene with Motion Blur

Figure 27-2. A Scene Without Motion Blur

The HLSL/Cg code in Listing 27-1 uses the previous equations in a full-screen post-processing pixel shader to compute the world-space position of the objects rendered at a given pixel, using the depth buffer and the inverse of the current view-projection matrix.

Listing 27-1. Shader Code That Extracts the Per-Pixel World-Space Positions of the Objects That Were Rendered to the Depth Buffer

```
// Get the depth buffer value at this pixel.
float zOverW = tex2D(depthTexture, texCoord);

// H is the viewport position at this pixel in the range -1 to 1.
float4 H = float4(texCoord.x * 2 - 1, (1 - texCoord.y) * 2 - 1,
zOverW, 1);

// Transform by the view-projection inverse.
float4 D = mul(H, g_ViewProjectionInverseMatrix);

// Divide by w to get the world position.
float4 worldPos = D / D.w;
```

Once we determine the world-space position, we can transform it by using the previous frame's view-projection matrix and take the difference in screen position to compute the pixel's velocity, as shown in Listing 27-2.

Listing 27-2. Shader Code That Computes the Per-Pixel Velocity Vectors That Determine the Direction to Blur the Image

```
// Current viewport position
float4 currentPos = H;

// Use the world position, and transform by the previous view-
// projection matrix.
float4 previousPos = mul(worldPos, g_previousViewProjectionMatrix);

// Convert to nonhomogeneous points [-1,1] by dividing by w.
previousPos /= previousPos.w;

// Use this frame's position and last frame's to compute the pixel
// velocity.
float2 velocity = (currentPos - previousPos)/2.f;
```

The method for acquiring the depth buffer for use as a texture varies from platform to platform and depends on the graphics API used. Some details on how to access the depth buffer as a texture are discussed in Gilham 2006. If the target hardware does not support sampling from depth buffers as textures, a depth texture may be generated by using multiple render targets and then outputting depth to a separate render target or outputting the depth value to the color buffer's alpha channel.

27.3 Performing the Motion Blur

Once we have the pixel velocities, we can sample along that direction in the color buffer, accumulating the color values to achieve the motion-blurred value, as shown in Listing 27-3.

Listing 27-3. Shader Code That Uses the Velocity Vector at the Current Pixel to Sample the Color Buffer Multiple Times to Achieve the Motion Blur Effect

```
// Get the initial color at this pixel.
float4 color = tex2D(sceneSampler, texCoord);

texCoord += velocity;

for(int i = 1; i < g_numSamples; ++i, texCoord += velocity)
{
  // Sample the color buffer along the velocity vector.
  float4 currentColor = tex2D(sceneSampler, texCoord);

  // Add the current color to our color sum.
  color += currentColor;
}

// Average all of the samples to get the final blur color.
float4 finalColor = color / numSamples;
```

We can see this technique in action in Figure 27-3. Notice how the terrain near the viewer is a lot blurrier than the terrain in the distance.

Figure 27-3. A Terrain with Our Full-Screen Motion Blur Effect
Notice how the parts of the scene that are farther away receive less of the blur.

27.4 Handling Dynamic Objects

This technique works perfectly for static objects because it only takes into account the movement of the camera. However, if more accuracy is needed to record the velocity of dynamic objects in the scene, we can generate a separate velocity texture.

To generate a velocity texture for rigid dynamic objects, transform the object by using the current frame's view-projection matrix and the last frame's view-projection matrix, and then compute the difference in viewport positions the same way as for the post-processing pass. This velocity should be computed per-pixel by passing both transformed positions into the pixel shader and computing the velocity there. This technique is described in the DirectX 9 SDK's motion blur sample (Microsoft 2006).

27.5 Masking Off Objects

Depending on the application, you might want to mask off certain parts of the scene so that they do not receive motion blur. For example, in a racing game, you might want to keep all the race cars crisp and detailed, rather than blurry. An easy way to achieve this is to render a mask to a separate texture or to the alpha channel of the color buffer and use this mask to determine what pixels should be blurred.

27.6 Additional Work

This technique for calculating the world-space position of objects in the scene based on the scene's depth buffer is very useful. We can use this technique to implement other graphics effects: Depth of field is an effect that fits nicely into this technique, as described in Gilham 2006, and scene fog can also be implemented as a post-processing step by using the depth buffer.

27.7 Conclusion

In this chapter, we discussed a method for retrieving the world-space position of objects by using the depth value stored in the depth buffer, and we showed how that information can be used as a basis for implementing motion blur in a game engine. Implementing motion blur as mostly a post-processing effect allows it to be easily integrated into an existing rendering engine while offering better performance than traditional multipass solutions.

27.8 References

Gilham, David. 2006. "Real-Time Depth-of-Field Implemented with a Post-Processing Only Technique." In *Shader X5*, edited by Wolfgang Engel, pp. 163–175. Charles River Media.

Microsoft Corporation. 2006. "DirectX 9.0 Programmer's Reference."

Chapter 28

Practical Post-Process Depth of Field

Earl Hammon, Jr.
Infinity Ward

28.1 Introduction

In this chapter we describe a depth-of-field (DoF) algorithm particularly suited for first-person games. At Infinity Ward, we pride ourselves on immersing players in a rich cinematic experience. Consistent with this goal, we developed a technique for *Call of Duty 4: Modern Warfare* that provides depth of field's key qualitative features in both the foreground and the background with minimal impact on total system performance or engine architecture. Our technique requires Shader Model 2.0 hardware.

28.2 Related Work

28.2.1 Overview

A rich body of work, dating back to Potmesil and Chakravarty 1981, exists for adding depth of field to computer-generated images. Demers (2004), in the original *GPU Gems* book, divides depth-of-field techniques into these five classes:

- *Ray-tracing techniques*, which send rays from over the whole area of the lens
- *Accumulation-buffer techniques*, which blend images from multiple pinhole cameras
- *Compositing techniques*, which merge multiple layers with different focus levels
- *Forward-mapped z-buffer techniques*, which scatter a pixel's color to its neighbors
- *Reverse-mapped z-buffer techniques*, which gather color samples from neighboring pixels

Ray tracing, accumulation buffer, and compositing can be considered "composition" techniques. Like Demers, we prefer z-buffer techniques (forward mapped or reverse mapped). As image-based algorithms, they are particularly suited to graphics hardware. Furthermore, z-buffer information is useful in other rendering effects, such as soft particles, because it amortizes the cost of generating a depth image. On the other hand, composition techniques are limited because they cannot be added easily to an existing graphics engine.

Z-buffer techniques are often extended to operate on a set of independent layers instead of on a single image. This process can reduce artifacts from incorrect bleeding and give proper visibility behind nearby objects that are blurred to the point of translucency.

28.2.2 Specific Techniques

Mulder and van Liere 2000 includes a fast DoF technique that splits the original image into those pixels in front of the focal plane and those behind. They build a set of blurred images from both sets, halving the resolution each time. Finally, they combine each of these blurred levels with the original scene by drawing a textured plane at the appropriate distance from the camera with depth testing enabled. Our technique also blends blurred images with the frame buffer, but we generate them in fewer passes and apply them to the final image with a single full-screen colored quad. We achieve higher efficiency by accepting more artifacts from blurring across depths.

Demers (2004) describes a gathering z-buffer technique that uses each pixel's circle of confusion (CoC) to blend between several downsampled versions of the original image. Our technique most closely matches this, but we also consider neighbors when we calculate a pixel's CoC, so that our technique also blurs foreground objects.

Scheuermann (2004) describes another gathering z-buffer technique that uses a Poisson filter to sample the neighborhood of a pixel based on its own CoC. He also uses the depth of the neighboring pixels to prevent foreground objects from bleeding onto unfocused background objects. This technique works well for blurring distant objects, but it doesn't extend well to blurring the foreground.

Křivánek et al. (2003) present a scattering z-buffer technique, using objects composed of point sprites that are scaled based on the point's CoC. They improve performance by using lower levels of detail for objects that are more out of focus. This is a good technique for point-sprite models. This could be extended to work as a post-process by treating each pixel of the screen as a point sprite, but doing so is computationally impractical.

Kass et al. (2006) achieve the blurring seen in DoF by modeling it as heat diffusion, where the size of the circle of confusion corresponds to the "heat" of the pixel. They further divide the scene into layers to draw objects behind an opaque foreground object that has become transparent because it was small relative to the camera aperture. Their technique achieves high quality with interactive performance in a prerendered scene, letting artists manipulate the DoF parameters used later in an offline render. However, the technique is too computationally intensive for dynamic scenes that must be rendered every frame.

28.3 Depth of Field

As the theoretical basis for our technique, we start from a virtual lens that focuses incoming light on an imaging plane. This lens is characterized by the focal length and the aperture. The focal length is the distance an imaging plane needs to be from the lens for parallel rays to map to a single point. The aperture is simply the diameter of the lens receiving light. The thin lens equation relates an object's distance from the lens u to the distance from the lens at which it is in focus v and the focal length of the lens f:

$$\frac{1}{u} + \frac{1}{v} = \frac{1}{f}.$$

The geometry of a simple lens is shown in Figure 28-1. The aperture radius of the lens is d. The point u_o is in focus for the imaging plane, which is at v_o. A point at u_n or u_f would be in focus if the imaging plane were at v_f or v_n, respectively, but both map to a circle with diameter c when the imaging plane is at v_o. This circle is known as the *circle of confusion*. The depth of field for a camera is the range of values for which the CoC is sufficiently small.

Using similar triangles, we find that

$$\frac{v_n - v_o}{v_n} = \frac{c}{d} = \frac{v_o - v_f}{v_f}.$$

So, for any point in space p that is focused at v_p, we can specify its circle of confusion by

$$c = d \times \left| \frac{v_p - v_o}{v_p} \right|.$$

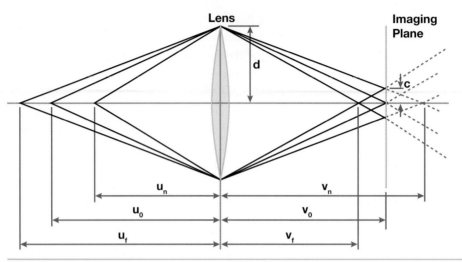

Figure 28-1. The Circle of Confusion for a Thin Lens

We can solve the thin lens approximation for v and substitute it into this equation to find the diameter of the circle of confusion for any point in space as a function of the camera's physical properties, as in Equation 1:

$$c = d \times \left| \frac{f}{v_o - f} \right| \times \left| 1 - \frac{v_o}{v_p} \right|. \tag{1}$$

We are primarily concerned with the qualitative properties of this equation to convey a sense of limited depth of field. Specifically, we note the following:

- A "pinhole" camera model sets d to 0. In this case, c is always 0, so every point in space is always in focus. Any larger value of d will cause parts of the image to be out of focus. All real lenses, including the human eye, have d greater than 0.
- There is an upper bound on the diameter of the circle of confusion for points beyond the focal point.
- There is no upper bound on the circle of confusion closer than the focal point.
- The circle of confusion increases much more rapidly in the foreground than in the background.

28.4 Evolution of the Algorithm

Clearly, blurring objects near the camera is crucial to any convincing depth-of-field algorithm. Our algorithm evolved through various attempts at convincingly blurring nearby objects.

28.4.1 Initial Stochastic Approach

We started from the technique described in Scheuermann 2004. We calculated each pixel's circle of confusion independently and used that to scale a circular Poisson distribution of samples from the original image. Like Scheuermann, we also read the depth for each sample point, rejecting those too close to the camera.

This provides a very convincing blur for objects beyond the focal plane. Unfortunately, objects in front of the focal plane still have sharp silhouettes. Nearby objects do not appear out of focus—they just seem to have low-quality textures. This poor texture detracts from the player's experience, so it would be better to restrict ourselves to blurring distant objects than to use this technique for blurring the foreground.

This technique for blurring foreground objects is represented in the top right image of Figure 28-2. Note that the character's silhouette is unchanged from the reference image. This screenshot used 33 sample positions for 66 texture lookups per pixel, but it still suffers from ringing artifacts, particularly around the chin strap, the collar, and the eyes. Contrast this with the soft silhouette and smooth blur in the bottom right image.

28.4.2 The Scatter-as-Gather Approach

We considered the problem of blurring the background solved at this point, so we directed our efforts to bleeding blurry foreground objects past their silhouettes. Our first algorithm did a gather from neighboring pixels, essentially assuming that each neighbor had a CoC that was the same as the current one. Logically, we would prefer each pixel to smear itself over its neighbors based on its own circle of confusion.

This selectively sized smearing is a scattering operation, which doesn't map well to modern GPUs. We inverted this scattering operation into a gather operation by searching the neighborhood of each pixel for pixels that scattered onto it. We again sampled with a Poisson distribution, but because we were searching for the neighboring pixels that bleed onto the center pixel, we always had to use the maximum circle of confusion.

Figure 28-2. A Character Rendered with Different Techniques for DoF
Top left: The reference image. Top right: Stochastic gather (66 texture lookups per pixel). Bottom left: Scatter as gather (128 texture lookups per pixel). Bottom right: This chapter's technique (9.625 texture lookups per pixel).

We found the CoC for each neighboring sample and calculated a weighted sum of only those samples that overlapped this pixel. Each sample's weight was inversely proportional to its area. We normalized the final color value by dividing by the sum of all used weights.

Unfortunately, this technique proved computationally and visually inadequate. We noticed that using less than about one-fourth of the pixels in the largest possible circle of confusion resulted in ugly ringing artifacts. This calculates to 24 sample points with 2 texture reads each for a maximum circle of confusion of only 5 pixels away (the diameter would be 11 pixels counting the center point). This cost could possibly be mitigated by using information about known neighbors to cull samples intelligently.

However, we abandoned this approach because it retained objectionable discontinuities between nearby unfocused pixels and more-distant focused pixels. To understand why this occurred, consider an edge between red source pixels with a large CoC and blue source pixels in focus. In the target image, the red pixels will have affected the blue pixels, but not vice versa. The unfocused red object will have a sharp silhouette against a purple background that fades to blue, instead of the continuous red-to-purple-to-blue transition we'd expect.

Two more problems with this method lead to the ugly behavior. First, the weight of each pixel should go smoothly to zero at the perimeter of the circle; without this, the output image will always have discontinuities where the blur radius changes. Second, the pixels cannot be combined using a simple normalized sum of their weights. To get the desired behavior, the contributing pixels need to be iterated from back to front, where this iteration's output color is a lerp from the previous iteration's output color to the current source pixel's color, based on the current source pixel's contribution weight. These two changes make this technique equivalent to rendering sorted depth sprites for each pixel with diameters equal to the pixel's CoC, essentially a post-process version of Křivánek et al. 2003. Unfortunately, they also make the pixel shader even more prohibitively expensive. Even with these fixes, the shader could not properly draw the scene behind any foreground objects that are blurred to transparency.

The bottom left image of Figure 28-2 was generated with this technique, using 64 sample points with a 12-pixel radius. The extra samples give this a better blur in the character's interior than the stochastic approach. However, 64 sample points are still too few for this blur radius, which leads to the ringing artifacts that can be seen on the antenna, neck, and helmet. Note that the silhouette still forms a harsh edge against the background; more samples wouldn't eliminate this.

28.4.3 The Blur Approach

At Infinity Ward we prioritize a quality user experience over an accurate simulation. That's why we abandoned physically based approaches when applying the circle of confusion for nearby objects in a continuous fashion. Instead, we decided to eliminate all discontinuities between focused objects and the unfocused foreground by using brute force, blurring them out of existence. The bottom right image in Figure 28-2 compares this technique to the previous approaches. The blur approach clearly has the best image quality, but it is also the fastest.

We apply a full-screen pass that calculates the radius of the circle of confusion for each foreground pixel into a render target. Pixels that are in focus or in the background use a CoC of zero. We then blur the CoC image to eliminate any edges. We use a Gaussian blur because it is computationally efficient and gives satisfactory results. We also downsample the CoC image to one-fourth the resolution along each axis as an optimization, so that the Gaussian blur affects only one-sixteenth of the total pixels in the frame.

This alone does not give the desired results for the silhouette of an unfocused object. If the foreground object is maximally blurred but the object behind it is not blurred at all, both objects will be approximately 50 percent blurred at their boundary. The foreground object should be 100 percent blurred along this edge. This does not look as bad as the previous discontinuities; however, it still looks odd when the blurriness of an edge on a foreground object varies based on the object behind it.

To fix this, we sized certain pixels—those located on either side of an edge between CoCs that had differing sizes—to always use the greater of the two diameters. However, a pixel has many neighbors, and we would rather avoid doing a search of all neighboring pixels. Instead, we only calculate each pixel's CoC and then use the blurred CoC image to estimate its neighboring pixel's CoC.

Consider an edge between two objects, each with uniform yet distinct circles of confusion having diameters D_0 and D_1. Clearly, in this case the blurred diameter D_B is given by

$$D_B = \tfrac{1}{2}(D_0 + D_1).$$

This equation also accurately gives the blurred diameter when the gradient of the diameter is the same on both sides of the edge, and for some other coincidental cases. We can get the current pixel's original diameter D_0 and blurred diameter D_B in two texture lookups. From these, we estimate D_1 by solving the previous equation:

$$D_1 \approx 2D_B - D_0.$$

Accordingly, we define our new diameter for the circle of confusion D by the equation

$$D = \max(D_0, 2D_B - D_0) = 2\max(D_0, D_B) - D_0.$$

Let D_1 be the larger circle of confusion. This equation will transition smoothly from a diameter of D_1 at the boundary between the two regions to D_0 at the limits of the blur radius inside region 0. This is exactly what we want.

The maximum function is continuous when its inputs are continuous. The D_0 input is not actually continuous, because it is the unblurred diameter for this pixel's circle of

Chapter 28   Practical Post-Process Depth of Field

confusion. This function was chosen to be continuous along certain straight edges. Most straight-edge boundaries match these assumptions quite well within the blur radius. However, there are some objectionable discontinuities, particularly at 90-degree corners, so we apply one last small blur to fix this issue.

Figures 28-3 and 28-4 illustrate this process applied to a sample image. Each row is a particular sample image. The first column is the unprocessed image, and the second column is the image with the filter applied without the final blur. The third column is the final blurred result. Pure white in the input image represents the maximum circle of confusion; pixels that are black are in focus.

The first image is a simple black-and-white scene. Visually, these letters are floating in space very near the camera. The filter works well overall, but there are still some sharp edges at the corners of the letters, particularly in the uppercase "I". Blurring the image gets rid of the hard edge. It still leaves a gradient that is steeper than ideal, but it is good enough for our purposes.

The second row applies a small Gaussian blur to the sample image of the first row before applying the filter. This corresponds to looking at an object at a glancing angle. This results in a clear outline around the original image after it has been filtered. The final blur significantly dampens this artifact, but it doesn't completely fix it.

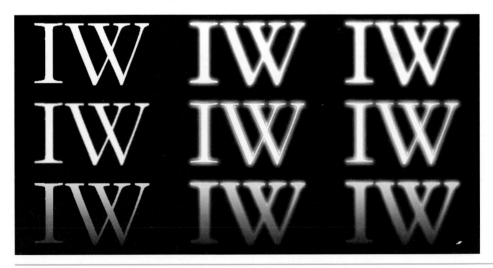

Figure 28-3. Foreground Circle of Confusion Radius Calculation Applied to Some Test Images
Top to bottom: Simple black-and-white text, the same text with a small blur applied, and the same text with a gradient applied. Left to right: Original image, filtered version of the original image, and blurred version of the filtered image.

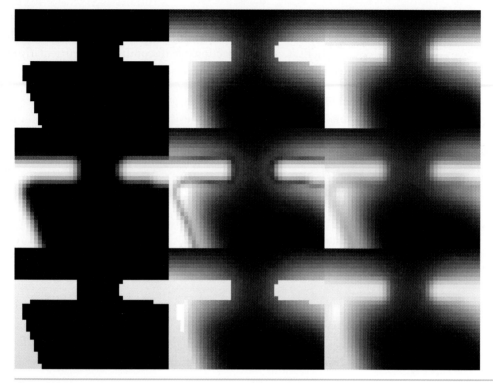

Figure 28-4. Zoom on the Top Left Corner of the "W" in Figure 28-3

The final row applies a gradient to the original image. This corresponds to the typical case of an object that gradually recedes into the distance. The radius for the circle of confusion is overestimated in "valleys" and underestimated in "peaks," but it is continuous and there are none of the really objectionable artifacts from the second row. Again, the final blur dampens this artifact. Note that the gradient within the text is preserved.

28.5 The Complete Algorithm

Our completed algorithm consists of four stages:

1. Downsample the CoC for the foreground objects.
2. Blur the near CoC image.
3. Calculate the actual foreground CoC from the blurred and unblurred images.
4. Apply the foreground and background CoC image in one last full-screen pass that applies a variable-width blur.

28.5.1 Depth Information

Our algorithm is implemented using DirectX 9 hardware, which does not allow reading a depth buffer as a texture. We get around this limitation by binding a 32-bit floating-point color buffer during our depth pre-pass. Although we do not require full 32-bit precision, we picked that format because it is the least common denominator across all of our target hardware.

The pixel shader during depth pre-pass merely passes the world-space distance from the vertex shader through to the render target. In the pixel shader, we kill transparent pixels for 1-bit alpha textures by using the HLSL `clip()` intrinsic function.

In calling our technique a "pure post-process that can easily be plugged into an existing engine," we assume that the engine already generates this information. Our performance impact analysis also assumes that this information is already available. Our technique requires more than just applying post-processing modifications to a rendering engine if this assumption is invalid.

28.5.2 Variable-Width Blur

We need a fast variable-width blur to apply the circle of confusion to the scene. We could use a Poisson disk as in the original stochastic approach based on Scheuermann 2004. However, we generate the blur by approaching it differently. We consider that each pixel has a function that gives it its color based on the CoC diameter. We then approximate this function using a piecewise linear curve between three different blur radii and the original unblurred sample.

The two larger blur radii are calculated in the RGB channels at the same time the down-sampled CoC is calculated in the alpha channel. The smallest blur radius is solved using five texture lookups, to average 17 pixels in a 5×5 grid, using the pattern in Figure 28-5.

Note that the center sample of this pattern reuses the texture lookup for the unblurred original pixel color.

This small blur is crucial for closely approximating the actual blur color. Without it, the image does not appear to blur continuously, but instead it appears to cross-fade with a blurred version of itself. We also found that a simple linear interpolation gave better results than a higher-polynomial spline because the splines tended to extrapolate colors for some pixels.

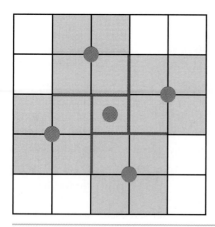

Figure 28-5. Sample Positions for Small Blur

28.5.3 Circle of Confusion Radius

We are given the distance of each pixel to the camera in a depth texture. We see from Equation 1 that an accurate model of the radius for the circle of confusion can be calculated from this using only a reciprocal and a multiply-add instruction, with the engine providing suitable scale and bias constants.

However, we again take advantage of the freedom in computer simulation to forego physical plausibility in favor of artistic control. Artistically, we want some depth range to be in focus, with specific amounts of blur before and beyond it. It is unclear how to convert this into physical camera dimensions. The most intuitive way to edit this is by using a piecewise linear curve, as in Figure 28-6. The artists specify the near and far blur radii and the start and end distances for each of the three regions. We disable blurring for any region that has degenerate values, so artists can blur only the foreground or only the background if they wish.

In practice, we pick a *world-near-end distance* and a *world-far-start distance* that enclose everything that the player is likely to find of interest. We then set the *world-near-start distance* based on the world-near-end distance. Similarly, we set the *world far-end distance* based on the world-far-start distance.

28.5.4 First-Person Weapon Considerations

Infinity Ward develops first-person shooter games. The player's weapon (view model) is very important in these games because it is always in view and it is the primary way

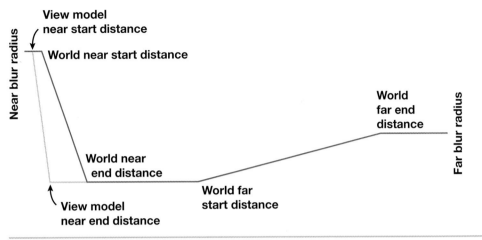

Figure 28-6. Graph of the Circle of Confusion

that the player interacts with the environment. DoF settings that looked good on the view model appeared to have no effect on the environment, while DoF settings that looked good on the nearby environment blurred the player's weapon excessively.

Our solution was to provide separate settings for the blur on the world and the player's view model. This makes no physical sense, but it provides a better experience for the player—perhaps because it properly conveys the effects of DoF whether the player is focusing on the important parts of the weapon or on the action in the environment. Each weapon configures its own near and far distances, with separate values used when the shooter aims with the weapon and when he or she holds it at the hip.

For this technique to work, we must know whether each pixel belongs to the view model or to the world. Our depth information is stored in a 32-bit floating-point render target. Using negative depths proved the most convenient way to get this bit of information. The normal lookup just requires a free absolute value modifier. This also leads to an efficient implementation for picking the near circle of confusion. We can calculate the near CoC for 4 pixels concurrently using a single `mad_sat` instruction. We calculate the near CoC for both the view model and the world in this way, and then we pick the appropriate CoC for all 4 pixels with a single `min` instruction.

28.5.5 The Complete Shader Listing

Most of the passes of our algorithm in Listing 28-1 are used to generate the near circle of confusion so that it is continuous and provides soft edges for foreground objects. We also want a large Gaussian blur radius, so we share GPU computation to concurrently calculate the blurred version of the scene and the near circle of confusion.

We specify the large blur radius in pixels at a normalized 480p resolution so that it is independent of actual screen resolution. However, the two small blurs are based on the actual screen resolution. We experimentally determined that the 17-tap small blur corresponds to a 1.4-pixel Gaussian blur at native resolution, and that the medium blur corresponds to a 3.6-pixel Gaussian blur at native resolution.

Listing 28-1. A Shader That Downsamples the Scene and Initializes the Near CoC

```
// These are set by the game engine.
// The render target size is one-quarter the scene rendering size.
sampler colorSampler;
sampler depthSampler;
const float2 dofEqWorld;
const float2 dofEqWeapon;
const float2 dofRowDelta;   // float2( 0, 0.25 / renderTargetHeight )
const float2 invRenderTargetSize;
const float4x4 worldViewProj;

struct PixelInput
{
  float4 position : POSITION;
  float2 tcColor0 : TEXCOORD0;
  float2 tcColor1 : TEXCOORD1;
  float2 tcDepth0 : TEXCOORD2;
  float2 tcDepth1 : TEXCOORD3;
  float2 tcDepth2 : TEXCOORD4;
  float2 tcDepth3 : TEXCOORD5;
};

PixelInput DofDownVS( float4 pos : POSITION, float2 tc : TEXCOORD0 )
{
  PixelInput pixel;

  pixel.position = mul( pos, worldViewProj );

  pixel.tcColor0 = tc + float2( -1.0, -1.0 ) * invRenderTargetSize;
  pixel.tcColor1 = tc + float2( +1.0, -1.0 ) * invRenderTargetSize;
  pixel.tcDepth0 = tc + float2( -1.5, -1.5 ) * invRenderTargetSize;
```

```
  pixel.tcDepth1 = tc + float2( -0.5, -1.5 ) * invRenderTargetSize;
  pixel.tcDepth2 = tc + float2( +0.5, -1.5 ) * invRenderTargetSize;
  pixel.tcDepth3 = tc + float2( +1.5, -1.5 ) * invRenderTargetSize;

  return pixel;
}

half4 DofDownPS( const PixelInput pixel ) : COLOR
{
  half3 color;
  half maxCoc;
  float4 depth;
  half4 viewCoc;
  half4 sceneCoc;
  half4 curCoc;
  half4 coc;
  float2 rowOfs[4];

  // "rowOfs" reduces how many moves PS2.0 uses to emulate swizzling.
  rowOfs[0] = 0;
  rowOfs[1] = dofRowDelta.xy;
  rowOfs[2] = dofRowDelta.xy * 2;
  rowOfs[3] = dofRowDelta.xy * 3;

  // Use bilinear filtering to average 4 color samples for free.
  color = 0;
  color += tex2D( colorSampler, pixel.tcColor0.xy + rowOfs[0] ).rgb;
  color += tex2D( colorSampler, pixel.tcColor1.xy + rowOfs[0] ).rgb;
  color += tex2D( colorSampler, pixel.tcColor0.xy + rowOfs[2] ).rgb;
  color += tex2D( colorSampler, pixel.tcColor1.xy + rowOfs[2] ).rgb;
  color /= 4;

  // Process 4 samples at a time to use vector hardware efficiently.
  // The CoC will be 1 if the depth is negative, so use "min" to pick
  // between "sceneCoc" and "viewCoc".
  depth[0] = tex2D( depthSampler, pixel.tcDepth0.xy + rowOfs[0] ).r;
  depth[1] = tex2D( depthSampler, pixel.tcDepth1.xy + rowOfs[0] ).r;
  depth[2] = tex2D( depthSampler, pixel.tcDepth2.xy + rowOfs[0] ).r;
  depth[3] = tex2D( depthSampler, pixel.tcDepth3.xy + rowOfs[0] ).r;
  viewCoc = saturate( dofEqWeapon.x * -depth + dofEqWeapon.y );
```

```
    sceneCoc = saturate( dofEqWorld.x * depth + dofEqWorld.y );
    curCoc = min( viewCoc, sceneCoc );
    coc = curCoc;

    depth[0] = tex2D( depthSampler, pixel.tcDepth0.xy + rowOfs[1] ).r;
    depth[1] = tex2D( depthSampler, pixel.tcDepth1.xy + rowOfs[1] ).r;
    depth[2] = tex2D( depthSampler, pixel.tcDepth2.xy + rowOfs[1] ).r;
    depth[3] = tex2D( depthSampler, pixel.tcDepth3.xy + rowOfs[1] ).r;
    viewCoc = saturate( dofEqWeapon.x * -depth + dofEqWeapon.y );
    sceneCoc = saturate( dofEqWorld.x * depth + dofEqWorld.y );
    curCoc = min( viewCoc, sceneCoc );
    coc = max( coc, curCoc );

    depth[0] = tex2D( depthSampler, pixel.tcDepth0.xy + rowOfs[2] ).r;
    depth[1] = tex2D( depthSampler, pixel.tcDepth1.xy + rowOfs[2] ).r;
    depth[2] = tex2D( depthSampler, pixel.tcDepth2.xy + rowOfs[2] ).r;
    depth[3] = tex2D( depthSampler, pixel.tcDepth3.xy + rowOfs[2] ).r;
    viewCoc = saturate( dofEqWeapon.x * -depth + dofEqWeapon.y );
    sceneCoc = saturate( dofEqWorld.x * depth + dofEqWorld.y );
    curCoc = min( viewCoc, sceneCoc );
    coc = max( coc, curCoc );

    depth[0] = tex2D( depthSampler, pixel.tcDepth0.xy + rowOfs[3] ).r;
    depth[1] = tex2D( depthSampler, pixel.tcDepth1.xy + rowOfs[3] ).r;
    depth[2] = tex2D( depthSampler, pixel.tcDepth2.xy + rowOfs[3] ).r;
    depth[3] = tex2D( depthSampler, pixel.tcDepth3.xy + rowOfs[3] ).r;
    viewCoc = saturate( dofEqWeapon.x * -depth + dofEqWeapon.y );
    sceneCoc = saturate( dofEqWorld.x * depth + dofEqWorld.y );
    curCoc = min( viewCoc, sceneCoc );
    coc = max( coc, curCoc );

    maxCoc = max( max( coc[0], coc[1] ), max( coc[2], coc[3] ) );

    return half4( color, maxCoc );
}
```

We apply a Gaussian blur to the image generated by `DofDownsample()`. We do this with code that automatically divides the blur radius into an optimal sequence of horizontal and vertical filters that use bilinear filtering to read two samples at a time. Additionally, we apply a single unseparated 2D pass when it will use no more texture lookups than two separated 1D passes. In the 2D case, each texture lookup applies four samples. Listing 28-2 shows the code.

Listing 28-2. A Pixel Shader That Calculates the Actual Near CoC

```
// These are set by the game engine.
sampler shrunkSampler;   // Output of DofDownsample()
sampler blurredSampler;  // Blurred version of the shrunk sampler

// This is the pixel shader function that calculates the actual
// value used for the near circle of confusion.
// "texCoords" are 0 at the bottom left pixel and 1 at the top right.
float4 DofNearCoc( const float2 texCoords )
{
  float3 color;
  float coc;
  half4 blurred;
  half4 shrunk;

  shrunk = tex2D( shrunkSampler, texCoords );
  blurred = tex2D( blurredSampler, texCoords );

  color = shrunk.rgb;
  coc = 2 * max( blurred.a, shrunk.a ) - shrunk.a;

  return float4( color, coc );
}
```

In Listing 28-3 we apply a small 3×3 blur to the result of `DofNearCoc()` to smooth out any discontinuities it introduced.

Listing 28-3. This Shader Blurs the Near CoC and Downsampled Color Image Once

```
// This vertex and pixel shader applies a 3 x 3 blur to the image in
// colorMapSampler, which is the same size as the render target.
// The sample weights are 1/16 in the corners, 2/16 on the edges,
// and 4/16 in the center.

sampler colorSampler;   // Output of DofNearCoc()
float2 invRenderTargetSize;

struct PixelInput
{
  float4 position : POSITION;
  float4 texCoords : TEXCOORD0;
};
```

```
PixelInput SmallBlurVS( float4 position, float2 texCoords )
{
  PixelInput pixel;
  const float4 halfPixel = { -0.5, 0.5, -0.5, 0.5 };

  pixel.position = Transform_ObjectToClip( position );
  pixel.texCoords = texCoords.xxyy + halfPixel * invRenderTargetSize;

  return pixel;
}

float4 SmallBlurPS( const PixelInput pixel )
{
  float4 color;

  color = 0;
  color += tex2D( colorSampler, pixel.texCoords.xz );
  color += tex2D( colorSampler, pixel.texCoords.yz );
  color += tex2D( colorSampler, pixel.texCoords.xw );
  color += tex2D( colorSampler, pixel.texCoords.yw );
  return color / 4;
}
```

Our last shader, in Listing 28-4, applies the variable-width blur to the screen. We use a premultiplied alpha blend with the frame buffer to avoid actually looking up the color sample under the current pixel. In the shader, we treat all color samples that we actually read as having alpha equal to 1. Treating the unread center sample as having color equal to 0 and alpha equal to 0 inside the shader gives the correct results on the screen.

Listing 28-4. This Pixel Shader Merges the Far CoC with the Near CoC and Applies It to the Screen

```
sampler colorSampler;       // Original source image
sampler smallBlurSampler;   // Output of SmallBlurPS()
sampler largeBlurSampler;   // Blurred output of DofDownsample()
float2 invRenderTargetSize;
float4 dofLerpScale;
float4 dofLerpBias;
float3 dofEqFar;
```

```
float4 tex2Doffset( sampler s, float2 tc, float2 offset )
{
  return tex2D( s, tc + offset * invRenderTargetSize );
}


half3 GetSmallBlurSample( float2 texCoords )
{
  half3 sum;
  const half weight = 4.0 / 17;

  sum = 0;   // Unblurred sample done by alpha blending
  sum += weight * tex2Doffset( colorSampler, tc, +0.5, -1.5 ).rgb;
  sum += weight * tex2Doffset( colorSampler, tc, -1.5, -0.5 ).rgb;
  sum += weight * tex2Doffset( colorSampler, tc, -0.5, +1.5 ).rgb;
  sum += weight * tex2Doffset( colorSampler, tc, +1.5, +0.5 ).rgb;
  return sum;
}


half4 InterpolateDof( half3 small, half3 med, half3 large, half t )
{
  half4 weights;
  half3 color;
  half  alpha;

  // Efficiently calculate the cross-blend weights for each sample.
  // Let the unblurred sample to small blur fade happen over distance
  // d0, the small to medium blur over distance d1, and the medium to
  // large blur over distance d2, where d0 + d1 + d2 = 1.
  // dofLerpScale = float4( -1 / d0, -1 / d1, -1 / d2, 1 / d2 );
  // dofLerpBias = float4( 1, (1 - d2) / d1, 1 / d2, (d2 - 1) / d2 );
  weights = saturate( t * dofLerpScale + dofLerpBias );
  weights.yz = min( weights.yz, 1 - weights.xy );

  // Unblurred sample with weight "weights.x" done by alpha blending
  color = weights.y * small + weights.z * med + weights.w * large;
  alpha = dot( weights.yzw, half3( 16.0 / 17, 1.0, 1.0 ) );
  return half4( color, alpha );
}
```

```
half4 ApplyDepthOfField( const float2 texCoords )
{
  half3 small;
  half4 med;
  half3 large;
  half depth;
  half nearCoc;
  half farCoc;
  half coc;

  small = GetSmallBlurSample( texCoords );
  med = tex2D( smallBlurSampler, texCoords );
  large = tex2D( largeBlurSampler, texCoords ).rgb;
  nearCoc = med.a;

  depth = tex2D( depthSampler, texCoords ).r;
  if ( depth > 1.0e6 )
  {
    coc = nearCoc; // We don't want to blur the sky.
  }
  else
  {
    // dofEqFar.x and dofEqFar.y specify the linear ramp to convert
    // to depth for the distant out-of-focus region.
    // dofEqFar.z is the ratio of the far to the near blur radius.
    farCoc = saturate( dofEqFar.x * depth + dofEqFar.y );
    coc = max( nearCoc, farCoc * dofEqFar.z );
  }

  return InterpolateDof( small, med.rgb, large, coc );
}
```

28.6 Conclusion

Not much arithmetic is going on in these shaders, so their cost is dominated by the texture lookups.

- Generating the quarter-resolution image uses four color lookups and 16 depth lookups for each target pixel in the quarter-resolution image, equaling 1.25 lookups per pixel in the original image.

- The small radius blur adds another four lookups per pixel.
- Applying the variable-width blur requires reading a depth and two precalculated blur levels, which adds up to three more lookups per pixel.
- Getting the adjusted circle of confusion requires two texture lookups per pixel in the quarter-resolution image, or 0.125 samples per pixel of the original image.
- The small blur applied to the near CoC image uses another four texture lookups, for another 0.25 samples per pixel in the original.

This equals 8.625 samples per pixel, not counting the variable number of samples needed to apply the large Gaussian blur. Implemented as a separable filter, the blur will typically use no more than two passes with eight texture lookups each, which gives 17 taps with bilinear filtering. This averages out to one sample per pixel in the original image. The expected number of texture lookups per pixel is about 9.6.

Frame-buffer bandwidth is another consideration. This technique writes to the quarter-resolution image once for the original downsample, and then another two times (typically) for the large Gaussian blur. There are two more passes over the quarter-resolution image—to apply Equation 1 and to blur its results slightly. Finally, each pixel in the original image is written once to get the final output. This works out to 1.3125 writes for every pixel in the original image.

Similarly, there are six render target switches in this technique, again assuming only two passes for the large Gaussian blur.

The measured performance cost was 1 to 1.5 milliseconds at 1024×768 on our tests with a Radeon X1900 and GeForce 7900. The performance hit on next-generation consoles is similar. This is actually faster than the original implementation based on Scheuermann 2004, presumably because it uses fewer than half as many texture reads.

28.7 Limitations and Future Work

When you use our approach, focused objects will bleed onto unfocused background objects. This is the least objectionable artifact with this technique and with post-process DoF techniques in general. These artifacts could be reduced by taking additional depth samples for the 17-tap blur. This should be adequate because, as we have seen, the background needs to use a smaller blur radius than the foreground.

The second artifact is inherent to the technique: You cannot increase the blur radius for near objects so much that it becomes obvious that the technique is actually a blur of the screen instead of a blur of the unfocused objects. Figure 28-7 is a worst-case example of this problem, whereas Figure 28-8 shows a more typical situation. The center image in Figure 28-8 shows a typical blur radius. The right image has twice that blur radius; even the relatively large rock in the background has been smeared out of existence. This becomes particularly objectionable as the camera moves, showing up as a haze around the foreground object.

The radius at which this happens depends on the size of the object that is out of focus and the amount of detail in the geometry that should be in focus. Smaller objects that are out of focus, and focused objects that have higher frequencies, require a smaller maximum blur radius. This could be overcome by rendering the foreground objects into a separate buffer so that the color information that gets blurred is only for the foreground objects. This would require carefully handling missing pixels. It also makes the technique more intrusive into the rendering pipeline.

Finally, we don't explicitly handle transparency. Transparent surfaces use the CoC of the first opaque object behind them. To fix this, transparent objects could be drawn after depth of field has been applied to all opaque geometry. They could be given an impression of DoF by biasing the texture lookups toward lower mipmap levels. Particle effects may also benefit from slightly increasing the size of the particle as it goes out of focus. Transparent objects that share edges with opaque objects, such as windows, may still have some objectionable artifacts at the boundary. Again, this makes the technique intrusive. We found that completely ignoring transparency works well enough in most situations.

Figure 28-7. The Worst-Case Scenario for Our Algorithm
Thin foreground geometry excessively blurs the high-frequency information in the background.

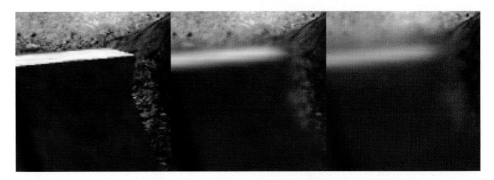

Figure 28-8. If the Blur Radius Is Too Large, the Effect Breaks Down
Left: The source image. Middle: A blur radius of 7.5. Right: A blur radius of 15.

28.8 References

Demers, Joe. 2004. "Depth of Field: A Survey of Techniques." In *GPU Gems*, edited by Randima Fernando, pp. 375–390. Addison-Wesley.

Kass, Michael, Aaron Lefohn, and John Owens. 2006. "Interactive Depth of Field Using Simulated Diffusion on a GPU." Technical report. Pixar Animation Studios. Available online at http://graphics.pixar.com/DepthOfField/paper.pdf.

Kosloff, Todd Jerome, and Brian A. Barsky. 2007. "An Algorithm for Rendering Generalized Depth of Field Effects Based On Simulated Heat Diffusion." Technical Report No. UCB/EECS-2007-19. Available online at http://www.eecs.berkeley.edu/Pubs/TechRpts/2007/EECS-2007-19.pdf.

Křivánek, Jaroslav, Jiří Žára, and Kadi Bouatouch. 2003. "Fast Depth of Field Rendering with Surface Splatting." Presentation at Computer Graphics International 2003. Available online at http://www.cgg.cvut.cz/~xkrivanj/papers/cgi2003/9-3_krivanek_j.pdf.

Mulder, Jurriaan, and Robert van Liere. 2000. "Fast Perception-Based Depth of Field Rendering." Available online at http://www.cwi.nl/~robertl/papers/2000/vrst/paper.pdf.

Potmesil, Michael, and Indranil Chakravarty. 1981. "A Lens and Aperture Camera Model for Synthetic Image Generation." In *Proceedings of the 8th Annual Conference on Computer Graphics and Interactive Techniques*, pp. 297–305.

Scheuermann, Thorsten. 2004. "Advanced Depth of Field." Presentation at Game Developers Conference 2004. Available online at http://ati.amd.com/developer/gdc/Scheuermann_DepthOfField.pdf.

PART V
PHYSICS SIMULATION

Physics simulation presents a high degree of data parallelism and is computationally intensive, making it a good candidate for execution on the GPU. What's more, the outcome of the simulation is often consumed by the GPU for visualization, so it makes sense to have it produced directly in graphics memory by the GPU too. This section assembles a few successful GPU implementations of various algorithms used in physics simulation. There are bound to be an increasing number of them in the future as GPUs become more versatile and powerful.

Video games, virtual reality systems, and computer-generated movies make heavy use of physically based simulations to increase the realism of their worlds. The first fundamental method used by physics engines to give life to the majority of the objects populating these worlds is *rigid body dynamics*. In **Chapter 29, "Real-Time Rigid Body Simulation on GPUs," Takahiro Harada** from the University of Tokyo proposes an implementation of rigid body dynamics on the GPU that represents a rigid body as a set of particles. This approach builds on the tremendous floating-point processing power of the GPU to provide a straight forward way of trading accuracy for speed. In addition, it extends naturally to nonrigid bodies, such as fluids, and allows rigid and nonrigid bodies to both move and interact in the same unified framework.

Water, fire, and smoke are other key elements that contribute to the vividness of virtual worlds, and fluid simulation is the best technique to achieve a high-quality implementation of these effects. In **Chapter 30, "Real-Time Simulation and Rendering of 3D Fluids," Keenan Crane** from the University of Illinois at Urbana-Champaign and **Ignacio Llamas** and **Sarah Tariq** from NVIDIA Corporation demonstrate that volumetric fluid simulation is a practical solution for today's games. The authors give a complete description, from GPU simulation to rendering, of how they used this approach in an actual game to achieve compelling visuals that blend and interact with the dynamic environment.

Of course, physics simulation is found in many domains other than computer graphics. In particular, the N-body problem—simulating a system of N bodies where each body exerts a force on all the other bodies—arises in areas as diverse as astrophysics, molecular dynamics, plasma physics, as well as radiosity rendering. In **Chapter 31, "Fast N-Body Simulation with CUDA," Lars Nyland** and **Mark Harris** from NVIDIA and **Jan Prins** from the University of North Carolina at Chapel Hill show how to best map this problem to the CUDA programming model. Not only that, they solve the problem so efficiently that their implementation outperforms an optimized CPU implementation many times over.

A very time-consuming step in most physics simulations is *collision detection*, so this undertaking is a primary target for optimization. Two chapters in our section take up this task and leverage CUDA to achieve significant speedups. In **Chapter 32, "Broad Phase Collision Detection with CUDA," Scott Le Grand** from NVIDIA focuses on the broad phase of collision detection, where pairs of objects that cannot possibly collide are quickly culled away. He presents a CUDA implementation of it based on parallel spatial subdivision. In particular, Le Grand exposes how to combine basic parallel programming techniques, such as parallel reduction and prefix sum, to come up with a CUDA implementation of radix sort—a key step of the overall algorithm. Next, in **Chapter 33, "LCP Algorithms for Collision Detection Using CUDA," Peter Kipfer** from Havok focuses on the narrow phase of collision detection, where exact collision detection is performed for each remaining pair of objects after the broad phase. Computing the distance between two convex polyhedra can be translated into a linear complementarity problem that he resolves through a parallel algorithm with a suitable implementation in CUDA.

The GPU can also accelerate data preprocessing, as illustrated by **Kenny Erleben** from the University of Copenhagen and **Henrik Dohlmann** from 3Dfacto R&D in **Chapter 34, "Signed Distance Fields Using Single-Pass GPU Scan Conversion of Tetrahedra."** Distance fields, which provide the distance from any point in space to the surface of an object, have applications in collision detection—in particular, between rigid and deformable bodies—but in many other fields as well, such as modeling, ray tracing, and path planning. In this chapter the authors describe an algorithm for computing distance fields that is amenable to a GPU implementation. They show how any programmable GPU can be used in a straightforward way to significantly speed it up. The latest generation of GPUs comes packed with new features that enable even more of the algorithm to be ported over.

Cyril Zeller, NVIDIA Corporation

Chapter 29

Real-Time Rigid Body Simulation on GPUs

Takahiro Harada
University of Tokyo

We can easily calculate realistic object motions and produce high-quality computer animations by using physically based simulation. For example, making an animation, by hand, of a falling chess piece is not difficult. However, it is very hard to animate several thousand falling chess pieces, as shown in Figure 29-1.

In the case of Figure 29-1, simulation is the only practical solution. Simulation remains computationally expensive, though, so any technique that can speed it up, such as the one we propose in this chapter, is welcome. As for real-time applications such as games, in which a user interacts with objects in the scene, there is no other alternative than simulation because the user interaction is unpredictable. Moreover, real-time applications are much more demanding because the simulation frame rate has to be at least as high as the rendering frame rate.

In this chapter, we describe how we use the tremendous computational power provided by GPUs to accelerate rigid body simulation. Our technique simulates a large number of rigid bodies entirely on the GPU in real time. Section 29.1 outlines our approach and Section 29.2 provides a detailed description of its implementation on the GPU.

Several studies use GPUs to accelerate physically based simulations, such as cellular automata (Owens et al. 2005), Eulerian fluid dynamics (Harris 2004), and cloth simulation (Zeller 2005). A common characteristic of these previous studies is that the connectivity of the simulated elements—either particles or grid cells—does not change

Figure 29-1. Real-Time Simulation Results of Chess Pieces and Tori
When 16,384 chess pieces and 10,922 tori are dropped, the simulation runs at 44 frames/sec and 68 frames/sec, respectively, including rendering time on a GeForce 8800 GTX.

during the simulation. However, our technique also works even if the connectivity between elements changes over time. We illustrate this in Section 29.3 by briefly discussing how it can be applied to other kinds of physically based simulations, such as granular materials, fluids, and coupling.

29.1 Introduction

The motion of a rigid body is computed by dividing motion into two parts:—translation and rotation—as shown in Figure 29-2. Translation describes the motion of the center of mass, whereas rotation describes how the rigid body rotates around the center of mass. A detailed explanation can be found in Baraff 1997.

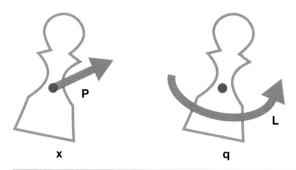

Figure 29-2. Translation and Rotation Parts of a Rigid Body Motion

29.1.1 Translation

The motion of the center of mass is easy to understand because it is the same as the motion of a particle. When a force **F** acts on a rigid body, this force can cause a variation of its linear momentum **P**. More precisely, the time derivative of **P** is equal to **F**:

$$\frac{d\mathbf{P}}{dt} = \mathbf{F}. \tag{1}$$

We obtain the velocity **v** of the center of mass from **P** and the rigid body's mass M, using the following formula:

$$\mathbf{v} = \frac{\mathbf{P}}{M}. \tag{2}$$

And the velocity is the time derivative of the position **x** of the center of mass:

$$\frac{d\mathbf{x}}{dt} = \mathbf{v}. \tag{3}$$

29.1.2 Rotation

A force **F** that acts at some point of a rigid body that is different from the center of mass can also cause a variation of the rigid body's angular momentum **L**. This variation depends on the relative position $\mathbf{r}$ of the acting point to the center of mass. More precisely, the time derivative of $\mathbf{L}$ is the torque that is the cross-product of $\mathbf{r}$ and $\mathbf{F}$:

$$\frac{d\mathbf{L}}{dt} = \mathbf{r} \times \mathbf{F}. \tag{4}$$

Then the angular velocity $\mathbf{w}$, whose norm is the spinning speed, is derived from the angular momentum $\mathbf{L}$:

$$\mathbf{w} = \mathbf{I}(t)^{-1}\mathbf{L}, \tag{5}$$

where the 3×3 matrix $\mathbf{I}(t)$ is the inertia tensor at time t and $\mathbf{I}(t)^{-1}$ is its inverse. The inertia tensor is a physical value of a rigid body, which indicates its resistance against rotational motion. Because the inertia tensor changes as the orientation of a rigid body changes, it must be reevaluated at every time step. To calculate $\mathbf{I}(t)^{-1}$, we have to introduce the rotation matrix $\mathbf{R}(t)$, which describes the orientation of a rigid body at time t. The appendix shows how to calculate a rotation matrix from a quaternion. $\mathbf{I}(t)^{-1}$ is obtained from the rotation matrix at time t as follows:

$$\mathbf{I}(t)^{-1} = \mathbf{R}(t)\mathbf{I}(0)^{-1}\mathbf{R}(t)^{T}. \tag{6}$$

Now that we have the angular velocity $\mathbf{w}$, the next step is to calculate the time derivative of the rigid body orientation with angular velocity $\mathbf{w}$. There are two ways to store orientation: using a rotation matrix or using a quaternion. We choose to use a quaternion, which is often employed for many reasons. The most important reason is that a rotation matrix accumulates nonrotational motion with time because a matrix represents not only rotation, but also stretch. Therefore, numerical errors that add up during repeated combinations of rotation matrices cause the rigid body to get distorted.

On the other hand, quaternions do not have degrees of freedom for nonrotational motion, and so the rigid body does not get distorted. Also, the quaternion representation is well suited to being implemented on the GPU because it consists of four elements. Thus, it can be stored in the RGBA channels of a pixel. A quaternion $\mathbf{q} = [s, v_x, v_y, v_z]$ represents a rotation of s radians about an axis (v_x, v_y, v_z). For simplicity, we write it as $\mathbf{q} = [s, \mathbf{v}]$, where $\mathbf{v} = (v_x, v_y, v_z)$. The variation of quaternion $d\mathbf{q}$ with angular velocity $\mathbf{w}$ is calculated as the following:

$$d\mathbf{q} = \left[\cos\left(\frac{\theta}{2}\right), \ \mathbf{a}\sin\left(\frac{\theta}{2}\right)\right], \tag{7}$$

where $\mathbf{a} = \mathbf{w}/|\mathbf{w}|$ is the rotation axis and $\theta = |\mathbf{w} \, dt|$ is the rotation angle.

Then the quaternion at time $t + dt$ is updated as follows:

$$\mathbf{q}(t + dt) = d\mathbf{q} \times \mathbf{q}(t). \tag{8}$$

29.1.3 Shape Representation

Now that we know how to calculate rigid body motions, the next step is to compute collision to deal with rigid body interactions. There are several ways to compute collision. In this subsection, we describe a method that is well suited to GPUs and real-time simulation.

In our method, collision detection is based not on the polygons that represent the rigid bodies, but on particles, as done by Bell et al. (2005) and Tanaka et al. (2006). A rigid body is represented by a set of particles that are spheres of identical size, as shown in Figure 29-3. To generate the particles inside a rigid body, we discretize space around the rigid body by defining a 3D grid that encloses it, and we assign one particle for each voxel inside the rigid body. Assuming that the rigid body is represented as a closed mesh, this can be done by casting rays parallel to some axis—usually one of the grid edges—and intersecting them with the mesh. As we progress along a ray, starting from outside the mesh and going from one voxel to the next, we track the number of times the ray intersects the mesh. If this number is odd, we mark each voxel as "inside" the rigid body.

The GPU can accelerate this computation—particle generation from a mesh—by using a technique called *depth peeling*. Depth peeling extracts depth images from 3D objects in depth order (Everitt 2001). When the object is orthographically projected in the direction of the axis, the first depth image extracted by depth peeling contains the depths of the first intersection points of each ray with the mesh (rays enter the mesh at

Figure 29-3. Particle Representations of a Chess Piece

these points). The second depth image contains the depths of the second intersection points of each ray with the mesh (rays exit the mesh at these points), and so on. In other words, *odd-numbered depth images* contain the depths of the entry points and *even-numbered depth images* contain the depths of the exit points.

After the extraction, a final rendering pass determines whether or not each voxel is located inside the rigid body. The render target is a flat 3D texture (as described later in Section 29.2.2). The fragment shader (FS) takes a voxel as input and looks up all depth images to determine if the voxel's depth falls between the depth of an odd-numbered image and the depth of an even-numbered image, in that order. If this is the case, the voxel is inside the object. Figure 29-4 illustrates this process.

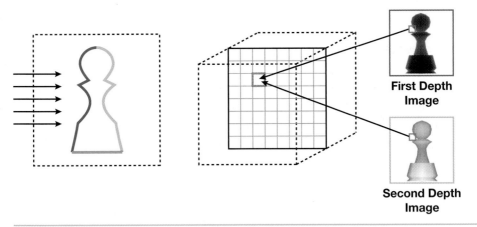

Figure 29-4. Particle Generation from a Polygon Model by Using Depth Peeling
Left: The blue curve indicates the first depth layer, and the green curve indicates the second depth layer when the object is projected from the direction indicated by the arrows. Right: Each voxel is tested to see whether it is inside the object or not, based on the depth images.

29.1.4 Collision Detection

Because we represent a rigid body as a set of particles, collision detection between rigid bodies with complicated shapes means we simply need to detect collisions between particles. When the distance between two particles is smaller than their diameter, collision occurs. A benefit of this particle representation is the controllability of simulation speed and accuracy. Increasing the resolution of particles increases computation cost—however, we get a more accurate representation of the shape and the accuracy of the simulation improves. Therefore, we can adjust the resolution, depending on the purpose. For example, for real-time applications where computation speed is important, we can lower the resolution.

However, the particle representation involves a larger number of elements, whose collisions must all be computed. If we employ a brute-force strategy, we have to check n^2 pairs for n particles. This approach is impractical, plus it is difficult to solve such a large problem in real time even with current GPUs. Thus, we use a three-dimensional uniform grid to reduce the computational burden. The grid covers the whole computational domain, and the domain is divided into voxels. The voxel index $\mathbf{g} = (g_x, g_y, g_z)$ of a particle at $\mathbf{p} = (p_x, p_y, p_z)$ is calculated as follows:

$$\mathbf{g} = \frac{(\mathbf{p} - \mathbf{s})}{d},$$

(9)

where $\mathbf{s} = (s_x, s_y, s_z)$ is the grid corner with smallest coordinates and d is the side length of a voxel.

Then the particle index is stored in the voxel to which the particle belongs, as shown in Figure 29-8. With the grid, particles that collide with particle i are restricted to (a) the particles whose indices are stored in the voxel that holds the index of particle i and (b) the 26 voxels adjacent to (that is, surrounding) the voxel that holds the index of particle i. The maximum number of particles stored in a voxel is finite (four particles in our implementation) because the interparticle forces work to keep the distance between particles equal to their diameter, as described later in Section 29.2.4. Consequently, the efficiency is improved from $O(n^2)$ to $O(n)$. Computation becomes most efficient when the side length of a voxel is set to the diameter of particles, because the number of voxels we have to search is the smallest: 3^2 in two dimensions and 3^3 in three dimensions.

29.1.5 Collision Reaction

The interparticle forces between colliding pairs are calculated by applying the *discrete element method* (DEM), which is a method for simulating granular materials (Mishra 2003). A repulsive force $\mathbf{f}_{i,s}$ modeled by a linear spring, and a damping force $\mathbf{f}_{i,d}$ modeled by a dashpot—which dissipates energy between particles—are calculated for a particle i colliding with a particle j as the following:

$$\mathbf{f}_{i,s} = -k\left(d - |\mathbf{r}_{ij}|\right)\frac{\mathbf{r}_{ij}}{|\mathbf{r}_{ij}|}$$

(10)

$$\mathbf{f}_{i,d} = \eta \mathbf{v}_{ij},$$

(11)

where k, η, d, $\mathbf{r}_{ij}$, and $\mathbf{v}_{ij}$ are the spring coefficient, damping coefficient, particle diameter, and relative position and velocity of particle j with respect to particle i, respectively. A shear force $\mathbf{f}_{i,t}$ is also modeled as a force proportional to the relative tangential velocity $\mathbf{v}_{ij,t}$:

$$\mathbf{f}_{i,t} = k_t \mathbf{v}_{ij,t},$$

(12)

where the relative tangential velocity is calculated as

$$\mathbf{v}_{ij,t} = \mathbf{v}_{ij} - \left(\mathbf{v}_{ij} \cdot \frac{\mathbf{r}_{ij}}{|\mathbf{r}_{ij}|}\right)\frac{\mathbf{r}_{ij}}{|\mathbf{r}_{ij}|}.$$

(13)

Then the force and torque applied to a rigid body are the sums of the forces exerted on all particles of the rigid body:

$$\mathbf{F}_c = \sum_{i \in RigidBody} \left(\mathbf{f}_{i,s} + \mathbf{f}_{i,d} + \mathbf{f}_{i,t}\right)$$

(14)

$$\mathbf{T}_c = \sum_{i \in RigidBody} \left(\mathbf{r}_i \times \left(\mathbf{f}_{i,s} + \mathbf{f}_{i,d} + \mathbf{f}_{i,t}\right)\right),$$

(15)

where $\mathbf{r}_i$ is the current relative position of particle i to the center of mass.

29.2 Rigid Body Simulation on the GPU

29.2.1 Overview

So far we have described the basic algorithm of rigid body simulation. In this section we explain how to implement this simulation on the GPU.

An iteration consists of the following five stages, which are shown in the flow chart in Figure 29-5.

1. Computation of particle values
2. Grid generation
3. Collision detection and reaction
4. Computation of momenta
5. Computation of position and quaternion

We do not describe basic GPGPU techniques; readers unfamiliar with these techniques can refer to references such as Harris 2004 and Harris 2005.

29.2.2 The Data Structure

To simulate rigid body motion on the GPU, we must store all the physical values for each rigid body as textures. The physical values can be stored in a 1D texture, but a 2D texture is often used because current GPUs have restrictions on the size of 1D textures.

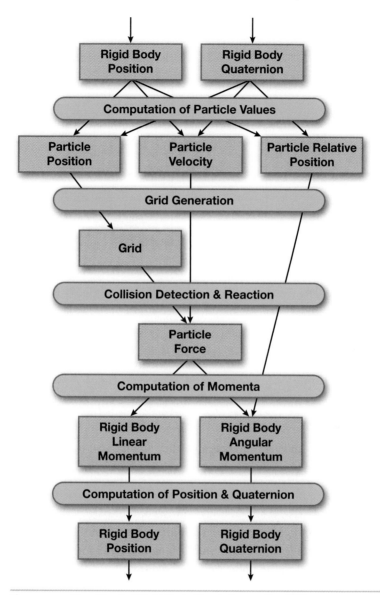

Figure 29-5. Flow Chart of Rigid Body Simulation on the GPU

An index is assigned to each rigid body. To store the physical values of each rigid body in a 2D texture, this index is converted to a 2D index and then the texture coordinates are calculated from the 2D index. Figure 29-6 illustrates this process. Each value of a rigid body is stored in the texel at the texture coordinates. For rigid bodies, we prepare textures for linear and angular momenta, position, and the orientation quaternion. Two

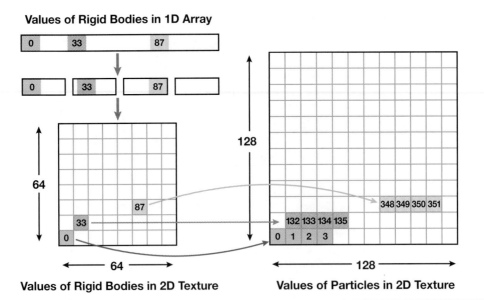

Figure 29-6. Data Structures of the Physical Values of Rigid Bodies and Their Particles
Left: Each rigid body is assigned an index (such as 0, 33, 87). We imagine the values of the rigid bodies as arranged one after the other in a 1D array in order of increasing index. However, these values are actually stored in a 2D texture by dividing the 1D array into partitions of equal size (matching the width of the texture) and by placing them in the texture. Right: Four particles are assigned to the rigid body of index 0 and their values are stored in a second texture, which contains the particle values. The indices of particles are calculated from the rigid body index.

textures are prepared for each value because they are updated by reading from one texture and then writing to the other texture.

We also need textures for the values of the particle's position, velocity, and relative position to the center of mass. If a rigid body consists of four particles, we need a texture four times larger than the textures of rigid bodies. The size of the textures is adjusted, depending on the number of particles that belong to a rigid body. The indices of the particles that belong to a rigid body are calculated from the rigid body index. As with the rigid body index, a particle index is converted into 2D texture coordinates (as shown in Figure 29-6). Because these particle values are dynamically derived from the physical values of rigid bodies, only one texture is enough to store each.

In addition to storing physical values, we need to allocate memory for the uniform grid on the GPU, which is the data structure that helps us search neighboring particles. We use a data layout called a *flat 3D texture*, in which the 3D grid is divided into a set of

2D grids arranged into a large 2D texture (Harris et al. 2003). We arrange the grid this way because GPUs did not support writing to slices of a 3D texture at the time of implementation. The NVIDIA GeForce 8 Series supports it, but there can still be performance advantages in using 2D textures.

To read and write a value in a grid, we need to convert the 3D grid coordinates to the 2D texture coordinates. Let the size of a 3D grid be $L_x \times L_y \times L_z$ and the number of 2D grids in the 2D texture be $D_x \times D_y$, as shown in Figure 29-7. The 2D texture coordinates (u, v) are calculated from the 3D grid coordinates (g_x, g_y, g_z) as follows:

$$u = g_x + L_x \left(g_z - D_x \left\lfloor \frac{g_z}{D_x} \right\rfloor \right) \tag{16}$$

$$v = g_y + L_y \left\lfloor \frac{g_x}{D_x} \right\rfloor . \tag{17}$$

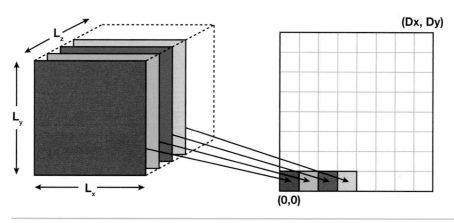

Figure 29-7. A Flat 3D Texture
A 3D grid is divided into a set of 2D grids and they are placed on a large 2D texture.

29.2.3 Step 1: Computation of Particle Values

Most of the following operations use the physical values of particles, so we should compute them first. The current relative position $\mathbf{r}_i$ of a particle i to the center of mass of rigid body j is derived from current quaternion $\mathbf{Q}_j$ and the initial relative position $\mathbf{r}_i^0$ of particle i:

$$\mathbf{r}_i = \mathbf{Q}_j \mathbf{r}_i^0 \mathbf{Q}^*_j . \tag{18}$$

Then the particle position $\mathbf{x}_i$ is computed from the position of the center of mass $\mathbf{X}_j$ and the relative position of the particle $\mathbf{r}_i$ as follows:

$$\mathbf{x}_i = \mathbf{X}_j + \mathbf{r}_i. \tag{19}$$

Particle velocity $\mathbf{v}_i$ is also computed with velocity $\mathbf{V}_j$ and angular velocity $\mathbf{W}_j$ of the rigid body as follows:

$$\mathbf{v}_i = \mathbf{V}_j + \mathbf{W}_j \times \mathbf{r}_i. \tag{20}$$

Storing the current relative positions of particles to a texture is necessary for some of the following steps of our simulation.

29.2.4 Step 2: Grid Generation

In this step we generate the uniform grid data structure. For each particle, we store the particle index at the pixel that corresponds to the voxel where the particle belongs. This operation cannot be performed in a fragment shader because it is a scattering operation (Buck 2005). Instead, we use a vertex shader (VS), which can write a value to an arbitrary position by rendering a vertex as a point primitive of size 1.

We prepare and assign vertices to each particle. In the VS, the particle position is read from the particle position texture, and the voxel index is calculated with Equation 9. Then the coordinates in the grid texture are calculated from the voxel index (as described in Section 29.2.2), the vertex position is set to the grid coordinates, and the color is set to the particle index. However, when we use this simple method, the grid is usually not generated correctly, because only one value is stored per pixel. Consequently, when there are several particles in a voxel, the procedure fails.

To solve this problem, we use a method—described in the following paragraph—that allows us to store, at most, four particles per voxel. Four particles per voxel is enough if the side length of a voxel is smaller than the particle diameter, and if the particles do not interpenetrate—which is our scenario because there is repulsive force between the particles. We set the side length of a voxel equal to the particle diameter; we noticed that overflow rarely occurs.

The method we use is similar to the stencil routing technique used by Purcell et al. (2003), but our method does not have to prepare complicated stencil patterns at every iteration. We prepare the vertices and arrange them, in advance, in ascending order of particle indices. Then, let us assume that there are four particles ending up in a voxel whose indices are p_0, p_1, p_2, and p_3, arranged in ascending order and rendered in this order. Our goal is to store these values, respectively, into the RGBA channels of a pixel, as shown in Figure 29-8, and we achieve this in four rendering passes. During each pass, we render all the vertices by using the VS described earlier, and then the FS outputs the particle index to the color as well as to the depth of the fragment. Using depth test, stencil test, and color masks, we select which index and channels to write to.

In the first pass, we want to write p_0 to the R channel. The vertex corresponding to p_0 has the smallest depth value among the four vertices, so we clear the depth of the buffer to the maximum value and set the depth test to pass smaller values. In the second pass, we want to write p_1 to the G channel. We do this by first setting the color mask so that the R channel is not overwritten during this pass. Then we use the same depth buffer as in the first pass without clearing it, and set the depth test to pass larger values. So p_0 will fail the depth test, but p_1, p_2, and p_3 will not. To write only p_1, we make p_2 and p_3 fail the stencil test by clearing the stencil buffer before rendering to zero, setting the stencil function to increment on depth pass, and setting the stencil test to fail when the stencil value is larger than one. This approach works because p_1 is rendered before p_2 and p_3. The settings of the third and fourth passes are identical to the settings of the second pass, except for the color mask. The RGA and RGB channels are masked in these two last passes, respectively. Also, the same depth buffer is used but never cleared, and the stencil buffer is used and cleared to zero before each pass. The pseudocode of grid generation is provided in Listing 29-1.

This method could be extended to store more than four particles per voxel by rendering to multiple render targets (MRTs).

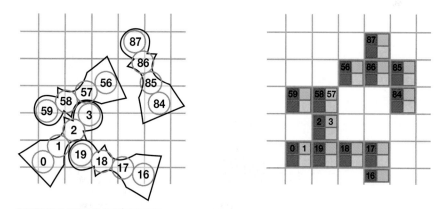

Figure 29-8. A Grid and Particle Indices in the Grid Texture
Left: The computational domain is divided into voxels, and particle indices are stored in the voxels.
Right: A voxel is stored as a pixel, and each channel of the pixel holds one particle index.

Listing 29-1. Pseudocode of Grid Generation

```
//=== 1 PASS
colorMask(GBA);
depthTest(less);
renderVertices();

//===2 PASS
colorMask(RBA);
depthTest(greater);
stencilTest(greater, 1);
stencilFunction(increment);
clear(stencilBuffer);
renderVertices();

//=== 3 PASS
colorMask(RGA);
clear(stencilBuffer);
renderVertices();

//=== 4 PASS
colorMask(RGB);
clear(stencilBuffer);
renderVertices();
```

29.2.5 Step 3: Collision Detection and Reaction

Particles that can collide with other particles are limited to colliding with the particles whose indices are stored (a) in the voxel of the uniform grid to which the particle belongs and (b) in the adjacent voxels, for a total of $3 \times 3 \times 3 = 27$ voxels. To detect the collisions of particle i, first we derive the grid coordinates of the particle from the position of particle i. Then indices stored in the 27 voxels are looked up from the grid texture. We detect collisions by calculating the distance of particle i to these particles.

We do not need to divide collision detection into broad and narrow phases in this collision detection technique. All we have to do is to compute a simple particle-particle distance. After collision is detected, the reaction forces between particles are calculated with Equations 10, 11, and 12. The computed collision force is written to the particle force texture. The collision detection and reaction can be executed in a single shader. The pseudocode is provided in Listing 29-2.

Listing 29-2. Pseudocode of Collision Detection and Reaction

```
gridCoordinate=calculateGridCoordinate(iParticlePosition);
FOREACH of the 27 voxels
  jIndex = tex2D(gridTexture, gridCoordinate);
  FOREACH RGBA channel C of jIndex
    jParticlePosition = tex2D(positionTexture, index2TexCrd(C));
    force += collision(iParticlePosition, jParticlePosition);
  END FOR
END FOR
```

29.2.6 Step 4: Computation of Momenta

After calculating the forces on particles, we use Equations 1 and 4 to compute momenta. Computing linear momentum variation of a rigid body requires adding up the forces that act on the particles that belong to the rigid body. This operation is done in a single fragment shader that is invoked once per rigid body. The FS reads the forces from the particle force texture and writes the calculated value to the linear momentum texture. If the number of particles per rigid body is large, we might be able to implement this sum more efficiently as a parallel reduction in multiple passes.

Similarly, computing the angular momentum variation requires the relative positions of particles to the center of mass, but these positions have already been computed in a previous step and stored in a texture. It is convenient to execute both computations in the same shader and output the results in multiple render targets, as shown in Listing 29-3.

Listing 29-3. Pseudocode for the Computation of Momenta

```
FOR all particles belonging to a rigid body
  particleIndex = particleStartIndex + i;
  particleTexCoord = particleIndex2TexCoord(particleIndex);
  linearMomentum += tex2D(forceOnParticle, particleTexCrd);
  angularMomentum += cross(tex2D(relativePosition, particleTexCrd),
  tex2D(forceOnParticle, particleTexCrd));
END FOR
```

29.2.7 Step 5: Computation of Position and Quaternion

Now that we have the current momenta in a texel assigned to each rigid body, we perform the position and quaternion updates like any other standard GPGPU operation.

The momenta and its previous position and quaternion are read from the texture, and the updated position and quaternion are calculated using Equations 3 and 8. This operation can also be performed in a single shader with MRTs.

29.2.8 Rendering

Each rigid body is associated with a polygon model and rendered using the position c_0 of the center of mass and quaternion q, calculated in Section 29.2.7. The vertex shader reads c_0 and q from textures based on the texture coordinates derived from the rigid body index, and then the current position of vertex r_t is calculated from the unrotated relative vertex position r_0 as follows:

$$r_t = c_0 + q r_0 q^* . \tag{21}$$

29.2.9 Performance

We have implemented the present method on an NVIDIA GeForce 8800 GTX and tested several scenes. In Figure 29-1, 16,384 chess pieces and 10,922 tori are dropped. In both simulations, 65,536 particles are used, and the simulations run at 168 iterations per second (ips) and 152 ips, respectively. When we render the scene at every iteration, the frame rates drop to 44 frames per second (fps) and 68 fps, respectively.

Figure 29-9 shows the results with rigid bodies that have much more complicated shapes: 963 bunnies and 329 teapots. The bunny consists of 68 particles, and the teapot consists of 199 particles. The total number of rigid particles is about 65,000 in these scenes. These simulations run at 112 ips and 101 ips, respectively. The particle representations used in these simulations are solid (that is, the inside of the model is filled with particles). If the particles are placed only on the surface, the simulation can be sped up and still work well. There are 55 particles on the surface of the bunny and 131 particles on the surface of the teapot. With the same number of rigid bodies but a smaller number of rigid particles, the simulations run at 133 ips and 148 ips, respectively. In all these rigid body simulations, the size of the uniform grid is 128^3.

Note that for large computational domains, a uniform grid is not the best choice for storing particle indices for rigid bodies. Rigid bodies do not distribute over the computational domain uniformly; therefore, many voxels contain no particle indices and graphics memory is wasted. In these cases, we would require a more efficient data structure—one that is dynamic, because the distribution of objects changes during the simulation.

Figure 29-9. Simulation Results of 963 Bunnies and 329 Teapots

29.3 Applications

As mentioned earlier, our technique works even if the connectivity between elements changes over time. The rigid body simulation explained in this chapter is an example of such a simulation in which the connectivity dynamically changes. In this section, we briefly discuss how it can be applied to other kinds of physically based simulations, such as granular materials, fluids, and coupling.

29.3.1 Granular Materials

The rigid body simulator presented in this chapter can be easily converted to a granular material simulator because the method used to compute the collision reaction force is based on the discrete element method, which has been developed for simulation of granular materials (Mishra 2003). Instead of using particle forces to update the momenta of rigid bodies, we use the particle forces to directly update the positions of the particles. Figure 29-10 (left) shows a result of the simulation. The simulation with 16,384 particles runs at about 285 ips.

29.3.2 Fluids

The rigid body simulator presented in this chapter can also be applied to fluid simulation. The momentum conservation equation of fluids is this:

$$\frac{D\mathbf{U}}{Dt} = -\frac{1}{\rho}\nabla P + \upsilon\nabla^2\mathbf{U} + \mathbf{F}. \tag{22}$$

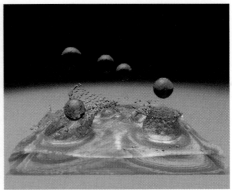

Figure 29-10. Particle-Based Simulations on GPUs
Left: A simulation result for granular materials. The particles are rendered with point sprites in real time. Right: A simulation result for fluid. The fluid is rendered by an offline renderer after the simulation.

We employ a particle-based method that discretizes fluids to a set of particles and solves the equation by calculating particle interaction forces. *Smoothed particle hydrodynamics* (SPH) is a particle-based method often used in computer graphics (details can be found in Müller et al. 2003). A physical value at particle position is calculated as a weighted sum of the values of neighboring particles. Therefore, we have to search for neighboring particles. The difficulty in implementing SPH on the GPU is that the neighborhood relationship among particles dynamically changes during the simulation (in other words, the connectivity among particles is not fixed).

Now that we know a way to generate a uniform grid on the GPU, we can search for neighboring particles dynamically. Although we search for neighboring particles once per iteration in the rigid body simulation, in the SPH simulation we have to search twice. First, we have to search for neighboring particles to compute the density. Then, the pressure force is derived from the densities of neighboring particles. Therefore, the computational cost is higher than for the rigid body simulation. However, we can obtain unprecedented performance with the GeForce 8800 GTX, as shown in Figure 29-10 (right). Here the particle positions are output to files, and then the fluid surface constructed from them, using marching cubes, is rendered by an offline renderer (Lorensen and Cline 1987). The simulation uses 1,048,576 fluid particles, with a uniform grid whose size is 256^3 and whose speed is about 1.2 ips. The speed is not fast enough for real-time applications, but a simulation with a few tens of thousands of fluid particles runs at about 60 frames/sec. Besides using this simulation for a real-time application, we can use it to accelerate offline simulations for high-quality animation productions and more. Finally, we are limited on the number of particles we can use because of the size of the GPU memory. With 768 MB of video memory, we can use up to about 4,000,000 fluid particles.

29.3.3 Coupling

We can use GPUs to accelerate not only a simple simulation, but also simulations in which several simulations are interacting with each other. The particle representation of rigid bodies described in this chapter makes it easy to couple it with particle-based fluid simulations. Figure 29-11 (top) shows a fluid simulation coupled with a rigid body simulation. The interaction forces are computed by treating particles belonging to rigid bodies as fluid particles and then using the forces to update the momenta of rigid bodies. Glasses are stacked and fluid is poured in from the top. After that, another glass is thrown into the stack. This simulation uses 49,153 fluid particles and runs at about 18 ips.

The techniques are not limited to particle-based simulations. In Figure 29-11 (bottom), we show the results of coupling particle-based fluid simulation and cloth simulation. We see that a mesh-based simulation can be integrated with a particle-based fluid simulation as well. Both the cloth and the fluid simulations are performed on the GPU, and the interaction is also computed on it. The simulations run at about 12 ips with 65,536 fluid particles, and each piece of cloth consists of 8,192 polygons. Videos of both simulations are available on this book's accompanying DVD.

29.4 Conclusion

In this chapter we have described techniques for implementing rigid body simulation entirely on the GPU. By exploiting the computational power of GPUs, we simulate a large number of rigid bodies, which was previously difficult to perform in real time. We showed that the present technique is applicable not only to rigid body simulation but also to several other kinds of simulations, such as fluids.

There is room for improving the accuracy of the rigid body simulation. For example, we could use the present particle-based collision detection technique as the broad phase and implement a more accurate method for the narrow phase.

We are sure that what we have shown in the application section is just a fraction of what is possible, and we hope that others will explore the possibility of GPU physics by extending the present techniques.

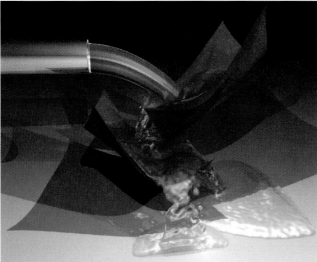

Figure 29-11. Coupling of Simulations
Top: A result of coupling rigid body and fluid simulation. Bottom: A result of coupling cloth and fluid simulation. An offline renderer is used to render these scenes.

29.5 Appendix

Rotation matrix $\mathbf{R}(t)$ is calculated with quaternion $\mathbf{q} = [s, v_x, v_y, v_z]$:

$$\mathbf{R}(t) = \begin{pmatrix} 1 - 2v_y^2 - 2v_z^2 & 2v_x v_y - 2sv_z & 2v_x v_z + 2sv_y \\ 2v_x v_y + 2sv_z & 1 - 2v_x^2 - 2v_z^2 & 2v_y v_z - 2sv_x \\ 2v_x v_z - 2sv_y & 2v_y v_z + 2sv_x & 1 - 2v_x^2 - 2v_y^2 \end{pmatrix}$$

The multiplication of quaternions $\mathbf{q}_0 = [s_0, \mathbf{v}_0]$ and $\mathbf{q}_1 = [s_1, \mathbf{v}_1]$ is

$$\mathbf{q}_0 \times \mathbf{q}_1 = [s_0 s_1 - \mathbf{v}_0 \cdot \mathbf{v}_1, \; s_0 \mathbf{v}_1 + s_1 \mathbf{v}_0 + \mathbf{v}_0 \times \mathbf{v}_1].$$

29.6 References

Baraff, David. 1997. "An Introduction to Physically Based Modeling: Rigid Body Simulation 1—Unconstrained Rigid Body Dynamics." SIGGRAPH '97 Course Notes.

Bell, Nathan, Yizhou Yu, and Peter J. Mucha. 2005. "Particle-Based Simulation of Granular Materials." In *Proceedings of the ACM SIGGRAPH/Eurographics Symposium on Computer Animation*, pp. 77–86.

Buck, Ian. 2005. "Taking the Plunge into GPU Computing." In *GPU Gems 2*, edited by Matt Pharr, pp. 509–519. Addison-Wesley.

Everitt, Cass. 2001. "Interactive Order-Independent Transparency." NVIDIA technical report. Available online at http://developer.nvidia.com/object/Interactive_Order_Transparency.html.

Harris, Mark J. 2004. "Fast Fluid Dynamics Simulation on the GPU." In *GPU Gems*, edited by Randima Fernando, pp. 637–665. Addison-Wesley.

Harris, Mark. 2005. "Mapping Computational Concepts to GPUs." In *GPU Gems 2*, edited by Matt Pharr, pp. 493–508. Addison-Wesley.

Harris, Mark, William Baxter, Thorsten Scheuermann, and Anselmo Lastra. 2003. "Simulation of Cloud Dynamics on Graphics Hardware." In *Proceedings of the SIGGRAPH/Eurographics Workshop on Graphics Hardware 2003*, pp. 92–101.

Lorensen, William E., and Harvey E. Cline. 1987. "Marching Cubes: A High Resolution 3D Surface Construction Algorithm." In *Proceedings of the 14th Annual Conference on Computer Graphics and Interactive Techniques*, pp. 163–169.

Mishra, B. K. 2003. "A Review of Computer Simulation of Tumbling Mills by the Discrete Element Method: Part 1—Contact Mechanics." *International Journal of Mineral Processing* 71(1), pp. 73–93.

Müller, Matthias, David Charypar, and Markus Gross. 2003. "Particle-Based Fluid Simulation for Interactive Applications." In *Proceedings of the 2003 ACM SIGGRAPH/Eurographics Symposium on Computer Animation*, pp. 154–159.

Owens, John, David Luebke, Naga Govindaraju, Mark Harris, Jens Krüger, Aaron Lefohn, and Timothy Purcell. 2005. "A Survey of General-Purpose Computation on Graphics Hardware." In *Proceedings of Eurographics 2005, State of the Art Reports*, pp. 21–51.

Purcell, Timothy J., Craig Donner, Mike Cammarano, Henrik-Wann Jensen, and Pat Hanrahan. 2003. "Photon Mapping on Programmable Graphics Hardware." In *Proceedings of the SIGGRAPH/Eurographics Workshop on Graphics Hardware 2003*, pp. 41–50.

Tanaka, Masayuki, Mikio Sakai, and Seiichi Koshizuka. 2006. "Rigid Body Simulation Using a Particle Method." In *ACM SIGGRAPH Research Posters*, no. 132.

Zeller, Cyril. 2005. "Cloth Simulation on the GPU." In *ACM SIGGRAPH Sketches*, no. 39.

The author would like to thank to Seiichi Koshizuka and Masayuki Tanaka for valuable advice and discussion.

Chapter 30

Real-Time Simulation and Rendering of 3D Fluids

Keenan Crane
University of Illinois at Urbana-Champaign

Ignacio Llamas
NVIDIA Corporation

Sarah Tariq
NVIDIA Corporation

30.1 Introduction

Physically based animation of fluids such as smoke, water, and fire provides some of the most stunning visuals in computer graphics, but it has historically been the domain of high-quality offline rendering due to great computational cost. In this chapter we show not only how these effects can be simulated and rendered in real time, as Figure 30-1 demonstrates, but also how they can be seamlessly integrated into real-time applications. Physically based effects have already changed the way interactive environments are designed. But fluids open the doors to an even larger world of design possibilities.

In the past, artists have relied on particle systems to emulate 3D fluid effects in real-time applications. Although particle systems can produce attractive results, they cannot match the realistic appearance and behavior of fluid simulation. Real time fluids remain a challenge not only because they are more expensive to simulate, but also because the volumetric data produced by simulation does not fit easily into the standard rasterization-based rendering paradigm.

Figure 30-1. Water Simulated and Rendered in Real Time on the GPU

In this chapter we give a detailed description of the technology used for the real-time fluid effects in the NVIDIA GeForce 8 Series launch demo "Smoke in a Box" and discuss its integration into the upcoming game *Hellgate: London*.

The chapter consists of two parts:

- Section 30.2 covers simulation, including smoke, water, fire, and interaction with solid obstacles, as well as performance and memory considerations.
- Section 30.3 discusses how to render fluid phenomena and how to seamlessly integrate fluid rendering into an existing rasterization-based framework.

30.2 Simulation

30.2.1 Background

Throughout this section we assume a working knowledge of general-purpose GPU (GPGPU) methods—that is, applications of the GPU to problems other than conventional raster graphics. In particular, we encourage the reader to look at Harris's chapter on 2D fluid simulation in *GPU Gems* (Harris 2004). As mentioned in that chapter, implementing and debugging a 3D fluid solver is no simple task (even in a traditional programming environment), and a solid understanding of the underlying mathematics and physics can be of great help. Bridson et al. 2006 provides an excellent resource in this respect.

Fortunately, a deep understanding of partial differential equations (PDEs) is not required to get some basic intuition about the concepts presented in this chapter. All PDEs presented will have the form

$$\frac{\partial}{\partial t} x = f(x, t),$$

which says that the rate at which some quantity x is changing is given by some function f, which may itself depend on x and t. The reader may find it easier to think about this relationship in the discrete setting of *forward Euler integration*:

$$x^{n+1} = x^n + f(x^n, t^n)\Delta t.$$

In other words, the value of x at the next time step equals the current value of x plus the current rate of change $f(x^n, t^n)$ times the duration of the time step Δt. (Note that superscripts are used to index the time step and do *not* imply exponentiation.) Be warned, however, that the forward Euler scheme is not a good choice numerically—we are suggesting it only as a way to *think* about the equations.

30.2.2 Equations of Fluid Motion

The motion of a fluid is often expressed in terms of its local *velocity* $\mathbf{u}$ as a function of position and time. In computer animation, fluid is commonly modeled as *inviscid* (that is, more like water than oil) and *incompressible* (meaning that volume does not change over time). Given these assumptions, the velocity can be described by the *momentum equation*:

$$\frac{\partial \mathbf{u}}{\partial t} = -(\mathbf{u} \cdot \nabla)\mathbf{u} - \frac{1}{\rho}\nabla p + \mathbf{f},$$

subject to the *incompressibility constraint*:

$$\nabla \cdot \mathbf{u} = 0,$$

where p is the pressure, ρ is the mass density, $\mathbf{f}$ represents any external forces (such as gravity), and ∇ is the differential operator:

$$\left[\begin{array}{ccc} \dfrac{\partial}{\partial x} & \dfrac{\partial}{\partial y} & \dfrac{\partial}{\partial z} \end{array}\right]^T.$$

To define the equations of motion in a particular context, it is also necessary to specify *boundary conditions* (that is, how the fluid behaves near solid obstacles or other fluids).

The basic task of a fluid solver is to compute a numerical approximation of **u**. This velocity field can then be used to animate visual phenomena such as smoke particles or a liquid surface.

30.2.3 Solving for Velocity

The popular "stable fluids" method for computing velocity was introduced in Stam 1999, and a GPU implementation of this method for 2D fluids was presented in Harris 2004. In this section we briefly describe how to solve for velocity but refer the reader to the cited works for details.

In order to numerically solve the momentum equation, we must *discretize* our domain (that is, the region of space through which the fluid flows) into computational elements. We choose an *Eulerian* discretization, meaning that computational elements are fixed in space throughout the simulation—only the values stored on these elements change. In particular, we subdivide a rectilinear volume into a regular grid of cubical cells. Each grid cell stores both scalar quantities (such as pressure, temperature, and so on) and vector quantities (such as velocity). This scheme makes implementation on the GPU simple, because there is a straightforward mapping between grid cells and voxels in a 3D texture. *Lagrangian* schemes (that is, schemes where the computational elements are *not* fixed in space) such as smoothed-particle hydrodynamics (Müller et al. 2003) are also popular for fluid animation, but their irregular structure makes them difficult to implement efficiently on the GPU.

Because we discretize space, we must also discretize *derivatives* in our equations: *finite differences* numerically approximate derivatives by taking linear combinations of values defined on the grid. As in Harris 2004, we store all quantities at cell centers for pedagogical simplicity, though a staggered MAC-style grid yields more-robust finite differences and can make it easier to define boundary conditions. (See Harlow and Welch 1965 for details.)

In a GPU implementation, cell attributes (velocity, pressure, and so on) are stored in several 3D textures. At each simulation step, we update these values by running computational *kernels* over the grid. A kernel is implemented as a pixel shader that executes on every cell in the grid and writes the results to an output texture. However, because

GPUs are designed to render into 2D buffers, we must run kernels once for each slice of a 3D volume.

To execute a kernel on a particular grid slice, we rasterize a single quad whose dimensions equal the width and height of the volume. In Direct3D 10 we can directly render into a 3D texture by specifying one of its slices as a render target. Placing the slice index in a variable bound to the SV_RenderTargetArrayIndex semantic specifies the slice to which a primitive coming out of the geometry shader is rasterized. (See Blythe 2006 for details.) By iterating over slice indices, we can execute a kernel over the entire grid.

Rather than solve the momentum equation all at once, we split it into a set of simpler operations that can be computed in succession: advection, application of external forces, and pressure projection. Implementation of the corresponding kernels is detailed in Harris 2004, but several examples from our Direct3D 10 framework are given in Listing 30-1. Of particular interest is the routine PS_ADVECT_VEL: this kernel implements *semi-Lagrangian* advection, which is used as a building block for more accurate advection in the next section.

Listing 30-1. Simulation Kernels

```
struct GS_OUTPUT_FLUIDSIM
{
  // Index of the current grid cell (i,j,k in [0,gridSize] range)
  float3 cellIndex : TEXCOORD0;

  // Texture coordinates (x,y,z in [0,1] range) for the
  // current grid cell and its immediate neighbors
  float3 CENTERCELL : TEXCOORD1;
  float3 LEFTCELL   : TEXCOORD2;
  float3 RIGHTCELL  : TEXCOORD3;
  float3 BOTTOMCELL : TEXCOORD4;
  float3 TOPCELL    : TEXCOORD5;
  float3 DOWNCELL   : TEXCOORD6;
  float3 UPCELL     : TEXCOORD7;
  float4 pos        : SV_Position; // 2D slice vertex in
                                   // homogeneous clip space
  uint RTIndex      : SV_RenderTargetArrayIndex; // Specifies
                                                 // destination slice
};
```

Listing 30-1 (*continued*). Simulation Kernels

```
float3 cellIndex2TexCoord(float3 index)
{
  // Convert a value in the range [0,gridSize] to one in the range [0,1].
  return float3(index.x / textureWidth,
                index.y / textureHeight,
                (index.z+0.5) / textureDepth);
}


float4 PS_ADVECT_VEL(GS_OUTPUT_FLUIDSIM in,
                     Texture3D velocity) : SV_Target
{
  float3 pos = in.cellIndex;
  float3 cellVelocity = velocity.Sample(samPointClamp,
                                        in.CENTERCELL).xyz;

  pos -= timeStep * cellVelocity;
  pos = cellIndex2TexCoord(pos);

  return velocity.Sample(samLinear, pos);
}


float PS_DIVERGENCE(GS_OUTPUT_FLUIDSIM in,
                    Texture3D velocity) : SV_Target
{
  // Get velocity values from neighboring cells.
  float4 fieldL = velocity.Sample(samPointClamp, in.LEFTCELL);
  float4 fieldR = velocity.Sample(samPointClamp, in.RIGHTCELL);
  float4 fieldB = velocity.Sample(samPointClamp, in.BOTTOMCELL);
  float4 fieldT = velocity.Sample(samPointClamp, in.TOPCELL);
  float4 fieldD = velocity.Sample(samPointClamp, in.DOWNCELL);
  float4 fieldU = velocity.Sample(samPointClamp, in.UPCELL);

  // Compute the velocity's divergence using central differences.
  float divergence =  0.5 * ((fieldR.x - fieldL.x)+
                             (fieldT.y - fieldB.y)+
                             (fieldU.z - fieldD.z));

  return divergence;
}
```

Listing 30-1 (*continued*). Simulation Kernels

```
float PS_JACOBI(GS_OUTPUT_FLUIDSIM in,
                Texture3D pressure,
                Texture3D divergence) : SV_Target
{
  // Get the divergence at the current cell.
  float dC = divergence.Sample(samPointClamp, in.CENTERCELL);

  // Get pressure values from neighboring cells.
  float pL = pressure.Sample(samPointClamp, in.LEFTCELL);
  float pR = pressure.Sample(samPointClamp, in.RIGHTCELL);
  float pB = pressure.Sample(samPointClamp, in.BOTTOMCELL);
  float pT = pressure.Sample(samPointClamp, in.TOPCELL);
  float pD = pressure.Sample(samPointClamp, in.DOWNCELL);
  float pU = pressure.Sample(samPointClamp, in.UPCELL);

  // Compute the new pressure value for the center cell.
  return(pL + pR + pB + pT + pU + pD - dC) / 6.0;
}

float4 PS_PROJECT(GS_OUTPUT_FLUIDSIM in,
                  Texture3D pressure,
                  Texture3D velocity): SV_Target
{
  // Compute the gradient of pressure at the current cell by
  // taking central differences of neighboring pressure values.
  float pL = pressure.Sample(samPointClamp, in.LEFTCELL);
  float pR = pressure.Sample(samPointClamp, in.RIGHTCELL);
  float pB = pressure.Sample(samPointClamp, in.BOTTOMCELL);
  float pT = pressure.Sample(samPointClamp, in.TOPCELL);
  float pD = pressure.Sample(samPointClamp, in.DOWNCELL);
  float pU = pressure.Sample(samPointClamp, in.UPCELL);
  float3 gradP = 0.5*float3(pR - pL, pT - pB, pU - pD);

  // Project the velocity onto its divergence-free component by
  // subtracting the gradient of pressure.
  float3 vOld = velocity.Sample(samPointClamp, in.texcoords);
  float3 vNew = vOld - gradP;

  return float4(vNew, 0);
}
```

Improving Detail

The semi-Lagrangian advection scheme used by Stam is useful for animation because it is unconditionally stable, meaning that large time steps will not cause the simulation to "blow up." However, it can introduce unwanted numerical smoothing, making water look viscous or causing smoke to lose detail. To achieve higher-order accuracy, we use a MacCormack scheme that performs two intermediate semi-Lagrangian advection steps. Given a quantity ϕ and an advection scheme A (for example, the one implemented by PS_ADVECT_VEL), higher-order accuracy is obtained using the following sequence of operations (from Selle et al. 2007):

$$\hat{\phi}^{n+1} = A\left(\phi^n\right)$$

$$\hat{\phi}^n = A^R\left(\hat{\phi}^{n+1}\right)$$

$$\phi^{n+1} = \hat{\phi}^{n+1} + \frac{1}{2}\left(\phi^n - \hat{\phi}^n\right).$$

Here, ϕ^n is the quantity to be advected, $\hat{\phi}^{n+1}$ and $\hat{\phi}^n$ are intermediate quantities, and ϕ^{n+1} is the final advected quantity. The superscript on A^R indicates that advection is reversed (that is, time is run backward) for that step.

Unlike the standard semi-Lagrangian scheme, this MacCormack scheme is not unconditionally stable. Therefore, a limiter is applied to the resulting value ϕ^{n+1}, ensuring that it falls within the range of values contributing to the initial semi-Lagrangian advection. In our GPU solver, this means we must locate the eight nodes closest to the sample point, access the corresponding texels *exactly at their centers* (to avoid getting interpolated values), and clamp the final value to fall within the minimum and maximum values found on these nodes, as shown in Figure 30-2.

Once the intermediate semi-Lagrangian steps have been computed, the pixel shader in Listing 30-2 completes advection using the MacCormack scheme.

Listing 30-2. MacCormack Advection Scheme

```
float4 PS_ADVECT_MACCORMACK(GS_OUTPUT_FLUIDSIM in,
                            float timestep) : SV_Target
{
    // Trace back along the initial characteristic - we'll use
    // values near this semi-Lagrangian "particle" to clamp our
    // final advected value.
    float3 cellVelocity = velocity.Sample(samPointClamp,
                                          in.CENTERCELL).xyz;
```

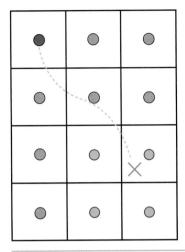

Figure 30-2. Limiter Applied to a MacCormack Advection Scheme in 2D
The result of the advection (blue) is clamped to the range of values from nodes (green) used to get the interpolated value at the advected "particle" (red) in the initial semi-Lagrangian step.

Listing 30-2 (*continued*). MacCormack Advection Scheme

```
float3 npos = in.cellIndex - timestep * cellVelocity;

// Find the cell corner closest to the "particle" and compute the
// texture coordinate corresponding to that location.
npos = floor(npos + float3(0.5f, 0.5f, 0.5f));
npos = cellIndex2TexCoord(npos);

// Get the values of nodes that contribute to the interpolated value.

// Texel centers will be a half-texel away from the cell corner.
float3 ht = float3(0.5f / textureWidth,
                   0.5f / textureHeight,
                   0.5f / textureDepth);

float4 nodeValues[8];
nodeValues[0] = phi_n.Sample(samPointClamp, npos +
                             float3(-ht.x, -ht.y, -ht.z));
nodeValues[1] = phi_n.Sample(samPointClamp, npos +
                             float3(-ht.x, -ht.y,  ht.z));
nodeValues[2] = phi_n.Sample(samPointClamp, npos +
                             float3(-ht.x,  ht.y, -ht.z));
nodeValues[3] = phi_n.Sample(samPointClamp, npos +
                             float3(-ht.x,  ht.y,  ht.z));
```

Listing 30-2 (*continued*). MacCormack Advection Scheme

```
nodeValues[4] = phi_n.Sample(samPointClamp, npos +
                        float3(ht.x, -ht.y, -ht.z));
nodeValues[5] = phi_n.Sample(samPointClamp, npos +
                        float3(ht.x, -ht.y,  ht.z));
nodeValues[6] = phi_n.Sample(samPointClamp, npos +
                        float3(ht.x,  ht.y, -ht.z));
nodeValues[7] = phi_n.Sample(samPointClamp, npos +
                        float3(ht.x,  ht.y,  ht.z));

// Determine a valid range for the result.
float4 phiMin = min(min(min(min(min(min(
    nodeValues[0],  nodeValues [1]), nodeValues [2]), nodeValues [3]),
    nodeValues[4]), nodeValues [5]), nodeValues [6]), nodeValues [7]);

float4 phiMax = max(max(max(max(max(max(max(
    nodeValues[0],  nodeValues [1]), nodeValues [2]), nodeValues [3]),
    nodeValues[4]), nodeValues [5]), nodeValues [6]), nodeValues [7]);

// Perform final advection, combining values from intermediate
// advection steps.
float4 r = phi_n_1_hat.Sample(samLinear, nposTC) +
        0.5 * (phi_n.Sample(samPointClamp, in.CENTERCELL) -
            phi_n_hat.Sample(samPointClamp, in.CENTERCELL));

// Clamp result to the desired range.
r = max(min(r, phiMax), phiMin);

return r;
}
```

On the GPU, higher-order schemes are often a better way to get improved visual detail than simply increasing the grid resolution, because math is cheap compared to bandwidth. Figure 30-3 compares a higher-order scheme on a low-resolution grid with a lower-order scheme on a high-resolution grid.

30.2.4 Solid-Fluid Interaction

One of the benefits of using real-time simulation (versus precomputed animation) is that fluid can interact with the environment. Figure 30-4 shows an example on one such scene. In this section we discuss two simple ways to allow the environment to act on the fluid.

Figure 30-3. Bigger Is Not Always Better!
Left: MacCormack advection scheme (applied to both velocity and smoke density) on a 128×64×64 grid. Right: Semi-Lagrangian advection scheme on a 256×128×128 grid.

A basic way to influence the velocity field is through the application of external forces. To get the gross effect of an obstacle pushing fluid around, we can approximate the obstacle with a basic shape such as a box or a ball and add the obstacle's average velocity to that region of the velocity field. Simple shapes like these can be described with an implicit equation of the form $f(x, y, z) \leq 0$ that can be easily evaluated by a pixel shader at each grid cell.

Although we could explicitly add velocity to approximate simple motion, there are situations in which more detail is required. In *Hellgate: London*, for example, we wanted smoke to seep out through cracks in the ground. Adding a simple upward velocity and smoke density in the shape of a crack resulted in uninteresting motion. Instead, we used the crack shape, shown inset in Figure 30-5, to define *solid obstacles* for smoke to collide and interact with. Similarly, we wanted to achieve more-precise interactions between smoke and an animated gargoyle, as shown in Figure 30-4. To do so, we needed to be able to affect the fluid motion with dynamic obstacles (see the details later in this section), which required a volumetric representation of the obstacle's interior and of the velocity at its boundary (which we also explain later in this section).

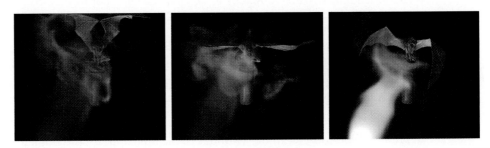

Figure 30-4. An Animated Gargoyle Pushes Smoke Around by Flapping Its Wings

Figure 30-5. Smoke Rises from a Crack in the Ground in the Game *Hellgate: London*
Inset: A slice from the obstacle texture that was used to block the smoke; white texels indicate an obstacle, and black texels indicate open space.

Dynamic Obstacles

So far we have assumed that a fluid occupies the entire rectilinear region defined by the simulation grid. However, in most applications, the fluid *domain* (that is, the region of the grid actually occupied by fluid) is much more interesting. Various methods for handling *static* boundaries on the GPU are discussed in Harris et al. 2003, Liu et al. 2004, Wu et al. 2004, and Li et al. 2005.

The fluid domain may change over time to adapt to dynamic obstacles in the environment, and in the case of liquids, such as water, the domain is constantly changing as the liquid sloshes around (more in Section 30.2.7). In this section we describe the scheme used for handling dynamic obstacles in *Hellgate: London*. For further discussion of dynamic obstacles, see Bridson et al. 2006 and Foster and Fedkiw 2001.

To deal with complex domains, we must consider the fluid's behavior at the *domain boundary*. In our discretized fluid, the domain boundary consists of the *faces* between cells that contain fluid and cells that do not—that is, the face *between* a fluid cell and a solid cell is part of the boundary, but the solid cell itself is not. A simple example of a domain boundary is a static barrier placed around the perimeter of the simulation grid to prevent fluid from "escaping" (without it, the fluid appears as though it is simply flowing out into space).

To support domain boundaries that change due to the presence of dynamic obstacles, we need to modify some of our simulation steps. In our implementation, obstacles are represented using an inside-outside voxelization. In addition, we keep a voxelized representation of the obstacle's velocity in solid cells adjacent to the domain boundary. This information is stored in a pair of 3D textures that are updated whenever an obstacle moves or deforms (we cover this later in this section).

At solid-fluid boundaries, we want to impose a *free-slip* boundary condition, which says that the velocities of the fluid and the solid are the same in the direction normal to the boundary:

$$\mathbf{u} \cdot \mathbf{n} = \mathbf{u}_{\text{solid}} \cdot \mathbf{n}.$$

In other words, the fluid cannot flow into or out of a solid, but it is allowed to flow freely along its surface.

The free-slip boundary condition also affects the way we solve for pressure, because the gradient of pressure is used in determining the final velocity. A detailed discussion of pressure projection can be found in Bridson et al. 2006, but ultimately we just need to make sure that the pressure values we compute satisfy the following:

$$\frac{\Delta t}{\rho \Delta x^2} \left(|F_{i,j,k}| p_{i,j,k} - \sum_{\mathbf{n} \in F_{i,j,k}} p_{\mathbf{n}} \right) = -d_{i,j,k},$$

where Δt is the size of the time step, Δx is the cell spacing, $p_{i,j,k}$ is the pressure value in cell (i, j, k), $d_{i,j,k}$ is the discrete velocity divergence computed for that cell, and $F_{i,j,k}$ is the set of *indices* of cells adjacent to cell (i, j, k) that contain fluid. (This equation is simply a discrete form of the pressure-Poisson system $\nabla^2 p = \nabla \cdot \mathbf{w}$ in Harris 2004 that respects solid boundaries.) It is also important that at solid-fluid boundaries, $d_{i,j,k}$ is computed using obstacle velocities.

In practice there's a very simple trick for making sure all this happens: any time we sample pressure from a neighboring cell (for example, in the pressure solve and pressure projection steps), we check whether the neighbor contains a solid obstacle, as shown in Figure 30-6. If it does, we use the pressure value from the center cell in place of the neighbor's pressure value. In other words, we nullify the solid cell's contribution to the preceding equation.

We can apply a similar trick for velocity values: whenever we sample a neighboring cell (for example, when computing the velocity's divergence), we first check to see if it contains a solid. If so, we look up the obstacle's velocity from our voxelization and use it in place of the value stored in the fluid's velocity field.

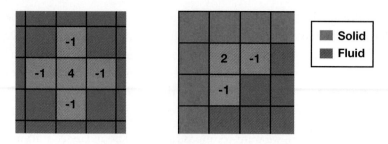

Figure 30-6. Accounting for Obstacles in the Computation of the Discrete Laplacian of Pressure
Left: A stencil used to compute the discrete Laplacian of pressure in 2D. Right: This stencil changes near solid-fluid boundaries. Checking for solid neighbors and replacing their pressure values with the central pressure value results in the same behavior.

Because we cannot always solve the pressure-Poisson system to convergence, we explicitly enforce the free-slip boundary condition immediately following pressure projection. We must also correct the result of the pressure projection step for fluid cells next to the domain boundary. To do so, we compute the obstacle's velocity component in the direction normal to the boundary. This value replaces the corresponding component of our fluid velocity at the center cell, as shown in Figure 30-7. Because solid-fluid boundaries are aligned with voxel faces, computing the projection of the velocity onto the surface normal is simply a matter of selecting the appropriate component.

If two opposing faces of a fluid cell are solid-fluid boundaries, we could average the velocity values from both sides. However, simply selecting one of the two faces generally gives acceptable results.

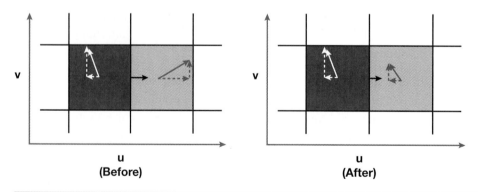

Figure 30-7. Enforcing the Free-Slip Boundary Condition After Pressure Projection
To enforce free-slip behavior at the boundary between a fluid cell (red) and a solid cell (black), we modify the velocity of the fluid cell in the normal (u) direction so that it equals the obstacle's velocity in the normal direction. We retain the fluid velocity in the tangential (v) direction.

Finally, it is important to realize that when very large time steps are used, quantities can "leak" through boundaries during advection. For this reason we add an additional constraint to the advection steps to ensure that we never advect any quantity into the interior of an obstacle, guaranteeing that the value of advected quantities (for example, smoke density) is always zero inside solid obstacles (see the PS_ADVECT_OBSTACLE routine in Listing 30-3). In Listing 30-3, we show the simulation kernels modified to take boundary conditions into account.

Listing 30-3. Modified Simulation Kernels to Account for Boundary Conditions

```
bool IsSolidCell(float3 cellTexCoords)
{
  return obstacles.Sample(samPointClamp, cellTexCoords).r > 0.9;
}


float PS_JACOBI_OBSTACLE(GS_OUTPUT_FLUIDSIM in,
                         Texture3D pressure,
                         Texture3D divergence) : SV_Target
{
  // Get the divergence and pressure at the current cell.
  float dC = divergence.Sample(samPointClamp, in.CENTERCELL);
  float pC = pressure.Sample(samPointClamp, in.CENTERCELL);

  // Get the pressure values from neighboring cells.
  float pL = pressure.Sample(samPointClamp, in.LEFTCELL);
  float pR = pressure.Sample(samPointClamp, in.RIGHTCELL);
  float pB = pressure.Sample(samPointClamp, in.BOTTOMCELL);
  float pT = pressure.Sample(samPointClamp, in.TOPCELL);
  float pD = pressure.Sample(samPointClamp, in.DOWNCELL);
  float pU = pressure.Sample(samPointClamp, in.UPCELL);

  // Make sure that the pressure in solid cells is effectively ignored.
  if(IsSolidCell(in.LEFTCELL)) pL = pC;
  if(IsSolidCell(in.RIGHTCELL)) pR = pC;
  if(IsSolidCell(in.BOTTOMCELL)) pB = pC;
  if(IsSolidCell(in.TOPCELL)) pT = pC;
  if(IsSolidCell(in.DOWNCELL)) pD = pC;
  if(IsSolidCell(in.UPCELL)) pU = pC;

  // Compute the new pressure value.
  return(pL + pR + pB + pT + pU + pD - dC) /6.0;
}
```

```
float4 GetObstacleVelocity(float3 cellTexCoords)
{
  return obstaclevelocity.Sample(samPointClamp, cellTexCoords);
}

float PS_DIVERGENCE_OBSTACLE(GS_OUTPUT_FLUIDSIM in,
                             Texture3D velocity) : SV_Target
{
  // Get velocity values from neighboring cells.
  float4 fieldL = velocity.Sample(samPointClamp, in.LEFTCELL);
  float4 fieldR = velocity.Sample(samPointClamp, in.RIGHTCELL);
  float4 fieldB = velocity.Sample(samPointClamp, in.BOTTOMCELL);
  float4 fieldT = velocity.Sample(samPointClamp, in.TOPCELL);
  float4 fieldD = velocity.Sample(samPointClamp, in.DOWNCELL);
  float4 fieldU = velocity.Sample(samPointClamp, in.UPCELL);

  // Use obstacle velocities for any solid cells.
  if(IsBoundaryCell(in.LEFTCELL))
    fieldL = GetObstacleVelocity(in.LEFTCELL);
  if(IsBoundaryCell(in.RIGHTCELL))
    fieldR = GetObstacleVelocity(in.RIGHTCELL);
  if(IsBoundaryCell(in.BOTTOMCELL))
    fieldB = GetObstacleVelocity(in.BOTTOMCELL);
  if(IsBoundaryCell(in.TOPCELL))
    fieldT = GetObstacleVelocity(in.TOPCELL);
  if(IsBoundaryCell(in.DOWNCELL))
    fieldD = GetObstacleVelocity(in.DOWNCELL);
  if(IsBoundaryCell(in.UPCELL))
    fieldU = GetObstacleVelocity(in.UPCELL);

  // Compute the velocity's divergence using central differences.
  float divergence =  0.5 * ((fieldR.x - fieldL.x) +
                             (fieldT.y - fieldB.y) +
                             (fieldU.z - fieldD.z));

  return divergence;
}
```

```
float4 PS_PROJECT_OBSTACLE(GS_OUTPUT_FLUIDSIM in,
                           Texture3D pressure,
                           Texture3D velocity): SV_Target
{
  // If the cell is solid, simply use the corresponding
  // obstacle velocity.
  if(IsBoundaryCell(in.CENTERCELL))
  {
    return GetObstacleVelocity(in.CENTERCELL);
  }

  // Get pressure values for the current cell and its neighbors.
  float pC = pressure.Sample(samPointClamp, in.CENTERCELL);
  float pL = pressure.Sample(samPointClamp, in.LEFTCELL);
  float pR = pressure.Sample(samPointClamp, in.RIGHTCELL);
  float pB = pressure.Sample(samPointClamp, in.BOTTOMCELL);
  float pT = pressure.Sample(samPointClamp, in.TOPCELL);
  float pD = pressure.Sample(samPointClamp, in.DOWNCELL);
  float pU = pressure.Sample(samPointClamp, in.UPCELL);

  // Get obstacle velocities in neighboring solid cells.
  // (Note that these values are meaningless if a neighbor
  // is not solid.)
  float3 vL = GetObstacleVelocity(in.LEFTCELL);
  float3 vR = GetObstacleVelocity(in.RIGHTCELL);
  float3 vB = GetObstacleVelocity(in.BOTTOMCELL);
  float3 vT = GetObstacleVelocity(in.TOPCELL);
  float3 vD = GetObstacleVelocity(in.DOWNCELL);
  float3 vU = GetObstacleVelocity(in.UPCELL);

  float3 obstV = float3(0,0,0);
  float3 vMask = float3(1,1,1);

  // If an adjacent cell is solid, ignore its pressure
  // and use its velocity.
  if(IsBoundaryCell(in.LEFTCELL)) {
    pL = pC; obstV.x = vL.x; vMask.x = 0; }
  if(IsBoundaryCell(in.RIGHTCELL)) {
    pR = pC; obstV.x = vR.x; vMask.x = 0; }
```

```
    if(IsBoundaryCell(in.BOTTOMCELL)) {
      pB = pC; obstV.y = vB.y; vMask.y = 0; }
    if(IsBoundaryCell(in.TOPCELL)) {
      pT = pC; obstV.y = vT.y; vMask.y = 0; }
    if(IsBoundaryCell(in.DOWNCELL)) {
      pD = pC; obstV.z = vD.z; vMask.z = 0; }
    if(IsBoundaryCell(in.UPCELL)) {
      pU = pC; obstV.z = vU.z; vMask.z = 0; }

    // Compute the gradient of pressure at the current cell by
    // taking central differences of neighboring pressure values.
    float gradP = 0.5*float3(pR - pL, pT - pB, pU - pD);

    // Project the velocity onto its divergence-free component by
    // subtracting the gradient of pressure.
    float3 vOld = velocity.Sample(samPointClamp, in.texcoords);
    float3 vNew = vOld - gradP;

    // Explicitly enforce the free-slip boundary condition by
    // replacing the appropriate components of the new velocity with
    // obstacle velocities.
    vNew = (vMask * vNew) + obstV;

    return vNew;
}

bool IsNonEmptyCell(float3 cellTexCoords)
{
    return obstacles.Sample(samPointClamp, cellTexCoords, 0).r > 0.0);
}

float4 PS_ADVECT_OBSTACLE(GS_OUTPUT_FLUIDSIM in,
                          Texture3D velocity,
                          Texture3D color) : SV_Target
{
    if(IsNonEmptyCell(in.CENTERCELL))
    {
      return 0;
    }
```

```
float3 cellVelocity = velocity.Sample(samPointClamp,
                                      in.CENTERCELL).xyz;
float3 pos = in.cellIndex - timeStep*cellVelocity;

float3 npos = float3(pos.x / textureWidth,
                     pos.y / textureHeight,
                     (pos.z+0.5) / textureDepth);

return color.Sample(samLinear, npos);
}
```

Voxelization

To handle boundary conditions for dynamic solids, we need a quick way of determining whether a given cell contains a solid obstacle. We also need to know the solid's velocity for cells next to obstacle boundaries. To do this, we *voxelize* solid obstacles into an "inside-outside" texture and an "obstacle velocity" texture, as shown in Figure 30-8, using two different voxelization routines.

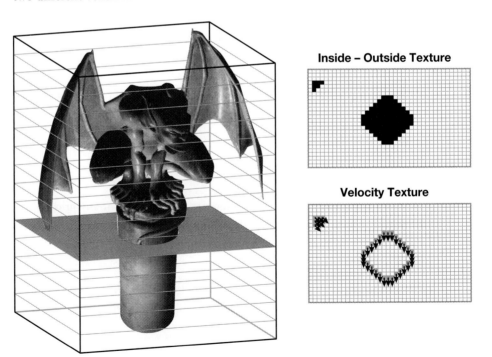

Figure 30-8. Solid Obstacles Are Voxelized into an Inside-Outside Texture and an Obstacle Velocity Texture

Inside-Outside Voxelization

Our approach to obtain an inside-outside voxelization is inspired by the *stencil shadow volumes* algorithm. The idea is simple: We render the input triangle mesh once into each slice of the destination 3D texture using an orthogonal projection. The far clip plane is set at infinity, and the near plane matches the depth of the current slice, as shown in Figure 30-9. When drawing geometry, we use a stencil buffer (of the same dimensions as the slice) that is initialized to zero. We set the stencil operations to *increment* for back faces and *decrement* for front faces (with wrapping in both cases). The result is that any voxel inside the mesh receives a nonzero stencil value. We then do a final pass that copies stencil values into the obstacle texture.[1]

As a result, we are able to distinguish among three types of cells: interior (nonzero stencil value), exterior (zero stencil), and interior but next to the boundary (these cells are tagged by the velocity voxelization algorithm, described next). Note that because this method depends on having one back face for every front face, it is best suited to watertight closed meshes.

Velocity Voxelization

The second voxelization algorithm computes an obstacle's velocity at each grid cell that contains part of the obstacle's boundary. First, however, we need to know the obstacle's velocity at each vertex. A simple way to compute per-vertex velocities is to store vertex positions $\mathbf{p}^{n-1}$ and $\mathbf{p}^n$ from the previous and current frames, respectively, in a vertex buffer. The instantaneous velocity $\mathbf{v}_i$ of vertex i can be approximated with the forward difference

$$\mathbf{v}_i = \frac{\mathbf{p}_i^n - \mathbf{p}_i^{n+1}}{\Delta t}$$

in a vertex shader.

Next, we must compute interpolated obstacle velocities for any grid cell containing a piece of a surface mesh. As with the inside-outside voxelization, the mesh is rendered once for each slice of the grid. This time, however, we must determine the intersection of each triangle with the current slice.

The intersection between a slice and a triangle is a segment, a triangle, a point, or empty. If the intersection is a segment, we draw a "thickened" version of the segment into the

---

1. We can also implement this algorithm to work directly on the final texture instead of using an intermediate stencil buffer. To do so, we can use additive blending. Additionally, if the interior is defined using the *even-odd rule* (instead of the *nonzero rule* we use), one can also use OpenGL's glLogicOp.

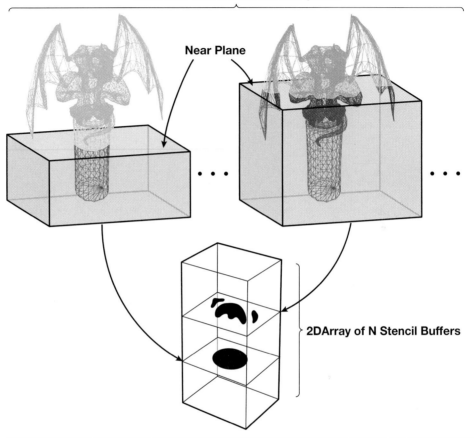

Render model N times with orthographic camera, each time with a different near plane.

Near Plane

2DArray of N Stencil Buffers

Figure 30-9. Inside-Outside Voxelization of a Mesh

slice using a quad. This quad consists of the two end points of the original segment and two additional points offset from these end points, as shown in Figure 30-10. The offset distance w is equal to the diagonal length of one texel in a slice of the 3D texture, and the offset direction is the projection of the triangle's normal onto the slice. Using linear interpolation, we determine velocity values at each end point and assign them to the corresponding vertices of the quad. When the quad is drawn, these values get interpolated across the grid cells as desired.

These quads can be generated using a geometry shader that operates on mesh triangles, producing four vertices if the intersection is a segment and zero vertices otherwise. Because geometry shaders cannot output quads, we must instead use a two-triangle

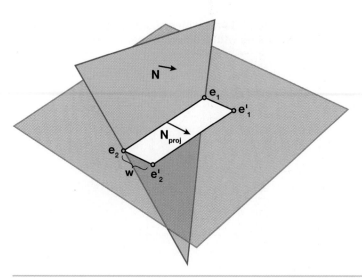

Figure 30-10. A Triangle Intersects a Slice at a Segment with End Points e_1 and e_2.
These end points are offset a distance w in the direction of the projected normal N_{proj} to get the other two vertices of the quad, e_1' and e_2'.

strip. To compute the triangle-slice intersection, we intersect each triangle edge with the slice. If exactly two edge-slice intersections are found, the corresponding intersection points are used as end points for our segment. Velocity values at these points are computed via interpolation along the appropriate triangle edges. The geometry shader GS_GEN_BOUNDARY_VELOCITY in Listing 30-4 gives an implementation of this algorithm. Figure 30-12 shows a few slices of a voxel volume resulting from the voxelization of the model in Figure 30-11.

Listing 30-4. Geometry Shader for Velocity Voxelization

```
// GS_GEN_BOUNDARY_VELOCITY:
// Takes as input:
//   - one triangle (3 vertices),
//   - the sliceIdx,
//   - the sliceZ;
// and outputs:
//   - 2 triangles, if intersection of input triangle with slice
//     is a segment
//   - 0 triangles, otherwise
// The 2 triangles form a 1-voxel wide quadrilateral along the
// segment.
```

Figure 30-11. Simplified Geometry Can Be Used to Speed Up Voxelization

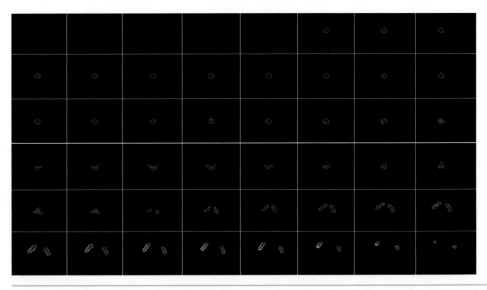

Figure 30-12. Slices of the 3D Textures Resulting from Applying Our Voxelization Algorithms to the Model in Figure 30-11.
The blue channel shows the result of the inside-outside voxelization (bright blue for cells next to the boundary and dark blue for other cells inside). The red and green channels are used to visualize two of the three components of the velocity.

Listing 30-4 (*continued*). Geometry Shader for Velocity Voxelization

```
[maxvertexcount (4)]
void GS_GEN_BOUNDARY_VELOCITY(
  triangle VsGenVelOutput input[3],
  inout TriangleStream<GsGenVelOutput> triStream)
{
  GsGenVelOutput output;
  output.RTIndex = sliceIdx;

  float minZ = min(min(input[0].Pos.z, input[1].Pos.z), input[2].Pos.z);
  float maxZ = max(max(input[0].Pos.z, input[1].Pos.z), input[2].Pos.z);
  if((sliceZ < minZ) || (sliceZ > maxZ))
    // This triangle doesn't intersect the slice.
    return;

  GsGenVelIntVtx intersections[2];
  for(int i=0; i<2; i++)
  {
    intersections[i].Pos = 0;
    intersections[i].Velocity = 0;
  }

  int idx = 0;
  if(idx < 2)
    GetEdgePlaneIntersection(input[0], input[1], sliceZ,
                             intersections, idx);
  if(idx < 2)
    GetEdgePlaneIntersection(input[1], input[2], sliceZ,
                             intersections, idx);
  if(idx < 2)
    GetEdgePlaneIntersection(input[2], input[0], sliceZ,
                             intersections, idx);

  if(idx < 2)
    return;

  float sqrtOf2 = 1.414; // The diagonal of a pixel
  float2 normal = sqrtOf2 * normalize(
    cross((input[1].Pos - input[0].Pos),
          (input[2].Pos - input[0].Pos)).xy);
```

Listing 30-4 (*continued*). Geometry Shader for Velocity Voxelization

```
for(int i=0; i<2; i++)
{
  output.Pos = float4(intersections[i].Pos, 0, 1);
  output.Velocity = intersections[i].Velocity;
  triStream.Append(output);

  output.Pos = float4((intersections[i].Pos +
                      (normal*projSpacePixDim)), 0, 1);
  output.Velocity = intersections[i].Velocity;
  triStream.Append(output);
}
triStream.RestartStrip();
}

void GetEdgePlaneIntersection(
  VsGenVelOutput vA,
  VsGenVelOutput vB,
  float sliceZ,
  inout GsGenVelIntVtx intersections[2],
  inout int idx)
{
  float t = (sliceZ - vA.Pos.z) / (vB.Pos.z - vA.Pos.z);
  if((t < 0) || (t > 1))
    // Line-plane intersection is not within the edge's end points
    // (A and B)
    return;

  intersections[idx].Pos = lerp(vA.Pos, vB.Pos, t).xy;
  intersections[idx].Velocity = lerp(vA.Velocity, vB.Velocity, t);
  idx++;
}
```

Optimizing Voxelization

Although voxelization requires a large number of draw calls, it can be made more efficient using *stream output* (see Blythe 2006). Stream output allows an entire buffer of transformed vertices to be cached when voxelizing deforming meshes such as skinned characters, rather than recomputing these transformations for each slice.

Additionally, instancing can be used to draw all slices in a single draw call, rather than making a separate call for each slice. In this case, the *instance ID* can be used to specify the target slice.

Due to the relative coarseness of the simulation grid used, it is a good idea to use a low level of detail mesh for each obstacle, as shown in Figure 30-11. Using simplified models allowed us to voxelize obstacles at every frame with little performance cost.

Finally, if an obstacle is transformed by a simple analytic transformation (versus a complex skinning operation, for example), voxelization can be precomputed and the *inverse* of the transformation can be applied whenever accessing the 3D textures. A simple example is a mesh undergoing rigid translation and rotation: texture coordinates used to access the inside-outside and obstacle velocity textures can be multiplied by the inverse of the corresponding transformation matrix to get the appropriate values.

30.2.5 Smoke

Although the velocity field describes the fluid's motion, it does not look much like a fluid when visualized directly. To get interesting visual effects, we must keep track of additional quantities that are pushed around by the fluid. For instance, we can keep track of density and temperature to obtain the appearance of smoke (Fedkiw et al. 2001). For each additional quantity ϕ, we must allocate an additional texture with the same dimensions as our grid. The evolution of values in this texture is governed by the same advection equation used for velocity:

$$\frac{\partial \phi}{\partial t} = -(\mathbf{u} \cdot \nabla)\phi.$$

In other words, we can use the same MacCormack advection routine we used to evolve the velocity.

To achieve the particular effect seen in Figure 30-4, for example, we inject a three-dimensional Gaussian "splat" into a *color* texture each frame to provide a source of "smoke." These color values have no real physical significance, but they create attractive swirling patterns as they are advected throughout the volume by the fluid velocity.

To get a more physically plausible appearance, we must make sure that hot smoke rises and cool smoke falls. To do so, we need to keep track of the fluid temperature T (which again is advected by $\mathbf{u}$). Unlike color, temperature values have an influence on the dynamics of the fluid. This influence is described by the *buoyant force*:

$$\mathbf{f}_{buoyancy} = \frac{Pmg}{R}\left(\frac{1}{T_0} - \frac{1}{T}\right)\mathbf{z},$$

where P is pressure, m is the molar mass of the gas, g is the acceleration due to gravity, and R is the universal gas constant. In practice, all of these physical constants can be treated as a single value and can be tweaked to achieve the desired visual appearance. The value T_0 is the ambient or "room" temperature, and T represents the temperature values being advected through the flow. $\mathbf{z}$ is the normalized upward-direction vector. The buoyant force should be thought of as an "external" force and should be added to the velocity field immediately following velocity advection.

30.2.6 Fire

Fire is not very different from smoke except that we must store an additional quantity, called the *reaction coordinate*, that keeps track of the time elapsed since gas was ignited. A reaction coordinate of one indicates that the gas was just ignited, and a coordinate of less than zero indicates that the fuel has been completely exhausted. The evolution of these values is described by the following equation (from Nguyen et al. 2002):

$$\frac{\partial}{\partial t}Y = -(u \cdot \nabla)Y - k.$$

In other words, the reaction coordinate is advected through the flow and decremented by a constant amount (k) at each time step. In practice, this integration is performed by passing a value for k to the advection routine (PS_ADVECT_MACCORMACK), which is added to the result of the advection. (This value should be nonzero only when advecting the reaction coordinate.) Reaction coordinates do not have an effect on the dynamics of the fluid but are later used for rendering (see Section 30.3).

Figure 30-14 (in Section 30.2.10) demonstrates one possible fire effect: a ball of fuel is continuously generated near the bottom of the volume by setting the reaction coordinate in a spherical region to one. For a more advanced treatment of flames, see Nguyen et al. 2002.

30.2.7 Water

Water is modeled differently from the fluid phenomena discussed thus far. With fire or smoke, we are interested in visualizing a density defined throughout the entire volume, but with water the visually interesting part is the *interface* between air and liquid.

Therefore, we need some way of representing this interface and tracking how it deforms as it is pushed around by the fluid velocity.

The *level set method* (Sethian 1999) is a popular representation of a liquid surface and is particularly well suited to a GPU implementation because it requires only a scalar value at each grid cell. In a level set, each cell records the *shortest signed distance* ϕ from the cell center to the water surface. Cells in the grid are classified according to the value of ϕ: if $\phi < 0$, the cell contains water; otherwise, it contains air. Wherever ϕ equals zero is exactly where the water meets the air (the *zero set*). Because advection will not preserve the distance field property of a level set, it is common to periodically *reinitialize* the level set. Reinitialization ensures that each cell does indeed store the shortest distance to the zero set. However, this property isn't needed to simply define the surface, and for real-time animation, it is possible to get decent results without reinitialization. Figure 30-1, at the beginning of this chapter, shows the quality of the results.

Just as with color, temperature, and other attributes, the level set is advected by the fluid, but it also affects the simulation dynamics. In fact, the level set *defines* the fluid domain: in simple models of water and air, we assume that the air has a negligible effect on the liquid and do not perform simulation wherever $\phi \geq 0$. In practice, this means we set the pressure outside of the liquid to zero before solving for pressure and modify the pressure only in liquid cells. It also means that we do not apply external forces such as gravity outside of the liquid. To make sure that only fluid cells are processed, we check the value of the level set texture in the relevant shaders and mask computations at a cell if the value of ϕ is above some threshold. Two alternatives that may be more efficient are to use z-cull to eliminate cells (if the GPU does not support dynamic flow control) (Sander et al. 2004) and to use a sparse data structure (Lefohn et al. 2004).

30.2.8 Performance Considerations

One major factor in writing an efficient solver is bandwidth. For each frame of animation, the solver runs a large number of arithmetically simple kernels, in between which data must be transferred to and from texture memory. Although most of these kernels exhibit good locality, bandwidth is still a major issue: using 32-bit floating-point textures to store quantities yields roughly half the performance of 16-bit textures. Surprisingly, there is little visually discernible degradation that results from using 16-bit storage, as is shown in Figure 30-13. Note that arithmetic operations are still performed in 32-bit floating point, meaning that results are periodically truncated as they are written to the destination textures.

In some cases it is tempting to store multiple cell attributes in a single texture in order to reduce memory usage or for convenience, but doing so is not always optimal in terms of memory bandwidth. For instance, suppose we packed both inside-outside and velocity information about an obstacle into a single RGBA texture. Iteratively solving the pressure-Poisson equation requires that we load inside-outside values numerous times each frame, but meanwhile the obstacle's velocity would go unused. Because packing these two textures together requires four times as many bytes transferred from memory as well as cache space, it may be wise to keep the obstacle's inside-outside information in its own scalar texture.

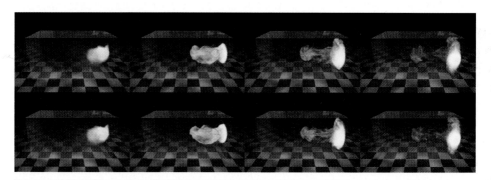

Figure 30-13. Smoke Simulated Using 16-Bit (*Top Row*) and 32-Bit (*Bottom Row*) Floating-Point Textures for Storage
Note that although some fine-scale detail differs between the two sequences, the overall motion is consistent.

30.2.9 Storage

Table 30-1 gives some of the storage requirements needed for simulating and rendering fluids, which amounts to 41 bytes per cell for simulation and 20 bytes per pixel for rendering. However, most of this storage is required only temporarily while simulating or rendering, and hence it can be shared among multiple fluid simulations. In *Hellgate: London*, we stored the exclusive textures (the third column of the table) with each instance of smoke, but we created global versions of the rest of the textures (the last column of the table), which were shared by all the smoke simulations.

Table 30-1. Storage Needed for Simulating and Rendering Fluids

	Total Space	Exclusive Textures	Shared Textures
Fluid Simulation	32 bytes per cell	12 bytes per cell	20 bytes per cell
		1×RGBA16 (velocity)	2×RGBA16 (temporary)
		2×R16 (pressure and density)	2×R16 (temporary)
Voxelization	9 bytes per cell	—	9 bytes per cell
			1×RGBA16 (velocity)
			1×R8 (inside-outside)
Rendering	20 bytes per pixel	—	20 bytes per pixel of off-screen render target
			1×RGBA32 (ray data)
			1×R32 (scene depth)

30.2.10 Numerical Issues

Because real-time applications are so demanding, we have chosen the simplest numerical schemes that still give acceptable visual results. Note, however, that for high-quality animation, more accurate alternatives are preferable.

One of the most expensive parts of the simulation is solving the pressure-Poisson system, $\nabla^2 p = \nabla \cdot \mathbf{u}^*$. We use the Jacobi method to solve this system because it is easy to implement efficiently on the GPU. However, several other suitable solvers have been implemented on the GPU, including the Conjugate Gradient method (Bolz et al. 2003) and the Multigrid method (Goodnight et al. 2003). Cyclic reduction is a particularly interesting option because it is direct and can take advantage of banded systems (Kass et al. 2006). When picking an iterative solver, it may be worth considering not only the overall rate of convergence but also the convergence rate of different *spatial frequencies* in the residual (Briggs et al. 2000). Because there may not be enough time to reach convergence in a real-time application, the distribution of frequencies will have some impact on the appearance of the solution.

Ideally we would like to solve the pressure-Poisson system exactly in order to satisfy the incompressibility constraint and preserve fluid volume. For fluids like smoke and fire, however, a change in volume does not always produce objectionable visual artifacts. Hence we can adjust the number of iterations when solving this system according to available resources. Figure 30-14 compares the appearance of a flame using different numbers of Jacobi iterations. Seen in motion, spinning vortices tend to "flatten out" a bit more when using only a small number of iterations, but the overall appearance is very similar.

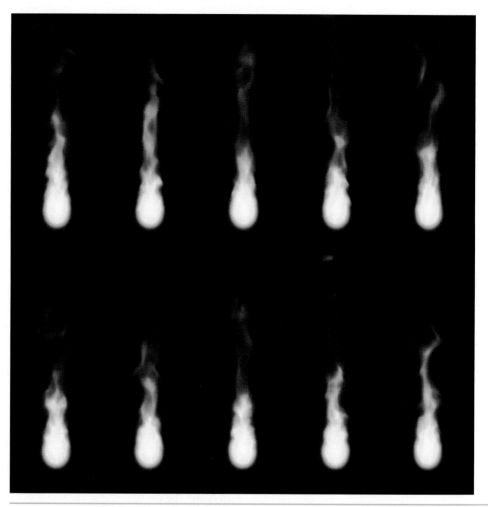

Figure 30-14. Fire Simulation Using 20 Jacobi Iterations (*Top Row*) and 1,000 Jacobi Iterations (*Bottom Row*) for the Pressure Solve

For a more thorough discussion of GPGPU performance issues, see Pharr 2005.

For liquids, on the other hand, a change of volume is immediately apparent: fluid appears to either pour out from nowhere or disappear entirely! Even something as simple as water sitting in a tank can potentially be problematic if too few iterations are used to solve for pressure: because information does not travel from the tank floor to the water surface, pressure from the floor cannot counteract the force of gravity. As a result, the water slowly sinks through the bottom of the tank, as shown in Figure 30-15.

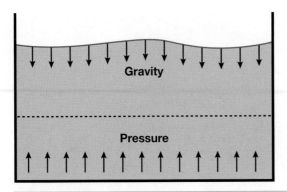

Figure 30-15. Uncorrected Water Simulation
Pressure pushing up from the bottom of the tank may not be able to counteract the force of gravity on the liquid's surface when using a small number of Jacobi iterations to solve for pressure.

Unfortunately, in a real-time application, it is not always possible to solve for p exactly (regardless of the particular solver used) because computation time is constrained by the target frame rate and the resource requirements of other concurrent processes. In simple situations where we know that the liquid should tend toward a static equilibrium, we can force the correct behavior by manipulating the level set in the following way:

$$\phi_{i,j,k}^{n+1} = \begin{cases} A\left(\phi^n\right)_{i,j,k} & \phi_{i,j,k}^{\infty} \geq 0 \\ (1-\beta)\,A\left(\phi^n\right)_{i,j,k} + \beta\phi_{i,j,k}^{\infty} & \phi_{i,j,k}^{\infty} < 0 \end{cases}$$

Here ϕ^{∞} is a level set whose zero set tells us what the surface *should* look like if we let the liquid settle for a long period of time. For example, the equilibrium level set for a tank of water would be simply $\phi^{\infty}(x, y, z) = y - h$, where y is the vertical distance from the bottom of the tank and h is the desired height of the water. See Figure 30-16.

The function A is the advection operator, and the parameter $\beta \in [0, 1]$ controls the amount of *damping* applied to the solution we get from advection. Larger values of β permit fewer solver iterations but also decrease the liveliness of the fluid. Note that this damping is applied only in regions of the domain where ϕ^{∞} is *negative*—this keeps splashes evolving outside of the domain of the equilibrium solution lively, though it can result in temporary volume *gain*.

Ultimately, however, this kind of nonphysical manipulation of the level set is a hack, and its use should be considered judiciously. Consider an environment in which the player scoops up water with a bowl and then sets the bowl down at an arbitrary location on a table: we do not know beforehand what the equilibrium level set should look like and hence cannot prevent water from sinking through the bottom of the bowl.

Chapter 30   Real-Time Simulation and Rendering of 3D Fluids

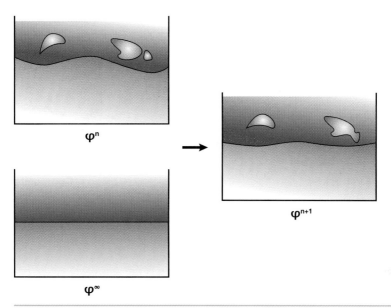

Figure 30-16. Combining Level Sets to Counter a Low Convergence Rate
To preserve fluid volume even under extreme performance constraints, the results of level set advection are combined with a known equilibrium level set ϕ^∞.

30.3 Rendering

30.3.1 Volume Rendering

The result of our simulation is a collection of values stored in a 3D texture. However, there is no mechanism in Direct3D or OpenGL for displaying this texture directly. Therefore we render the fluid using a *ray-marching* pixel shader. Our approach is very similar to the one described in Scharsach 2005.

The placement of the fluid in the scene is determined by six quads, which represent the faces of the simulation volume. These quads are drawn into a deferred shading buffer to determine where and how rays should be cast. We then render the fluid by marching rays through the volume and accumulating densities from the 3D texture, as shown in Figure 30-17.

Volume Ray Casting

In order to cast a ray, we need to know where it enters the volume, in which direction it is traveling, and how many samples to take. One way to get these values is to perform several ray-plane intersections in the ray-marching shader. However, precomputing these values and storing them in a texture makes it easier to perform proper compositing and

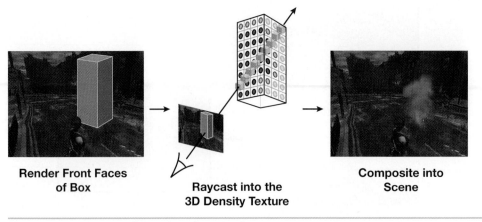

| Render Front Faces of Box | Raycast into the 3D Density Texture | Composite into Scene |

Figure 30-17. A Conceptual Overview of Ray Casting

clipping (more on this later in this section), which is the approach we use here. As a pre-pass, we generate a screen-size texture, called the *RayData* texture, which encodes, for every pixel that is to be rendered, the entry point of the ray in texture space, and the depth through the volume that the ray traverses. To get the depth through the volume, we draw first the back faces of the volume with a shader that outputs the distance from the eye to the fragment's position (in view space) into the alpha channel. We then run a similar shader on the front faces but enable subtractive blending using Equation 1. Furthermore, to get the entry point of the ray, we also output into the RGB channel the texture-space coordinates of each fragment generated for the front faces.

$$OutputColor.rgb = SourceColor.rgb$$
$$OutputColor.a = DestinationColor.a - SourceColor.a$$

(1)

To render the volume, we draw a full-screen quad with a ray-marching shader. This shader looks up into the *RayData* texture to find the pixels that we need to ray-cast through, and the ray entry point and marching distance through the volume for those pixels. The number of samples that the ray-marching shader uses is proportional to the marching distance (we use a step size equal to half a voxel). The ray direction is given by the vector from the eye to the entry point (both in texture space). At each step along the ray, we sample values from the texture containing the simulated values and blend them front to back according to Equation 2. By blending from front to back, we can terminate ray casting early if the color saturates (we exit if *FinalColor.a* > 0.99). For a more physically based rendering model, see Fedkiw et al. 2001.

$$FinalColor.rgb \mathrel{+}= SampleColor.rgb \times SampleColor.a \times (1 - FinalColor.a)$$

$$FinalColor.a \mathrel{+}= SampleColor.a \times (1 - FinalColor.a)$$

(2)

Compositing

There are two problems with the ray-marching algorithm described so far. First, rays continue to march through the volume even if they encounter other scene geometry. See the right side of Figure 30-18 for an illustration. Second, rays are traced even for parts of the volume that are completely occluded, as the left side of Figure 30-18 shows. However, we can modify our computation of volume depth such that we march through only relevant parts of the grid.

Previously we used the distance to the back faces of the volume to determine where ray marching should terminate. To handle obstacles that intersect the volume, we instead use the minimum of the *back-face distance* and the *scene distance* (that is, the distance between the eye and the closest obstacle in the scene). The scene distance can be calculated by reading the scene depth and reverse projecting it back to view space to find the distance from the eye to the scene. If the depth buffer cannot be read as a texture in a pixel shader, as is the case in Direct3D 10 when using multisample antialiasing, this distance can be computed in the main scene rendering pass using multiple render targets; this is the approach we use.

To deal with cases in which the scene geometry completely occludes part of the volume, we compare the front-facing fragments' distance to the *scene distance*. If the front-face distance is greater than the scene distance (that is, the fragment is occluded), we output

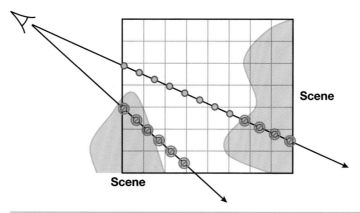

Figure 30-18. Rays Are Clipped According to Scene Depth to Account for Occlusion

a large negative value in the red channel. This way, the final texture-space position computed for the corresponding texel in the *RayData* texture will be outside the volume, and hence no samples will be taken along the corresponding ray.

Clipping

We also need to modify our ray-marching algorithm to handle the cases in which the camera is located *inside* the fluid volume and the camera's near plane clips parts of the front faces of the volume, as shown in Figure 30-19.

In regions where the front faces were clipped, we have no information about where rays enter the volume, and we have incorrect values for the volume depth.

To deal with these regions, we mark the pixels where the back faces of the volume have been rendered but not the front faces. This marking is done by writing a negative color value into the green channel when rendering the back faces of the fluid volume to the *RayData* texture. Note that the *RayData* texture is cleared to zero before either front or back faces are rendered to it. Because we do not use the RGB values of the destination color when rendering the front faces with alpha blending (Equation 1), the pixels for which the green channel contains a negative color after rendering the front faces are those where the back faces of the fluid volume were rendered but not the front (due to

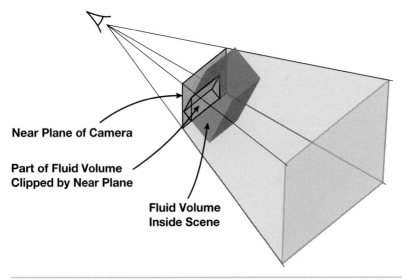

Near Plane of Camera

Part of Fluid Volume Clipped by Near Plane

Fluid Volume Inside Scene

Figure 30-19. Part of the Fluid Volume May Be Clipped by the Near Plane
In areas where the front faces of the fluid volume get clipped by the near plane of the camera, we have incorrect information for ray marching.

clipping). In the ray-casting shader, we explicitly initialize the position of these marked pixels to the appropriate texture-space position of the corresponding point on the near plane. We also correct the depth value read from the *RayData* texture by subtracting from it the distance from the eye to the corresponding point on the near plane.

Filtering

The ray-marching algorithm presented so far has several visible artifacts. One such artifact is *banding*, which results from using an integral number of equally spaced samples. This artifact is especially visible when the scene inside the fluid volume has rapidly changing depth values, as illustrated in Figure 30-20.

To suppress it, we take one more sample than necessary and weigh its contribution to the final color by *d/sampleWidth*, as shown in Figure 30-21. In the figure, *d* is the difference between the scene distance at the fragment and the total distance traveled by the ray at the last sample, and *sampleWidth* is the typical step size along the ray.

Banding, however, usually remains present to some degree and can become even more obvious with high-frequency variations in either the volume density or the mapping between density and color (known as the *transfer function*). This well-known problem is addressed in Hadwiger 2004 and Sigg and Hadwiger 2005. Common solutions include increasing the sampling frequency, jittering the samples along the ray direction, or using higher-order filters when sampling the volume. It is usually a good idea to combine several of these techniques to find a good performance-to-quality trade-off. In *Hellgate: London*, we used trilinear jittered sampling at a frequency of twice per voxel.

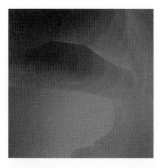 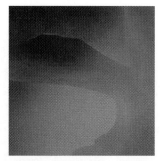

Figure 30-20. Dealing with Banding
Using scene depth can cause banding artifacts (left), which can be solved using weighted sampling (right).

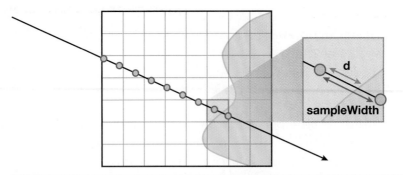

Figure 30-21. Reducing Banding by Taking an Additional Weighted Sample
Taking an additional weighted sample can help reduce banding artifacts such as those seen in Figure 30-20.

Off-Screen Ray Marching

If the resolution of the simulation grid is low compared to screen resolution, there is little visual benefit in ray casting at high resolution. Instead, we draw the fluid into a smaller off-screen render target and then composite the result into the final image. This approach works well except in areas of the image where there are sharp depth discontinuities in scene geometry, as shown in Figure 30-22, and where the camera clips the fluid volume.

This issue is discussed in depth by Iain Cantlay in Chapter 23 of this book, "High-Speed, Off-Screen Particles." In *Hellgate: London*, we use a similar approach to the one presented there: we draw most of the smoke at a low resolution but render pixels in problematic areas at screen resolution. We find these areas by running an edge-

Figure 30-22. Fixing Artifacts Introduced by Low-Resolution Off-Screen Rendering
Left: Ray marching at a low resolution and upsampling can cause artifacts near sharp silhouettes. Center: Detecting these features and rendering the corresponding fragments at higher resolution. Right: The resulting artifact-free image.

detection filter on the *RayData* texture computed earlier in this section. Specifically, we run a Sobel edge-detection filter on the texture's alpha channel (to find edges of obstacles intersecting the volume), red channel (to find edges of obstacles occluding the volume), and green channel (to find the edges where the near plane of the camera clips the volume).

Fire

Rendering fire is similar to rendering smoke except that instead of blending values as we march, we *accumulate* values that are determined by the reaction coordinate Y rather than the smoke density (see Section 30.2.6). In particular, we use an artist-defined 1D texture that maps reaction coordinates to colors in a way that gives the appearance of fire. A more physically based discussion of fire rendering can be found in Nguyen et al. 2002.

The fire volume can also be used as a light source if desired. The simplest approach is to sample the volume at several locations and treat each sample as a point light source. The reaction coordinate and the 1D color texture can be used to determine the intensity and color of the light. However, this approach can lead to severe flickering if not enough point samples are used, and it may not capture the overall behavior of the light. A different approach is to downsample the texture of reaction coordinates to an extremely low resolution and then use *every* voxel as a light source. The latter approach will be less prone to flickering, but it won't capture any high-frequency lighting effects (such as local lighting due to sparks).

30.3.2 Rendering Liquids

To render a liquid surface, we also march through a volume, but this time we look at values from the level set ϕ. Instead of integrating values as we march, we look for the first place along the ray where $\phi = 0$. Once this point is found, we shade it just as we would shade any other surface fragment, using $\nabla\phi$ at that point to approximate the shading normal. For water, it is particularly important that we do not see artifacts of the grid resolution, so we use tricubic interpolation to filter these values. Figure 30-1 at the beginning of the chapter demonstrates the rendered results. See Sigg and Hadwiger 2005 and Hadwiger et al. 2005 for details on how to quickly intersect and filter volume isosurface data such as a level set on the GPU.

Refraction

For fluids like water, there are several ways to make the surface appear as though it refracts the objects behind it. Ray tracing is one possibility, but casting rays is expensive, and there may be no way to find ray intersections with other scene geometry. Instead, we use an approximation that gives the impression of refraction but is fast and simple to implement.

First, we render the objects behind the fluid volume into a background texture.

Next, we determine the nearest ray intersection with the water surface at every pixel by marching through the volume. This produces a pair of textures containing hit locations and shading normals; the alpha value in the texture containing hit locations is set to zero if there was no ray-surface intersection at a pixel, and set to one otherwise. We then shade the hit points with a refraction shader that uses the background texture. Finally, foreground objects are added to create the final image.

The appearance of refraction is achieved by looking up a pixel in the background image near the point being shaded and taking its value as the refracted color. This refracted color is then used in the shading equation as usual. More precisely, this background pixel is accessed at a texture coordinate $\mathbf{t}$ that is equal to the location $\mathbf{p}$ of the pixel being shaded offset by a vector proportional to the projection of the surface normal $\mathbf{N}$ onto the image plane. In other words, if $\mathbf{P}_h$ and $\mathbf{P}_v$ are an orthonormal basis for the image plane oriented with the viewport, then

$$\mathbf{t} = \mathbf{p} - \beta(\mathbf{N} \cdot \mathbf{P}_h, \ \mathbf{N} \cdot \mathbf{P}_v),$$

where $\beta > 0$ is a scalar parameter that controls the severity of the effect. The vectors $\mathbf{P}_v$ and $\mathbf{P}_h$ are defined by

$$\mathbf{P}_v = \frac{\mathbf{z} - (\mathbf{z} \cdot \mathbf{V})\mathbf{V}}{\|\mathbf{z} - (\mathbf{z} \cdot \mathbf{V})\mathbf{V}\|}$$

$$\mathbf{P}_h = \mathbf{P}_v \times \mathbf{V},$$

where $\mathbf{z}$ is up and $\mathbf{V}$ is the view direction.

The effect of applying this transformation to the texture coordinates is that a convex region of the surface will magnify the image behind it, a concave region will shrink the image, and flat (with respect to the viewer) regions will allow rays to pass straight through.

30.4 Conclusion

In this chapter, we hope to have demonstrated that physically based fluid animation is a valuable tool for creating interactive environments, and to have provided some of the basic building blocks needed to start developing a practical implementation. However, this is by no means the end of the line: we have omitted discussion of a large number of possible directions for fluid animation, including melting (Carlson et al. 2002), visco-elastic fluids (Goktekin et al. 2004), and multiphase flows (Lossasso et al. 2006). We have also omitted discussion of a number of interesting data structures and algorithms, such as sparse level sets (Lefohn et al. 2004), which may significantly improve simulation performance; or mesh-based surface extraction (Ziegler et al. 2006), which may permit more efficient rendering of liquids.

30.5 References

Blythe, David. 2006. "The Direct3D 10 System." In *ACM Transactions on Graphics (Proceedings of SIGGRAPH 2006)* 25(3), pp. 724–734.

Bolz, J., I. Farmer, E. Grinspun, and P. Schröder. 2003. "Sparse Matrix Solvers on the GPU: Conjugate Gradients and Multigrid." In *ACM Transactions on Graphics (Proceedings of SIGGRAPH 2003)* 22(3), pp. 917–924.

Bridson R., R. Fedkiw, and M. Muller-Fischer. 2006. "Fluid Simulation." SIGGRAPH 2006 Course Notes. In *ACM SIGGRAPH 2006 Courses*.

Briggs, William L., Van Emden Henson, and Steve F. McCormick. 2000. *A Multigrid Tutorial*. Society for Industrial and Applied Mathematics.

Carlson, M., P. Mucha, R. Van Horn, and G. Turk. 2002. "Melting and Flowing." In *Proceedings of the ACM SIGGRAPH/Eurographics Symposium on Computer Animation*.

Fang, S., and H. Chen. 2000. "Hardware Accelerated Voxelization." *Computers and Graphics* 24(3), pp. 433–442.

Fedkiw, R., J. Stam, and H. W. Jensen. 2001. "Visual Simulation of Smoke." In *Proceedings of SIGGRAPH 2001*, pp. 15–22.

Foster, N., and R. Fedkiw. 2001. "Practical Animation of Liquids." In *Proceedings of SIGGRAPH 2001*.

Goktekin, T. G., A.W. Bargteil, and J. F. O'Brien. 2004. "A Method for Animating Viscoelastic Fluids." In *ACM Transactions on Graphics (Proceedings of SIGGRAPH 2004)* 23(3).

Goodnight, N., C. Woolley, G. Lewin, D. Luebke, and G. Humphreys. 2003. "A Multigrid Solver for Boundary Value Problems Using Programmable Graphics Hardware." In *Proceedings of the SIGGRAPH/Eurographics Workshop on Graphics Hardware 2003*, pp. 102–111.

Hadwiger, M. 2004. "High-Quality Visualization and Filtering of Textures and Segmented Volume Data on Consumer Graphics Hardware." Ph.D. Thesis.

Hadwiger, M., C. Sigg, H. Scharsach, K. Buhler, and M. Gross. 2005. "Real-time Raycasting and Advanced Shading of Discrete Isosurfaces." In *Proceedings of Eurographics 2005*.

Harlow, F., and J. Welch. 1965. "Numerical Calculation of Time-Dependent Viscous Incompressible Flow of Fluid with Free Surface." *Physics of Fluids* 8, pp. 2182–2189.

Harris, Mark J. 2004. "Fast Fluid Dynamics Simulation on the GPU." In *GPU Gems*, edited by Randima Fernando, pp. 637–665. Addison-Wesley.

Harris, Mark, William Baxter, Thorsten Scheuermann, and Anselmo Lastra. 2003. "Simulation of Cloud Dynamics on Graphics Hardware." In *Proceedings of the SIGGRAPH/Eurographics Workshop on Graphics Hardware 2003*, pp. 92–101.

Kass, Michael, Aaron Lefohn, and John Owens. 2006. "Interactive Depth of Field Using Simulated Diffusion on a GPU." Technical report. Pixar Animation Studios. Available online at http://graphics.pixar.com/DepthOfField/paper.pdf.

Krüger, Jens, and Rüdiger Westermann. 2003. "Linear Algebra Operators for GPU Implementation of Numerical Algorithms." In *ACM Transactions on Graphics (Proceedings of SIGGRAPH 2003)* 22(3), pp. 908–916.

Lefohn, A. E., J. M. Kniss, C. D. Hansen, and R. T. Whitaker. 2004. "A Streaming Narrow-Band Algorithm: Interactive Deformation and Visualization of Level Sets." *IEEE Transactions on Visualization and Computer Graphics* 10(2).

Li, Wei, Zhe Fan, Xiaoming Wei, and Arie Kaufman. 2005. "Flow Simulation with Complex Boundaries." In *GPU Gems 2*, edited by Matt Pharr, pp. 747–764. Addison-Wesley.

Liu, Y., X. Liu, and E. Wu. 2004. "Real-Time 3D Fluid Simulation on GPU with Complex Obstacles." *Computer Graphics and Applications*.

Lossasso, F., T. Shinar, A. Selle, and R. Fedkiw. 2006. "Multiple Interacting Liquids." In *ACM Transactions on Graphics (Proceedings of ACM SIGGRAPH 2006)* 25(3).

Müller, Matthias, David Charypar, and Markus Gross. 2003. "Particle-Based Fluid Simulation for Interactive Applications." In *Proceedings of the 2003 ACM SIGGRAPH/Eurographics Symposium on Computer Animation*, pp. 154–159.

Nguyen, D., R. Fedkiw, and H. W. Jensen. 2002. "Physically Based Modeling and Animation of Fire." In *ACM Transactions on Graphics (Proceedings of SIGGRAPH 2002)* 21(3).

Pharr, Matt, ed. 2005. "Part IV: General-Purpose Computation on GPUs: A Primer." In *GPU Gems 2.* Addison-Wesley.

Sander, P. V., N. Tatarchuk, and J. Mitchell. 2004. "Explicit Early-Z Culling for Efficient Fluid Flow Simulation and Rendering." ATI Technical Report.

Scharsach, H. 2005. "Advanced GPU Raycasting." In *Proceedings of CESCG 2005.*

Selle, A., R. Fedkiw, B. Kim, Y. Liu, and J. Rossignac. 2007. "An Unconditionally Stable MacCormack Method." *Journal of Scientific Computing* (in review). Available online at http://graphics.stanford.edu/~fedkiw/papers/stanford2006-09.pdf.

Sethian, J. A. 1999. *Level Set Methods and Fast Marching Methods: Evolving Interfaces in Computational Geometry, Fluid Mechanics, Computer Vision, and Materials Science.* Cambridge University Press.

Sigg, Christian, and Markus Hadwiger. 2005. "Fast Third-Order Texture Filtering." In *GPU Gems 2*, edited by Matt Pharr, pp. 307–329. Addison-Wesley.

Stam, Jos. 1999. "Stable Fluids." In *Proceedings of SIGGRAPH 99*, pp. 121–128.

Wu, E., Y. Liu, and X. Liu. 2004. "An Improved Study of Real-Time Fluid Simulation on GPU." In *Computer Animation and Virtual Worlds* 15(3–4), pp. 139–146.

Ziegler, G., A. Trevs, C. Theobalt, and H.-P. Seidel. 2006. "GPU PointList Generation using HistoPyramids." In *Proceedings of Vision Modeling & Visualization 2006.*

Chapter 31

Fast N-Body Simulation with CUDA

Lars Nyland
NVIDIA Corporation

Mark Harris
NVIDIA Corporation

Jan Prins
University of North Carolina at Chapel Hill

31.1 Introduction

An N-body simulation numerically approximates the evolution of a system of bodies in which each body continuously interacts with every other body. A familiar example is an astrophysical simulation in which each body represents a galaxy or an individual star, and the bodies attract each other through the gravitational force, as in Figure 31-1. N-body simulation arises in many other computational science problems as well. For example, protein folding is studied using N-body simulation to calculate electrostatic and van der Waals forces. Turbulent fluid flow simulation and global illumination computation in computer graphics are other examples of problems that use N-body simulation.

The *all-pairs* approach to N-body simulation is a brute-force technique that evaluates all pair-wise interactions among the N bodies. It is a relatively simple method, but one that is not generally used on its own in the simulation of large systems because of its $O(N^2)$ computational complexity. Instead, the all-pairs approach is typically used as a kernel to determine the forces in close-range interactions. The all-pairs method is combined with a faster method based on a far-field approximation of longer-range forces, which is valid only between parts of the system that are well separated. Fast N-body

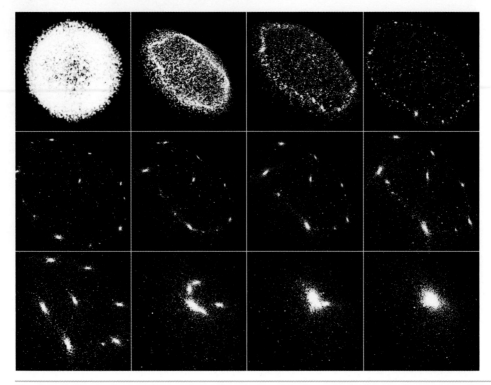

Figure 31-1. Frames from an Interactive 3D Rendering of a 16,384-Body System Simulated by Our Application
We compute more than 10 billion gravitational forces per second on an NVIDIA GeForce 8800 GTX GPU, which is more than 50 times the performance of a highly tuned CPU implementation.

algorithms of this form include the Barnes-Hut method (BH) (Barnes and Hut 1986), the fast multipole method (FMM) (Greengard 1987), and the particle-mesh methods (Hockney and Eastwood 1981, Darden et al. 1993).

The all-pairs component of the algorithms just mentioned requires substantial time to compute and is therefore an interesting target for acceleration. Improving the performance of the all-pairs component will also improve the performance of the far-field component as well, because the balance between far-field and near-field (all-pairs) can be shifted to assign more work to a faster all-pairs component. Accelerating one component will offload work from the other components, so the entire application benefits from accelerating one kernel.

In this chapter, we focus on the all-pairs computational kernel and its implementation using the NVIDIA CUDA programming model. We show how the parallelism available in the all-pairs computational kernel can be expressed in the CUDA model and how various parameters can be chosen to effectively engage the full resources of the NVIDIA GeForce 8800 GTX GPU. We report on the performance of the all-pairs N-body kernel for astrophysical simulations, demonstrating several optimizations that improve performance. For this problem, the GeForce 8800 GTX calculates more than 10 billion interactions per second with $N = 16{,}384$, performing 38 integration time steps per second. At 20 flops per interaction, this corresponds to a sustained performance in excess of 200 gigaflops. This result is close to the theoretical peak performance of the GeForce 8800 GTX GPU.

31.2 All-Pairs N-Body Simulation

We use the gravitational potential to illustrate the basic form of computation in an all-pairs N-body simulation. In the following computation, we use bold font to signify vectors (typically in 3D). Given N bodies with an initial position $\mathbf{x}_i$ and velocity $\mathbf{v}_i$ for $1 \leq i \leq N$, the force vector $\mathbf{f}_{ij}$ on body i caused by its gravitational attraction to body j is given by the following:

$$\mathbf{f}_{ij} = G\frac{m_i m_j}{\left\|\mathbf{r}_{ij}\right\|^2} \cdot \frac{\mathbf{r}_{ij}}{\left\|\mathbf{r}_{ij}\right\|},$$

where m_i and m_j are the masses of bodies i and j, respectively; $\mathbf{r}_{ij} = \mathbf{x}_j - \mathbf{x}_i$ is the vector from body i to body j; and G is the gravitational constant. The left factor, the *magnitude* of the force, is proportional to the product of the masses and diminishes with the square of the distance between bodies i and j. The right factor is the *direction* of the force, a unit vector from body i in the direction of body j (because gravitation is an attractive force).

The total force $\mathbf{F}_i$ on body i, due to its interactions with the other $N - 1$ bodies, is obtained by summing all interactions:

$$\mathbf{F}_i = \sum_{\substack{1 \leq j \leq N \\ j \neq i}} \mathbf{f}_{ij} = Gm_i \cdot \sum_{\substack{1 \leq j \leq N \\ j \neq i}} \frac{m_j \mathbf{r}_{ij}}{\left\|\mathbf{r}_{ij}\right\|^3}.$$

As bodies approach each other, the force between them grows without bound, which is an undesirable situation for numerical integration. In astrophysical simulations, collisions between bodies are generally precluded; this is reasonable if the bodies represent galaxies that may pass right through each other. Therefore, a *softening factor* $\varepsilon^2 > 0$ is added, and the denominator is rewritten as follows:

$$\mathbf{F}_i \approx Gm_i \cdot \sum_{1 \leq j \leq N} \frac{m_j \mathbf{r}_{ij}}{\left(\left\|\mathbf{r}_{ij}\right\|^2 + \varepsilon^2\right)^{3/2}}.$$

Note the condition $j \neq i$ is no longer needed in the sum, because $\mathbf{f}_{ii} = 0$ when $\varepsilon^2 > 0$. The softening factor models the interaction between two Plummer point masses: masses that behave as if they were spherical galaxies (Aarseth 2003, Dyer and Ip 1993). In effect, the softening factor limits the magnitude of the force between the bodies, which is desirable for numerical integration of the system state.

To integrate over time, we need the acceleration $\mathbf{a}_i = \mathbf{F}_i / m_i$ to update the position and velocity of body i, and so we simplify the computation to this:

$$\mathbf{a}_i \approx G \cdot \sum_{1 \leq j \leq N} \frac{m_j \mathbf{r}_{ij}}{\left(\left\|\mathbf{r}_{ij}\right\|^2 + \varepsilon^2\right)^{3/2}}.$$

The integrator used to update the positions and velocities is a leapfrog-Verlet integrator (Verlet 1967) because it is applicable to this problem and is computationally efficient (it has a high ratio of accuracy to computational cost). The choice of integration method in N-body problems usually depends on the nature of the system being studied. The integrator is included in our timings, but discussion of its implementation is omitted because its complexity is $O(N)$ and its cost becomes insignificant as N grows.

31.3 A CUDA Implementation of the All-Pairs N-Body Algorithm

We may think of the all-pairs algorithm as calculating each entry $\mathbf{f}_{ij}$ in an $N \times N$ grid of all pair-wise forces.[1] Then the total force $\mathbf{F}_i$ (or acceleration $\mathbf{a}_i$) on body i is obtained from the sum of all entries in row i. Each entry can be computed independently, so there is $O(N^2)$ available parallelism. However, this approach requires $O(N^2)$ memory

---

1. The relation between reciprocal forces $\mathbf{f}_{ji} = -\mathbf{f}_{ij}$ can be used to reduce the number of force evaluations by a factor of two, but this optimization has an adverse effect on parallel evaluation strategies (especially with small N), so it is not employed in our implementation.

and would be substantially limited by memory bandwidth. Instead, we serialize some of the computations to achieve the data reuse needed to reach peak performance of the arithmetic units and to reduce the memory bandwidth required.

Consequently, we introduce the notion of a computational *tile*, a square region of the grid of pair-wise forces consisting of p rows and p columns. Only $2p$ body descriptions are required to evaluate all p^2 interactions in the tile (p of which can be reused later). These body descriptions can be stored in shared memory or in registers. The total effect of the interactions in the tile on the p bodies is captured as an update to p acceleration vectors.

To achieve optimal reuse of data, we arrange the computation of a tile so that the interactions in each row are evaluated in sequential order, updating the acceleration vector, while the separate rows are evaluated in parallel. In Figure 31-2, the diagram on the left shows the evaluation strategy, and the diagram on the right shows the inputs and outputs for a tile computation.

In the remainder of this section, we follow a bottom-up presentation of the full computation, packaging the available parallelism and utilizing the appropriate local memory at each level.

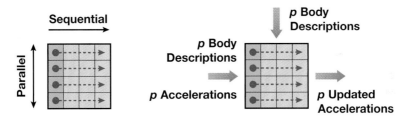

Figure 31-2. A Schematic Figure of a Computational Tile
Left: Evaluation order. Right: Inputs needed and outputs produced for the p^2 interactions calculated in the tile.

31.3.1 Body-Body Force Calculation

The interaction between a pair of bodies as described in Section 31.2 is implemented as an entirely serial computation. The code in Listing 31-1 computes the force on body i from its interaction with body j and updates acceleration $\mathbf{a}_i$ of body i as a result of this interaction. There are 20 floating-point operations in this code, counting the additions, multiplications, the sqrtf() call, and the division (or reciprocal).

```
__device__ float3
bodyBodyInteraction(float4 bi, float4 bj, float3 ai)
{
    float3 r;

    // r_ij  [3 FLOPS]
    r.x = bj.x - bi.x;
    r.y = bj.y - bi.y;
    r.z = bj.z - bi.z;

    // distSqr = dot(r_ij, r_ij) + EPS^2  [6 FLOPS]
    float distSqr = r.x * r.x + r.y * r.y + r.z * r.z + EPS2;

    // invDistCube =1/distSqr^(3/2)  [4 FLOPS (2 mul, 1 sqrt, 1 inv)]
    float distSixth = distSqr * distSqr * distSqr;
    float invDistCube = 1.0f/sqrtf(distSixth);

    // s = m_j * invDistCube [1 FLOP]
    float s = bj.w * invDistCube;

    // a_i =  a_i + s * r_ij [6 FLOPS]
    ai.x += r.x * s;
    ai.y += r.y * s;
    ai.z += r.z * s;

    return ai;
}
```

We use CUDA's `float4` data type for body descriptions and accelerations stored in GPU device memory. We store each body's mass in the w field of the body's `float4` position. Using `float4` (instead of `float3`) data allows *coalesced* memory access to the arrays of data in device memory, resulting in efficient memory requests and transfers. (See the *CUDA Programming Guide* (NVIDIA 2007) for details on coalescing memory requests.) Three-dimensional vectors stored in local variables are stored as `float3` variables, because register space is an issue and coalesced access is not.

31.3.2 Tile Calculation

A tile is evaluated by p threads performing the same sequence of operations on different data. Each thread updates the acceleration of one body as a result of its interaction with

p other bodies. We load p body descriptions from the GPU device memory into the shared memory provided to each *thread block* in the CUDA model. Each thread in the block evaluates p successive interactions. The result of the tile calculation is p updated accelerations.

The code for the tile calculation is shown in Listing 31-2. The input parameter myPosition holds the position of the body for the executing thread, and the array shPosition is an array of body descriptions in shared memory. Recall that p threads execute the function body in parallel, and each thread iterates over the same p bodies, computing the acceleration of its individual body as a result of interaction with p other bodies.

Listing 31-2. Evaluating Interactions in a *p×p* Tile

```
__device__  float3
tile_calculation(float4 myPosition, float3 accel)
{
  int i;
  extern __shared__  float4[] shPosition;

  for (i = 0; i < blockDim.x; i++) {
    accel = bodyBodyInteraction(myPosition, shPosition[i], accel);
  }
  return accel;
}
```

The G80 GPU architecture supports concurrent reads from multiple threads to a single shared memory address, so there are no shared-memory-bank conflicts in the evaluation of interactions. (Refer to the *CUDA Programming Guide* (NVIDIA 2007) for details on the shared memory broadcast mechanism used here.)

31.3.3 Clustering Tiles into Thread Blocks

We define a thread block as having p threads that execute some number of tiles in sequence. Tiles are sized to balance parallelism with data reuse. The degree of parallelism (that is, the number of rows) must be sufficiently large so that multiple warps can be interleaved to hide latencies in the evaluation of interactions. The amount of data reuse grows with the number of columns, and this parameter also governs the size of the transfer of bodies from device memory into shared memory. Finally, the size of the tile also determines the register space and shared memory required. For this implementation, we have used square tiles of size p by p. Before executing a tile, each thread fetches one body into shared memory, after which the threads synchronize. Consequently, each tile starts with p successive bodies in the shared memory.

Figure 31-3 shows a thread block that is executing code for multiple tiles. Time spans the horizontal direction, while parallelism spans the vertical direction. The heavy lines demarcate the tiles of computation, showing where shared memory is loaded and a barrier synchronization is performed. In a thread block, there are N/p tiles, with p threads computing the forces on p bodies (one thread per body). Each thread computes all N interactions for one body.

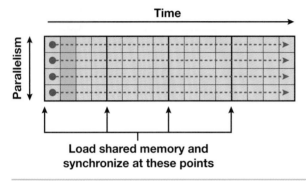

Figure 31-3. The CUDA Kernel of Pair-Wise Forces to Calculate
Multiple threads work from left to right, synchronizing at the end of each tile of computation.

The code to calculate N-body forces for a thread block is shown in Listing 31-3. This code is the CUDA kernel that is called from the host.

The parameters to the function `calculate_forces()` are pointers to global device memory for the positions `devX` and the accelerations `devA` of the bodies. We assign them to local pointers with type conversion so they can be indexed as arrays. The loop over the tiles requires two synchronization points. The first synchronization ensures that all shared memory locations are populated before the gravitation computation proceeds, and the second ensures that all threads finish their gravitation computation before advancing to the next tile. Without the second synchronization, threads that finish their part in the tile calculation might overwrite the shared memory still being read by other threads.

```
__global__ void
calculate_forces(void *devX, void *devA)
{
  extern __shared__ float4[] shPosition;

  float4 *globalX = (float4 *)devX;
  float4 *globalA = (float4 *)devA;
  float4 myPosition;
  int i, tile;
  float3 acc = {0.0f, 0.0f, 0.0f};
  int gtid = blockIdx.x * blockDim.x + threadIdx.x;

  myPosition = globalX[gtid];

  for (i = 0, tile = 0; i < N; i += p, tile++) {
    int idx = tile * blockDim.x + threadIdx.x;
    shPosition[threadIdx.x] = globalX[idx];
    __syncthreads();
    acc = tile_calculation(myPosition, acc);
    __syncthreads();
  }
  // Save the result in global memory for the integration step.
  float4 acc4 = {acc.x, acc.y, acc.z, 0.0f};
  globalA[gtid] = acc4;
}
```

31.3.4 Defining a Grid of Thread Blocks

The kernel program in Listing 31-3 calculates the acceleration of *p* bodies in a system, caused by their interaction with all *N* bodies in the system. We invoke this program on a *grid* of thread blocks to compute the acceleration of all *N* bodies. Because there are *p* threads per block and one thread per body, the number of thread blocks needed to complete all *N* bodies is N/p, so we define a 1D grid of size N/p. The result is a total of *N* threads that perform *N* force calculations each, for a total of N^2 interactions.

Evaluation of the full grid of interactions can be visualized as shown in Figure 31-4. The vertical dimension shows the parallelism of the 1D grid of N/p independent thread blocks with p threads each. The horizontal dimension shows the sequential processing of N force calculations in each thread. A thread block reloads its shared memory every p steps to share p positions of data.

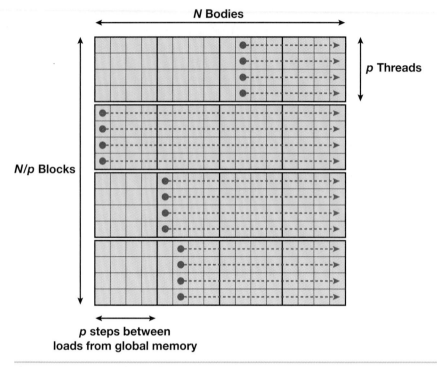

N Bodies

p Threads

N/p Blocks

**p steps between
loads from global memory**

Figure 31-4. The Grid of Thread Blocks That Calculates All N^2 Forces
Here there are four thread blocks with four threads each.

31.4 Performance Results

By simply looking at the clocks and capacities of the GeForce 8800 GTX GPU, we observe that it is capable of 172.8 gigaflops (128 processors, 1.35 GHz each, one floating-point operation completed per cycle per processor). Multiply-add instructions (MADs) perform two floating-point operations every clock cycle, doubling the potential performance. Fortunately, the N-body code has several instances where MAD instructions are generated by the compiler, raising the performance ceiling well over 172.8 gigaflops.

Conversely, complex instructions such as inverse square root require multiple clock cycles. The *CUDA Programming Guide* (NVIDIA 2007) says to expect 16 clock cycles per warp of 32 threads, or four times the amount of time required for the simpler operations. Our code uses one inverse-square-root instruction per interaction.

When comparing gigaflop rates, we simply count the floating-point operations listed in the high-level code. By counting the floating-point operations in the `bodyBody-Interaction` code (Listing 31-1), we see nine additions, nine multiplications, one square root, and one division. Division and square root clearly require more time than addition or multiplication, and yet we still assign a cost of 1 flop each,[2] yielding a total of 20 floating-point operations per pair-wise force calculation. This value is used throughout the chapter to compute gigaflops from interactions per second.

31.4.1 Optimization

Our first implementation achieved 163 gigaflops for 16,384 bodies. This is an excellent result, but there are some optimizations we can use that will increase the performance.

Performance Increase with Loop Unrolling

The first improvement comes from *loop unrolling*, where we replace a single body-body interaction call in the inner loop with 2 to 32 calls to reduce loop overhead. A chart of performance for small unrolling factors is shown in Figure 31-5.

We examined the code generated by the CUDA compiler for code unrolled with 4 successive calls to the body-body interaction function. It contains 60 instructions for the 4 in-lined calls. Of the 60 instructions, 56 are floating-point instructions, containing 20 multiply-add instructions and 4 inverse-square-root instructions. Our best hope is that the loop will require 52 cycles for the non-inverse-square-root floating-point instructions, 16 cycles for the 4 inverse-square-root instructions, and 4 cycles for the loop control, totaling 72 cycles to perform 80 floating-point operations.

If this performance is achieved, the G80 GPU will perform approximately 10 billion body-body interactions per second (128 processors at 1350 MHz, computing 4 body-body interactions in 72 clock cycles), or more than 200 gigaflops. This is indeed the performance we observe for $N > 8192$, as shown in Figure 31-6.

---

2. Although we count `1.0/sqrt(x)` as two floating-point operations, it may also be assumed to be a single operation called "`rsqrt()`" (Elsen et al. 2006). Doing so reduces the flop count per interaction to 19 instead of 20. Some researchers use a flop count of 38 for the interaction (Hamada and Iitaka 2007); this is an arbitrary conversion based on an historical estimate of the running time equivalent in flops of square root and reciprocal. It bears no relation to the actual number of floating-point operations.

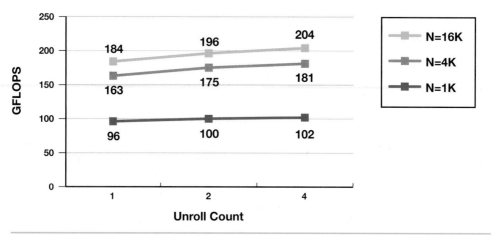

Figure 31-5. Performance Increase with Loop Unrolling
This graph shows the effect of unrolling a loop by replicating the body of the loop 1, 2, and 4 times for simulations with 1024, 4096, and 16,384 bodies. The performance increases, as does register usage, until the level of multiprogramming drops with an unrolling factor of 8.

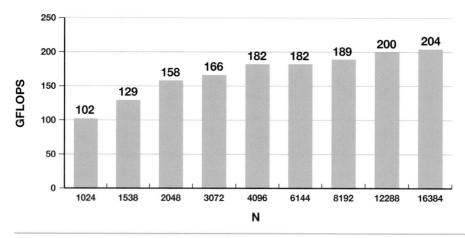

Figure 31-6. Performance Increase as *N* Grows
This graph shows observed gigaflop rates for varying problem sizes, where each pair-wise force calculation is considered to require 20 floating-point operations. There are evident inefficiencies when N < 4096, but performance is consistently high for N ≥ 4096.

Performance Increase as Block Size Varies

Another performance-tuning parameter is the value of p, the size of the tile. The total memory fetched by the program is N^2/p for each integration time step of the algorithm, so increasing p decreases memory traffic. There are 16 multiprocessors on the

GeForce 8800 GTX GPU, so p cannot be arbitrarily large; it must remain small enough so that N/p is 16 or larger. Otherwise, some multiprocessors will be idle.

Another reason to keep p small is the concurrent assignment of thread blocks to multiprocessors. When a thread block uses only a portion of the resources on a multiprocessor (such as registers, thread slots, and shared memory), multiple thread blocks are placed on each multiprocessor. This technique provides more opportunity for the hardware to hide latencies of pipelined instruction execution and memory fetches. Figure 31-7 shows how the performance changes as p is varied for $N = 1024$, 4096, and 16,384.

Improving Performance for Small N

A final optimization that we implemented—using multiple threads per body— attempts to improve performance for $N < 4096$. As N decreases, there is not enough work with one thread per body to adequately cover all the latencies in the GeForce 8800 GTX GPU, so performance drops rapidly. We therefore increase the number of active threads by using multiple threads on each row of a body's force calculation. If the additional threads are part of the same thread block, then the number of memory requests increases, as does the number of warps, so the latencies begin to be covered again. Our current register use limits the number of threads per block to 256 on the 8800 GTX GPU (blocks of 512 threads fail to run), so we split each row into q segments, keeping $p \times q \leq 256$.

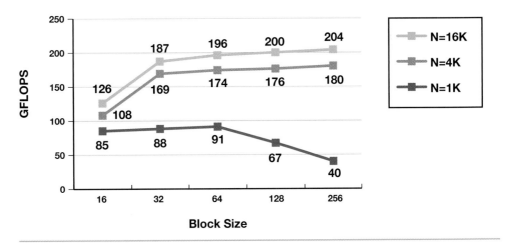

Figure 31-7. Performance as Block Size Varies
This graph shows how performance changes as the tile size p changes, for N = 1024, 4096, and 16,384. Larger tiles lead to better performance, as long as all 16 multiprocessors are in use, which explains the decline for N = 1024.

Splitting the rows has the expected benefit. Using two threads to divide the work increased performance for $N = 1024$ by 44 percent. The improvement rapidly diminishes when splitting the work further. And of course, for $N > 4096$, splitting had almost no effect, because the code is running at nearly peak performance. Fortunately, splitting did not reduce performance for large N. Figure 31-8 shows a graph demonstrating the performance gains.

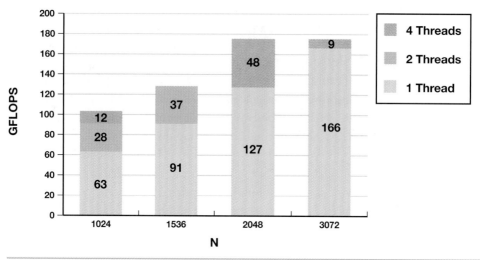

Figure 31-8. Performance Increase by Using Multiple Threads per Body
This chart demonstrates that adding more threads to problems of small N improves performance. When the total force on one body is computed by two threads instead of one, performance increases by as much as 44 percent. Using more than four threads per body provides no additional performance gains.

31.4.2 Analysis of Performance Results

When we judge the performance gain of moving to the GeForce 8800 GTX GPU, the most surprising and satisfying result is the speedup of the N-body algorithm compared to its performance on a CPU. The performance is much larger than the comparison of peak floating-point rates between the GeForce 8800 GTX GPU and Intel processors. We speculate that the main reason for this gain is that Intel processors require dozens of unpipelined clock cycles for the division and square root operations, whereas the GPU has a single instruction that performs an inverse square root. Intel's Streaming SIMD Extensions (SSE) instruction set includes a four-clock-cycle $1/\text{sqrt}(x)$ instruction (vector and scalar), but the accuracy is limited to 12 bits. In a technical report from Intel (Intel 1999), a method is proposed to increase the accuracy over a limited domain, but the cost is estimated to be 16 clock cycles.

31.5 Previous Methods Using GPUs for N-Body Simulation

The N-body problem has been studied throughout the history of computing. In the 1980s several hierarchical and mesh-style algorithms were introduced, successfully reducing the $O(N^2)$ complexity. The parallelism of the N-body problem has also been studied as long as there have been parallel computers. We limit our review to previous work that pertains to achieving high performance using GPU hardware.

In 2004 we built an N-body application for GPUs by using Cg and OpenGL (Nyland, Harris, and Prins 2004). Although Cg presented a more powerful GPU programming language than had previously been available, we faced several drawbacks to building the application in a graphics environment. All data were either read-only or write-only, so a double-buffering scheme had to be used. All computations were initiated by drawing a rectangle whose pixel values were computed by a shader program, requiring $O(N^2)$ memory. Because of the difficulty of programming complex algorithms in the graphics API, we performed simple brute-force computation of all pair-wise accelerations into a single large texture, followed by a parallel sum reduction to get the vector of total accelerations. This sum reduction was completely bandwidth bound because of the lack of on-chip shared memory. The maximum texture-size limitation of the GPU limited the largest number of bodies we could handle (at once) to 2048. Using an out-of-core method allowed us to surpass that limit.

A group at Stanford University (Elsen et al. 2006) created an N-body solution similar to the one described in this chapter, using the BrookGPU programming language (Buck et al. 2004), gathering performance data from execution on an ATI X1900 XTX GPU. They concluded that loop unrolling significantly improves performance. They also concluded that achieving good performance when $N < 4096$ is difficult and suggest a similar solution to ours, achieving similar improvement. The Stanford University group compares their GPU implementation to a highly tuned CPU implementation (SSE assembly language that achieves 3.8 gigaflops, a performance metric we cannot match) and observe the GPU outperforming the CPU by a factor of 25. They provide code (written in BrookGPU) and analyze what the code and the hardware are doing. The

GPU hardware they used achieves nearly 100 gigaflops. They also remind us that the CPU does half the number of force calculations of the GPU by using the symmetry of $\mathbf{f}_{ij} = -\mathbf{f}_{ji}$.

Since the release of the GeForce 8800 GTX GPU and CUDA, several implementations of N-body applications have appeared. Two that caught our attention are Hamada and Iitaka 2007 and Portegies Zwart et al. 2007. Both implementations mimic the Gravity Pipe (GRAPE) hardware (Makino et al. 2000), suggesting that the GeForce 8800 GTX GPU replace the GRAPE custom hardware. Their N-body method uses a multiple time-step scheme, with integration steps occurring at different times for different bodies, so the comparison with these two methods can only be done by comparing the number of pair-wise force interactions per second. We believe that the performance we have achieved is nearly two times greater than the performance of the cited works.

31.6 Hierarchical N-Body Methods

Many practical N-body applications use a hierarchical approach, recursively dividing the space into subregions until some criterion is met (for example, that the space contains fewer than k bodies). For interactions within a leaf cell, the all-pairs method is used, usually along with one or more layers of neighboring leaf cells. For interactions with subspaces farther away, far-field approximations are used. Popular hierarchical methods are Barnes-Hut (Barnes and Hut 1986) and Greengard's fast multipole method (Greengard 1987, Greengard and Huang 2002).

Both algorithms must choose how to interact with remote leaf cells. The general result is that many body-cell or cell-cell interactions require an all-pairs solution to calculate the forces. The savings in the algorithm comes from the use of a multipole expansion of the potential due to bodies at a distance, rather than from interactions with the individual bodies at a distance.

As an example in 3D, consider a simulation of 2^{18} bodies (256 K), decomposed into a depth-3 octree containing 512 leaf cells with 512 bodies each. The minimum neighborhood of cells one layer deep will contain 27 leaf cells, but probably many more will be used. For each leaf cell, there are at least $27 \times 512 \times 512$ pair-wise force interactions to compute. That yields more than 7 million interactions per leaf cell, which in our implementation would require less than 1 millisecond of computation to solve. The total time required for all 512 leaf cells would be less than a half-second.

Contrast this with our all-pairs implementation[3] on an Intel Core 2 Duo[4] that achieves about 20 million interactions per second. The estimated time for the same calculation is about 90 seconds (don't forget that the CPU calculates only half as many pair-wise interactions). Even the high-performance implementations that compute 100 million interactions per second require 18 seconds. One way to alleviate the load is to deepen the hierarchical decomposition and rely more on the far-field approximations, so that the leaf cells would be populated with fewer particles. Of course, the deeper tree means more work in the far-field segment.

We believe that the savings of moving from the CPU to the GPU will come not only from the increased computational horsepower, but also from the increased size of the leaf cells, making the hierarchical decomposition shallower, saving time in the far-field evaluation as well. In future work we hope to implement the BH or FMM algorithms, to evaluate the savings of more-efficient algorithms.

31.7 Conclusion

It is difficult to imagine a real-world algorithm that is better suited to execution on the G80 architecture than the all-pairs N-body algorithm. In this chapter we have demonstrated three features of the algorithm that help it achieve such high efficiency:

- Straightforward parallelism with sequential memory access patterns
- Data reuse that keeps the arithmetic units busy
- Fully pipelined arithmetic, including complex operations such as inverse square root, that are much faster clock-for-clock on a GeForce 8800 GTX GPU than on a CPU

The result is an algorithm that runs more than 50 times as fast as a highly tuned serial implementation (Elsen et al. 2006) or 250 times faster than our portable C implementation. At this performance level, 3D simulations with large numbers of particles can be run interactively, providing 3D visualizations of gravitational, electrostatic, or other mutual-force systems.

---

3. Our implementation is single-threaded, does not use any SSE instructions, and is compiled with gcc. Other specialized N-body implementations on Intel processors achieve 100 million interactions a second (Elsen et al. 2006).

4. Intel Core 2 Duo 6300 CPU at 1.87 GHz with 2.00 GB of RAM.

31.8 References

Aarseth, S. 2003. *Gravitational N-Body Simulations*. Cambridge University Press.

Barnes, J., and P. Hut. 1986. "A Hierarchical O(n log n) Force Calculation Algorithm." *Nature* 324.

Buck, I., T. Foley, D. Horn, J. Sugerman, K. Fatahalian, M. Houston, and P. Hanrahan. 2004. "Brook for GPUs: Stream Computing on Graphics Hardware." In *ACM Transactions on Graphics (Proceedings of SIGGRAPH 2004)* 23(3).

Darden, T., D. York, and L. Pederson. 1993. "Particle Mesh Ewald: An N log(N) Method for Ewald Sums in Large Systems." *Journal of Chemical Physics* 98(12), p. 10089.

Dehnen, Walter. 2001. "Towards Optimal Softening in 3D N-body Codes: I. Minimizing the Force Error." *Monthly Notices of the Royal Astronomical Society* 324, p. 273.

Dyer, Charles, and Peter Ip. 1993. "Softening in N-Body Simulations of Collisionless Systems." *The Astrophysical Journal* 409, pp. 60–67.

Elsen, Erich, Mike Houston, V. Vishal, Eric Darve, Pat Hanrahan, and Vijay Pande. 2006. "N-Body Simulation on GPUs." Poster presentation. Supercomputing 06 Conference.

Greengard, L. 1987. *The Rapid Evaluation of Potential Fields in Particle Systems*. ACM Press.

Greengard, Leslie F., and Jingfang Huang. 2002. "A New Version of the Fast Multipole Method for Screened Coulomb Interactions in Three Dimensions." *Journal of Computational Physics* 180(2), pp. 642–658.

Hamada, T., and T. Iitaka. 2007. "The Chamomile Scheme: An Optimized Algorithm for N-body Simulations on Programmable Graphics Processing Units." *ArXiv Astrophysics e-prints*, astro-ph/0703100, March 2007.

Hockney, R., and J. Eastwood. 1981. *Computer Simulation Using Particles*. McGraw-Hill.

Intel Corporation. 1999. "Increasing the Accuracy of the Results from the Reciprocal and Reciprocal Square Root Instructions Using the Newton-Raphson Method." Version 2.1. Order Number: 243637-002. Available online at http://cache-www.intel.com/cd/00/00/04/10/41007_nrmethod.pdf.

Intel Corporation. 2003. *Intel Pentium 4 and Intel Xeon Processor Optimization Reference Manual*. Order Number: 248966-007.

Johnson, Vicki, and Alper Ates. 2005. "NBodyLab Simulation Experiments with GRAPE-6a and MD-GRAPE2 Acceleration." *Astronomical Data Analysis Software and Systems XIV P3-1-6*, ASP Conference Series, Vol. XXX, P. L. Shopbell, M. C. Britton, and R. Ebert, eds. Available online at http://nbodylab.interconnect.com/docs/P3.1.6_revised.pdf.

Makino, J., T. Fukushige, and M. Koga. 2000. "A 1.349 Tflops Simulation of Black Holes in a Galactic Center on GRAPE-6." In *Proceedings of the 2000 ACM/IEEE Conference on Supercomputing*.

NVIDIA Corporation. 2007. *NVIDIA CUDA Compute Unified Device Architecture Programming Guide*. Version 0.8.1.

Nyland, Lars, Mark Harris, and Jan Prins. 2004. "The Rapid Evaluation of Potential Fields Using Programmable Graphics Hardware." Poster presentation at GP^2, the ACM Workshop on General Purpose Computing on Graphics Hardware.

Portegies Zwart, S., R. Belleman, and P. Geldof. 2007. "High Performance Direct Gravitational N-body Simulations on Graphics Processing Unit." *ArXiv Astrophysics e-prints*, astro-ph/0702058, Feb. 2007.

Verlet, J. 1967. "Computer Experiments on Classical Fluids." *Physical Review* 159(1), pp. 98–103.

Chapter 32

Broad-Phase Collision Detection with CUDA

Scott Le Grand
NVIDIA Corporation

Collision detection among many 3D objects is an important component of physics simulation, computer-aided design, molecular modeling, and other applications. Most efficient implementations use a two-phase approach: a *broad phase* followed by a *narrow phase*. In the broad phase, collision tests are conservative—usually based on bounding volumes only—but fast in order to quickly prune away pairs of objects that do not collide with each other. The output of the broad phase is the potentially colliding set of pairs of objects. In the narrow phase, collision tests are exact—they usually compute exact contact points and normals—thus much more costly, but performed for only the pairs of the potentially colliding set. Such an approach is very suitable when a lot of the objects are actually not colliding—as is the case in practice—so that many pairs of objects are rejected during the broad phase.

In this chapter, we present a GPU implementation of broad-phase collision detection ("broad phase," for short) based on CUDA that is an order of magnitude faster than the CPU implementation.

32.1 Broad-Phase Algorithms

The brute-force implementation of broad phase for n objects consists in conducting $n(n-1)/2$ collision tests. Thus it has a complexity of $O(n^2)$. Alternative algorithms, such as *sort and sweep* (described in Section 32.1.1) or *spatial subdivision* (described in

Section 32.1.2), achieve an average complexity of $O(n \log n)$ (their worst-case complexity remains $O(n^2)$). In Section 32.1.3, we outline the complications arising from a parallel implementation of spatial subdivision and how we deal with them. Our CUDA implementation of parallel spatial subdivision is described in Section 32.2.

32.1.1 Sort and Sweep

One approach to the broad phase, as mentioned, is the sort and sweep algorithm (Witkin and Baraff 1997). In this approach, the bounding volume of each object i is projected onto the x, y, or z axis, defining the one-dimensional collision interval $[b_i, e_i]$ of the object along this axis; b_i marks the beginning of the collision interval, and e_i marks its end. Two objects whose collision intervals do not overlap cannot possibly collide with each other, leading to the algorithm that follows. The two markers of each object are inserted into a list with $2n$ entries (two markers for each object). Next, this list is sorted in ascending order. Finally, the list is traversed from beginning to end. Whenever a b_i marker is found in the list, object i is added to a list of active objects. Whenever an e_i marker is found, object i is removed from the list of active objects. Collision tests for object i are performed only between object i and all objects currently in the list of active objects at the moment when object i itself is added to this list of active objects. An example with three objects is illustrated in Figure 32-1.

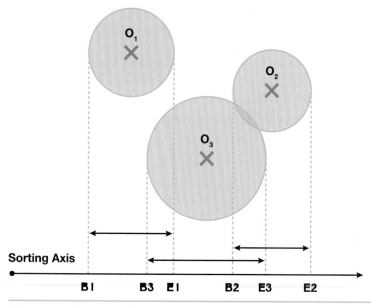

Figure 32-1. The Sort and Sweep Algorithm for Three Objects
Because object 1's collision interval does not overlap with object 2's collision interval, the only pairs of objects left after broad phase are (object 1, object 3) and (object 2, object 3).

Sort and sweep is simple to implement, and it is a great starting point for a broad-phase collision detection algorithm. Additionally, due to spatial coherency between one frame of simulation and the next, one can often use an $O(n^2)$ sort such as insertion sort in an efficient manner to accelerate the algorithm, because of its improved $O(n)$ performance when applied to mostly sorted lists.

32.1.2 Spatial Subdivision

Spatial subdivision is an alternative to sort and sweep. Spatial subdivision partitions space into a uniform grid, such that a grid cell is at least as large as the largest object. Each cell contains a list of each object whose centroid is within that cell. A collision test between two objects is then performed only if they belong to the same cell or to two adjacent cells. Alternatively—and this is the approach taken in the rest of the chapter— one can assign to each cell the list of all objects whose bounding volume intersects the cell. In this case, an object can appear in up to 2^d cells, where d is the dimension of the spatial subdivision (for example, $d = 3$ for a 3D world), as illustrated in Figure 32-2.

A collision test between two objects is performed only if they appear in the same cell and at least one of them has its centroid in this cell. For example, in Figure 32-3, a collision test is performed between objects o_1 and o_2 because both have their centroids in cell 1, and between objects o_2 and o_3 because both appear in cell 5 and o_3 has its centroid in cell 5. But no collision test is performed between o_2 and o_4 because although both appear in cell 2, neither of their centroids is in cell 2.

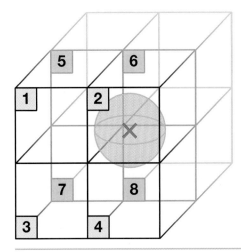

Figure 32-2. A Bounding Sphere in 3D Space Overlapping the $2^3 = 8$ Possible Cells

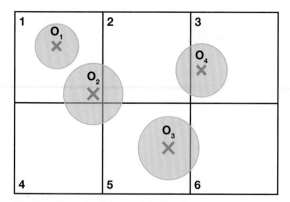

Figure 32-3. An Example of 2D Spatial Subdivision of Four Objects

The simplest implementation of spatial subdivision creates a list of object IDs along with a hashing of the cell IDs in which they reside, sorts this list by cell ID, and then traverses swaths of identical cell IDs, performing collision tests between all objects that share the same cell ID.

The necessity for a cell to be at least as big as the bounding volume of the largest object can cause unnecessary computation where there is great disparity in size between all of the objects. One such example would be a large planet surrounded by thousands of much smaller asteroids. Hierarchical grids (Mirtich 1996) address this issue, but they are beyond the scope of this chapter.

32.1.3 Parallel Spatial Subdivision

Parallelizing spatial subdivision complicates the algorithm a bit. The first complication arises from the fact that a single object can be involved in more than one collision test simultaneously if it overlaps multiple cells and these cells are processed in parallel. Therefore, some mechanism must exist to prevent two or more computational threads from updating the state of the same object at the same time. To deal with this issue, we exploit the spatial separation of the cells. Because each cell is guaranteed to be at least as large as the bounding volume of the largest object in a computation, then it is guaranteed that as long as each cell processed during a computational pass is separated from every other cell being processed at the same time by at least one intervening cell, then only one cell containing each object will be updated at once. In 2D, this means that there must be four computational passes to cover all possible cells, which is illustrated in Figure 32-4: all cells with the same numeric label (1 to 4), or *cell type*, can be processed in the same pass. This figure illustrates a simple case wherein object 2 has two potential collisions that must be processed separately. In 3D, eight passes are required as the repeating unit in 2D changes from a repeating 2×2 square of cells numbered 1 to 4 to a repeating 2×2×2 cube of cells numbered 1 to 8, as illustrated in Figure 32-5.

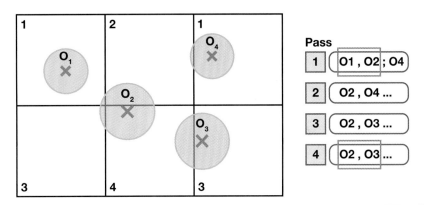

Figure 32-4. Separating Potential Collisions into 2^d Separate Lists
This process ensures that the two potential collision pairs involving object 2 will be processed sequentially in different lists. Object 2's state can then be updated sequentially within an individual pass.

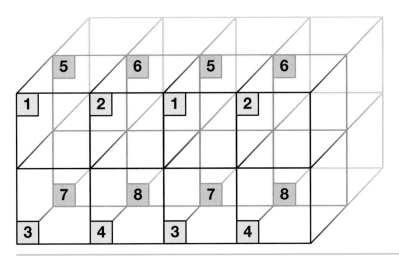

Figure 32-5. Spatial Subdivision Cells That Can Be Processed in Parallel in 3D
Cells with the same numeric code or cell type can be processed safely in parallel.

There are two special cases that modify the need for ordering cell traversal. First, in the event that we are not changing the state of the objects but only performing collision tests, these 2^d passes can be collapsed into a single pass. And second, in the event that we are using this collision system to perform Jacobi versus Gauss-Seidel physics integration (Erleben et al. 2005), we can also handle all cells in one pass. In that case, though, there is the caveat that each object has 2^d velocity impulse outputs (one corresponding to each of the 2^d collision cells it could occupy) that are summed together for each object after collision processing is complete.

Another complication arising from parallel execution is that we must avoid performing the same collision test between two objects multiple times. This can happen if the two objects occupy an overlapping set of cells and their centroids are not in the same cell.

We deal with this possibility by doing the following:

1. Associating to each object a set of $d + 2^d$ control bits; d bits hold the type of the cell where its centroid resides, or its *home cell*; 2^d bits specify the types of the cells intersected by its bounding volume.

2. Scaling the bounding sphere of each object by sqrt(2) and ensuring that the grid cell is at least 1.5 times as large as the scaled bounding sphere of the largest object.

Before performing a collision test between two objects during pass T, we first find out if one of the objects' home cell type, say T', is both less than T and among the cell types that are common to both objects (obtained by ANDing their 2^d control bits). If this is the case, we can skip the test because either the objects share a cell of type T', in which case the test has already been performed during pass T'; or they do not share a cell of type T', in which case their bounding volumes cannot possibly overlap because of point 2 we just mentioned. The first case is illustrated by objects o_1 and o_2 in Figure 32-6. The test is skipped in pass T = 3 because both objects share cell types 1 and 3, and o_2's home cell type is T' = 1. Skipping the test is indeed safe because it has already been performed in pass 1. The second case is illustrated by objects o_3 and o_4 in Figure 32-6. The test is skipped in pass T = 4 because both objects share cell types 3 and 4, and o_4's home cell type is T' = 3. Skipping the test is indeed safe because both objects cannot possibly collide: They overlap different cells of type 3, so their centroids are separated by a distance greater than the diameter of the largest object.

32.2 A CUDA Implementation of Spatial Subdivision

In this section, we provide the details of our implementation using CUDA. In Section 32.2.1, we describe how we store the list of object IDs and cell IDs in device memory. In Section 32.2.2, we show how we build the list of cell IDs from the object's bounding

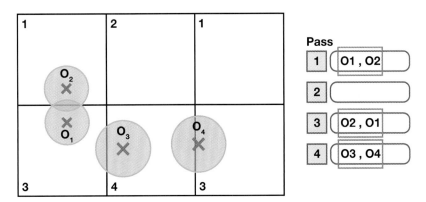

Figure 32-6. Control Bits and Large Enough Cells Allow Us to Avoid Performing the Same Collision Test Between Two Objects Multiple Times

boxes. In Section 32.2.3, we provide an in-depth description of the algorithm we use to sort the list. In Section 32.2.4, we show how we build an index table so that we can traverse this sorted list, as outlined in Section 32.2.5, and schedule pairs of objects for more-rigorous collision detection during the narrow phase. All the figures illustrating the whole process throughout this section correspond to the example in Figures 32-7 and 32-8.

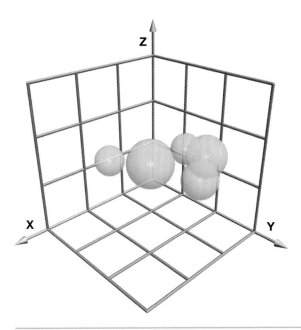

Figure 32-7. A Set of Objects Superimposed on the Uniform Grid That Partitions 3D Space

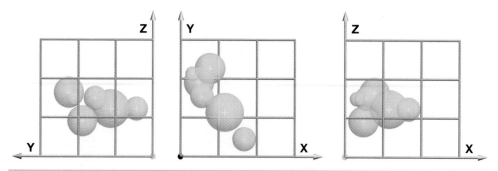

Figure 32-8. The Same Objects from Figure 32-7 Projected on the Three Different Planes

32.2.1 Initialization

The attributes of each object are its ID (which is used to access additional object properties such as its bounding volume during low-level collision tests and construction of the cell ID array discussed next), its control bits (used to store various bit states, such as the home cell type and other occupied cell types, as mentioned at the end of Section 32.1.2), and up to 2^d IDs of the cells covered by its bounding volume. The most natural way of storing these is as an array of structures. To reduce bandwidth requirements when sorting this array, though, it is preferable to store these attributes in two separate arrays of $(n \times 2^d)$ elements each:

- The first array, the *cell ID array*, contains the cell IDs of the first object followed by the cell IDs of the second object, and so on.

- The second array, the *object ID array*, contains the object IDs and control bits for each object, once for each cell it occupies.

It is implicitly assumed in the rest of the description of the algorithm that each time the elements of the cell ID array are reordered, the elements of the object ID array are reordered the same way.

32.2.2 Constructing the Cell ID Array

Once sufficient storage has been allocated, the first step in performing collision detection is to populate the cell ID array. For a given object, there may be cells that overlap with its bounding volume but are not its home cell, or *H cell*. We call such overlapping cells the *phantom cells*, or *P cells*, of that object. As indicated earlier, if a cell is a P cell for one object and a P cell for another object, then these objects can never collide in this cell because the centroids of the two objects in question are separated by at least one intervening cell, and by design, the cell diameter is at least twice the radius of the largest object.

The H cell ID of each object is simply a hash of its centroid's coordinates. A typical 3D hash would resemble this:

```
GLuint hash = ((GLuint)(pos.x / CELLSIZE) << XSHIFT) |
              ((GLuint)(pos.y / CELLSIZE) << YSHIFT) |
              ((GLuint)(pos.z / CELLSIZE) << ZSHIFT);
```

Here, `pos` represents the position of the object; `CELLSIZE` is the dimension of the cells; and `XSHIFT`, `YSHIFT`, and `ZSHIFT` are predefined constants determining how many bits are assigned to the hash of each dimension's coordinate. This hash is stored in the cell ID array as the first cell ID for each object. Simultaneously, the corresponding element in the object ID array is updated with the object ID, and we set a control bit to indicate that this is the object's H cell.

Next, the P cell IDs of each object are stored in the cell ID array by testing to see if its bounding volume overlaps any of its H cell's $3^d - 1$ immediate neighbors. Given that the cell size is at least as large as the largest bounding volume, an object can touch only 2^d cells at once. This means that an object has one H cell and that it can have up to $2^d - 1$ P cells. If the object has fewer than $2^d - 1$ P cells, the extra cell IDs are marked as `0xffffffff` to indicate they are not valid.

The creation of these H and P cell IDs is performed for each object by one thread. To accommodate for the case in which there are more objects than threads, each thread handles multiple objects. More precisely, thread j of thread block i handles objects $iB + j$, $iB + j + nT$, $iB + j + 2nT$, and so on, where B is the number of threads per block and T is the total number of threads.

Figure 32-9 illustrates the result of cell ID array construction.

After all cell IDs have been created, we need to count them to compute their total number for use during the creation of the collision cell list in Section 32.2.4. The most efficient way to add multiple values together on a parallel machine is through a parallel reduction. In CUDA, the threads of a thread block can cooperate through shared memory, yielding a very fast implementation of parallel reduction. (See Chapter 39 of this book, "Parallel Prefix Sum (Scan) with CUDA," for all the details.) Therefore, we first calculate the number of cell IDs created by each thread block. This count is written out for each block to global memory. Once all blocks have finished this process, a single block is launched to add the results of the preceding blocks.

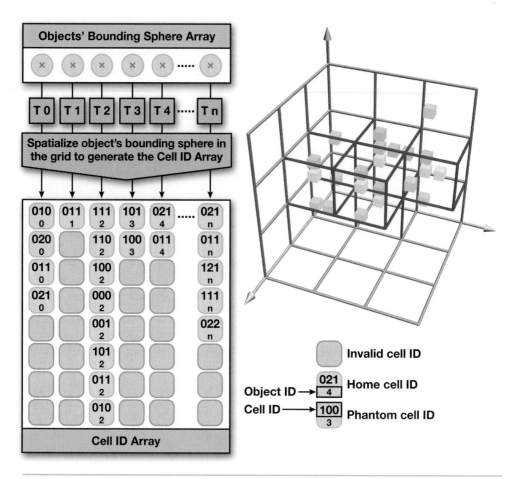

Figure 32-9. Initial Contents of the Cell ID Array for the Objects of Figure 32-7 After Construction

32.2.3 Sorting the Cell ID Array

Next, the cell ID array is sorted by cell ID. Of course, each cell ID appears multiple times in the array in general—each time there is more than one bounding volume that intersects a cell. We want elements with the same cell ID to be sorted by cell ID type (H before P), because this simplifies the collision cell processing of Section 32.2.5, where we iterate over all H cell IDs against the total of all H and P cell IDs. Because we have already ordered the cell ID array first by object ID and second by cell ID type (H or P), the choice of sort algorithm is therefore limited to a stable sort. A stable sort guarantees that at the end of the sorting process, identical cell IDs remain in the same order that they were in at the beginning of it. Figure 32-10 illustrates the sorting process applied to the cell ID array of Figure 32-9.

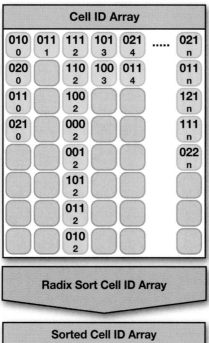

Figure 32-10. The Radix Sort Algorithm Applied to the Cell ID Array
The cell IDs are ordered by cell and type. The invalid cell IDs are pushed to the end of the array.

We first outline the radix sort algorithm and then describe our parallel implementation in detail.

The Radix Sort Algorithm

A radix sort sorts keys—in our case, the 32-bit cell IDs—with B bits by groups of L bits within them—where $L < B$—in as many successive passes as there are groups (Sedgewick 1992). For example, a common radix sort on 32-bit keys would set L to 8, resulting in a four-pass radix sort, because B/L is equal to 4 in that case.

The most surprising feature of a radix sort is that it sorts low-order bits before higher-order bits. The aforementioned stability of a radix sort guarantees that this unexpected direction of sorting works; that is, keys already sorted by their lowest 8 bits will not lose this ordering when the keys are subsequently sorted by higher-order bits during future passes.

Each sorting pass of a radix sort proceeds by masking off all bits of each key except for the currently active set of L bits, and then it tabulates the number of occurrences of each of the 2^L possible values that result from this masking. The resulting array of *radix counters* is then processed to convert each value into offsets from the beginning of the array. In other words, each value of the table is replaced by the sum of all its preceding values; this operation is called a *prefix sum*. Finally, these offsets are used to determine the new positions of the keys for this pass, and the array of keys is reordered accordingly.

The Parallel Radix Sort Algorithm

Each pass takes a cell ID array as input and outputs the reordered elements to another cell ID array. The input array for the first pass is the cell ID array built in Section 32.2.2; both input and output arrays are swapped after each pass, except after the last one. The final output array is used as input to the next step, described in Section 32.2.4.

A pass is implemented in three phases, each corresponding to one kernel invocation. These phases are described in the next three subsections.

Phase 1: Setup and Tabulation

The first phase of a serial radix sort pass involves counting the number of occurrences of each radix value in the list of keys. This means that the algorithm requires a minimum of $Num\_Radices = 2^L$ 32-bit radix counters. This phase is parallelized by spreading the work across the Num_Blocks CUDA thread blocks and assigning to each CUDA thread a portion of the input cell ID array. Each thread is then responsible for counting the number of occurrences of each radix value within its assigned portion.

Each thread requires its own set of counters, or else threads could potentially corrupt each other's counters. Therefore, over the entire process, a parallelized radix sort requires

$$Num\_Blocks \times Num\_Threads\_Per\_Block \times Num\_Radices$$

counters, where *Num_Threads_Per_Block* is the number of threads per block.

The obvious location for these counters is in the shared memory of each multiprocessor. On a GeForce 8800 GTX, there is 16 K of shared memory available per multiprocessor. A small portion of it is used for block housekeeping, so this leaves room for just under 4,096 32-bit counters per multiprocessor. This imposes constraints on both *L* and *Num_Threads_Per_Block*. Additionally, it is desirable that *Num_Threads_Per_Block* is a multiple of 64. If we were to use 256 threads, a quick division of just under 4,096 32-bit counters by 256 threads per thread block reveals that there would be room for only 16 counters per thread. This would limit *L* to 4, for a total of eight passes.

To reduce the number of passes, we therefore have to share counters among threads. For this, we divide each thread block in groups of *R* threads (making for *Num_Groups_Per_Block* = *Num_Threads_Per_Block*/*R* thread groups per block) such that threads within the same group share the same *Num_Radices* counters. In our case, it works out that *R* is best equal to 16, allowing us to choose *L* equal to 8 and perform an 8-bit radix sort with 192 threads per thread block, for a total of 12 thread groups per block. In doing so, we reduce the number of passes to four and we nearly double the performance of the sort algorithm. Indeed, the additional calculations required for sharing counters are present only in kernels that are memory bound, and therefore they impart a very small performance penalty.

To avoid read-after-write or write-after-read conflicts between threads of the same thread group, we have to construct a serialized increment of the radix counters for each thread group. This process is outlined in Figure 32-11. Each group of threads passes through this block sequentially, and each uniquely increments each counter without any chance of overwrites by other threads.

To maintain the stability of the sort, threads need to write data to the output array in the same order as they appear in the input array. The most straightforward way to achieve this is to have both successive thread blocks and successive threads themselves process successive data segments of the input array.

Therefore, we first assign successive segments of the input array to successive thread blocks, as illustrated in Figure 32-12. Empirical analysis has indicated that using one

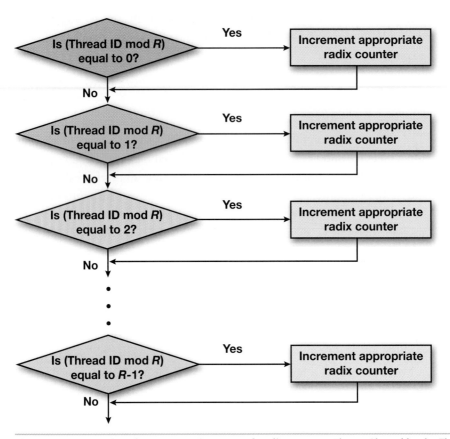

Figure 32-11. Flow Chart for Incrementing a Set of Radix Counters That Is Shared by the Threads Within a Thread Group

thread block per multiprocessor performs best. Therefore, because we are targeting the GeForce 8800 GTX with its 16 multiprocessors, we use *Num_Blocks* = 16 thread blocks; but the extension to a GPU with more multiprocessors is straightforward.

Similarly, within a thread block, as illustrated in Figure 32-13, we assign to successive thread groups successive segments of the section of the input array assigned to the block.

Within a thread group, threads read data in an interleaved way, though, as illustrated in Figure 32-14. This is to make sure that global memory reads are coalesced. To maintain the stability of the sort, we will thus have to serialize the writes to global memory by each thread of a group when it happens in phase 3.

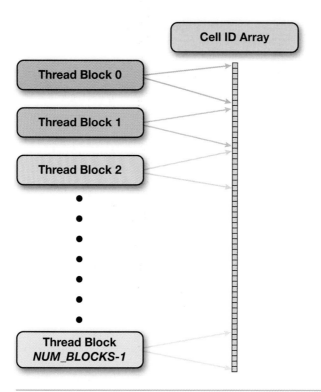

Figure 32-12. Mapping Between the Thread Blocks and the Input Cell ID Array

Given this mapping between the threads and the cell ID input array, the index of the first cell ID read by each thread during tabulation is the following:

$$\left(blockIdx.x \times Num\_Groups\_Per\_Block + \frac{threadIdx.x}{R} \right) \times Num\_Elements\_Per\_Group + (threadIdx.x \% R),$$

where *Num_Elements_Per_Group* is the size of the data segment assigned to each thread group. Each thread then jumps in increments of *R* until it reaches the end of its thread group's data segment.

The radix counters are laid out in shared memory first by radix, second by thread block, and third by thread group, as illustrated in Figure 32-15. At the end of the tabulation, we must combine the radix counters of each thread block. Because this requires inter-thread-block synchronization, this can only be done by saving to global memory the counters computed by each block in this phase and calling another kernel; this is therefore left for the next phase.

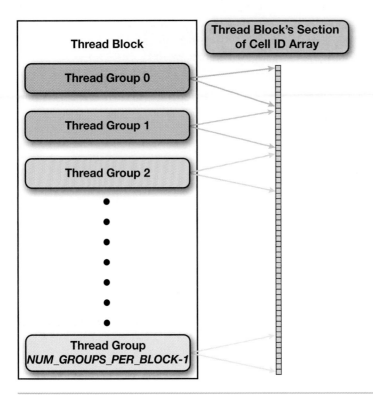

Figure 32-13. Mapping Between the *Num_Groups_Per_Block* Thread Groups of a Thread Block and the Section of the Input Cell ID Array Assigned to This Block

Phase 2: Radix Summation

In phase 3, the input cell ID array will get read by each block in the same way as in phase 1, and each block will output its assigned cell IDs to the right location in the output cell ID array. These locations are determined by offsets in the output cell ID array, and to calculate these offsets, we need the following:

1. For each radix, the prefix sum of each of its radix counters (so, one prefix sum per line of Figure 32-15)

2. For each radix, the total sum of its radix counters

3. The prefix sum of the *Num_Radices* total sums computed in step 2

The prefix sum from step 3 gives the offsets in the output cell ID array of each section of cell ID with the same radix. The prefix sums from step 1 give the offsets in each of these sections of the subsection where each block will write its assigned cell IDs. In phase 2, we compute steps 1, 2, and part of 3 as detailed now.

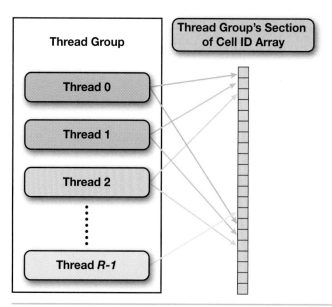

Figure 32-14. Mapping Between the R Threads of a Thread Group and the Section of the Input Cell ID Array Assigned to This Group

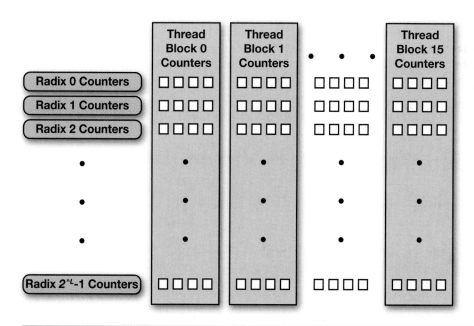

Figure 32-15. The Memory Layout of Radix Counters
Ordered first by radix, second by thread block, and third by thread group.

The work is broken down among the blocks by having each block take care of $Num\_Radices\_Per\_Block = Num\_Radices/Num\_Blocks$ radices—so, 16 radices in our case, as illustrated in Figure 32-16.

There are as many radix counters per radix as there are thread groups; in other words, $Num\_Groups = Num\_Blocks \times Num\_Groups\_Per\_Block$ radix counters per radix. So, each block allocates Num_Groups 32-bit values in shared memory. It then iterates through its $Num\_Radices\_Per\_Block$ assigned radices, and for each of them, the following operation is performed by all threads of the block:

1. The Num_Groups counters of the radix are read from global memory to shared memory.

2. The prefix sum of the Num_Groups counters is performed.

3. The Num_Groups counters in global memory are overwritten with the result of the prefix sum.

4. The total sum of the Num_Groups counters is computed by simply adding together the value of the last counter before the prefix sum to its value after the prefix sum.

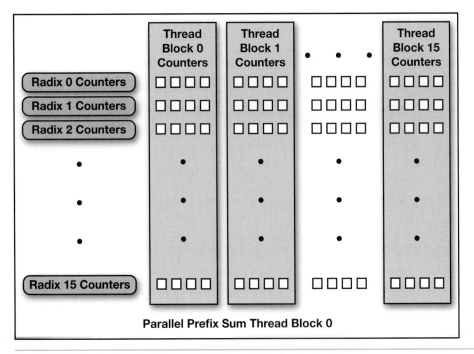

Figure 32-16. Radix Counters Processed by Thread Block 0 During Phase 2

Chapter 32   Broad-Phase Collision Detection with CUDA

In step 1, the reads are organized such that threads with consecutive IDs read consecutive counters in memory to get proper memory coalescing.

In step 2, a work-efficient parallel implementation of prefix sum in CUDA is employed, such as the one described in detail in Chapter 39. As explained in this chapter, in order to limit bank conflicts as much as possible, the shared memory array containing the *Num_Groups* counters needs to be padded appropriately (and therefore more memory must be allocated).

Each block also allocates an array of *Num_Radices_Per_Block* 32-bit values in shared memory to hold the prefix sum of the *Num_Radices_Per_Block* total sums computed in step 4. This prefix sum is performed simply by adding the total sum computed at the end of iteration N to element $N - 1$ of the array.

So at the end of this phase, each thread block has performed a prefix sum on its assigned *Num_Radices_Per_Block* counters, as illustrated in Figure 32-17, but in order to obtain absolute offsets in the output cell ID array, the total sum of all preceding thread blocks needs to be added to each element of this prefix sum. Because this requires inter-thread-block synchronization, this can only be done by saving to global memory the prefix sum computed by each block in this phase and then calling another kernel; this is therefore left for the next phase.

Phase 3: Reordering

The final phase of each pass is used to reorder the input cell ID array based on the radix tabulation performed in phases 1 and 2.

As mentioned at the end of phase 2, each block must first finish the work—partially done in phase 2—of computing the prefix sum of the *Num_Radices* radix counters in order to get absolute offsets in the output cell ID array. For this, it loads from global memory to shared memory the *Num_Blocks* prefix sums (each of them being composed of *Num_Radices_Per_Block* values) computed by each block in phase 2, performs a parallel prefix sum on the last values of each of these prefix sums, and uses it to offset each value of each prefix sum appropriately. The parallel prefix sum performed here is repeated by each block and is inefficient in that it uses only *Num_Blocks* threads, but it is very fast because it requires few operations.

Next, each block loads its *Num_Groups_Per_Block* × *Num_Radices* radix counters from global memory to shared memory (so, one of the *Num_Blocks* columns of Figure 32-17) and offsets each of them with the appropriate absolute offsets previously computed.

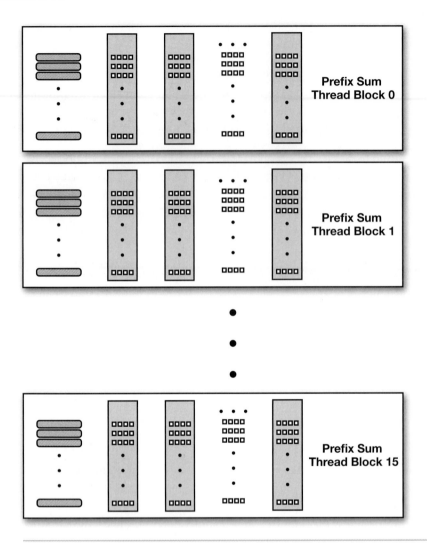

Figure 32-17. Overall Layout of the Parallel Prefix Sum Involved in Radix Summation
Each thread block computes a prefix sum of a section of the radix counters involved in phase 1.

Finally, each thread block reads from global memory the same section of the input cell ID array it read in phase 1, in the same order, and for each cell ID, it does the following:

1. Reads the value of the radix counter corresponding to the thread group and radix of the cell ID.

2. Writes the cell ID to the output cell ID array at the offset indicated by the radix counter

3. Increments the radix counter

The write and increment operations of steps 2 and 3, respectively, must be serialized for each thread of a half-warp, as illustrated in Figure 32-18; this is necessary both to avoid any shared and global memory hazards between threads of the same half-warp and to maintain the order of cell IDs with the same radix.

Step 2 produces extremely scattered and thus uncoalesced writes to global memory, causing a roughly 50 percent performance penalty, but the low pass count of the overall algorithm more than makes up for it.

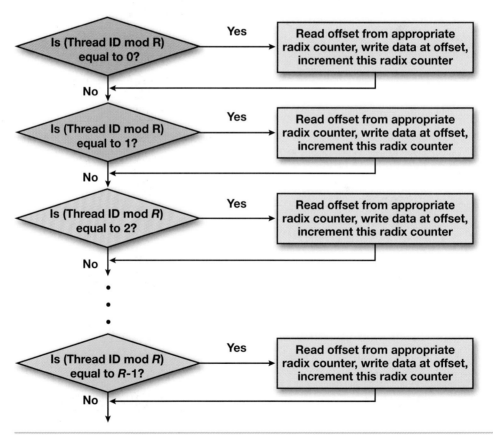

Figure 32-18. Increments of Radix Counters in Shared Memory and Writes to Global Memory Need to Be Serialized for Each Thread of a Half-Warp

32.2.4 Creating the Collision Cell List

A *collision cell* is a cell that requires processing in the narrow phase. In other words, it is a cell that contains more than one object. The list of all the collision cells is created from the sorted cell ID array as follows. The sorted cell ID array is scanned for changes of cell ID, the occurrence of which marks the end of the list of occupants of one cell and the beginning of another. To parallelize this task, we give each thread of each thread block a roughly equal segment of the cell ID array to scan for transitions. Because we want both the beginning and the end of each swath of identical cell IDs to be found by the same thread, each thread scans past the end point of its assigned segment for a final transition and skips its first transition under the assumption that it will be located and recorded by a preceding thread. The only exception is for the first thread of the first thread block, which handles the beginning of the cell ID array and so does not skip its first transition. Also, because we computed the number of valid cells in Section 32.2.2, we can ignore all invalid cell IDs from here on.

The sorted cell ID array is actually scanned twice. The first time, we count the number of objects each collision cell contains and convert them into offsets in the array through a parallel prefix sum in several passes, much like what we have done in phase 2 of the radix sort. The second time, we create entries for each collision cell in a new array. Each collision cell's entry records its start, the number of H occupants, and the number of P occupants, as shown in Figure 32-19. As explained in Section 32.1.3, these cells are also optionally divided into 2^d different lists of noninteracting cells, and the collision processing proceeds with 2^d passes, each of which focuses on one of these lists.

32.2.5 Traversing the Collision Cell List

Each collision cell list is then traversed, and collision cells are assigned for processing on a per-thread basis, as illustrated in Figure 32-20. In applications such as molecular dynamics or particle simulation, potential collisions can be processed immediately, allowing the traversal to serve as narrow-phase collision detection. For higher-level simulation, the traversal just records all collisions that pass bounding volume overlap for more detailed processing in a subsequent narrow phase; such simulations are beyond the scope of this chapter.

Because there is only one thread per collision cell, full utilization of the GPU is achieved only if there are thousands of collision cells to process. This issue becomes more pronounced during Gauss-Seidel physics processing, wherein the collision cells are processed during eight individual passes.

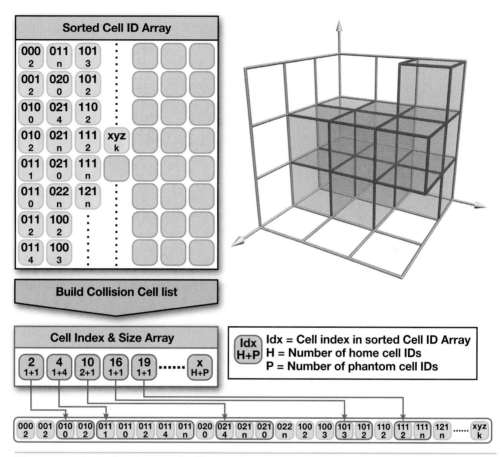

Figure 32-19. Scanning the Sorted Cell ID List for Transitions in Order to Locate Collision Cells

32.3 Performance Results

We tested the algorithm with Gauss-Seidel physics on typical configurations of 3,072 to 30,720 dispersed but potentially colliding objects. For the latter, broad phase prunes 450,000,000 potential collisions down to approximately 203,000 on average, and we obtained a frame rate of around 79 frames/sec on a GeForce 8800 GTX. This is approximately 26 times faster than a CPU implementation that was written at the same time as a relative performance benchmark. As illustrated in Figure 32-21, as we decrease object count, frame rate improves dramatically, to a peak of 487 frames/sec with 3,072 objects.

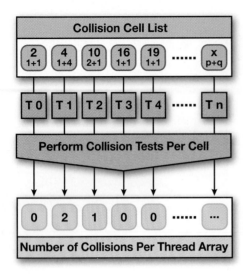

Figure 32-20. Thread Layout for Processing Individual Collision Cells on a Per-Thread Basis
If performing physics, process the collisions. If performing collision detection, record them to an array with a collision counter per thread.

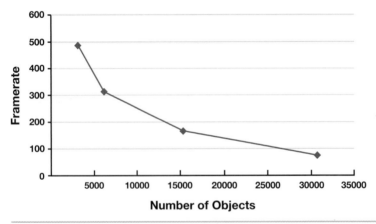

Figure 32-21. Frame Rate as a Function of Object Count for Gauss-Seidel Physics

Figure 32-22 illustrates the total amount of time spent in each phase of the algorithm. It is clear that the cell ID array sort and collision cell traversal consume the most time, thus making them the obvious targets for future optimization.

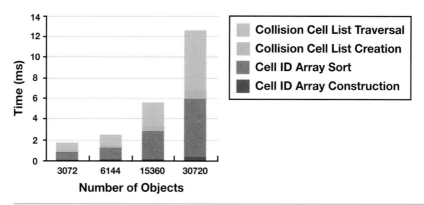

Figure 32-22. Total Time Spent in Each Phase for Gauss-Seidel Physics

32.4 Conclusion

In this chapter, we have shown that CUDA is a great platform for high-speed collision detection. Future work will focus on sharing collision cell processing between multiple threads and on exploring alternative approaches to spatial subdivision.

32.5 References

Erleben, Kenny, Joe Sporring, Knud Henriksen, and Henrik Dohlmann. 2005. *Physics-Based Animation.* Charles River Media. See especially pp. 613–616.

Mirtich, Brian. 1996. "Impulse-Based Dynamic Simulation of Rigid Body Systems." Ph.D. thesis. Department of Computer Science, University of California, Berkeley.

Sedgewick, Robert. 1992. *Algorithms in C++.* Addison-Wesley. See especially pp. 133–144.

Witkin, A., and D. Baraff. 1997. "An Introduction to Physically Based Modeling: Rigid Body Simulation II—Nonpenetration Constraints." SIGGRAPH 1997 Course 19.

The author would like to thank Samuel Gateau for his many helpful figures and for showing the author his way around Office 2007, and Cyril Zeller for proofreading above and beyond the call of duty.

Chapter 33

LCP Algorithms for Collision Detection Using CUDA

Peter Kipfer
Havok

An environment that behaves correctly physically is central to the immersive experience of a computer game. In some games, the player is even forced to interact with objects in the scene in a way that is critical to succeeding in the game level. Physics simulation therefore has become a mission-critical software component for game developers. The main challenge for developing game physics is minimizing the processor usage of the simulation, because the available resources are already heavily loaded with game AI, asset handling, animation, and graphics preprocessing. What complicates the situation further is that all these components depend on a consistent representation of the physics world and heavily depend on being able to query information from it.

In this chapter, we use CUDA to accelerate convex collision detection, and we study a parallel implementation of Lemke's algorithm (also called the complementary pivot algorithm) (Lemke 1965) for the *linear complementarity problem* (LCP). Important LCP applications are linear and quadratic programming, two-person games, boundary-value problems, and the determination of the convex hull of points in a plane. A parallel version of the algorithm was first proposed by Thompson (1987) with near-linear speedup for low numbers of processors.

33.1 Parallel Processing

A natural approach to speed up the calculations needed for a particular simulation is to split up the work to multiple processors. Modern computer systems have several programmable units. The main CPU nowadays features multiple execution cores, and specialized parallel algorithms on graphics hardware have become important building blocks for highly responsive simulations.

There is a huge amount of literature on parallel computing. CUDA provides an environment that has many of the standard parallelization features used on multi-CPU computers. It is thus worth investigating existing parallel algorithms for their suitability to run efficiently on the current GPU generation. This will allow us to perhaps dynamically shift workload between processing units, which is still tedious with previous-generation GPUs because of restricted functionality. NVIDIA's current generation of GPUs has changed from a rather rigid four-component vector processor to a scalar architecture featuring several SIMD multiprocessors. The GPU still is very specific in terms of its memory access patterns. While parallel CPU threads usually communicate over main memory, the current generation of GPUs move the shared memory block nearer to the ALUs. This has implications for the communication and synchronization granularity necessary for an efficient algorithm. Existing parallel algorithms therefore must be adapted to this change.

In this chapter, we examine the opportunities presented by the new CUDA programming environment for advanced solver techniques in the context of physics simulation. The involved numerics have not been a major problem on the previous GPU generation, but the missing flexibility with respect to memory addressing and limited output bandwidth have prevented many algorithms from running efficiently on the GPU. The CUDA environment solves these problems and provides additional features vital for concurrent processing: thread synchronization as well as thread-shared and thread-local storage. These enhancements allow us to bring a class of algorithms to the GPU that would have been impossible to implement before: multithreaded cooperative parallel programs.

33.2 The Physics Pipeline

The processing pipeline for rigid body physics is usually split into three major blocks: broad phase, narrow phase, and resolution phase. Each phase has a specific task to solve and needs a different view of the participating objects to be simulated.

The broad phase does a coarse and quick check to determine which of the objects can experience a collision at all. It produces a pair list of potential collision partners. For fast comparisons, very simple data structures are used, such as bounding spheres or axis-aligned bounding boxes, as shown in Figure 33-1a. The general understanding, furthermore, is that most of the time, the motion of the objects per simulated time step is small compared to their bounding box size. Algorithms that can exploit this coherence are readily available (such as sweep-and-prune).

The narrow phase obtains the collision pair list and for every pair, using their actual geometry, it checks whether the two partners are colliding. This phase can get arbitrarily complex, so in the context of real-time physics simulation, the participating colliding shapes are usually restricted to being convex. For nonconvex shapes, only the convex hull will then be used for collision detection. In most cases this is good enough—for example if the concavities are small or constitute object parts where you don't want a game character to go anyway, such as the exhaust pipes of a spacecraft or other irrelevant places. To improve collision quality and performance, we can decompose big or concave objects into convex pieces. A game object therefore might hold a simplified collision geometry that is different from the one displayed. In this chapter we investigate a narrow-phase algorithm for determining the distance between two convex objects. For the two objects in Figure 33-1b, the contact point marked with the yellow star is detected, and its location is calculated and stored with the collision pair.

Finally, the resolution phase computes forces according to the result of the narrow phase for pushing penetrating objects apart at every contact point. Because an object might collide with several others, appropriate handling of multiple contacts has to be done.

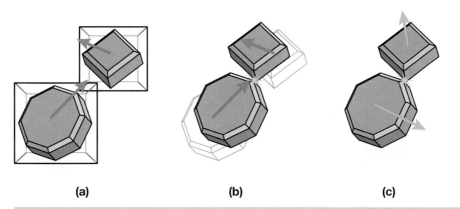

(a)   (b)   (c)

Figure 33-1. The Three Main Phases of the Processing Pipeline for Rigid Body Physics
(a) Broad phase. (b) Narrow phase. (c) Collision resolution phase.

The resulting contact forces and velocities, shown as green arrows in Figure 33-1c, together with body properties (such as inertias) are then inserted into the formulas for rigid body motion, and the objects are integrated in time.

33.3 Determining Contact Points

The problem of determining contact points is covered in an immense amount of literature. The algorithms can be divided into two main groups. First, finding contact points from time t_0 to t_1 can be viewed as a single, continuous function of time. Here, the basic problem is to determine the time of first contact. Alternatively, the problem can be considered discretely, at a sequence of time increments $t_0 < t_0 + \Delta\tau_1 < t_0 + \Delta\tau_2 < \ldots < t_0 + \Delta\tau_n < t_1$. Here, given the positions of bodies at time $t_0 + \Delta\tau_i$, the bodies have to be tested for interpenetration. Figure 33-2 compares the two approaches. The continuous approach on the bottom can consider, for example, the intersection of the swept volume of the object from time t_0 to t_1 with other objects in the scene analytically to solve for ∂_0, the time of first contact. The discrete approach in this case would simply check for overlap at the three positions.

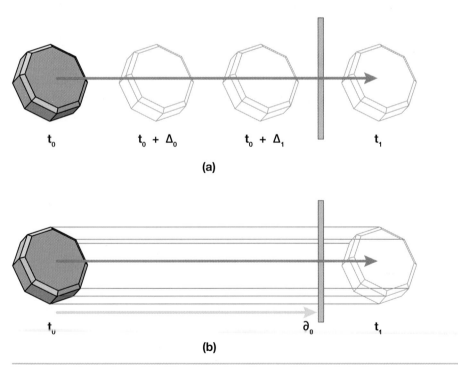

t_0 $t_0 + \Delta_0$ $t_0 + \Delta_1$ t_1

(a)

t_0 ∂_0 t_1

(b)

Figure 33-2. Comparison of the Discrete and Continuous Collision Detection Approaches

     Chapter 33   LCP Algorithms for Collision Detection Using CUDA

33.3.1 Continuum Methods

The first approach assumes a specified motion of bodies over some time interval. Algorithms for determining the first collision between rigid polyhedral objects with constant angular velocity have been described in the literature using roots of (low-order) polynomials. However, for the general case of arbitrary trajectories of rigid convex polyhedra, no closed-form solution for the time of first contact exists, and iterative numerical methods are used to determine it.

Because the continuum methods assume a specified motion path of the bodies over time, they cannot solve the contact-point problem globally, because such a path is exactly what the simulator is trying to compute. Used over appropriately short time intervals, they however guarantee that collisions between objects are not missed, as for example happens with the discrete method in Figure 33-2. These continuum methods, especially those based on interval analysis, are complicated to implement and are not currently as fast as the discrete methods.

33.3.2 Discrete Methods (Coherence Based)

The second approach involves the geometric analysis of bodies at a point in time. The goal is to solve a single, static instance of the problem with optimal asymptotic time complexity. The most prominent algorithm here is the Gilbert-Johnson-Keerthi distance algorithm, which computes the minimum distance between convex polyhedra with n vertices. The algorithm has a complexity between $O(n)$ and $O(n \log n)$, depending on stability optimizations present. For the problem of determining disjointness of two convex polyhedra with n vertices (without regard to the distance between them), a simpler $O(n)$ algorithm based on linear programming is available.

Unfortunately, the small asymptotic time complexity comes at the price of large runtime constants. However, the involved algorithms offer good potential for parallel processing. In this chapter, we develop such a parallel solution using CUDA.

33.3.3 Resolving Contact Points

After determining when and where objects contact each other, we need to enforce non-interpenetration constraints. There are two basic approaches for preventing interpenetration between contacting objects without friction. The first approach, also called the *penalty method*, models contacts by placing a damped spring at each contact point, between the two contacting bodies. Interpenetration is allowed between the bodies at a contact point, but as the amount of interpenetration increases at a contact point, a repulsive restoring, or penalty, force acts between the objects, pushing them apart. The penalty method is a very attractive model, because it is extremely simple to implement and numerically simple. In particular, exploiting parallelism for GPU implementations on previous-generation hardware is rather straightforward.

The second approach computes constraint forces that are designed to exactly cancel any external accelerations that would result in interpenetration. This method requires solving nonlinear systems of equations. The CUDA solver developed in this chapter can be used for computing such forces. It results in simulations where interpenetration is completely eliminated (within numerical tolerances).

33.4 Mathematical Optimization

33.4.1 Linear Programming

Let's take a look at a simple optimization problem. We want to know whether or not two 2D polygons intersect. Consider the two triangles from Ericson 2005 given in Figure 33-3. The interior of each triangle can be described as an intersection of the half-spaces defined by its edges.

Triangle A is described by these three half-space equations:

$$-u + v \leq -1, \quad -u - 4v \leq -1, \quad 4u + v \leq 19$$

and triangle B is given as the following:

$$-4u + v \leq 0, \quad u - 4v \leq 0, \quad u + v \leq 5.$$

In matrix notation this gives inequality constraints $\mathbf{Ax} \leq \mathbf{b}$ and an objective function $\mathbf{c}^T \mathbf{x}$ to be maximized, where $\mathbf{c}$ is a vector of constants. Because any point that is common to both triangles is a witness of their collision, the objective function can be chosen arbitrarily, for example $\mathbf{c} = (1, 0, \ldots, 0)$. To solve the system for a maximum of x using the simplex algorithm, we introduce slack variables $\mathbf{s}$ to turn the inequalities into equalities—that is, for the inequality in every component i of the vector $\mathbf{x} : A_i x_i \leq b_i$, we write $A_i x_i + s_i = b_i$. The slack variable $\mathbf{s}$ thus takes the difference to fulfill the equality. For this simple case, direct solution methods or even exhaustive testing of the half-spaces might be faster, but the presented idea is general enough to support arbitrary convex polyhedra. This is important for a physics engine, to allow queries between any objects in the simulation.

The given linear programming problem answers the question whether two objects overlap or not. So in case an overlap is detected, the physics simulation is actually in an

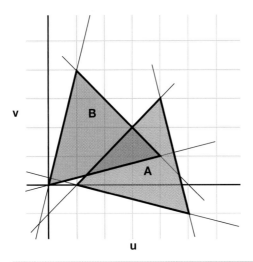

Figure 33-3. Two Intersecting Triangles

invalid state with penetrating rigid bodies. This has to be avoided, and therefore we'd like to perform a distance query between separated objects. This, however, cannot be answered using the current process.

33.4.2 The Linear Complementarity Problem

One important observation in linear programming is that for every maximization problem, there is a dual minimization problem. The strong duality principle states that you can optimize either the original or the dual problem to arrive at the same value. The consequence of this is that the slack variables of the original and the dual problems are related (*complementary slackness*). The vector of slack variables of the original problem is $\mathbf{s} = \mathbf{b} - \mathbf{Ax} \geq 0$; the vector of the dual problem is $\mathbf{u} = \mathbf{A}^T \mathbf{y} - \mathbf{c}$. Therefore we can conclude that we have found an optimal solution only if either $x_j = 0$ or $u_j = 0$ or either $y_i = 0$ or $s_i = 0$. The idea now is to combine both the original and the dual problems into what is called a *complementarity problem*.

In linear algebra, the linear complementarity problem is formulated as follows:

$$\mathbf{w} = \mathbf{Mz} + \mathbf{q} \geq 0, \qquad \mathbf{w} \geq 0, \mathbf{z} \geq 0, \mathbf{z}^T \mathbf{w} = 0, \tag{1}$$

where $\mathbf{M}$ is a real n-dimensional matrix and $\mathbf{q}$ is a given vector in $\mathbb{R}^n$. Because of the last restriction, either $w_i = 0$ or $z_i = 0$ for $i = 1, \ldots, n$, hence the name "complementarity problem." Apart from the trivial solution $\mathbf{z} = 0$, $\mathbf{w} = \mathbf{q}$, if $\mathbf{M}$ is a P-matrix, it can be shown that this system has either a unique optimal solution or is unsolvable. In mathematics, a *P-matrix* is a square matrix with every principal minor greater than zero. Using the complementary slackness, our linear optimization problem from Equation 1 can be written as an LCP:

$$\mathbf{w} = \begin{bmatrix} \mathbf{u} \\ \mathbf{s} \end{bmatrix}, \quad \mathbf{M} = \begin{bmatrix} 0 & \mathbf{A}^T \\ -\mathbf{A} & 0 \end{bmatrix}, \quad \mathbf{z} = \begin{bmatrix} \mathbf{x} \\ \mathbf{y} \end{bmatrix}, \quad \mathbf{q} = \begin{bmatrix} -\mathbf{c} \\ \mathbf{b} \end{bmatrix}.$$

Note how this implicitly optimizes the objective function, because the solution vector of the LCP is the optimal feasible vector of the original and the dual problems.

33.4.3 Quadratic Programming

For our purpose of determining the distance between two objects, the objective function contains a quadratic term in addition to the linear term—that is, $f(\mathbf{x}) = \mathbf{x}^T \mathbf{S} \mathbf{x} - \mathbf{c}^T \mathbf{x}$, and we are therefore faced with a problem of quadratic programming. The constraints are still linear, $g(\mathbf{x}) = (\mathbf{A}\mathbf{x} - \mathbf{b}, -\mathbf{x}) \leq 0$, so we can use the LCP representation to solve it using the Karush-Kuhn-Tucker (KKT) conditions: Recall from calculus that a differentiable function has extreme points where its first derivative is zero. The KKT conditions state the same for the optimization problem as follows:

$$g(\mathbf{x}) \leq 0, \quad \nabla f(\mathbf{x}) + \mathbf{u}^T \Gamma = 0, \qquad \text{for } \mathbf{u} \geq 0 \text{ and } \mathbf{u} \circ g(\mathbf{x}) = 0, \tag{2}$$

where $\nabla f(\mathbf{x})$ is the gradient of f and Γ is the derivative matrix of $\mathbf{g}$. The feasible points of this equation system are the local minima of the optimization problem. If we now additionally restrict f to be a convex function, we have a convex quadratic programming problem, and the following convenient statements are true:

- If a local minimum exists, then it is a global minimum.
- The set of all (global) minima is convex.
- If the function f is strictly convex, then there exists at most one minimum.

In the context of physics simulation, for the two convex quadratic programming applications of calculating the distance between two convex polyhedra and for solving for impulse forces for resting contacts, we are therefore guaranteed to find the global optimal solution if it exists.

33.5 The Convex Distance Calculation

Let's do a simple example and determine the squared distance between two triangles in 2D. If $\mathbf{P}_0$ is a point inside the first triangle and $\mathbf{P}_1$ is a point inside the second triangle, then we'd like to minimize the squared distance

$$\mathbf{x} = \begin{bmatrix} \mathbf{P}_0 \\ \mathbf{P}_1 \end{bmatrix}, \qquad f(\mathbf{x}) = |\mathbf{P}_0 - \mathbf{P}_1|^2 = \begin{bmatrix} \mathbf{P}_0^T & \mathbf{P}_1^T \end{bmatrix} \begin{bmatrix} \mathbf{I} & -\mathbf{I} \\ -\mathbf{I} & \mathbf{I} \end{bmatrix} \begin{bmatrix} \mathbf{P}_0 \\ \mathbf{P}_1 \end{bmatrix} = \mathbf{x}^T \mathbf{S} \mathbf{x},$$

where $\mathbf{I}$ is the 2D identity matrix. The matrix $\mathbf{S}$ therefore has diagonal blocks $\mathbf{I}$ and off-diagonal blocks $-\mathbf{I}$, and its eigenvalues are $\lambda = 0$ and $\lambda = 2$, hence it is symmetric and positive-semidefinite and the LCP will either be unsolvable or return an optimal solution. The constraints of the problem are that the two points must be inside the triangles. We can express that using the half-space inequalities from the preceding linear programming example. The minimum obviously is then reached for points lying on the triangle edges. Using the definition from Equation 2, we set up the LCP problem shown in Equation 3.

The blue part of Equation 3 is the matrix $2\mathbf{S}$, the orange part is $\mathbf{A}^T$, and the green part is $-\mathbf{A}$. Note that the solution $\mathbf{z}$ vector conveniently contains the two optimal contact points in its first four components. This matrix is expanded easily for higher dimensions and more constraints, making it easy to formulate a canonical system for solving for the distance between convex polyhedra in 3D. Also note that the participating polyhedra do not need to have the same number of faces nor do they need the faces to be triangular.

Equation 3. An Example LCP Problem

$$\mathbf{M} = \begin{bmatrix} 2 & 0 & -2 & 0 & a_{x_0}^0 & a_{x_1}^0 & a_{x_2}^0 & 0 & 0 & 0 \\ 0 & 2 & 0 & -2 & a_{y_0}^0 & a_{y_1}^0 & a_{y_2}^0 & 0 & 0 & 0 \\ -2 & 0 & 2 & 0 & 0 & 0 & 0 & a_{x_0}^1 & a_{x_1}^1 & a_{x_2}^1 \\ 0 & -2 & 0 & 2 & 0 & 0 & 0 & a_{y_0}^1 & a_{y_1}^1 & a_{y_2}^1 \\ -a_{x_0}^0 & -a_{y_0}^0 & 0 & 0 & 0 & 0 & 0 & 0 & 0 & 0 \\ -a_{x_1}^0 & -a_{y_1}^0 & 0 & 0 & 0 & 0 & 0 & 0 & 0 & 0 \\ -a_{x_2}^0 & -a_{y_2}^0 & 0 & 0 & 0 & 0 & 0 & 0 & 0 & 0 \\ 0 & 0 & -a_{x_0}^1 & -a_{y_0}^1 & 0 & 0 & 0 & 0 & 0 & 0 \\ 0 & 0 & -a_{x_1}^1 & -a_{y_1}^1 & 0 & 0 & 0 & 0 & 0 & 0 \\ 0 & 0 & -a_{x_2}^1 & -a_{y_2}^1 & 0 & 0 & 0 & 0 & 0 & 0 \end{bmatrix} \qquad \mathbf{z} = \begin{bmatrix} P_{0_x} \\ P_{0_y} \\ P_{1_x} \\ P_{1_y} \\ 0 \\ 0 \\ 0 \\ 0 \\ 0 \\ 0 \end{bmatrix}, \quad \mathbf{q} = \begin{bmatrix} 0 \\ 0 \\ 0 \\ 0 \\ b_0^0 \\ b_1^0 \\ b_2^0 \\ b_0^1 \\ b_1^1 \\ b_2^1 \end{bmatrix}.$$

33.5.1 Lemke's Algorithm for Solving the LCP

Lemke's algorithm operates on an equivalent, augmented linear complementarity problem by adding an artificial variable z_0:

$$\mathbf{w} = \mathbf{Mz} + ez_0 + \mathbf{q} \geq 0, \quad w_0 = z_0, \quad (\mathbf{z}, z_0) \geq 0, \quad (\mathbf{z}, z_0)^T (\mathbf{w}, w_0) = 0. \quad (4)$$

A basic feasible point, which is a basic vector such that $(\mathbf{w}, w_0, \mathbf{z}, z_0) \geq 0$, is immediately available. A solution $(\mathbf{z}, z_0)$ $(\mathbf{w}, w_0)$ is said to be *almost complementary* if it is feasible and $z_i w_i = 0$ for all $i = 0, \ldots, n$ except for at most one i. The algorithm now moves (at every nondegenerate step) from a basic vector for Equation 4 to a new one maintaining the property of almost complementarity between $(\mathbf{z}, z_0)$ and $(\mathbf{w}, w_0)$ until either a complementary basic feasible solution for Equation 4 is obtained or an unbounded ray is detected. In every step, a Gauss-Jordan-elimination pivoting operation is performed. The current basis is modified by bringing into the basis a new variable and dropping a variable from the current set. The new entering variable is uniquely determined by the complementary pivot rule (that is, pick the variable that is complementary to the variable that just left the basis). The variable to drop from the basis is determined by the minimum ratio test of the simplex algorithm.

We refer the reader to Murty 1988 for details and definitions as well as the convergence of the algorithm. The algorithm features a method for preventing pivoting cycles and always terminates in a finite number of steps for important classes of matrices $\mathbf{M}$, such as positive semidefinite matrices and matrices with positive entries.

33.6 The Parallel LCP Solution Using CUDA

From the example in Equation 3 and Lemke's algorithm for parallelization, it immediately becomes clear that we can parallelize the pivoting algorithm for the matrix. In particular, we can update the columns of the matrix concurrently, provided that the pivot column is available. Following Thompson 1987, we partition the matrix $\mathbf{M}$ among CUDA threads by rows; that is, each thread is responsible for one of the rows of the matrix $\mathbf{M}$. The right-hand-side vector $\mathbf{q}$ is available to all threads, and a list of current basic and nonbasic variables is maintained.

At the beginning of each iteration, the pivot column is determined by the complementary pivot rule. Each thread independently computes the pivot row using the minimum ratio test and updates its portion of the matrix. This can be done in parallel, because each thread has an updated copy of the right-hand-side vector $\mathbf{q}$ and can compute the current pivot column. For optimization, the pivot column is computed in thread-shared memory of the multiprocessor.

33.6.1 Implementation of the Solver

The CUDA LCP solver has three main tasks:

1. Select the pivot element

2. Solve for the selected equation variable

3. Check for termination

A solution has to be computed for every collision pair. Computing each solution is independent of each other. We therefore map the collision pair list to CUDA's compute grid. Each block has as many threads as there are equations in the LCP. Because the threads can communicate partial results, solving the LCP equations can be done in a cooperative manner by the threads. Figure 33-4 gives an overview of the processing.

The number of equations needed to set up the specific LCP problem for convex distance calculation depends on the dimension of the domain and the number of half-spaces. We

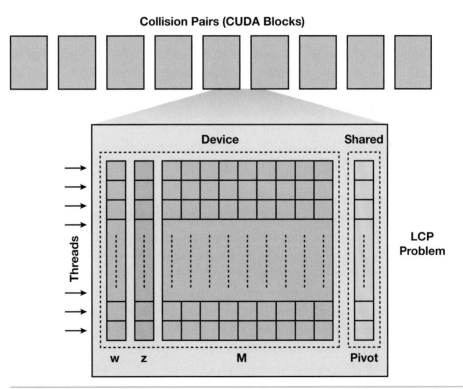

Figure 33-4. CUDA Processing of the LCP Problem
When solving for a specific pivot equation, all threads compute the pivot column vector in shared memory and then process the equation the thread is responsible for, represented by one matrix row.

get one equation per dimension of each of the two points' distances and one for each participating half-space constraint. For calculating the distance between two triangles in 2D, this amounts to $2 \times 2 + 3 + 3 = 10$ equations (see Equation 3). If arbitrary polygons are participating, obviously the number of constraints varies. To run the entire pair list as a CUDA grid, however, the number of threads per block must be the same for all blocks. We handle this by storing the number of equations per block and let excessive threads idle. This is more efficient than calling the kernel for each block separately, and it can be programmed very easily because each thread knows its cardinality. Note that this would have been very difficult to solve on previous GPU architectures. The number of threads needed for this approach quickly reaches quite large numbers. This has been a problem for past implementations on multiprocessor machines. For CUDA, however, this approach is ideal, because the GPU is optimized for handling high thread counts. To solve for the 3D distance between two convex objects with 60 faces each, we need 129 threads. This is a reasonable number for a CUDA kernel. Object descriptions easily get even more complicated when dealing with convex decompositions of concave objects.

The entire grid can therefore be covered by the same kernel. This is a very powerful feature, and we take advantage of that by implementing the control loop over the three steps previously mentioned also in the kernel. We therefore do not need to read back any intermediate status. When the kernel returns, each of the blocks will have either computed a solution or flagged itself as unsolvable. The implementation of the second step takes care of producing a contiguous list of results (see Figures 33-5 and 33-6), which allows us to download it efficiently in one batch.

Selecting the Pivot Element

The choice of the next pivot element is governed by the minimum ratio test of the simplex algorithm. It states that the objective function gets the most improvement by removing the variable from the basic set that has the smallest ratio of the constant term of the polynomial to the variable coefficient. Because each variable is represented by a matrix row, this amounts to checking the ratios of all rows and selecting the smallest one. Because we are solving an LCP here, we additionally have to be careful to choose the correct complementary variable, depending on the basic/nonbasic state of the equation. We also need to handle the special case in which the artificial variable z_0 is not a basic variable. This is the first step the solver will take. We can implement it by simply choosing the smallest (negative) constant term. At least one constant term must be negative initially or else we start with a solution. If all of the negative constant terms are different, pick the equation with the smallest (negative) ratio of constant term to the coefficient of z_0. If several equations contain the smallest negative constant term, pick the one with the highest coefficient, because that one is the coefficient for the largest power of the polynomial (this is the *least-index rule* [Bland 1977]).

The processing of the ratios offers several opportunities for parallel work. Figure 33-5 shows the processing paths of the CUDA algorithm. The thread layout described in the previous section ensures that we have one thread for each equation available—that is, for each matrix row. The control flow in Figure 33-5 therefore is executed on all threads in parallel. The threads are synchronized for three major blocks. First, it is established whether or not z_0 is a basic variable. This controls the following search. The second block builds a list of valid coefficients for every variable in parallel. After synchronizing again, all threads now can access identical information about the state of the equation system, because the z_0 basic flag and the valid candidates are in shared memory. The third block now can determine the equation that has the smallest constant-to-variable-coefficient ratio. Then, the found pivot variable is written back to device memory. Because this information is computed in shared memory, all threads of the block have the same view of the current state of the LCP.

Solving for the Selected Equation Variable

Solving for the selected variable is straightforward to parallelize with CUDA. Again, we have one thread per equation available. Each thread brings one element of the pivot column into fast shared memory and also reads its coefficients. This efficiently utilizes the available bandwidth. Because shared memory is limited, this part repeats for the z, w, and constant coefficients sequentially, as shown in Figure 33-6. Note that we actually do not do this for sharing the equation coefficients between the threads, but the modifications to them do incur several arithmetic operations, and the shared memory access is much faster than working in device memory. This is a huge advantage over previous GPU architectures.

Each thread also creates the replacement equation (that is, the variable to solve for). Then it pivots its equation using the correct complementary variable. One of the threads, however, will be the one serving the pivot row. This thread simply replaces the row with the computed replacement equation.

The final step is to check if we have reached a solution. All threads check whether they represent z_0 as a basic variable. The flags are collected in shared memory, and after a

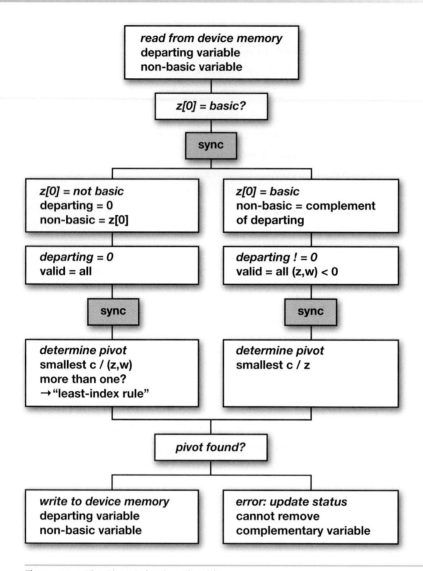

Figure 33-5. The Pivot Selection Algorithm

synchronization point, all threads of the block know whether this LCP is solved. In that case, a status variable is updated accordingly to signal completion to the host program. Note that we do not need the entire **z** vector for our application. We are interested only in the points P_0 and P_1 that form the solution. They are therefore written to a packed solution array. For our small 2D LCP problem in Equation 3, the first four entries contain the two 2D solution points (see the setup of matrix **M**).

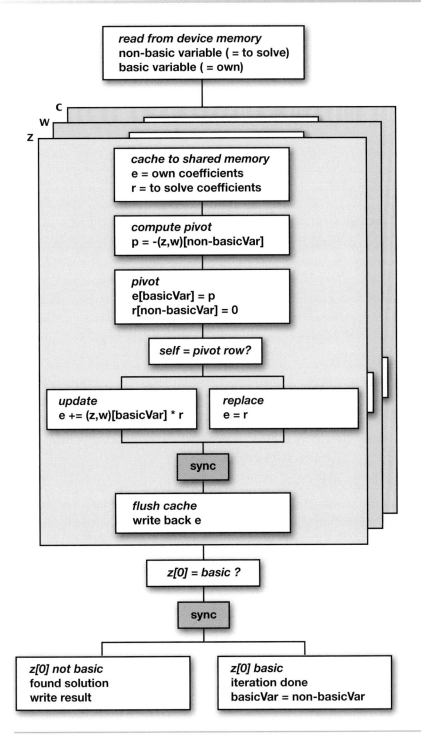

Figure 33-6. Solving for the Selected Equation

33.7 Results

The presented LCP method is very versatile for discrete (coherence-based) contact-point methods. It can be used for determining contact points for convex polyhedra and for calculating constrained contact forces. Its matrix nature lends itself particularly well to highly parallel systems and can be mapped efficiently to the GeForce 8800 architecture.

For examining the performance of the CUDA LCP solver, we employ CUDA's profiling tool. Table 33-1 shows a breakdown of typical timings obtained on a GeForce 8800 GTX for some convex object types. This GPU has 16 multiprocessors, whose processing units run at 1350 MHz. In each simulated time step, the LCP matrix M must be built, because to be able to compute the distance, we need the objects' world-space positions. As the objects are moving around, the plane inequalities must be recomputed. Then the pivoting iteration alternates between solving for an equation and determining the next one to solve for. In theory, this requires at most pivoting for every equation once. Because of numerical precision, this process can take a few more iterations. In practice, however, the iteration count stays well below the dimension of M most of the time.

Using the CUDA environment, we are now able to write highly dynamic algorithms for the GPU. The pivot selection and the routine for solving for a selected equation are such algorithms. Table 33-1 documents the variation in measured execution time for these routines. This is a considerable step forward in GPU processing. The setup routine does not benefit from dynamic control flow, because the number of constraints to compute is constant in each scenario.

The code as provided in the demo application on this book's DVD can execute three collision-pair resolution kernels per multiprocessor. A publicly available LCP solver for the CPU can be found in Eberly 2004. If we apply some memory optimizations, it can

Table 33-1. Performance Numbers for the CUDA LCP Solver
In microseconds per collision pair for selected complexities of convex objects.

	6-Sided	12-Sided	24-Sided
Setup • Build half-space descriptions • Assemble M and q • Initialize z and w	1.5	3.1	4.8
Select next pivot equation	0.04 0.2	0.06 0.6	0.16 1.6
Solve equation	0.1 – 1.0	0.2 – 3.9	0.3 – 6.2

resolve about 21,000 distance queries per second for six-sided convex objects on a 3.0 GHz Pentium 4. The CUDA LCP solver demo computes about 69,000 queries per second on a GeForce 8800 GTX.

Figure 33-7 shows the accompanying demo in action. The LCP solver implementation is used for determining distances between convex objects in the narrow-phase processing step. The resting contact force calculation and the time integration step are simple standard implementations. They could also be moved to GPU processing using CUDA.

Figure 33-7. The Demo Application

33.8 References

Baraff, David. 1993. "Non-penetrating Rigid Body Simulation." In *State of the Art Reports of EUROGRAPHICS '93*, Eurographics Technical Report Series.

Bland, R. G. 1977, "New Finite Pivoting Rules for the Simplex Method." *Mathematics of Operations Research* 2, pp. 103–107.

Cottle, R. W., and G. Dantzig. 1968. "Complementarity Pivot Theory of Mathematical Programming." *Linear Algebra and Its Applications* 1, pp. 103–125.

Dantzig, G. B. 1963. *Linear Programming and Extensions*. Princeton University Press.

Eberly, D. H. 2004. *Game Physics*. Morgan Kaufmann.

Ericson, Christer. 2005. *Real-Time Collision Detection*. Morgan Kaufmann.

Lemke, C. E. 1965. "Bimatrix Equilibrium Points and Mathematical Programming." *Management Science* 11, pp. 681–689.

Murty, K. G. 1988. *Linear Complementarity, Linear and Nonlinear Programming*. Heldermann Verlag.

Thompson, K. 1987. "A Parallel Pivotal Algorithm for Solving the Linear Complementarity Problem." Technical Report 707, Computer Sciences Department, University of Wisconsin.

Chapter 34

Signed Distance Fields Using Single-Pass GPU Scan Conversion of Tetrahedra

Kenny Erleben
University of Copenhagen

Henrik Dohlmann
3Dfacto R&D

34.1 Introduction

In this chapter we address the practicalities in computing a signed distance field. We present a method that accelerates the computation by using graphics hardware. Our method is simple to implement and offers a trade-off between performance and quality.

34.1.1 Overview of Signed Distance Fields

A signed distance field is represented as a grid sampling of the closest distance to the surface of an object represented as a polygonal model. Usually the convention of using negative values inside the object and positive values outside the object is applied. Signed distance fields are very attractive in computer graphics and related fields. Often they are used for collision detection in cloth animation (Bridson et al. 2003), multibody dynamics (Guendelman et al. 2003), deformable objects (Fisher and Lin 2001), mesh generation (Molino et al. 2003), motion planning (Hoff et al. 1999), and sculpting (Bærentzen 2001).

However, fast and robust signed distance field computation is often either a performance bottleneck, because of high-resolution fields, or a nearly impossible task because of degeneracies in input meshes. Thus, computation can be tedious and time-consuming. For example, a naive implementation on a CPU can take hours, even days, to complete for high-resolution grids (256^3 resolution or greater).

Methods for computing distance fields on graphics hardware fall into two different approaches: *distance meshing* or *scan conversion of bounded volumes*. Section 34.7 gives a short survey of these and other approaches.

34.1.2 Overview of Our Method

Our approach is a novel scan conversion method. In addition to being GPU-accelerated, our method fixes the leaking artifacts sometimes produced by the prism scan (Sigg et al. 2003) and characteristic scan conversion (CSC) (Mauch 2003) methods. It is therefore able to handle "inconsistent meshes" (Bischoff et al. 2005), which are polygonal models that have holes, flipped surfaces, overlapping faces, and worse. In practice, these polygonal models are often encountered on object surfaces that are modeled by an animator or obtained by scanning or segmentation.

More precisely, our method does not need any scan line and combines the novel fragment program from prism scan with the pseudonormal method (Aanæs and Bærentzen 2003). Thus, it is single-pass and avoids any sign errors of other scan conversion algorithms. Note that the correct sign computation in the fragment program relies on the angle-weighted pseudonormals of the vertices and edges; if these pseudonormals cannot be computed correctly, there is no guarantee that the method will compute the proper sign of the distance field.

In the prism scan and CSC methods, the signed distance is computed within a narrow-band shell along the surface of objects. The size of the shell is user specified. Our method, too, is limited by a narrow-band size. Previous methods often used narrow-band sizes of three to five voxels. These small narrow-band sizes can hide computation errors at farther distances, so we use narrow-band sizes on the order of 30 to 50 voxels.

34.2 Leaking Artifacts in Scan Methods

Characteristic scan conversion uses a subdivision of space, which is inspired by Voronoi regions. More precisely, a bounded volume, or *characteristic polyhedron*, is created for each feature of the polygonal model (that is, the vertex, edge, and face) such that it encloses the set of the voxels that is closer to this feature than any other features. The union of all these potentially overlapping bounded volumes defines the narrow-band shell.

To avoid aliasing artifacts from discretization, we slightly enlarge the bounded volumes. Each feature's bounded volume is then scan-converted, and for each voxel that is inside the volume, its signed distance to the feature is computed. For any voxel inside the narrow-band shell, the signed distance to the object is then chosen. From all the signed distances to some feature previously computed for this voxel, this signed distance is chosen as the one with minimum absolute value.

Prism scan works similarly, except that no bounded volumes are created for the edges and vertices; instead, a single type of bounded volume—a tower prism—is created for each face.

Both methods sometimes produce *leaking artifacts*, whereby the sign of the distance computed for some voxels is wrong. These artifacts come from the following three sources.

34.2.1 The Plane Test

Both scan methods—distance meshing and scan conversion of bounded volumes—use a plane test to determine the sign of the distance function, as illustrated in Figure 34-1. As shown in this figure, this usage may lead to an incorrect computation of the sign.

The figure shows a cross section of a polygonal model focused on two faces, A and B. A and B are shown together with the bounded volume around A, in which the signed distance is calculated. In the dashed-red area, the points are closest to A and the sign will therefore become positive. This is clearly wrong. The points in the dashed-red region are located inside the object, so the sign should be negative. The sign will be correct in the green-dashed region. If the planes alone are used to determine the distance, the distance will be wrong in both the red-dashed and in the green-dashed areas.

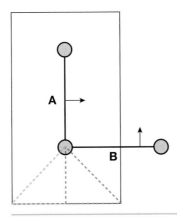

Figure 34-1. Plane Test Sign Error

In the characteristic scan conversion method, this problem is worse because the characteristic polyhedra are enlarged to avoid aliasing. So for a face, the distance of voxels outside the face's Voronoi region is also computed with respect to the face plane. This means that the dashed lines shown in Figure 34-1 will produce voxels with distances close to zero inside Voronoi regions of the neighboring faces. Prism scan performs a case analysis of voxels in enlarged regions and will only suffer from a wrong sign computation.

Figure 34-2 shows real-life examples of these problems. As is the case for all such examples in this chapter, for better visualization, we cut the isosurface by a plane such that the inside and outside parts are shown in blue and red colors, respectively. Figure 34-5, in the next section, shows the results of using our method.

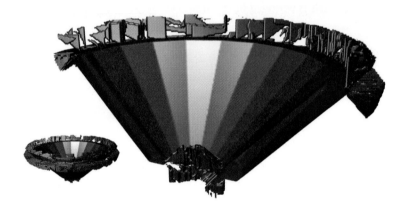

Figure 34-2. Leaking Due to the Plane Test Problem
A zero-level-set isosurface visualization of a real-life example. Note the noisy shape around the sharp ridges of the model. The unclipped isosurface is shown in the lower left corner.

34.2.2 How a Bounding Volume Is Constructed

The second source of leaking artifacts lies in the way bounding volumes are constructed, as shown in Figure 34-3. The narrow-band shells have different widths on opposite sides of a thin region, which causes the inside region of one side to extend beyond the outside region on the opposite side. For the configuration shown in the figure, the bounding region of the top face extrudes below the bounding region of the bottom face. This results in the small gray area in the figure, where the distance becomes negative. In Figure 34-4, a real-life example is shown.

Our method, which is described in Section 34.3, is capable of handling these two first sources of leaking artifacts—use of a plane test and how a bound volume is constructed—as shown in Figure 34-5.

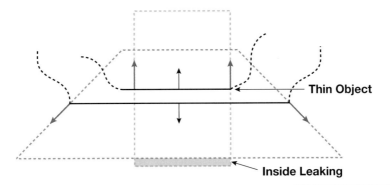

Figure 34-3. A Cross Section of a Mesh with Thin Structure, Shown Together with Their Bounding Regions

The top face has a bounding region (green), and the bottom face has a bounding region (red).

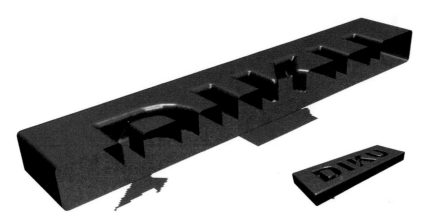

Figure 34-4. Leaking by Construction

A zero-level-set isosurface visualization of a real-life example. Note the noisy blue parts outside the isosurface. In the lower right corner, the unclipped isosurface is shown.

Figure 34-5. Results Produced with Our Tetrahedra GPU Scan Method

A zero-level-set isosurface visualization showing how our method handles the real-life examples from Figures 34-2 and 34-4. Notice that no leaking is present.

34.2.3 Folds in the Polygonal Model

The last source of leaking artifacts is due to folds present in the polygonal model. Although both scan methods rely on the model's surface to be a perfect two-manifold, this condition is not sufficient to avoid sign problems. In fact, if the surface contains folds, then the orientation of a triangle face can be flipped.

A fold typically overlaps other triangles in the mesh, with its inside pointing in the same direction as the other triangles' outsides. If the folded triangle's outside has an absolute distance to a voxel that is less than the absolute distance to the overlapped triangles, the distance value computed will have the wrong sign and distance. A special case of this problem occurs when the folded triangle and the overlapped triangles have the same absolute distance. In this scenario, the sign that's selected depends upon the scan order, and this order can give some weird-looking errors, where the distance is correct but the sign is wrong. This situation creates a strange leaking effect. Figure 34-6 illustrates the mesh topology of a fold, and Figure 34-7 shows a real-life example.

Folds cannot be handled by a single-pass algorithm. Our method could be extended with a second pass to deal with sign problems caused by folding, as done in Houston et al. 2006.

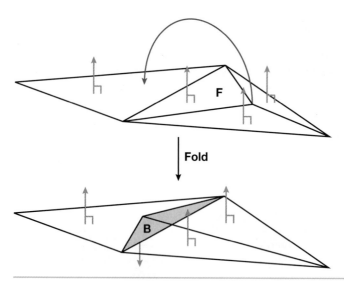

Figure 34-6. The Mesh Topology of a Fold
A planar mesh is folded so that the back side, B, of a triangle, instead of the front side, F, is turning outside.

Figure 34-7. Leaking by Folding
A zero-level-set isosurface visualization of a real-life example. Note the noisy tentacles of the model. The upper right corner shows the original mesh using two-sided lighting. The red face on the nose is flipped.

34.3 Our Tetrahedra GPU Scan Method

Given a surface of an object as a collection of triangles, we compute the signed distance within a user-specified narrow-band shell.

Our approach, the tetrahedra (T4) GPU scan method, uses a shell made of tetrahedra: that is, only tetrahedral volumes are considered. Section 34.3.1 describes how we compute the shell from the mesh triangles on the CPU. Several tetrahedra are computed per triangle, and each of these tetrahedra bounds a region of space containing a subset of the grid voxels. For each of these voxels, the signed closest distance to the triangle is computed on the GPU.

To ensure complete coverage, we make sure the generated tetrahedra covers the Voronoi regions of the mesh within a specified narrow-band distance. Thus, the generated tetrahedra from a triangle must cover all voxels of the Voronoi region of the triangle. The union of generated tetrahedra from a one-ring neighborhood of a vertex must, likewise, cover the Voronoi region of the vertex. In addition, the union of tetrahedra from two neighboring triangles of an edge must cover the Voronoi region of that edge. Our tetrahedra generation method generates tetrahedra so that there are large overlaps in the Voronoi regions of vertices and edges.

Using tetrahedra allows us to employ a fast tetrahedron slicer to compute the intersections of the shell with the grid voxels. The technique of slicing tetrahedra is well known from volume visualization and is extremely efficient. It is thus cheaper than doing a 3D scan conversion of more-complex prisms, cones, or wedges.

To determine the voxels lying inside each tetrahedron, we move a z-plane in the direction of the positive z axis. At each z-slice of the regular grid, we halt the z-plane and find the cross sections between the tetrahedra and the z-plane, as described in Section 34.3.2. A *status set* contains all the tetrahedra that intersect the z-slice at any given step. We adopted a simple sweep-line algorithm (de Berg et al. 1997) to quickly find all tetrahedra that intersect the z-plane. This algorithm requires the tetrahedra to be sorted by increasing z-value. As an alternative, we could use the occlusion query method from Sud et al. 2004.

Having found the cross sections, we render them and use a GPU fragment program to compute the signed distances, as described in Section 34.3.3. The fragment program outputs the signed distance to the color buffer and outputs the absolute value of the signed distance to the depth buffer. A depth test is set up so that the final result in the color buffer is the signed distance with minimum absolute value, as wanted. Before moving to the next z-slice of the regular grid, we read back the computed distance values from the frame buffer and store them in an internal data structure. Listing 34-1 shows the overall steps of the T4 GPU scan method.

Listing 34-1. Pseudocode for Our T4 GPU Scan Conversion Method

```
algorithm T4-GPU-scan()
  for z = min z plane to max z plane
    foreach tetrahedra t that intersects the z plane
      find cross-section with z
      render cross section
    next t
    read back distance values
  next z
end algorithm
```

Note that we could have created the shell during the scan conversion to minimize storage usage. However, in our implementation we have chosen to keep the shell creation as a separate stage for better modularity of the implementation.

Our shell creation method has linear time complexity, $O(n)$, in the number of triangle faces, n, because it iterates once over the triangle faces, and it generates a fixed number of tetrahedra for each triangle face. The initialization of the sweep line (the z-sorting of the tetrahedra) has $O(n \log n)$ time complexity, although the actual scan conversion can be expected to have linear complexity in the number of generated tetrahedra.

Observe that we make one render pass for each z-increment. Also, we make one render call per cross section. Currently, cross-section geometry is transferred to the GPU using OpenGL's immediate mode. We could optimize this step considerably by using vertex arrays and geometry shaders for creating the cross sections. This will be the subject of future work.

34.3.1 Computing the Shell

The shell is computed by iterating over the mesh triangles and generating five tetrahedra per triangle.

Using the longest edge, **e**, and the orthogonal height vector, **h**, a tight-fitting rectangle can be placed in the plane of the triangle. From now on, the rectangle is enlarged by the user-specified narrow-band size, ε. Finally, the four vertices of the rectangle are extruded an ε-distance outward and inward along the face normal, **n,** to produce an enclosing *oriented bounding box* (OBB) around the triangle face. Figure 34-8 illustrates the steps involved.

The OBB is then directly decomposed into five tetrahedra. This step is simple to implement and nearly impossible to get wrong. It ensures complete coverage of the narrow band, although large parts may stick outside or overlap. Thus, simplicity comes at a performance degradation.

The shell creation method makes no assumption about the mesh and can be used for unstructured meshes with all kinds of degeneracies. Note that any kind of tetrahedral shell generation method could be used in our scan conversion method, such as the adaptive thin tetrahedral shell mesh (Erleben et al. 2005), which allows a trade-off between simplicity of creation and efficiency of scan conversion.

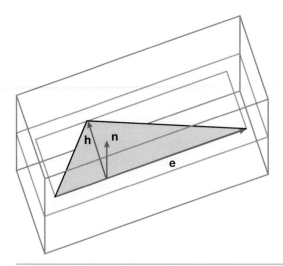

Figure 34-8. Fitting an Oriented Bounding Box Around a Triangle Face

34.3.2 Computing the Cross Section of a Tetrahedron

To calculate the cross section of a tetrahedron by using z-plane, we sort the four points of the tetrahedron by increasing z-value. This method allows a very simple algorithm to find the number of intersections and to create polygons to be processed by the fragment program.

Consider Figure 34-9. If the z-plane under consideration is below the lowest point in the tetrahedron, there will be no intersections. Similarly, if the z-plane is above the highest point in the tetrahedron, there will be no intersections, as shown in Figure 34-9.

There are only three topologically distinct ways a z-plane can actually slice the tetrahedron:

1. **The z-plane lies below p_1.** In this case the plane cuts the lines $p_0 p_3$, $p_0 p_1$, and $p_0 p_2$ (case A in the figure).

2. **The z-plane lies between p_1 and p_2.** In this case the plane cuts the lines $p_0 p_3$, $p_1 p_3$, $p_1 p_2$, and $p_0 p_2$ (case B in the figure).

3. **The z-plane lies above p_2.** In this case the plane cuts the lines $p_0 p_3$, $p_1 p_3$, and $p_2 p_3$ (case C in the figure).

In case B, the polygon will always be convex, which can be seen by drawing all the possible configurations of a tetrahedron and considering the order in which the plane cuts the four lines. A tetrahedron that is sliced in only one point, or sliced along a line,

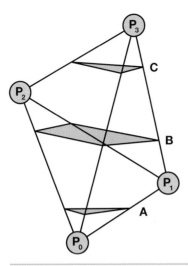

Figure 34-9. The Possible Different Topological Slicings of a Tetrahedron

has no area and should not be considered. The slicing algorithm we described ensures this never happens. The polygons might be clockwise or counterclockwise, so a post-process might be necessary to ensure proper orientation. However, the T4 GPU scan method does not need this property.

34.3.3 Computing Signed Distance Using Angle-Weighted Pseudonormals

A novel fragment program was introduced in Sigg et al. 2003, which calculated the distance to a triangle. We describe here the case analysis used to determine the distance, together with our extension that calculates the correct sign through use of angle-weighted pseudonormals.

The triangle is used to create a local triangle frame consisting of vectors **r**, **s**, and **t**, as shown in Figure 34-10.

The **t** vector is set to the face normal, **n**. Next, the longest edge of the triangle is found, and vertices are numbered counterclockwise with respect to the face normal. By convention, the longest edge is always going from vertex 0 to vertex 1, as shown in Figure 34-11. The origin of the triangle frame is computed by projecting vertex 2 onto the longest triangle edge. Next, **r** is computed as the unit vector from the origin to vertex 1, and **s** as the unit vector from the origin to vertex 2.

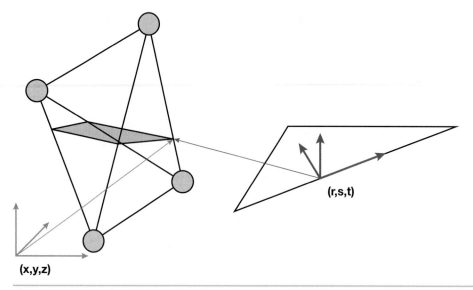

Figure 34-10. A Local Triangle Frame for a Triangle in the Mesh and a Related Cross Section

The coordinates of the cross section of the tetrahedron are converted to the local triangle frame and sent to the GPU as texture coordinates $\mathbf{p} = (r, s, t)$, where r, s, and t are the local triangle coordinates with respect to the $\mathbf{r}$, $\mathbf{s}$, and $\mathbf{t}$ vectors, respectively.

The triangle is analyzed to produce three lengths, as shown in Figure 34-11: the height, h; the length, a, from the origin of the triangle frame to vertex $\mathbf{v}_1$; and the length, b, from the origin to vertex $\mathbf{v}_0$.

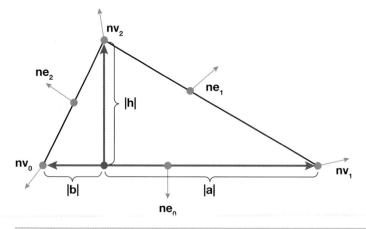

Figure 34-11. A Local Triangle with Lengths a, b, and h, and Pseudonormals

Further, the six angle-weighted pseudonormals for the vertices ($\mathbf{n}_{v_0}$, $\mathbf{n}_{v_1}$, and $\mathbf{n}_{v_2}$) and edges ($\mathbf{n}_{e_0}$, $\mathbf{n}_{e_1}$, and $\mathbf{n}_{e_2}$) are calculated and transformed to the local triangle frame by using a rotation matrix constructed from unit column vectors, as follows:

$$\mathbf{n}' = \left[\frac{\mathbf{a}}{\|\mathbf{a}\|} \quad \frac{\mathbf{h}}{\|\mathbf{h}\|} \quad \frac{\mathbf{n}}{\|\mathbf{n}\|} \right]^T \mathbf{n},$$

where $\mathbf{n}'$ is the transformed normal of $\mathbf{n}$. These pseudonormals and the three lengths are sent to the GPU as texture coordinates.

The first thing that happens on the GPU is a reduction of the problem to the half-plane, where $r \geq 0$. That is, if r is negative, we flip the data such that $r = -r$, $a = b$, $\mathbf{n}_{v_1} = \mathbf{n}_{v_0}$, and $\mathbf{n}_{e_1} = \mathbf{n}_{e_2}$. This considerably reduces further analysis.

A primed coordinate system with coordinates r' and s' is used in the case analysis. The origin of the primed coordinate system is vertex 2, and the r' axis is the vector from vertex 2 to vertex 1. The s' axis is simply the hat of the r' axis. Note that the primed coordinate system does not have unit axis vectors. r' and s' are derived from r and s, and a case analysis is performed according to regions shown in Figure 34-12.

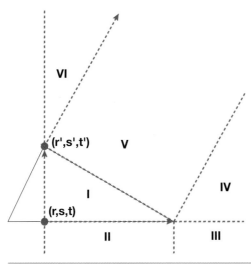

Figure 34-12. Regions Used in the Case Analysis for the Triangle
Notice the two coordinate frames that are used: the local triangle frame (r, s, t) and the primed coordinate frame (r', s', t').

From the case analysis, we can compute the distance to the closest feature and determine the corresponding pseudonormal. The sign can be computed using the pseudonormal of the closest feature, $\mathbf{n(c)}$, and some point, $\mathbf{c}$, on the closest feature, as the sign of

$$d = \mathbf{n(c)} \cdot (\mathbf{p} - \mathbf{c}),$$

as described in Bærentzen and Aanæs 2005.

The complete Cg program for the signed distance field computation is shown in Listing 34-2.

Listing 34-2. Cg Program Using Case Analysis and Pseudonormals to Correctly Compute the Sign

```
void main(
    in float3 local      : TEXCOORD0,
    in float3 triangle   : TEXCOORD1,
    in float3 nv0        : TEXCOORD2,
    in float3 nv1        : TEXCOORD3,
    in float3 nv2        : TEXCOORD4,
    in float3 ne0        : TEXCOORD5,
    in float3 ne1        : TEXCOORD6,
    in float3 ne2        : TEXCOORD7,
    out float4 dist      : COLOR0,
    out float  absDist   : DEPTH,
    const uniform float narrowbandSize)
{
    // Copy to temporaries.
    float   a = triangle.x;
    float   b = triangle.y;
    float   h = triangle.z;
    float   r = local.x;
    float   s = local.y;
    float   t = local.z;
    float3 nv = nv1;
    float3 ne = ne1;

    // Normalize to half-space r >= 0.
    if (r < 0) {
        r = -r;
        a =  b;
        nv = nv0;
        ne = ne2;
    }
    // Transform to the primed coordinate frame.
    float lensqr = (a * a + h * h);
    float rprime = (a * r + h * h - h * s) / lensqr;
    float sprime = (a * s + h * r - h * a) / lensqr;
```

Listing 34-2 (*continued*). Cg Program Using Case Analysis and Pseudonormals to Correctly Compute the Sign

```
// Case analysis
// Default to region I
float3 c = float3(0, 0, 0);
float3 n = float3(0, 0, 1);
if (s < 0) {
  // Region III or II
  c.x = a;
  n = (r > a) ? nv : ne0;
}
else if (sprime > 0) {
  if (rprime < 0) {
    // Region VI
    c.y = h;
    n = nv2;
  }
  else {
    // Region IV or V
    c.x = a;
    n = (rprime > 1) ? nv : ne;
  }
}
// IV, V, VI
rprime = max(max(- rprime,0), rprime - 1);
// I, V
sprime = max(sprime,0);
// II, III
r      = max(r-a,0);

// Compute the distance.
float tmp = (s < 0) ? (r * r + s * s)
                    : ((rprime * rprime + sprime * sprime) * lensqr);
absDist = sqrt(tmp + t * t);

// Compute the sign.
float sign_tst = sign(dot(n, local - c));
dist = float4(sign_tst * absDist, local);

// Depth buffer is clamped to 0..1, so we rescale.
absDist /= narrowbandSize;
}
```

34.4 Results

All measurements in Figures 34-13 and 34-14 were performed on a 2.4 GHz Pentium 4 with 4 GB of RAM, running Gentoo Linux with an NVIDIA GeForce 6800 GT with 256 MB of RAM. We used a narrow-band size corresponding to 10 percent of the maximum mesh extent, so roughly to an order of 30 to 50 voxels. All timings are in seconds and plotted in Figures 34-13 and 34-14. As expected, all figures show linear complexity in the mesh size.

Figure 34-13 shows the CPU time overhead. Clearly, the lookup operations into our tetrahedra mesh data structure are bottlenecks in our implementation. Why? Because all our mesh data structures are designed for making topological operations easy, not for quickly retrieving information. The second most expensive operations are local triangle initialization, slicing, surface mesh lookup of vertex coordinates and normals, and transformation of normals. Except for the mesh vertex and normal lookup, these operations

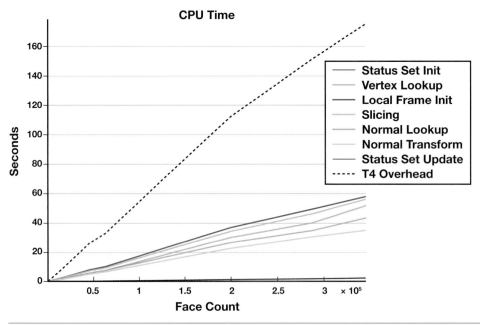

Figure 34-13. The Time to Process the Geometry on the CPU for the OBB Shell Creation Method
Status set initialization (Status Set Init) and updating (Status Set Update) correspond to handling the set of intersecting tetrahedra used in the sweep-line method. Tetrahedral vertices are looked up (T4 Overhead) and each tetrahedron is sliced (Slicing) to produce cross sections. We look up vertices (Vertex Lookup) and normals (Normal Lookup) of the surface mesh. Afterward, the local triangle frame is initialized (Local Frame Init) and a normal transformation is done (Normal Transform).

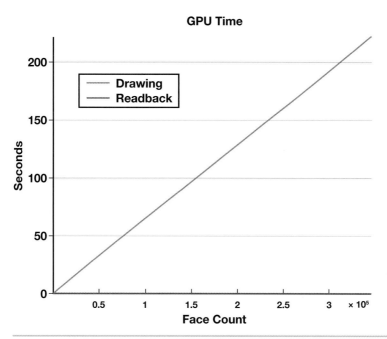

Figure 34-14. The Time to Process the Geometry on the GPU

could be offloaded to the GPU by using vertex and geometry shaders. Figure 34-14, which charts the GPU time overhead, shows that the fragment program is computationally the most expensive part and outweighs the frame buffer readback for large mesh sizes.

In Figure 34-15, we show a few of our signed distance field results. The left column shows the sign computation, the middle column shows the signed distance field, and the right column has the mesh superimposed. Note that no leaking is present and that the signed distance field appears smooth everywhere.

Figure 34-16 compares the running times of a CPU implementation of our method and our GPU implementation. Various meshes of different sizes were scan-converted into 256^3 grids by using a narrowband size of roughly 20 pixels, which corresponds to 10 percent of the mesh extent. These tests were done on a Dell Precision M90, with Intel Core Duo, 2.33 GHz, and 2 GB of RAM, running Windows XP and having an NVIDIA Quadro FX 2500 graphics card with 512 MB of RAM. On average, the GPU version gives a speedup factor of 6. The CPU version exploits random access to the memory, so there is no need to use the scan line; instead, tetrahedra slices are rendered directly into the 3D grids in the CPU memory.

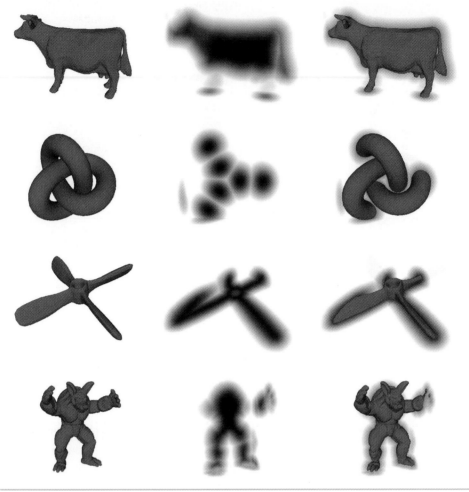

Figure 34-15. Sign Verification and Signed Distance Field Results
The first column shows isosurface extractions, the second column shows cuts through the distance map, and the third column combines the first two columns.

34.5 Conclusion

We have presented an approach for scan conversion of signed distance fields that offers these features:

- It is based on a single type of simple geometry: a tetrahedron.
- It uses pseudonormals to handle correct sign computations.

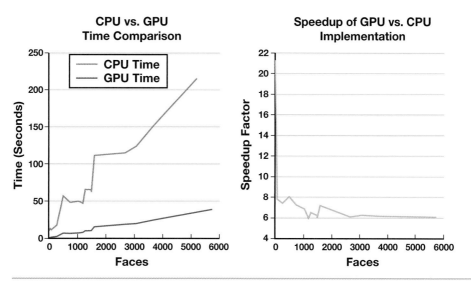

Figure 34-16. Performance Comparison
Left: A comparison of CPU and GPU running times of different mesh sizes, using 256^3 grids and narrowband size of 20 pixels (corresponding to 10 percent mesh extent). Right: The actual GPU speedup factor, which averages 6.

- Part of it lends itself naturally to a GPU implementation, yielding an average speedup factor of 6.

We have also presented a shell generation method that is simple to understand and easy to implement. Put together, our work yields a flexible, simple, and efficient system for computing signed distance fields.

34.6 Future Work

Future work includes improvements to the algorithm itself and to its GPU implementation.

34.6.1 Improvements to the Algorithm

Fast methods that generate more tight-fitting tetrahedral shell meshes could be used to boost performance. Indeed, the OBB creation method clearly yields good quality. However, because of the large OBBs extending far beyond the narrow-band size and having large overlaps, redundant and unneeded computations are done during the scan conversion.

Next, although we have presented a shell generation method that doesn't rely on pseudonormals, the fragment program actually needs the pseudonormals. This may be a disadvantage for several degenerate meshes that have redundant vertices, creating open boundaries that meet but are not topologically connected. So, future work could focus on the dependence on pseudonormals—for instance, by figuring out an algorithm capable of computing meaningful pseudonormals for degenerate meshes. Other than that, the method is capable of handling open boundaries, even overlapping faces.

34.6.2 Improvements to Our Implementation

Our GPU implementation could be much improved to achieve even higher speedups.

First, we could replace OpenGL's immediate mode by using vertex buffer objects to obtain better triangle batching. Second, the scan-line method could be moved onto the GPU by using occlusion queries to quickly determine the set of tetrahedra that intersects the current z-plane. Third, the multiple readbacks that occur for every z-slice could be reduced to a single readback by creating a flattened 3D texture (that is, a 2D texture containing all z-slices of the signed distance field and having uniforms to indicate offsets into the flattened texture for each render pass). These three improvements would still keep the implementation backward-compatible with all graphics cards that support programmable GPUs.

In addition, on more recent GPUs we could use a vertex texture fetch to set up the actual tetrahedral slicing in a vertex program and to generate the tetrahedral geometries in geometry shaders.

34.7 Further Reading

The brute-force approach to computing distance fields can be described as "For each voxel, compute the closest distance to the faces in a polygonal model." Acceleration techniques exist, such as only querying voxels against a bounding volume hierarchy, or reversing the iteration to iterate over bounding volumes around faces.

A straightforward parallelization of the naive approach is possible by reversing the order of iteration; that is, for each face, compute the distance to all voxels, as was done in Hoff et al. 1999. The authors mesh the distance function of a vertex, edge, or face and render it directly to the depth buffer. For volumes, this is done in a slice-by-slice manner, and the distance field is read back from the depth buffer. Any distance metric can be used, but signs are not handled. The simplicity of this method is attractive, although it requires tessellating elliptical cones and hyperboloid sheets in 3D. Obviously, the tessellation causes discretization errors in the distance computation, but the errors can be controlled. This approach is termed *distance meshing*.

Scan conversion algorithms using the GPU have become quite popular. Here various external regions, which bound the space of points lying closer to a geometric feature than any other geometric feature, are scan-converted. These methods require the construction of bounded volumes that are scan-converted slice by slice using a CPU-based scan-line method extended for 3D volumes. Previous CPU methods used a two-pass strategy to resolve the sign issue. In Aanæs and Bærentzen 2003, angle-weighted pseudonormals were used to determine the correct sign, which allows for a single pass only.

In Mauch 2003, the characteristic scan conversion algorithm was presented, and three different kinds of characteristic polyhedra were used: a prism (for faces), a cone (for vertices), and a wedge (for edges). Although this algorithm is conceptually easy to understand, it's not clear how the curved surfaces of the cones and wedges should be tessellated. To avoid aliasing, you must enlarge the polyhedra; however, the author did not describe the possible errors in the computations caused by voxels getting caught on the wrong side of the surface. This artifact is described in detail in Section 34.2.

Sigg et al. 2003 presented an optimized GPU version of CSC together with a more aggressive scan conversion method, named *prism scan*. Prisms are constructed for faces only, reducing the number of bounded volumes that need to be scan-converted. Also, a novel fragment program was presented for computing the signed distances of the rasterized voxels. Prism scan suffers from the same sign problems as CSC, because only the face planes are used to determine the sign, as explained in detail in Section 34.2. These sign errors may seem innocent because they occur rarely for small-sized narrow-bands and smooth curved objects. However, if narrow-band size is increased and objects with sharp ridges and valleys are scan-converted, the sign errors immediately blow up as huge areas of discontinuities where the wrong side of the surface is leaked into the other side.

Both prism scan and CSC are limited by a user-specified narrow-band size.

Both these methods rely on the input surface mesh to be a perfect two-manifold. When working with real-world models, we find that this is often not the case, so we must often resort to a mesh reconstruction (Nooruddin and Turk 2003).

Sud et al. 2004 presents several performance improvements for computing distance fields on graphics hardware. The two main contributions are a culling method based on occlusion queries and a conservative clamping computation based on the spatial coherency of the distance field.

To summarize, methods for computing distance fields on graphics hardware fall into two different approaches: distance meshing and scan conversion of bounded volumes. In Hsieh and Tai 2005, a hybrid of these two approaches is presented for the 2D case.

Other approaches involve solving the eikonal equation by using, for instance, a two-stage fast-marching method (Sethian 1999a). Whereas the scan conversion methods we just described compute exact signed distance fields, fast-marching methods usually have a discretization error of order $O(1)$, but higher-order accurate versions do exist (Sethian 1999b). Other methods deal with the computation of distance fields, such as Danielsson's distance field algorithm (Danielsson 1980). Danielsson uses a four-pass scan method to propagate distance information on a regular 2D grid. This method, which can be extended to 3D, somewhat resembles the fast-marching method.

Frisken et al. (2000) take a different approach by introducing adaptive distance fields.

34.8 References

Aanæs, H., and J. A. Bærentzen. 2003. "Pseudo-normals for Signed Distance Computation." In *Proceedings of Vision, Modeling, and Visualization 2003.*

Bærentzen, J. A. 2001. "Manipulation of Volumetric Solids, with Application to Sculpting." Ph.D. dissertation, IMM, Technical University of Denmark.

Bærentzen, J. A., and H. Aanæs. 2005. "Signed Distance Computation Using the Angle Weighted Pseudo-normal." *Transactions on Visualization and Computer Graphics* 11(3), pp. 243–253.

Bischoff, S., D. Pavic, and L. Kobbelt. 2005. "Automatic Restoration of Polygon Models." *ACM Transactions on Graphics* 24(4), pp. 1332–1352.

Bridson, R., S. Marino, and R. Fedkiw. 2003. "Simulation of Clothing with Folds and Wrinkles." In *Proceedings of the 2003 ACM SIGGRAPH/Eurographics Symposium on Computer Animation*, pp. 28–36.

Danielsson, P. E. 1980. "Euclidean Distance Mapping." *Computer Graphics and Image Processing* 14, pp. 227–248.

de Berg, M., M. van Kreveld, M. Overmars, and O. Schwarzkopf. 1997. *Computational Geometry: Algorithms and Applications.* Springer-Verlag.

Erleben, K., H. Dohlmann, and J. Sporring. 2005. "The Adaptive Thin Shell Tetrahedral Mesh." *The Journal of WSCG* 13, pp. 17–24.

Fisher, S., and M. C. Lin. 2001. "Deformed Distance Fields for Simulation of Non-penetrating Flexible Bodies." In *Proceedings of the Eurographics Workshop on Computer Animation and Simulation*, pp. 99–111.

Frisken, S. F., R. N. Perry, A. P. Rockwood, and T. R. Jones. 2000. "Adaptively Sampled Distance Fields: A General Representation of Shape for Computer Graphics." In *Proceedings of the 27th Annual Conference on Computer Graphics and Interactive Techniques*, pp. 249–254.

Guendelman, E., R. Bridson, and R. Fedkiw. 2003. "Nonconvex Rigid Bodies with Stacking." In *ACM Transactions on Graphics (Proceedings of SIGGRAPH 2003)* 22(3).

Hasselgren, J., T. Akenine-Möller, and L. Ohlsson. 2005. "Conservative Rasterization." In *GPU Gems 2*, edited by Matt Pharr, pp. 677–690. Addison-Wesley.

Hoff III, K. E., J. Keyser, M. Lin, D. Manocha, and T. Culver. 1999. "Fast Computation of Generalized Voronoi Diagrams Using Graphics Hardware." In *Proceedings of the 26th Annual Conference on Computer Graphics and Interactive Techniques*, pp. 277–286.

Houston, B., M. B. Nielsen, C. Batty, O. Nilsson, and K. Museth. 2006. "Hierarchical RLE Level Set: A Compact and Versatile Deformable Surface Representation." *ACM Transactions on Graphics* 25(1), pp. 151–175.

Hsieh, H.-H., and W.-K. Tai. 2005. "A Simple GPU-Based Approach for 3D Voronoi Diagram Construction and Visualization." *Simulation Modelling Practice and Theory* 13(8), pp. 681–692.

Mauch, S. 2003. "Efficient Algorithms for Solving Static Hamilton-Jacobi Equations." Ph.D. dissertation, California Institute of Technology.

Molino, N., R. Bridson, J. Teran, and R. Fedkiw. 2003. "A Crystalline, Red Green Strategy for Meshing Highly Deformable Objects with Tetrahedra." *International Meshing Roundtable* 12, pp. 103–114.

Nooruddin, F. S., and G. Turk. 2003. "Simplification and Repair of Polygonal Models Using Volumetric Techniques." *IEEE Transactions on Visualization and Computer Graphics* 9(2), pp. 191–205.

O'Rourke, J. 1998. *Computational Geometry in C*, 2nd ed. Cambridge University Press.

Sethian, J. A. 1999a. *Level Set Methods and Fast Marching Methods: Evolving Interfaces in Computational Geometry, Fluid Mechanics, Computer Vision, and Materials Science.* Cambridge University Press.

Sethian, J. A. 1999b. "Fast Marching Methods." *SIAM Review* 41(2), pp. 199–235.

Sigg, C., R. Peikert, and M. Gross. 2003. "Signed Distance Transform Using Graphics Hardware." In *Proceedings of IEEE Visualization*, pp. 83–90.

Sud, A., M. A. Otaduy, and D. Manocha. 2004. "DiFi: Fast 3D Distance Field Computation Using Graphics Hardware." In *Proceedings of Eurographics* 23(3).

In *GPU Gems 3*, we continue to showcase work that uses graphics hardware for nongraphics computation. As each new generation provides significantly greater computing power and programmability, GPUs are increasingly attractive targets for general-purpose computation, or what is commonly called *GPGPU* or *GPU Computing*. As a result, researchers and developers in academia and industry continue to develop new GPU algorithms for tasks such as sorting, database operations, image processing, and linear algebra. In many cases, the principal motivation for using the GPU is the prospect of high performance at a relatively low cost.

GPU programming tools have evolved dramatically over the past few years. Recently, NVIDIA launched a new set of tools for GPU Computing with the introduction of its CUDA technology. CUDA provides a flexible programming model and C-like language for implementing data-parallel algorithms on the GPU. What's more, NVIDIA's CUDA-compatible GPUs have additional hardware features specifically designed to boost performance and give users more control over how algorithms are mapped to the GPU. In many ways, CUDA is an important step forward in widening the domain of algorithms that can benefit from GPU performance. This part of the book contains a mix of new applications using CUDA, in addition to graphics-based GPGPU using languages like Cg.

We begin this section with a look at the role of GPUs in network security. For network virus detection systems, there is a tradeoff between fast, expensive solutions using specialized processors and low-cost alternatives based on commodity CPUs. In **Chapter 35, "Fast Virus Signature Matching on the GPU," Elizabeth Seamans** of Juniper Networks and **Thomas Alexander** of Polytime present a high-performance, GPU-based virus scanning library. The system uses the GPU as a fast filter to quickly identify possible virus signatures for thousands of data objects in parallel. The performance of their library suggests that the GPU is now a viable platform for cost-effective, high-performance network security processing.

In **Chapter 36, "AES Encryption and Decryption on the GPU," Takeshi Yamanouchi** of SEGA Corporation describes his work on implementing encryption algorithms on the GPU. AES (Advanced Encryption Standard) is the current standard for block cipher encryption, and, like many encryption algorithms, it relies heavily on integer operations. The author describes how to use the integer-processing capabilities of NVIDIA's GeForce 8800 GPUs to accelerate AES encryption and decryption.

Many software systems, including particle physics simulators and stochastic ray tracers, rely on Monte Carlo methods to efficiently solve problems involving complex, multidimensional functions. Fast and accurate random number generation is a critical component of all Monte Carlo simulations. In **Chapter 37, "Efficient Random Number Generation and Application Using CUDA," Lee Howes** and **David Thomas** of Imperial College London present methods for generating random numbers using CUDA to exploit the massive parallelism and arithmetic performance of the GPU. They describe the relative advantages of two fast algorithms for generating Gaussian random numbers—techniques that are particularly useful in financial simulations for pricing stock options.

Companies in the oil and gas industry depend on accurate seismic surveys of the Earth to identify subsurface oil reservoirs. The challenge is that most seismic data sets are many terabytes in size and it takes enormous amounts of computing power to convert the raw data into useful survey images. In **Chapter 38, "Imaging Earth's Subsurface Using CUDA," Bernard Deschizeaux** and **Jean-Yves Blanc** of CGGVeritas describe a CUDA implementation of several time-critical algorithms within their industrial seismic processing pipeline. Their CUDA implementation achieves significant performance improvements over the latest generation of CPUs, and the authors discuss the possibility of building clusters of GPUs to accelerate large seismic processing problems.

A number of commonly used algorithms in computer science involve a simple operation called *all-prefix-sum*, or *scan*. For each value in an array of data, the scan operation computes the sum of all preceding values. In **Chapter 39, "Parallel Prefix Sum (Scan) with CUDA," Mark Harris** of NVIDIA and **Shubhabrata Sengupta** and **John D. Owens** of University of California, Davis, describe an efficient CUDA implementation of a parallel scan algorithm and provide results for applications such as stream compaction and radix sort. This chapter is also a good reference for developers to learn CUDA programming and optimization strategies.

The Gaussian function is one of the most widely used filter kernels in image and signal processing. The exponential term makes the Gaussian expensive to evaluate dynamically, so in practice it is common to precompute a table of coefficients. In **Chapter 40, "Incremental Computation of the Gaussian," Ken Turkowski** of Adobe Systems presents a method to quickly evaluate the Gaussian on the fly using a technique similar to polynomial forward differencing. By replacing differences with quotients, this algorithm incrementally computes Gaussian coefficients. For a GPU implementation, this approach eliminates a texture lookup in the pixel shader, which can result in faster filtering performance.

Chapter 41, "Using the Geometry Shader for Compact and Variable-Length GPU Feedback," completes this section by describing how to use a new hardware feature in DirectX 10-compliant GPUs to implement algorithms that cannot be implemented efficiently using pixel or vertex shaders. The geometry shader is an extra stage in the GPU rendering pipeline that is capable of executing algorithms with variable, data-dependent input and output. This capability is particularly useful for computer vision applications that analyze images to identify geometric shapes. In this chapter, **Franck Diard** of NVIDIA presents geometry shader implementations of several algorithms, including histogram building and corner detection.

This section provides a small sampling of recent work on GPGPU techniques. Even with rapidly evolving architectures and programming tools like NVIDIA's CUDA, GPUs remain fairly specialized for data-parallel computation. However, it is clear that many important algorithms in scientific computing and other fields have enough parallelism to benefit from GPU performance, and it's likely that new algorithms will emerge as GPUs become more general and easier to program. As the chapters in this section demonstrate, the price/performance ratio of graphics processors is a potentially disruptive force in high-performance, and other, computing industries.

Nolan Goodnight, NVIDIA Corporation

Chapter 35

Fast Virus Signature Matching on the GPU

Elizabeth Seamans
Juniper Networks

Thomas Alexander
Polytime

35.1 Introduction

The Internet, with its constantly improving data communications infrastructure, moves vast amounts of data every second. To process data at a low latency and high throughput, networking equipment vendors use dedicated hardware. At the 4 Gb/s to 40 Gb/s level, processing is done using expensive, purpose-built application-specific integrated circuits. From the 100 Mb/s to 4 Gb/s level, processing is usually performed using a combination of general-purpose CPUs, network processors, and field-programmable gate arrays (FPGAs). Processing throughput below 100 Mb/s is performed using either an x86 CPU or an embedded processor.

Specialized network processors and FPGAs are flexible, and new algorithms and services can be deployed on edge routers or security appliances built using either technology. However, the low unit volumes force manufacturers to price these devices at many times the cost of producing them, to recoup the R&D dollars.

In this chapter we explore the potential of using the parallelism of commodity-priced graphics processors as network coprocessors. Although GPUs are designed principally for real-time 3D graphics, network processing and graphics processing have a lot in common.

Network processing and graphics processing share these important characteristics:

- They involve highly data-parallel algorithms, with requirements for a small but very high speed memory subsystem.
- They offer the ability to use large numbers of multithreaded processors to hide DRAM latency.
- They offer a fast interconnection bus to stream large volumes of data.

To illustrate this comparison, Figures 35-1 and 35-2 show the main attributes of a high-end network processor from Intel (IXP2800) and a high-end GPU from NVIDIA.

The motivation for this work is to see if the GPU has sufficient functionality to act as a network processor and, if it does, to leverage its commodity pricing to build routing and security appliances with a disruptive price/performance profile. Network security is probably the most demanding of data packet processing operations. Every byte, and potentially a combination of neighboring bytes, has to be processed multiple times. The

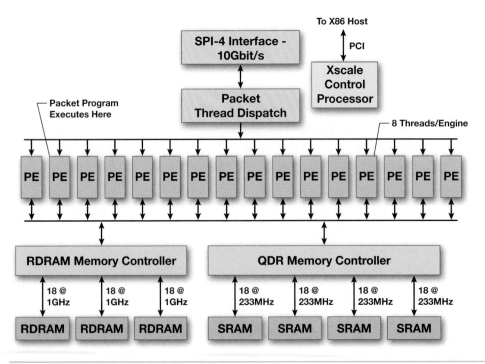

Figure 35-1. An Intel IXP2800 Network Processor
Many small processors accept packets from a high-bandwidth interface and perform independent work.

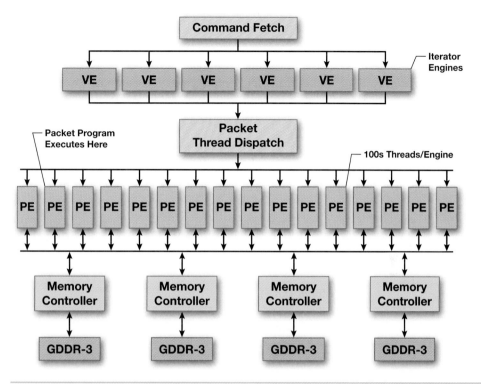

Figure 35-2. A High-End NVIDIA GPU
Many small engines accept data from a high-bandwidth interface and perform independent work.

processing involves bit manipulations and many lookups into several multi-megabyte databases. For example, virus detection requires pattern matching at multi-gigabit rates to achieve acceptable throughput.

To address this performance requirement, we present a prototype virus scanning system partially implemented on a modern graphics processor. The results we obtained indicate that GPUs now have the necessary computing, memory, and interface functionality to be compelling network offload engines.

35.2 Pattern Matching

Network security processing for virus detection relies extensively on pattern matching to determine if the data in packets is harmful and how to process the information. Pattern matching algorithms analyze pieces of the network data stream and compare data patterns (*signatures*) against a database of known viruses. These signature patterns can be fairly complex, composed of different-size strings, wild characters, range constraints, and sometimes recursive forms.

Typically, the processing and memory bottleneck in network processing engines is the performance of pattern matching computations at gigabit rates over many tens of thousands of signatures. The different signature lengths, wild characters, and range constraints require each input byte to be read and processed many times. In addition, many bytes of state are kept in flight while the matching operation is being done. Figure 35-3 gives an example of comparing the input data against a virus signature.

To achieve sufficient processing throughput for high-performance networks, data streams must be analyzed in parallel using *intrapacket scanning* (bytes within a packet are processed in parallel) or by using the *interpacket* approach (multiple packets are processed simultaneously). These methods provide different benefits and limitations, and we experiment with both types of parallelism for our GPU-based virus detection system.

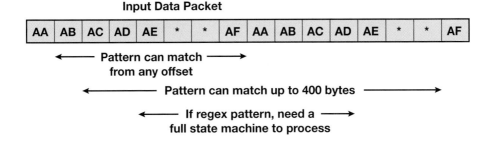

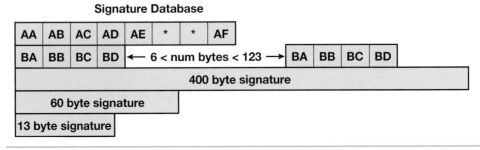

Figure 35-3. Matching a Virus Signature Against Packet Data

35.2.1 A Data-Scanning Library

We developed a library to support applications with data objects, such as packets or files, of varying sizes and requirements. The library accepts a data buffer and a data object description from the application. It inspects the data buffer and compares it against a static database of fixed-character, or *exact-match*, signature strings as a first step toward supporting full regular-expression signatures. Our library returns information to the application about any matches it detected.

We used the open-source antivirus application ClamAV, along with its virus signature database, as a demonstration application. ClamAV detects virus signatures in files of various types and sizes. Its signature database holds around 30,000 exact-match virus signatures whose sizes range between a few bytes to several hundred bytes. In the original algorithm, ClamAV processes one file at a time before it begins the next file, using the following steps:

1. Determine the file type.
2. Perform any necessary preprocessing (such as decompression).
3. Read the file data into a data buffer until the buffer is full or the end of the file is reached.
4. Find the signature matches for fixed-character signature strings.
5. Repeat steps 3 and 4 until the end of the file is reached.
6. Report the result for the file.

These steps place specific requirements on any virus detection library, including the stipulation that the library use GPU acceleration. In addition the library must be able to handle files that are much smaller than the data buffer, or file memory footprints that span multiple data buffers. Also, it must properly identify signature matches for different file types.

35.3 The GPU Implementation

As a data-parallel processor, the GPU excels at algorithmic tasks with regular, fixed-size input and output data sets. Therefore, to best utilize the GPU for virus detection, we need to focus on highly parallel portions of the pipeline and use the CPU for more-variable and serial execution tasks. In this way, we employ the GPU as a high-speed filter before completing the signature-matching work on the CPU. The GPU uses a small number of bytes to determine whether there is a likely match against a signature in the database, and the CPU verifies any possible matches.

The GPU maintains a version of the signature database, which it uses to detect possible signature matches in the input data. We create the GPU database by identifying 2 consecutive bytes from each signature and using them as an index into a 64,000-entry array, where each index is mapped to, at most, one signature. The array stores the 4 bytes in the signature immediately preceding the 2-byte key. A thread on the GPU reads a single 2-byte value from the input data and uses it as an index into the database array. It fetches the 4-byte tag and compares the tag against the 4 bytes of data immediately preceding the 2-byte value in the input data. In this way, every consecutive 2-byte value from the input data is read and compared to the signature database.

Figure 35-4 shows how a GPU thread performs the packet filtering operation. Listing 35-1 gives the Cg code for reading 2-byte values from the input buffer and generating 4-byte tags for comparison against the database array. Listing 35-2 gives the Cg code for signature pattern matching on the GPU where, if there is a match, we write the corresponding bytes to the output buffer.

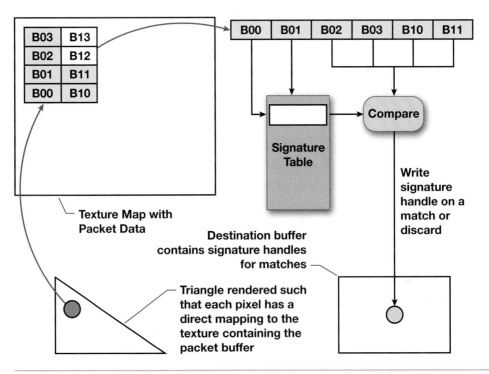

Figure 35-4. Filtering Packet Data on the GPU

```
void get_words(in float4 in_pos,
  out float4 w0,
  out float4 w1,
  out float4 tag0,
  out float4 tag1,
  const uniform samplerRECT pkt_buffer)
{
  // Read the data from the packet buffer.
  float4 p = texRECT(pkt_buffer, pos.xy);
  float4 p_p, n_p;
  float2 pindex = float2(pos.x-1, pos.y);
  float2 nindex = float2(pos.x+1, pos.y);

  // Check boundary case and perform address wraping if needed.
  // PKT_MAP_X_SZ is the packet buffer size.
  if (pos.x == 0)
    pindex = float2(PKT_MAP_X_SZ-1, pos.y-1);
  if (pos.x == PKT_MAP_X_SZ-1)
    nindex = float2(0, pos.y+1);

  // Read the second word from the packet buffer.
  float4 p_p = texRECT(pkt_buf, pindex);
  float4 n_p = texRECT(pkt_buf, nindex);

  // Pack data and check for 2-word alignment.
  if (floor(fmod(in_pos.x, 2.0))) {
    w0 = float4(p.w, p.x, 0, 0);
    tag0 = float4(p.z, p_p.w, p_p.x, p.y);
    w1 = float4(n_p. z, p.w, 0, 0);
    tag1 = float4(p.y, p.z, p_p.w, p.x);
  } else {
    w0 = float4(p.y, p.z, 0, 0);
    tag0 = float4(p_p.x, p_p.y, p_p.z, p_p.w);
    w1 = float4(p.x, p.y, 0, 0);
    tag1 = float4(p_p.w, p_p.x, p_p.y, p.z);
  }
}
```

Listing 35-2. Cg Code for Virus Signature Matching on the GPU

```
void signature_match(in float4 fragid : WPOS,
  out float4 output_value : COLOR0,
  const uniform samplerRECT pkt_buffer,
  const uniform samplerRECT g_table)
{
  float4 word0, word1, tag0, tag1;

  // Read 2 words from the packet buffer and create tag.
  get_words(fragid, word0, word1, tag0, tag1, pkt_buffer);

  // Use the word values to index the virus pattern table.
  float4 h0 = texRECT(g_table, word0.xy * 256);
  float4 h1 = texRECT(g_table, word1.xy * 256);

  // Check if all 4 of the bytes match.
  float all_match0 = all(h0 == tag0);
  float all_match1 = all(h1 == tag1);

  output_value = float4(0, 0, 0, 0);

  // Discard this output if there are no matches.
  if (!(all_match0 || all_match1))
    discard;

  output_value.xy = all_match0 * word0.xy;
  output_value.zw = all_match1 * word1.xy;
}
```

We draw a quad primitive to execute the GPU threads with proper input addresses for reading consecutive 2-byte pairs from the input buffer. For example, if Thread A reads bytes $[i, j]$, then Thread B reads bytes $[j, k]$, and so on until the entire buffer is processed. If a thread detects a match, it writes a 2-byte signature identifier into the write buffer at the relative offset of the input segment. Because the identifier is 2 bytes long, the write buffer is twice the size of the input buffer and a result for input location i is written at offset $2i$. This GPU workload gives each thread a short, regular execution path to take advantage of the single-instruction, multiple-data characteristics of the GPU.

The GPU threads are oblivious to the data objects in the data buffer. This allows the threads to operate independently and avoid any decision making regarding object boundaries in the data buffer. The CPU simply transfers the input data to the GPU and receives back an integer value indicating the number of possible signature matches in the buffer. The CPU is then responsible for completing the signature match verification for each result and mapping it to a particular data object.

We changed the ClamAV application to fill the data buffer completely before beginning the scan. In our version, ClamAV performs steps 1 to 3 from Section 35.2.1 until the data buffer is full and passes the full buffer and the relevant object descriptions to our library. The application fills the input data buffer before submitting it to the library, so the buffer can hold multiple files, a single complete file, a portion of a file, or some combination of these. ClamAV gives our library enough information to enable it to track multipart files, and it replicates enough data (as many bytes as the longest signature) between files to ensure that signature data spanning two buffers will be matched accurately.

We divided the work between the CPU and the GPU, so our library needs to transfer each data buffer it receives to the GPU and wait for processing to complete before using the results. Because the application and library execute in the context of the same software thread, the CPU might stand idle while the data is transferred and processed by the GPU. To keep the CPU busy, we pipelined the work by rotating among multiple data buffers. This way, almost all executions on the CPU can be performed in parallel with the GPU processing, and vice versa. The one section that can't be processed in parallel—transferring the result buffer back from the GPU if there are matches—is serialized only as an artifact of our implementation.

35.4 Results

We compared the execution of the open-source ClamAV antivirus application executing its own exact-match algorithm on the CPU against the same application calling out to our scanning library.

We point out that the original ClamAV application performs two additional steps: it detects matches against its approximately 2,000 regular-expression signatures, and it computes the MD5 hash for every file and compares it to a database of approximately 8,000 hash values. These functions are beyond the scope of the algorithm we describe here, and we removed them from our ClamAV application before comparing the performance.

The graph in Figure 35-5 shows the speedup obtained with our GPU-based approach for a range of signature tag matches in an 8 MB data file. The hardware used for these comparisons is a 3 GHz Intel Pentium 4 with an NVIDIA GeForce 7800 GTX. If no signature tags match (the first data point on the curves), the GPU implementation outperforms the CPU by 27×. When the GPU finds matching tags in the input data, the performance drops sharply because of the overhead incurred when the result buffer is copied back to the CPU.

The match rates represent the percentage of 64-byte segments in the input data that contain a valid signature tag. The speedup drops from 17× to 11× as the match rate increases because the CPU must do additional verification work. The two curves compare the effects of the number of individual signatures matched. As the number of matches goes up *and* the number of individual signatures identified grows, performance degrades noticeably because thousands of randomly ordered individual signature strings are fetched into the CPU caches for comparison.

In a practical setting, most input data for real systems contain few, if any, signature matches, so the speedup from the GPU is significant. However, it would be useful to mitigate the performance effects of signature tag matches not only for the infrequent case where full virus signatures are matched, but also for cases where the GPU reports false positives—that is, the data contains the signature tag but not the full signature.

When the CPU must verify the GPU results, it incurs three kinds of overhead: the time to copy the GPU result buffer back to the CPU, the processing time to walk through the

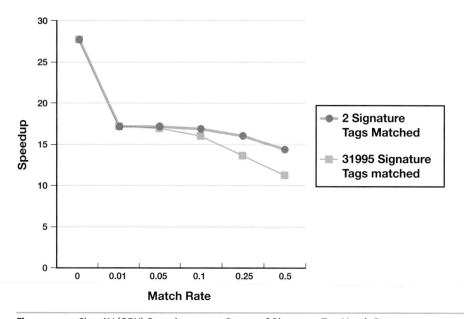

Figure 35-5. ClamAV (GPU) Speedup over a Range of Signature Tag Match Rates

result buffer, and the time to verify each positive result. Although the results reported in Figure 35-5 conflate the effects of all three overheads, the bar chart in Figure 35-6 helps to set them apart. The "No tags matched" bars compare the original zero-match case with, and without, the result buffers being copied to the CPU. For low match rates, almost all the additional overhead is incurred by the buffer transfers.

The "Tags matched, CPU intervention" bars compare two techniques for reducing CPU processing time for high match rates, demonstrated on the worst case (50 percent match rate and 31,995 signature tags) from Figure 35-5. In the first approach, the CPU compares the total number of results written to the buffer against a threshold value. If the results exceed the threshold, the CPU opts to declare the entire block of input data as bad (or suspect) without verifying the matches, thereby avoiding the result copy and the processing. This option is useful for input blocks of one object or a group of related objects (such as packets in a stream). In the second approach, the CPU copies the result buffer and processes it while tallying the results returned for each object in the buffer. Once an object exceeds a threshold, the CPU marks the object and skips over its remaining results; at the start of the next object, the CPU begins processing again.

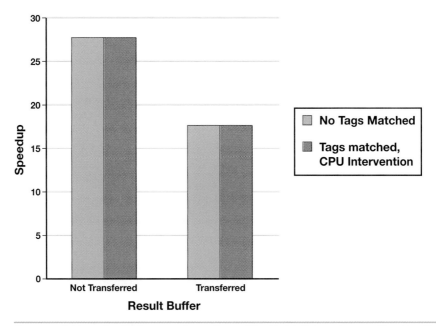

Figure 35-6. Managing Performance for 50 Percent Tag Match Rate and 31,995 Signature Tags Matched

For the outcome we present here, each 512-byte segment of input data is designated as an individual object. Although the result copy still reduces the gain from 27× to 17×, the reduced number of result buffer reads of signature verifications no longer degrades the performance. This conclusion is consistent with our observations that although the CPU and GPU execute in parallel, the workload on the GPU is much greater than that on the CPU in the zero-match case, leaving the CPU frequently idle.

Our implementation does not pipeline the write-buffer transfer, and neither the CPU nor the GPU can perform work during that time. A multithreaded system could avoid some of that overhead by allowing the CPU to continue executing while the transfer is taking place. The CPU processing overhead, which can degrade performance for high match rates, can be diminished by halting work on a particular data object or group of related objects as long as it is acceptable to report some number of false positives.

35.5 Conclusions and Future Work

Our implementation of a fast data-scanning library suggests the GPU can be effectively employed for accelerating virus signature detection over real networks. Although we have successfully exploited the power of the GPU to act as a pattern filter, our simple algorithm is not very scalable in three key areas. For example, it supports, at most, 64,000 signatures (the size of the GPU signature array), which is problematic for larger virus databases. In addition, it requires each signature to have a unique 6-byte sequence of characters (including a unique 2-byte array index), and this requirement obviously limits the space of viruses we can detect. Finally, it supports only fixed-character signatures.

If we change the GPU signature data structure to hold more signatures, it will occupy a larger footprint and possibly require more memory reads to navigate the structure. Both these changes can potentially degrade memory performance. Alternatively, we could make the GPU filter coarser by mapping individual GPU array entries to multiple signatures. In this scheme, the CPU would disambiguate between signatures; however, this approach returns some of the signature-matching work to the CPU, which could degrade the CPU cache performance and throughput and, in some cases, slow the performance of the full system.

Our algorithm would easily extend to support the simple regular-expression signatures found in the ClamAV database, but most of the effort would occur on the CPU. ClamAV regular-expression signatures have fixed-character segments separated by a variable number of wildcard characters, but they do not include recursion. We can use the GPU to identify probable matches of the fixed-character segments as it does now. Then we could use the CPU to execute the remaining work by verifying that each segment in the signature has a probable match and that each segment match is a true positive. After verifying these matches, the CPU would run a coarse-grained state machine to determine whether the signature is completely matched. This way, the GPU is not responsible for speculatively reading a large number of input data bytes or for keeping state across multiple data buffers.

35.6 References

The Clam AV software we used is available at http://www.clamav.org.

Chapter 36

AES Encryption and Decryption on the GPU

Takeshi Yamanouchi
SEGA Corporation

In this chapter, we take up integer stream processing on the GPU, which has been at best a difficult task to do on the GPU up to now.

Traditionally the GPU has been used almost exclusively for floating-point operations, because integer operations could only be done using the mantissa of floats; thus, processes that required bitwise logical operations were impossible. Another issue was that we had to render the output of the GPU to textures or pixel buffers before we could get to our results. Therefore, to process streaming data, we needed to write tricky graphics code.

However, with the advent of the new GeForce 8 Series GPU, several new extensions and functions have been introduced to GPU programming. First, the new integer-processing features include not only the arithmetic operations but also the bitwise logical operations (such as AND and OR) and the right/left shift operations. Second, array variables are flexible enough that they can be used in place of texture fetching to store constant tables. And finally, with the new "transform feedback mode," it is now possible to store our results without the need to render to textures or pixel buffers.

In this chapter we present an application of these new features by implementing Advanced Encryption Standard (AES) (NIST 2001) encryption and decryption on the GPU. Unlike previous attempts (Cook et al. 2005) and precisely thanks to these new features, our implementation shows significant performance gains over CPU implementations.

In addition, within the AES system, we consider several block-cipher modes of operation (Dworkin 2001) that demonstrate the practical cases where the GPU can be used to optimize performance through parallel processing, and other cases where it cannot.

36.1 New Functions for Integer Stream Processing

For our implementation of the AES encryption system, we use the new OpenGL extensions provided by NVIDIA in the GeForce 8 Series (NVIDIA 2006, OpenGL.org 2007). In this section we briefly introduce some of these extensions.

36.1.1 Transform Feedback Mode

Transform feedback mode is a new OpenGL mode of operation. In this mode the GPU can send its output to a buffer before the rasterization stage. This way we can store the output of the shaders into buffer objects as vertex attributes. Figure 36-1 illustrates the process.

Rendering in transform feedback mode is like regular rendering from buffer objects except for the following differences:

- The GL's `target` parameter is changed to GL_TRANSFORM_FEEDBACK_BUFFER_NV.
- We need to specify the output attributes and whether each of them is output into a separate buffer object or they are all output interleaved into a single buffer object.
- The output buffer must be bound through special new API calls such as `glBind-BufferRangeNV()`, and so on.
- Primitive draw calls have to be enclosed between `glBeginTransformFeedbackNV()` and `glEndTransformFeedbackNV()` calls in a similar fashion to `glBeginQuery()` and `glEndQuery()`.
- Rasterization can also be optionally disabled, as we do in this chapter, because we do not need any other subsequent pipeline stages. This is done through the following call: `glEnable(GL_RASTERIZER_DISCARD_NV)`.

36.1.2 GPU Program Extensions

We use two of the new features introduced in the assembly instruction set.

First, when declaring a register, we can either specify its type, such as FLOAT or INT, or just leave it typeless. We can also specify a type for each executed instruction that declares how the instruction should interpret its operands. This is done by using the type

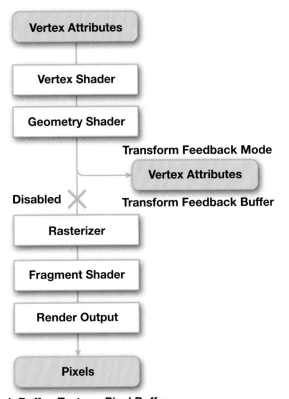

Vertex Attributes

Vertex Shader

Geometry Shader

Transform Feedback Mode

Vertex Attributes

Disabled ✕ **Transform Feedback Buffer**

Rasterizer

Fragment Shader

Render Output

Pixels

Back Buffer, Texture, Pixel Buffer

Figure 36-1. The Transform Feedback Mode Processing Pipeline

indicators following the opcodes. These type indicators are `.F` for float, `.S` for signed int, and `.U` for unsigned int:

```
TEMP  r0, r1, r2;        // typeless registers
MOV.U r0, 0x3f800000;    // r0 = 1.0f
MAD.F r1, r0, 2, -1;     // r1 = 1.0f
MAD.S r2, r0, 2, -1;     // r2 = 0x7effffff
```

Second, we can declare variables as arrays and index into them using registers. Arrays advantageously replace textures as a means to store the results of complex calculation.

```
INT PARAM tab[] = { {1, 2, 3, 4}, {5, 6, 7, 8} };
INT TEMP r0;
MOV.S r0, 0;
MOV.S r0.x, tab[r0.x].x;  // r0.x = 1
MOV.S r0,   tab[r0.x];    // r0 = { 5, 6, 7, 8 }
```

Finally, GPU program parameters, vertex attributes, and textures can now be of integer type.

36.2 An Overview of the AES Algorithm

The AES algorithm is currently the standard block-cipher algorithm that has replaced the Data Encryption Standard (DES). Back in 1997 the National Institute of Standards and Technology (NIST) made a public call for new cipher algorithms that could replace the DES. A rough summary of the requirements made by NIST for the new AES were the following:

- Symmetric-key cipher
- Block cipher
- Support for 128-bit block sizes
- Support for 128-, 192-, and 256-bit key lengths

Finally in October 2000, the Rijndael algorithm was chosen as the basis for the new standard encryption algorithm (Hironobu 2001). The original Rijndael algorithm also supported both fixed-size and variable-size bit cipher blocks. However, currently the Federal Information Processing Standards specification for the AES algorithm supports only the fixed-size, 128-bit blocks.

The operation of the AES algorithm is shown in Figure 36-2. The encryption step uses a key that converts the data into an unreadable ciphertext, and then the decryption step

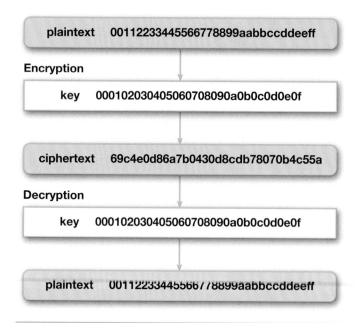

Figure 36-2. AES Cipher Operation

uses the same key to convert the ciphertext back into the original data. This type of key is a *symmetric key*; other algorithms require a different key for encryption and decryption.

The precise steps involved in the algorithm can be seen in Figure 36-3. The process is relatively simple, but some brief cryptographic explanations are necessary to understand what is going on. In cryptography, algorithms such as AES are called *product ciphers*. For this class of ciphers, encryption is done in *rounds*, where each round's processing is accomplished using the same logic. Moreover, many of these product ciphers, including AES, change the cipher key at each round. Each of these round keys is determined by a *key schedule*, which is generated from the cipher key given by the user.

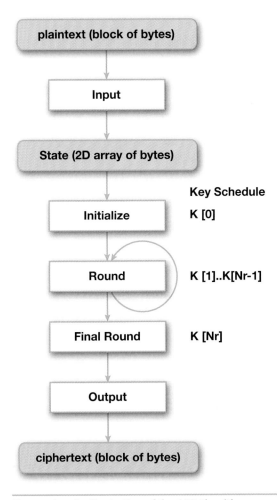

Figure 36-3. An Illustration of the AES Algorithm

Generally speaking, the strength of an encryption by product ciphers can be heightened by increasing the number of rounds used to process the data. The AES standard specifies that the number of rounds is determined by the length of the cipher key, as shown in Figure 36-4.

Key Length	Number of Rounds
128	10
192	12
256	14

Figure 36-4. Key Length and the Number of Rounds

36.3 The AES Implementation on the GPU

Now that we know what the AES algorithm is supposed to do, let's see what its implementation looks like as a vertex program. The code given throughout this chapter uses C-style macros and comments to improve readability of the assembly language. These— like those in the ROT8 macro shown in Listing 36-1—get filtered out using the standard C preprocessor.

Listing 36-1. Head of the AES Cipher Vertex Program

```
!!NVvp4.0
/*
 * aes.vpt -- AES encryption and decryption
 * Author Yamanouchi_Takeshi@sega.co.jp
 */

// input, output
ATTRIB  state_in  = vertex.attrib[0];
OUTPUT  state_out = result.texcoord[0];

// macros
INT TEMP  _tmp0, _tmp1;     // macro work

#define ROT8(_arg) \
   SHL.U  _tmp0, _arg, 8; \
   SHR.U  _arg, _arg, 24; \
   OR  _arg, _arg, _tmp0
```

In this application we expand the cipher key using the CPU and store the key schedule in the GPU program-local parameters. Besides the key schedule, other arguments and tables can also be stored directly in advance to improve performance, as shown in Listing 36-2.

Listing 36-2. Program Parameters for Arguments and Constant Tables

```
// parameters
// cipher mode, 0:encrypt, 1:decrypt
INT PARAM mode      = program.local[MODE];
// number of rounds
INT PARAM num_round = program.local[NUM_ROUND];
// key schedule for encryption
INT PARAM enc_key[15] = { program.local[ENC_KEY_BEGIN..ENC_KEY_END] };
// key schedule for decryption
INT PARAM dec_key[15] = { program.local[DEC_KEY_BEGIN..DEC_KEY_END] };
//(x,y,z,w)=(s_box, inv_s_box, mix_col, inv_mix_col)
INT PARAM aes_tab[256] = { program.env[0..255] };
```

36.3.1 Input/Output and the State

AES encryption operates over a two-dimensional array of bytes, called *the state*. During the input step, we slice our data into sequential blocks of 16 bytes and unpack it into 4×4 arrays that we push onto the GPU's registers. Finally, during the output step, we pack these 4×4 arrays back into sequential blocks of 16 bytes and stream the results back to the transform feedback buffer, as shown in Figure 36-5.

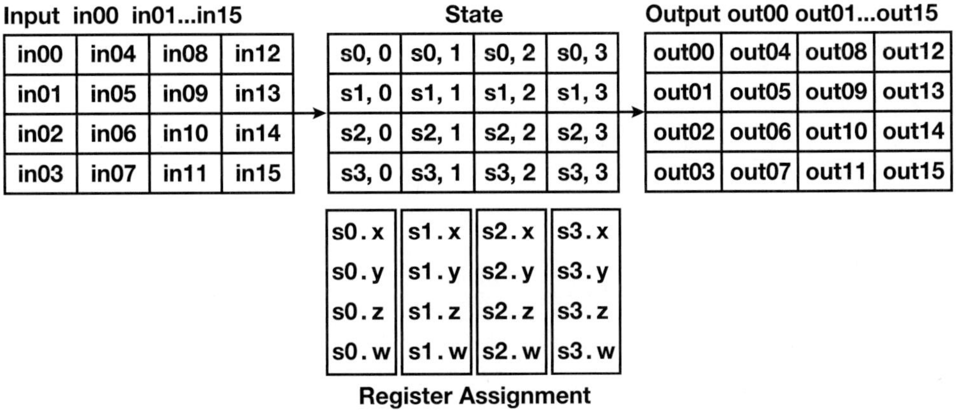

Input in00 in01...in15			
in00	in04	in08	in12
in01	in05	in09	in13
in02	in06	in10	in14
in03	in07	in11	in15

State			
s0, 0	s0, 1	s0, 2	s0, 3
s1, 0	s1, 1	s1, 2	s1, 3
s2, 0	s2, 1	s2, 2	s2, 3
s3, 0	s3, 1	s3, 2	s3, 3

Output out00 out01...out15			
out00	out04	out08	out12
out01	out05	out09	out13
out02	out06	out10	out14
out03	out07	out11	out15

s0.x	s1.x	s2.x	s3.x
s0.y	s1.y	s2.y	s3.y
s0.z	s1.z	s2.z	s3.z
s0.w	s1.w	s2.w	s3.w

Register Assignment

Figure 36-5. Input, State, Output, and Register Assignment for the Streamed Data

The code fragments in Listing 36-3 go into the details for these steps. First we define our packing and unpacking methods as macros. Then we have an unpack_state_in: subroutine, which unpacks the input into the current state matrix, and a pack_state_out: subroutine, which packs the current state matrix back to the output stream.

The registers for state_in and state_out consist of four components of 32-bit integers each, giving us the standard AES block size of 128 bits for processing.

Listing 36-3. The State and Input (Unpack)/Output (Pack) Subroutine

```
// registers
INT TEMP  s0, s1, s2, s3;        // state
#define UNPACK(_res, _arg) \
  SHR  _res.w, _arg, 24; \
  SHR  _res.z, _arg, 16; \
  SHR  _res.y, _arg,  8; \
  MOV.U  _res.x, _arg; \
  AND  _res, _res, 0xff

#define PACK(_res, _arg) \
  SHL  _tmp0.w, _arg.w, 24; \
  SHL  _tmp0.z, _arg.z, 16; \
  SHL  _tmp0.y, _arg.y,  8; \
  OR  _tmp0.w, _tmp0.w, _tmp0.z; \
  OR  _tmp0.w, _tmp0.w, _tmp0.y; \
  OR  _res, _tmp0.w, _arg.x

unpack_state_in:
  // arg0: round key
  XOR  tmp, state_in, arg0;
  UNPACK(s0, tmp.x);
  UNPACK(s1, tmp.y);
  UNPACK(s2, tmp.z);
  UNPACK(s3, tmp.w);
  RET;

pack_state_out:
  // arg0: round key
  PACK(tmp.x, s0);
  PACK(tmp.y, s1);
  PACK(tmp.z, s2);
  PACK(tmp.w, s3);
  XOR  state_out, tmp, arg0;
  RET;
```

36.3.2 Initialization

During the initialization stage, we do an *AddRoundKey* operation, which is an XOR operation on the state by the round key, as determined by the key schedule. In our case, we perform unpacking and round key addition together in the unpack_state_in: subroutine.

36.3.3 Rounds

A round for the AES algorithm consists of four operations: the *SubBytes* operation, the *ShiftRows* operation, the *MixColumns* operation, and the previously mentioned AddRoundKey operation.

The SubBytes Operation

The SubBytes operation substitutes bytes independently, in a black-box fashion, using a nonlinear substitution table called the *S-box*, as shown in Figure 36-6.

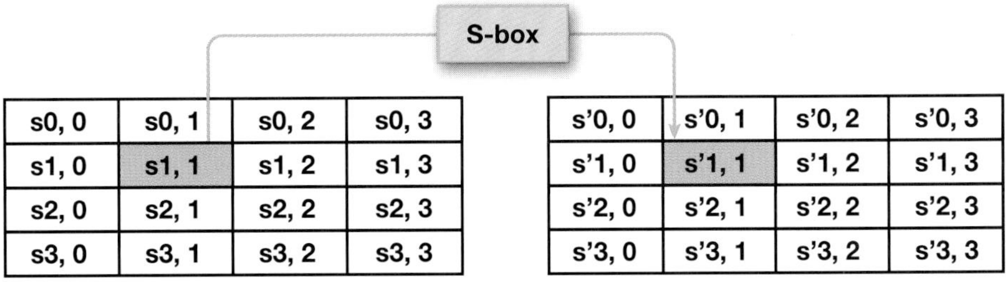

Figure 36-6. The SubBytes Operation

The S-box is a uniform table calculated in advance and stored into the GPU program.env parameters as aes_tab[] (see the code in Listing 36-2). In our implementation we store the encryption table in the aes_tab[].x values, and the transformation table used for decryption in the aes_tab[].y values, as you can see in Listing 36-4.

Listing 36-4. SubBytes for the First Row of the State

```
sub_bytes_shift_rows:
  // first row
  MOV.U  s0.x,  aes_tab[s0.x].x;   // aes_tab[].x: s_box
  MOV.U  s1.x,  aes_tab[s1.x].x;
  MOV.U  s2.x,  aes_tab[s2.x].x;
  MOV.U  s3.x,  aes_tab[s3.x].x;
```

The ShiftRows Operation

The ShiftRows operation shifts the last three rows of the state cyclically, effectively scrambling row data, as shown in Figure 36-7.

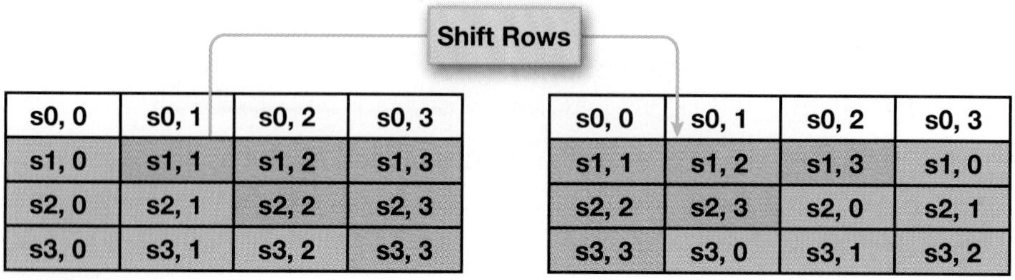

Shift Rows

s0, 0	s0, 1	s0, 2	s0, 3
s1, 0	s1, 1	s1, 2	s1, 3
s2, 0	s2, 1	s2, 2	s2, 3
s3, 0	s3, 1	s3, 2	s3, 3

s0, 0	s0, 1	s0, 2	s0, 3
s1, 1	s1, 2	s1, 3	s1, 0
s2, 2	s2, 3	s2, 0	s2, 1
s3, 3	s3, 0	s3, 1	s3, 2

Figure 36-7. The ShiftRows Operation

One simple optimization we can do is to combine the SubBytes and ShiftRows operations into a single subroutine that we call sub_bytes_shift_rows:. The continuation of the code from the previous section that combines both operations as one is shown in Listing 36-5.

Listing 36-5. SubBytes and ShiftRows for the Second, Third, and Fourth Rows

```
// second row
MOV.U   tmp.x,  aes_tab[s0.y].x;
MOV.U   s0.y,   aes_tab[s1.y].x;
MOV.U   s1.y,   aes_tab[s2.y].x;
MOV.U   s2.y,   aes_tab[s3.y].x;
MOV.U   s3.y,   tmp.x;
// third row
MOV.U   tmp.x,  aes_tab[s0.z].x;
MOV.U   s0.z,   aes_tab[s2.z].x;
MOV.U   s2.z,   tmp.x;
MOV.U   tmp.x,  aes_tab[s1.z].x;
MOV.U   s1.z,   aes_tab[s3.z].x;
MOV.U   s3.z,   tmp.x;
// fourth row
MOV.U   tmp.x,  aes_tab[s3.w].x;
MOV.U   s3.w,   aes_tab[s2.w].x;
MOV.U   s2.w,   aes_tab[s1.w].x;
MOV.U   s1.w,   aes_tab[s0.w].x;
MOV.U   s0.w,   tmp.x;

RET;
```

Chapter 36   AES Encryption and Decryption on the GPU

The MixColumns Operation

The next step is the MixColumns operation, which has the purpose of scrambling the data of each column. This operation is done by performing a matrix multiplication upon each column vector, as shown in Figure 36-8.

Because the multiplication is over a finite field of the AES, we cannot use the usual MUL operation. The closure of the finite field is within a byte range. So we store the results of the multiplication by (0x2, 0x1, 0x1, 0x3) in the aes_tab[].z values. The resulting bytes are packed into a 32-bit integer in little-endian form, such as 0x03010102.

The resulting transformation matrix is shifted by columns; therefore, the results are rotated by the ROT8()..ROT24() macros. Finally, we add them together by XOR'ing and unpacking into the state, as seen in Listing 36-6.

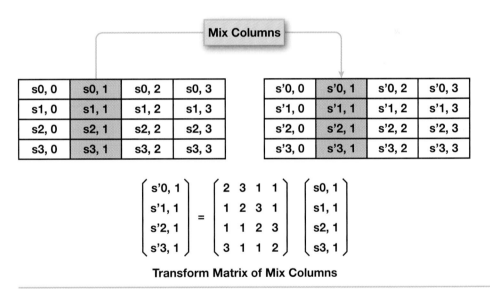

Transform Matrix of Mix Columns

Figure 36-8. The MixColumns Operation

Listing 36-6. MixColumns and AddRoundKey

```
mix_columns_add_round_key:
  // arg0: round key
  MOV.U  mix0.x, aes_tab[s0.x].z;  // aes_tab[].z: mix_col
  MOV.U  mix0.y, aes_tab[s1.x].z;
  MOV.U  mix0.z, aes_tab[s2.x].z;
  MOV.U  mix0.w, aes_tab[s3.x].z;
```

Listing 36-6 (*continued*). MixColumns and AddRoundKey

```
MOV.U   mix1.x, aes_tab[s0.y].z;
   . . .
MOV.U   mix3.w, aes_tab[s3.w].z;

ROT8 (mix1);
ROT16 (mix2);
ROT24 (mix3);

XOR   tmp, arg0, mix0;   // add round key
XOR   tmp, tmp, mix1;
XOR   tmp, tmp, mix2;
XOR   tmp, tmp, mix3;

UNPACK(s0, tmp.x);
UNPACK(s1, tmp.y);
UNPACK(s2, tmp.z);
UNPACK(s3, tmp.w);

RET;
```

During decryption, the multiplication results are stored in the `aes_tab[].w` values of the table. The coefficients are (0xe, 0x9, 0xd, 0xb).

In brief, all components of the `aes_tab[]` at this point are as follows:

- x holds the encryption S-box data.
- y holds the decryption S-box data.
- z holds the encryption MixColumns data.
- w holds the decryption MixColumns data.

The AddRoundKey Operation

This operation determines the current round key from the key schedule, where the register `arg0` serves as the argument. As an optimization we can also combine the Mix-Columns and AddRoundKey operations into a single subroutine named `mix_columns_add_round_key:`.

The code in Listing 36-7 is the encryption loop. Note that the cost of control flow operations has significantly decreased in the GeForce 8 Series; so much so that unrolling the loop—which would have further complicated the code—is unnecessary to obtain good performance.

Listing 36-7. AES Encryption Loop

```
encrypt:
  // input & first round
  MOV.U  arg0, enc_key[0];
  CAL  unpack_state_in;

  // loop round
  SUB.S  cnt.x, num_round.x, 1;
  MOV.S  cnt.y, 1;
  REP.S  cnt.x;
    CAL  sub_bytes_shift_rows;
    MOV.U  arg0, enc_key[cnt.y];
    CAL  mix_columns_add_round_key;
    ADD.S  cnt.y, cnt.y, 1;
  ENDREP;

  // final round & output
  CAL  sub_bytes_shift_rows;
  MOV.U  arg0, enc_key[cnt.y];
  CAL  pack_state_out;
  RET;
```

36.3.4 The Final Round

The final round has no MixColumns operation. The AddRoundKey operation is combined with packing into a single subroutine called `pack_state_out`: in a similar fashion to what we did for initialization.

36.4 Performance

Now that we have a working AES implementation, let us measure the performance of GPU-based encryption. The decryption is omitted because it performs the same as the encryption in the AES algorithm. Our tests were performed on a test machine with the following specifications:

- CPU: Pentium 4, 3 GHz, 2 MB Level 2 cache
- Memory: 1 GB
- Video: GeForce 8800 GTS 640 MB
- System: Linux 2.6, Driver 97.46

36.4.1 Variable Batch Size

The data to be encrypted, or *plaintext*, is sent to and processed by the GPU in batches of identical size. A minimum batch size is required to reduce the CPU overhead of many draw calls and reach maximum throughput. Our tests show that the minimum size is around 256 KB, as illustrated in Figure 36-9, which plots throughput as a function of batch size. These results have been obtained by processing a plaintext of 128 MB and averaging measurements from ten runs. The blue line shows the speed of data transfer alone, and the red line also includes data encryption.

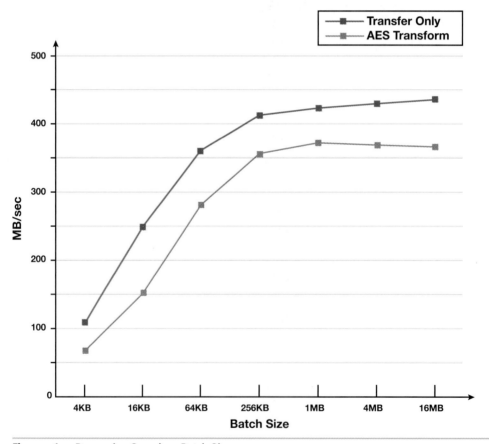

Figure 36-9. Processing Speed vs. Batch Size

36.4.2 Comparison to CPU-Based Encryption

The `openssl` command has benchmarks for determining the speed of their cipher algorithms on the CPU. We measured the speed of these CPU-based encryptions on the same test machine, and we got results of about 55 MB/sec using the same AES algorithm. Our GPU-based encryption is thus about 6.5 times faster for a 256 KB batch size. For a 16 KB batch size, the GPU still outperforms the CPU by 3 times. This demonstrates that the GPU is suitable for tasks such as AES cipher processing.

36.5 Considerations for Parallelism

There are some considerations to be made based on the mode of operation for our block ciphers that affect suitability for parallelism. In this section, we look at a few different modes and how they may affect suitability for parallel processing.

36.5.1 Block-Cipher Modes of Operation

Electronic Code Book Mode

The encrypting operation of each block is called the *electronic code book* (ECB) mode. In ECB encryption, each block is operated upon independently, as shown in Figure 36-10.

This mode of operation makes it possible to compute ciphertexts in parallel, and it was the mode of operation used for all the tests in Section 36.4.

In ECB mode, the same bit blocks will always generate the same ciphertext. But although the ciphertext is not directly readable, there is a possibility that the content can be guessed based on the resulting pattern. Figure 36-11 shows a 256×256 texture encrypted in ECB mode, and although it cannot be directly read, there is an evident pattern in the cipher texture.

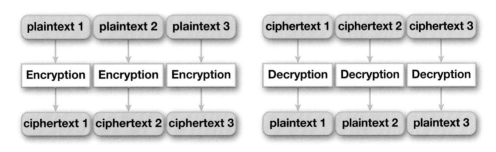

Figure 36-10. ECB Mode Encryption and Decryption

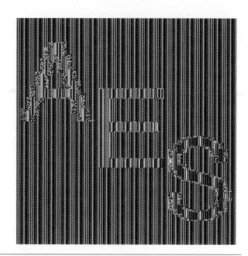

Figure 36-11. Plain Texture and Cipher Texture in ECB Mode

Cipher-Block Chaining Mode

The *cipher-block chaining* (CBC) mode overcomes the ECB mode's weakness by chaining each cipher into the next block. This is done by chaining (XOR'ing) our current plaintext block with the previously encrypted block. The first block has no previous block, so we use an *initial vector* (IV) instead that is passed during initialization along with the symmetric key for decryption. See Figure 36-12.

In CBC mode, because plaintexts are scrambled before encryption, the ciphertext pattern never appears in the final result. So we cannot see the "AES" letters in Figure 36-13 as we could in Figure 36-11.

However, because CBC mode needs the ciphertexts of each previous step to process the next step, it is not possible to begin the encryption of a block until its previous block has been encrypted. So we can't hope for parallel processing during the encryption stage of this mode.

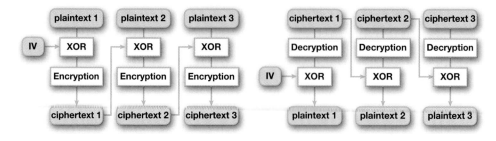

Figure 36-12. CBC Mode Encryption and Decryption

Figure 36-13. The Cipher Texture in CBC Mode

36.5.2 Modes for Parallel Processing

Decryption in CBC Mode

As we just mentioned, in CBC mode, encryption cannot be processed in parallel because it requires the results of each previous step. However, fortunately we can decrypt our results using parallel processing. This is because after encryption, we already know the states of all the previous ciphertext blocks and the IV needed for decryption.

The gain to be obtained here is that we often need to do more decryption than encryption, and many times decryption is required to have higher throughput speeds, such as when preprocessing and storing cipher textures encrypted in CBC mode into distribution files; these files can then be decrypted in parallel during loading without any noticeable delays.

Counter Mode

Nevertheless, there are cases when fast encryption is highly desirable, such as for secure communications, where the parallel processing of the encryption stage would greatly speed up the overall performance. In these cases, *counter* (CTR) mode can be used. The CTR algorithm's procedure is shown in Figure 36-14. First, we make the input block by indexing the current block, called a *counter block*. We then encrypt it using the symmetric key, and XOR'ing with the original plaintext block.

The decryption for CTR can be done following the same steps. Thus we can encrypt and decrypt each cipher block independently, giving us the benefit of true parallelization.

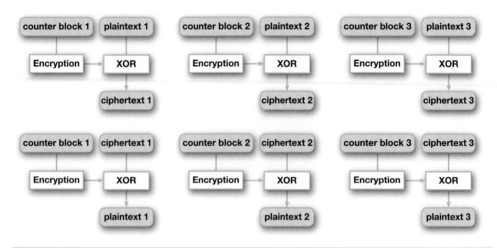

Figure 36-14. CTR Mode Encryption and Decryption

36.6 Conclusion and Future Work

Thanks to new capabilities added to the GPU, we can now truly perform integer stream processing. As a showcase, we presented an implementation for an AES system that relies heavily on integer processing, and we demonstrated that the GPU can outperform the CPU for this algorithm.

Our implementation is OpenGL-based, but another way to program the latest generation of NVIDIA GPUs is to use CUDA (NVIDIA 2007). As future work, we plan to implement the same algorithm using CUDA and compare performance against the OpenGL implementation.

Another direction of future work is to find other novel areas besides AES encryption that could benefit from GPU parallel processing power.

36.7 References

Cook, Debra L., John Ioannidis, Angelos D. Keromytis, and Jake Luck. 2005. "CryptoGraphics: Secret Key Cryptography Using Graphics Cards." In *RSA Conference, Cryptographer's Track* (CT-RSA), pp. 334–350.

Dworkin, M. 2001. "Recommendation for Block Cipher Modes of Operation: Methods and Techniques." NIST Special Publication 800-38A. Available online at http://csrc.nist.gov/publications/nistpubs/800-38a/sp800-38a.pdf.

Hironobu, Suzuki. 2001. "Memorandum of DES and AES." Available online (in Japanese only) at http://h2np.net/hironobu/docs/DES_and_AES.pdf.

NIST. 2001. "Advanced Encryption Standard (AES)." FIPS Publication 197. Available online at http://csrc.nist.gov/publications/fips/fips197/fips-197.pdf.

NVIDIA Corporation. 2006. "NVIDIA OpenGL Extension Specifications for the GeForce 8 Series Architecture (G8x)." Available online at http://developer.download.nvidia.com/opengl/specs/g80specs.pdf.

NVIDIA Corporation. 2007. "NVIDIA Compute Unified Device Architecture." http://developer.nvidia.com/cuda/.

OpenGL.org. 2007. "OpenGL Extension Registry." http://www.opengl.org/registry/.

Chapter 37

Efficient Random Number Generation and Application Using CUDA

Lee Howes
Imperial College London

David Thomas
Imperial College London

Monte Carlo methods provide approximate numerical solutions to problems that would be difficult or impossible to solve exactly. The defining characteristic of Monte Carlo simulations is the use of multiple independent trials, each driven by some stochastic (random) process. The results of the independent trials are then combined to extract the average answer, relying on the Law of Large Numbers, which states that as more trials are combined, the average answer will converge on the true answer. The independent trials are inherently parallelizable, and they typically consist of dense numeric operations, so GPUs provide an almost ideal platform for Monte Carlo simulations.

However, a key component within Monte Carlo simulations is the random number generators (RNGs) that provide the independent stochastic input to each trial. These generators must meet the conflicting goals of being extremely fast while also providing random number streams that are indistinguishable from a true random number source. There is an extensive body of literature devoted to random number generation in CPUs, but the most efficient of these make fundamental assumptions about processor architecture and performance: they are often not appropriate for use in GPUs. Previous work such as Sussman et. al. 2006 has investigated random number generation in older generations of GPUs, but the latest generation of completely programmable GPUs has different characteristics, requiring a new approach.

In this chapter, we discuss methods for generating random numbers using CUDA, with particular regard to generation of Gaussian random numbers, a key component of many financial simulations. We describe two methods for generating Gaussian random numbers, one of which works by transforming uniformly distributed numbers using the Box-Muller method, and another that generates Gaussian distributed random numbers directly using the Wallace method. We then demonstrate how these random number generators can be used in real simulations, using two examples of valuing exotic options using CUDA. Overall, we find that a single GeForce 8 GPU generates Gaussian random numbers 26 times faster than a Quad Opteron 2.2 GHz CPU, and we find corresponding speedups of 59× and 23× in the two financial examples.

37.1 Monte Carlo Simulations

Monte Carlo approaches were introduced by Ulam and von Neumann in the 1940s with the aim of simulating nuclear reactions (Metropolis 1987). A simple example of a Monte Carlo solution to a problem is for calculating π. Take a square and inscribe within it a circle that touches each edge of the square. We know that if the radius of the circle is r, then the area of the circle is πr^2, and the area of the square is $4r^2$. If we can calculate the ratio, p, of the circle area to the square area, then we can calculate π:

$$p = \frac{\pi r^2}{4r^2}$$

$$p = \frac{\pi}{4}$$

$$\pi = 4p$$

We can calculate the ratio p using Monte Carlo methods by generating n independent random points that are uniformly distributed within the square. Some fraction k of the points will lie within the circle, thus we have $p \approx k/n$, leading to $\pi \approx 4k/n$. Figure 37-1 shows random points placed within a circle, with $n = 20$, 200, and 2,000, shown as blue circles, red crosses, and green points, respectively, providing estimates of π as 3.4, 3.18, and 3.158. As the number of points increases, the accuracy improves, giving estimates of 3.1492 for $n = 2 \times 10^4$ and 3.1435 for $n = 2 \times 10^5$.

Clearly this is an inefficient way to calculate π: the rate of increase in accuracy is low (accuracy is usually proportional to the square root of the number of trials) and is much

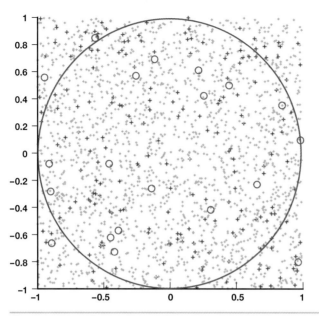

Figure 37-1. Random Points Within a Square to Calculate Pi

less efficient than standard iterative methods. However, it does demonstrate three reasons why Monte Carlo methods are so popular:

1. It is very easy to understand how the method works, which is often not the case with the algorithm for the corresponding exact solution (assuming one exists).

2. It is very easy to implement, with the main hurdle being the generation of random numbers.

3. Monte Carlo methods are inherently parallelizable.

This last point is a major advantage, allowing Monte Carlo solutions to easily scale to multiple nodes in a networked cluster, or to multiple processors within a CPU or GPU.

A more realistic example of Monte Carlo methods is in finance. Here the approach is to capture a subset of market variables—for example, the price S_0 of an equity at time 0—then choose an artificial stochastic model that appears to model previous equity paths reasonably well. The most commonly used model is geometric Brownian motion, where the final price of the stock at time t is modeled as $S_t = S_0 e^{\mu + \sigma N}$, where N is a random sample from the Gaussian distribution (Wilmott 2006).

A programmatic estimator of the average stock price would then be as shown in Listing 37-1. The goal of the random runs is to produce an approximation to the behavior of the historical market and use the results to judge the probability of making a profit. This is similar to the π computation example, where the system tends toward the probability of a point being within the circle, and that probability is directly related to the ratio of areas. This method allows us to find solutions for a wide class of financial models for which there are no analytical solutions.

Listing 37-1. Estimating the Average Stock Price

```
float sum=0;
for(unsigned i=0;i<N;i++){
    sum += S0 * exp(mu+sigma*RandN());
}
return sum/N;
```

The Monte Carlo approach is trivially parallelizable across multiple processors, and it is often called embarrassingly parallel. There are five major steps:

1. Assign each processing element a random sequence. Each processing element must use a different random number sequence, which should be uncorrelated with the sequences used by all other processors.

2. Propagate the simulation parameters (for example, S_0) to all processing elements, and tell them how many simulation runs to execute.

3. Generate random number streams for use by each processing element.

4. Execute the simulation kernel on the processing elements in parallel.

5. Gather the simulation outputs from each processing element and combine them to produce the approximate results.

In many traditional architectures, the difficult part is step 4, writing an efficient implementation of the simulation kernel, because a faster kernel allows more simulated trials to be executed within a given time and so will provide a more accurate answer. However, in a GPU, the mathematically heavy simulation kernel is often relatively easy to implement. The real challenge is to manage the assignment of different random number streams to processors, and to generate those random number streams efficiently. Figure 37-2 shows the division of processing among processors at a high level.

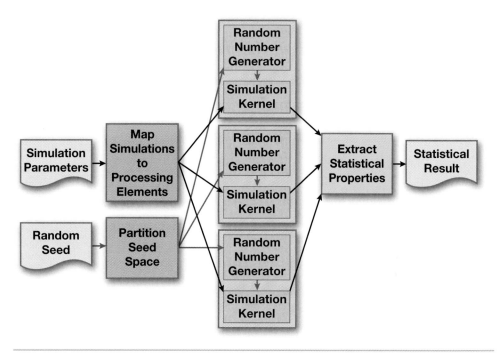

Figure 37-2. Dividing the Simulation Space Among Multiple Executions of the Simulation Kernel
By dividing the simulation space among multiple executions of the simulation kernel, we can efficiently use parallel hardware and increase simulation throughput.

37.2 Random Number Generators

37.2.1 Introduction

Random number generators can be classified into three groups, according to the source of their "randomness":

- **True random number generators (TRNGs).** This type uses a physical source of randomness to provide truly unpredictable numbers. TRNGs are mainly used for cryptography, because they are too slow for simulation purposes.

- **Quasirandom number generators (QRNGs).** These generators attempt to evenly fill an n-dimensional space with points, without clustering or grouping of points. Although QRNGs are used in Monte Carlo simulations, we do not consider them in this chapter.

- **Pseudorandom number generators (PRNGs).** The most common type of random number generator, PRNGs are designed to look as random as a TRNG, but can be implemented in deterministic software because the state and transition function can be predicted completely. In this chapter, we consider only this type of generator.

An orthogonal classification of random number generators is organized according to the distribution of the numbers that are produced. Commonly encountered library functions, such as C's rand(), sample from the uniform distribution, meaning that within some range of numbers, each value is equally likely to occur.

However, many Monte Carlo simulations actually need different distributions; common examples are the normal, log-normal, and exponential distributions. The main method used for producing samples from nonuniform distributions is first to generate uniform random numbers, and then to apply a transform to convert the uniform numbers into samples from the desired nonuniform distribution.

To give an example, a standard exponential variate E has the cumulative distribution function (CDF) $F_E(x) = P[x < E] = 1 - e^{-x}$. The CDF maps a sample x from the exponential distribution back to the probability of a value less than x occurring, where the probability is a value between 0 and 1. Thus if E is exponentially distributed, then $P[x < E]$ will be uniformly distributed. This leads to the *inversion method*: if we know that $F_E(x)$ converts from the exponential distribution to the uniform distribution, then logically $F_E^{-1}(p)$ will convert from the uniform distribution to the exponential distribution. Thus if a random variate U is uniformly distributed, then $F_E^{-1}(p) = -\log(1 - U)$ will be exponentially distributed.

Although inverting the CDF is a conceptually simple method, it is often too computationally expensive to use. In the preceding exponential example, a call to log() is required for every random number. This may be acceptable, but in many cases the inverse may be much more complicated, or in some cases there may not even be a closed-form solution. This is the case for the Gaussian distribution, one of the most important distributions, so significant effort has been devoted to investigating alternative methods for transforming the uniform distribution. Rather than use the direct inverse CDF transform, these methods use mathematical identities and statistical tricks to convert from the uniform distribution, for example by using pairs of uniform random numbers.

We then see two main general requirements that we wish PRNGs to satisfy:

- **A long period.** Every deterministic generator must eventually loop, but the goal is to make the loop period as long as possible. There is a strong argument that if n random samples are used across all nodes in a simulation, then the period of the generator should be at least n^2.

- **Good statistical quality**. The output from the generator should be practically indistinguishable from a TRNG of the required distribution, and it should not exhibit any correlations or patterns. Poor generator quality can ruin the results of Monte Carlo applications, and it is critical that generators are able to pass the set of theoretical and empirical tests for quality that are available. Numerous statistical tests are available to verify this requirement (Knuth 1969, Marsaglia 1995, L'Ecuyer 2006).

In this chapter, we consider two methods for generating Gaussian random numbers that are particularly well suited to the new class of GPUs. The first uses the traditional technique of generating uniform random numbers, then applying a transform to produce the Gaussian distribution. The second uses a newer technique to generate random numbers directly, without needing a uniform random source. We then look at the use of these generators within two Monte Carlo simulations for exotic option valuation.

37.2.2 Uniform-to-Gaussian Conversion Generator

The traditional method for producing Gaussian random numbers requires two components: a uniform PRNG and a transform to the Gaussian distribution. There are many choices for both components, so here we briefly discuss the requirements for each, and provide a brief analysis of the main choices. We will then select two components based on the unique requirements of GPU architectures.

Besides meeting the general requirements of uniform PRNGs discussed in Section 37.2.1, the parallel nature of GPUs imposes two additional requirements:

- **The ability to generate different substreams on parallel nodes.** Each node must be given a different portion of the random stream with no overlap.

- **No correlations between substreams on different nodes.** The substreams must appear to be completely independent streams of random numbers.

Available Uniform PRNGs

Linear Congruential Generator

The classic generator is the *linear congruential generator* (LCG) (Knuth 1969), which uses a transition function of the form $x_{n+1} = (ax_n + c) \bmod m$. The maximum period of the generator is m (assuming the triple (a, c, m) has certain properties), but this means that in a 32-bit integer, the period can be at most 2^{32}, which is far too low. LCGs also have known statistical flaws, making them unsuitable for modern simulations.

Multiple Recursive Generator

A derivative of the LCG is the *multiple recursive generator* (MRG), which additively combines two or more generators. If n generators with periods $m_1, m_2, \ldots, m_n$ are combined, then the resulting period is $\mathrm{LCM}(m_1, m_2, \ldots, m_n)$, thus the period can be at most $m_1 x$, $m_2 x, \ldots, m_n x$. These generators provide both good statistical quality and long periods, but the relatively prime moduli require complex algorithms using 32-bit multiplications and divisions, so they are not suitable for current GPUs (NVIDIA 2007, Section 6.1.1.1).

Lagged Fibonacci Generator

A generator that is commonly used in distributed Monte Carlo simulations is the *lagged Fibonacci generator* (Knuth 1969). This generator is similar to an LCG but introduces a delayed feedback, using the transition function $x_{n+1} = (x_n \otimes x_{n-k}) \bmod m$, where $\otimes$ is typically addition or multiplication. However, to achieve good quality, the constant k must be large. Consequentially k words of memory must be used to hold the state. Typically k must be greater than 1000, and each thread will require its own state, so this must be stored in global memory. We thus reject the lagged Fibonacci method but note that it may be useful in some GPU-based applications, because of the simplicity and small number of registers required.

Mersenne Twister

One of the most widely respected methods for random number generation in software is the *Mersenne twister* (Matsumoto and Nishimura 1998), which has a period of $2^{19,937}$ and extremely good statistical quality. However, it presents problems similar to those of the lagged Fibonacci, because it has a large state that must be updated serially. Thus each thread must have an individual state in global RAM and make multiple accesses per generator. In combination with the relatively large amount of computation per generated number, this requirement makes the generator too slow, except in cases where the ultimate in quality is needed.

Combined Tausworthe Generator

Internally, the Mersenne twister utilizes a binary matrix to transform one vector of bits into a new vector of bits, using an extremely large sparse matrix and large vectors. However, there are a number of related generators that use much smaller vectors, of the order of two to four words, and a correspondingly denser matrix. An example of this kind of generator is the *combined Tausworthe generator*, which uses exclusive-or to combine the results of two or more independent binary matrix derived streams, providing a stream of longer period and much better quality. Each independent stream is generated using TausStep, shown in Listing 37-2, in six bitwise instructions. For example, the four-component LFSR113 generator from L'Ecuyer 1999 requires $6 \times 4 + 3 = 27$ instructions, producing a stream with a period of approximately 2^{113}.

Listing 37-2. A Single Step of the Combined Tausworthe Generator

```
// S1, S2, S3, and M are all constants, and z is part of the
// private per-thread generator state.
unsigned TausStep(unsigned &z, int S1, int S2, int S3, unsigned M)
{
   unsigned b=(((z << S1) ^ z) >> S2);
   return z = (((z & M) << S3) ^ b);
}
```

However, our statistical tests show that even the four-component LFSR113 produces significant correlations across 5-tuples and 6-tuples, even for relatively small sample sizes.

A Hybrid Generator

The approach we propose is to combine the simple combined Tausworthe with another kind of generator; if the periods of all the components are co-prime, then the resulting generator period will be the product of all the component periods, and the statistical defects of one generator should hide those of the other.

We have already mentioned LCG-based generators but dismissed them because of the prime moduli needed to create MRGs. However, if we use a single generator with a modulus of 2^{32}, we gain two important properties: (1) The modulus is applied for free in LCGStep, shown in Listing 37-3, due to the truncation in 32-bit arithmetic. (2) The resulting period of 2^{32} is relatively prime to all the component periods of a combined Tausworthe, thus the two can be combined to create a much longer period generator.

Listing 37-3. A Simple Linear Congruential Generator

```
// A and C are constants
unsigned LCGStep(unsigned &z, unsigned A, unsigned C)
{
    return z=(A*z+C);
}
```

The specific combination we chose is the three-component combined Tausworthe "taus88" from L'Ecuyer 1996 and the 32-bit "Quick and Dirty" LCG from Press et al. 1992, as shown in Listing 37-4. Both provide relatively good statistical quality within each family of generators, and in combination they remove all the statistical defects we observed in each separate generator. The generator state comprises four 32-bit values, and it provides an overall period of around 2^{121}. The only restrictions on the initial state are that the three Tausworthe state components should be greater than 128; other than that, the four state components can be initialized to any random values. Each thread should receive a different set of four state values, which should be uncorrelated and for convenience can be supplied using a CPU-side random number generator. For cases in which a significant fraction of the entire random stream will be used (for example, more than 2^{64}), it is possible to use stream skipping to advance each of the four state components, ensuring independent random streams; however, that case is out of the scope of this chapter.

Listing 37-4. Combining the LCG and Tausworthe into an Improved Generator

```
unsigned z1, z2, z3, z4;

float HybridTaus()
{
    // Combined period is lcm(p1,p2,p3,p4) ~ 2^121
    return 2.3283064365387e-10 * (                // Periods
        TausStep(z1, 13, 19, 12, 4294967294UL) ^  // p1=2^31-1
        TausStep(z2, 2, 25, 4, 4294967288UL) ^    // p2=2^30-1
        TausStep(z3, 3, 11, 17, 4294967280UL) ^   // p3=2^28-1
        LCGStep(z4, 1664525, 1013904223UL)        // p4=2^32
    );
}
```

KISS

Another well-respected hybrid generator is the KISS family (L'Ecuyer 2006) from Marsaglia. These combine three separate types of generator: an LCG, a shift-based generator similar to the Tausworthe, and a pair of multiply-with-carry generators. Although this generator also gives good statistical quality, it requires numerous 32-bit multiplications, which harm performance (NVIDIA 2007, Section 6.1.1.1) on current-generation hardware, offering only 80 percent of the Tausworthe's performance.

37.2.3 Types of Gaussian Transforms

We now turn to the transformation from the uniform to Gaussian distribution. Again, there are many techniques to choose from, because the Gaussian distribution is so important.

The Ziggurat Method

The fastest method in software is the *ziggurat method* (Marsaglia 2000). This procedure uses a complicated method to split the Gaussian probability density function into axis-aligned rectangles, and it is designed to minimize the average cost of generating a sample. However, this means that for 2 percent of generated numbers, a more complicated route using further uniform samples and function calls must be made. In software this is acceptable, but in a GPU, the performance of the slow route will apply to all threads in a warp, even if only one thread uses the route. If the warp size is 32 and the probability of taking the slow route is 2 percent, then the probability of any warp taking the slow route is $(1 - 0.02)^{32}$, which is 47 percent! So, because of thread batching, the assumptions designed into the ziggurat are violated, and the performance advantage is destroyed.

The Polar Method

Many other methods also rely on looping behavior similar to that of the Ziggurat and so are also not usable in hardware. The *polar method* (Press et. al. 1992) is simple and relatively efficient, but the probability of looping per thread is 14 percent. This leads to an expected 1.6 iterations per generated sample turning into an expected 3.1 iterations when warp effects are taken into account.

The Box-Muller Transform

Because GPUs are so sensitive to looping and branching, it turns out that the best choice for the Gaussian transform is actually the venerable Box-Muller transform, code for which can be seen in Listing 37-5. This takes two uniform samples u0 and u1 and transforms them into two Gaussian distributed samples n0 and n1, using the relations:

$$r_0 = \sin(2\pi u_0)\sqrt{-2\log(u_1)},$$
$$r_1 = \cos(2\pi u_0)\sqrt{-2\log(u_1)}.$$

Listing 37-5. The Box-Muller Transform

```
float2 BoxMuller()
{
    float u0=HybridTaus (), u1=HybridTaus ();
    float r=sqrt(-2 log(u0));
    float theta=2*PI*u1;

    return make_float2(r*sin(theta),r*cos(theta));
}
```

The Box-Muller approach has been largely discarded in software, in particular because it requires the evaluation of sine and cosine for every sample that is produced. However, it offers a number of important advantages for a GPU implementation with batched threads, the most obvious of which is that it has no branching or looping: there is only a single code path. It also does not require any table lookups, or the large numbers of constants found in some methods. It still has a fairly high computational load, but fortunately this is what GPUs are good at: straight-line code, loaded with math. In addition, our results suggest that the high-speed sine and cosine functions present on the GPU offer satisfactory results, largely negating the performance downsides of the Box-Muller approach.

37.2.4 The Wallace Gaussian Generator

The *Wallace Gaussian generator* (Wallace 1996, Brent 2003) is a novel method that is able to generate Gaussian samples directly, without using a uniform generator first. The central idea is to take a pool of k random numbers that are already Gaussian distributed and then apply a transform to the pool, such that another pool is produced that is also Gaussian. After each transform the pool can be output to supply random numbers. The key requirement is to make the output of the transform as uncorrelated with the input as possible, while still preserving the distribution properties.

Ideally each new pool would be produced by applying a different orthogonal $k{\times}k$ matrix to the previous pool. An orthogonal matrix is one that preserves the sum of squares in the pool, or put another way: if the input pool is taken as a k-dimensional vector, then an orthogonal matrix would preserve the Euclidean length of that vector. Common examples of orthogonal matrices include the identity matrix and size-preserving affine transforms such as reflection and rotation.

However, there is a computational problem, because generating a random $k{\times}k$ orthogonal matrix is very expensive—orders of magnitude more expensive than just generating k Gaussian-distributed numbers using traditional techniques. Instead, the approach used is to construct an orthogonal transform using lots of much smaller orthogonal transforms, for example by using $2{\times}2$ orthogonal matrices, such as 2D rotations. Applying $k/2$ 2D rotations will preserve the length of the overall k vector, but it is much cheaper to implement. The drawback is that the degree of mixing between passes is much lower: using a full $k{\times}k$ matrix, each value in the new pool can be influenced by every value in the old pool, but if $2{\times}2$ matrices are used, then each value in the new pool depends on at most two values in the old pool.

Two techniques can mitigate this lack of mixing. The first applies a random permutation to the pool before applying the blocked transform, so that after a sufficient number of passes, each element of the new pool will be dependent on all elements of a previous pool. The second simply transforms the pool multiple times before using the pool to output numbers. Both methods have their drawbacks, because a full random permutation is expensive to set up, and performing multiple passes obviously takes more time. In practice, a combination of both is often used, performing a small number of passes and using a somewhat random permutation of the pool in each pass.

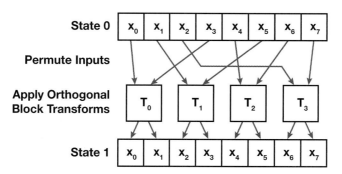

Figure 37-3. A Single Step of the Wallace Transform
Combining a permutation of the pool with an orthogonal transformation on each block.

Permuting the Pool

Mapping the Wallace algorithm into a GPU presents a number of challenges. The most important requirement is that the random permutation must be sufficiently random. In tests we found that the quality of this permutation was a key factor in producing good-quality random numbers: using simple nonrandom permutations produced random numbers that failed statistical tests. In light of these tests, we determined that producing a random permutation was much more important than reducing bank conflicts, so we can ignore conflicts when designing the algorithm.

The only critical requirement for the permutation is that it must be exactly that, a permutation. No pool value can be read twice during a pass (and so logically, no pool value can be ignored). During the reading stage, each thread must read d samples from a pool of k samples. We can thus define the problem as creating a random mapping from $1..k \rightarrow 1..d \times 1..k/d$. Earlier we mentioned the LCG, which provides a method for specifying a maximum period generator in the range $[0, m)$. If we choose $m = k/d$, we can use this as the basis of a high-quality random permutation.

We already have a unique per-thread value, the thread id, which is a value in $[0, m)$. Now, if we take the thread id and feed it into a mod-m LCG, each thread will still have a unique identifier, but the ordering will have changed pseudorandomly. Note that this LCG provides low statistical quality; however, we found that in this context, low quality is not a problem. Applying the LCG again would result in a new mapping, but each thread would still have a unique identifier in the range $[0, m)$. The combination of the address permutation and the blockwise orthogonal transformation forms the basis of the transformation process. When we combine an individual Wallace transform step with a loop to perform repeated internal transformations as part of an overall visible transformation, we obtain the code in Listing 37-6, where `TransformBlock` performs the matrix operation on the data, in this case using a Walsh-Hadamard matrix (Wallace 1996).

Listing 37-6. Transforming the Wallace Pool Using a Defined Number of Passes and a Walsh-Hadamard Matrix on Each Set of Values

This uses a defined number of passes and a Walsh-Hadamard matrix on each set of values. The size of the block to execute a matrix on can be varied but for optimality should use registers, and hence we have manually unrolled the computation here.

```
void Transform()
{
    // K, and M are binary powers.
    const unsigned K=...;   // Size of pool
    const unsigned M=K/D;   // Number of threads, and LCG modulus
```

Listing 37-6 (*continued*). Transforming the Wallace Pool

```
float block_0, block_1 , block_2 , block_3;
for( int pass = 0; pass < POOL_PASSES; pass++ ) {
  // Read the pool in using a pseudorandom permutation.
  unsigned s=tid;
  // M is a binary power, don't need %.
  // s is being recomputed as an LCG.
  s = (s*A+B) & (M-1); block_0=pool[(s<<3)+0];
  s = (s*A+B) & (M-1); block_1=pool[(s<<3)+1];
  s = (s*A+B) & (M-1); block_2=pool[(s<<3)+2];
  s = (s*A+B) & (M-1); block_3=pool[(s<<3)+3];

  // All pool values must be read before any are written.
  __syncthreads();

  // Perform in-place 4x4 orthogonal transform on block.
  TransformBlock(block);

  // Output the blocks in linear order.
  s=tid;
  pool[s]=block_0; s+=NT;
  pool[s]=block_1; s+=NT;
  pool[s]=block_2; s+=NT;
  pool[s]=block_3; s+=NT;
  }
}

__device__ void TransformBlock(float *b)
{
  float t=(b[0]+b[1]+b[2]+b[3])/2;
  b[0]=b[0]-t;
  b[1]=b[1]-t;
  b[2]=t-b[2];
  b[3]=t-b[3];
}
```

Initializing the Pool

Initialization of the random number pool is necessarily a separate process from the Wallace generator itself and hence requires a separate random number generator. This initialization can be performed on the CPU: for example, by using the ziggurat method in concert with a Mersenne twister. Although this generator will not be as fast as the GPU-based Wallace generator, it needs to provide only the seed values for the Wallace pools; once the threads start executing, they require no further seed values. In fact, the software can take advantage of this by generating the next set of seed values while the GPU threads work from the previous set of seed values.

The Wallace approach to random number generation conveys two main advantages over other approaches:

1. Direct generation of normally distributed values
2. A state pool that can be operated on fully in parallel, allowing high utilization of processor-local shared memory resources

37.2.5 Integrating the Wallace Gaussian Generator into a Simulation

Listing 37-7 demonstrates how the Wallace transform can be combined with code to perform repeated passes and to output multiple random numbers per execution into global memory. It is, of course, no problem to replace the global memory output with the use of the values within a simulation. Because we have generated multiple random numbers in each thread (the entire matrix size at a minimum), we can use these repeatedly within the transform, taking the appropriate pool value from shared memory as needed.

Listing 37-7. Using the Wallace Generator to Output into Memory

Note that an array of chi^2 correction values is required to maintain statistical properties of the output data. A small performance improvement can be obtained by moving this data into constant memory (around 5 percent in this case), thanks to caching. Constant memory is limited in size and hence care must be taken with this adjustment.

```
__device__ void generateRandomNumbers_wallace(
  unsigned seed,   // Initialization seed
  float *chi2Corrections,   // Set of correction values
  float *globalPool,   // Input random number pool
  float *output   // Output random numbers
){
  unsigned tid=threadIdx.x;
  // Load global pool into shared memory.
  unsigned offset = __mul24(POOL_SIZE, blockIdx.x);
  for( int i = 0; i < 4; i++ )
    pool[tid+THREADS*i] = globalPool[offset+TOTAL_THREADS*i+tid];

  __syncthreads();
```

```
const unsigned lcg_a=241;
const unsigned lcg_c=59;
const unsigned lcg_m=256;
const unsigned mod_mask = lcg_m-1;
seed=(seed+tid)&mod_mask ;

// Loop generating outputs repeatedly
for( int loop = 0; loop < OUTPUTS_PER_RUN; loop++ )
{
  Transform();
  unsigned intermediate_address;
  i_a = __mul24(loop,8*TOTAL_THREADS)+8*THREADS *
    blockIdx.x + threadIdx.x;
  float chi2CorrAndScale=chi2Corrections[
    blockIdx.x * OUTPUTS_PER_RUN + loop];
  for( i = 0; i < 4; i++ )
    output[i_a + i*THREADS]=chi2CorrAndScale*pool[tid+THREADS*i];
}
}
```

In integrating the Wallace with a simulation, we begin to see limitations. If the simulation requires a large amount of shared memory, then the Wallace method might be inappropriate for integration, because it also has a shared memory requirement. Of course, it can still output to global memory and have a simulation read that data as discussed earlier, but performance is likely to be lower. We also see limits on the number of registers we can use, because the larger computation complexity of combining the Wallace transform with the simulation loops increases the register requirement. Reducing the number of threads operating is one solution to this problem, and because the computation is very arithmetic heavy with the integrated Wallace generator having a lower number of threads, it need not be a severe performance limitation, with the benefits of integration outweighing the problems of a low thread count.

37.3 Example Applications

To evaluate the ideas in the previous section, we now look at two different Monte Carlo simulation kernels. Both are used for valuing options, but they have different computational and (in particular) storage characteristics. The goal of both these algorithms is to attempt to place a price on an option, which is simply a contract that one party may choose to exercise (or not). For example, the contract may say "In two months' time, party A has the *option* to buy 1 share of stock S for $50.00 from party B." Here we would call $50.00 the *strike price* of the option, and stock S is *the underlying*, because it is the thing on which the option is based.

This contract obviously has a nonnegative monetary value to party A: If in two months' time, stock S is trading at more than $50.00, then A can exercise the option, buying the stock from B at the cheaper price, then immediately selling it on the open market. If it is trading at less than $50.00, then A chooses not to exercise the option, and so makes no profit (nor loss). The problem for party B is to place a price on the contract *now*, when B sells the option to party A, taking into account all possible outcomes from the contract.

The most common model for stocks is that of the log-normal random walk, which assumes that the percentage change in a stock's price follows the Gaussian distribution. This preserves the two most important characteristics of stocks: prices are never negative, and the magnitude of stock price fluctuations is proportional to the magnitude of the stock price. Under this model party B can estimate the probability distribution of the price of stock S and try to estimate B's expected loss on the option. This expected loss then dictates the price at which B should sell the option to A.

These simple options can be priced in a number of ways: through the closed-form Black-Scholes pricing formula, finite-difference methods, binomial trees, or Monte Carlo simulation. In a Monte Carlo pricing simulation, the expected loss is estimated by generating thousands of different potential prices for S in two months' time, using random samples from the log-normal distribution. The average loss over all these potential stock prices is then used as the price of the option. See Wilmott 2006 for more technical details and the underlying theory; and for a GPU-based implementation of option pricing, see Colb and Pharr 2005.

However, there also exist much more complex options than simple calls (options to buy) and puts (options to sell), often called *exotic options*. These may specify a complex payoff function over multiple underlyings, constructed by party A to hedge against some specific set of market circumstances, which party B will then sell as a one-off contract. It is often impossible to find any kind of closed-form solution for the option price, and the multiasset nature of the contract makes tree and finite-difference methods impractical. This leaves Monte Carlo simulation as the only viable choice for pricing many exotic options.

37.3.1 Asian Option

The first application is an Asian option (Wilmott 2006) on the maximum of a basket of two underlyings. An Asian option uses the average price of the underlying to determine the final strike price, so the price depends on both where the underlying price ends up and what path it took to get there. In this case we will be considering an option on the maximum of two underlyings, following a log-normal random walk, and having a known correlation structure. Note that we ignore some details such as discounting and concentrate only on the computation.

The initial state of the basket is $S_0 = (a_0, b_0)$. The assets in the basket have a known correlation structure σ, which is a 2×2 matrix of covariances that describes the tendency of movements in one asset to be reflected in movements of another asset. For example, the stock price of XXX is highly correlated with that of YYY, so when one increases in value, the other is also likely to, and vice versa. The correlation structure σ can be reduced to three constants $s_{a,a}$, $s_{b,b}$, and $s_{a,b}$, and with the addition of two constants m_a and m_b to allow for trend growth, the evolution of the assets proceeds as follows:

$$a_{t+1} = a_t e^{\mu_a + N_1 \sigma_{a,a}}$$

$$b_{t+1} = b_t e^{\mu_b + N_1 \sigma_{a,b} + N_2 \sigma_{b,b}}$$

$$s_{t+1} = \max\left(a_{t+1}, b_{t+1}\right).$$

The option payoff P is then defined in the following equation:

$$\overline{S} = \frac{1}{T} \sum_1^T s_t$$

$$P = \max\left(\overline{S} - s_T, 0\right).$$

Figure 37-4 displays an example of the behavior of the correlated assets, and Listing 37-8 provides the code for a single path of the Asian basket simulation.

Listing 37-8. Code for a Single Path of the Asian Basket Simulation

```
__device__  float AsianBasket(
  unsigned T, float A_0, float B_0,
  float MU_A, float SIG_AA,
  float MU_B, float SIG_AB, float SIG_BB)
{
  float a=A_0, b=B_0, s=0, sum=0;
```

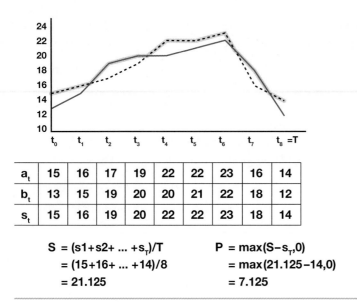

a_t	15	16	17	19	22	22	23	16	14
b_t	13	15	19	20	20	21	22	18	12
s_t	15	16	19	20	22	22	23	18	14

$$S = (s1+s2+ \ldots +s_T)/T \qquad P = \max(S-s_T,0)$$
$$= (15+16+ \ldots +14)/8 \qquad = \max(21.125-14,0)$$
$$= 21.125 \qquad = 7.125$$

Figure 37-4. Example of One Run of the Asian Basket Simulation

Listing 37-8 (*continued*). Code for a Single Path of the Asian Basket Simulation

```
for(unsigned t=0;t<T;t++){
    float ra=RNORM();
    float rb=RNORM();

    a*=exp(MU_A+ra*SIG_AA);
    b*=exp(MU_B+ra*SIG_AB+rb*SIG_BB);

    s=max(a,b);
    sum+=s;
}

return max(sum/T-s,0);
}
```

37.3.2 Variant on a Lookback Option

The second application is a variant on a *lookback option* (Wilmott 2006), with some special features. Specifically, the payoff is determined by the sum of the positive differences between the asset price at each time step, and the final asset price. This can be thought of as drawing a horizontal line across the asset path from the terminal price and using the area above the line and below the path as the payoff. Thus, if $s_0 \ldots s_T$ is the path of the asset, the payoff P will be the following:

$$P = \sum_{0}^{T-1} \max\left(s_t s_T, 0\right).$$

This option requires that the entire evolution of the path be stored, because the payoff can be determined only when the final price is known.

We also use a more complex type of asset price model in this option, called a *GARCH model*. This model incorporates the idea of time-varying volatility: basically, the idea that the size of the asset movement depends in part on the size of the most recent movement. This is often seen when a large change in a stock price is followed by another large change, while in more stable periods, the size of a change is lower. The asset path is modeled as follows:

$$\sigma_{t+1} = \sqrt{A_0 + A_1 \sigma_t^2 + A_2 \varepsilon_t^2}$$
$$\varepsilon_{t+1} = N \sigma_{t+1}$$
$$s_{t+1} = s_t e^{\mu + \varepsilon}_{t+1}.$$

Figure 37-5 demonstrates the movement and relevant asset values, and Listing 37-9 provides the code for a single path of the lookback option simulation. When used in practice, the single-path functions shown in Listings 37-8 and 37-9 are called repeatedly such that results from a set of different simulation paths are combined into mean and variance results, as shown in Listing 37-10.

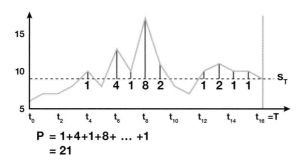

Figure 37-5. Movement of the Asset

Listing 37-9. Code for a Single Path of the Lookback Option Simulation

```
// (MAX_T%WARP_SIZE)==0
const unsigned MAX_T;

__device__ float LookbackDiff(
  unsigned T,
  float VOL_0, float EPS_0,
  float A_0, float A_1, float A_2
  float MU
)
{
  __shared__ float path[NUM_THREADS*MAX_T];
  float vol=VOL_0, eps=EPS_0;
  float s=S0;
  int base=__mul24(tid,MAX_T)-NUM_THREADS;

  // Choose a random asset path.
  for(unsigned t=0;t<T;t++){
    // Store the current asset price.
    base=base+NUM_THREADS;
    path[base]=s;

    // Calculate the next asset price.
    vol=sqrt(A_0+A_1*vol*vol+A_2*eps*eps);
    eps=RNORM()*vol;
    s=s*exp(MU+eps);
  }

  // Look back at path to find payoff.
  float sum=0;
  for(unsigned t=0;t<T;t++){
    base=base-NUM_THREADS;
    sum+=max(path[base]-s,0);
  }

  return sum;
}
```

Listing 37-10. Making Use of the Individual Simulation Kernels

Results from the kernel runs are combined into mean and variance results, which can then be returned. We have left the parameters to `SimKernel()` *vague here, to generalize over the two kernels described in Listings 37-8 and 37-9.*

```
// Extract a thread-specific seed from the array of seeds.
__device__ void InitRNORM(seeds);

// Produce a random number from the thread's stream
// based on whichever generator we are using.
__device__ float RNORM();

// Execute the simulation kernel using calls to RNORM().
__device__ float SimKernel(parameters);

__global__ float2 MonteCarloThread(seed, parameters)
{
  InitRNORM(seeds);

  float mean=0, varAcc=0;
  for(float i=1;i<=PATHS_PER_SIM;i++){
    // Simulate one path.
    float res=SimKernel(parameters);

    // Now update mean and variance in
    // numerically stable way.
    float delta=res-mean;
    mean+=delta/i;
    varAcc+=delta*(res-mean);
  }
  float variance=S/(PATHS_PER_SIM-1);

  return make_float2(mean,variance);
}
```

37.3.3 Results

We have implemented the hybrid Tausworthe RNG with Box-Muller and the Wallace Gaussian RNG in CUDA and show the raw RNG performance results in the first column (labeled "Raw RNG") in Table 37-1. The results are measured in millions of Gaussian samples produced across the entire GPU every second (MSamples/s). The

Wallace generator provides more than 5 billion samples per second, achieving a rate 1.2 times that of the hybrid Tausworthe generator. However, the Wallace transform also uses a large amount of shared memory to store the pool, in this case 2,048 words. This leaves only 2,048 words available to be used within simulation code; so in cases where simulations require all the shared memory, the slower Tausworthe generator must be used.

Also included in the table are performance results for all four processors of a 2.2 GHz Quad Opteron, using a combination of the Mersenne twister uniform generator and Ziggurat transform. The GPU-based Wallace generator provides a speedup of 26 times over the quad-CPU machine, but this measures only raw RNG speed: it is also important to be able to do something with these random numbers.

Columns two and three of Table 37-1 show the performance of simulations for the two exotic options presented in the previous section. As well as the two GPU and one GPU based mentioned earlier, two further rows are included, both labeled "Constant RNG." In these cases the random number generator was removed, while taking care to ensure the rest of the simulation code is not optimized out, thus giving an idea of the ratio of time spent generating random numbers to time spent using them.

The performance figures are reported in MSteps/s, which is a measure of the number of simulation time steps that can be processed per second. For example, in the Asian option, each step corresponds to one iteration of the inner loop of Listing 37-8. When measuring the performance of the Asian option, each simulation executed 256 time steps, with 256 threads per block; so completing one block per second would provide 65 KSteps/s. In the lookback case, the number of time steps is limited by the amount of shared memory that can be dedicated to each thread. We used 512 threads per block; thus the lookback option was limited to 8 time steps per simulation.

In the Asian case, we see that the Wallace generator provides only a modest improvement of 1.06 times, compared to the Tausworthe/Box-Muller generators. The relative slowdown appears to be due to interactions between the Wallace code and simulation kernel code, possibly due to register allocation conflicts. Even so, the performance is 59 times that of the software implementation.

In the lookback case, the Wallace cannot be used because the shared memory is needed by the simulation kernel, and performance is much lower than that of the Asian option. Interestingly, the software implementation exhibits the opposite performance: the lookback is significantly faster than the Asian. However, a 23 times improvement in speed is seen by using the GPU rather than CPU-based solution.

Table 37-1. Performance Results for the Discussed Random Number Generators and Simulations
The Constant RNG row represents the case where no real random numbers are being produced and the values are being taken directly from variables such that the simulation code is not optimized away. The Raw RNG column denotes the random number executing in isolation directly into memory with no simulation being driven.

		Raw RNG (MSamples/s)	Asian (MSteps/s)	Lookback (MSteps/s)
GPU	**Tausworthe plus Box-Muller**	4,327	1,769	1,147
	Wallace	5,274	1,877	—
	Constant RNG	—	5,177	2,908
Quad Opteron	**Ziggurat plus Mersenne Twister**	206	32	50
	Constant RNG	—	44	64
	Speedup	**26**	**59**	**23**

37.4 Conclusion

Modern GPU hardware is highly capable of use in financial simulation. In this chapter, we have discussed approaches for generating random numbers for these kinds of simulation. Wallace's method provides good performance while maintaining a high quality of random numbers, as shown by statistical analysis. Due to resource limitations, trade-offs are necessary, so the Wallace approach will not be the appropriate method to use in all situations. These trade offs should be manageable in most situations, and the use of CUDA and the GPU hardware for financial simulation should be a viable option in the future.

37.5 References

Brent, Richard P. 2003, "Some Comments on C. S. Wallace's Random Number Generators." *The Computer Journal.*

Colb, C., and M. Pharr. 2005. "Options Pricing on the GPU." In *GPU Gems 2*, edited by Matt Pharr, pp. 719–731. Addison-Wesley.

Knuth, D. 1969. *The Art of Computer Programming, Volume 2: Seminumerical Algorithms.* Addison-Wesley.

L'Ecuyer, P. 1996. "Maximally Equidistributed Combined Tausworthe Generators." *Mathematics of Computation.*

L'Ecuyer, P. 1999. "Tables of Maximally Equidistributed Combined LFSR Generators." *Mathematics of Computation.*

L'Ecuyer, P. 2006. "TestU01: A C Library for Empirical Testing of Random Number Generators." *ACM Transactions on Mathematical Software.*

Marsaglia, George. 1995. "The Diehard Battery of Tests of Randomness." http://www.stat.fsu.edu/pub/diehard/.

Marsaglia, George. 2000. "The Ziggurat Method for Generating Random Variables." *Journal of Statistical Software.*

Matsumoto, M. and T. Nishimura. 1998. "Mersenne Twister: A 623-Dimensionally Equidistributed Uniform Pseudorandom Number Generator." *ACM Transactions on Modeling and Computer Simulation.*

Metropolis, N. 1987. "The Beginning of the Monte Carlo Method." *Los Alamos Science.*

NVIDIA Corporation. 2007. *NVIDIA CUDA Compute Unified Device Architecture Programming Guide.* Version 0.8.1.

Press, W. H., S. A. Teukolsky, W. T. Vetterling, and B. P. Flannery. 1992. *Numerical Recipes in C.* Second edition. Cambridge University Press.

Sussman, M., W. Crutchfield, and M. Papakipos. 2006. "Pseudorandom Number Generation on the GPU." *Graphics Hardware.*

Wallace, C. S. 1996. "Fast Pseudorandom Generators for Normal and Exponential Variates." *ACM Transactions on Mathematical Software.*

Wilmott, P. 2006. *Paul Wilmott on Quantitative Finance.* Wiley.

Chapter 38

Imaging Earth's Subsurface Using CUDA

Bernard Deschizeaux
CGGVeritas

Jean-Yves Blanc
CGGVeritas

38.1 Introduction

The main goal of earth exploration is to provide the oil and gas industry with knowledge of the earth's subsurface structure to detect where oil can be found and recovered. To do so, large-scale seismic surveys of the earth are performed, and the data recorded undergoes complex iterative processing to extract a geological model of the earth. The data is then interpreted by experts to help decide where to build oil recovery infrastructure.

The state-of-the-art algorithms used in seismic data processing are evolving rapidly, and the need for computing power increases dramatically every year. For this reason, CGGVeritas has always pioneered new high-performance computing (HPC) technologies, and in this work we explore GPUs and NVIDIA's CUDA programming model to accelerate our industrial applications.

The algorithm we selected to test CUDA technology is one of the most resource-intensive of our seismic processing applications, usually requiring around a week of processing time on a latest-generation CPU cluster with 2,000 nodes. To be economically sound at its full capability for our industry, this algorithm must be an order of magnitude faster. At present, only GPUs can provide such a performance breakthrough.

After much analysis and testing, we were able to develop a fully parallel prototype using GPU hardware to speed up part of our processing pipeline by more than a factor of ten. In this chapter, we present the algorithms and methodology used to implement this seismic imaging application on a GPU using CUDA. It should be noted that this work is not an academic benchmark of the CUDA technology—it is a feasibility study for the industrial use of GPU hardware in clusters.

38.2 Seismic Data

A seismic survey is performed by sending compression waves into the ground and recording the reflected waves to determine the subsurface structure of the earth. In the case of a marine survey, like the one shown in Figure 38-1, a ship tows about ten cables equipped with recording systems called hydrophones that are positioned 25 meters apart. Also attached to the ship is an air gun used as the source of the compression waves.

To acquire seismic data, the ship fires the air gun every 50 meters, and the resulting compression waves propagate through the water to the sea floor and beyond into the subsurface of the earth. When a wave encounters a change of velocity or density in the

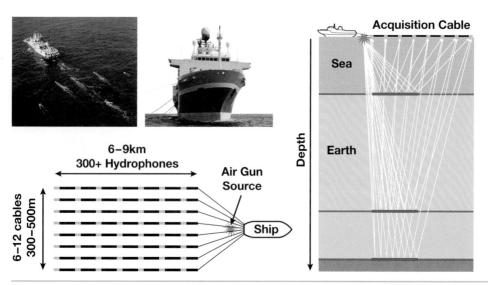

Figure 38-1. Marine Seismic Data Acquisition
A vessel fires an air gun to generate a compression wave that propagates down to the earth and generates reflection waves recorded by hydrophones attached to cables behind the ship

earth media, it splits in two, one part being reflected back to the surface while the other is refracted, propagating further into the earth (see Figure 38-1). Therefore, each layer of the subsurface produces a reflection of the wave that is recorded by the hydrophones. Because sound waves propagate through water at about 2,500 m/s and through the earth at 3,000 to 5,000 m/s, recording reflection waves for about four seconds after the shot provides information on the earth down to a depth of about 10 to 20 km.

A typical marine survey covers a few hundred square kilometers, which represents a few million shots and several terabytes of recorded data. Processing this amount of data for many studies in parallel is the core business of CGGVeritas processing centers through-out the world. Due to its very low initial signal-to-noise ratio and the large data size, seismic data processing is extremely demanding in terms of processing power. As illus-trated by the image in Figure 38-2, CGGVeritas computing facilities consist of PC clusters of several thousand nodes, providing more than 300 teraflops of computing power and petabytes of disk space.

To support increasing survey sizes and processing complexity, our computing power needs to grow by more than a factor of two every year (see the graph in Figure 38-2). Further-more, heat limitations have forced CPU manufacturers to limit future clock frequencies to around 4 GHz. Increasing the size of clusters in data centers can be realistic for only a short period of time, and this problem enforces the need for new technologies. Therefore,

 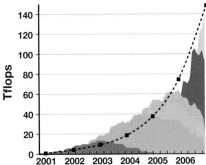

Figure 38-2. Computing Capability Is a Critical Aspect of Our Domain
Our growing trend presented here, color coded according to each different hardware, shows that whenever the technology was available (before 2005), our growth more than doubled every year. The dashed curve gives a reference for exponential growth. As CPU clock frequencies reach a limit, we start to fall below this curve, and only the use of new hardware like GPUs allows us to maintain necessary computing power.

we believe mastering new computing technologies such as general-purpose computing on GPUs is critically important for the future of seismic data processing.

38.3 Seismic Processing

The goal of seismic processing is to convert terabytes of survey data into a 3D volume description of the earth's subsurface structure. A typical data set contains billions of vectors of a few thousand values each, where each vector represents the information recorded by a detector at a specific location and specific wave shot.

The first step in seismic data processing is to correctly position all survey data within a global geographic reference frame. In a marine survey, for instance, we need to take into account the tidal and local streams that shift the acquisition cables from their theoretical straight-line position, and we also need to include any movement of the ship's position. All of the data vectors must be positioned inside a 100 km^2 region at a resolution of 1 meter. Many different positioning systems, both relative and global, are used during data acquisition, and all such position information is included in this processing step.

After correcting the global position for all data elements, the next step is to apply signal processing algorithms to normalize the signal over the entire survey and to increase the signal-to-noise ratio. Here we correct for any variation in hydrophone sensitivity that can lead to nonhomogeneous response between different parts of the acquisition cables. Band-limited deconvolution algorithms are used to verify the known impulse response of the overall acquisition process. Various filtering and artifact removal steps are also performed during this phase. The main goal of this step is to produce data that coherently represents the physics of the wave reflection for a standard, constant source.

The last and the most important and time-consuming step is designed to correct for the effects of changing subsurface media velocity on the wave propagation through the earth. Unlike other echoing systems such as radar, our system has no information about the propagation velocity of the media through which the compression waves travel. Moreover, the media are not homogeneous, causing the waves to travel in curves rather than straight lines, as shown in Figure 38-3a. Therefore, the rather simple task for radar of converting the time of the echo arrival into the distance of the reflection is, in the seismic domain, an extremely complex, inverse problem. To further complicate the

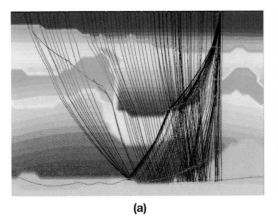 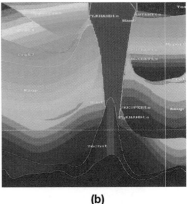

(a)   (b)

Figure 38-3. Ray Tracing for a Single Reflector (*Bottom*) Through the Earth, Modeled by a Velocity Field Display in Color
(a) We can clearly see how velocity variations bend the rays even for a rather smooth velocity model. (b) In some cases, the velocity changes are extremely complex and nonhomogeneous, and the wave propagation is extremely difficult to model, especially because we would need to compute billions of rays.

process, more than one reflection occurs after a wave shot, so the recorded signal can in fact be a superposition of many different reflections coming from different places.

Because the velocity field is initially unknown, we generally start by assuming a rather simple velocity model. Then the migration process gives us a better image of the earth's subsurface that allows us to refine the velocity field. This iterative process finally converges toward our best approximation to the exact earth reflectivity model.

At the end of the processing, the 3D volume of data is far cleaner and easier to understand. Some attributes can be extracted to help geologists interpret the results. Typically the impedance of the media is one of those attributes, as well as the wave velocity, the density, and the anisotropy. Figure 38-4 gives an overview of what the data looks like before and after the processing sequence. Also shown is an attribute map representing the wave velocity at a particular depth of the seismic survey. Different rock types have different velocities, so velocity is a good indicator to look for specific rocks such as sand. In the particular case of Figure 38-4c, low velocities (in blue) are characteristic of sand, here from an old riverbed. As a rock, sand is very porous and is typically a good location to prospect for oil.

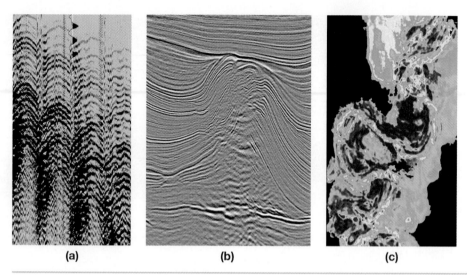

(a)	(b)	(c)

Figure 38-4. A Seismic Processing Example

(a) Raw data recorded during a land survey in Germany showing the poor signal-to-noise ratio and the lack of calibration. (b) A vertical section of about 10 km wide and 5 km deep in the final 3D result shows the layered structure of the earth. (c) This map represents an attribute extracted at a particular depth from a final seismic data set. This attribute is used to distinguish between sand and shale rocks (blue versus green) around a winding shape, which is the remaining channel imprint of a 70-million-year-old river buried under 10 km of earth.

38.3.1 Wave Propagation

For a perfect theoretical seismic data set, the recorded signal $\mathbf{r}_x$ of the wave propagation from a specific source $\mathbf{S}_i$ recorded by a hydrophone $\mathbf{G}_j$ after a reflection of amplitude $\mathbf{R}_x$ at the 3D location $\mathbf{x}(x, y, z)$ can be expressed as follows:

$$\mathbf{r}_x = \mathbf{P}_{xj}^V \left(\mathbf{R}_x \cdot \mathbf{P}_{ix}^V \left(\mathbf{W}_s \right) \right), \tag{1}$$

where $\mathbf{W}_s$ is the source signal, $\mathbf{P}_{ix}$ is the operator that propagates the wave from the source position $\mathbf{i}$ to the reflection position $\mathbf{x}$ through the velocity field $\mathbf{V}$, and $\mathbf{P}_{xj}$ is the operator that propagates the reflected wave from $\mathbf{x}$ to the recorder position $\mathbf{j}$.

To model the complete seismic recording by one receiver, we need to integrate the Equation 1 for all possible reflection positions—that is, integrate on the whole 3D volume of $\mathbf{x}$ values:

$$\mathbf{S}_j - \int_x \left[\mathbf{P}_{xj}^V \left(\mathbf{R.C}_{earth} \left(\mathbf{x} \right) \cdot \mathbf{P}_{ix}^V \left(\mathbf{W}_s \right) \right) \right], \tag{2}$$

where $\mathbf{S}_j$ is the seismic recording at position $\mathbf{j}$ and $\mathbf{RC}_{earth}$ is the reflectivity model of the earth we are looking for. The complexity should be apparent now, because each of the hundreds of millions of data vectors may include information from the whole earth area in a way that depends on the velocity field. Note that in practice the velocity is around a few kilometers per second. Thus if we record wave reflection for a few seconds, only the earth approximately 10 km around the receiver position will contribute to the signal.

It is not realistic to use a brute-force approach to solve this inverse problem, but it can be simplified if we use the property of the propagation operator: $\mathbf{P}_{ij}(\mathbf{P}_{ji}(\mathbf{a})) = \mathbf{I}$. That is, propagation from source to reflection point and back to the source position should give the initial result (that is, there should be no dissipation). From Equation 1 we can see that

$$\mathbf{P}_{jx}^{V}(\mathbf{r}_x) = \mathbf{P}_{jx}^{V}\left(\mathbf{P}_{xj}^{V}\left(\mathbf{R}_x.\mathbf{P}_{ix}^{V}(\mathbf{W}_s)\right)\right) = \mathbf{R}_x.\mathbf{P}_{ix}^{V}(\mathbf{W}_s). \tag{3}$$

And if we consider all the possible contributions to a specific record—that is, summing up all contributions for all $\mathbf{x}$ locations—we can write this:

$$\int_x \mathbf{P}_{jx}^{V}(S_j) = \int_x \left[RC_{earth}(\mathbf{x}).\mathbf{P}_{ix}^{V}(W_s)\right] = RC_{earth} \otimes \int_x \left[\mathbf{P}_{ix}^{V}(W_s)\right]. \tag{4}$$

Hence, the recorded seismic signal $\mathbf{S}_j$, taken as a source and propagated through the earth at all possible $\mathbf{x}$ locations, is equal to the earth reflectivity model convolved by the initial source shot propagated to any possible reflection position in the earth. It is then clear that if we correlate both sides of this equation by

$$\int_x \left[\mathbf{P}_{ix}^{V}(W_s)\right]$$

and sum up information from all receivers for each source, we may extract the earth reflectivity model:

$$RC_{earth} = \sum_s \left[\int_x \mathbf{P}_{ix}^{V}(W_s) * \sum_j \int_x \mathbf{P}_{jx}^{V}(S_j)\right],$$

where $*$ is the correlation operator, and using

$$\int_x \left[\mathbf{P}_{ix}^{V}(W_s)\right] * \int_x \left[\mathbf{P}_{ix}^{V}(W_s)\right] = 1.$$

Hence, if we propagate the source wave through the earth to all reachable positions $\mathbf{x}$, and correlate the result with the recorded data back-propagated to the same $\mathbf{x}$ location, we only have to sum up results for all sources and all receivers to obtain the earth reflectivity model. Note that in practice we need to take into account the dispersive effect of the propagation, as well as the fact that the data is band limited. Also, because the velocity field is initially unknown, we need to start with an initial guess (based on expert knowledge of the area) to compute a first reflection model and then refine our velocity field by interpreting the results in terms of the geological structure. (See Yilmaz 2001 and Sherifs 1984 for more information.)

38.3.2 Seismic Migration Using the SRMIP Algorithm

In the case of the CGGVeritas algorithm, called SRMIP, that we want to develop using CUDA, the wave propagation is performed using a finite-difference algorithm applied in the frequency domain.

As presented earlier, the seismic data is composed of a succession of wave shots. Each wave shot is recorded as a 3D volume (x, y, t) where x and y represent the receiver location and t the recording time. This data is transformed into frequency planes by applying a Fast Fourier Transform on the time axis. For each frequency plane, we want to propagate the source wave (called the *downgoing wave*) and the seismic data (called the *upgoing wave*) from the surface (depth $= 0$) to the maximum depth we want to image. The propagation (also called *downward extrapolation*) is carried out from one depth to the next by applying spatial convolution using finite-length filters.

The SRMIP algorithm relies on a method to take advantage of the circular symmetry of the wave propagator filter: the radial response of the filter is expanded as a polynomial in the Laplacian, which is approximated by the sum of two 1D filters (approximating the second derivative k_x^2 and k_y^2):

$$L = \sum_{n=0}^{n=N_{L_x}} d_x(n)\cos(n\Delta x k_x) + \sum_{n=0}^{n=N_{L_y}} d_y(n)\cos(n\Delta y k_y)$$

and approximate the exact extrapolation operator:

$$G_0(L) = \exp\left[i\Delta z\left(\frac{\mathbf{w}^2}{\mathbf{v}^2 - L}\right)^{\frac{1}{2}}\right]$$

by a polynomial $G(L)$:

$$G(L) = \sum_{n=0}^{n-N} b_{\mathbf{w}/\mathbf{v}}(n)L^n,$$

where $\mathbf{w}$ is the frequency considered, $\mathbf{v}$ the velocity, and L the Laplacian.

Because we want to extrapolate the wave in an iterative way for all depth values starting from the surface, the choice of the filter parameterization is critical for the stability of the results. To optimize the coefficients of the polynomials, we use the L_∞ norm, because the stability condition is expressed more easily in this norm. In our SRMIP algorithm, we use an expression of the extrapolator using Chebyshev polynomials (see Soubaras 1996 and Hall 1991 for details):

$$G(L) = \sum_{n=0}^{n=N} t_{\mathbf{w}/c}(n)T_n(L),$$

where $T_n(x)$, the Chebyshev polynomial of degree n, is defined by $T_n(x) = \cos(n \arccos x)$ and can be recursively computed using the formula:

$$T_n(x) = 2xT_{n-1}(x) - T_{n-2}(x).$$

The degree of the polynomial expansion (that is, the parameter N) is about 15, which means that to propagate the wave from one depth to the next we need to apply a Chebyshev polynomial of Laplacian filter 15 times, recursively.

The pseudocode given in Listing 38-1 shows the implementation of the extrapolator to propagate the wave from one depth to the next. For obvious efficiency reasons, the iterative calculation of the Chebyshev polynomial is computed directly and applied to every point of the input wave grid, saving an operation in the internal loop.

The SRMIP algorithm has a high degree of parallelism. This is because the basic operation is a simple 1D convolution with a constant short filter (approximating the second derivative). The fact that the Chebyshev recursion is not intrinsically parallel is not in this case a problem, because the parallelism is achieved across independent grid elements. Note that for a parallel implementation, some potential improvements that decrease the number of operations at the cost of a more complex data structure—such as making the degree of the polynomials or the length of the second derivative filters vary with the frequency—are not automatically advantageous.

Figure 38-5 gives an example of results obtained by applying the SRMIP algorithm to seismic data. Beyond the general quality improvement, we can see that the results are particularly improved where the earth structure is complex. For instance, the salt body in the top of the earth section has a very high velocity compared to the other surrounding rocks. Therefore, before migration, all data below the salt is not properly focused and appears almost random. After migration, as the propagation within different velocity media has been properly handled, the earth structure below the salt appears.

Listing 38-1. Pseudocode of the Extrapolator

The input `Wave` *grid is convolved recursively with two 1D Laplacian filters to produce the propagated* `Wave1` *grid at the next depth.*

```
T(x,y)  = Wave(x,y);
TT(x,y) =Laplacian⊗Wave(x,y);
Wave1(x,y) = a_{w/v}(1,x,y)*T(x,y)  + a_{w/v}(2,x,y)*TT(x,y);
for (n = 2; n < NMAX; n++)
{
    // Compute the Chebyshev polynomial TTT
    // using the two previous stored values TT and T.
    TTT(x,y)=2*Laplacian⊗TT(x,y)-T(x,y);

    // Add the contribution of the iteration to the results.
    Wave1(x,y) += a_{w/v}(n,x,y)*TTT(x,y);

    // Store Chebyshev results for next iteration.
    T(x,y)  = TT(x,y);
    TT(x,y)= TTT(x,y);
};
```

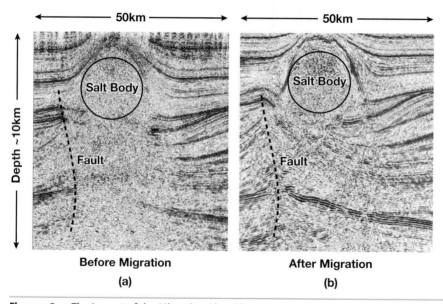

Before Migration

(a)

After Migration

(b)

Figure 38-5. The Impact of the Migration Algorithm on a Data Set
(a) The high-velocity salt body blurs the image below. (b) After migration, information below the salt is correctly focused and reveals the earth's structure.

38.4 The GPU Implementation

Selecting algorithms for GPU implementation can be difficult, especially without experience in GPU programming. In our seismic processing sequence, there are several important considerations. For example, the algorithms we port to the GPU are part of an industrial application already running in parallel on a large cluster. Therefore, our goal is an application running on the same kind of cluster but with graphics cards installed in every node. Furthermore, a significant part of the application that deals with all cluster parallelization and efficient data management cannot be changed to accommodate the GPU programming model.

The pseudocode in Listing 38-2 illustrates another consideration. Clearly, the overall benefit of GPU acceleration is limited by the percentage of total execution time attributed to each computational kernel. This code shows the general structure of the SRMIP program that runs independently on every node of the cluster. Each instance of the program (one per processor core) processes a group of seismic shots in sequence and produces a contribution to the final image. Profiling the program with standard parameters shows that 65 percent of the CPU time is consumed in the wave propagation, while all the interpolation routines used 20 percent, and the final correlation and summation use 5 percent. The interpolation step has been added to reduce processing time for the wave propagation. Therefore, it is possible that this step could be removed, depending on how much we accelerate the wave propagation.

Listing 38-2. Pseudocode of the Algorithm Showing the Main Loops and Steps of the Process

```
// uwave = upward wave; dwave = downward wave
// Frequency loop ~ 1000 iterations
for (freq = 0; freq < freq_max; freq++)
{
  Read_frequency_plane(uwave,dwave,nx,ny);

  // Depth loop ~ 1000 iterations
  for (z = 0; z < depth_max; z = z+dz)
  {
    Read_velocity_scalar_field(velocity,nx,ny,z);

    // Propagate uwave and dwave from z to z+dz
    // by applying N time (N~15) Laplacian operator.
    for (i=0; i < N ; i++)
    {
      convolution(uwave,velocity,nx,ny,z,dz);
      convolution(dwave,velocity,nx,ny,z,dz);
    }
```

```
    // Interpolate uwave and dwave between z and z +dz.
    interpolate_wave_over_dz(uwave,velocity,nx,ny,z,z+zd);
    interpolate_wave_over_dz(dwave,velocity,nx,ny,z,z+zd);

    for (zz = z; zz < Z+dz; z++)
    {
      // Interpolate uwave and dwave on output grid.
      Interpolat_xy(uwave,nx,nx,zz,fnx,fny,final_uwave);
      Interpolat_xy(dwave,nx,nx,zz,fnx,fny,final_dwave);

      // Convolve the two waves and sum results.
      sum_udwave(final_uwave,final_dwave,fnx,fny,zz,result);
    }
  }
}
```

In addition to focusing GPU implementation efforts on the most time-consuming parts of our application, it is equally if not more important to consider the amount of parallelism inherent in our algorithms. Indeed, the CUDA programming model is designed to let users exploit the massive data-parallel processing power of the GPU, so to achieve high performance, we have to choose algorithms with significant data parallelism. In the case of the SRMIP algorithm, the typical grid size we need to process is 400×400 elements, which is determined by the spatial extent of the wave propagation. The data grids correspond to 25 m spacing within a 100 km² region, which results in parallelism of roughly 160,000 independent operations. This is more than enough to make efficient use of modern GPUs.

38.4.1 GPU/CPU Communication

A potential problem for GPU-based seismic processing is the cost of GPU/CPU communication. Looking at the general trend of hardware evolution, we predict the GPU will roughly double in performance every year. However, for data transfer between the CPU and GPU (currently using PCIe), the increase in performance is far less impressive. We can expect the PCIe bandwidth to increase by 2× every two or three years at best. Therefore, if we want to design implementations that scale with future GPU performance, we have to avoid potential communication bottlenecks.

By analyzing the data flow of our code and taking into account the large memory available on NVIDIA Quadro FX 5600 hardware (1.5 GB), we were able to develop a communication schema where almost all the relevant data is stored on the GPU. As shown in Listing 38-3, frequency planes are sent one by one to the GPU, which then computes the two waves to be propagated for all depths and interpolates the results in the *x*, *y*, and *z* directions. Only the final result after summing all contribution will have to be sent back to the CPU.

Listing 38-3. Pseudocode Showing the Proposed Communication Scheme

```
// Frequency loop ~ 1000 iterations
for (freq=0; freq < freq_max; freq++)
{
  Read_frequency_plan(uwave,dwave,nx,ny);

  // Send frequency plan (~2 x 1.3 MB).
  Send_freqplan_to_GPU(uwave,dwave,nx,ny);
  // Depth loop ~ 1000 iterations
  for (z=0; z < depth_max; z=z+dz){
    Read_velocity_field(velocity,nx,ny,z);
    // Send velocity field (~0.6 MB).
    Send_Velocity_to_GPU(velocity,nx,ny);
    for (i=0; i < N ; i++)
    {
      convolution(uwave...); //(on the GPU)
      convolution(dwave...); //(on the GPU)
    }
    interpolate_wave_over_dz(uwave...); //(on the GPU)
    interpolate_wave_over_dz(dwave...); //(on the GPU)
    for (zz = z; zz < Z+dz; z++)
    {
      // Interpolate uwave and dwave on output grid.
      Interpolat_xy(uwave...); //(on the GPU)
      Interpolat_xy(dwave...); //(on the GPU)
      // Convolve the two waves and sum results.
      sum_udwave(uwave,dwave...); //(on the GPU)
    }
  }
}
// Get back results (~1.3 GB)
Receive_image_result(result,nx,ny,nz);
```

According to our profiling, the CPU time to compute one depth value is about 30 ms, and the total time of the depth loop is about half a minute. Taking that into account, we can easily compute the throughput needed by our communication scheme and check that we are within PCIe bandwidth limits. Even the velocity transfer (in the inner loop) is around 20 MB/s, which is far below the communication bottleneck even if the GPU implementation is an order of magnitude more efficient than the CPU version.

The 1.5 GB of memory on the NVIDIA Quadro FX 5600 is of great advantage here. Considering that standard cluster nodes have only a few gigabytes of memory to be shared between two to four processor cores, most of the data set handled in memory by one core on the CPU should fit in the GPU memory.

38.4.2 The CUDA Implementation

NVIDIA's CUDA technology provides a flexible programming environment that allows us to address each of the considerations outlined in the last section. After analyzing our core algorithm and the global framework of the GPU, we split our 12 most compute-intensive CPU routines into four separate kernels to be implemented using CUDA. The four kernels more or less correspond to the four routines shown in the pseudocode in Listing 38-3.

All four target algorithms perform local computations on a grid by applying a small operator to every grid element. We divide the computational grid into 2D tiles that map nicely to CUDA's grid of thread blocks. Each kernel loads a tile of grid data from global memory and caches the data in shared memory for further processing. The main advantage of shared memory is its extremely high bandwidth compared to global GPU memory. For three of the kernels, we load the data directly from GPU memory using standard arrays. For the wave propagation algorithm, we use CUDA's texture extensions as a read path to GPU memory. By using texture, we take advantage of hardware caching and automatic boundary handling, which is otherwise difficult and costly to implement in the kernel code. Because the convolution kernel is applied recursively, storing an extra copy of the outputs back into a texture was necessary between iterations.

The GPU code for our algorithms is quite straightforward, because CUDA is a C-based language. However, the G80 architecture has several performance constraints that make optimization somewhat complicated. For example, G80 has 8,000 32-bit registers per multiprocessor, which limits the register count for each kernel. For example, if a kernel executes on 256 threads running in parallel, each thread can use only 32 registers before reaching the limit. In many cases, it is necessary to optimize around this problem in one of two ways. First, we can simply reduce the kernel complexity (that is, the code size) to decrease register pressure and complete the algorithm using multiple passes. The second, and many times more successful, approach is to adjust the number of threads in a thread block. In this case, the range of useful thread counts is limited not only by the available registers but also by the fact that we need enough threads to hide memory latency (for example, global loads).

Our experience implementing kernels in CUDA is that the most efficient thread configuration partitions threads differently for the load phase and the processing phase. The load phase is usually constrained by the need to access the device memory in a coalesced way, which requires a specific mapping between threads and data elements. During processing, however, we try to organize the workload in such a way that threads do as much processing as possible—at least around 30 operations per byte of data loaded.

38.4.3 The Wave Propagation Kernel

As previously mentioned, our processing time is dominated by the wave propagation operator. Practically, the wave at a given depth is extrapolated to the next depth using the iterative process described in Section 38.3.2 and Listing 38-1. The iteration loop executes on the CPU; the GPU kernel is mainly in charge of the convolution of the wave grid by the Laplacian filter. In addition, at each iteration, the velocity field at each grid position is used to index into a lookup table and scale the input wave by the polynomial coefficients.

Figure 38-6 provides a graphic illustration of how we partition CUDA threads for data loading and convolution with the cross-shaped filter kernel. For loading, warps for a thread block are distributed across a 2D tile region of the computational grid. We use a tile size of 48×32 elements and thread block dimensions of 48×8, so threads with the same y component spread out such that each thread reads four complex frequency coefficients in a vertical column. The data covered by each tile represents a portion of the actual frequency plane as well as a support region (that is, the boundary elements) determined by the cross-filter radius. After storing the tile in shared memory, we synchronize all threads in the block and move to the processing phase. The radius of the convolution filter is four elements, so the output tile is 40×24. Therefore, we redistribute the thread warps so that each thread computes filtered results for three elements. This approach allows us to use all threads in the block for loading and most threads for processing. The less efficient alternative would be to disable more threads before processing, so that each thread outputs four elements.

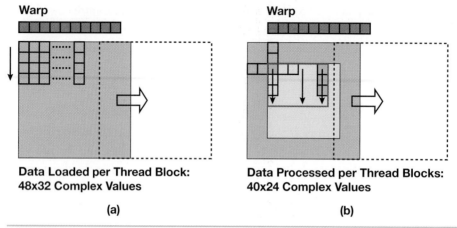

Warp

Data Loaded per Thread Block:
48x32 Complex Values

(a)

Warp

Data Processed per Thread Blocks:
40x24 Complex Values

(b)

Figure 38-6. Two Thread Organization Strategies for the Convolution Kernel
For data loading, 48×8 thread blocks load 48×32 tiles of complex values. This means each thread loads four values in a column from global memory and writes them to shared memory. For the processing phase, the output tile is 40×24 elements (disregarding the filter support region). In this case, each thread performs a convolution for three output elements in a column.

In addition to giving us an efficient mapping between threads and elements for the load and processing phases, the 48×32 tile size fits nicely within certain resource constraints in the GPU. For example, the G80 architecture has 16 KB of shared memory per multi-processor. Our tile size (for complex data) takes about 12 KB, so this configuration uses a majority of the shared memory for filtering. A slightly smaller tile size that still uses more than half the available shared memory is less efficient because it prevents multiple thread blocks from running in parallel. Another advantage of this tile size involves coalescing constraints for global memory. In general, it is easier to reason about alignment requirements for fast memory access if the thread block width is a multiple of the SIMD width of the GPU, which for G80 is 16 threads. Finally, it is important to have enough threads in the machine to hide memory latencies, and a 48×8 thread block gives 384 threads, which, in our experience, is plenty of parallelism for G80.

Listing 38-4 shows CUDA C code for the wave propagation kernel used in our SRMIP algorithm. The structure of the code reflects the thread configuration discussed previously. See the comments for a description of the constant terms used in the code. As explained previously, for this kernel we load the input data using CUDA's 2D texture extension. We also read the lookup table through 2D texture, because we need to get efficient, almost random, access to the polynomial coefficients. The cross-shaped filter is stored in CUDA's constant memory.

```
__global__ void Convo(float2 *odata1, float2 *odata2,
                      int id, int nx, int ny)
{
  // TW is the logical tile width (40 elements).
  // TH is the logical tile height (24 elements).
  // RW is the tile width including the filter support region.
  // IT is the number of input elements per thread (4).
  // OT is the number of output elements per thread (3).
  // FR is the convolution filter radius (4 elements).

  // Compute local and global thread locations.
  int ltidx = threadIdx.x;
  int ltidy = threadIdx.y * IT;
  int gtidx = blockIdx.x * TW + ltidx - FR;
  int gtidy = blockIdx.y * TH + ltidy - FR;
  int tltid = ltidy * RW + ltidx;

  float2 term;
  int i;
  // Each thread reads 4 input values from global memory.
  // The loop is for clarity and should be unrolled for efficiency.
  for (i = 0; i < 4; i++) {
    term = texfetch(itexref, gtidx, gtidy + i);
    smem[tltid     ] = term.x;
    smem[tltid + IO] = term.y;
    tltid += RW;
  }

  __syncthreads();

  // Each thread compute results for 3 output values.
  if (ltidx < TW) {
    int rtlt = (threadIdx.y * OT + FR) * RW + (ltidx + FR);
    int itlt = rtlt + IO;
    int gthx = blockIdx.x * TW + ltidx;
    int gthy = blockIdx.y * TH + threadIdx.y * OT;
    int rind = gthy * nx + gthx;
    int index;
    float vel, floorvel, residus;
    float2 term0, term1, temp, temp2;
```

```
// Compute one element for 3 consecutive lines.
if (gthx < nx) {
  // The loop is for clarity and should be unrolled for efficiency.
  for (i = 0; i < 3; i++) {
    if (gthy < ny) {
      temp    = texfetch(otexref, gthx , gthy);
      temp.x = (smem[rtlt-    4] + smem[rtlt+    4])*coeff_X[4] +
               (smem[rtlt-    3] + smem[rtlt+    3])*coeff_X[3] +
               (smem[rtlt-    2] + smem[rtlt+    2])*coeff_X[2] +
               (smem[rtlt-    1] + smem[rtlt+    1])*coeff_X[1] +
               (smem[rtlt-4*RW] + smem[rtlt+4*RW])*coeff_Y[4] +
               (smem[rtlt-3*RW] + smem[rtlt+3*RW])*coeff_Y[3] +
               (smem[rtlt-2*RW] + smem[rtlt+2*RW])*coeff_Y[2] +
               (smem[rtlt-  RW] + smem[rtlt+  RW])*coeff_Y[1] +
                smem[rtlt      ]*(coeff_X[0]+coeff_Y[0]) - temp.x;
      temp.y = (smem[itlt-    4] + smem[itlt+    4])*coeff_X[4] +
               (smem[itlt-    3] + smem[itlt+    3])*coeff_X[3] +
               (smem[itlt-    2] + smem[itlt+    2])*coeff_X[2] +
               (smem[itlt-    1] + smem[itlt+    1])*coeff_X[1] +
               (smem[itlt-4*RW] + smem[itlt+4*RW])*coeff_Y[4] +
               (smem[itlt-3*RW] + smem[itlt+3*RW])*coeff_Y[3] +
               (smem[itlt-2*RW] + smem[itlt+2*RW])*coeff_Y[2] +
               (smem[itlt-  RW] + smem[itlt+  RW])*coeff_Y[1] +
                smem[itlt      ]*(coeff_X[0]+coeff_Y[0]) - temp.y;
      vel      = texfetch(vtexref, gthx, gthy);
      floorvel = floorf(vel);
      index    = floorvel;
      term0    = texfetch(ltexref, index, id);
      term1    = texfetch(ltexref, index + 1, id);
      residus  = vel - floorvel;
      term0.x  = term0.x + residus*(term1.x - term0.x);
      term0.y  = term0.y + residus*(term1.y - term0.y);
      temp2    = texfetch(olktexref, gthx, gthy);
      temp2.x += term0.x*temp.x - term0.y*temp.y;
      temp2.y += term0.x*temp.y + term0.y*temp.x;
      odata1[rind] = temp2;
      odata2[rind] = temp;
    }
    rtlt += RW; itlt += RW;
    gthy++; rind += nx;
  }
 }
 }
 }
}
```

38.5 Performance

Because of its strategic importance, our wave migration system uses highly optimized CPU code, especially on Intel platforms. Therefore, our GPU-to-CPU performance comparison uses a solid reference on the CPU. However, it should be noted that, because CPU performance for this algorithm does not scale linearly with the number of cores (mainly because of memory access bottlenecks), we compare our GPU kernel to a latest-generation CPU with only one core enabled.

Using a synthetic data set with typical input parameters, our CUDA kernels achieve performance ranging from 8× to 15× over the optimized CPU code. In addition, the kernels perform equally well on real seismic data sets, where the CUDA code is fully integrated into our industrial processing sequence. However, it is important to note that we have not tested the GPU implementation with the full range of input parameters used with the CPU version. The main reason is that the GPU code is designed for a specific problem size and thread configuration, while the CPU can more easily adapt to different kinds of user parameters and data characteristics. Even still, the GPU performance is a significant improvement by any measure.

Including all the kernels in the industrial parallel application is an ongoing process, and many issues still remain to be solved. The algorithm is so time-consuming that even with a speedup of 15×, a few graphics cards will not meet our processing needs. A cluster solution is mandatory, and on the hardware side, the question of how to design a cluster including GPUs is still open. What speedup the overall application will finally achieve and for what hardware price is our main strategic concern for the future.

38.6 Conclusion

With NVIDIA's CUDA technology, we now have access to a powerful data-parallel programming model and language for exploring scientific computing on the GPU. Once mastered, the flexibility of CUDA can be a real advantage when considering the huge variability of algorithm behavior and data size within the scientific domain. Most important, the CUDA implementation of our most expensive seismic algorithm is more than an order of magnitude faster than its CPU version.

In the long term, CPUs are expected to continue to follow Moore's Law due to the rise of multicore architectures, while GPUs should be able to roughly double in floating-point performance twice a year. Another attractive aspect of GPUs is their fast memory, which outperforms the regular DDR or FBDIMM memory typically used by CPUs.

This proved to be very important for all of our algorithms, because they are already memory limited on the normal cluster solution. The main drawback with GPUs is the transfer speed through PCIe, and bus performance is not expected to increase as rapidly as GPU performance.

There are several factors to consider before building a GPU-based seismic processing cluster. First, it is simply not practical to deploy a large-scale cluster built with racked workstations, because it is neither dense enough nor cost-effective. At this point, two paths can be explored: (1) Classical 1U servers with PCIe slots and a companion external package (such as NVIDIA's Quadro Plex) containing the GPUs or (2) a form factor that includes one or more GPUs on the motherboard. Second, because GPUs need CPUs for control, it's important to choose CPUs for each node that are powerful enough to manage the GPU without becoming a bottleneck. Also, there is the issue of whether PCIe bandwidth is enough to drive one or more GPUs per cluster node. Finally, given the scale and processing time of our algorithms, fault-tolerant hardware is critical in order to recover from failures and avoid wasting days of processing time. Future generations of GPUs will need this feature to be viable for inclusion in our processing centers.

Although there are many open questions about how graphics processors can be used in a large-scale cluster, our work in this chapter shows that GPUs definitely have the potential to disrupt the current seismic processing ecosystem.

38.7 References

Hall, D. 1991. "3-D Depth Migration via McClellan Transforms." *Geophysics* 36, pp. 99–114.

Sherifs, R. E., ed. 1984. *Encyclopedic Dictionary of Exploration Geophysics*. Society of Exploration Geophysicists.

Soubaras, R. 1996. "Explicit 3-D Migration Using Equiripple Polynomial Expansion and Laplacian Synthesis." *Geophysics* 61, pp. 1386–1393.

Yilmaz, O. 2001. *Seismic Data Analysis: Processing, Inversion, and Interpretation of Seismic Data (Investigations in Geophysics, No. 10)*. Society of Exploration Geophysicists.

Chapter 39

Parallel Prefix Sum (Scan) with CUDA

Mark Harris
NVIDIA Corporation

Shubhabrata Sengupta
University of California, Davis

John D. Owens
University of California, Davis

39.1 Introduction

A simple and common parallel algorithm building block is the *all-prefix-sums* operation. In this chapter, we define and illustrate the operation, and we discuss in detail its efficient implementation using NVIDIA CUDA. Blelloch (1990) describes all-prefix-sums as a good example of a computation that seems inherently sequential, but for which there is an efficient parallel algorithm. He defines the all-prefix-sums operation as follows:

The all-prefix-sums operation takes a binary associative operator $\oplus$ with identity I, and an array of n elements

$$[a_0, a_1, \ldots, a_{n-1}],$$

and returns the array

$$[I, a_0, (a_0 \oplus a_1), \ldots, (a_0 \oplus a_1 \oplus \ldots \oplus a_{n-2})].$$

For example, if $\oplus$ is addition, then the all-prefix-sums operation on the array

$$[3\ 1\ 7\ 0\ 4\ 1\ 6\ 3]$$

would return

$$[0\ 3\ 4\ 11\ 11\ 15\ 16\ 22].$$

The all-prefix-sums operation on an array of data is commonly known as *scan*. We use this simpler terminology (which comes from the APL programming language [Iverson 1962]) for the remainder of this chapter. The scan just defined is an *exclusive* scan, because each element *j* of the result is the sum of all elements up to but *not including j* in the input array. In an *inclusive* scan, all elements *including j* are summed. An exclusive scan can be generated from an inclusive scan by shifting the resulting array right by one element and inserting the identity. Likewise, an inclusive scan can be generated from an exclusive scan by shifting the resulting array left and inserting at the end the sum of the last element of the scan and the last element of the input array (Blelloch 1990). For the remainder of this chapter, we focus on the implementation of exclusive scan and refer to it simply as "scan" unless otherwise specified.

There are many uses for scan, including, but not limited to, sorting, lexical analysis, string comparison, polynomial evaluation, stream compaction, and building histograms and data structures (graphs, trees, and so on) in parallel. For example applications, we refer the reader to the survey by Blelloch (1990). In this chapter, we cover summed-area tables (used for variable-width image filtering), stream compaction, and radix sort.

In general, all-prefix-sums can be used to convert certain sequential computations into equivalent, but parallel, computations, as shown in Figure 39-1.

Sequential	Parallel
`out[0] = 0;`	`forall j in parallel do`
`for j from 1 to n do`	`    temp[j] = f(in[j]);`
`    out[j] = out[j-1] + f(in[j-1]);`	`all_prefix_sums(out, temp);`

Figure 39-1. A Sequential Computation and Its Parallel Equivalent

39.1.1 Sequential Scan and Work Efficiency

Implementing a sequential version of scan (that could be run in a single thread on a CPU, for example) is trivial. We simply loop over all the elements in the input array and add the value of the previous element of the input array to the sum computed for the previous element of the output array, and write the sum to the current element of the output array.

```
out[0] := 0
for k := 1 to n do
    out[k] := in[k-1] + out[k-1]
```

This code performs exactly n adds for an array of length n; this is the minimum number of adds required to produce the scanned array. When we develop our parallel version of scan, we would like it to be *work-efficient*. A parallel computation is work-efficient if it does asymptotically no more work (add operations, in this case) than the sequential version. In other words the two implementations should have the same *work complexity*, $O(n)$.

39.2 Implementation

The sequential scan algorithm is poorly suited to GPUs because it does not take advantage of the GPU's data parallelism. We would like to find a parallel version of scan that can utilize the parallel processors of a GPU to speed up its computation. In this section we work through the CUDA implementation of a parallel scan algorithm. We start by introducing a simple but inefficient implementation and then present improvements to both the algorithm and the implementation in CUDA.

39.2.1 A Naive Parallel Scan

The pseudocode in Algorithm 1 shows a first attempt at a parallel scan. This algorithm is based on the scan algorithm presented by Hillis and Steele (1986) and demonstrated for GPUs by Horn (2005). Figure 39-2 illustrates the operation. The problem with Algorithm 1 is apparent if we examine its work complexity. The algorithm performs $O(n \log_2 n)$ addition operations. Remember that a sequential scan performs $O(n)$ adds. Therefore, this naive implementation is not work-efficient. The factor of $\log_2 n$ can have a large effect on performance.

Algorithm 1. A Sum Scan Algorithm That Is Not Work-Efficient

```
1:  for d = 1 to log₂ n do
2:      for all k in parallel do
3:          if k ≥ 2ᵈ then
4:              x[k] = x[k − 2ᵈ⁻¹] + x[k]
```

Algorithm 1 assumes that there are as many processors as data elements. For large arrays on a GPU running CUDA, this is not usually the case. Instead, the programmer must divide the computation among a number of *thread blocks* that each scans a portion of the array on a single multiprocessor of the GPU. Even still, the number of processors in a multiprocessor is typically much smaller than the number of threads per block, so the hardware automatically partitions the "for all" statement into small parallel batches

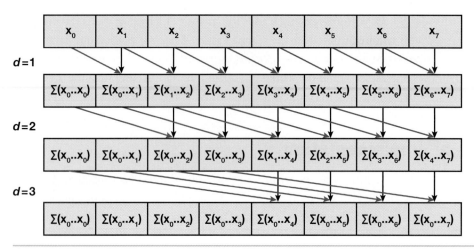

Figure 39-2. The Naive Scan of Algorithm 1
Performing a scan of n elements using O(n log n) add operations. It is demonstrated here on an array of eight elements.

(called *warps*) that are executed sequentially on the multiprocessor. An NVIDIA 8 Series GPU executes warps of 32 threads in parallel. Because not all threads run simultaneously for arrays larger than the warp size, Algorithm 1 will not work, because it performs the scan in place on the array. The results of one warp will be overwritten by threads in another warp.

To solve this problem, we need to double-buffer the array we are scanning using two temporary arrays. Pseudocode for this is given in Algorithm 2, and CUDA C code for the naive scan is given in Listing 39-1. Note that this code will run on only a single thread block of the GPU, and so the size of the arrays it can process is limited (to 512 elements on NVIDIA 8 Series GPUs). Extension of scan to large arrays is discussed in Section 39.2.4.

Algorithm 2. A Double-Buffered Version of the Sum Scan from Algorithm 1

1: **for** $d = 1$ to $\log_2 n$ **do**
2:     **for all** k in parallel **do**
3:         **if** $k \geq 2^d$ **then**
4:             $x[out][k] = x[in][k - 2^{d-1}] + x[in][k]$
5:         **else**
6:             $x[out][k] = x[in][k]$

Listing 39-1. CUDA C Code for the Naive Scan Algorithm

This version can handle arrays only as large as can be processed by a single thread block running on one multiprocessor of a GPU.

```
__global__ void scan(float *g_odata, float *g_idata, int n)
{
  extern __shared__ float temp[]; // allocated on invocation
  int thid = threadIdx.x;
  int pout = 0, pin = 1;
  // Load input into shared memory.
  // This is exclusive scan, so shift right by one
  // and set first element to 0
  temp[pout*n + thid] = (thid > 0) ? g_idata[thid-1] : 0;
  __syncthreads();
  for (int offset = 1; offset < n; offset *= 2)
  {
    pout = 1 - pout; // swap double buffer indices
    pin = 1 - pout;
    if (thid >= offset)
      temp[pout*n+thid] += temp[pin*n+thid - offset];
    else
      temp[pout*n+thid] = temp[pin*n+thid];
    __syncthreads();
  }
  g_odata[thid] = temp[pout*n+thid1]; // write output
}
```

39.2.2 A Work-Efficient Parallel Scan

Our implementation of scan from Section 39.2.1 would probably perform very badly on large arrays due to its work-inefficiency. We would like to find an algorithm that would approach the efficiency of the sequential algorithm, while still taking advantage of the parallelism in the GPU. Our goal in this section is to develop a work-efficient scan algorithm for CUDA that avoids the extra factor of $\log_2 n$ work performed by the naive algorithm. This algorithm is based on the one presented by Blelloch (1990). To do this we will use an algorithmic pattern that arises often in parallel computing: *balanced trees*. The idea is to build a balanced binary tree on the input data and sweep it to and from the root to compute the prefix sum. A binary tree with n leaves has $d = \log_2 n$

levels, and each level d has 2^d nodes. If we perform one add per node, then we will perform $O(n)$ adds on a single traversal of the tree.

The tree we build is not an actual data structure, but a concept we use to determine what each thread does at each step of the traversal. In this work-efficient scan algorithm, we perform the operations in place on an array in shared memory. The algorithm consists of two phases: the *reduce phase* (also known as the *up-sweep phase*) and the *down-sweep phase*. In the reduce phase, we traverse the tree from leaves to root computing partial sums at internal nodes of the tree, as shown in Figure 39-3. This is also known as a parallel reduction, because after this phase, the root node (the last node in the array) holds the sum of all nodes in the array. Pseudocode for the reduce phase is given in Algorithm 3.

Algorithm 3. The Up-Sweep (Reduce) Phase of a Work-Efficient Sum Scan Algorithm (After Blelloch 1990)

1: **for** $d = 0$ to $\log_2 n - 1$ **do**
2:     **for all** $k = 0$ to $n - 1$ by 2^{d+1} in parallel **do**
3:         $x[k + 2^{d+1} - 1] = x[k + 2^d - 1] + x[k + 2^{d+1} - 1]$

In the down-sweep phase, we traverse back down the tree from the root, using the partial sums from the reduce phase to build the scan in place on the array. We start by inserting zero at the root of the tree, and on each step, each node at the current level passes its own value to its left child, and the sum of its value and the former value of its left child to its right child. The down-sweep is shown in Figure 39-4, and pseudocode is given in Algorithm 4. CUDA C code for the complete algorithm is given in Listing 39-2. Like the naive scan code in Section 39.2.1, the code in Listing 39-2 will run on only a single

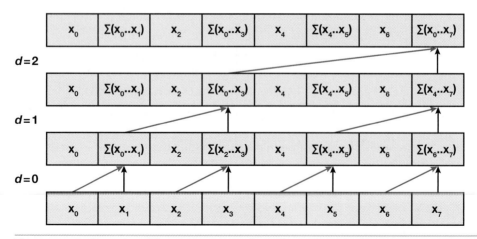

Figure 39-3. An Illustration of the Up-Sweep, or Reduce, Phase of a Work-Efficient Sum Scan Algorithm

thread block. Because it processes two elements per thread, the maximum array size this code can scan is 1,024 elements on an NVIDIA 8 Series GPU. Scans of larger arrays are discussed in Section 39.2.4.

Algorithm 4. The Down-Sweep Phase of a Work-Efficient Parallel Sum Scan Algorithm (After Blelloch 1990)

1: $x[n - 1] \leftarrow 0$
2: **for** $d = \log_2 n - 1$ down to 0 **do**
3:     **for all** $k = 0$ to $n - 1$ by 2^{d+1} in parallel **do**
4:         $t = x[k + 2^d - 1]$
5:         $x[k + 2^d - 1] = x[k + 2^{d+1} - 1]$
6:         $x[k + 2^{d+1} - 1] = t + x[k + 2^{d+1} - 1]$

The scan algorithm in Algorithm 4 performs $O(n)$ operations (it performs $2 \times (n - 1)$ adds and $n - 1$ swaps); therefore it is work-efficient and, for large arrays, should perform much better than the naive algorithm from the previous section. Algorithmic efficiency is not enough; we must also use the hardware efficiently. If we examine the operation of this scan on a GPU running CUDA, we will find that it suffers from many shared memory bank conflicts. These hurt the performance of every access to shared memory and significantly affect overall performance. In the next section, we look at some simple modifications we can make to the memory address computations to recover much of that lost performance.

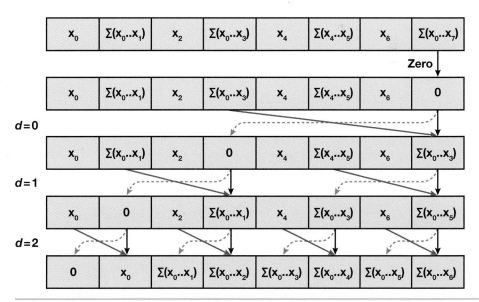

Figure 39-4. An Illustration of the Down-Sweep Phase of the Work-Efficient Parallel Sum Scan Algorithm
Notice that the first step zeroes the last element of the array.

Listing 39-2. CUDA C Code for the Work-Efficient Sum Scan of Algorithms 3 and 4.

The highlighted blocks are discussed in Section 39.2.3.

```
__global__ void prescan(float *g_odata, float *g_idata, int n)
{
    extern __shared__ float temp[]; // allocated on invocation
    int thid = threadIdx.x;
    int offset = 1;
```
A
```
    temp[2*thid] = g_idata[2*thid]; // load input into shared memory
    temp[2*thid+1] = g_idata[2*thid+1];
    for (int d = n>>1; d > 0; d >>= 1) // build sum in place up the tree
    {
        __syncthreads();
        if (thid < d)
        {
```
B
```
            int ai = offset*(2*thid+1)-1;
            int bi = offset*(2*thid+2)-1;
            temp[bi] += temp[ai];
        }
        offset *= 2;
    }
```
C
```
    if (thid == 0) { temp[n - 1] = 0; } // clear the last element
    for (int d = 1; d < n; d *= 2) // traverse down tree & build scan
    {
        offset >>= 1;
        __syncthreads();
        if (thid < d)
        {
```
D
```
            int ai = offset*(2*thid+1)-1;
            int bi = offset*(2*thid+2)-1;
            float t = temp[ai];
            temp[ai] = temp[bi];
            temp[bi] += t;
        }
    }
    __syncthreads();
```
E
```
    g_odata[2*thid] = temp[2*thid]; // write results to device memory
    g_odata[2*thid+1] = temp[2*thid+1];
}
```

39.2.3 Avoiding Bank Conflicts

The scan algorithm of the previous section performs approximately as much work as an optimal sequential algorithm. Despite this work-efficiency, it is not yet efficient on NVIDIA GPU hardware, due to its memory access patterns. As described in the *NVIDIA CUDA Programming Guide* (NVIDIA 2007), the shared memory exploited by this scan algorithm is made up of multiple banks. When multiple threads in the same warp access the same bank, a bank conflict occurs unless all threads of the warp access the same address within the same 32-bit word. The number of threads that access a single bank is called the *degree* of the bank conflict. Bank conflicts cause serialization of the multiple accesses to the memory bank, so that a shared memory access with a degree-n bank conflict requires n times as many cycles to process as an access with no conflict. On NVIDIA 8 Series GPUs, which execute 16 threads in parallel in a half-warp, the worst case is a degree-16 bank conflict.

Binary tree algorithms such as our work-efficient scan double the stride between memory accesses at each level of the tree, simultaneously doubling the number of threads that access the same bank. For deep trees, as we approach the middle levels of the tree, the degree of the bank conflicts increases, and then it decreases again near the root, where the number of active threads decreases (due to the `if` statement in Listing 39-2). For example, if we are scanning a 512-element array, the shared memory reads and writes in the inner loops of Listing 39-2 experience up to 16-way bank conflicts. This has a significant effect on performance.

Bank conflicts are avoidable in most CUDA computations if care is taken when accessing `__shared__` memory arrays. We can avoid most bank conflicts in scan by adding a variable amount of padding to each shared memory array index we compute. Specifically, we add to the index the value of the index divided by the number of shared memory banks. This is demonstrated in Figure 39-5. We start from the work-efficient scan code in Listing 39-2, modifying only the highlighted blocks A through E. To simplify the code changes, we define a macro CONFLICT_FREE_OFFSET, shown in Listing 39-3.

Listing 39-3. Macro Used for Computing Bank-Conflict-Free Shared Memory Array Indices

```
#define NUM_BANKS 16
#define LOG_NUM_BANKS 4

#define CONFLICT_FREE_OFFSET(n) \
    ((n) >> NUM_BANKS + (n) >> (2 * LOG_NUM_BANKS))
```

The blocks A through E in Listing 39-2 need to be modified using this macro to avoid bank conflicts. Two changes must be made to block A. Each thread loads two array elements from the __global__ array g_idata into the __shared__ array temp. In the original code, each thread loads two adjacent elements, resulting in the interleaved indexing of the shared memory array, incurring two-way bank conflicts. By instead loading two elements from separate halves of the array, we avoid these bank conflicts. Also, to avoid bank conflicts during the tree traversal, we need to add padding to the shared memory array every NUM_BANKS (16) elements. We do this using the macro in Listing 39-3 as shown in Listing 39-4. Note that we store the offsets to the shared memory indices so that we can use them again at the end of the scan, when writing the results back to the output array g_odata in block E.

Listing 39-4. Modifications to the Work-Efficient Scan Code to Avoid Shared Memory Bank Conflicts

Block A:
```
int ai = thid;
int bi = thid + (n/2);

int bankOffsetA = CONFLICT_FREE_OFFSET(ai)
int bankOffsetB = CONFLICT_FREE_OFFSET(bi)

temp[ai + bankOffsetA] = g_idata[ai]
temp[bi + bankOffsetB] = g_idata[bi]
```

Blocks B and D are identical:
```
int ai = offset*(2*thid+1)-1;
int bi = offset*(2*thid+2)-1;
ai += CONFLICT_FREE_OFFSET(ai)
bi += CONFLICT_FREE_OFFSET(bi)
```

Block C:
```
if (thid==0) { temp[n - 1 + CONFLICT_FREE_OFFSET(n - 1)] = 0;}
```

Block E:
```
g_odata[ai] = temp[ai + bankOffsetA];
g_odata[bi] = temp[bi + bankOffsetB];
```

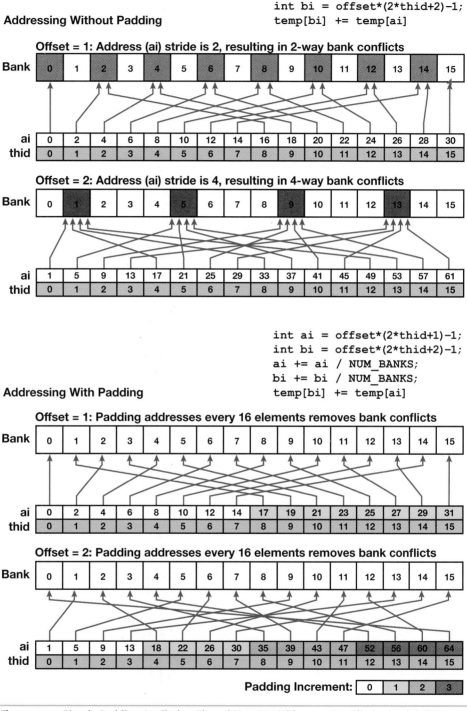

Figure 39-5. Simple Padding Applied to Shared Memory Addresses Can Eliminate High-Degree Bank Conflicts During Tree-Based Algorithms Like Scan
The top of the diagram shows addressing without padding and the resulting bank conflicts. The bottom shows padded addressing with zero bank conflicts.

39.2.4 Arrays of Arbitrary Size

The algorithms given in the previous sections scan an array inside a single thread block. This is fine for small arrays, up to twice the maximum number of threads in a block (since each thread loads and processes two elements). On NVIDIA 8 Series GPUs, this limits us to a maximum of 1,024 elements. Also, the array size must be a power of two. In this section, we explain how to extend the algorithm to scan large arrays of arbitrary (non-power-of-two) dimensions. This algorithm is based on the explanation provided by Blelloch (1990).

The basic idea is simple. We divide the large array into blocks that each can be scanned by a single thread block, and then we scan the blocks and write the total sum of each block to another array of block sums. We then scan the block sums, generating an array of block increments that that are added to all elements in their respective blocks. In more detail, let N be the number of elements in the input array, and B be the number of elements processed in a block. We allocate N/B thread blocks of $B/2$ threads each. (Here we assume that N is a multiple of B, and we extend to arbitrary dimensions in the next paragraph.) A typical choice for B on NVIDIA 8 Series GPUs is 128. We use the scan algorithm of the previous sections to scan each block i independently, storing the resulting scans to sequential locations of the output array. We make one minor modification to the scan algorithm. Before zeroing the last element of block i (the block of code labeled B in Listing 39-2), we store the value (the total sum of block i) to an auxiliary array SUMS. We then scan SUMS in the same manner, writing the result to an array INCR. We then add INCR[i] to all elements of block i using a simple uniform add kernel invoked on N/B thread blocks of $B/2$ threads each. This is demonstrated in Figure 39-6. For details of the implementation, please see the source code available at http://www.gpgpu.org/scan-gpugems3/.

Handling non-power-of-two dimensions is easy. We simply pad the array out to the next multiple of the block size B. The scan algorithm is not dependent on elements past the end of the array, so we don't have to use a special case for the last block.

39.2.5 Further Optimization and Performance Results

After optimizing shared memory accesses, the main bottlenecks left in the scan code are global memory latency and instruction overhead due to looping and address computation instructions. To better cover the global memory access latency and improve overall effi-

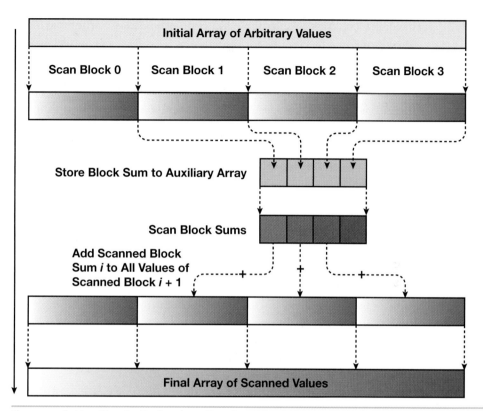

Figure 39-6. Algorithm for Performing a Sum Scan on a Large Array of Values

ciency, we need to do more computation per thread. We employ a technique suggested by David Lichterman, which processes eight elements per thread instead of two by loading two `float4` elements per thread rather than two `float` elements (Lichterman 2007). Each thread performs a sequential scan of each `float4`, stores the first three elements of each scan in registers, and inserts the total sum into the shared memory array. With the partial sums from all threads in shared memory, we perform an identical tree-based scan to the one given in Listing 39-2. Each thread then constructs two `float4` values by adding the corresponding scanned element from shared memory to each of the partial sums stored in registers. Finally, the `float4` values are written to global memory. This approach, which is more than twice as fast as the code given previously, is a consequence of Brent's Theorem and is a common technique for improving the efficiency of parallel algorithms (Quinn 1994).

To reduce bookkeeping and loop instruction overhead, we unroll the loops in Algorithms 3 and 4. Because our block size is fixed, we can completely unroll these loops, greatly reducing the extra instructions required to traverse the tree in a loop.

Our efforts to create an efficient scan implementation in CUDA have paid off. Performance is up to 20 times faster than a sequential version of scan running on a fast CPU, as shown in the graph in Figure 39-7. Also, thanks to the advantages provided by CUDA, we outperform an optimized OpenGL implementation running on the same GPU by up to a factor of seven. The graph also shows the performance we achieve when we use the naive scan implementation from Section 39.2.1 for each block. Because both the naive scan and the work-efficient scan must be divided across blocks of the same number of threads, the performance of the naive scan is slower by a factor of $O(\log_2 B)$, where B is the block size, rather than a factor of $O(\log_2 n)$. Figure 39-8 compares the performance of our best CUDA implementation with versions lacking bank-conflict avoidance and loop unrolling.

The scan implementation discussed in this chapter, along with example applications, is available online at http://www.gpgpu.org/scan-gpugems3/.

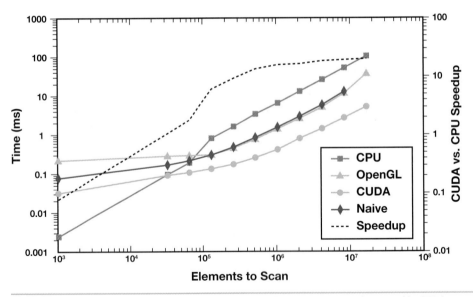

Figure 39-7. Performance of the Work-Efficient, Bank-Conflict-Free Scan Implemented in CUDA Compared to a Sequential Scan Implemented in C++, and a Work-Efficient Implementation in OpenGL
The CUDA and OpenGL scans were executed on an NVIDIA GeForce 8800 GTX GPU, and the sequential scan on a single core of an Intel Core Duo Extreme 2.93 GHz processor.

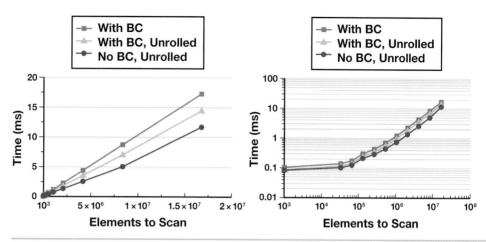

Figure 39-8. Comparison of Performance of the Work-Efficient Scan Implemented in CUDA with Optimizations to Avoid Bank Conflicts and to Unroll Loops
On the left is linear scale, on the right a log scale of the same results. "With BC" is our implementation with bank conflicts. "With BC, Unrolled" is our implementation with bank conflicts and unrolled loops. "No BC, Unrolled" is our bank-conflict-free version with unrolled loops. Both optimizations provide significant speedups: for the 16M-element scan, both optimizations together give a 47 percent speedup. The scans were executed on an NVIDIA GeForce 8800 GTX GPU.

39.2.6 The Advantages of CUDA over the OpenGL Implementation

Prior to the introduction of CUDA, several researchers implemented scan using graphics APIs such as OpenGL and Direct3D (see Section 39.3.4 for more). To demonstrate the advantages CUDA has over these APIs for computations like scan, in this section we briefly describe the work-efficient OpenGL inclusive-scan implementation of Sengupta et al. (2006). Their implementation is a hybrid algorithm that performs a configurable number of reduce steps as shown in Algorithm 5. It then runs the double-buffered version of the sum scan algorithm previously shown in Algorithm 2 on the result of the reduce step. Finally it performs the down-sweep as shown in Algorithm 6.

Algorithm 5. The Reduce Step of the OpenGL Scan Algorithm

```
1:  for d = 1 to log₂ n do
2:      for all k = 1 to n/2ᵈ − 1 in parallel do
3:          a[d][k] = a[d − 1][2k] + a[d − 1][2k + 1]
```

Algorithm 6. The Down-Sweep Step of the OpenGL Scan Algorithm

1: **for** $d = \log_2 n - 1$ down to 0 **do**
2:    **for all** $k = 0$ to $n/2^d - 1$ in parallel **do**
3:       **if** $i > 0$ **then**
4:          **if** $k \bmod 2 \neq 0$ **then**
5:             $a[d][k] = a[d+1][k/2]$
6:          **else**
7:             $a[d][i] = a[d+1][k/2 - 1]$

The OpenGL scan computation is implemented using pixel shaders, and each a [d] array is a two-dimensional texture on the GPU. Writing to these arrays is performed using render-to-texture in OpenGL. Thus, each loop iteration in Algorithm 5 and Algorithm 2 requires reading from one texture and writing to another.

The main advantages CUDA has over OpenGL are its on-chip shared memory, thread synchronization functionality, and scatter writes to memory, which are not exposed to OpenGL pixel shaders. CUDA divides the work of a large scan into many blocks, and each block is processed entirely on-chip by a single multiprocessor before any data is written to off-chip memory. In OpenGL, all memory updates are off-chip memory updates. Thus, the bandwidth used by the OpenGL implementation is much higher and therefore performance is lower, as shown previously in Figure 39-7.

39.3 Applications of Scan

As we described in the introduction, scan has a wide variety of applications. In this section, we cover three applications of scan: stream compaction, summed-area tables, and radix sort.

39.3.1 Stream Compaction

Stream compaction is an important primitive in a variety of general-purpose applications, including collision detection and sparse matrix compression. In fact, stream compaction was the focus of most of the previous GPU work on scan (see Section 39.3.4). Stream compaction is the primary method for transforming a heterogeneous vector, with elements of many types, into homogeneous vectors, in which each element has the same type. This is particularly useful with vectors that have some elements that are interesting and many elements that are not interesting. Stream compaction produces a smaller vector with only interesting elements. With this smaller vector, computation is more efficient, because we compute on only interesting elements, and thus transfer costs, particularly between the GPU and CPU, are potentially greatly reduced.

Informally, stream compaction is a filtering operation: from an input vector, it selects a subset of this vector and packs that subset into a dense output vector. Figure 39-9 shows an example. More formally, stream compaction takes an input vector v_i and a predicate p, and outputs only those elements in v_i for which $p(v_i)$ is true, preserving the ordering of the input elements. Horn (2005) describes this operation in detail.

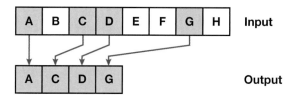

Figure 39-9. Stream Compaction Example
Given an input vector, stream compaction outputs a packed subset of that vector, choosing only the input elements of interest (marked in gray).

Stream compaction requires two steps, a scan and a scatter.

1. The first step generates a temporary vector where the elements that pass the predicate are set to 1 and the other elements are set to 0. We then scan this temporary vector. For each element that passes the predicate, the result of the scan now contains the destination address for that element in the output vector.

2. The second step scatters the input elements to the output vector using the addresses generated by the scan.

Figure 39-10 shows this process in detail.

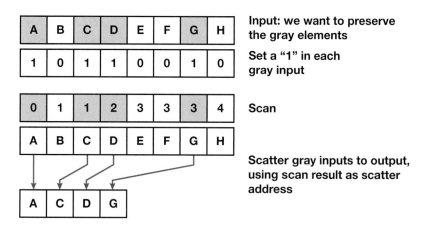

Input: we want to preserve the gray elements

Set a "1" in each gray input

Scan

Scatter gray inputs to output, using scan result as scatter address

Figure 39-10. Scan and Scatter
Stream compaction requires one scan to determine destination addresses and one vector scatter operation to place the input elements into the output vector.

The GPUs on which Horn implemented stream compaction in 2005 did not have scatter capability, so Horn instead substituted a sequence of gather steps to emulate scatter. To compact n elements required $\log n$ gather steps, and while these steps could be implemented in one fragment program, this "gather-search" operation was fairly expensive and required more memory operations. The addition of a native scatter in recent GPUs makes stream compaction considerably more efficient. Performance of our stream compaction test is shown in Figure 39-11.

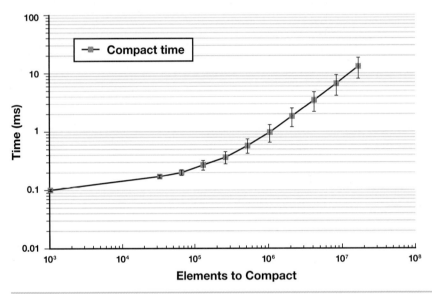

Figure 39-11. Performance of Stream Compaction Implemented in CUDA on an NVIDIA GeForce 8800 GTX GPU
The scattered writes performed by stream compaction result in noncoalesced global memory writes. Therefore performance decreases linearly with an increasing number of compacted elements. The graph shows the mean compaction time for each input size, with error bars showing the minimum (output is 10 percent of input) and the maximum (output is 90 percent of input) compaction time.

39.3.2 Summed-Area Tables

A summed-area table (SAT) is a two-dimensional table generated from an input image in which each entry in the table stores the sum of all pixels between the entry location and the lower-left corner of the input image. Summed-area tables were introduced by Crow (1984), who showed how they can be used to perform arbitrary-width box filters on the input image. The power of the summed-area table comes from the fact that it can be used to perform filters of different widths at every pixel in the image in constant time per pixel. Hensley et al. (2005) demonstrated the use of fast GPU-generated summed-area tables for interactive rendering of glossy environment reflections and refractions. Their implementation on GPUs used a scan operation equivalent to the naive implementation in Section 39.2.1. A work-efficient implementation in CUDA allows us to achieve higher performance. In this section we describe how summed-area tables can be computed using scans in CUDA, and we demonstrate their use in rendering approximate depth of field.

To compute the summed-area table for a two-dimensional image, we simply apply a sum scan to all rows of the image followed by a sum scan of all columns of the result. To do this efficiently in CUDA, we extend our basic implementation of scan to perform many independent scans in parallel. Thanks to the "grid of thread blocks" semantics provided by CUDA, this is easy; we use a two-dimensional grid of thread blocks, scanning one row of the image with each row of the grid. Modifying scan to support this requires modifying only the computation of the global memory indices from which the data to be scanned in each block are read. Extending scan to also support scanning columns would lead to poor performance, because column scans would require large strides through memory between threads, resulting in noncoalesced memory reads (NVIDIA 2007). Instead, we simply transpose the image after scanning the rows, and then scan the rows of the transposed image.

Generating a box-filtered pixel using a summed-area table requires sampling the summed-area table at the four corners of a rectangular filter region, $s_{ur}, s_{ul}, s_{ll}, s_{lr}$. The filtered result is then

$$s_{filter} = \frac{s_{ur} - s_{ul} - s_{lr} + s_{ll}}{w \times h},$$

where w and h are the width and height of the filter kernel, and s_{ur} is the upper-right corner sample, s_{ll} is the lower-left corner sample, and so on (Crow 1977). We can use this technique for variable-width filtering, by varying the locations of the four samples we use to compute each filtered output pixel.

Figure 39-12 shows a simple scene rendered with approximate depth of field, so that objects far from the focal length are blurry, while objects at the focal length are in focus. In the first pass, we render the teapots and generate a summed-area table in CUDA from the rendered image using the technique just described. In the second pass, we render a full-screen quad with a shader that samples the depth buffer from the first pass and uses the depth to compute a blur factor that modulates the width of the filter kernel. This determines the locations of the four samples taken from the summed-area table at each pixel.

Figure 39-12. Approximate Depth of Field Rendered by Using a Summed-Area Table to Apply a Variable-Size Blur to the Image Based on the Depth of Each Pixel
Notice that the first, third, and fourth closest teapots are blurry, while the second closest teapot is in focus.

Rather than write a custom scan algorithm to process RGB images, we decided to use our existing code along with a few additional simple kernels. Computing the SAT of an RGB8 input image requires four steps. First we de-interleave the RGB8 image into three separate floating-point arrays (one for each color channel). Next we scan all rows of each array in parallel. Then the arrays must be transposed and all rows scanned again (to scan the columns). This is a total of six scans of *width* × *height* elements each. Finally, the three individual summed-area tables are interleaved into the RGB channels of a 32-bit floating-point RGBA image. Note that we don't need to transpose the image again, because we can simply transpose the coordinates we use to look up into it. Table 39-1 shows the time spent on each of these computations for two image sizes.

Table 39-1. Performance of Our Summed-Area Table Implementation on an NVIDIA GeForce 8800 GTX GPU for Two Different Image Sizes

Resolution	(De)interleave (ms)	Transpose (ms)	6 Scans (ms)	Total (ms)
512×512	0.44	0.23	0.97	1.64
1024×1024	0.96	0.84	1.70	3.50

39.3.3 Radix Sort

Previous GPU-based sorting routines have primarily used variants of bitonic sort (Govindaraju et al. 2006, Greß and Zachmann 2006), an efficient, oblivious sorting algorithm for parallel processors. The scan primitive can be used as a building block for another efficient sorting algorithm on the GPU, *radix sort*.

Our implementation first uses radix sort to sort individual chunks of the input array. Chunks are sorted in parallel by multiple thread blocks. Chunks are as large as can fit into the shared memory of a single multiprocessor on the GPU. After sorting the chunks, we use a parallel bitonic merge to combine pairs of chunks into one. This merge is repeated until a single sorted array is produced.

Step 1: Radix Sort Chunks

Radix sort is particularly well suited for small sort keys, such as small integers, that can be expressed with a small number of bits. At a high level, radix sort works as follows. We begin by considering one bit from each key, starting with the least-significant bit. Using this bit, we partition the keys so that all keys with a 0 in that bit are placed before all keys with a 1 in that bit, otherwise keeping the keys in their original order. See Figure 39-13. We then move to the next least-significant bit and repeat the process.

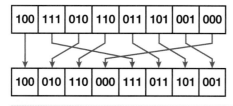

Figure 39-13. Radix Sort
The split *operation permutes its input such that the "false" elements are packed to the left of the output and the "true" elements are packed to the right. Here we split the input based on the value of the least-significant bit.*

Thus for *k*-bit keys, radix sort requires *k* steps. Our implementation requires one scan per step.

The fundamental primitive we use to implement each step of radix sort is the `split` primitive. The input to `split` is a list of sort keys and their bit value b of interest on this step, either a true or false. The output is a new list of sort keys, with all false sort keys packed before all true sort keys.

We implement `split` on the GPU in the following way, as shown in Figure 39-14.

1. In a temporary buffer in shared memory, we set a 1 for all false sort keys (b = 0) and a 0 for all true sort keys.

2. We then scan this buffer. This is the `enumerate` operation; each false sort key now contains its destination address in the scan output, which we will call f. These first two steps are equivalent to a stream compaction operation on all false sort keys.

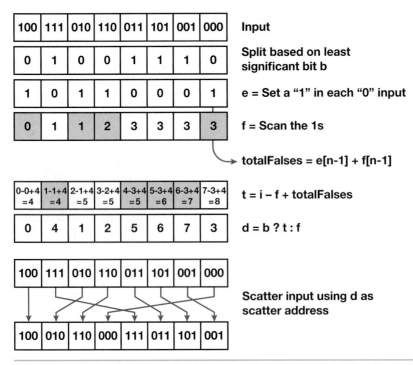

Figure 39-14. The `split` Operation Requires a Single Scan and Runs in Linear Time with the Number of Input Elements

3. The last element in the scan's output now contains the total number of false sort keys.[1] We write this value to a shared variable, `totalFalses`.

4. Now we compute the destination address for the true sort keys. For a sort key at index i, this address is `t = i - f + totalFalses`. We then select between `t` and `f` depending on the value of `b` to get the destination address `d` of each fragment.

5. Finally, we scatter the original sort keys to destination address `d`. The scatter pattern is a perfect permutation of the input, so we see no write conflicts with this scatter.

With `split`, we can easily implement radix sort. We begin by loading a block-size chunk of input from global memory into shared memory. We then initialize our current bit to the least-significant bit of the key, split based on the key, check if the output is sorted, and if not shift the current bit left by one and iterate again. When we are done, we copy the sorted data back to global memory. With large inputs, each chunk is mapped to a thread block and runs in parallel with the other chunks.

Step 2: Merge Sorted Chunks

After each block-size chunk is sorted, we use a recursive merge sort to combine two sorted chunks into one sorted chunk. If we have b sorted chunks of size n, we require $\log_2 b$ steps of merge to get one final sorted output at the end. On the first step, we perform $b/2$ merges in parallel, each on two n-element sorted streams of input and producing $2n$ sorted elements of output. On the next step, we do $b/4$ merges in parallel, each on two $2n$-element sorted streams of input and producing $4n$ sorted elements of output, and so on.

Our merge kernel must therefore operate on two inputs of arbitrary length located in GPU main memory. At a high level, our implementation keeps two buffers in shared memory, one for each input, and uses a parallel bitonic sort to merge the smallest elements from each buffer. It then refills the buffers from main memory if necessary, and repeats until both inputs are exhausted. All reads from global memory into shared memory and all writes to global memory are coherent and blocked; we also guarantee that each input element is read only once from global memory and each output element is written only once.

In our merge kernel, we run p threads in parallel. The most interesting part of our implementation is the computation and sorting of the p smallest elements from two sorted sequences in the input buffers. Figure 39-15 shows this process. For p elements, the output of the pairwise parallel comparison between the two sorted sequences is bitonic and can thus be efficiently sorted with $\log_2 p$ parallel operations.

---

1. Actually, we have to add an additional 1 to this value if the last sort key was false.

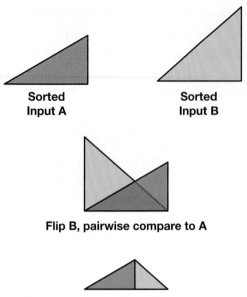

Sorted Input A

Sorted Input B

Flip B, pairwise compare to A

Smallest element in each comparison yields smallest p elements overall in a bitonic sequence

Figure 39-15. Merging Two Sorted Subsequences into One Sorted Sequence Is an Efficient Operation
The second sequence is flipped and compared against the first sequence in parallel; the smallest element from each comparison will be included in the output. The result of the parallel comparison is bitonic and can be sorted efficiently.

39.3.4 Previous Work

Scan was first proposed in the mid-1950s by Iverson as part of the APL programming language (Iverson 1962). Blelloch was one of the primary researchers to develop efficient algorithms using the scan primitive (Blelloch 1990), including the scan-based radix sort described in this chapter (Blelloch 1989).

On the GPU, the first published scan work was Horn's 2005 implementation (Horn 2005). Horn's scan was used as a building block for a nonuniform stream compaction operation, which was then used in a collision-detection application. Horn's scan implementation had $O(n \log n)$ work complexity. Hensley et al. (2005) used scan for summed-area-table generation later that year, improving the overall efficiency of Horn's implementation by pruning unnecessary work. Like Horn's, however, the overall work complexity of Hensley et al.'s technique was also $O(n \log n)$.

The first published $O(n)$ implementation of scan on the GPU was that of Sengupta et al. (2006), also used for stream compaction. They showed that a hybrid work-efficient ($O(n)$ operations with $2n$ steps) and step-efficient ($O(n \log n)$ operations with n steps) implementation had the best performance on GPUs such as NVIDIA's GeForce 7 Series. Sengupta et al.'s implementation was used in a hierarchical shadow map algorithm to compact a stream of shadow pages, some of which required refinement and some of which did not, into a stream of only the shadow pages that required refinement. Later that year, Greß et al. (2006) also presented an $O(n)$ scan implementation for stream compaction in the context of a GPU-based collision detection application. Unlike previous GPU-based 1D scan implementations, Greß et al.'s application required a 2D stream reduction, which resulted in fewer steps overall. Greß et al. also used their scan implementation for stream compaction, in this case computing a stream of valid overlapping pairs of colliding elements from a larger stream of potentially overlapping pairs of colliding elements.

39.4 Conclusion

The scan operation is a simple and powerful parallel primitive with a broad range of applications. In this chapter we have explained an efficient implementation of scan using CUDA, which achieves a significant speedup compared to a sequential implementation on a fast CPU, and compared to a parallel implementation in OpenGL on the same GPU. Due to the increasing power of commodity parallel processors such as GPUs, we expect to see data-parallel algorithms such as scan to increase in importance over the coming years.

39.5 References

Blelloch, Guy E. 1989. "Scans as Primitive Parallel Operations." *IEEE Transactions on Computers* 38(11), pp. 1526–1538.

Blelloch, Guy E. 1990. "Prefix Sums and Their Applications." Technical Report CMU-CS-90-190, School of Computer Science, Carnegie Mellon University.

Crow, Franklin. 1984. "Summed-Area Tables for Texture Mapping." In *Computer Graphics (Proceedings of SIGGRAPH 1984)* 18(3), pp. 207–212.

Govindaraju, Naga K., Jim Gray, Ritesh Kumar, and Dinesh Manocha. 2006. "GPUTeraSort: High Performance Graphics Coprocessor Sorting for Large Database Management." In *Proceedings of the 2006 ACM SIGMOD International Conference on Management of Data*, pp. 325–336.

Greß, Alexander, and Gabriel Zachmann. 2006. "GPU-ABiSort: Optimal Parallel Sorting on Stream Architectures." In *Proceedings of the 20th IEEE International Parallel and Distributed Processing Symposium*.

Greß, Alexander, Michael Guthe, and Reinhard Klein. 2006. "GPU-Based Collision Detection for Deformable Parameterized Surfaces." *Computer Graphics Forum* 25(3), pp. 497–506.

Hensley, Justin, Thorsten Scheuermann, Greg Coombe, Montek Singh, and Anselmo Lastra. 2005. "Fast Summed-Area Table Generation and Its Applications." *Computer Graphics Forum* 24(3), pp. 547–555.

Hillis, W. Daniel, and Guy L. Steele, Jr. 1986. "Data Parallel Algorithms." *Communications of the ACM* 29(12), pp. 1170–1183.

Horn, Daniel. 2005. "Stream Reduction Operations for GPGPU Applications." In *GPU Gems 2*, edited by Matt Pharr, pp. 573–589. Addison-Wesley.

Iverson, Kenneth E. 1962. *A Programming Language*. Wiley.

Lichterman, David. 2007. Course project for UIUC ECE 498 AL: Programming Massively Parallel Processors. Wen-Mei Hwu and David Kirk, instructors. http://courses.ece.uiuc.edu/ece498/al/.

NVIDIA Corporation. 2007. *NVIDIA CUDA Compute Unified Device Architecture Programming Guide*. Version 0.8.1.

Quinn, Michael J. 1994. *Parallel Computing: Theory and Practice*, 2nd ed. McGraw-Hill.

Sengupta, Shubhabrata, Aaron E. Lefohn, and John D. Owens. 2006. "A Work-Efficient Step-Efficient Prefix Sum Algorithm." In *Proceedings of the Workshop on Edge Computing Using New Commodity Architectures*, pp. D-26–27.

Chapter 40

Incremental Computation of the Gaussian

Ken Turkowski
Adobe Systems

We present an incremental method for computing the Gaussian at a sequence of regularly spaced points, with the cost of one vector multiplication per point. This technique can be used to implement image blurring by generating the Gaussian coefficients on the fly, avoiding an extra texture lookup into a table of precomputed coefficients.

40.1 Introduction and Related Work

Filtering is a common operation performed on images and other kinds of data in order to smooth results or attenuate noise. Usually the filtering is linear and can be expressed as a convolution:

$$b_k = \sum_{i=-N}^{N} a_{k-i} h_i, \tag{1}$$

where a_i is an input sequence, b_i is an output sequence, and h_i is the *kernel* of the convolution.

One of the most popular filtering kernels is the Gaussian:

$$G(x) = e^{-\frac{x^2}{2\sigma^2}}, \tag{2}$$

where σ is a parameter that controls its width. Figure 40-1 shows a graph of this function for $\sigma = 1$.

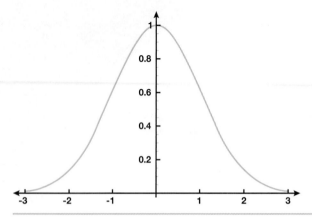

Figure 40-1. Gaussian with $\sigma = 1.0$

When used for images in 2D, this function is both separable and radially symmetric:

$$H(x,\ y) = e^{-\frac{x^2+y^2}{2\sigma^2}} = G(x)G(y) = G\left(\sqrt{x^2 + y^2}\right). \tag{3}$$

We can take advantage of this symmetry to considerably reduce the complexity of the computations.

Gaussian blurring has a lot of uses in computer graphics, image processing, and computer vision, and the performance can be enhanced by utilizing a GPU, because the GPU is well suited to image processing (Jargstorff 2004). The fragment shader for such a computation is shown in Listing 40-1.

In Listing 40-1, acc implements the summation in Equation 1, coeff is one of the coefficients h_i in the kernel of the convolution, texture2D() is the input sequence a_{k-i}, and gl_FragColor is one element of the output sequence b_k.

The coefficient computations involve some relatively expensive operations (an exponential and a division), as well as some cheaper multiplications. The expensive operations can dominate the computation time in the inner loop. An experienced practitioner can reduce the coefficient computations to

```
coeff = exp(-u * u);
```

but still, there is the exponential computation on every pixel.

One approach to overcome these expensive computations would be to precompute the coefficients and look them up in a texture. However, there are already two other texture fetches in the inner loop, and we would prefer to do some computations while waiting for the memory requests to be fulfilled.

Chapter 40 Incremental Computation of the Gaussian

Listing 40-1.

```
uniform sampler2D inImg;    // source image
uniform float     sigma;    // Gaussian sigma
uniform float     norm;     // normalization, e.g. 1/(sqrt(2*PI)*sigma)
uniform vec2      dir;      // horiz=(1.0, 0.0), vert=(0.0, 1.0)
uniform int       support;  // int(sigma * 3.0) truncation
void main()
{
  vec2 loc = gl_FragCoord.xy;      // center pixel cooordinate
  vec4 acc;                        // accumulator
  acc = texture2D(inImg, loc);     // accumulate center pixel
  for (i = 1; i <= support; i++) {
    float coeff = exp(-0.5 * float(i) * float(i) / (sigma * sigma));
    acc += (texture2D(inImg, loc - float(i) * dir)) * coeff; // L
    acc += (texture2D(inImg, loc + float(i) * dir)) * coeff; // R
  }
  acc *= norm;                     // normalize for unity gain
  gl_fragColor = acc;
}
```

Another approach would be to compute the Gaussian using one of several polynomial or rational polynomial approximations that are chosen based on the range of the argument. However, range comparisons are inefficient on a GPU, and the table of polynomial coefficients would most likely need to be stored in a texture, so this is less advantageous than the previous approach.

Our approach is to compute the coefficients *on the fly*, taking advantage of the coherence between adjacent samples to perform the computations *incrementally* with a small number of simple instructions. The technique is analogous to polynomial forward differencing, so we take a moment to describe that technique first.

40.2 Polynomial Forward Differencing

Suppose we wish to evaluate a polynomial

$$p(t) = c_0 + c_1 t + c_2 t^2 + \ldots + c_{N-1} t^{N-1} \qquad (4)$$

M times at regular intervals δ starting at t_0, that is,

$$\{t_0, \ t_0 + \delta, \ t_0 + 2\delta, \ \ldots, \ t_0 + (M-1)\delta\}.$$

We hope to use the coherence between successive values to decrease the amount of computation at each point. We know that, for a linear (that is, second order) polynomial $L(t) = at + b$, the difference between successive values is constant:

$$L(t + \delta) - L(t) = [a(t + \delta) + b] - [at + b]$$

$$= at + a\delta + b - at - b \tag{5}$$

$$= a\delta,$$

which results in the following *forward-differencing* algorithm to compute a sequence of linear function values at regular intervals dt, starting at a point t_0:

```
p0 = a * t0 + b;
p1 = a * dt;
for (i = 0; i < LENGTH; i++) {
   DoSomethingWithTheFunctionValue(p0);
   p0 += p1;
}
```

We extend this algorithm to an N-order polynomial by taking higher-order differences and maintaining them in N variables whose values at iteration i are denoted as

$$p_0^{(i)}(t_0), \ p_1^{(i)}(t_0), \ \dots, \ p_{N-1}^{(i)}(t_0).$$

These N variables are initialized as the repeated differences of the polynomial evaluated at successive points:

$$p_0^{(0)}(t_0) = p(t_0)$$

$$p_1^{(0)}(t_0) = p_0^{(0)}(t_0 + \delta) - p_0^{(0)}(t_0) \tag{6}$$

$$\vdots$$

$$p_{N-1}^{(0)}(t_0) = p_{N-2}^{(0)}(t_0 + \delta) - p_{N-2}^{(0)}(t_0).$$

That is, we first take differences of the polynomial evaluated at regular intervals, and then we take differences of those differences, and so on. It should come as no surprise that the Nth difference is zero for an Nth-order polynomial, because the differences are related to derivatives, and the Nth derivative of an Nth-order polynomial is zero. Moreover, the $(N-1)$th difference (and derivative) is constant.

At each iteration i, the N state variables are updated by incrementing $p_k^{(i)}(t_0)$ by $p_{k+1}^{(i)}(t_0)$:

$$p_k^{(i+1)}(t_0) = p_k^{(i)}(t_0) + p_{k+1}^{(i)}(t_0).$$

The value of the polynomial at $t_0 + i\delta$ is then given by $p_0^{(i)}(t_0)$.

For example, to incrementally generate a cubic polynomial

$$p(t) = c_0 + c_1 t + c_2 t^2 + c_3 t^3, \tag{7}$$

we initialize the forward differences as such:

$$p_0^{(0)}(t_0) = p(t_0)$$

$$p_1^{(0)}(t_0) = p_0^{(0)}(t_0 + \delta) - p_0^{(0)}(t_0)$$

$$p_2^{(0)}(t_0) = p_1^{(0)}(t_0 + \delta) - p_1^{(0)}(t_0) \tag{8}$$

$$p_3(t_0) = p_2^{(0)}(t_0 + \delta) - p_2^{(0)}(t_0),$$

where $p_0^{(0)}$ is the value of the polynomial at the initial point, $p_1^{(0)}$ and $p_2^{(0)}$ are the first and second differences at the initial point, and p_3 is the constant second difference. Note that we have dropped the iteration superscript on p_3 because it is constant.

To evaluate the polynomial at $t_0 + \delta$ by the method of forward differences, we increment p_0 by p_1, p_1 by p_2, and p_2 by p_3:

$$p_0^{(1)} = p_0^{(0)} + p_1^{(0)}$$

$$p_1^{(1)} = p_1^{(0)} + p_2^{(0)} \tag{9}$$

$$p_2^{(1)} = p_2^{(0)} + p_3$$

and the value is given by $p_0^{(1)}$.

Similarly, the value of the polynomial at $t_0 + 2\delta$ is computed from the previous forward differences:

$$p_0^{(2)} = p_0^{(1)} + p_1^{(1)}$$

$$p_1^{(2)} = p_1^{(1)} + p_2^{(1)} \tag{10}$$

$$p_2^{(2)} = p_2^{(1)} + p_3,$$

and so on. Note that in the case of a cubic polynomial, we can use a single state vector to store the forward differences. Utilizing the powerful expressive capabilities of GLSL, we can implement the state update *in one instruction*:

```
p.xyz += p.yzw;
```

where we have initialized the forward-difference vector as follows:

```
p = f(vec4(t, t+d, t+2*d, t+3*d));
p.yzw -= p.xyz;
p.zw  -= p.yz;
p.w   -= p.z;
```

Note that this method can be used to compute arbitrary functions, not just polynomials. Forward-differencing is especially useful for rendering in 2D and 3D graphics using scan-conversion techniques for lines and polygons (Foley et al. 1990). *Adaptive* forward differencing was developed in a series of papers (Lien et al. 1987, Shantz and Chang 1988, and Chang et al. 1989) for evaluating and shading cubic and NURBS curves and surfaces in floating-point and fixed-point arithmetic. Klassen (1991a) uses adaptive forward differencing to draw antialiased cubic spline curves. Turkowski (2002) renders cubic and spherical panoramas in real time using forward differencing of piecewise polynomials adaptively approximating transcendental functions.

Our initialization method corresponds to the Taylor series approximation. More accurate approximations over the desired domain can be achieved by using other methods of polynomial approximation, such as Lagrangian interpolation or Chebyshev approximation (Ralston and Rabinowitz 1978).

40.3 The Incremental Gaussian Algorithm

When we apply the forward-differencing technique to the Gaussian, we get poor results, as shown in Figure 40-2.

The orange curve in Figure 40-2 is the Taylor series approximation at 0, and the green curve is a polynomial fit to the points {0.0, 1.0, 2.0}. The black curve is the Gaussian. The fundamental problem is that polynomials get larger when their arguments do, whereas the Gaussian gets smaller.

The typical numerical analysis approach is to instead use a rational polynomial of the form

$$r(t) = \frac{n_0 + n_1 t + n_2 t^2 + \ldots + n_{N-1} t^{N-1}}{d_0 + d_1 t + d_2 t^2 + \ldots + d_{D-1} t^{D-1}}. \tag{11}$$

We can also use forward differencing to compute the numerator and the denominator separately, but we still have to divide them at each pixel. This algorithm does indeed

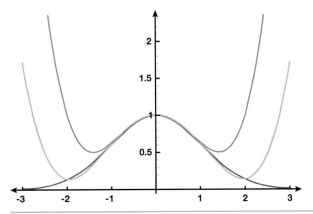

Figure 40-2. Gaussian Approximated by a Polynomial

produce a better approximation and has the desired asymptotic behavior. This is a good technique for approximating a wide class of functions, but we can take advantage of the exponential nature of the Gaussian to yield a method that is simpler and faster. It turns out that we have such an algorithm that shares the simplicity of forward differencing if we replace differences by quotients.

Given the Gaussian

$$G(t) = e^{-\frac{t^2}{2\sigma^2}} \tag{12}$$

we evaluate the quotient of successive values

$$G_1(t) = \frac{G(t+\delta)}{G(t)} = e^{-\frac{\delta^2}{2\sigma^2}} e^{-\frac{\delta t}{\sigma^2}}$$

$$\tag{13}$$

$$G_2(t) = \frac{G_1(t+\delta)}{G_1(t)} = e^{-\frac{\delta^2}{\sigma^2}}$$

and we find that the second quotient is constant, whereas the first quotient is exponential, as illustrated in Figure 40-3.

The next quotient would yield another constant: 1. These properties have a nice analogy to those of forward differencing, where quotients take the place of differences, and a quotient of 1 takes the place of a difference of 0.

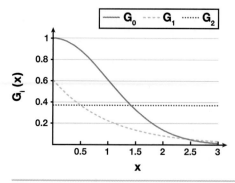

Figure 40-3. Gaussian with First and Second Quotients

Note that there are two factors in the first quotient: one is related purely to the sampling spacing δ, and the other is an attenuation from $t = 0$. In fact, when we set $t = 0$, we get

$$G_0(0) = 1$$

$$G_1(0) = \frac{G(\delta)}{G(0)} = e^{-\frac{\delta^2}{2\sigma^2}}$$

(14)

$$G_2(0) = \frac{G_1(\delta)}{G_1(0)} = e^{-\frac{\delta^2}{\sigma^2}} = (G_1(0))^2.$$

Only one exponential evaluation is needed to generate any number of regularly spaced samples starting at zero. The entire Gaussian is characterized by one attenuation factor, as shown in Listing 40-2.

Listing 40-2.

```
#ifdef USE_SCALAR_INSTRUCTIONS // suitable for scalar GPUs

float g0, g1, g2;
g0 = 1.0 / (sqrt(2.0 * PI) * sigma);
g1 = exp(-0.5 * delta * delta / (sigma * sigma));
g2 = g1 * g1;

for (i = 0; i < N; i++) {
  MultiplySomethingByTheGaussianCoefficient(g0);
  g0 *= g1;
  g1 *= g2;
}
```

Listing 40-2 (*continued*).

```
#else // especially for vector architectures

float3 g;
g.x = 1.0 / (sqrt(2.0 * PI) * sigma);
g.y = exp(-0.5 * delta * delta / (sigma * sigma));
g.z = g.y * g.y;

for (i = 0; i < N; i++) {
  MultiplySomethingByTheGaussianCoefficient(g.x);
  g.xy *= g.yz;
}
#endif // USE_VECTOR_INSTRUCTIONS
```

The Gaussian coefficients are generated with just one vector multiplication per sample. A vector multiplication is one of the fastest instructions on the GPU.

40.4 Error Analysis

The incremental Gaussian algorithm is exact with exact arithmetic. In this section, we perform a worst-case error analysis, taking into account (1) errors in the initial coefficient values, which are due to representation in single-precision IEEE floating-point (that is, $a(1 + \varepsilon)$) and (2) error that is due to floating-point multiplication ($ab(1 + \varepsilon)$). Then we determine how the error grows with each iteration.

Let the initial relative error of any of the forward quotient coefficients be a stochastic variable ε so that its floating-point representation is

$$a(1 + \varepsilon) \tag{15}$$

instead of a, because it is approximated in a finite floating-point representation. For single-precision IEEE floating-point, for example,

$$|\varepsilon| \leq \tfrac{1}{2} \text{ULP} \approx 6 \times 10^{-8}.$$

The product of two finite-precision numbers c and d is

$$cd(1 + \varepsilon) \tag{16}$$

instead of cd because the product will be truncated to the word length. Putting this together, we find that the relative error of the product of two approximate variables a and b is

$$[a(1 + \varepsilon_a)][b(1 + \varepsilon_b)](1 + \varepsilon_c) = ab(1 + \varepsilon_a + \varepsilon_b + \varepsilon_c + \varepsilon_a\varepsilon_b + \varepsilon_b\varepsilon_c + \varepsilon_c\varepsilon_a + \varepsilon_a\varepsilon_b\varepsilon_c) \tag{17}$$

$$\approx ab(1 + \varepsilon_a + \varepsilon_b + \varepsilon_c).$$

Thus, the errors accumulate. As is traditional with error analysis, we drop the higher-order terms in ε, because they are much less significant.

The relative error for the coefficients is shown in Table 40-1, computed simply by executing the incremental Gaussian algorithm with the error accumulation just given. Here, we do *two* exponential computations: one for the first-order quotient g_1 and one for the second-order quotient g_2, to maximize the precision.

The error in g_1 increases linearly, because it is incremented by the constant g_2 every iteration. The error in g_0 also accumulates the error in g_1, so it grows quadratically. The error for g_0 can then be expressed as a polynomial function of n:

$$E(n) = \left(1 + n + n^2\right)\varepsilon. \tag{18}$$

If the initial error ε is $1/2$ of the least significant bit of a single-precision floating-point number and we wish the coefficients to have a relative error of $1/256$, then the parenthesized quantity in the Equation 18 should be less than 2^{17}. This suggests $n \le 361$.

Typically, however, practitioners truncate the Gaussian at 3σ, where

$$G(3\sigma) = e^{-\frac{(3\sigma)^2}{2\sigma^2}} = e^{-\frac{9}{2}} \approx 0.01111. \tag{19}$$

The error in the last evaluation (at 3σ), relative to the central coefficient is still only

$$\frac{\varepsilon_{3\sigma}}{\varepsilon_0} = \frac{0.01111 \times 2^{17} \times \varepsilon}{2^{24}\varepsilon} = 8.68 \times 10^{-5}, \tag{20}$$

when we compute it with 361 forward products. If we are willing to have a maximum error of $1/256$ relative to the *central* coefficient (as opposed to the error relative to the *fringe* coefficient), then we can go up to 3,435 samples. When these coefficients are used to implement a convolution kernel, this is the kind of accuracy that we need.

We have a different situation if we choose to do only *one* exponential computation for the first quotient and compute the second difference from the first. In this case the error in the second quotient is doubled, as shown in Table 40-2.

The error for g_0 in this scenario is

$$E(n) = \left(1 + \tfrac{1}{2}n + \tfrac{3}{2}n^2\right)\varepsilon \tag{21}$$

with the maximum number of iterations for 8-bit accuracy 295 or 2,804, depending on whether the relative accuracy desired is relative to the fringe or the central coefficients, respectively.

Table 40-1. Growth in Coefficient Error			
Iteration	g_0 Error	g_1 Error	g_2 Error
0	ε	ε	ε
1	3ε	3ε	ε
2	7ε	5ε	ε
3	13ε	7ε	ε
4	21ε	9ε	ε
.	.	.	.
.	.	.	.
.	.	.	.

Table 40-2. Growth in Coefficient Error When g_2 Is Computed from g_1

Iteration	g_0 Error	g_1 Error	g_2 Error
0	ε	ε	2ε
1	3ε	4ε	2ε
2	8ε	7ε	2ε
3	16ε	10ε	2ε
4	27ε	13ε	2ε
.	.	.	.
.	.	.	.
.	.	.	.

For image-blurring applications, the fringe error relative to the central coefficient is of primary concern. Even when we compute g_2 from g_1, the limitation of $3\sigma \le 2804$, or $\sigma \le 934$ is not restrictive (because applications with $\sigma > 100$ are rare), so it suffices to compute only the g_1 coefficient as an exponential, and g_2 as its square.

40.5 Performance

Processor performance has increased substantially over the past decade, so that arithmetic logic unit (ALU) operations are executed faster than accessing memory, by one to three orders of magnitude. As a result, algorithms on modern computer architectures benefit from replacing table lookups with relatively simple computations, especially when the tables are relatively large.

The incremental computation algorithm is noticeably faster on the GPU and CPU than looking up coefficients in a table. While GPU performance highly depends on the capabilities of the hardware, the GPU vendor, the driver version, and the operating system version, we can conservatively say that the technique yields at least a 15 percent performance improvement.

Another aspect of performance is whether a particular blur filter can fit on the GPU. The incremental Gaussian blur algorithm may appear to be small, but the GPU driver will increase the number of instructions dramatically, under certain circumstances. In particular, some GPUs do not have any looping primitives, so the driver will automatically unroll the loop. The maximum loop size (that is, the Gaussian radius) is then limited by the number of ALU instructions or texture lookup instructions. This algorithm will then reduce the number of texture lookups to increase the maximum blur radius.

Graphics hardware architecture is constantly evolving. While texture access is relatively slow compared to arithmetic computations, some newer hardware (such as the GeForce 8800 Series) incorporates up to 16 *constant buffers* of 16K floats each, with the same access time as a register. The incremental Gaussian algorithm may not yield any higher performance than table lookup using such constant buffers, but it may not yield lower performance either. The incremental Gaussian algorithm has the advantage that it can be deployed successfully on a wide variety of platforms.

40.6 Conclusion

We have presented a very simple technique to evaluate the Gaussian at regularly spaced points. It is not an approximation, and it has the simplicity of polynomial forward differencing, so that only one vector instruction is needed for a coefficient update at each point on a GPU.

The method of *forward quotients* can accelerate the computation of any function that is the exponential of a polynomial. Modern computers can perform multiplications as fast as additions, so the technique is as powerful as forward differencing. This method opens up incremental computations to a new class of functions.

40.7 References

Chang, Sheue-Ling, Michael Shantz, and Robert Rocchetti. 1989. "Rendering Cubic Curves and Surfaces with Integer Adaptive Forward Differencing." In *Computer Graphics (Proceedings of SIGGRAPH 89)*, pp. 157–166.

Foley, James D., Andries van Dam, Steven K. Feiner, and John F. Hughes. 1990. *Computer Graphics: Principles and Practice*. Addison-Wesley.

Jargstorff, F. 2004. "A Framework for Image Processing." In *GPU Gems*, edited by Randima Fernando, pp. 445–467. Addison-Wesley.

Klassen, R. Victor. 1991a. "Drawing Antialiased Cubic Spline Curves." *ACM Transactions on Graphics* 10(1), pp. 92–108.

Klassen, R. Victor. 1991b. "Integer Forward Differencing of Cubic Polynomials. Analysis and Algorithms." *ACM Transactions on Graphics* 10(2), pp. 152–181.

Lien, Sheue-Ling, Michael Shantz, and Vaughan Pratt. 1987. "Adaptive Forward Differencing for Rendering Curves and Surfaces." *Computer Graphics (Proceedings of SIGGRAPH 87)*, pp. 111–118.

Ralston, Anthony, and Philip Rabinowitz. 1978. *A First Course in Numerical Analysis*, 2nd ed. McGraw-Hill.

Shantz, Michael, and Sheue-Ling Chang 1988. "Rendering Trimmed NURBS with Adaptive Forward Differencing." *Computer Graphics (Proceedings of SIGGRAPH 88)*, pp. 189–198.

Turkowski, Ken. 2002. "Scanline-Order Image Warping Using Error-Controlled Adaptive Piecewise Polynomial Approximation." Available online at http://www.worldserver.com/turk/computergraphics/AdaptPolyFwdDiff.pdf.

I would like to thank Nathan Carr for encouraging me to write a chapter on this algorithm, and Paul McJones for suggesting a contribution to GPU Gems. Gavin Miller, Frank Jargstorff and Andreea Berfield provided valuable feedback for improving this paper. I would like to thank Frank Jargstorff for his evaluation of performance on the GPU.

Chapter 41

Using the Geometry Shader for Compact and Variable-Length GPU Feedback

Franck Diard
NVIDIA Corporation

41.1 Introduction

Although modern graphics hardware is designed for high-performance computer graphics, the GPU is being increasingly used in other domains, such as image processing and technical computing, to take advantage of its massively parallel architecture.

Several generations of GPUs have incrementally delivered better instruction sets with branching and texture fetches for fragment programs, making the GPU a fantastic machine to execute data-parallel algorithms. On the other hand, algorithms with dynamic output such as compression or data searching are not well mapped to the GPU.

With a high-level shading language like Cg, programming the GPU is now very easy. However, GPU shader programs run in very constrained contexts: vertex shading and pixel shading. These execution environments are designed for performance and are not very helpful for more conventional serial or dynamic programming.

In this chapter, we demonstrate how to use the geometry shader (GS) unit of Microsoft's DirectX 10 (DX10)-compliant graphics hardware (Microsoft 2007) to implement some algorithms with variable input and output on the GPU. Introduced as an extra stage between vertex processing and fragment processing, the geometry shader adds or deletes some elements in the geometry stream sent to the rendering pipeline. However, by using this unit in a way that differs from its original purpose, we can exploit the GPU to implement a broad class of general-purpose algorithms beyond the normal usage of processing geometry.

41.2 Why Use the Geometry Shader?

The geometry shader is unique because it can be programmed to accomplish some tasks that neither the vertex shader (VS) nor the pixel shader (PS) units can perform efficiently. This capability allows a new class of commodity algorithms to be performed on the GPU. For example, in the computer vision domain, this new programming technique can be used to avoid reading back images on the GPU. By sending back only a few scalars to system memory, the GS can increase throughput and scalability.

Suppose we would like to write some shading code executed by the GPU that scans a texture input and writes a number $2n + 1$ of real numbers in the frame buffer, where n is computed dynamically while reading the contents of the input texture. The algorithm output is a set of 2D locations—pairs of x and y scalars—in addition to the number of pairs as a scalar.

This output cannot be implemented with a pixel shader for two reasons:

- A pixel shader repeats the same algorithm for all the pixels of the output buffer, and this size is not known in advance.
- A fragment processor working on a pixel from the output buffer has no visibility to the context of other threads that are processing other pixels (adjacent or not), so no global/adaptive decision can be taken.

Vertex shaders are also not very helpful for this kind of algorithm. Let's take a compressor program, for example, that is working on an input stream of data. By sending one geometry primitive (such as a flat triangle), the vertex program can loop over the input data and compress. However, the program will have to pass exactly one triangle to the rasterizer to write different bytes (the compressed codes) to the output buffer. This is not possible, because the program will write the same code to all the pixels rasterized by the geometry element.

So although a vertex shader can run a program that collects statistics on the input data by fetching texels, it has only two options:

- It can kill the primitive (which is useless).
- It can forward down the pipeline a primitive for which rasterization will write the same code on all corresponding pixels. To be able to write n different codes to the output buffer, the VS would have to receive n elements of geometry. But then n vertex shader programs would run, all doing the same thing and unable to make any adaptive decisions because they run in separate GPU threads, isolated from each other.

41.3 Dynamic Output with the Geometry Shader

The geometry shader, in contrast to the fragment or vertex shader, is able to output variable-length results based on adaptive, data-dependent execution. In a single pass, the GS can analyze input data (for example, the contents of a texture) and output a variable-length code (many scalars can be emitted by a single GS thread). In this way, the GS unit is able to implement small algorithms for which the following is true:

- The output size is not known in advance.
- The output size is known, but the size spans several pixels.

It's possible to execute these algorithms by sending a single vertex to the GS. If some input data can be passed in as static Cg program parameters in the color, this vertex is processed in a single GPU thread. This thread can build statistics, fetch as many texels as needed, perform math operations, plus write a variable-length output by emitting an adaptive number of scalars.

The GS unit can write its results in two ways:

- By emitting vertices for which the rasterizer will write the scalar values at any location in the render target.
- By emitting scalars that are incrementally added to a stream-out buffer, a DX10 feature that redirects the output of the GS unit into a 1D buffer in GPU-accessible memory. (For more information, refer to the DX10 specification [Microsoft 2007].)

The geometry shader is able to write arbitrary blobs to an output buffer at any location (1D or 2D) and at any rate (the number of scalar outputs per input vertex) by passing data packets to the rasterizer. In Figure 41-1, the GS emits and transmits vertices down the rendering pipeline as the GS program progresses. The 2D coordinates are set by the GS program, which keeps incrementing the x coordinate each time it emits values to be written.

If the output of the program is sent to the frame buffer, these few bytes of output can be read back with the glReadPixels() function. If the render target is in system memory, the rasterizer will write only a few bytes to system memory, where the CPU can retrieve the bits directly. This approach provides good bus optimization compared to moving the whole input data to system memory for the CPU to analyze.

The "position" and "color" (a packet of scalars) of these emitted vertices are computed by the GS program and given to the rasterizer. The x and y coordinates of the vertices tell the rasterizer where to write the scalars that are stored in the frame buffer's color packet. For this to work, the codes emitted by the GS have to be untouched by the transform and clipping unit, so the model/view transforms are set to "identity," with no filtering, pixel shader usage, or lighting effects allowed.

The stream-out feature of DX-compliant hardware can also be used for output. In this case, the GS program does not have to track the 2D location of the pixels being output. The stream-out feature is compact because it does not use the "location" components; however, this feature may be less convenient because it is only an incremental output in

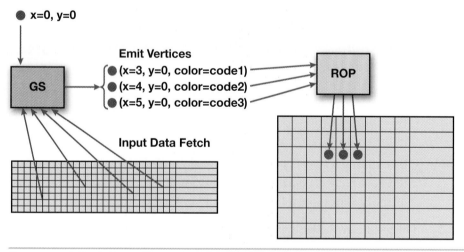

Figure 41-1. A Single Vertex Sent to the GS Emits Several Vertices
These vertices write different codes at different locations in the render target.

a linear buffer. This stream-out buffer also needs to be changed for each GS thread, which is not efficient when we expect several GS threads to execute in parallel. If the stream-out's output is stored directly at some 2D position in the frame buffer, it can be readily used as an input texture to the next processing stage, which is useful when we're implementing on-the-fly texture compression.

If the CPU needs to retrieve the number of codes that were output, it can read the quantity from a known position in the output data, such as the first scalar written at the end of the GS thread when the exact number of emitted codes is known. Or, it can retrieve the quantity through an occlusion query.

41.4 Algorithms and Applications

41.4.1 Building Histograms

Building fast histograms efficiently is useful in many image-processing algorithms, including contrast correction and tone-mapping high-dynamic-range (HDR) images. The output of a histogram computation is a fixed-size data set, where the size typically matches the range of the input. For example, the histogram of an 8-bit-luminance image is an array of 256 scalar values. The size of the output would preclude an implementation through a pixel shader program because the output would span several pixels. The GS implementation, like the one shown in Listing 41-1, is simply done using a Cg program (version 2.0).

Listing 41-1. Building a Histogram in a Geometry Shader

```
POINT void histoGS( AttribArray<float4> position : POSITION,
                    AttribArray<float4> color : COLOR,
                    uniform samplerRECT texIn)
{
  float h[256], lum, i, j;
  float3 c;

  for (int j=0; j<256; j++) h[j] = 0; //Histogram init

  float sx=color[0].x, sy=color[0].y; //Read block size from
                                      //vertex color.

  // Compute the luminance value for this pixel.
  c.x=255.0*0.30; c.y=255.0*0.59; c.z=255.0*0.11;
```

Listing 41-1 (*continued*). Building a Histogram in a Geometry Shader

```
for (j=0; j<sy; j++)
  for (i=0; i<sx;  i++)
  {
      lum=dot(texRECT(texIn, float2(i, j)).xyz, c.xyz);
      h[lum]++;
  }

  // Write the histogram out.
  float4 outputPos : POSITION = position[0];
  outputPos.x=0; outputPos.y=0;

  for (int j=0; j<64; j++)
  {
    outputPos.x = -1 + j/128.0;  // Moving the output pixel
    emitVertex(outputPos, float4(h[j*4], h[j*4+1],
              h[j*4+2], h[j*4+3]) : COLOR);
  }
}
```

As we can see in Listing 41-1, the GS will build this histogram in one pass and output the results in the floating-point render target (type GL_FLOAT_RGBA_NV). Also, the GS keeps track of the *x* coordinate of the emitted pixels.

The trigger in this case is a simple OpenGL program, which needs some special setup because what we pass in as colors are just full-range floating-point numbers in and out of shading programs, as shown in Listing 41-2.

Listing 41-2. OpenGL Setup to Avoid Clamping

```
glClampColorARB(GL_CLAMP_VERTEX_COLOR_ARB, FALSE);
glClampColorARB(GL_CLAMP_FRAGMENT_COLOR_ARB, FALSE);
glClampColorARB(GL_CLAMP_READ_COLOR_ARB, FALSE);
```

It's possible to send only one vertex to produce a GS thread that can read the entire input image and output the histogram values in one pass. However, the GPU is inherently parallel, so we can increase performance if we execute this histogram computation on several GS threads, with each thread working on a partition of the input image. This technique is easily performed by sending several vertices to trigger more GS threads.

The color of each vertex contains the coordinates and bounds of the input area. Each GS thread can be programmed to output its histogram to *n* different locations in the frame buffer (256 scalars = 64 RGBA32F pixels each). The outputs can then be read back on the CPU ($n \times 256$ floats) and summed. There is, however, room for a little optimization. Because the output histogram bins are simply added together, we can program the n threads to output their results in the same frame-buffer location and enable the GL_BLEND function with GL_ONE/GL_ONE as arguments. This way, the floating-point values are summed up automatically and only one vector of 256 floats needs to be read back to the CPU.

Figure 41-2 illustrates a GS histogram algorithm using multiple threads, where each thread handles a separate partition of the input image and all the threads write results to the same output array.

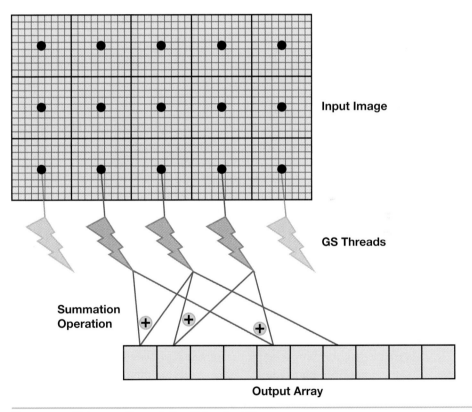

Figure 41-2. Histogram Computation Using the GS
One thread per vertex (one vertex per block) can work in parallel because the raster operator unit will automatically sum their output in the frame buffer.

41.4.2 Compressors

The GS programming technique described for histograms can also be used by DXT-like compression schemes, where the size of the output blobs is known in advance. DXT is a compression algorithm that takes a 4×4-pixel block as input. The two most representative colors are chosen and output as two 16-bit (565) color values In addition, sixteen 2-bit indices are output to be used for lookup in a table that contains the two chosen colors and two interpolated colors. The input is 128 bytes and the output is 16 bytes, so the algorithm provides a 6:1 lossy compression (if alpha is discarded).

A GS program can fetch 16 pixels and then write 16 bytes to the frame buffer. This program can use multiple GPU threads at the same time because blocks of input data are independent. In fact, a pixel shader is able to implement a regular DXT compressor because it has a fixed-size output of 8 bytes, and the compressed tile can be written with one pixel with color components of type GL_UNSIGNEDINT32. But a PS cannot be used for compression algorithms—such as for some DCT compression blocks that require writing more than 128 bits of output.

Variable-Length Output

So far we have presented GS algorithms for fixed-size output. However, the pixel shader on modern GPUs is also effective for handling variable-length types of algorithms, especially image processing on a 2D array of pixels. In contrast, computer vision algorithms typically produce variable-length output.

Although some vision applications have been ported to the PS, they are generally more difficult to accelerate because of the differences between 3D graphics and vision in terms of input and output spaces.

- 3D graphics rendering takes a variable-length, compact, and parametric representation as an input (such as vertices, light positions, textures, and geometry) and outputs a fixed-size matrix of pixels.

- Computer vision algorithms take a static matrix of pixels as an input and output a variable-length, compact, and parametric representation of lines or estimates of the camera position, for example. These results are then fed back to some other device (most likely the CPU) for further action.

The inability of the GPU to efficiently carry out processing stages that require variable-length output has hampered its adoption in the field of computer vision. Previous GPU implementations containing many vision algorithms used the PS for regular, data-parallel processing, and then the image buffers were copied back to system memory through the bus for further processing on the CPU (refer to Fung 2005 for more examples of computer vision algorithms on the GPU). These extra steps have the negative side effects of saturating the bus, increasing the system memory footprint, increasing the CPU load, and stalling the GPU.

In the following sections, we describe how the GS unit can be used for algorithms with variable-length output, making the GPU a more viable compute target for computer vision.

41.4.3 The Hough Transform

The Hough transform, a classical computer vision algorithm for detecting straight lines in an image, is often used to help robots identify basic geometry for navigation or industrial quality control. In short, the algorithm builds a map of all lines—represented with the pair (θ, d) ($\theta \in [0, 2\pi[$ and $d \geq 0$)—that can exist in an image. One pair (x, y) in image space matches a continuous sinusoidal curve in Hough space, representing all the lines that go through this point. One pair (θ, d) in Hough space matches a line in the image space.

Fung et al. 2005 proposed a GPU implementation of a line detection algorithm based on the Hough transform. However, in their framework, the CPU is still involved in some processing stages, such as searching for maxima in a Hough map. GS programming allows for mapping all stages of a line's detection program to run on the GPU.

A basic line detection algorithm using the Hough transform can be programmed as follows:

1. The video GPU hardware unit decodes a frame and writes it in the frame buffer.
2. A pixel shader pass applies convolution kernels with thresholds to identify the pixels that have a large gradient.
3. A pixel shader pass computes a Hough map (see details later in this section).
4. A geometry shader pass looks for n local maxima in the Hough map, identifying n parametric lines in the initial image and writing the dynamic output, made of line coordinates.

The benefit of this GS-based approach is that only a few bytes of data representing the n lines are copied back to the CPU—a good savings in bandwidth and significant CPU offloading.

Figure 41-3b shows a Hough map computed from Figure 41-3a.

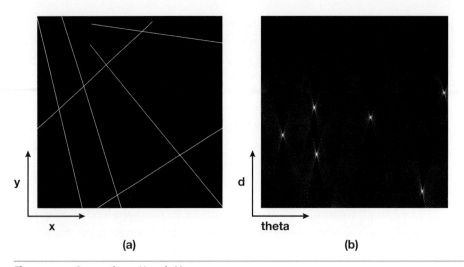

y

x

(a)

d

theta

(b)

Figure 41-3. Generating a Hough Map
(a) The input image with some lines to be detected. (b) The Hough map, where the location of maximum values identifies the orientation and the location of lines.

The next step is to run an algorithm to search for maximum values in this map without reading back the image on the CPU. That is easily done using a small GS program (triggered by sending one vertex) that will look for local maxima and emit, for each maximum, four scalars containing the line parameters. In this example, the full algorithm will output six points to be read back by the CPU. To get more parameters, the GS program can fetch the pixels from the input image that belong to this line and count the ones that are lit, thus computing the start position and length of each segment.

The implementation developed by Fung et al. 2005 goes from image space to Hough space, using the VS to plot the sinusoidal curve made of m vertices per pixel of interest. The source image needs to be in system memory and scanned by the CPU (m is the number of samples of θ) to send a large number of vertices to the GPU.

There is, however, a simple way to build this map completely on the GPU side with a PS program that is triggered by drawing just a single quad covering the whole rendering target. This approach goes from Hough space to image space. Figure 41-4 shows a point in the Hough map that corresponds to a line in the image space.

The pixel shader code (included on this book's accompanying DVD) finds all the image pixels that belong to a line represented by a point in the Hough map. So for each sample of the Hough map, a PS program is run by rendering a single quad. This program intersects the line with the image rectangle and rasterizes the line, fetching the

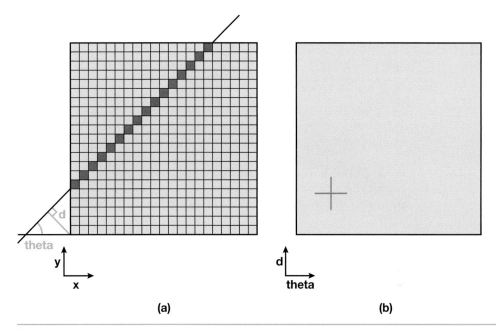

Figure 41-4.
The rasterized line (a) corresponding to a (θ, d) pair in the Hough space (b).

texels and summing them up to write a single float number (the vote) into the render target (the Hough map). When this process using the PS unit is complete, we use a simple GS program that scans the entire Hough map and outputs a 2D location (two scalars per point) for each local maximum. When the search is over, the number of output points is written to the output buffer, where the CPU program can retrieve it. The first two components of the pixels contain the position of the local maxima in the Hough map. Listing 41-3 provides the GS program that dynamically outputs the location of local maxima.

Listing 41-3. GS Program That Dynamically Outputs the Location of Local Maxima

```
POINT void outputMaxPositionsGS(AttribArray<float4> position : POSITION,
                                AttribArray<float4> color : COLOR,
                                uniform samplerRECT texIn,
                                uniform float BlockSize)
{
  int index=1;
  float sx=color[0].x, sy=color[0].y; // Read block size from
                                      // vertex color.
  float4 outputPos : POSITION = position[0];  outputPos.y=0;
```

```
    for (int j=0; j<sy; j++)
      for (int i=0; i<sx;  i++)
        if(texRECT(texIn, float2(i, j)).r==1.0)
          {
            outputPos.x = -1 + index/128;
            emitVertex(outputPos, float4(i, j, 0, 0) : COLOR);
            index++;
          }
    // Outputting the number of points found
    outputPos.x = -1 ;
    emitVertex(outputPos, float4(index-1, 0, 0, 0) : COLOR);
  }
```

In Listing 41-3 the input data to the GS program has been preprocessed to increase efficiency. We first ran a pixel shader, as shown in Listing 41-4, that, for each pixel, finds the local maximum of all the pixels in the neighborhood and outputs a value of 1 if the current pixel is the maximum, 0 otherwise. The GS code (in Listing 41-3) is very lean for the highest efficiency because, by default, it will run on only one GPU thread.

Listing 41-4. PS Program That Searches for Local Maxima (Preparation for GS)

```
float4 findMaxFirstPassPS(float2 uv : TEX0,
                          uniform samplerRECT texIn) : COLOR
{
  float lum, max;
  float2 t, tcenter;
  float4 valueOut = float4(0, 0, 0, 1);

  for (int j=-KSIZE; j<KSIZE+1; j++) // KSIZE is the size of the window.
  {
    t[1]=uv[1]+j;
    for (int i=-KSIZE; i<KSIZE+1; i++)
    {
      t[0]=uv[0]+i;
      lum=texRECT(texIn, t).r;
      if (lum>max)
      {
        max=lum;
        tcenter=t;
      }
    }
  }
}
```

```
if (tcenter.x==uv.x && tcenter.y==uv.y)
  valueOut = float4(1, 0, 0, 0);

return valueOut;
}
```

41.4.4 Corner Detection

Another classical computer vision technique is *corner detection* for tracking points of interest. This algorithm can also be implemented efficiently using the GS unit. In general, an input image is processed by a set of convolution kernels, which are very well executed in parallel by PS units. Many filters are used for feature extraction (Canny 1986, Trajkovic and Hedley 1998, Tomasi and Kanade 1991, and Harris and Stephens 1988), and the GPU pixel shaders are very efficient at handling these computationally intensive tasks. The final result of the algorithm is a generally dynamic set of 2D positions.

Implementations of these algorithms (for example, Sinha et al. 2006) usually include a readback of temporary buffers of floating-point data that contain image gradients, eigenvalues, and so forth on the CPU to generate the list of 2D points representing the corners. The number of corners is not known in advance, but it is computed by analyzing local neighborhoods of coefficients. The GS is particularly well suited to accelerating this step because it offers dynamic and compact feedback to the CPU.

Figure 41-5 shows an example of corner detection. To increase parallel processing, we can divide the input space into several subrectangles, each processed by a GS thread that writes its dynamic output in different lines (that is, different y coordinates of the emitted vertices) in the frame buffer.

41.5 Benefits: GPU Locality and SLI

The main advantage of moving data analysis to the GPU is data locality (reducing CPU/GPU exchanges) and CPU offloading. Additionally, if the results of a given algorithm (such as computer vision on live video) are only a few vectors, the performance can scale linearly with the number of GPUs, because CPU processing is not increased significantly by adding GPUs. Figure 41-6 shows a sample configuration with four GeForce 8800 GTX GPUs connected using the SLI interconnect.

Figure 41-5. The Output of a Corner Detection Algorithm
In the algorithm the GS is used to output a variable number of corners (represented by red dots).

Consider the case where the input data is the result of hard drive video decoding. Multiple GPUs decode the incoming video stream in parallel into their respective frame buffers. Once every *g* frames, each GPU will use the pixel engine to run some image filtering algorithm. Then each will use a GS program to look for some features in the filtered data. This method is optimal because each GPU will send back only a few bytes to system memory, which the CPU will process quickly because it is fully available. If instead we process some stages on the CPU, we will benefit a lot less from SLI scalability because the CPU and bus can saturate and become a bottleneck. Multiple GPU decoding helps even more in some SLI appliances such as the NVIDIA Quadro Plex because the GPUs share the same PCIe path to system memory.

In this case of a video application, using the GS unit to run quick and simple programs works particularly well with the video engine because the programs can run in parallel and the data they work on is shared in the frame buffer with no extra copies.

Figure 41-6. NVIDIA SLI System Loaded with Four GeForce 8800 GTX GPUs
This system offers 3 GB of frame-buffer storage and 2.1 teraflops of processing power.

41.6 Performance and Limits

41.6.1 Guidelines

It's nice having a single execution thread to program algorithms that need to compute statistics before generating variable-length output. On the other hand, using a single execution thread reduces the efficiency of the GPU. Whenever possible, GS algorithms should partition the input space and use multiple threads to exploit the massive parallelism of the GPU. In addition, all per-pixel computations should be done as a preprocess using pixel shaders and stored in a temporary buffer. This way, even a single GS thread working on some data preprocessed by the PS is likely to perform better than if we transferred the image data through the bus back to system memory and processed the image on the CPU.

According to the DirectX 10 specification, the maximum number of scalars that can be written by a GS is 1,024 (4,096 bytes). Based on this limit, the input space has to be divided and processed by different GS threads so that each thread does not emit more than 1,024 scalars. So, if the algorithm permits, it is also beneficial to increase the number of GS threads in order to decrease per-thread output requirements.

Finally, depending on the GPU, GS programs can be optimized by grouping texture fetches and math operations. For example, when we scan an input texture, it is better to traverse the texture in tiles such as 64×64 (this varies with hardware), rather than linearly, to take advantage of the texture cache.

41.6.2 Performance of the Hough Map Maxima Detection

In this section we compare implementing a GPU-CPU algorithm that looks for local maxima in a 1024×1024 Hough map to implementing an algorithm that is completely GPU based. The complete program performs the following steps:

1. Load the source image on the GPU.
2. Compute the Hough map using a pixel shader.
3. Find the local maxima:
   a. Run a search for local maximum inside 7×7-pixel neighborhoods.
   b. Scan the intermediate buffer for local maxima output following step 3a.

Table 41-1 shows frame rates and bus utilization for two GPU configurations (one and four GPUs) and two implementations of the algorithm (CPU and GPU). The CPU implementation runs step 3b on the CPU, including a readback in system memory of the output of step 3a. As the numbers show, the complete GPU implementation (steps 3a and 3b), with its minimal feedback, is significantly faster and scales well with the number of GPUs.

Table 41-1. Comparison Between the CPU and GPU Implementations of the Hough Map Local Maxima Detection for One GPU and Four GPUs
The hardware for these experiments is a GeForce 8800 GTX and an Intel Core 2 2.4 GHz.

	Frame Rate	Bus Bandwidth	Frame Rate (4 GPUs)	Bus Bandwidth (4 GPUs)
CPU	58 fps	232 MB/s	58 fps	232 MB/s
GPU	170 fps	<1MB/s	600 fps	<1MB/s

41.7 Conclusion

We have demonstrated the basics of the geometry shading unit and shown how it can be used to provide large or variable-length output within GPU threads, or both. Our techniques allow executing some algorithms on the GPU that were traditionally implemented on the CPU, to provide compact and dynamic feedback to an application.

The capabilities of the GS unit allow some multistage computer vision algorithms to remain completely on the GPU, maximizing bus efficiency, CPU offloading, and SLI scaling.

41.8 References

Canny, J. F. 1986. "A Computational Approach to Edge Detection." *IEEE Transactions on Pattern Analysis and Machine Intelligence* 8(6), pp. 679–698.

Fung, James. 2005. "Computer Vision on the GPU." In *GPU Gems 2*, edited by Matt Pharr, pp. 649–665. Addison-Wesley.

Fung, James, Steve Mann, and Chris Aimone. 2005. "OpenVIDIA: Parallel GPU Computer Vision." In *Proceedings of the ACM Multimedia 2005*, pp. 849–852.

Harris, Chris, and Mike Stephens. 1988. "A Combined Corner and Edge Detector." In *Proceedings of Fourth Alvey Vision Conference*, pp. 147–151.

Microsoft Corporation. 2007. DirectX Web site. http://www.microsoft.com/directx/.

Sinha, Sudipta N., Jan-Michael Frahm, Marc Pollefeys, and Yakup Genc. 2006. "GPU-Based Video Feature Tracking and Matching." Technical Report 06-012, Department of Computer Science, UNC Chapel Hill.

Tomasi, C., and T. Kanade. 1991. "Detection and Tracking of Point Features." Technical Report CMU-CS-91-132, Carnegie Mellon University.

Trajkovic, M., and M. Hedley. 1998. "Fast Corner Detection." *Image and Vision Computing* 16, pp. 75–87.

Index

axis-aligned bounding boxes (AABBs)
    shadow volumes, 252–253
    transformation matrices, 210–211

B

B-splines, 544
back color in bidirectional lighting, 434–435
back-face distance in volume rendering, 667
baking normal maps. *See* normal maps
balanced trees, 855
banding in volume rendering, 669–670
bandwidth
    3D fluid effects, 660–661
    deferred shading, 451–452
    seismic data processing, 844
    volumetric light scattering, 279, 284
bank conflicts, 859–861
Barnes-Hut method (BH), 678, 692
base color
    animated crowd rendering, 50
    procedural terrains, 34
baskets in Asian options, 823–824
batch size in AES encryption, 798
Beckmann distribution texture, 302–304
Beer's Law, 300
bendBranch function, 116
bending vegetation animation, 116, 373–374,
    376–378
Bézier control points, 549–551
Bézier convex hulls
    antialiasing, 557
    overlapping triangles, 555
Bézier form in TrueType data, 544
Bézier patches, 100–101
BH (Barnes-Hut method), 678, 692
biasing in shadow maps, 160, 164–166
bidirectional lighting, 434–435
bidirectional reflectance distribution function
        (BRDF)
    factoring, 301
    Fresnel reflectance, 300–301
    importance sampling, 460, 462, 465
    skin rendering, 295, 299–305
    texture-space diffusion, 333–335

bidirectional surface-scattering reflectance distribu-
        tion function (BSSRDF), 344
bidirectional transmittance distribution function
        (BTDF), 344
bilinear filtering, 380
bilinear interpolation, 174
billboards, 482–483
binary bounding-volume hierarchy (BVH), 252–
    254
binary searches
    cone step mapping, 416, 425
    relief mapping, 409–410, 413–415
    true impostors, 484–486
binary trees, 855, 859
binomial trees, 822
BioSpec model, 344–345
bit depth, 445, 451, 515–516
bit masking, 445
bitwise operations
    encryption and decryption, 785
    polygon generation, 9
    random number generators, 813
Black-Scholes pricing formula, 822
black values in gamma correction, 531
blend shapes
    DirectX 10 features, 56
    HLSL buffer templates, 60–66
    introduction, 53–55
    mathematics, 56
    meshes, 56–57
    performance, 66–67
    samples, 66
    stream-out, 56–60
blending
    deferred shading, 450–451
    frame-buffer, 199
    particle systems, 520–521
    vegetation shading, 378
Blinn-Phong modeling, 295
block ciphers, 788, 799–801
blockers with variance shadow maps, 172,
    179
blocks
    N-body simulation performance, 688–690
    procedural terrains, 8, 12–13, 20–29, 35
bloom filters, 342

blurring
    depth-of-field. *See* depth-of-field (DoF)
    Gaussian. *See* incremental Gaussian computation
    subsurface scattering, 314
    texture-space diffusion, 316–319
    variance shadow maps, 178
bodies
    deferred shading, 430
    rigid. *See* rigid body simulation
body-body force calculations, 681–682
`bodyBodyInteraction` function, 682, 687
border color in parallel-split shadow maps, 217,
        230
boundaries in 3D fluid effects, 636
    dynamic obstacles, 644–651
    voxelization, 651–658
boundary cages, 492–493
bounding boxes
    LCP algorithms, 725
    oriented, 749–750
    shadow volumes, 252–253
    transformation matrices, 210–211
bounding volumes
    scan conversion, 744–745
    sort and sweep, 698
BoundingBox class, 210
box lights, 435
Box-Muller transforms, 806, 815–816
`BoxMuller` function, 816
branch animation, 110–113
BRDF (bidirectional reflectance distribution func-
        tion)
    factoring, 301
    Fresnel reflectance, 300–301
    importance sampling, 460, 462, 465
    skin rendering, 295, 299–305
    texture-space diffusion, 333–335
Brent's Theorem, 863
broad-phase collision detection, 697
    algorithms, 697–698
    performance, 719–721
    rigid body, 624
    sort and sweep, 698–699
    spatial subdivision, 699–702
Brownian motion, 807
BSSRDF (bidirectional surface-scattering
        reflectance distribution function), 344

BTDF (bidirectional transmittance distribution
        function), 344
buffers
    3D fluid effects, 652–653
    adaptive mesh refinement, 96–97, 99
    blend shapes, 56, 60–66
    cinematic relighting, 196
    deferred shading, 440–444, 453
    extracting object positions from, 576–579
    geometry shader unit, 897–898
    incremental Gaussian computation, 888
    linearity, 541
    motion blur, 576–579
    parallel prefix sums (scans), 854, 865, 869
    parallel-split shadow maps, 221
    particle systems, 523–524, 526
    point-based metaball visualization, 146
    procedural terrains, 9, 12, 27–28
    radix sorts, 872
    shadow volumes, 240, 242
    sparse matrix multiplication, 199
    tree rendering, 117
    virus signature matching, 778–779
bump mapping
    trees, 70
    triplanar texturing, 30
buoyant force in smoke effects, 658–659
bus utilization in geometry shader unit, 906
BVH (binary bounding-volume hierarchy), 252–
        254

C

`calculate_forces` function, 684–685
`CalculateCropMatrix` function, 211, 213–214
`calculateGridCoordinate` function, 625
calibrated monitors, 538
camera-aligned quads, 199
camera view in particle systems, 514
Carmack's reverse, 242
Cartesian space in importance sampling, 465
cascaded shadow mapping (CSM), 81
cases in procedural terrains, 9–10
CBC (cipher-block chaining) mode, 800–802
CDF (cumulative distribution function), 462–464
cell ID arrays, 704, 707–708
    constructing, 704–706

correlation operators, 837
correlation structures, 823
counter blocks, 801
counter modes, 801–802
counters
    radix, 708–717
    shadow volumes, 240
coupled reflection models, 332–333
coupling in rigid body simulation, 629–630
covariance matrix, 355
CPU
    adaptive refinement patterns, 99
    cinematic relighting, 200
    encryption, 799
    instancing, 42
`CreateAABB` function, 210
`createGather` function, 186–187
crepuscular rays, 276–277, 283
crop matrix transformation
    matrices, 210
    parallel-split shadow maps, 227
cross-fading in alpha to coverage, 85–86
cross sections of tetrahedra, 750–751
cross-shaped filter kernels, 845–846
crowd rendering. *See* animated crowd rendering
Crysis. *See* vegetation
CSC (characteristic scan conversion), 742, 744
CSM (cascaded shadow mapping), 81
CSM (cone step mapping), 409–410
    algorithm, 415–416
    relaxed. *See* relaxed cone stepping (RCS)
CTR (counter) mode, 801
cube maps
    parallel-split shadow maps, 230–232
    point light shadow maps, 435
    ray tracing layered distance maps, 392
    reflections and refractions, 389, 398, 400
cubic splines, 546–552
CUDA programming model
    broad-phase collision detection. *See* broad-phase
        collision detection
    LCP collision detection. *See* LCP (linear comple-
        mentarity problem) algorithms
    N-body simulation. *See* N-body simulation
    parallel prefix sums (scans). *See* parallel prefix
        sums (scans)
    random numbers. *See* random numbers
    subsurface imaging. *See* seismic data processing

cumulative distribution function (CDF), 462–464
curved surfaces in UV distortion, 321
curves in vector art
    cubic, 547–548
    loop, 553–554
    quadratic, 555, 558–559
    serpentine, 552
cusps, vector art, 554
cyclic reduction in 3D fluid effects, 662

D

`D3D10_CPU_ACCESS_WRITE` function, 62
`D3D10_USAGE_DYNAMIC` function, 62
D3DX effects, 430
damping
    3D fluid effects, 664
    collision reaction, 617
    trunk animation, 109
data acquisition pipeline in Universal Capture,
    350–352
data buffers in virus signature matching, 778–779
Data Encryption Standard (DES), 788
data loading in seismic data processing, 845
data patterns in virus signature matching, 773–775
data-scanning libraries, 774–775
Dawn character, 54–57
dawn light, 437
`ddx` function, 87
`ddy` function, 87
decay in volumetric light scattering, 278–279
decoding matrices from textures, 45
decompression in principal component analysis,
    358–360
`DecompressPcaColor` function, 365–370
decryption. *See* AES (Advanced Encryption Stan-
    dard) encryption and decryption
deep frame buffers, 196
deferred shading, 429
    alpha-blended geometry, 450–451
    background, 430–431
    depth and normal buffers, 440–445
    dynamic branching, 449–450
    edge detection, 442–444
    forward shading support, 431–434
    introduction, 429–430
    issues, 450–453

H

Haar wavelets, 185
  2D transforms, 197
  compression, 189
  gather samples, 187
hair in deferred shading, 451
Hammersley sequence, 465
hand-painted 2D textures, 18
hard-edged shadows, 178
hardware gradients, 557
hardware texture filtering, 158
harmonics in importance sampling, 470
hash buckets, 132
hash function, 134
hash index tables, 132–133
hashes
  constraining particles, 132–135
  point-based visualization of metaballs, 145
heat diffusion, 585
height
  cone step mapping, 417
  silhouette clipping, 72–76
  silhouette edge antialiasing, 87
hemispherical lighting, 432
Hessian polynomials, 551
hiding multiple render target data, 446–447
hierarchical grids, 700
hierarchical N-body simulation methods, 692–693
hierarchical occlusion culling technique, 252–254.
    See also shadow volumes
hierarchical trees, 258
high dynamic range (HDR) images
  deferred shading, 452
  illumination, 459
  linearity, 533
  SpeedTree rendering, 85
  sum-of-Gaussians diffusion profiles, 320
high-frequency pinching artifacts, 261
high-speed, off-screen particles. *See* particles and
    particle systems
histograms, 895–897
histoGS function, 895–896
Hit function, 397
HLSL
  blend shapes, 56, 60–66
  quaternion library in, 115–116
home cells in spatial subdivisions, 704–706

homogeneous curve parameterization, 548
Hough maps, 906
Hough transform, 899–903
hybrid random number generators, 813–815
HybridTaus function, 814
hydrophones, 832–833, 836

I

IEC standard for gamma, 539
illumination. *See* lights and lighting
illumination integrals in importance sampling, 460
image quality in particle systems, 525–526
image synthesis in reflections and refractions, 388
imaging Earth subsurface. *See* seismic data
    processing
implicit surfaces
  defining, 128
  visualization, 125
implicitization, 543
importance sampling
  introduction, 459
  mapping and distortion, 469–470
  material functions, 462–465
  mipmap filtered samples, 466–470
  performance, 470–473
  quasirandom low-discrepancy sequences, 465–
    466
  rendering formulation, 459–460
impostors, true, 481
  algorithm and implementation details, 482–487
  introduction, 481–482
  performance, 487–489
inclusive scans, 852
incompressibility constraints, 635
incompressible fluids, 635
inconsistent meshes, 742
incremental Gaussian computation, 877
  algorithm, 882–885
  error analysis, 885–887
  introduction and related work, 877–879
  performance, 887–888
  polynomial forward differencing, 879–882
independent bit depth in deferred shading, 451
index buffers
  adaptive mesh refinement, 96–97, 99
  deferred shading, 453

K

k-means clustering, 187

Karush-Kuhn-Tucker (KKT) conditions, 730

`keepImportantCoeffs` function, 191

Kelemen/Szirmay-Kalos specular function, 302–304

kernels
3D fluid effects, 636–637, 646–647, 660
Core Image image-processing, 564
implicit surfaces, 128
incremental Gaussian computation, 877
metaballs, 124
parallel prefix sums (scans), 873
parallel solution to LCP, 734
repulsion force equation, 136
seismic data processing, 845–848
sum-of-Gaussians diffusion profiles, 320

keys
encryption, 788–790
radix sorts, 871–873

KISS random number generators, 815

KKT (Karush-Kuhn-Tucker) conditions, 730

`KS_Skin_Specular` function, 302

`KSTextureCompute` function, 302

L

Lafortune BRDF, 465

lagged Fibonacci generators, 812

Lagrangian interpolation, 882

Lagrangian schemes for 3D fluid effects, 636

Lambertian emission, 192

Laplacian filters, 839

Law of Large Numbers, 805

layered distance maps, 387, 390–396

layers
particles, 513
skin, 296–297

LCGs (linear congruential generators), 812, 814–815

`LCGStep` function, 814

LCP (linear complementarity problem) algorithms, 723
contact points, 726–728
convex distance calculation, 731–732
mathematical optimization, 728–730
parallel processing, 724
parallel solution, 732–737
performance, 738–739
physics pipeline, 724–726

leaf cells in N-body simulation, 692

`LeafShadingBack` function, 382

`LeafShadingFront` function, 382

leaking artifacts, 742–747

Leanne character, 353–362

leapfrog-Verlet integrators, 680

least-index rule, 735

leaves
detail bending, 374, 376
lighting, 81–84
self-shadowing, 77–81
shading, 378

Lemke's algorithm, 723, 732

`length` function, 170

length of encryption keys, 790

lenses in depth-of-field, 585–586

lerping
color variations, 50
texture seams, 331
translucent shadow maps, 339–340
two-sided lighting, 82

level-of-detail (LOD)
alpha to coverage cross-fading, 85–86
animated crowd rendering, 39, 49–50
importance sampling, 468
instancing, 42
mipmaps, 534
procedural terrains, 35–36
silhouette clipping, 76–77
wind animations, 107–108

level sets
3D fluid effects, 664–665
water effects, 660

LFSR113 generators, 813

libraries, data-scanning, 774–775

lift in branch animation, 111

light bleeding, 166–169

light polarization, 305

light-seam reduction, 71–72

light shafts, 276–277, 283

light-space perspective shadow maps (LiSPSMs), 204

lights and lighting
ambient occlusion. *See* ambient occlusion

M

S

turbulence
  branch animation, 111
  trunk animation, 109
two-sided lighting, 82–83
2D textures
  procedural terrains, 18
  relief mapping, 413

U

UcapWindow structure, 365
Uncanny Valley hypothesis, 350
undersampling artifacts, 400
undershooting in ray tracing layered distance maps,
    391, 393–394
uniform distributions, 463
uniform grids
  normal maps, 494–496
  rigid body simulation, 628
  spatial subdivisions, 699, 703–704
uniform PRNGs, 812–815
uniform split schemes, 207–209
uniform-to-Gaussian conversion generators, 811–
    815
Universal Capture (UCap), 349
  animated textures. *See* animated textures
  conclusion, 363–370
  data acquisition pipeline, 350–352
  introduction, 349–350
  sequencing performances, 363
UNPACK macro, 792
unpack_state_in routine, 792–793
unrolling loops in N-body simulation, 687–688
up-sweep phase in parallel prefix sums (scans), 856
upgoing waves in seismic data processing, 838
UVs and UV distortion
  edge detection, 442
  procedural terrains, 29
  texture-space diffusion, 320–322
  true impostors, 482–483

V

v2gConnector structure, 26
variable batch size in AES encryption, 798
variable-length output, 898–899

variable principal component analysis, 360
variable-width blur, 593–594
variance in animated facial textures, 352, 354
variance shadow maps (VSMs), 157, 161–162
  biasing, 164–166
  filtering, 162–164
  implementation, 171–172
  light bleeding, 166–169
  numeric stability, 169–171
  parallel-split shadow maps, 232
  soft shadows, 172–173
  summed-area. *See* summed-area variance shadow
      maps (SAVSMs)
vector art
  antialiasing, 556–558
  code, 558–559
  cubic splines, 546–552
  cusps, 554
  introduction, 543–544
  loop curves, 553–554
  quadratic curves, 555, 558–559
  quadratic splines, 544–546
  serpentine curves, 552
  triangulation, 555–556
vectors
  3D fluid effects, 636
  wind animation, 106–107
vegetation
  animation, 373
    detail bending, 376
    implementation, 374–375
    procedural, 373–374
    sine waves, 375–376
    SpeedTree. *See* SpeedTree rendering
    wind. *See* wind animation
  shading, 378–379
    ambient lighting, 379–380
    edge smoothing, 380
    implementation, 381–382
velocity
  3D fluid effects, 635–639, 643, 645–646, 652
  all-pairs N-body simulation, 680
  rigid body simulation, 613–614, 617–618,
      622
  seismic data processing, 834–837
  smoke effects, 658–659
velocity constraint equation, 128–131
velocity voxelization, 652–657

informIT

Addison-Wesley Warranty on the DVD

Addison-Wesley warrants the enclosed DVD to be free of defects in materials and faulty workmanship under normal use for a period of ninety days after purchase (when purchased new). If a defect is discovered in the DVD during this warranty period, a replacement DVD can be obtained at no charge by sending the defective DVD, postage prepaid, with proof of purchase to:

> **Disc Exchange**
> **Addison-Wesley**
> **Pearson Technology Group**
> **75 Arlington Street, Suite 300**
> **Boston, MA 02116**
> **Email: AWPro@aw.com**

Addison-Wesley makes no warranty or representation, either expressed or implied, with respect to this software, its quality, performance, merchantability, or fitness for a particular purpose. In no event will Addison-Wesley, its distributors, or dealers be liable for direct, indirect, special, incidental, or consequential damages arising out of the use or inability to use the software. The exclusion of implied warranties is not permitted in some states. Therefore, the above exclusion may not apply to you. This warranty provides you with specific legal rights. There may be other rights that you may have that vary from state to state. The contents of this DVD are intended for personal use only.

NVIDIA Statement on the Software

The source code provided is freely distributable, so long as the NVIDIA header remains unaltered and user modifications are detailed. NVIDIA makes no warranty or representation that the techniques described herein are free from any Intellectual Property claims. The reader assumes all risk of any such claims based on his or her use of these techniques.

NO WARRANTY

THE SOFTWARE AND ANY OTHER MATERIALS PROVIDED BY NVIDIA ON THE ENCLOSED DVD ARE PROVIDED "AS IS." NVIDIA DISCLAIMS ALL WARRANTIES, EXPRESS, IMPLIED OR STATUTORY, INCLUDING, WITHOUT LIMITATION, THE IMPLIED WARRANTIES OF TITLE, MERCHANTABILITY, FITNESS FOR A PARTICULAR PURPOSE AND NONINFRINGEMENT.

LIMITATION OF LIABILITY

NVIDIA SHALL NOT BE LIABLE TO ANY USER, DEVELOPER, DEVELOPER'S CUSTOMERS, OR ANY OTHER PERSON OR ENTITY CLAIMING THROUGH OR UNDER DEVELOPER FOR ANY LOSS OF PROFITS, INCOME, SAVINGS, OR ANY OTHER CONSEQUENTIAL, INCIDENTAL, SPECIAL, PUNITIVE, DIRECT OR INDIRECT DAMAGES (WHETHER IN AN ACTION IN CONTRACT, TORT OR BASED ON A WARRANTY), EVEN IF NVIDIA HAS BEEN ADVISED OF THE POSSIBILITY OF SUCH DAMAGES. THESE LIMITATIONS SHALL APPLY NOTWITHSTANDING ANY FAILURE OF THE ESSENTIAL PURPOSE OF ANY LIMITED REMEDY. IN NO EVENT SHALL NVIDIA'S AGGREGATE LIABILITY TO DEVELOPER OR ANY OTHER PERSON OR ENTITY CLAIMING THROUGH OR UNDER DEVELOPER EXCEED THE AMOUNT OF MONEY ACTUALLY PAID BY DEVELOPER TO NVIDIA FOR THE SOFTWARE OR ANY OTHER MATERIALS.

DVD System Requirements

The system requirements for each chapter's sample vary widely, but for optimal performance, we recommend that you use a Shader Model 4.0-class GPU such as an NVIDIA GeForce 8 Series, G8X-based NVIDIA Quadro FX, or newer graphics processor. In addition, you may need to upgrade your graphics driver. You will need Microsoft Visual Studio to open up some of the provided projects. OpenGL, GLUT, and DirectX are also required to view all the examples. Many of the executable demos will run only on PCs running Microsoft Windows.

More information and updates are available at:
developer.nvidia.com/gpugems3
www.awprofessional.com